W9-DFS-992

Handbook of
Applied Behavior
Analysis

Dedication

One can read Baer, Wolf, and Risley (1968, 1987) to find the still-current dimensions of applied behavior analysis. An appreciation of these dimensions is necessary, but not sufficient, for the development of skilled applied behavior analysts (nor was it argued to be). That is, the effective training of applied behavior analysts does not occur solely through didactic instruction of the behavioral literature, but also through the mentorship process. Such mentoring requires a sort of assiduousness and devotion that is far too high a cost for most to pay, as it means that training applied behavior analysts must be your life. We dedicate this book to the devoted professor who mentored us, as well as over 50 other doctoral-level applied behavior analysts...Jon S. Bailey, Ph.D.

Handbook of Applied Behavior Analysis

Edited by

John Austin

and

James E. Carr

Western Michigan University

Foreword by Beth Sulzer-Azaroff

CONTEXT PRESS
Reno, Nevada

Publisher's Note

This publication is designed to provide accurate and authoritative information in regard to the subject matter covered. It is sold with the understanding that the publisher is not engaged in rendering psychological, financial, legal, or other professional services. If expert assistance or counseling is needed, the services of a competent professional should be sought.

Distributed in Canada by Raincoast Books

Copyright © 2000 by Context Press

Cotext Press is a division of New Harbinger Publications, Inc.
5674 Shattuck Avenue
Oakland, CA 94609
www.newharbinger.com

All Rights Reserved
Printed in the United States of America

Library of Congress Cataloging-in-Publication Data
Handbook of applied behavior analysis / edited by John Austin and James E. Carr;
    foreword by Beth Sulzer-Azaroff.
        p. cm.
    Includes bibiiographical references
    ISBN-13: 978-1-878978-34-9
    ISBN-10: 1-878978-34-9
        1. Behavioral assessment. 2. Behavioral modification. I. Austin, John, 1969-
            II. Carr, James E.
    RC473.B43 H36 2000
    616.89'075--dc21

                                                                          00-052362

---

11 10 09
10 9 8 7 6 5 4 3 2

Introduction

John Austin and James E. Carr
Western Michigan University

The primary goal of this text is to provide a survey of over a dozen areas in which behavioral principles have been applied. We do not intend this to be a procedural manual, but rather a reference for those interested in an overview of behavioral applications. We refer to the text as a "handbook" because of its breadth. However, many areas in which quality behavioral work is being conducted have not been included in this version of the text. We hope to highlight some of those areas (e.g., behavioral gerontology) in a future edition.

The primary target audiences for this text are academic behavior analysts and graduate students. However, we also hope that practitioners find the research reviews informative. The text is organized into two general sections. Chapters 1 through 11 focus on "clinical" areas in which behavioral principles have been applied. Chapters 12 through 19 generally cover organizational and instructional areas. The final chapter is a perspective on the future of applied behavior analysis. Each chapter surveys the previous and contemporary research in its domain of interest, and includes directions for future research in the area. We have each used a pre-printed version of this text to teach graduate-level survey courses in applied behavior analysis. The content and level of writing seem to be well suited for graduate courses. In addition, each chapter includes 10 reading objectives to facilitate instructional use.

We thank the following individuals for their assistance in editing and reviewing chapters for this book: Sean Coriaty, Debra Fredericks, Brian Gaunt, Scott Harrington, David Hatfield, Tom Higbee, Kate Kellum, and David Wilder.

We look forward to receiving feedback on this text so that we may produce a better version in the future. Please address correspondence to Dr. John Austin or Dr. James E. Carr at Department of Psychology, Western Michigan University, Kalamazoo, MI 49008-5052 (E-mail: john.austin@wmich.edu and jim.carr@wmich.edu).

Foreword

Beth Sulzer-Azaroff
Professor Emeritus
University of Massachusetts

We were there in the beginning. It was the fall of 1956; easy to remember because I was pregnant with my first child, David. Edward Sulzer, my late husband, had been discharged from the US army in June and returned to Columbia University to study clinical psychology. Previously, I had been teaching in inner-city elementary schools and studying school psychology.

One day Ed came home and excitedly told me about a new invention, the air crib (*Ladies' Home Journal*, 1945). One of his professors, either Keller or Schoenfeld, had described this safe, comfortable, infant environment during a class on learning. Although Ed had become acquainted with Murray Sidman and Lawrence Stoddard while stationed at Walter Reed Hospital, that course was Ed's first systematic exposure to behavioral psychology and he was finding it intriguing. It seemed so compatible with his hard science background as an undergraduate at the University of Chicago. The long and short of it was that when David was born, his bed was an air crib, and Ed and I had become very intrigued by behavior analysis.

By the early sixties, our second son, Richard had outgrown the air crib. Ed was a member of the University of Minnesota Medical School faculty and I had entered a doctoral program in psychology. About that time, an applied behavioral literature was beginning to emerge. As a field, we began to use and report on the newly evolving behavioral therapy methods applied to our clinical populations. I actively studied the research literature spinning out from Skinner's (1958) provocative paper on teaching.

Not much had been published yet: a few papers and Skinner's books. I did have the good fortune to serve as a teaching assistant in Kenneth McCorquodale's superb course on behavior analysis. The text was *The Analysis of Behavior*, the one Holland and Skinner programmed in 1961. It included many everyday examples of the principles of behavior in action. In those early years it was largely by word-of-mouth, however, that we found out what others were doing. One highlight was a conference Ed and some of his colleagues organized on the topic of behavior modification. Other experts visited the University of Minnesota to give talks or short courses. Among others, the people who we had the pleasure of meeting were Jack Michael, Nathan Azrin, Sidney Bijou, Ivar Lovaas, Jay Birnbrauer, and the great B.F. Skinner himself.

If one were to attempt to characterize the behavior modification/therapy/ analysis of the late fifties and early sixties, probably it could best be labeled *piecemeal*. Most practitioners were addressing specific individual or small-group behavioral challenges: delayed learning in the "retarded," aberrations among "psychotic," "neurotic" and "autistic" clients, problems with eating, studying, interpersonal relations and so on. We learned from each other about how to apply differential reinforcement to reduce problem performances and shape and increase adaptive behaviors, while keeping loose - by today's standards - measures of progress. It seemed to be this creative combination of applying procedures based on principles of learning and behavioral measurement that so many of us found attractive. The procedures helped behavior to improve and the measures informed us of such successes.

By the time I had completed my doctoral studies in 1965, just ahead of my third child, Lenore, Nathan Azrin enticed Ed to join the faculty at Southern Illinois University (SIU). His task there was to organize the first full-scale graduate training program in behavior modification in the country. In concert with Azrin's Behavior Research Laboratory at Anna State Hospital, the program shortly attained true excellence. It attracted as faculty, students, and visitors, some of yesterday and today's world leaders in the field. Concurrently I joined the SIU faculty of the School of Education and immediately began teaching, practicing, and doing research in behavior analysis. Texts for my courses included, at various times, the ones by Holland and Skinner (1961), Staats and Staats (1963), Ullmann and Krasner (1965), Krasner and Ullmann (1965), and Reese's (1966) gem entitled, *The Analysis of Human Operant Behavior*. Along with several films made by other people, I used Reese's superb film series demonstrating what behavior analysis was and how it operated.

By then, behavior modification was becoming recognized as a reputable field of scholarship and practice. *Journal of the Experimental Analysis of Behavior* included some reports of successful application, while *Journal of Experimental Child Psychology* included several studies conducted with children. Division 25 (Experimental Analysis of Behavior) had been organized within the American Psychological Association, which had begun to include applied activities in its program.

What seemed to appeal to so many was the evolving rigor of the field. Researchers and practitioners alike adopted as a convention the kinds of scientific tactics recommended by Sidman (1960), emphasizing methods for enhancing the validity of results and reliability of data collection. By the late sixties, interobserver agreement checks, conducted independently by multiple observers, as well as formal experimental strategies, tended to be included in published studies.

During this time, the field also began to expand in terms of the kinds of clients it served and the number of personnel that were trained. Although the preponderance of client populations included those with developmental delays, "psychoses," and "neuroses," we began to see increasing numbers of reports of studies involving more general populations: young children, students in the regular classroom, people with habits they found annoying or detrimental to their health, and ordinary people at work and in the community. These efforts were led by personnel trained in rehabilitation, child development, psychology, psychiatry, and social work at Southern Illinois University and beyond: at Universities in Kansas, Michigan, Illinois, Hawaii, South Africa, England, Australia, and elsewhere.

The day in 1968 the *Journal of Applied Behavior Analysis (JABA)* made its debut we knew the field had established its own identity. Codified in the first issue were its definition and defining features (Baer, Wolf, & Risley, 1968). Clearly, the subject of applied behavior analysis was socially meaningful behavior that could be rigorously defined and objectively detected and measured. The relation between changes in the management of independent variables and any systematic behavioral changes was to be analyzed by designing methods to screen out possible confounding variables.

It took little time for additional journals, such as *Behavior Therapy, Journal of Behavior Therapy and Experimental Psychiatry, School Applications of Learning Theory,* and others to come upon the scene. By the early seventies, new, more specialized texts in speech and language, clinical and school applications (e.g., *Behavior Modification Procedures for School Personnel* by Sulzer & Mayer, 1972) also began to be produced. From that point on, the field's bibliography rapidly expanded. Just as a case in point, our book included about 150 references. When we revised it in 1977, (*Applying Behavior Analysis Procedures with Children and Youth* by Sulzer-Azaroff & Mayer), despite intentionally limiting our coverage to children, families and those serving them, there were about 800 references. The revision in 1991, broadened to include organizational factors (*Behavior Analysis for Lasting Change*) had about 1,200. Then we called it quits!

The story of the field's evolution continues, as Bailey so lucidly describes in the chapter (Ch. 20) titled "A Futurist Perspective for Applied Behavior Analysis." Professional societies increased, along with journals, specialty meetings, as well as other outlets for the ever-enlarging volume of work. Long ago it became impossible to keep up with it all. Fortunately, now the American Psychological Association helps us out by publishing sets of abstracts in *PsycSCAN: Behavior Analysis and Therapy.* It lists about 2,300 records each year.

Beyond sheer numbers, though, several other features appear to distinguish the field as it continues to evolve. Constrained by space limitations, many, but not all, are explored in this text. A few of these features include the following.

Widening Areas of Application

Health is a big thrust. The role of behavioral medicine had so much potential for preventing and treating illness that some of its practitioners formed their own separate *Society for Behavioral Medicine.* Successful pilot work in preventing and treating cardiovascular problems, diabetes, and injuries, among others, needed to be expanded and large-scale controlled field trials were undertaken, many with the support of the National Institutes of Health. Scholars like Nathan Azrin and many others have continued to conduct controlled field studies in treating noxious habits, and alcohol and substance abuse.

In this volume, we see some timely examples. Jacobs discusses brain-injury rehabilitation" in Chapter 9. Alavosius' chapter (15) titled "Behavioral Approaches to Organizational Safety" describes his company's elegant combination of the best of organizational system design, performance management, and other behavior-analytic principles and procedures to improve the wellbeing of workers employed in many small businesses. In "Behavioral Pediatrics: The Confluence of Applied Behavior Analysis and Pediatric Medicine" (Ch. 7), Blum and Friman tell us how pharmaceutical and behavioral treatment can work in tandem to treat sleep, bowel, bladder and other common children's health problems. Additionally, beyond attempting to seek out the contingencies maintaining habit disorders, Miltenberger and Woods (Ch. 6) describe how habit reversal techniques can be used successfully to treat those like tic disorders, nail biting, hair pulling, among others.

General and special education is another important area. New behavior-based technologies of teaching, such as Precision Teaching (Lindsley, 1992), Direct Instruction (Becker & Carnine, 1981), Personalized System of Instruction (Keller, 1968) and others were engineered, put to the test and found powerfully effective. Kent Johnson has integrated these methods along with others in his *Morningside Teaching Model.* Johnson's students become fluent not only in rote learning of tool subjects but also higher levels of analyses and creative problem solving to the extent that they double and triple their former rates of progress (Johnston & Layng, 1992). In this book, Jennifer Austin (Ch. 19) tells us about how some of those behavioral methods are used in college classrooms, while Brethower (Ch. 18) describes what concepts are and how to teach them. He also describes the contingencies supporting and impeding effective education in school and business.

Tools to help teachers develop their own behavior-based instructional strategies and to manage and motivate students continue to develop (see for example Sulzer-Azaroff & Mayer, 1986 *Behavior Analysis in Education* by Sulzer-Azaroff et al., 1987). Many pupil personnel specialists, such as counselors and school psychologists, are being trained to employ behavior-analytic principles and procedures in their work. In Chapter 5, entitled "Behavior Analysis and School Psychology," Ervin and Ehrhardt describe how behavior analysis is incorporated within six areas of school psychological application: consultation, assessment, direct and indirect intervention, supervision, research, and program evaluation.

Educating students who face major challenges, such as impaired developmental, sensory, and brain function, requires precision in programming. The fact that behavior-analytic methodology, ideally suited to this demand, has become the strategy of choice with these populations, can be seen by thumbing through the journals and textbooks on special education. Examples are elaborated on throughout this book.

Business and service organizations concerned with increasing efficiency, employee satisfaction and well being, and quality and profit have been turning to behavior analysis in growing numbers. Facets explored in this volume include various models and algorithms for analyzing and diagnosing organizational performance (e.g., Ch. 14 by John Austin). Williams' chapter (16) contributes here by defining and providing a course of action within "Behavioral Consultation."

Martin and Tkachuk's chapter (17) on "Behavioral Sport Psychology" illustrates another area of application. He describes how he and his colleagues have used imagery, self-talk, goal setting, and feedback to improve athletic performance. Increasing attention to the analysis of verbal behavior enables the design of curricula supportive of "cognitive learning," including effective concept formation of the type that Brethower discusses in his chapter (18) on training. Behavior analysis has been practiced in numerous other areas including family and community issues, social and recreational activities, economic decision making, and just about any facet in which learning, feeling, thinking and doing are of concern.

Scientists operating in the basic research laboratory are making new discoveries and refining others relevant to applied concerns. Included are the work on stimulus equivalence and other methods for promoting fine discrimination learning, momentum building, the construction of complex behavioral chains, and many others. In this book, Poling, Dickinson, Austin, and Normand (Ch. 13) concentrate on a few aspects of this element when they summarize the work on pay for performance and other facets of "Basic and Applied Research in Organizational Management."

Bridges are being built between basic and applied work, like that on establishing fluency and building momentum (Mace, 1996). These bridging actions promote the kinds of striking progress that Johnson and Layng (1992) are accomplishing in education, as well as expanding our understanding of the kinds of problems Carr, Coriaty and Dozier (Ch. 4) address in their chapter titled "Current Issues in the Function-Based Treatment of Aberrant Behavior in Individuals with Developmental Disabilities."

New applied strategies are being fashioned all the time. Beyond those that originate in the laboratory, many are based on extrapolations from combinations or refinements of other applied methods. One instance is the habit reversal technique, originally detailed by Azrin and Nunn (1973) and described in this volume by Miltenberger and Woods (Ch. 6). This especially effective strategy includes a number of behavioral procedures: awareness training, practicing competing responses, occasional relaxation training, and social consequences. Martin and Tkachuk's (Ch. 17) use of such techniques as imagery, self-talk, goal setting, and feedback derive from earlier work on applications of stimulus control, verbal learning, and reinforcement tactics. Practices, which Poling, Dickinson, Austin, and Normand (Ch. 13) and Reid and Parsons (Ch. 12) describe in their chapters on organizational behavior management share analogous roots.

Efforts are directed toward *assessing the ecological context* to determine what variables are likely to be in place to sustain improved performance. We recognize that the people and the organizations they comprise will adhere to a practice only if contingencies of reinforcement are favorable. Reid and Parsons (Ch. 12) suggest turning to self-management and other tactics to provide powerful supportive consequences. Although not necessarily optimal techniques, because they involve little cost in terms of time and effort, the self-management practices are likely to continue.

A closely related facet is the growing recognition of the importance of *contextual variation* and how it can impact the nature of specific functional relations within those contexts. One instance is the way the "culture of an organization" (i.e., the network of macro-contingencies) can establish certain events as either reinforcers or punishers under specific circumstances. Several of the elements of the Alavosius COST program (see Ch. 15), such as assessing the safety culture, are of relevance here. If taking careful safety precautions is thought to be a form of prissiness in one setting, but highly valued in another, that could differentially affect the safe response-consequence relation.

Some also have begun to examine how other predictable factors can constrain or facilitate durable behavior change and how to manage them to optimize outcome. A case in point is the way Lifter, Sulzer-Azaroff, Anderson, and Cowdery (1993) analyzed how developmental factors might influence whether or how slowly or rapidly a youngster might acquire a particular play skill. Many of the discoveries of fields beyond behavior analysis, such as human development, social and biological psychology, and other behavioral sciences have much to contribute here. Just consider the context set by a screaming crowd at a sports event or a field of battling soldiers for a hint about how the relation between certain behaviors (screaming, killing) and their consequences are altered. To realize the futility of failing to consider developmental factors, try teaching ducklings to follow a moving inanimate object after they have passed the "critical period" for imprinting.

Focus on assessment and analyses keeps expanding. Although we realized that behavior did not take place in a vacuum and any persistent response must have a function, it took a while for the field to develop sound methods for systematically assessing the particular function of certain destructive behaviors. Frea and Vittimberga (Ch. 11) discuss how functional assessments inform our selection of teaching goals and the environmental conditions that need to be in place to support change. Today, instead of simply employing reductive procedures to try to eliminate disruptive and destructive behaviors, as Miltenberger and Woods (Ch. 6) caution and Iwata, Kahng, Wallace, and Lindberg (Ch. 3) details in their chapter on functional assessment, we approach the issue systematically. Iwata and colleagues outline why and how to conduct functional analyses, emphasizing the use of rigorous analytic designs like the multielement and others. When such precision is not feasible, the authors suggest ways to make do in the interim by means of indirect methods such as A-B-C assessments, scatter plots, and interviews. At least such methods permit us to begin to hypothesize about conditions likely to be supporting the problem.

Just as we have learned to look toward the more distal conditions that impact upon behavior, and how behavior is affected by its consequences, we also are becoming more sensitive to the *ecological impact* of behavior change upon the environment. Ervin and Ehrhardt (Ch. 5) caution school psychologists to select interventions that are "ecological" in nature. Teach a formerly non-verbal youngster to use the colloquial speech of his typically developing peers, or a sexually active teen to practice safe sex, and his family may find itself punished by those behaviors and retaliate accordingly. Today, as Frea and Vittimberga (Ch. 11) emphasize in discussing the issue of "goodness of fit," we try to check out the objective with those whose lives will be affected by such major changes.

Refined, new, and different experimental analytic methods come on the scene from time to time. The withdrawal and reversal designs, delineated by Baer et al. (1968), were the standard from the start. As circumstances demanded, these methods have been broadened to include multiple probes, multi-elements, and diverse other ways for evaluating the functional impact of variables upon patterns of behavior. Today the generality of effects previously determined through individual and small-group functional analyses are being put to the test in large field trials. Sometimes, too, it seems eminently reasonable to examine any indirect effects by means of correlational data, of the sort Alavosius (Ch. 15) reports for the impact of his COST program.

Consideration of individual rights, has intensified along with concern for societal values and "customer" satisfaction. Publications such as that by Stolz (1976) on ethics of social and educational interventions, the Association for Advancement of Behavior Therapy ethical guidelines, and other organizational policies supplement those of the American Psychological Association. A number of years ago, Wolf (1978) reminded us about the importance of social validity in selecting our objectives and methods, while in this current volume, Jennifer Austin (Ch.19) talks about our need to find ways to gain wide-scale acceptance of demonstrably effective teaching methods. Functional analyses of the variables affecting large-scale consumer choice remain to be examined, probably constrained by the cost of such investigations.

Behavior analysts have begun reaching out to the public. While we bemoan the failure of society to adopt the "proven" methods of behavior analysis, Bailey's (Ch. 20) futurist perspective aptly accuses us of failing to do what we can to accomplish that purpose. Indeed, studies of consumer choice can contribute here. Bailey also mentions communicating in the language of the lay person as a valuable approach, citing several recent books written for that audience. Others too, are coming on the scene, including a couple by Aubrey Daniels, designed for the business audience, and one I recently completed, a mystery-adventure fable incorporating the full model for addressing behavioral safety challenges in the workplace (Sulzer-Azaroff, 1998a). Professionally sophisticated audio-visual materials, like those Aubrey Daniels, Scott Geller, and Tom Krause have developed for audiences interested in teaching personnel about behavioral applications to improve workplace performance, also get our points across quite effectively. The Cambridge Center for Behavioral Studies has taken on as its mission transferring the methods and results of behavior-analytic research to the public. It communicates its messages via forums, user conferences and over the web (*www.behavior.org*).

These efforts, however, take place primarily at the antecedent end which, as we know, are far less powerful than those related to the response-consequence contingency. The challenge is to engineer ways for our consumers to behave in accord with these concepts; ways that can rapidly prove of value to them. That the authors of the present book are sensitive to this point is apparent in that they, like *JABA* and many behavior-analytic textbooks, have included study questions covering key concepts. As my co-authors and I have regularly done (e.g., Sulzer-Azaroff, 1998b) many textbook developers in our field also have prepared study guides and activity manuals as ancillary materials and mechanisms to stimulate active reader responding.

The internet provides us with a remarkable communication tool and can afford us the opportunity to provide the immediate knowledge of results that Skinner itemized as a powerful feature of programmed instruction so many decades ago. Among others, West Virginia University, University of South Florida, Florida International University, and Temple University currently offer general and specialty courses for college credit over the internet.

Today it is obvious that no single textbook can do it all (i.e., present fundamental principles of behavior, research, and analytic methods, conceptual and philosophical issues, along with a survey of procedural examples). The broad-brush depiction of what is happening in the field of behavior analysis in books like the present one serves behavior analysts well by updating them on recent trends and practices. Now, at the dawn of a new millennium, our challenge is to transfer this information to the public. They will be empowered thereby, by enabling them to use the science and technology of behavior analysis to better their lives.

References

Azrin, N. H., & Nunn, R. G. (1973). Habit-reversal: A method of eliminating nervous habits and tics. *Behaviour Research and Therapy, 11,* 619-628.

Baby in a box. (1945, October). *Ladies' Home Journal,* pp. 30-31, 135-36, 138.

Baer, D. M., Wolf, M. M., & Risley, T. R. (1968). Some current dimensions of applied behavior analysis. *Journal of Applied Behavior Analysis, 1,* 91-97.

Becker, W. C., & Carnine, D. W. (1981). Direct instruction: A behavior theory model of comprehensive educational intervention with the disadvantaged. In S. W. Bijou & R. Ruiz (Eds.), *Behavior modification: Contributions to education* (pp. 145-210). Hillsdale, NJ: Lawrence Erlbaum Associates.

Holland, J., & Skinner, B. F. (1961). *The analysis of behavior.* New York: McGraw Hill.

Johnson, K. R., & Layng, T. V. J. (1992). Breaking the structuralist barrier: Literacy and numeracy with fluency. *American Psychologist, 47,* 1475-1490.

Keller, F. S. (1968). Good-bye, teacher.... *Journal of Applied Behavior Analysis, 1,* 79-89.

Krasner, L. A., & Ullmann, L. P. (Eds.). (1965). *Research in behavior modification: New developments and implications.* New York: Holt, Rinehart, & Winston.

Lifter, K., Sulzer-Azaroff, B., Anderson, S. R., & Cowdery, G. E. (1993). Teaching play activities to preschool children with disabilities: The importance of developmental considerations. *Journal of Early Intervention, 17,* 139-159.

Lindsley, O. R. (1992). Precision teaching: Discovery and effects. *Journal of Applied Behavior Analysis, 25,* 51-58.

xiv

Mace, F. C. (1996). In pursuit of general behavioral relations. *Journal of Applied Behavior Analysis, 29,* 557-563.

Reese, E. P. (1966). *The analysis of human operant behavior.* Dubuque, IA: William C. Brown.

Sidman, M. (1960). *Tactics of scientific research.* New York: Basic Books.

Skinner, B. F. (1958). Teaching machines. *Science, 128,* 969-977.

Staats, A. W., & Staats, C. K. (1963). *Complex human behavior.* New York: Holt, Rinehart, & Winston.

Stolz, S. B. (1976). Ethics of social and educational interventions: Historical context and a behavior analysis. In T. A. Brigham & A. C. Catania (Eds.), *Analysis of behavior: Social and educational processes.* New York: Irving-Neiburg Wiley.

Sulzer, B., & Mayer, G. R. (1972). *Behavior modification procedures for school personnel.* New York: Dryden Press.

Sulzer-Azaroff, B. (1998a). *Who killed my daddy?: A behavioral safety story.* Cambridge, MA: Cambridge Center for Behavioral Studies.

Sulzer-Azaroff, B. (1998b). *Activities manual for "Who killed my daddy?: A behavioral safety story".* Cambridge, MA: Cambridge Center for Behavioral Studies.

Sulzer-Azaroff, B., Drabman, R. M., Greer, R. D., Hall, R. V., Iwata, B. A., & O'Leary, S. G. (Eds.). (1987). *Behavior analysis in education.* Lawrence, KS: The Society for the Experimental Analysis of Behavior.

Sulzer-Azaroff, B., & Mayer, G. R. (1991). *Behavior analysis for lasting change.* Fort Worth, TX: Harcourt Brace.

Sulzer-Azaroff, B., & Mayer, G. R. (1977). *Applying behavior analysis procedures with children and youth.* New York: Holt, Rinehart, & Winston.

Sulzer-Azaroff, B., & Mayer, G. R. (1986). *Achieving educational excellence using behavioral strategies.* New York: Holt, Rinehart, & Winston. Reprinted in 1994 in three volumes by Western Image, P.O. Box 427, San Marcos, CA 92079-0247.

Ullmann, L. P., & Krasner, L. A. (Eds). (1965). *Case studies in behavior modification.* New York: Holt, Rinehart, & Winston.

Wolf, M. M. (1978). Social validity: The case for subjective measurement or how applied behavior analysis is finding its heart. *Journal of Applied Behavior Analysis, 11,* 203-214.

Table of Contents

Chapter 1

Stimulus Preference and Reinforcer Assessment Applications

Martin T. Ivancic
Western Carolina Center

The practice of assessing reinforcers includes a large portion of the work of behavior analysis. That is, almost any procedure that in application increases a behavior or in removal decreases a behavior is either a demonstration of the effect of a reinforcer or a demonstration of some dimension of that reinforcer's effect. The applied history of reinforcer assessment has involved searching for conditions that produce optimal effects for changing an individual's behavior that are durable, as well as efficient to conduct. Often, such procedures have addressed the behavioral excesses or deficiencies of the population of people with developmental disabilities, but this is probably more an artifact of this group's extreme need for effective treatment than an indication of who can benefit from a reinforcer assessment procedure.

What is currently understood about behavior-change interventions has been discovered by analyzing the conditions under which the future frequency of behavior is changed (Skinner, 1953; 1966). That is, target responses have been observed to change in some measurable, predictable way only when specified conditions are present. Observing this effect repeatedly across time, with other responses, in different settings, or with other individuals supports the belief that these are the conditions responsible for the repeated change (Baer, Wolf, & Risley, 1968; 1987). There are three interlocking variables, broadly referred to as the "contingencies of reinforcement" or the "three-term contingency" that are considered in explaining how environmental conditions relate to behavior changes for a particular organism. These conditions include that which has occurred prior to, during, and following the occurrence of a target response (Skinner, 1966; 1969).

The stimulus change that occurs following a response and is demonstrated to increase the frequency of that response is known as "reinforcement" (see Michael, 1993a for more detail). This stimulus change, the third component of the three-term contingency, has become a major focus of applied behavior-change procedures. The use of reinforcers to change behavior has probably become popular because of its general effectiveness and because of the relative simplicity of utilizing only one component of the complex behavior-change process. Hence, surveys of behavioral consequences known as reinforcer assessments have become frequently and successfully used as tools for determining optimal behavior change programming by identifying particular stimuli to be used as reinforcers.

However, if this chapter were to focus exclusively on reviewing procedures that simply surveyed potentially effective behavioral consequences, there would be a danger in proliferating the mistaken idea that a given stimulus change following a response changes that behavior regardless of the situation (and behavior) that is used (for a discussion of the "trans-situational hypothesis," see Meehl, 1950; Timberlake & Farmer-Dougan, 1991). The fact remains that a behavioral consequence acts as a reinforcer to change behavior only as it functions within the interlocking variables of its contingencies, including the organism's current status or history of such change (i.e., conditions prior to the response) and the response itself. Although behavior has often been changed without addressing these other conditions, the change cannot be understood to have occurred without the function of all three of these variables. In fact, there are often situations in the practice of changing behavior in which simply applying a specific consequence following a behavior does not result in the predicted behavior change. In these situations, it becomes important to appreciate how research has demonstrated the effects of other variables related to establishing a stimulus as a reinforcer. These variables will be reviewed under this topic of reinforcer assessment. To summarize, in order to avoid the tendency to believe different qualities and/or intensities of behavioral consequences have their own independent effects, this chapter will include research not only on popular survey reinforcer assessment procedures, but also on antecedent and response variables as they relate to behavioral deficits and excesses in order to more completely understand the effects of reinforcers identified in standard reinforcer assessments.

Standard Reinforcer Assessments

Early Surveys

Surveys used to identify stimuli with potential reinforcing effects began with investigations of edibles and manipulatables (Bijou & Sturges, 1959; Ferster & DeMeyer, 1962), but soon sensory stimuli, based on a wealth of basic research (Kish, 1966), were included in these investigations. One reason sensory stimulation was initially included in research for people with developmental disabilities was evidence there was better responding to sensory stimulation by people with more severe developmental disabilities than by higher functioning individuals (Cantor & Hottel, 1955; Ohwaki, Brahlek, & Stayton, 1973; Stevenson & Knights, 1961). Also, sensory stimulation was shown to be more durable (Bailey & Meyerson, 1969) than commonly used consumables which were candidates for rapid satiation (Rincover & Newsom, 1985). Some early examples of sensory reinforcer assessments addressed receptors related to audition (Remington, Foxen, & Hogg, 1977), touch (Rehagen & Thelen, 1972), vision (Rynders & Friedlander, 1972), vibration (Murphy & Doughty, 1977), and vestibular stimulation (Sellick & Over, 1980) as well as social stimulation (Harzem & Damon, 1976), food, and manipulatables.

Pace, Ivancic, Edwards, Iwata, and Page (1985) took an important step in the systematic advancement of reinforcer assessment technology by offering an assessment that not only surveyed a reasonable variety of stimuli, but also used the stimuli identified as preferred as reinforcers to change socially relevant behavior (e.g., increased compliance). This two-part procedure of first identifying preferences and then demonstrating their behavior-change effects became the framework from which a technology of reinforcer assessment began to develop. The first part, the stimulus preference assessment, is a fairly efficient review of a number of potentially reinforcing stimuli to determine which stimuli are most (and least) preferred. The second part, the reinforcer evaluation, uses one or more of these stimuli in some design to demonstrate their reinforcing effects.

Stimulus Preference Assessments

Stimulus preference assessments are conducted by making presentations of available stimuli and observing for approach or preference responding. When stimuli are presented singly, avoidance or non-preference is sometimes measured (Pace et al., 1985). Approach responding is generally defined as "a voluntary movement toward the stimulus, maintaining eye contact with the stimulus for at least three seconds, exhibiting a positive facial expression, or making a positive vocalization within five seconds of the stimulus presentation" (Green et al., 1988). Avoidance of a non-preferred stimulus is typically defined as "exhibiting a negative vocalization, pushing the stimulus away, or making a movement away from the stimulus within five seconds of the presentation" (Green et al., 1988).

Some preference assessments have utilized duration of contact between simultaneously available materials as the measurement of preference (Favell & Cannon, 1976). Others have used trial presentation because explicit presentation of a stimulus item not only allows multiple stimuli to be assessed in a relatively short period of time, but also offers an opportunity to insure the participant comes in contact with the available stimulus. All direct-observation preference assessments utilize a procedure to insure contact with the stimulus either in a noncontingent application before each assessment trial (Green et al., 1988) or in a post-trial application after which a second presentation is made on trials when no response occurred to the first presentation (Fisher et al., 1992; Pace et al., 1985).

Presenting two stimuli at once (Fisher et al., 1992; Witryol & Fischer, 1960) has proven to differentiate between preferred stimuli much better than the single-stimulus presentation method (e.g., Pace et al., 1985). To be more descriptive, if money were a preferred stimulus, single presentations of a dime or a dollar would likely generate identical absolute rates of approach responding. However, the proportion of approach responding when a choice between the dime and the dollar is given (i.e., presenting them together) is likely to be more sensitive in demonstrating that preference for the dollar is greater than for the dime (for a more thorough discussion of choice responding, see Fisher & Mazur, 1997). In addition, the paired-choice procedure has been shown to be more sensitive in showing difference in preference for visually impaired people who appeared to be predisposed to manipulate all presented objects (Paclawskyj & Vollmer, 1995). The single-stimulus presentation preference assessment is the simplest procedure to provide but often yields an overestimate of preference (Fisher et al., 1992). However, the single-stimulus assessment may still be useful to identify preferences for individuals who show clear differential choice, for individuals who have difficulty responding to a choice occasion (Ivancic & Bailey, 1996), or when non-preferred stimuli are the focus of the investigation (Fisher et al., 1994).

Single-stimulus presentation procedures have used from 10 trials per stimulus (Pace et al., 1985) to 30 trials per stimulus (Green et al., 1988; Green, Reid, Canipe, & Gardner, 1991) to assess preference. Paired-stimulus presentation procedures (also referred to as choice, concurrent operant, and or forced-choice assessments) offer each stimulus with every other stimulus (Fisher et al., 1992). Stimulus presentations are typically counterbalanced for stimulus item and presentation position to control for sequence or position preferences.

In an attempt to increase the efficiency of conducting the stimulus preference assessment, procedures offering multiple-stimulus presentations (more than two) have been used to assess preferences (DeLeon & Iwata, 1996; Windsor, Piche, & Locke, 1994). When DeLeon and Iwata removed previously chosen items from multiple-stimulus arrays, this multiple-stimulus presentation without replacement format (MSWO) was found to provide rankings of stimulus preference similar to procedures in which stimuli were presented in pairs. In addition, the MSWO format, which presented the stimuli in a group and only five times each, was more efficient than the others. Reporting this efficiency, Fisher and Mazur (1997) suggested that the most important clinical advancement of the MSWO procedure may not be in its overall efficiency, but that a similar procedure could be used before or during training sessions by offering a participant to select one or two potential reinforcers from an array of several (cf. Mason, McGee, Farmer-Dougan, & Risley, 1989) thereby taking advantage of any momentary state of motivation for available stimuli. However, even though presenting a large array of stimuli may be an efficient stimulus preference assessment for some, there is still a physical limit to the number of stimuli an individual can attend to at once, and this may be even more true when used with people who have the most severe disabilities.

An important part of stimulus preference assessments is offering a convincing representation of the stimuli with reinforcer potential for an individual. Pace et al. (1985) made an apparent attempt to survey the universe of stimuli available by offering 16 different stimuli that addressed seven sensory modalities (i.e., visual, auditory, olfactory, gustatory, tactile, thermal, vestibular) and social stimulation. Others have chosen stimuli most likely to be found available and most easily provided (Green et al., 1988). It is possible that further investigations into different qualities of stimulation or receptors may produce preferred stimulation currently not included in standard assessments. For example, sensory assessments (e.g., Reisman & Hanschu, 1992) may include activities which stimulate joints via deep muscle receptors (e.g., "pushes against [things]", "holds arms flexed"), which have been demonstrated as reinforcers (Favell, McGimsey, Jones, & Cannon, 1981; Foxx & Dufrense, 1984), but have not yet been included in standard stimulus preference assessments. Nevertheless, increasing the number of stimuli utilized in a stimulus preference assessment increases the effort to conduct it and likely decreases the probability of completing the assessment. In addition, no assessment can presume to include the potentially infinite number of stimuli available.

Efforts to simplify the process of stimulus preference assessments by use of a standard list of stimuli found that staff opinion was not as accurate in identifying preferences compared to more formal assessments (Green et al., 1988). However, there has been agreement with more formal assessments on stimuli that staff report a participant likes the most (Green et al., 1991). Further, Fisher, Piazza, Bowman, and Amari (1996) found stimuli identified by caregivers in their Reinforcer Assessment for Individuals with Severe Disabilities (RAISD) were *more* potent reinforcers than those identified in standard reinforcer assessments. The RAISD is a structured interview that uses general sensory domains as guidelines to ask familiar staff members questions about an individual's preferences.

Bowman, Fisher et al., (1997) reported that the 15 to 20 minutes required to use the RAISD, combined with an MSWO assessment, could allow accurate identification of preferences for a person in less than an hour. The authors suggested that such an efficient technology should begin to make stimulus preference assessments, which are largely conducted only in clinics and hospitals now, available for everyday use in schools and residential facilities. Still, it appears that for a clinician who does not have the advantage of interviewing familiar caregivers, more standardized assessments may still be reasonably successful in identifying a reinforcer for an individual by presenting lists of commonly available, easy-to-provide stimuli (Green et al., 1991).

There may be a tendency for a clinician to use a person's failure to show preference in a reinforcer assessment as an indication that this individual is untrainable. Of course, this is not true. A person could never be proven untrainable merely by showing an inability to respond to a given procedure (for a related discussion see Baer, 1981) unless every procedure had been used and all stimuli had been assessed. That is, claiming one set of stimuli were not useful in training an individual is very different from saying no stimuli could be used to train that person.[1] Failure to identify a reinforcer for an individual represents exactly that – a situation in which a person was not trained with a given procedure.

Preference assessment limitations. Much of the work with preference assessments has been shaped by individuals with extreme needs who failed to show reinforcer effects (e.g., Green et al., 1991). Ivancic and Bailey (1996) provided reinforcer assessments to 10 individuals determined to have chronic training deficits. None of these participants showed reinforcer effects, despite the use of common switch-activated responses (leaf or panel switches) that required minimal effort (range, 57-341 g of force), and were "bridged" with automatic auditory and visual feedback to decrease any delay between the switch response and the manually delivered consequence. In addition, it was reported that the individuals who failed to show reinforcer effects in this study, as a group, showed minimal movement (Experiment 2) (see also Giacino & Zasler, 1995). It may come as no surprise that individuals who show minimal overt responding may also show difficulty demonstrating the effect of reinforcement based on increasing overt behavior.

The trainability question for these individuals could be pursued by selecting a different variety of stimuli or further minimizing the effort of the response or some other aspect of the behavior change process. However, a more rational solution to addressing the needs of these individuals, given their minimal responsiveness, may be to rely on responses currently available in their repertoires to increase contact with stimulation that can be identified as preferred.

Utilizing a technology which recently demonstrated forms of approach responding (e.g., smiling and laughing) as "happiness" indices (Green & Reid, 1996), others have increased happiness indices for people with chronic training problems, but not minimal responsiveness (Ivancic, Barrett, Simonow, & Kimberly, 1997). It appears that stimulus preference assessments may be used to identify preferred stimulation that may or may not be able to function as reinforcers, but may hold value to noncontingently enrich the environment of a person who has difficulty operating independently in the environment.

For those who do show preferences in single- and paired-stimulus assessments, an approach response of 80% of the opportunities has been used as a general guideline for use in subsequent reinforcer evaluations (Fisher et al., 1992; Green et al., 1988; Pace et al., 1985). Nevertheless, others have shown that stimuli that are eventually shown to be effective as reinforcers may show a very low approach (i.e., may be displaced) in multiple-stimulus formats due to particularly strong preferences (e.g., food) unless arrangements are made to separate these overpowering stimuli from others that are being assessed (DeLeon, Iwata, & Roscoe, 1997).

Reinforcer Evaluations

A preference assessment makes no contribution to a reinforcer assessment unless the stimuli identified as preferred can be used to change behavior (i.e., used as reinforcers). Relative to the efficiency of most preference assessments, reinforcer evaluations are more effortful to conduct, per stimulus, given the need for a design (e.g., reversal, multielement) to analyze whether the stimulus actually changed behavior. In addition, the effects of the reinforcer in applied research are judged by a socially significant standard of behavior change (Baer, et al., 1968; 1987). A separate requirement of social significance is not typically required for responses emitted in a preference assessment.

Pace et al. (1985) used preferred stimuli following simple requests (e.g., percentage of trials with compliance) in evaluating their preferred stimuli as reinforcers. Green et al. (1991) measured mean (reduced) prompt level during skill acquisition training trials to evaluate their reinforcers. However, as the different variables of reinforcer assessment procedures began to be investigated, the effort of the response during the reinforcer evaluation became more minimal and standard, hence less socially significant, in order to reveal the effect of the stimulus without being confounded by the effort of the response. For example, Fisher et al. (1992) evaluated the reinforcing effect of preferred stimuli by using easily trained *in-square* or *in-chair* behavior in a free-operant (unprompted) situation in which engaging in the targeted response resulted in receiving the associated stimulus under evaluation. Subsequent research has added a no-consequence area to this procedure to control for area preference (e.g., Fisher, Thompson, Piazza, Crosland, & Gotjen, 1997). Consistent choice between the two areas offering different stimulus opportunities shows the relative reinforcing value of each stimulus. Others have used free operant responding of minimal effort with microswitches (Ivancic & Bailey, 1996) or head turning (Piazza, Fisher, Hanley, Hilker, & Derby, 1996) to evaluate preferred stimuli as reinforcers.

Using a RAISD interview and a paired-choice assessment to identify preferred stimuli, and in-chair/in-square responding in the reinforcer evaluation, Piazza, Fisher, Hagopian, Bowman, and Toole (1996) showed that relative rankings of high, medium, and low-preference stimuli predicted reinforcer efficacy. That is, stimuli showing the highest preference consistently functioned as reinforcers (compared to medium- and low-preference stimuli), medium-preferred stimuli sometimes functioned as reinforcers, and low-preference stimuli rarely did. Nevertheless, other work has shown that highly preferred stimuli may be ineffective in reducing high-rate problem behaviors, thus indicating that the identification of reinforcers for simple behaviors such as those mentioned above may not adequately predict reinforcer effectiveness for other behaviors (Piazza, Fisher, Hanley et al., 1996).

Alternative Procedures for Identifying Reinforcer Effects

Reinforcer surveys evaluate different qualities of stimulus consequences to determine reinforcement value. However, the "interlocked" nature of the contingencies of reinforcement indicate that the effect of a stimulus consequence on a given response is not only *related* to the other contingencies, but the effects of one contingency can constrain or facilitate the effect of another. That is, a given behavioral consequence can be more or less effective by the action of the other contingencies. Michael (1993b) called the antecedent conditions to a given response that are responsible for momentary changes in the effectiveness of that stimulus consequence an *establishing operation*[2], and considered the effect of the establishing operation so important he identified it as the "fourth" term in the three-term contingency of operant relations. Applied research explicitly identified as addressing establishing operations will be reviewed in the rest of this chapter, as well as important work identifying the effectiveness of stimuli within choice methodologies. In addition, applied work will be mentioned characterizing response changes in relation to different reinforcement schedules and response rates.

Establishing Operations

One antecedent condition that obviously affects the momentary effectiveness of a reinforcer is the continuum of deprivation and satiation of a stimulus. In animal research, the use of ongoing schedules of food and water consumption are commonly used techniques for maintaining the effectiveness of stimuli used as reinforcers. Naturally occurring events are rarely, if ever, disrupted in applied research.

However, it has recently been demonstrated that reinforcers are more and less effective at different moments during a routine day. Vollmer and Iwata (1991) demonstrated the differential effectiveness of food, music, and attention during periods of satiation and deprivation. This study suggests that the judicious scheduling of training sessions, or events just prior to training sessions may be important procedures (i.e., establishing operations) for increasing the effectiveness of the stimuli used as reinforcers. Another study has shown that unequal durations of consequences provided during functional analyses made attention, which was a functionally relevant stimulus for disruptive behavior, more effective (Fisher, Piazza, & Chiang, 1996).

Smith, Iwata, Goh, and Shore (1995) showed how individuals exhibiting escape-maintained self-injury emitted more behavior when (a) new tasks were presented (novelty) compared to the same task (for two participants), (b) sessions lasted longer relative to shorter sessions (for five participants), and (c) more instructions were presented during sessions (for two participants). The authors suggested that identifying the functional properties of behavior problems (e.g., escape) can lead to selection of an antecedent procedure, or a combination of procedures (e.g., decreasing novelty and shortening sessions), based on those functions which can, not only treat the problem, but contribute to our knowledge of behavior processes.

Using Choice Procedures to Assess Basic Processes

Recently, a proliferation in the use of the choice procedures as assessment tools has resulted in many extensions of the work identifying individual reinforcement sensitivities for several variables including reinforcer quality, reinforcer delay, schedule of reinforcement, and response effort (Horner & Day, 1991; Mace & Roberts, 1993; Neef, Mace, & Shade, 1993). The choice situation in which each response alternative is made distinctive (Nevin & Mace, 1994) and responding is allocated to the available reinforcers (Fisher & Mazur, 1997) is considered to be most representative of responding that occurs in the natural environment (McDowell, 1988). Fisher and Mazur, who provide an extensive review of the basic and "bridge" research (i.e., basic research findings demonstrated in applied settings) toward the clinical use of choice methods, suggested that the commonly used procedure of differential reinforcement be conceptualized as a choice between concurrently available reinforcement. In such a paradigm, a participant can choose either an inappropriate (often dangerous or harmful) response or a more appropriate alternative, and the clinician has the opportunity to arrange contingencies that favor the alternative response.

Choice-Making Procedures to Increase Life Quality

Choice procedures have not only been useful in the assessment of stimulus preference, but the making of that choice is considered an important component in the quality of life for disabled people (Felce & Perry, 1995). Such applications make important advances, not only in helping improve reinforcer effectiveness, but also in clarifying what is meant by words such as "quality of life."

While an individual's choice between stimulus alternatives is presumed by some (Bannerman, Sheldon, Sherman, & Harchik, 1990) and assessed by others (e.g., Dyer, Dunlap, & Winterling, 1990) to have more value than when one's reinforcers are selected by another, other investigations do not always show an absolute value for choice (Kahng, Iwata, DeLeon, & Worsdell, 1997; Parsons, Reid, Reynolds, & Bumbarger, 1990). Lerman et al. (1997) found, for six people with severe disabilities, reinforcer choice did not improve their task performance when reinforcer items in the no-choice situation (yoked to the rate provided in the choice condition) were assessed as highly preferred. Fisher et al. (1997) investigated whether the effect of choice making occurred because choosing brought opportunities to choose more highly valued consequences or because choice-making itself had high value. To determine this, the authors taught three children with developmental disabilities to press three distinctive switches. The first two switches resulted in reinforcement and the third did not (extinction), controlling for automatically reinforced switch responding. In Experiment 1, after teaching participants to respond on variable-interval (VI) schedules, the authors compared the responding allocated to the three switches when the first switch was followed by a choice between highly preferred stimuli and the second switch was followed by no-choice of these same highly preferred stimuli yoked to the rate of reinforcement in the previous choice session. Participants always chose the switch associated with the choice of highly preferred stimulation. In Experiment 2, the consequences to switch activating were changed so that the first switch gave the participants a choice between two less preferred stimuli and the second switch provided various no-choice amounts of the more highly preferred stimuli. In this experiment participants responded more in the no-choice condition. That is, when stimuli available through the choice and no-choice options were equated (Experiment 1), participants preferred to select their reinforcers themselves, but when higher quality reinforcers were available through the no-choice option (Experiment 2), they preferred to have the therapist select their reinforcer for them.

Regardless of the absolute value of choice, choice may become an important component to valid treatment selection by determining an individual's preference for treatment alternatives. Hanley, Piazza, Fisher, Contrucci, and Maglieri (1997), using a concurrent-chain procedure with three switches, determined client preference (Phase 3) by rates of responding on the switches (the initial link of the chain). The first two switches each activated two minutes of different reductive treatments (the terminal links in the chain) and the third was a control (extinction). One reductive treatment was noncontingent attention (NCR), which was previously determined to maintain the participants' destructive behavior, and the other was a communicative response requesting that functionally relevant stimulus (attention), which had been previously taught in functional communication training (FCT) sessions. Again, the noncontingent stimulus was yoked to the rate of communication in the previous FCT session. Hanly et al. found their participants activated the switch producing the FCT consequences more than the NCR switch, even though NCR treatment was determined to be just as effective in reducing the destructive behavior (Phase 2). Interestingly, even though the FCT procedure might have been considered to be more effortful for the two participants, both eventually preferred the treatment when they requested the stimulus (FCT) rather than receiving it noncontingently. Peck et al. (1996) also used FCT within a choice paradigm to demonstrate client preference for treatments. In this study, toddlers reliably chose higher quality, longer duration rewards of stimulus consequences functionally related to their problem behavior regardless of the treatment. Functional stimuli included attention for three participants and escape for two others. The choice situation was set up between the communicative response and a neutral response because the problem responses were life threatening (e.g, pulling out gastric tubes).

Reinforcer-Reinforcer Relations

A relatively new area of applied behavior-analytic study involves a topic referred to as "behavioral economics" (see Green & Kagel, 1987; 1990; 1996), in which the effect of a reinforcer is conceptualized as an event in which responding is "ex-changed" for reinforcers (Tustin, 1994). In typical behavior-economic research, relations between two concurrently available reinforcers are inferred from changes in the rate of reinforcement with one response requirement (i.e., price) when the response requirement of the alternative reinforcer remains the same. One reinforcer is said to "substitute" for the other if the unchanged reinforcer's rate decreases when the new reinforcer is introduced. The newly introduced reinforcer is said to "complement" the other if the unchanged reinforcer rate increases (or changes with) that of the newly introduced stimulus (Green & Freed, 1993; Iwata & Michael, 1994).

Tustin (1994), using the button on a joystick as the response, measured choice for two concurrently available sensory stimuli on a changing schedule of response requirements or pay rates (fixed-ratio 1, 2, 5, 10, & 20). Across the various schedule requirements, Tustin found one individual (Participant 2) for which a stimulus was preferred over (i.e., substituted for) another at low requirements but showed a reverse preference at higher requirements. DeLeon, Iwata, Goh, and Worsdell (1997) found similar preference switches at high and low schedule requirements with similar (but not dissimilar) concurrently available stimuli. This led the authors to suggest that, in order to identify effective reinforcers for some individuals it may be necessary to conduct preference assessments with response requirements similar to those being utilized in training protocols.

Tustin's (1994) third participant illustrated a preference for constant stimuli over complex stimuli with higher response requirements. Several past studies have indicated that people with developmental disabilities (e.g., autism) preferred varied stimulation to constant stimulation (Egel, 1980; 1981). However, Bowman, Piazza, Fisher, Hagopian, and Kogan (1997) found that when seven children with develop-mental disabilities were given the choice between a constant stimulus assessed to be the most highly preferred on a preference assessment or a varied one of three stimuli of "slightly lower" quality from that preference assessment, 3 out of 7 participants responded more to the constant stimulus alternative in the reinforcer evaluation.

The natural clinical extension of a choice between reinforcing alternatives would be to reduce a problematic behavior by identifying a reinforcing alternative that substituted for the maintaining reinforcer. There are frequent examples in the literature showing competition with problem behaviors by introducing alternative stimulation (e.g., Davenport & Berkson, 1963; Favell, McGimsey, & Schell, 1982), particularly when that stimulation has been assessed as functioning to maintain the problem behavior (Ringdahl, Vollmer, Marcus, & Roane, 1997). This suggests one functional definition of "environmental enrichment" as the provision of a stimulus assessed as highly preferred, and an important category of stimuli to review would be those stimuli that function to maintain high-rate (often inappropriate) behavior (see Berg & Wacker, 1991).

Using the conceptualization of reinforcer substitution, Shore, Iwata, DeLeon, Kahng, and Smith (1997) showed stimulus objects that decreased stereotypic self-injurious behavior (assessed to be controlled by automatic reinforcement) when continuously and concurrently available with the self-injury. However, reductions in self-injury did not occur when those same stimuli were presented in a differential reinforcement of zero rates procedure. In addition, the authors showed that when the effort to obtain the object was changed by tying the object to a string and requiring a movement forward to manipulate or mouth the object, even slight changes caused the preference for the object for all three participants to switch to self injury.

A final topic regarding reinforcer-reinforcer relations is the phenomenon of conjugate reinforcement schedules (for a review see Rovee-Collier & Gekoski, 1979). Conjugate reinforcement schedules increase or decrease the quality/intensity of a consequence as a function of increased or decreased responding. This requires a consequence which can be gradated such as vibration (Nunes, Murphy, & Doughty, 1980), movies or television (Greene & Hoates, 1969; Switzky, & Haywood, 1973), or sound (Lovitt, 1968a; 1968b), and an easily repeated response such as a switch pulling (Nunes et al.), switch pressing (Lindsley, 1956), or motion (Switzky & Haywood). The conjugate schedule is ideal for showing not only preference quality, but the preferred intensity of that reinforcement as well.

Response-Response Relations

One commonly used reinforcer assessment increases a response by making a higher probability response contingent upon a lower probability response (Premack, 1959; 1965). Charlop, Kurtz, and Casey (1990) used higher probability inappropriate motor and vocal stereotypic behaviors as contingent responses for task performance to increase these appropriate behaviors above that obtained with food and other reinforcers, with no negative side effects (e.g., increases in aberrant behavior).

Timberlake and Farmer-Dougan (1991) suggested a much more complex arrangement of using one behavior to reinforce another behavior known as "disequilibrium." Specifically, after determining the free-operant rates of any two behaviors (e.g., coloring and math work), the disequilibrium inequality describes how one of those behaviors can be used to increase the other (i.e., act as reinforcement) if the ratio between the instrumental response (the response being increased, labeled *I*) and the contingent response (the response made contingent upon the instrumental response, labeled *C*) is *greater* in the contingency than the ratio is in their free-operant baseline rates (the baseline rates of the instrumental response and the contingent responses, labeled *i* and *c*, respectively). That is, the instrumental response will increase if the ratio between the instrumental and contingent response in the arranged contingency is relatively greater than the free-operant ratio (I/C>i/c). This procedure has also been referred to as "response deprivation" (e.g., Konarski, Johnson, Crowell, & Whitman, 1980). Similarly, there should be a decrease in the instrumental response if the ratio between the instrumental response and the contingent response is relatively *less* than the free-operant ratio (I/C< i/c). This procedure has also been referred to as "response satiation" (e.g., Realon & Konarski, 1993). In examining the advantages and disadvantages of the disequilibrium approach to reinforcement, Timberlake and Farmer-Dougan suggested that although this inequality equation leads to a more complex explanation of reinforcer effects, development of this approach could lead to a more accurate explanation for some current circumstances of reinforcement, increased predictability of reinforcer effects, and increased flexibility in the practice of behavior control in applied setting (for applied implications see Iwata & Michael, 1994).

Directions for Future Research

There is clearly room for more research in determining preference via hard and software technology. For example, the development of mechanical devices allowing less effortful motor responses (e.g., Dewson & Whiteley, 1987) or overt physiological responses such as heart rate (e.g., Jones, Hux, Morton-Anderson, & Knepper, 1994) may reveal preferences of people with minimal response repertoires for whom no successful preference assessments have been previously possible. In addition, the use of computer programming to arrange reinforcement schedules (e.g, Fisher, Thompson et al., 1997), conjugate schedule requirements (e.g., Nunes et al. 1980), and response-schedule predictions (i.e., disequilibrium theory) should allow these technologies to be available to more individuals.

As work identifying behavior-change conditions to alleviate problems of individuals who show extreme deficits and excesses develops, it is reasonable to believe other uses of reinforcer assessment for people without disabilities may increase. There appears to be room for improvement in motivational variables used in the technology of education (Geller, 1992), including the use of programmed instruction (Keller, 1968; Skinner, 1968). Very little work has been conducted showing how reinforcers are conditioned (e.g., Watson, Orser, & Sanders, 1968). In particular, the conditioned effect of social reinforcement (Fisher, Ninness, Piazza, & Owen-DeSchryver, 1996; Harzem & Damon, 1976) is a conspicuously under-researched variable of behavior change given the pervasiveness of its use and the ease with which it can be delivered.

Finally, the choice study described in this chapter in which participants selected their own reductive procedures (e.g., Hanley et al., 1997) stands to be a very important technique for the future of reinforcer identification technology. What better justification for an effective treatment could there be than a treatment chosen by its recipient?

Notes

[1] See Hagen (1997) for a discussion of the problems associated with attempting to prove the null hypothesis.

[2] This is a tremendous simplification of the effect of an establishing operation. Michael (1993b) carefully points out the immediate (evocative) and delayed (function altering) effects of establishing operations. In addition, he points out 23 multiple behavioral effects that can occur from environmental events and be characterized along three dichotomous categories of behavioral principles including (a) respondent vs. operant, (b) evocative vs. function-altering, and (c) learned vs. unlearned (Michael, 1995). Michael (1995) makes a compelling case for considering these 23 behavioral effects information with which every student of behavior analysis should be familiar.

Reading Objectives

1. Describe the presentation method attributed to the absolute and relative preference assessment results?
2. What is provided by the reinforcer evaluation that the preference assessment alone does not provide?
3. What three specific situations make the use of the single-presentation method most appropriate for a given participant?
4. Generating "happiness" indices is not an operant reinforcement procedure because the stimulus comes *before* the response. What behavior process does this most likely represent?
5. What are at least two advantages in conceptualizing reinforcement effects in terms of their behavioral function?
6. What makes choice procedures naturally relevant?
7. What condition for each response alternative helps to insure a sensitive demonstration of preference?
8. What specific significance is the term "establishing operation" given in the conceptualization of behavioral effects?
9. The disequilibrium inequality is frequently mischaracterized as the absolute rate of a high probability behavior reinforcing the absolute rate of a low probability behavior, but the contingency is one of relative rates. What is the contingent condition in which a high probability response would *not* reinforce a lower probability response?
10. What word best describes the interrelation between the contingencies of reinforcement? What does it suggest?

I thank Duke Schell and Ed Konarski for their helpful comments on parts of the chapter.

References

Baer, D. M. (1981). A hung jury and a Scottish decision: "Not proven." *Analysis and Intervention in Developmental Disabilities, 1*, 91-97.

Baer, D. M., Wolf, M. M., & Risley, T. R. (1968). Some current dimensions of applied behavior analysis. *Journal of Applied Behavior Analysis, 1*, 91-97.

Baer, D. M., Wolf, M. M., & Risley, T. R. (1987). Some still-current dimensions of applied behavior analysis. *Journal of Applied Behavior Analysis, 20*, 313-327.

Bailey, J. S., & Meyerson, L. (1969). Vibration as a reinforcer with a profoundly retarded child. *Journal of Applied Behavior Analysis, 2*, 135-137.

Bannerman, D. J., Sheldon, J. B., Sherman, J. A., & Harchik, A. E. (1990). Balancing the right to habilitation with the right to personal liberties: The rights of people with developmental disabilities to eat too many doughnuts and take a nap. *Journal of Applied Behavior Analysis, 23*, 79-89.

Berg, W. K., & Wacker, D. P. (1991). The assessment and evaluation of reinforcers for individuals with severe mental handicap. In B. Remington (Ed.), *The challenge of severe mental handicap: A behavior analytic approach* (pp. 25-45). Chichester, England: John Wiley & Son.

Bijou, S. W., & Sturges, P. T. (1959). Positive reinforcers for experimental studies with children – consumables and manipulatables. *Child Development, 30*, 151-170.

Bowman, L. G., Fisher, W. W., Piazza, C. C., Hagopian, L. P., Kuhn, D. E., & Kurtz, P. F. (1997, May). *Choice paradigms for identifying reinforcers and assessing their relative reinforcement value.* Paper presented at the annual meeting of the Association for Behavior Analysis, Chicago, IL.

Bowman, L. G., Piazza, C. C., Fisher, W. W., Hagopian, L. P., & Kogan, J. S. (1997). Assessment for preference for varied versus constant reinforcers. *Journal of Applied Behavior Analysis, 30*, 451-458.

Cantor, G. N., & Hottel, J. V. (1955). Discrimination learning in mental defectives as a function of the magnitude of food reward and intelligence level. *American Journal of Mental Deficiency, 60*, 380-384.

Charlop, M. H., Kurtz, P. F., & Casey, F. G. (1990). Using aberrant behaviors as reinforcers for autistic children. *Journal of Applied Behavior Analysis, 23*, 163-181.

Davenport, R. K., & Berkson, G. (1963). Stereotyped movements in mental defectives. *American Journal of Mental Deficiency, 67*, 879-882.

DeLeon, I. G., & Iwata, B. A. (1996). Evaluation of a multiple-stimulus presentation format for assessing reinforcer preferences. *Journal of Applied Behavior Analysis, 29*, 519-533.

DeLeon, I. G., Iwata, B. A., Goh, H., & Worsdell, A. S. (1997). Emergence of reinforcer preference as a function of schedule requirements and stimulus similarity. *Journal of Applied Behavior Analysis, 30*, 439-449.

DeLeon, I. G., Iwata, B. A., & Roscoe, E. M. (1997). Displacement of leisure reinforcers by food during preference assessments. *Journal of Applied Behavior Analysis, 30*, 475-484.

Dewson, M. R. J., & Whiteley, J. H. (1987). Sensory reinforcement of head-turning with nonambulatory, profoundly mentally retarded persons. *Research in Developmental Disabilities, 8*, 413-426.

Dyer, K., Dunlap, G., & Winterling, V. (1990). Effects of choice making on the serious behaviors of students with severe handicaps. *Journal of Applied Behavior Analysis, 23*, 515-524.

Egel, A. L. (1981). Reinforcer variation: Implications for motivating developmentally disabled children. *Journal of Applied Behavior Analysis, 14*, 345-350.

Egel, A. L. (1980). The effects of constant vs. varied reinforcer presentation on responding by autistic children. *Journal of Experimental Child Psychology, 30*, 455-463.

Felce, D., & Perry, J. (1995). Quality of life: Its definition and measurement. *Research in Developmental Disabilities, 16*, 51-74.

Ferster, C. B., & DeMeyer, M. K. (1962). A method for the experimental analysis of the behavior of autistic children. *American Journal of Orthopsychiatry, 32*, 89-98.

Favell, J. E., & Cannon, P. R. (1976). Evaluation of entertainment materials for severely retarded persons. *American Journal of Mental Deficiency, 81*, 357-361.

Favell, J. E., McGimsey, J., Jones, M. L., & Cannon, P. R. (1981). Physical restraint as positive reinforcement. *American Journal of Mental Deficiency, 85*, 425-432.

Favell, J. E., McGimsey, J., & Schell, R. (1982). Treatment of self-injury by providing alternative sensory activities. *Analysis and Intervention in Developmental Disabilities, 2*, 83-104.

Fisher, W. W., & Mazur, J. E. (1997). Basic and applied research on choice responding. *Journal of Applied Behavior Analysis, 30*, 387-410.

Fisher, W. W., Ninness, H. A. C., Piazza, C. C., & Owen-DeSchryver, J. S. (1996). On the reinforcing effects of the content of social attention. *Journal of Applied Behavior Analysis, 29*, 235-238.

Fisher, W. W., Piazza, C. C., Bowman, L. G., & Amari, A. (1996). Integrating caregiver report with a systematic choice assessment to enhance reinforcer identification. *American Journal on Mental Retardation, 101*, 15-25.

Fisher, W., Piazza, C. C., Bowman, L. G., Hagopian, L. P., Owens, J. C., & Slevin, I. (1992). A comparison of two approaches for identifying reinforcers for persons with severe and profound disabilities. *Journal of Applied Behavior Analysis, 25*, 491-498.

Fisher, W. W., Piazza, C. C., Bowman, L. G., Kurtz, P. F., Sherer, M. R., & Lachman, S. R. (1994). A preliminary evaluation of empirically derived consequences for the treatment of pica. *Journal of Applied Behavior Analysis, 27*, 447-457.

Fisher, W. W., Piazza, C. C., & Chiang, C. L. (1996). Effects of equal and unequal reinforcer duration during functional analysis. *Journal of Applied Behavior Analysis, 29*, 117-120.

Fisher, W. W., Thompson, R. H., Piazza, C. C., Crosland, K., & Gotjen, D. (1997). On the relative reinforcing effects of choice and differential consequences. *Journal of Applied Behavior Analysis, 30*, 423-438.

Foxx, R. M., & Dufrense, D. (1984). "Harry": The use of physical restraint as a reinforcer, timeout from restraint, and fading restraint in treating a self-injurious man. *Analysis and Intervention in Developmental Disabilities, 4*, 1-13.

Geller, E. S. (Ed.). (1992). The educational crisis: Issues, perspectives, solutions [Monograph 7]. *Journal of Applied Behavior Analysis, 25*, 13-97.

Giacino, J. T., & Zasler, N. D. (1995). Outcome following severe brain injury: The comatose, vegetative, and minimally responsive patient. *Journal of Head Trauma Rehabilitation, 10*, 40-56.

Green, C. W., & Reid, D. H. (1996). Defining, validating, and increasing happiness indices among people with profound multiple disabilities. *Journal of Applied Behavior Analysis, 29*, 67-78.

Green, C. W., Reid, D. H., Canipe, V. S., & Gardner, S. M. (1991). A comprehensive evaluation of reinforcer identification processes for persons with profound multiple handicaps. *Journal of Applied Behavior Analysis, 24*, 537-552.

Green, C. W., Reid, D. H., White, L. K., Halford, R. C., Brittain, D. P., & Gardner, S. M. (1988). Identifying reinforcers for persons with profound handicaps: Staff opinion versus systematic assessment of preferences. *Journal of Applied Behavior Analysis, 21*, 31-43.

Green, L., & Freed, D. E. (1993). The substitutability of reinforcers. *Journal of the Experimental Analysis of Behavior, 60*, 141-158.

Green, L., & Kagel, J. H. (1987). *Advances in behavioral economics* (Vol. 1). Norwood, NJ: Ablex.

Green, L., & Kagel, J. H. (1990). *Advances in behavioral economics* (Vol. 2). Norwood, NJ: Ablex.

Green, L., & Kagel, J. H. (1996). *Advances in behavioral economics* (Vol. 3). Norwood, NJ: Ablex.

Greene, R. J., & Hoats, D. L. (1969). Reinforcing capabilities of television distortion. *Journal of Applied Behavior Analysis, 2*, 139-141.

Hagen, R. L. (1997). In praise of the Null Hypothesis Statistical Test. *American Psychologist, 52*, 15-24.

Hanley, G. P., Piazza, C. C., Fisher, W. W., Contrucci, S. A., & Maglieri, K. A. (1997). Evaluation of client preference for function-based treatment packages. *Journal of Applied Behavior Analysis, 30*, 459-473.

Harzem, P., & Damon, S. G. (1976). Comparative study of reinforcing stimuli: Imitative responses and general behavior of two retarded adults. *Psychological Reports, 39*, 503-513.

Horner, R. H., & Day, H. M. (1991). The effects of response efficiency on functionally equivalent competing behaviors. *Journal of Applied Behavior Analysis, 24*, 719-732.

Ivancic, M. T., & Bailey, J. S. (1996). Current limits to reinforcer identification for some persons with profound multiple disabilities. *Research in Developmental Disabilities, 17*, 77-92.

Ivancic, M. T., Barrett, G. T., Simonow, A., & Kimberly, A. (1997). A replication to increase happiness indices among some people with profound multiple disabilities. *Research in Developmental Disabilities, 18*, 79-89.

Iwata, B. A., & Michael, J. L. (1994). Applied implications of theory and research on the nature of reinforcement. *Journal of Applied Behavior Analysis, 27*, 183-193.

Jones, R., Hux, M. S., Morton-Anderson, A., & Knepper, L. (1994). Auditory stimulation effects on a comatose survivor of traumatic brain injury. *Archives of Physical Medicine and Rehabilitation, 75*, 164-171.

Kahng, S., Iwata, B. A., DeLeon, I. G., & Worsdell, A. S. (1997). Evaluation of the "control over reinforcement" component in functional communication training. *Journal of Applied Behavior Analysis, 30*, 267-277.

Keller, F. S. (1968). "Good-bye teacher..." *Journal of Applied Behavior Analysis, 1*, 79-89.

Kish, G. B. (1966). Studies of sensory reinforcement. In W. K. Honig (Ed.), *Operant behavior: Areas of research and application* (109-159). Englewood Cliffs, NJ: Prentice-Hall.

Konarksi, E. A., Johnson, M. R., Crowell, C. R., & Whitman, T. L. (1980). Response deprivation and reinforcement in applied settings: A preliminary analysis. *Journal of Applied Behavior Analysis, 13*, 595-609.

Lerman, D. C., Iwata, B. A., Rainville, B., Adelinis, J. D., Crosland, K., & Kogan, J. (1997). Effects of reinforcement on task responding in individuals with developmental disabilities. *Journal of Applied Behavior Analysis, 30*, 411-422.

Lindsley, O. R. (1956). Operant conditioning methods to research in chronic schizophrenia. *Psychiatric Research Reports, 5*, 118-139.

Lovitt, T. C. (1968a). Operant preferences of retarded and normal males for rates of narration. *Psychological Record, 18*, 205-214.

Lovitt, T. C. (1968b). Free-operant assessment of musical preference. *Journal of Experimental Child Psychology, 6*, 361-367.

Mace, F. C., & Roberts, M. L. (1993). Factors affecting selection of behavioral interventions. In J. Reiche & D. Wacker (Eds.), *Communicative alternatives to challenging behavior: Integrating functional assessment and intervention strategies* (pp.113-133). Baltimore: Paul H. Brookes.

Mason, S. A., McGee, G. G., Farmer-Dougan, V., & Risley, T. R. (1989). A practical strategy for ongoing reinforcer assessment. *Journal of Applied Behavior Analysis, 22*, 171-179.

McDowell, J. J. (1988). Matching theory in natural human environments. *The Behavior Analyst, 11*, 95-109.

Meehl, P. E. (1950). On the circularity of the Law of Effect. *Psychological Bulletin, 45*, 52-75.

Michael, J. (1993a). *Concepts and principles of behavior analysis.* Kalamazoo, MI: Society for the Advancement of Behavior Analysis.

Michael, J. (1993b). Establishing operations. *The Behavior Analyst, 16*, 191-206.

Michael, J. (1995). What every student of behavior analysis ought to learn: A system for classifying multiple effects of behavioral variables. *The Behavior Analyst, 18*, 273-284.

Murphy, R. J., & Doughty, N. R. (1977). Establishment of controlled arm movements in profoundly retarded students using contingent vibratory stimulation. *American Journal of Mental Deficiency, 82*, 212-216.

Neef, N. A., Mace, F. C., & Shade, D. (1993). Impulsivity in students with serious emotional disturbance: The interactive effects of reinforcer rate, delay, and quality. *Journal of Applied Behavior Analysis, 26*, 37-52.

Nevin, J. A., & Mace, F. C. (1994). The ABC's of *JEAB*, September, 1993. *Journal of Applied Behavior Analysis, 27*, 561-565.

Nunes, D. L., Murphy, R. J., & Doughty, N. R. (1980). An interlocking progressive-ratio procedure for determining the reinforcer preferences of multihandicapped children. *Behavior Research of Severe Developmental Disabilities, 1*, 161-174.

Ohwaki, S., Brahlek, J. A., & Stayton, S. E. (1973). Preference for vibratory and visual stimuli in mentally retarded children. *American Journal of Mental Deficiency, 77*, 733-736.

Pace, G. M., Ivancic, M. T., Edwards, G. L., Iwata, B. A., & Page, T. J. (1985). Assessment of stimulus preference and reinforcer value with profoundly retarded individuals. *Journal of Applied Behavior Analysis, 18*, 249-255.

Paclawskyj, T. R., & Vollmer, T. R. (1995). Reinforcer assessment for children with developmental disabilities and visual impairments. *Journal of Applied Behavior Analysis, 28*, 219-224.

Parsons, M. B., Reid, D. M., Reynolds, J., & Bumbarger, M. (1990). Effects of chosen versus assigned jobs on the work performance of persons with severe handicaps. *Journal of Applied Behavior Analysis, 23*, 253-258.

Peck, S. M., Wacker, D. P., Berg, W. K., Cooper, L. J., Brown, K. A., Richman, D., McComas, J. J., Frischmeyer, P., & Millard, T. (1996). Choice-making treatment of young children's severe behavior problems. *Journal of Applied Behavior Analysis, 29*, 263-290.

Piazza, C. C., Fisher, W. W., Hagopian, L. P., Bowman, L. G., & Toole, L. (1996). Using choice assessment to predict reinforcer effectiveness. *Journal of Applied Behavior Analysis, 29*, 1-9.

Piazza, C. C., Fisher, W. W., Hanley, G. P., Hilker, K., & Derby, K. M. (1996). A preliminary procedure for predicting the positive and negative effects of reinforcement-based procedures. *Journal of Applied Behavior Analysis, 29*, 137-152.

Premack, D. (1959). Toward empirical behavioral laws: Instrumental positive reinforcement. *Psychological Review, 66*, 219-233.

Premack, D. (1965). Reinforcement theory. In D. Levine (Ed.), *Nebraska Symposium on Motivation* (pp. 123-180). Lincoln, NE: University of Nebraska Press.

Realon, R. E., & Konarski, E. A. (1993). Using decelerative contingencies to reduce the self-injurious behavior of people with multiple handicaps: The effects of Response satiation? *Research in Developmental Disabilities, 14*, 341-357.

Rehagen, N. J., & Thelen, M. K. (1972). Vibration as positive reinforcement for retarded children. *Journal of Abnormal Psychology, 80*, 162-167.

Reisman, J. E., & Hanschu, B. (1992). *Sensory Integration Inventory - Revised*. Hugo, MN: PDP Press.

Remington, R. E., Foxen, T., & Hogg, J. (1977). Auditory reinforcement in profoundly retarded multiply handicapped children. *American Journal on Mental Deficiency, 82*, 299-304.

Rincover, A., & Newsom, C. D. (1985). The relative motivational properties of sensory and edible reinforcers in teaching autistic children. *Journal of Applied Behavior Analysis, 18*, 237-248.

Ringdahl, J. E., Vollmer, T. R., Marcus, B. A., & Roane, H. S. (1997). An analogue evaluation of environmental enrichment: The role of stimulus preference. *Journal of Applied Behavior Analysis, 30*, 203-216.

Rovee-Collier, C. K., & Gekoski, M. J. (1979). The economics of infancy: A review of conjugate reinforcement. *Advances in Child Development and Behavior, 13*, 195-255.

Rynders, J. E., & Friedlander, B. Z. (1972). Preferences in institutionalized severely retarded children for selected visual stimulus material presented as operant reinforcement. *American Journal on Mental Deficiency, 76*, 568-573.

Sellick, K. J., & Over, R. (1980). Effects of vestibular stimulation on motor development of cerebral-palsied children. *Developmental Medicine and Child Neurology, 22*, 476-483.

Shore, B. A., Iwata, B. A., DeLeon, I. G., Kahng, S., & Smith, R. G. (1997). An analysis of reinforcer substitutability using object manipulation and self-injury as competing responses. *Journal of Applied Behavior Analysis, 30*, 21-41.

Skinner, B. F. (1953). *Science and human behavior*. New York: The Macmillan Company.

Skinner, B. F. (1966). Operant behavior. In W. K. Honig (Ed.), *Operant behavior: Areas of research and application* (pp. 12-32). New York: Appleton-Century-Crofts.

Skinner, B. F. (1968). *The technology of teaching*. New York: Meredith Corporation.

Skinner, B. F. (1969). *Contingencies of reinforcement: A theoretical analysis*. New York: Appleton-Century-Crofts.

Smith, R. G., Iwata, B. A., Goh, H., & Shore, B. A. (1995). Analysis of establishing operations for self-injury maintained by escape. *Journal of Applied Behavior Analysis, 28*, 515-535.

Stevenson, H. W., & Knights, R. M. (1961). Effect of visual reinforcement on the performance of normal and retarded children. *Perceptual and Motor Skills, 13*, 119-126.

Switzky, H. N., & Haywood, C. (1973). Conjugate control of motor activity in mentally retarded persons. *American Journal of Mental Deficiency, 77*, 567-570.

Timberlake, W., & Farmer-Dougan, V. A. (1991). Reinforcement in applied settings: Figuring out ahead of time what will work. *Psychological Bulletin, 110,* 379-391.

Tustin, R. D. (1994). Preference for reinforcers under varying schedule arrangements: A behavioral economic analysis. *Journal of Applied Behavior Analysis, 27,* 597-606.

Vollmer, T. R., & Iwata, B. A. (1991). Establishing operations and reinforcement effects. *Journal of Applied Behavior Analysis, 24,* 279-291

Watson, L. S., Orser, R., & Sanders, C. (1968). Reinforcement preferences of severely mentally retarded children in a generalized reinforcement context. *American Journal of Mental Deficiency, 72,* 748-756.

Windsor, J., Piche, L. M., & Locke, P. A. (1994). Preference testing: A comparison of two presentation methods. *Research in Developmental Disabilities, 15,* 439-455.

Witryol, S. L., & Fischer, W. F. (1960). Scaling children's incentives by the method of paired comparisons. *Psychological Reports, 7,* 471-474.

Chapter 2

Behavioral Acquisition by Persons With Developmental Disabilities

Anthony J. Cuvo and Paula K. Davis
Southern Illinois University

The application of behavioral principles to promote the acquisition of behavior by persons with mental retardation and other developmental disabilities dates back half a century. Some of the landmark studies capture the target behaviors, behavioral principles and procedures, and research methods that were of interest to the pioneers of applied behavior analysis. In one of the earliest studies, the "operant conditioning of a vegetative human organism" was investigated (Fuller, 1949, p. 587). The acquisition and extinction of arm raising by an 18-year-old male with profound mental retardation was studied. Other target behaviors for acquisition in those early studies included visual discrimination and differentiation (Barrett & Lindsley, 1962), academic behavior (Birnbrauer, Bijou, Wolf, & Kidder, 1965), vocalizations in a mute child (Kerr, Meyerson, & Michael, 1965), and verbal behavior (Salzinger, Feldman, Cowan, & Salzinger, 1965).

During the past quarter century, the research literature demonstrating effective applications of behavioral principles to the instruction of persons with mental retardation has grown exponentially, such that strategies derived from applied behavior analysis represent the dominant approach in special education and adult habilitation. The recent issue of *Behavior Analysis in Developmental Disabilities* (Iwata et al., 1997) presents a selected collection of reprints from *Journal of Applied Behavior Analysis* of "classic" and "cutting edge" articles, according to its editors. Among the topics related to behavioral acquisition included in the volume are self-care and daily living skills, language acquisition and communication, leisure and recreation, academic performance, vocational skills, community preparation, as well as health, safety, and bio-behavioral applications. These topics represent the major domains of behavior acquisition for persons with mental retardation during the past several decades.

Shifts in the philosophy of habilitation (e.g., normalization, inclusion, self-determination), bolstered by supportive legislation (e.g., Individuals with Disabilities Education Act, 1990) and litigation (*Halderman v. Pennhurst*, 1977) during the past 40 years, have resulted in the movement of persons with mental retardation from life-long institutionalization in public residential facilities to life in the community where they live, go to school, go to work, and take part in other activities that the community has to offer (e.g., eating in restaurants, taking public transportation, engaging in recreational activities). Although the evolving philosophy and law enabled people with mental retardation and other developmental disabilities to find new lives in community alternatives to institutions, it has been behavior analysis that has provided the necessary scientific framework for a technology of instruction that helps people with disabilities function effectively in the community.

Although the literature on behavior acquisition for persons with mental retardation is vast, there are common elements that can be illustrated in an instructional model used by Cuvo and his associates in a program of research that originated in 1973. The model was developed in the context of behavior analysis of community living skills (Cuvo & Davis, 1983); however, it has general relevance to acquisition by persons with mental retardation. That model will be summarized because it presents the major components that must be considered by behavior analysts and others interested in acquisition. The key components of the model relevant to acquisition of all target behaviors are those pertaining to stimulus control and its transfer. [For a more complete description of the model, see Cuvo and Davis (1983). Cuvo and Davis (1998) provides a detailed description of stimulus control procedures and a discussion of problems in the transfer of stimulus control.]

A Model for the Acquisition of Functional Community Living Skills
Preliminary Steps to Behavioral Program Development
Assess the Learner's Environment of Community Functioning

An approach that guides assessment and training of community referenced skills is based on the demands of adult life in the community. An initial step is to conduct an "ecological inventory," a systematic method of identifying and cataloging skills needed by people to function in a socially integrated fashion in their community (Brown et al., 1979). Strategies for assessing the demands for living in the community include performing direct observations in the community settings where learners will live and work, as well as conducting interviews with individuals who play a significant role in the lives of persons with disabilities.

Assess the Learner's Community Living Skills

After the ecological inventory has been completed, learners should be assessed to determine which living skills are and are not in their behavioral repertoires. The assessment could be either a broad-based general assessment of many skills or a focused evaluation of certain high priority skills essential for providing key reinforcers.

Select Instructional Goals and Objectives

The results of the community-based assessment are likely to reveal that learners lack a number of skills necessary to function independently in the community. The ones that increase learners' options and independence from service providers should have the highest priority as instructional goals (Brown & Snell, 1993). Other variables to consider when selecting instructional goals and objectives include whether or not the skill would be: (a) used frequently, (b) used across different stimulus conditions, (c) maintained by natural environmental conditions, and (d) appropriate for the learner's non-disabled peers.

Consider Legal and Ethical Issues

Prior to implementing a behavior analysis program, legal and ethical issues must be considered. In addition to adhering to the requirements of all pertinent statutes, litigation, and administrative policies, a behavior analyst must determine whether there are special risks involved in teaching community living skills (e.g., pedestrian and public transportation skill training involves safety considerations).

Task Specification and Analysis

When specifying tasks to be trained, behavior analysts must consider natural stimulus and response variations associated with community settings, as well as the requirements to live adaptively in those settings when defining instructional objectives. Will learners have a functional community living skill if they respond to a limited stimulus class or must they be able to respond to a broader stimulus class? Will a single response be appropriate or should a larger response class be taught?

After the task has been specified, it is a common practice to develop a task analysis for behavioral chains. Task analyses have two primary uses (Moyer & Dardig, 1978). First, the written sequence of steps could serve as an assessment instrument (e.g., a checklist with each step scored to indicate correct or incorrect independent performance). A second use is to specify responses and their sequence to be trained. Task analyses, therefore, serve both an evaluation and training function.

The steps of a task analysis should reflect the requirements of the pertinent instructional objective. The conditions, behavior, and criterion statements that comprise the instructional objective should be incorporated in the task analyses, as appropriate. The test of the adequacy of how well a task analysis has been written comes in its use with learners. Revising a task analysis tends to be idiosyncratic to individual learners and their specific errors.

Task Sequencing

After one or more tasks have been specified and analyzed, the next instructional design questions are how to teach responses within tasks, and how to sequence multiple tasks for training.

Teaching a Single Response Chain

Whole task instruction. A review of published research on community living skills training shows that the majority of experiments have employed the whole or total task sequence to teach the links or responses within chains. Learners are instructed through all steps of the entire task analysis each session in a forward sequence until the terminal behavior has been performed.

Chaining. Instead of allowing a learner to move through the whole task without mastering one or more links in the chain each session, a chaining procedure would require training only one response to criterion at a time. In forward chaining, training is delivered only for the first step and continues until the learner reaches criterion on that step. Subsequently, the learner performs the first step and receives training on the second step until reaching criterion. Training continues in this cumulative fashion until all steps have been mastered. Backward chaining follows the same general strategy as forward chaining except that the order proceeds cumulatively from the last to the first response in the chain.

Teaching Multiple Discriminations and Chains

When teaching persons to respond to multiple examples from a single instructional class (i.e., members of the same stimulus class), should the various examples be taught sequentially to criterion or should they be taught simultaneously? When teaching several tasks from different instructional classes (i.e., responding to different stimulus classes), should the tasks be taught concurrently or sequentially? Would learning be maintained if previously mastered responses were integrated with new responses to be acquired? Should learners receive massed, spaced, or distributed practice on responses to be learned? Although researchers have posed these task sequencing methodological questions using somewhat different terminology, these issues have a common conceptual framework and empirical database. The research on teaching multiple tasks and multiple training examples will be considered.

Distribution of trials. The temporal distribution of training trials has been classified as massed, distributed, and spaced. Research appears to favor the distributed trials approach to instruction in which training trials on one task are interspersed with training trials on one or more other tasks. Distributed practice should result in fewer training trials to attain an acquisition criterion, and less instructional time for tasks, especially those that are more difficult (Mulligan, Guess, Holvoet, & Brown, 1980).

Interspersal training. Another effective task sequencing procedure has been termed "interspersal training," which involves mixing training trials of items on which learners have performed at or above criterion with items on which they have performed below criterion (Neef, Iwata, & Page, 1977). Interspersal training should help maintain performance on responses for which learners have reached criterion.

General case instruction. Multiple training and testing exemplars are taught concurrently rather than sequentially. Guidelines for selecting exemplars include: (a) define the instructional class, (b) define the range of relevant stimulus and response variation within that class, and (c) select examples from the instructional class for use in teaching and testing (Horner, Sprague, & Wilcox, 1982). Horner and McDonald (1982) demonstrated the superiority of general case instruction compared to single instance instruction for a vocational task.

Stimulus equivalence methodology. Research on stimulus equivalence has demonstrated a methodology for using match-to-sample tasks to train a few conditional relations, and then test for the emergence of new untrained conditional relations (Sidman, 1971). New conditional relations that may emerge following training of a few conditional relations are also called equivalence relations if reflexive, symmetric, and transitive relational properties are demonstrated. This approach has been fruitful in expanding the number of members of stimulus classes to which persons with mental retardation respond. Stimulus equivalence methodology, as the general case approach, has utility in this instructional model by broadening the stimulus classes to which learners will respond before emitting behavioral chains.

The Training Environment

Dimensions of the Training Environment

The training environment is composed of several physical or interpersonal dimensions, each of which can vary.

Physical setting. One dimension is the physical setting in which instruction takes place. At one end of the training setting continuum is the natural location where people typically perform community living skills (e.g., grocery store). At the other end of the continuum are artificial settings where discriminative stimuli and response topographies may be quite different from those in the natural setting (e.g., classrooms). Intermediate along this continuum are simulated (analog) settings that are structurally designed to approximate discriminative stimuli in natural settings (e.g., classroom area arranged like a store).

Instructional materials. A second component of the training environment is the instructional material used in the physical setting. Analogous to the setting dimension, instructional materials can also vary along a continuum from natural to simulated. In natural settings, instructional materials typically would be the actual or natural stimuli. In contrast, artificial instructional materials are physically quite dissimilar to natural materials (e.g., worksheets). Modified natural materials fall between natural and artificial materials with respect to their representation of natural discriminative stimuli. For example, actual telephones may be used to teach dialing, but they may not be plugged into wall jacks during the initial stages of training.

The trainer. A third dimension of the training environment is the instructor. Traditionally, human service professionals (e.g., public school teachers) or paraprofessionals (e.g., public residential facility direct care workers) have been the trainers. Sometimes, however, learners' peers, with or without disabilities, may have a major role to play in instruction. Another level on the trainer dimension is self-management, when antecedents and consequences are manipulated by individuals to influence their own behavior (Browder & Shapiro, 1985).

Trainer-learner ratio. The fourth dimension of the training environment is the trainer-to-learner ratio, an interpersonal dimension. Individual learner instruction is characterized by one trainer providing antecedent cues and response consequences to one learner. Group instruction, which involves one trainer and multiple learners, can be not only effective, but also more efficient than individual instruction (Reid & Favell, 1984).

Stimulus Control

The process of instruction involves using procedures to bring the learner under the stimulus control of natural community discriminative stimuli and consequences. Stimulus control is accomplished initially by the trainer using various prompts to occasion the target responses, and then providing reinforcing stimuli after those responses. The instructional prompts and consequences that have been used to promote stimulus control of community living skills will be discussed.

Instructional Prompts

Verbal instruction. Verbal instructions have been implemented along a continuum from less-to-more explicit response specification. Providing the least response specificity are nonspecific verbal prompts such as asking, "What is next?" (Cuvo, Jacobi, & Sipko, 1981). A more controlling discriminative stimulus along the verbal prompting continuum is a succinct statement specifying the response to be performed (e.g., the next step of a task analysis). Although verbal instructions typically have been provided in person by the trainer, they also have been delivered by audiotape (Alberto, Sharpton, Briggs, & Stright, 1986).

Visual cues. Another category of instructional prompt is the visual cue. One of the most frequently employed forms is the picture prompt (e.g., pictorial representations of the steps of a task analysis). Physical gestures (e.g., pointing or manual motions by a trainer simulating the response the learner should make) also have been employed as visual cues.

Modeling. In the vast majority of the community living skills training research, service providers (e.g., public residential facility employees, graduate student experimenters, public school teachers) have functioned as live models. Also, peers with (Wacker & Berg, 1984) and without disabilities (Blew, Schwartz, & Luce, 1985) have served as models. Rather than using live modeling, an alternative has been to employ videotaped modeling. An alternative to either live or videotaped human models has been the use of dolls or figures as models to teach community living skills. These objects have been manipulated to demonstrate responses learners should make in a simulation related to community living (Page, Iwata, & Neef, 1976).

Physical prompts. The most controlling type of prompting involves the trainer grasping the participants' relevant body parts and manipulating them to occasion the appropriate response. Physical prompts can be on a continuum that ranges from full prompting to light touches that occasion responding.

Permanent prompts. Permanent prompts may be especially useful when persons with limited behavioral repertoires are learning complex skills, or for individuals with physical or sensory disabilities. These prompts are used continuously without transfer of stimulus control to more natural discriminative stimuli. Examples of permanent prompts or prosthetic devices include a personal telephone directory of emergency telephone numbers and picture recipe cookbooks.

Consequences

In order for the initially neutral antecedent stimuli described above to become discriminative for responding, it is necessary that responses emitted be followed by differential reinforcement. A variety of consequences has been used to positively reinforce community living skill responses (e.g., verbal and visual performance feedback, social, edibles, money, tokens).

Transfer of Stimulus Control

To the degree that stimuli and response topographies in both the training and natural environments are similar, generalization may readily occur (Striefel & Owens, 1980). This is an argument for training in natural environments. To the degree that stimuli in the natural environment differ from those in the training setting, there may be a failure to generalize, either in whole or in part. One of the major challenges facing behavior analysts, therefore, is to transfer stimulus control from the training environment to the environment of ultimate functioning.

Fading, particularly prompt fading, has been used most frequently as a transfer of stimulus control procedure in the community living skills literature. Qualitatively different prompts have been sequenced to bring community living responses under stimulus control. The sequence frequently cited in the literature, termed "system of least prompts," orders instructional prompts from lesser to greater artificial control (Snell & Brown, 1993). In addition to fading across qualitatively different types of prompts, some studies have reported fading within a prompt type (e.g., various levels of modeling).

Prompt delay also has been used to transfer stimulus control in community living research. Transfer is accomplished by programming either a constant or an increasing delay between presentation of the natural discriminative stimulus first and then the trainer's prompt (Snell & Gast, 1981; Striefel & Owens, 1980). Over trials, learners begin to respond to the natural discriminative stimuli and transfer of stimulus control takes place.

Skill Maintenance

After learners have acquired community living skills, behavior analysts should assess and program, as necessary, for the maintenance of that behavior in the environment of ultimate functioning. A common practice has been to hope that the behavior will maintain and provide additional instruction contingent on response problems. Alternatively, instructional procedures can be implemented during original training itself to help insure response maintenance (e.g., fading the instructional program, transferring from contrived to natural reinforcers, interspersal training, overlearning, permanent prompts, self-management).

Recent Research

The behavioral model of skill acquisition described above has been employed in research conducted by the present authors for more than 20 years. In recent years, focus has shifted from determining whether we can teach functional skills to people with developmental disabilities to investigating variables that promote more effective and efficient instruction of those skills. In this section, selected studies will be presented to illustrate efforts to make this behavioral model of skill acquisition more effective and efficient. Studies will focus on community living, academic, and self-determination skills.

Community Living Skills Instruction

Promoting Stimulus Control with Textual Prompts

As stated in the instructional model, task analyses have been used as assessment instruments to evaluate learner performance, as well as to specify the behavioral chain for instruction. Most typically, trainers have task analyses on a clipboard and score responses as they are emitted by learners during assessment and training. The specific steps of the task analyses generally are not disclosed to learners. For learners with limited behavioral repertoires, this manner of assessment and instruction with task analyses may be appropriate.

For learners with more advanced behavioral repertoires, including reading skills, the traditional procedure may not be very efficient. It might be more efficient to disclose all the steps of the task analysis to learners and present them a written listing of the steps to be performed. That was the hypothesis of a series of studies investigating whether stimulus control could be achieved by learners using written task analyses as self-administered textual prompts. The role of the trainer was initially confined to teaching learners how to use one set of task analyses as prompts, and then providing response contingent feedback.

In addition, another research question inquired about the degree of specificity of the written steps (i.e., generic vs. specific) required for promoting effective stimulus control. Would people with mild disabilities respond appropriately with generic task analyses, which included statements about outcomes to achieve, or would learners require greater response description in the steps of task analyses? Furthermore, would we be able to promote effective stimulus control using the written task analyses as self-administered prompts without trainer feedback? Could the written prompts be used for self-management of instruction without having the trainer in the immediate vicinity to provide systematic performance feedback?

These research questions were investigated with three groups of young adult rehabilitation clients with mild disabilities performing functional community living tasks (i.e., cleaning an oven and stove, and doing laundry; Cuvo, Davis, O'Reilly, Mooney, & Crowley, 1992). Participants' IQs ranged from 69 to 84, and reading grade equivalents ranged from 3.5 to 8.0. The first group was used to evaluate whether written, generic task analyses and end-of-session feedback would be sufficient to promote stimulus control or whether it was necessary to employ more specific task analyses. This research was conducted in the context of a multiple-baseline design across two kitchen-cleaning tasks for individual participants. Results showed that performance with the generic task analyses and end-of-session feedback did not result in socially meaningful improvement over baseline. When the written, specific task analyses were administered with end-of-session feedback, learners reached the acquisition criterion quickly. These findings suggest that learning would be facilitated by using greater procedural specificity of written prompts, along with end-of-session feedback.

With the above finding, the effect of the specific task analysis and feedback on acquisition was systematically replicated on a second group, with the addition of generalization probes to untrained exemplars of kitchen appliances in novel settings. Results confirmed that self-administered specific textual prompts and end-of-session feedback were effective instructional procedures, and that participants demonstrated generalization by cleaning additional appliances without prompts and feedback.

In an effort to extend the use of textual prompts for self-management, the third group was given specific textual prompts to use as antecedent cues. The trainer was not physically present in the setting and end-of-session feedback was not provided. Results showed that prompts without feedback resulted in partial acquisition, but it was necessary to add feedback to the textual prompts for participants to attain the acquisition criterion. The results support a basic principle of behavior analysis; prompts without consequences do not promote effective stimulus control.

In a subsequent study, the utility of providing learners with mild disabilities written task analyses to be used as self-administered textual prompts was further investigated (McAdam & Cuvo, 1994). The main research question was whether participants who were trained to use a set of textual prompts for one task would respond appropriately without training when given novel task analyses for different tasks. To enhance stimulus control and the utility of the task analyses as self-administered prompts, the task analyses were enhanced compared to traditional ones.

In this research, each step of the self-management task analyses consisted of three written sub-steps: (a) an antecedent step, (b) a behavioral step, and (c) a self-evaluation step. The purpose of the antecedent step was to orient participants to natural discriminative stimuli for the subsequent response step. An example of an antecedent step was "Find refrigerator side walls." These antecedent sub-steps also prompted an overt response to help insure that participants attended to these textual stimuli (e.g., "When you have found refrigerator side walls, circle 'yes'"). This served a self-monitoring function. Response sub-steps described the behavior to be occasioned by the preceding antecedent sub-step (e.g., "Wipe refrigerator side walls from top to bottom using a sponge and warm soapy water. Wipe refrigerator side walls until all dirt is gone"). Self-evaluation sub-steps prompted participants to evaluate and correct, if necessary, their performance on the preceding step (e.g., "Did you wipe refrigerator side walls from top to bottom using a sponge and warm soapy water? Did you wipe refrigerator side walls until all dirt was gone? If not, do so now"). Self-evaluation steps also contained the overt response instruction (e.g., "If you wiped refrigerator side walls from top to bottom using a sponge and warm soapy water until all dirt was gone, circle 'yes'").

Initially, modeling, corrective verbal feedback, and contingent descriptive praise were employed to train participants to use a written task analysis to perform one home maintenance task (e.g., clean toilet). Subsequently, participants were tested on their use of different task analyses for novel tasks combined with end-of-session general feedback (e.g., "Good job Bill. You cleaned the toilet correctly"). No direct training was provided on these novel task analyses. Results indicated that the written task analyses served as self-administered written prompts and, along with general feedback, provided stimulus control for the second and third tasks. This research on textual prompts (Cuvo et al., 1992; McAdam & Cuvo, 1994) provides evidence that persons with mild disabilities may be able to use written task analyses with only general end-of-session feedback to perform functional community living tasks after they have been trained how to use the textual prompts.

Behavioral Acquisition using a Personalized System of Instruction

Another method that may be efficient for teaching learners with more advanced behavioral repertoires, especially if the learners can read and write, is a personalized system of instruction (PSI). With PSI, learners proceed at their own rate through the course material and progress to new material only after mastering the previous material (Keller, 1968). Instructors provide repeated testing, scoring, and tutoring. Zencius, Davis, and Cuvo (1990) investigated whether PSI would be effective in teaching adults with mild disabilities to write checks, make deposits, and reconcile bank statements. Two groups of rehabilitation clients between the ages of 18 and 23 served as participants. Six of the participants had IQs between 70 and 84. Both of the remaining participants were of average intelligence; one had cerebral palsy and one had a diagnosis of psychoneurosis.

Each participant received a PSI workbook divided into three instructional units, one for each of three banking tasks to be trained. Each unit began with systematic written instructions and visual models for completing that unit's task. To promote skill generalization, the models sampled the range of check, deposit, and reconciliation problems that the learners were likely to encounter when handling a checking account. The procedure was derived from general case instruction. In addition to the models, the workbook also contained problems requiring skills trained in that unit, which were interspersed with skills trained in previous units to promote response maintenance.

Participants worked individually in a group with other students and progressed through the instructional units at their own pace. The instructor circulated around the room, providing feedback to participants on all problems completed since the previous observation. Praise was given for correct responses and errors were corrected in one of two ways. If the instructor observed the participant make an error, he used a system of least prompts (i.e., nonspecific verbal instruction, specific verbal instruction, a gesture plus specific verbal instruction, modeling plus specific verbal instruction) to transfer stimulus control to natural discriminative stimuli. Errors the instructor did not directly observe were corrected only with specific verbal instructions.

All participants demonstrated rapid acquisition of the monetary skills, demonstrating mastery of each unit in 3 to 7 trials per unit. All except two participants maintained those skills at an 8-to-10-week follow-up assessment. The two who did not maintain recouped the skills with brief remedial training. Additionally, all four who were assessed for generalization performed the skills in the community (e.g., bank, grocery store, post office). This study suggests that PSI can be effective for teaching persons with mild disabilities. It may be especially suitable for those skills whose natural stimuli can be presented textually and whose natural responses are written.

Cumulative versus Interspersal Task Sequencing

In a follow-up to the PSI research described above, a study was conducted to determine the effectiveness of two different task-sequencing procedures (Cuvo, Davis, & Gluck, 1991). Task sequencing referred to the order in which training and test trials of the instructional package were presented. In this study, 20 young adults with mild disabilities (IQs ranged from 60 to 80) were taught seven money management tasks (e.g., depositing money into a savings account, withdrawing cash from a savings account, using money orders) using self-paced instructional books and training procedures similar to those described above.

In this study, however, the manner in which the 56 workbook practice problems was presented was manipulated to determine whether sequencing of the problems affected learning. In the cumulative workbook, when a new task was introduced, participants initially completed four practice problems from that task, and then additional practice problems from all previously trained tasks. In contrast, the interspersal workbook presented practice problems that reviewed previously trained tasks integrated with, rather than after, practice problems from the new task. Results showed that both task-sequencing methods produced statistically significant improvements in performance and that gains were maintained at one-week and one-month follow-up assessments. Both methods were highly and equally, effective, probably because they incorporated maintenance training with acquisition training.

Teaching Complex Discriminations

Persons with mental retardation and other disabilities have faced a history of discrimination. Their rights often have been defended by family members, friends, attorneys, and rehabilitation professionals (Herr, 1983). In one of the first studies to demonstrate that people with mild mental disabilities can learn self-advocacy skills, eight men and women with a variety of mild disabilities (i.e., mild mental retardation, psychiatric disabilities, cerebral palsy, learning disabilities) were taught to discriminate whether or not their rights had been violated and, if so, to engage in the necessary steps to redress the rights violation (Sievert, Cuvo, & Davis, 1988).

Training occurred in two stages. In the first stage, participants were taught to discriminate whether a rights violation had occurred. A list of 30 legal rights and their accompanying conditions was developed. The rights represented four general categories: personal (e.g., right to marry), community (e.g., right to minimum wage), human service (e.g., right to look at one's own records), and consumer rights (e.g., right to buy safe products). For each of the 30 specific rights, scenarios were developed that described hypothetical interpersonal situations in which participants were denied a request. In some of the situations, the request was justifiably denied because a condition was not met (e.g., did not pay a fee when applying for a marriage license). In other situations, the request was not justifiably denied.

Discrimination training consisted of the verbal presentation of a scenario in which a right was or was not violated. Participants were expected to determine whether a violation had occurred and to explain why or why not. Praise was provided for correct answers; verbal instructions and modeling were provided when errors occurred. Instruction began with the first general rights category. After participants received interspersal training on all rights within that category, training on the second rights category was provided followed by practice on all specific rights within that category. This was followed by interspersal training in which scenarios from the first and second rights category were presented in arbitrary order for practice and feedback. Training continued in this fashion until all four general rights categories and their specific rights had been trained. After legal rights discrimination training, participants were taught a behavioral chain to redress rights violations. Instructional procedures included written instructions, videotaped modeling, behavioral rehearsal, verbal feedback, and praise.

Participants in this study learned to discriminate and respond to up to 200 hypothetical situations in which their rights were and were not violated. In addition, they learned a general complaint response to possible rights violations. With only one exception, participants demonstrated generalization to four role-play situations in the community.

Academic Tasks

Effect of Response Practice Variables on Learning Spelling and Sight Vocabulary

In a series of four experiments, Cuvo and colleagues (Cuvo, Ashley, Marso, Zhang, & Fry, 1995) investigated the effect of several response practice variables on the learning of spelling and sight vocabulary by young adult rehabilitation clients and adolescents in special education classes. The first experiment involved a component analysis of the "cover-write" method for teaching spelling to adults whose IQs ranged from 70 to 85 and whose spelling grade equivalent ranged from 2.8 to 3.7. The cover-write procedure involved 10 steps in which the learner looked at a word whose spelling was to be learned, said it, printed it twice, covered the model and printed it again, checked the spelling, and repeated this process of writing with the model both present and covered. There were two major research questions: (a) whether an equivalent amount of written practice would be just as effective with the model always visible (i.e., write method), and (b) whether oral practice would be as effective as written practice (i.e., oral method). Results showed rapid acquisition with no meaningful differences for all three conditions. This suggested that practice and reinforcement were the essential components of the cover write procedure, and that oral and written practice were equally effective. The covering component was not associated with enhanced learning over and above response practice.

If practice and reinforcement were the key variables, how much practice is necessary? Experiment 2 compared three levels of written practice of words (i.e., 5, 10, 15 times) for students with mild or moderate mental retardation. Results showed no difference in this response practice variable; more practice did not result in more rapid acquisition or better maintenance. Writing the words 15 times was not a more effective instructional technique than writing them 5 or 10 times. Experiments 3 and 4 further tested the effects of amount of practice and relevance of practice to the words to be learned. Students with behavior disorders were administered a spelling task (Experiment 3), and students with mild or moderate mental retardation were administered a sight vocabulary task (Experiment 4). Contingent on response errors for each task, students practiced the words to be learned either one or five times, or an irrelevant word not to be learned five times. Again, results showed that additional relevant practice (i.e., 5 times) did not facilitate learning and irrelevant practice was as effective as relevant practice. Taken as a whole, this series of experiments suggests a parsimonious procedure of limited response practice and positive reinforcement for the tasks and populations studied.

Effect of Community versus Classroom Instruction on Learning Sight Words

Instruction of persons with mental retardation traditionally has taken place in classroom settings, with the hope that these students would subsequently respond appropriately to natural discriminative stimuli and consequences outside the classroom. In recent years, proponents of community based instruction have argued that teaching should take place in natural community environments, in large part, to increase the probability that students would respond appropriately in those settings. If training occurs in natural environments, one does not have to hope for generalization from the classroom to the community. It is an empirical question, however, whether students would generalize from school to community settings. If generalization were to occur, then it may be more efficient to train in school rather than deal with transportation and student supervision issues that arise when teaching in the community.

This issue was the focus of a study in which functional sight words were taught to students with mild and moderate mental retardation under three conditions (Cuvo & Klatt, 1992). Students received instruction either in the natural environment where the words occurred (e.g., stores at a mall), in school with a videotaped presentation of the words as they appeared in the community, or in school with traditional flashcard instruction. Students not only had to read the words, but also state what they would do if they saw that word. The latter attempted to measure comprehension of the word. In each condition, a constant prompt-delay procedure was used to transfer stimulus control from the trainer's prompt to the natural textual stimuli.

Results showed rapid acquisition in all three training conditions and generalization from the flashcard and videotape conditions to the community sites. Although there may be social arguments in favor of community-based instruction, this research demonstrated that two forms of school-based instruction were as effective as community based instruction for teaching functional sight vocabulary to students with mild and moderate mental retardation.

Effect of Stimulus Equivalence Instruction on Learning an Arithmetic Operation

Research on stimulus equivalence during the past two decades has provided a means of training academic skills such as reading (Mackay, 1985; Sidman, 1971), spelling (Stromer, Mackay, & Stoddard, 1992), and pre-math (Green, 1993). Research on math skills was extended by Lynch and Cuvo (1995) using match-to-sample tasks to teach conditional relations between quantities represented as printed fraction ratios (e.g., 1/4), equivalent printed decimals (e.g., 0.25), and their pictorial counterparts (e.g., 1/4 or .25 presented as 25 shaded squares of a 100-square grid). Participants were fifth-and sixth-grade students who were experiencing difficulty with math. Post-test performance by all participants indicated the emergence of equivalence relations between fractions represented as ratios, decimals, and pictures. The conditional training procedures facilitated the emergence of 12 stimulus equivalence classes. All participants matched decimals to counterpart fraction ratios and fraction ratios to equivalent decimals. Limited generalization of fraction-decimal relations emerged. The results replicated previous stimulus equivalence research showing that teaching a few relations directly provided for the emergence of many relations without additional training.

Self-determination

The studies reviewed in the academic and community living skills areas were selected for inclusion in this chapter to illustrate a variety of the components in the behavioral model of skill acquisition. The studies reviewed now are included to provide an application of the model to a novel task, self-determination, a community living skill that has been the subject of much discussion but little experimental research. Self-determination has been defined as "the capacity to choose and to have those choices be the determinants of one's own actions" (Deci & Ryan, 1985, p. 38), and it is a strong predictor of quality of life (Wehmeyer & Schwartz, 1997). People with mental retardation who are more self-determined experience a higher quality of life than those who are less self-determined.

Most people with developmental disabilities have the ability to express their preferences and participate in daily decision making (Williams, 1991), but they may not be given opportunities to do so. A survey of the self-determination of people with mental retardation revealed that the opportunity to participate in decisions was related to the importance of the decisions (Wehmeyer & Metzler, 1995). For example, they were more likely to participate in decisions about what to wear than where to live. Despite the fact that choosing where to live is one of the major decisions that adults make, residential placement decisions are often made by persons who are legally responsible and reflect the caregivers' preferences rather than those of the person who will live in the residence (Turnbull, Turnbull, Bronicki, Summers, & Roeder-Gordon, 1989).

Two recent studies have demonstrated that people with mental retardation can be active participants in the decision about where to live (Faw, Davis, & Peck, 1996; Foxx, Faw, Taylor, Davis, & Fulia, 1993). Institutionalized adults with mental retardation were assessed to determine their preferences with respect to characteristics of group homes in the community (e.g., having a private room, using the telephone anytime). After the preference testing was completed, they received small photo albums that had pictures of their strongest preferences. Using the photo albums as visual prompts, they were taught to go on group-home tours and ask questions about the availability of their preferences in the homes, to report that information to their social workers when they returned to the institution after the tours (Faw et al.; Foxx et al.), and to decide whether that home was a good place to live (Faw et al.).

Training procedures in both studies were based on the instructional model outlined above. The procedures used in Faw et al. (1996) will be described to illustrate the research. A 31-step task analysis was developed for testing and training purposes. It included 10 steps pertaining to asking preference questions when touring group homes, 10 steps pertaining to asking for clarification if the answer to a preference question was vague, 10 steps for reporting the information obtained to the social worker at the end of the tour, and the final step requiring the participant to make a decision about the home that had just been toured.

Prior to training, the institutionalized participants were assessed in community group homes and in vacant homes on their facility grounds that were similar to community homes. The assessments revealed that participants had skill deficits in determining whether their preferences were available in the homes and deciding whether they would like to live in the homes. Based on these results, training on the 31 steps of the task analysis was provided.

On the first day of training, which took place in a conference room, participants were presented individualized preference booklets that had pictures of their 10 highest preferences. Under each picture was a corresponding question (e.g., "Could I use the phone anytime?") and boxes labeled "yes," "no," and "maybe." Participants were also given evaluation worksheets that showed a picture of a home and a sidewalk consisting of 20 squares that ended at the front door of the home. The 10 squares of the sidewalk closest to the home were shaded. Each "yes," "maybe," or "no" answer regarding a preference question resulted in 2, 1, or 0 squares of the sidewalk marked with an "X," respectively. If any shaded portion of the sidewalk contained an "X," participants were taught to make the decision that the home would be a good place for them to live because the home had at least half of their preferences.

Next, the trainer modeled how to perform all 31 steps of the task analysis. Specifically, he demonstrated how to use the photo booklet to ask preference questions, to score responses, to request clarification for vague answers, and to use the evaluation worksheet to evaluate the home.

After the trainer modeled the steps, training trials were conducted with participants individually using a total-task format. Each trial began by the trainer role-playing the completion of a group-home tour and asking participants whether they had any questions. The participant was then given the opportunity to ask questions and clarify ambiguous answers as the trainer continued to role play the group-home director who would answer questions. After the participants had asked all 10 questions, the trainer played the role of social worker and the participant completed the evaluation worksheet including the determination of whether the home would be a good place to live.

During each training session, participants were given the opportunity to perform each step of the task analysis with no assistance. If a participant made an error or did not respond, a system of least prompts was used. A general prompt ("What's the next step?") was initially used. If that prompt did not evoke the response, a verbal description of the correct response was provided. If the participant still did not respond correctly, the trainer modeled the correct response and repeated the verbal direction. Descriptive feedback was provided immediately after each step regardless of the level of prompt necessary to cue performance. Additionally, general feedback and praise were provided at the end of each training trial. Criterion for completion of training was performance of 100% of all of the steps of the task analysis with no help across four consecutive trials over a period of no less than three days.

After training criterion was met, participants were tested individually at the vacant homes on the facility grounds and at community group homes. The assessments were conducted identically to those in baseline, except that during post-test assessments participants were allowed to use their preference booklets and evaluation worksheets. Prior to training, participants did not independently complete the steps of the task analysis when taken on tours of group homes in the community or when participating in simulated tours. After training, all participants improved their performance substantially and maintained their skills at a 1-month follow-up assessment.

Both self-determination studies revealed that people with mental retardation can identify preferences and can be active participants in decisions about where to live. In a similar fashion, preference information can be used to assist persons access a desired lifestyle in their current living arrangement (Faw et al., 1997). Using the preference identification procedures described above, three people with mental retardation living in a state facility selected their 10 highest preferences. Using role playing, modeling, instruction, and feedback, they were taught to direct their own interdisciplinary team meeting by beginning the meeting, reporting their preferences using a picture booklet, asking if they could access their preferences, recording the answer in the booklet, and then ending the meeting. Before identifying their preferences and learning to conduct their own meetings, participants asked 0 to 4 of their preference questions. After training, the three participants asked all 10 questions regarding their preferences.

Additional data from that study revealed that by changing the focus of the meeting from the traditional reporting of assessment information by professionals to discussion about the preferences of the person, the types of interactions occurring during the meetings changed considerably. Specifically, before treatment only 17%

of interactions were between team members and the individual. After the individuals were taught to direct their own meetings and express their preferences, the team and individuals interacted 57% of the time.

Areas For Future Study

Self-determination

Although self-determination is a strong predictor of a person's quality of life (Wehmeyer & Schwartz, 1997), little empirical research has been conducted in the area. Future research could extend the studies described above in at least two ways. First, the Faw et al. (1996) study could be replicated when teaching people with developmental disabilities to make other similar decisions that have long term consequences (e.g., choosing between jobs as a stocker or fast-food worker) and those that are expected to be relatively stable over time.

A second area of research would extend knowledge by teaching a more complex decision-making skill. In the Faw et al. (1996) study, persons with mental retardation learned to follow a simple model: express preferences, ask questions regarding those preferences, summarize the information obtained, and make a data-based decision. Participants were taught only how to decide if the home they toured was a good place for them to live based on the availability of their preferences. Future research could teach participants how to compare several homes with the intent of choosing one as the most suitable. That same method could then be evaluated to determine its effectiveness in teaching people how to make other decisions requiring comparisons between preferred items.

Self-Advocacy

Two of the studies described above illustrated that persons with developmental disabilities can be their own advocates. In Sievert et al. (1988), participants learned to discriminate between situations in which their rights were and were not violated and how to redress those violations if appropriate. In Faw et al. (1997), participants learned to lead the interdisciplinary team meeting in which training and service objectives were established for their habilitation plan. These studies demonstrated that persons with developmental disabilities can learn to advocate for their preferences (Faw et al., 1997) and rights (Sievert et al.).

Future research should focus on the interpersonal problem solving that is required when attempts at self-advocacy are unsuccessful. For example, in a habilitation-planning meeting, if a person with developmental disabilities makes a request that the interdisciplinary team does not honor, how should the person respond? In this example, persons with developmental disabilities need to be taught complex social skills that permit them to negotiate with team members until both sides are satisfied with the outcomes. Much of the research in the social skills area has focused on relatively simple skills that are unlikely to be sufficient to address the requirements of complex, ongoing interactions such as those described above or those required in other complex interpersonal situations (e.g., at work, on dates). Such complex social interactions often require social skills used in combination with problem solving skills in which one weighs the outcome of various social responses and engages in the chosen response. Research into the most effective and efficient manner of teaching complex interpersonal problem solving skills that generalize across situations within and across settings is needed.

Teaching Complex Equivalence Relations

Another manner that research on behavioral acquisition and generalization could be extended is to employ stimulus equivalence methodology to form more complex equivalence classes that promote the functioning of persons with mental retardation. Research during the past quarter-century has focused on equivalence classes primarily related to basic academic tasks (e.g., reading, spelling, pre-math). Few studies have been relevant to community living, such as applications of stimulus equivalence procedures to teach monetary skills to persons with mental retardation (Stoddard, Brown, Hurlbert, Manoli, & McIlvane, 1989) and name-face matching to adults with brain injuries (Cowley, Green, & Braunling-McMorrow, 1992).

Stimulus equivalence methodology could be extended to promote the development of a variety of other complex stimulus classes related to the functioning of persons with mental retardation. It is highly adaptive for individuals to respond to stimulus classes with several members rather than single members of a potential class. For example, equivalence relations among the spoken word, equivalent written stimulus, and the actual physical stimulus would be most helpful for stimuli related to food, its purchase, and preparation. A person living in a group home may be verbally asked to buy bananas, read the word in a recipe, see a picture of it in a specially constructed picture recipe, and then locate and buy bananas at the grocery store. A related more complex equivalence class might entail the various foods that comprise nutritional food groups (e.g., grain, meat). The class includes various foods that are members of the same class, and the category label for that class. People with mental retardation may learn substitutable foods within a class (e.g., various fruits), and to discriminate members of one class from members of another class with stimulus equivalence methods.

People with mental retardation also may have difficulty responding to subtle affective or emotional stimuli, such as facial expressions or equivalent verbal stimuli of happiness, sadness, anger, disgust, fear, and surprise. Consequently, these facial stimuli may remain neutral and individuals fail to come under their control. As a result, they may not respond in a contextually appropriate manner to others, such as housemates or staff members in a group home. In addition, individuals with mental retardation should be taught to emit verbal and nonverbal responses that cue these emotions so that others may respond appropriately to them. Affective or emotional stimuli, such as those cited above, could be taught and formed using stimulus equivalence methods. Researchers are encouraged to consider these more complex domains for the extension of stimulus equivalence methodology.

Reading Objectives

1. State the dominant approach for behavioral acquisition by persons with developmental disabilities.
2. Describe the essential components of the behavioral model of functional community living skills.
3. Describe how stimulus control is accomplished.
4. Describe and give examples of commonly used instructional prompts.
5. Explain the role of consequences in establishing stimulus control.
6. Describe procedures to transfer stimulus control from trainer-delivered prompts to naturally occurring discriminative stimuli.
7. Describe recent research that illustrates behavioral acquisition of community living skills.
8. Describe recent research that illustrates behavioral acquisition of academic skills.
9. Describe recent research that illustrates behavioral acquisition of self-determination skills.
10. Describe three areas of behavioral acquisition in which future research could be conducted.

References

Alberto, P. A., Sharpton, W. R., Briggs, A., & Stright, M. H. (1986). Facilitating task acquisition through the use of a self-operated auditory prompting system. *Journal of the Association for the Severely Handicapped, 11,* 85-91.

Barrett, B. H., & Lindsley, O. R. (1962). Deficits in acquisition of operant discrimination and differentiation shown by institutionalized retarded children. *American Journal of Mental Deficiency, 67,* 424-436.

Birnbrauer, J. S., Bijou, S. W., Wolf, M. M., & Kidder, J. D. (1965). Programed instruction in the classroom. In L. P. Ullmann & L. Krasner (Eds.), *Case studies in behavior modification* (pp. 358-363). New York: Holt, Rinehart, and Winston, Inc.

Blew, P. A., Schwartz, I. S., & Luce, S. C. (1985). Teaching functional community skills to autistic children using nonhandicapped peer tutors. *Journal of Applied Behavior Analysis, 18,* 337-342.

Browder, D. M., & Shapiro, E. S. (1985). Applications of self-management to individuals with severe handicaps: A review. *Journal of the Association for Persons with Severe Handicaps, 10,* 200-208.

Brown, F., & Snell, M. E. (1993). Meaningful assessment. In M. E. Snell (Ed.), *Instruction of students with severe disabilities* (4th ed.; pp. 61-98). New York: Merrill.

Brown, L., Branston, M. B., Hamre-Nietupski, A., Pumpian, I., Certo, N., & Gruenewald, L. (1979). A strategy for developing chronological age-appropriate and functional curricular content for severely handicapped adolescents and young adults. *Journal of Special Education, 13,* 81-90.

Cowley, B. J., Green, G., & Braunling-McMorrow, D. (1992). Using stimulus equivalence procedures to teach name-face matching to adults with brain injuries. *Journal of Applied Behavior Analysis, 25,* 461-475.

Cuvo, A. J., Ashley, K. M., Marso, K. J., Zhang, B. L., & Fry, T. A. (1995). Effect of response practice variables on learning spelling and sight vocabulary by persons with intellectual disabilities. *Journal of Applied Behavior Analysis, 28,* 155-173.

Cuvo, A. J., & Davis, P. K. (1998). Establishing and transferring stimulus control: Teaching people with developmental disabilities. In J. K. Luiselli & M. J. Cameron (Eds.), *Antecedent control: Innovative approaches to behavioral support* (pp. 347-369). Baltimore: Paul H. Brookes.

Cuvo, A. J., & Davis, P. K. (1983). Behavior therapy and community living skills. In M. Hersen, R. M. Eisler, & P. M. Miller (Eds.), *Progress in behavior modification* (Vol. 14; pp. 125-172). New York: Academic Press.

Cuvo, A. J., Davis, P. K., & Gluck, M. S. (1991). Cumulative and interspersal task sequencing in self-paced training for persons with mild handicaps. *Mental Retardation, 6,* 335-342.

Cuvo, A. J., Davis, P. K., O'Reilly, M. F., Mooney, B. M., & Crowley, R. (1992). Promoting stimulus control with textual prompts and performance feedback for persons with mild disabilities. *Journal of Applied Behavior Analysis, 25,* 477-489.

Cuvo, A. J., Jacobi, L., & Sipko, R. (1981). Teaching laundry skills to mentally retarded students. *Education and Training of the Mentally Retarded, 16,* 54-64.

Cuvo, A. J., & Klatt, K. P. (1992). The effects of in vivo, videotape, and flashcard instruction of community referenced sight words on students with mental retardation. *Journal of Applied Behavior Analysis, 25,* 499-512.

Deci, E. L., & Ryan, R. M. (1985). *Intrinsic motivation and self-determination in human behavior.* New York: Plenum.

Faw, G. D., Davis, P. K., McCord, B., Troutman, L., Holden, M., & Livesay, J. (1997, May). *Teaching people with mental retardation to self-direct their habilitation planning meetings.* Poster presented at the annual meeting of the Association for Behavior Analysis, Chicago, IL.

Faw, G. D., Davis, P. K., & Peck, C. (1996). Increasing self-determination: Teaching people with mental retardation to evaluate residential options. *Journal of Applied Behavior Analysis, 29,* 173-188.

Foxx, R. M., Faw, G. D., Taylor, S., Davis, P. K., & Fulia, R. (1993). "Would I be able to . . .?" Teaching clients to assess the availability of their community living preferences. *American Journal of Mental Retardation, 98,* 235-248.

Fuller, P. R. (1949). Operant conditioning of a vegetative human organism. *American Journal of Psychology, 62,* 587-590.

Green, G. (1993). Stimulus control technology for teaching number/quantity equivalences. *Proceedings of the 1992 conference of the National Association for Autism (Australia)* (pp. 51-63). Melbourne, Australia: Victoria Autistic Children's and Adults' Association, Inc.

Halderman v. Pennhurst, 446 F. Supp. 1295 (E.D.P.A. 1977).

Herr, S. S. (1983). *Rights and advocacy for retarded people.* Lexington, MA: D.C. Heath and Co.

Horner, R. H., & McDonald, R. S. (1982). Comparison of single instance and general case instruction in teaching a generalized vocational skill. *Journal of the Association for Persons with Severe Handicaps, 8,* 7-20.

Horner, R. H., Sprague, J., & Wilcox, B. (1982). General case programming for community activities. In B. Wilcox & G. T. Bellamy (Eds.), *Design of high school programs for severely handicapped students* (pp. 61-98). Baltimore: Paul H. Brookes.

Iwata, B. A., Bailey, J. S., Neef, N. A., Wacker, D. P., Repp, A. C., & Shook, G. L. (1997). *Behavior analysis in developmental disabilities* (2nd ed.). Lawrence, KS: Society for the Experimental Analysis of Behavior.

Keller, F. S. (1968). "Good-bye, teacher." *Journal of Applied Behavior Analysis, 1,* 79-89.

Kerr, N., Meyerson, L., & Michael, J. (1965). A procedure for shaping vocalizations in a mute child. In L. P. Ullmann & L. Krasner (Eds.), *Case studies in behavior modification* (pp. 366-370). New York: Holt, Rinehart, and Winston, Inc.

Lynch, D. C., & Cuvo, A. J. (1995). Instruction of fraction-decimal relations via stimulus equivalence. *Journal of Applied Behavior Analysis, 28,* 115-126.

Mackay, H. A. (1985). Stimulus equivalence in rudimentary reading and spelling. *Analysis and Intervention in Developmental Disabilities, 5,* 373-387.

McAdam, D., & Cuvo, A. J. (1994). Textual prompts as an antecedent cue self-management strategy for persons with mild disabilities. *Behavior Modification, 18,* 47-65.

Moyer, J. R., & Dardig, J. C. (1978). Practical task analyses for special educators. *Teaching Exceptional Children, 11,* 1-16.

Mulligan, M., Guess, D., Holvoet, J., & Brown, F. (1980). The Individualized Curriculum Sequencing model (I): Implications for research on massed, distributed, or spaced trial training. *Journal of the Association for the Severely Handicapped, 5,* 325-336.

Neef, N. A., Iwata, B. A., & Page, T. J. (1977). The effects of known item interspersal on acquisition and retention of spelling and sight reading words. *Journal of Applied Behavior Analysis, 10,* 738.

Page, T. J., Iwata, B. A., & Neef, N. A. (1976). Teaching pedestrian skills to retarded persons: Generalization from the classroom to the natural environment. *Journal of Applied Behavior Analysis, 9,* 433-444.

Reid, D. H., & Favell, J. E. (1984). Group instruction with persons who have severe disabilities: A critical review. *Journal of the Association for Persons with Severe Handicaps, 9,* 167-177.

Salzinger, K., Feldman, R. S., Cowan, J. E., & Salzinger, S. (1965). Operant conditioning of verbal behavior of two young speech-deficient boys. In L. Krasner & L. P. Ullmann (Eds.), *Research in behavior modification* (pp. 82-105). New York: Holt, Rinehart, and Winston, Inc.

Sidman, M. (1971). Reading and auditory-visual equivalences. *Journal of Speech and Hearing Research, 14,* 5-13.

Sievert, A. L., Cuvo, A. J., & Davis, P. K. (1988). Training self-advocacy skills to adults with mild handicaps. *Journal of Applied Behavior Analysis, 21,* 299-309.

Snell, M. E., & Brown, F. (1993). Instructional planning and implementation. In M. E. Snell (Ed.), *Instruction of students with severe disabilities* (4th ed.; pp. 99-151). New York: Merrill.

Snell, M. E., & Gast, D. L. (1981). Applying the time delay procedure to the instruction of the severely handicapped. *Journal of the Association for the Severely Handicapped, 6,* 3-14.

Stoddard, L. T., Brown, J., Hurlbert, B., Manoli, C., & McIlvane, W. J. (1989). Teaching money skills through stimulus class formation, exclusion, and component matching methods: Three case studies. *Research in Developmental Disabilities, 10,* 413-439.

Striefel, S., & Owens, C. R. (1980). Transfer of stimulus control procedures: Applications to language acquisition training with the developmentally handicapped. *Behavior Research of Severe Developmental Disabilities, 1,* 307-331.

Stromer, R., Mackay, H. A., & Stoddard, L. T. (1992). Classroom applications of stimulus equivalence technology. *Journal of Behavioral Education, 2,* 225-256.

Turnbull, H. R., III, Turnbull, A. P., Bronicki, G. J., Summers, J. A., & Roeder-Gordon, C. (1989). *Disability and the family: A guide to decisions for adulthood.* Baltimore: Paul H. Brookes.

Wacker, D. P., & Berg, W. (1984). Use of peer instruction to train a complex photocopying task to moderately and severely retarded adolescents. *Analysis and Intervention in Developmental Disabilities, 4,* 219-234.

Wehmeyer, M. L., & Metzler, C. A. (1995). How self-determined are people with mental retardation? The National Consumer Survey. *Mental Retardation, 33,* 111-119.

Wehmeyer, M. L., & Schwartz, M. (1997). Self-determination and positive adult outcomes: A follow-up study of youth with mental retardation or learning disabilities. *Exceptional Children, 63,* 245-255.

Williams, R. (1991). Choices, communication, and control: A call for expanding them in the lives of people with severe disabilities. In L. H. Meyer, C. A. Peck, & L. Brown (Eds.), *Critical issues in the lives of people with severe disabilities* (pp. 543-544). Baltimore: Paul H. Brookes.

Zencius, A. H., Davis, P. K., & Cuvo, A. J. (1990). A personalized system of instruction for teaching checking account skills to adults with mild disabilities. *Journal of Applied Behavior Analysis, 23,* 245-252.

Chapter 3

The Functional Analysis Model of Behavioral Assessment

Brian A. Iwata, Sung Woo Kahng, Michele D. Wallace, and Jana S. Lindberg

University of Florida

The term "functional analysis," when used in reference to behavior, denotes empirical demonstrations of "cause and effect relationships" between environment and behavior (Skinner, 1953). Thus, whether the goal of intervention is to increase or decrease the frequency of behavior, a functional analysis identifies the variables responsible for change (Baer, Wolf, & Risley, 1968). However, there is an important distinction to be made between response acquisition and reduction. Whereas responses "to be established" do not exist and, hence, have no *current* function, those already present are usually influenced by some feature(s) of the environment. Results of over 30 years of research on the treatment of behavior disorders such as aggression, noncompliance, property destruction, and self-injurious behavior (SIB) indicate that these responses are, by and large, learned performances. As such, they are acquired and maintained through an individual's history of interaction with the physical and social environment in the form of reinforcement contingencies. Techniques designed to identify these sources of reinforcement comprise an area of assessment that is unique to the treatment of behavior disorders and is known as "functional analysis methodology" or "functional assessment." This chapter describes the basic elements of functional analysis methodology and reviews research on its development and extension, discusses alternative approaches to assessment, and identifies several areas for future research.

The Learned Functions of Behavior Disorders

There is strong evidence that most behavior problems are maintained by the same contingencies that account for the development of non-pathological behavior patterns. Briefly, these are positive and negative reinforcement, which, for the purpose of treatment development, are often further delineated based on the source of reinforcement for the behavior.

Positive Reinforcement

Social reinforcement. The occurrence of a behavior problem often sets the occasion for immediate reaction by those nearby. Aggression, tantrums, property destruction, and SIB commonly produce social consequences in the form of reprimands, response interruption, comfort, or attempts to engage the individual in an alternative activity. Such reactions often seem unavoidable and may even interrupt the behavior temporarily; however, each of these contingent social interactions may function as positive reinforcement and maintain behavior over time. For example, it has been shown that SIB can dramatically increase when it is followed by comforting statements made by caregivers (Lovaas & Simmons, 1969), and that aggression and disruption can be maintained in the same manner (Mace, Page, Ivancic, & O'Brien, 1986). These and similar findings suggest that many well-intentioned efforts to stop behavior have the inadvertent effect of strengthening it.

Automatic reinforcement. Some behavior problems seem to persist in the absence of social reinforcement. For example "aerophagia" or air swallowing (Barrett, McGonigle, Ackles, & Brukhart, 1987), bruxism (Heller & Strang, 1973), rumination (Johnston, Greene, Rawal, Vazin, & Winston, 1991), some cases of SIB (Cowdery, Iwata, & Pace, 1990), and a variety of repetitive behaviors collectively described as "stereotyped acts" (Baumeister & Forehand, 1973) have been observed to occur independent of social context. Theories about the specific source of maintenance for such behaviors have ranged from perceptual stimulation as reinforcement for ritualistic behavior in autistic individuals (Lovaas, Newsom, & Hickman, 1987) to endogenous opioids as reinforcement for SIB (Cataldo & Harris, 1982). A common feature among many of these accounts is the assertion that behavior directly produces its own reinforcement. These types of nonsocial contingencies have been described more generally as "automatic" reinforcement (Skinner, 1969; Vaughan & Michael, 1982). As a functional description, automatic reinforcement reveals little about the specific reinforcer that maintains behavior. Nevertheless, it focuses our attention on the identification of those reinforcers by emphasizing the learned nature of behavior and it provides a convenient means for distinguishing between social and nonsocial contingencies.

Negative Reinforcement

Social reinforcement. Another type of social consequence for problem behavior is the termination of ongoing activity. Individuals who engage in dangerous forms of behavior such as aggression often are not required to complete assigned work or attend class because they are so disruptive; they may even be sent home or to "time out" as a means of "punishment." Such consequences may, in fact, reduce the frequency of behavior to the extent they result in a loss of positive reinforcement. It is possible, however, that the contingent termination or postponement of certain activities may function as escape or avoidance and strengthen behavior through negative reinforcement (see Iwata, 1987, for an extensive review of this topic). For example, it has been shown that both time out (Solnick, Rincover, & Peterson, 1977) and extinction in the form of "ignoring" (Iwata, Pace, Cowdery, & Miltenberger, 1994) can maintain behavior problems if the contingency produces escape from work. Noncompliance, a common form of escape, may be ineffective for individuals who have severe behavioral deficits because it merely results in further exposure to aversive stimulation in the form of remedial training, as well as in further loss of positive reinforcement due to repeated errors. Under such conditions, the inadvertent shaping of more intolerable behaviors (e.g., aggression, SIB) may occur.

Automatic reinforcement. When experiencing the pain of a toothache or the itching caused by an insect bite, we usually rub or scratch our skin at the site of the discomfort, and we often attribute causation to the antecedent condition (e.g., the toothache "causes" the rubbing). Although the event that occasions behavior is important, it is not responsible for behavioral maintenance. Rather, the aversive stimulation we experience from a toothache is an "establishing operation" (EO) that makes its termination reinforcing (see Michael, 1982, 1993, for extensive discussions). Responses such as jaw rubbing that directly alleviate pain are maintained by negative reinforcement that is an automatic response product. When these behaviors are ineffective, we resort to more elaborate alternatives, such as taking medication or calling the dentist to arrange an appointment. But when such alternatives are not available, the previous responses persist and may increase in intensity or duration. This source of reinforcement may account for observed correlations between specific medical conditions and certain forms of SIB. For example, head banging has been associated with ear infections in children (DeLissovoy, 1963).

The Role of Functional Analysis Methodology in Practice, Research, and Prevention

A long-standing tradition in the fields of both psychology and psychiatry is the classification and treatment of behavior disorders based on shared topographical characteristics—presenting symptoms—such as such as "hyperactivity," "aggression," or "delusional speech." However, as the above discussion suggests, topography reveals little about the conditions that contribute to behavioral maintenance because divergent forms of behavior can be produced by the same contingency; likewise, the same behavior can be maintained by different contingencies. Placing greater emphasis on function rather than on form may allow us to determine when different problems can be treated similarly and, more important, when the same problem must be treated differently. For example, if we find that an individual's tantrums, aggression, and property destruction are all maintained by contingent attention, perhaps the same intervention strategy (e.g., time out and differential reinforcement of other behavior; DRO) would be effective in managing all of the behaviors. By contrast, if tantrums are maintained by attention, but aggression and destruction are maintained by escape, time out would effectively reduce tantrums but it would serve as negative reinforcement for aggression and destruction.

The systematic use of functional analysis methodology as an assessment tool may also yield general benefits with respect to practice, prevention, and research. (Iwata, Vollmer, & Zarcone, 1990). The identification of behavioral function improves our ability to develop effective treatment programs in four ways. First, it allows us to specify the antecedent conditions (EOs, discriminative stimuli; S^Ds) under which behavior occurs and to alter them so that problem behavior is less likely. Second, a functional analysis identifies the source of reinforcement that must be eliminated in order to produce extinction or, alternatively, what must be done to minimize reinforcement. Third, the same reinforcer that currently maintains the behavior problem may be used to establish and strengthen alternative behaviors. Finally, results of a functional analysis will identify those reinforcers and/or treatment components that are irrelevant.

Functional analysis methodology may also contribute to methodological refinement in research on treatment development and comparison. Results from studies conducted over the past 20 years have shown some degree of inconsistency with the use of almost every reinforcement-based approach to behavior reduction; however, the conditions responsible for failure have not been analyzed thoroughly. It is likely that some interventions were simply not designed properly (e.g., lean DRO schedules) and that others were not implemented consistently. Another possibility is that the intervention was unrelated to the function of the target behavior. By conducting functional analyses during the treatment development phase, researchers will be able to avoid one source of treatment failure. As a result, future research should yield a classification of treatment procedures whose effectiveness is demonstrated for specific functions of behavior (Iwata, Vollmer, Zarcone, & Rodgers, 1993).

Finally, an accumulation of data on the conditions under which behavior problems occur may lead to more careful examination of "at-risk" environments—those in which behavior problems do not presently occur but are likely in the future. The presence of conditions such as deprivation from attention (the EO for attention-maintained behavior), and others known to influence the occurrence of behavior problems can serve as the basis for prevention.

Assessment of Behavioral Function

Over the past 10 years, research on functional analysis methodologies has become one of the most active areas of investigation in our field (e.g., see the special issue of *Journal of Applied Behavior Analysis, 27*(2), 1994) and has yielded a wide range of assessment procedures. For purposes of discussion, current approaches may be classified under three general categories, which are distinguished on the basis of the method used for collecting data and the conditions under which observation is done. Functional analyses involve manipulation of suspected maintaining variables using experimental methodology to demonstrate control over responding. Descriptive analyses involve direct observation of behavior, typically under naturalistic conditions, in the absence of manipulation. Finally, indirect methods involve gathering information about behavioral function in the absence of direct observation. The second and third approaches are approximations to the first because they do not delineate functional relationships. However, all three approaches will be discussed in this chapter because each has certain advantages that may contribute to a comprehensive assessment of behavioral function.

Functional (Experimental) Analysis

Historical Developments

Although results from a number of studies published during the mid-1960s through the 1970s suggested that a variety of behavior disorders might be learned responses, three sets of studies are noteworthy because they were systematic investigations of distinct environmental influences. The earliest demonstration that a pathological behavior could be maintained by reinforcement was reported by Lovaas, Freitag, Gold, and Kassorla (1965), who observed that a child's SIB worsened when therapists made sympathetic statements contingent on its occurrence. In a subsequent study, Lovaas and Simmons (1969) exposed another child who engaged in SIB to conditions involving deprivation from attention, continuous attention, or attention contingent only upon SIB, and observed the highest response rates under the contingent attention condition. These results showed not only that SIB could be maintained by positive reinforcement, but also that it could be extinguished through deprivation and reduced through noncontingent reinforcement. In another series of studies, it was shown that SIB (Carr, Newsom, & Binkoff, 1976) and aggression (Carr, Newsom, & Binkoff, 1980) occurred more frequently under a "demand" condition relative to a "no-demand" condition, suggesting that a different contingency—negative reinforcement in the form of escape—could also maintain problem behavior. Finally, Berkson and Mason (1963, 1965) observed an important environmental relationship that did not involve the manipulation of social contingencies. They demonstrated that individuals with mental retardation engaged in higher rates of "stereotyped" movements when they were environmentally deprived than when they had access to leisure materials.

Although the above studies were designed as demonstrations of the effects of specific variables on specific responses, as a group they provided experimental analyses of behavioral maintenance and illustrated the influence of social-positive reinforcement, social-negative reinforcement, and (indirectly) automatic-positive reinforcement across a range of behavior disorders. In doing so, they also provided a model for identifying behavioral sensitivity to a given contingency by measuring behavior when it is exposed to conditions in which a variable of interest is present (test condition) versus absent (control condition).

A General Paradigm

The experimental logic demonstrated in the above studies was extended by Iwata, Dorsey, Slifer, Bauman, and Richman (1994/1982), who proposed a general model for concurrently assessing behavioral sensitivity to a variety of contingencies. They arranged three test conditions, each designed to contain an S^D, an EO, and a source of reinforcement for behavior maintained by a given contingency, and a fourth condition designed to be a control

In the social disapproval or attention condition, a therapist who was present (S^D) ignored a participant throughout the session (EO). However, when the participant engaged in the target behavior, which was SIB, the therapist reacted by delivering a reprimand and/or a statement of concern and by providing physical contact in some form, such as response blocking (positive reinforcement). Throughout the session the participant had free access to leisure materials, so that behavior maintained by automatic reinforcement might be suppressed. In the demand or escape condition, the therapist (S^D) repeatedly presented instructional trials (EO) to the participant. Although correct responses were praised, the test contingency involved termination of instruction in the form of a brief time out contingent on the occurrence of SIB (negative reinforcement). In the alone condition, the participant was observed while alone in a room that was devoid of stimulating materials. Given the *absence* of any stimuli associated with social reinforcement, and also the absence of materials whose manipulation might serve as a source of reinforcement, persistence of behavior in this condition could not be attributed to either attention or escape and, through elimination, was probably maintained by automatic reinforcement. Finally, the play condition involved free access to leisure materials throughout the session, the absence of demands, and frequent attention delivered by the therapist. Thus, the

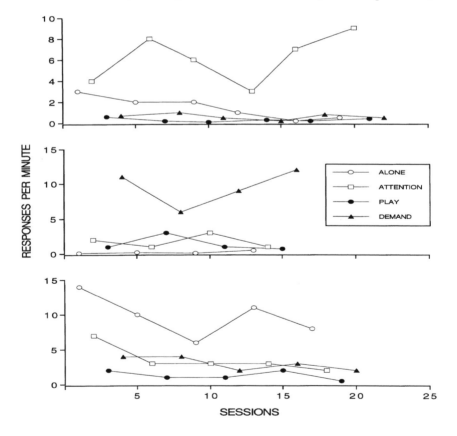

Figure 1. Examples of functional analysis data reflecting different behavioral functions.

EOs, as well as the contingencies, for social reinforcement (both attention and escape) were absent from the play condition and were replaced with frequent access to play materials and attention.

The authors exposed 9 individuals who engaged in SIB to the above conditions during repeated 15-minute sessions, arranged in a multielement design. Results showed differential response patterns across conditions for 6 of the 9 participants, and at least one individual showed evidence of maintenance by each of the test conditions. Thus, the methodology seemed well suited to the assessment of a behavior disorder that might be maintained by different sources of reinforcement, and was it used in subsequent studies to develop treatment procedures for SIB maintained by social-positive reinforcement (Vollmer, Iwata, Zarcone, Smith, & Mazaleski, 1993a), social-negative reinforcement (Iwata, Pace, Kalsher, Cowdery, & Cataldo, 1990), and automatic-positive reinforcement (Cowdery et al., 1990). In a large-scale analysis of data for 152 individuals who were exposed to this functional analysis methodology, differential or uniformly high levels of responding were observed in over 90% of the data (Iwata et al., 1994). Figure 1 presents samples of data collected during functional analyses reflecting different sources of reinforcement.

Procedural and Methodological Variations

The general methodology described above has been replicated and extended in a large number of studies on the assessment and/or treatment of a wide range of behavior disorders, including aggression (Mace et al., 1986), noncompliance (Lalli, Casey, & Kates, 1995; Reimers et al., 1993), pica (Piazza, Hanley, & Fisher, 1996), stereotypy (Mace, Browder, & Lin, 1987; Wehmeyer, Bourland, & Ingram, 1993), tantrums (Vollmer, Northrup, Ringdahl, LeBlanc, & Chauvin, 1996), and vocal tics (Carr, Taylor, Wallander, & Reiss, 1996). These and other studies are noteworthy, not only for demonstrating the robustness of the functional analysis approach to assessment, but also for incorporating numerous variations in procedure or methodology.

Parametric influences. Test conditions in a functional analysis typically involve the delivery of reinforcement on a continuous (fixed-ratio [FR] 1) schedule, based on the assumption that exposure to contingencies per se will produce response differentiation. Occasionally, however, intermittent schedules have been used during assessment (e.g., Mace & Lalli, 1991), because it has been shown that response rates may be higher when reinforcement is not delivered following every occurrence (Lovaas et al., 1965). Other parametric manipulations that have been shown to influence behavior during functional analyses include reinforcement duration (Fisher, Piazza, & Chiang, 1996), delay to reinforcement (Horner & Day, 1991), rate of demand presentation, and session duration (Smith, Iwata, Goh, & Shore, 1995).

Characteristics of the EO, response, and reinforcer. Qualitative characteristics of stimuli and responses have been altered in several studies and have been shown, independent of consequences, to affect behavior. For example, increases in escape behavior have been observed under conditions involving the presentation of more difficult (Carr & Durand, 1985) or novel (Smith et al., 1995) tasks, and increases in attention-maintained behavior have been observed when a third individual was present and receiving attention from the therapist (Mace, Webb, Sharkey, Mattson, & Rosen, 1988). Results of these studies illustrate the idiosyncratic nature of EOs in that certain types of aversive stimulation (or deprivation), but not others, may occasion behavior. Similar results have been shown with differing "qualities" of reinforcement (Fisher, Ninness, Piazza, & Owen-DeSchryver, 1996; Peck et al., 1996).

Additional test condition. Aside from parametric and qualitative variations, the most notable modification in functional analysis methodology in recent years has been the addition of a test condition in which access to a "tangible" or material reinforcer is delivered contingent occurrences of the target behavior (Piazza et al., 1996; Shirley, Iwata, Kahng, Mazaleski, & Lerman, 1997; Wacker et al., 1990). In this condition, access to a tangible reinforcer is confounded with attention because the therapist delivers the item. However, selective control can be demonstrated if response rates under the tangible condition are higher than those observed under an attention condition.

Experimental design. The multielement design has been used most often during functional analyses because it allows comparisons across multiple conditions to be made efficiently and it eliminates the possibility of lengthy exposure to a single condition, which may affect behavior in a subsequent condition. Occasionally, however, the multielement design may pose difficulty if conditions are not easily discriminated; for this reason, the reversal design is also used (Carr & Durand, 1985; Vollmer, Iwata, Duncan, & Lerman, 1993). But the reversal design is not well suited to multiple comparisons because increased rates of responding under one condition require a return to baseline (the control condition) before proceeding to another test condition. An alternative to both designs has been called the sequential or pairwise "test-control" design and involves a combination of multielement and reversal formats (Iwata, Duncan, Zarcone, Lerman, & Shore, 1994). In this design, test conditions are ordered sequentially as in a reversal design, but a continuous baseline is provided by alternating test and control sessions in a multielement design. Figure 2 illustrates each of these three design formats with a sets of data reflecting the same maintaining variable (attention)

Length of assessment. In single-subject designs, observations of behavior continue until changes in level, trend, or variability can be established. Thus, the length of assessment cannot be specified at the outset. For example, in the large scale-study based on 152 functional analyses reported by Iwata et al. (1994), it was found that the length of assessment ranged from 8 to 66 sessions (2 to 16.5 hours). When severe restrictions are placed on the amount of time available for assessment (e.g., during consultations or outpatient visits), functional analyses of this type may be impractical. In an attempt to retain the highest degree of objectivity possible under such conditions, Wacker and colleagues (Cooper, Wacker, Sasso, Reimers, & Donn, 1990; Derby et al., 1992; Northup et al., 1991; Wacker et al., 1990) have reported in a number of studies the use of a "brief functional analysis," which typically can be conducted in about half a day. The procedure entails only one or two repetitions

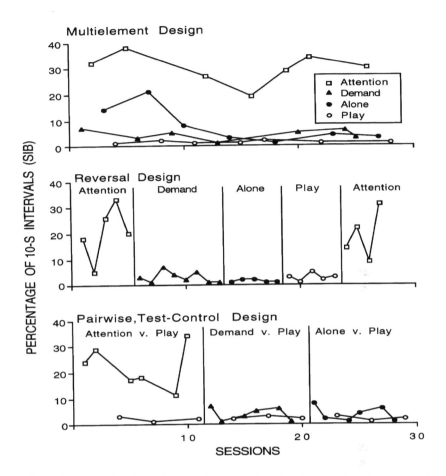

Figure 2. Examples of experimental designs used during functional analyses. From Iwata et al. (1994), p. 223. Copyright 1994 by the Society for the Experimental Analysis of Behavior, Inc. Reprinted by permission of the author.

of selected test and control conditions, and session length is usually limited to 5 minutes. Response differentiation under such conditions requires immediate discrimination and control by the relevant contingencies. If this can be achieved, however, there is clear verification of behavioral function. An additional feature usually included in the brief functional analysis is the use of probes to evaluate the effects of one or more treatment options. In summarizing the results obtained from 79 cases in which assessment was completed within a 90-minute time period, Derby et al. reported that occurrences of target behavior were observed in 63% of the sample and that, of these, response differentiation was observed in 74%, for an overall "hit rate" of 46.6%. Although this outcome is less favorable than that reported with more extended functional analyses (Iwata et al., 1994), it nevertheless represents a major advance over other models of outpatient assessment, in which there is usually no attempt to validate information obtained solely through verbal report.

Analysis of antecedent events. Identification of behavioral function typically requires that an individual be exposed to the reinforcement contingencies suspected of maintaining behavior, such as contingent attention, access to materials, or escape from demands. In several studies, however, (Durand & Carr, 1987, 1991, 1992), individuals have been exposed only to variations in antecedent events across assessment conditions. Manipulations consisted of access to more- or less-frequent noncontingent attention and assignment of easy or difficult work tasks, with the same consequences delivered for occurrences of problem behavior across all conditions. This arrangement exemplifies a paradigm in which an individual is exposed to the EO relevant to a given contingency but not the contingency itself (e.g., difficult tasks are presented but escape is not allowed). Under such conditions, extinction would be expected to occur; therefore, response differentiation must be observed immediately. Moreover, the occurrence of behavior under a given antecedent condition may not reflect the influence of the hypothesized contingency. It has been observed, for example, that behavior problems occurring in a demand context were maintained by access to attention (Rortvedt & Miltenberger, 1994; Vollmer, Iwata, Smith, & Rodgers, 1992). Thus, what appeared to be EOs for escape (demands) were, instead, either EOs or discriminative stimuli for attention seeking.

Hierarchical methodology. Given the availability of several arrangements for conducting a functional analysis, Vollmer, Marcus, Ringdahl, and Roane (1995) recommended a hierarchical approach to assessment consisting of the following components. A brief analysis is first conducted and, if differential responding is observed immediately, treatment is begun. If data are undifferentiated, assessment continues according to a multielement design until differential responding is observed, at which time treatment is begun. If responding is still undifferentiated, the possibility that behavior will maintain independent of environmental circumstances can be determined by observing behavior during a series of alone or "no interaction" sessions. If behavior persists, treatment appropriate to an automatic reinforcement function is begun. Finally, decreases in responding under the alone condition suggest the influence of extinction (for behavior maintained by attention) or the absence of aversive stimulation (for behavior maintained by escape), which may not have been detected during the multielement phase due to lack of discrimination, multiple treatment interference, or related problems. Therefore, assessment would continue using a reversal design. Using this approach with 20 individuals who engaged in a variety of behavior problems, Vollmer et al. were able to complete the assessment with 4 individuals during the brief analysis, 4 more during the extended analysis, 5 more following exposure to alone sessions, and 2 more using the reversal design. Thus, the approach appears to represent an efficient means for progressing from simple to more complex assessments only when circumstances require it.

Data analysis. The traditional method used for analyzing results from single-subject analyses consists of visual inspection of graphed data. However, Hagopian et al. (1997) et al. argued that visual inspection of data arrays from multielement designs containing four or more conditions, which are not commonly found in behavioral research, present a number of interpretive problems. To alleviate these difficulties, they developed a series of structured criteria for making decisions about behavioral function, based on a comparison of response patterns across conditions with respect to differences in level and trend. They found that training individuals to apply these rules during the examination of functional analysis data improved interrater agreement from 46% to 81%. Another variation in data analysis was suggested by Vollmer, Iwata, Zarcone, Smith, and Mazaleski (1993b). Noting that certain trends in responding that may occur within a session can be obscured by overall session rates, they suggested that data from initial sessions, if undifferentiated, be plotted on a within-session basis (e.g., as minute-by-minute values). For example, within-session extinction effects would produce relatively high response rates at the beginning of a session but low rates near the end. The overall session rate would not reflect this change, but examination of response rates throughout the session would allow its detection.

Critique

The major strength of functional analysis methodology is its ability to identify environmental determinants of behavior through a demonstration of functional relationships. In addition, the high degree of precision and flexibility that are inherent characteristics of this type of analysis make it well suited to the identification of complex relationships such as multiple control (behavior maintained by more than one source of reinforcement), and to the isolation of subtle influences over behavior (e.g., the effects of intermittent schedules or idiosyncratic reinforcers). In short, the results obtained from a functional analysis allow for the development of truly individualized treatment plans based on sound assessment data. For this reason, functional analysis methodology has been widely adopted by applied behavior analysis researchers whose interest is the assessment and treatment of behavior disorders, and its use is becoming more common in clinical practice.

One unique feature of a functional analysis is that its results may suggest some immediate strategies to effect behavior change even though their use may not be practical for long-term implementation. For example, high rates of escape behavior in the presence of demands are usually associated with low rates of behavior during other conditions (e.g., play or alone), suggesting that the behavior might be eliminated quickly by reducing exposure to demanding situations until such time that other interventions can be developed.

Finally, because results of a functional analysis allow the development of treatment components aimed at eliminating the source of behavioral maintenance, a higher degree of success might be achieved using reinforcement-based approaches to behavior reduction, thereby reducing the situations in which punishment might be considered (Iwata et al., 1994).

The methodology does, however, pose some problems. The most common limitations raised in the literature are that assessment is too time consuming and requires a high level of expertise (Durand & Crimmins, 1988; Spreat & Connelly, 1996). It is possible that the length of assessment can be minimized through the use of several strategies noted above (e.g., the brief functional analysis or examination of within-session response patterns). Nevertheless, it is clear that conducting any type of functional analysis will require more time than that allotted to the traditional clinical interview. The question is whether equally valid conclusions about behavioral maintenance can be reached through other means. The issue of clinical expertise is a legitimate one; implementation of functional analyses requires the ability to deliver antecedent and consequent events in a rather precise manner. However, the inability to do so may also preclude the implementation of most behavioral treatment procedures, which require the very same skills.

There are some inherent limitations of functional analysis methodology. First, the assessment process may increase the risk of the behavior problem beyond acceptable limits. Under such conditions, it is possible that assessment of behaviors that form members of the same response class (or alternative behaviors) may provide insight into behavioral maintenance (Peck et al., 1996). Second behavior disorders maintained by alleviation of painful conditions (automatic-negative reinforcement) are not amenable to assessment. Although it is theoretically possible to arrange a suitable test condition for such behavior, it would be ethically unacceptable to do so except under highly unusual circumstances. Third, low-frequency behavior problems pose difficulty for all assessment techniques. It is, of course, possible that a behavior problem occurs at a low rate because the naturally occurring conditions that occasion and maintain it are not experienced frequently. If so, their inclusion in a functional analysis should have the effect of increasing rate of the behavior. If not, the only alternative to assessment is the descriptive analysis (see next section). Finally, it is possible that a maintaining variable may elude detection or, alternatively, that although a source of reinforcement is identified for behavior, it is not the source that accounts for behavioral maintenance in the natural environment. The first problem may be solved through additional analysis; the second may be addressed by conducting naturalistic observations to determine if what is observed during assessment can be found elsewhere. It should be noted, however, that sensitivity of a behavior problem to any source of reinforcement is valuable information because it suggests conditions under which behavior might worsen.

Descriptive Analysis

Descriptive analysis involves direct observation of behavior under naturally occurring (uncontrolled) conditions. This approach has a long-standing tradition in our field, and its development was heavily influenced by Bijou, Peterson, and Ault (1968). In proposing a methodology for quantifying the results of direct observation, Bijou et al. described a system to "tag" behavioral events in time, which included the following components: (a) objective definitions of behavior and environment, (b) a coding system and rules for observations, (c) a quantitative method for summarizing the data, and (d) assessment of interobserver agreement. The fact that data can be collected, not only on the behavior of interest, but also on a number of contiguous environmental events, has opened the possibility of using descriptive analyses as a tentative basis for making hypotheses about behavioral function. The basic assumption underlying such hypotheses is that correlational relationships are suggestive of functional relationships—the higher the degree of correspondence (correlation) between events A and B, the higher the likelihood that these events are related causally. In other words, events that frequently precede problem behavior may reflect the influence of EOs (e.g., deprivation from attention or the presentation of aversive stimulation in the form of demands); whereas events that frequently follow problem behavior may be suggestive of maintaining contingencies (e.g., the delivery of attention as positive reinforcement or the termination of instructional demands as negative reinforcement).

The principal components of a descriptive analysis are easily understood (see above) and have become the basis for measurement in most research conducted in applied behavior analysis. Observations are conducted in one or more environmental contexts, and occurrences of behavior are recorded in relationship to events that precede and follow it. Although many variations of the descriptive analysis are possible and have been reported in the literature, most can be classified as belonging to one of three types. The most common form involves continuous observation of multiple events using frequency, interval, or time sampling procedures. Approximations to continuous observation include ABC (antecedent-behavior-consequence) narrative recording and the scatter plot technique.

Continuous Observation (Frequency, Interval, and Time-Sample Recording)

Based on the work of Bijou et al. (1968), most current approaches to descriptive analysis involve continuous (or near continuous) observation of behavior and the recording of stimulus and response codes either as frequencies or as the presence/ absence of events during brief time periods (e.g., 10 seconds) using interval or time sampling techniques. These methods have been used to collect data on a wide range of behaviors across a variety of settings. For example, Wahler (1975) used interval recording to identify events that were correlated with the occurrence of disruptive behaviors at home and at school, and Epstein, Parker, McCoy, and McGee (1976) used time sampling to identify differences in eating patterns between obese and non-obese children.

Results obtained through descriptive analysis may show that the presence or absence of behavior covaries with global and somewhat static features of the environment. For example, Ninness, Fuerst, and Rutherford (1995) observed that the disruptive behavior of two boys occurred more often in the absence of supervision; and Baumeister, MacLean, Kelly, and Kasari (1980) and Schroeder et al. (1982) found that stereotypic and/or SIB behaviors tended to occur more often in the absence of stimulating leisure materials. Relationships such as these, although correlational in nature, point to aspects of the environment that might be easily modified and subsequently evaluated, again using descriptive analyses.

The analysis of transient events, such as patterns of social interaction, may also be accomplished by examining raw data from descriptive analyses, but only if correlations between events are extremely large (e.g., if occurrences of one person's specific behavior reliably precede or follow another person's specific behavior). This outcome is unlikely under most circumstances because (a) many interactional sequences may involve a variety of different behaviors, such that there are relatively few occurrences of specific responses, (b) influential antecedent events may not always precede the target behavior (e.g., demands may not always precede episodes of aggression), and (c) influential consequences may not always follow the target behavior due to their inconsistent delivery. For these reasons, the interpretation of descriptive data often requires further analysis by way of conditional probabilities, which isolate pairs (or clusters) of events from the ongoing behavioral stream and determine the likelihood that one event was either preceded or followed by another event. It is the conditional probabilities of events, rather than their overall occurrence, that suggest the existence of a contingency (i.e., a functional relationship).

Examples of both frequency-of-occurrence and conditional probability analysis can be found in two recent studies. Mace and Belfiore (1990) conducted a descriptive analysis of a woman's repetitive stereotypic behaviors via 10-second interval recording. They noted that its most frequent antecedents were two types of interaction (demand and no demand) and that its most frequent consequences were disapproval and continued instruction. These data suggested the possibility that stereotypy was maintained by social reinforcement. However, there was some discrepancy between antecedent and consequent events. If stereotypy was maintained by attention as a consequence, the antecedent delivery of demands was functionally unrelated to the behavior. By contrast, if stereotypy was maintained by escape from demands, it must have been maintained on a highly intermittent schedule because social interaction typically followed the behavior. The authors subsequently conducted a functional analysis, which showed that stereotypy was maintained by escape. In a later study, Mace and Lalli (1991) conducted a descriptive analysis of an individual's delusional speech and examined the data by way of conditional probabilities: (a) the likelihood of bizarre speech following a given antecedent, (b) the likelihood of a given consequence following bizarre speech during a task, and (c) the likelihood of a given consequence following bizarre speech during non-interaction times. Results suggested that bizarre speech probably served a social function and was maintained by either attention or escape. The authors then conducted a functional analysis, which showed that the behavior was maintained by attention.

The studies by Mace and Belfiore (1990) and Mace and Lalli (1991) are important in they demonstrated different ways in which descriptive data could be analyzed in an attempt to identify behavioral function. Results of both studies also showed that the descriptive analysis identified a social function for the target behaviors, thereby serving as a guide in the construction of a subsequent functional analysis. However, the descriptive analysis did not seem well suited to the identification of positive versus negative reinforcement. This apparent limitation was verified by Lerman and Iwata (1993), who conducted independent descriptive and functional analyses of the SIB of 6 individuals. Using outcomes of the functional analysis as standards for comparison, they found that the descriptive analysis was useful in determining whether behavior was maintained by social versus automatic reinforcement, but that it did discriminate well between attention and escape as sources of social reinforcement.

Another method for analyzing descriptive data is to calculate overall conditional probabilities across sessions (Repp & Karsh, 1994). Finally, there are a variety of statistical techniques based on leg-sequential analysis (Emerson et al., 1995; Wehby, Symons, & Shores, 1995), whose description is beyond the scope of this presentation. Results of the Emerson et al. study are noteworthy because, unlike Lerman and Iwata (1993), they observed correspondence between results of descriptive and functional analyses in 12 of the 14 cases for which both methods identified a behavioral function.

The obvious strength of descriptive analysis based on continuous recording is the high degree of precision afforded by quantitative data collection; the measures are often identical to those used in a functional analysis. Second, although some amount of training is required to yield reliable data, the basic methodology is easily understood and is widely used for establishing behavioral baselines and for evaluating treatment effects. Third, assessment can be done under more or less naturalistic conditions without having to induce control over environmental context. Finally, correlational relationships may actually reflect causal relationships. To the extent that this is true, results obtained from descriptive analyses may provide an adequate basis for program development.

One limitation inherent to the descriptive analysis the fact that correlational relationships exists to the extent that the temporal contiguity of two events is highly likely; therefore, relative frequencies of occurrence are the data of interest. For this reason, the descriptive analysis may not be sensitive to the influence of intermittent schedules. If behavior is not reliably followed a particular consequence, as is the case when behavior problems produce attention or escape only when they become intolerable, a low conditional probability may result. Under such conditions, a functional relationship may go undetected. The opposite problem may occur when behavior problems are followed by consequences that do not function as reinforcers. For example, institutional policies may dictate that teachers or therapists must intervene whenever behavior problems occur. If so, an analysis of conditional probabilities will suggest that a large proportion of behavior problems are maintained by attention. For these reasons, correlational relationships may not predict functional relationships, and the conclusions based on descriptive analyses should be made cautiously. Finally, the time required to conduct a thorough descriptive analysis may equal or exceed that required to conduct a functional analysis. For example, in the few studies in which both types of analysis were conducted (Lerman & Iwata, 1993; Mace & Lalli, 1991; Sasso et al., 1992), the time requirements were comparable.

ABC Narrative Recording

An efficient alternative to continuous observation, especially for behaviors occurring at relatively low frequencies, involves collecting data only when the behavior of interest is observed. On those occasions, the observer notes the occurrence of behavior and of the events that immediately preceded and followed it (see Figure 3 as an example of a data sheet). This pattern of observation, antecedent-behavior-consequence, has given rise the generic term "ABC" recording that is also sometimes applied to continuous observation procedures. Bijou et al. (1968) illustrated the use of ABC narrative recording during continuous observations. Their purpose was merely to collect samples of behavior, which would be used to develop response definition codes for collecting quantitative data using interval observation procedures. Nevertheless, the basic ABC narrative format has remained a common method for capturing behavioral sequences as they occur. A collection of such sequences across time may indicate that certain events are more likely than others to occur in close temporal contiguity with the target behavior.

Although ABC recording is described in most textbooks on applied behavior analysis (e.g., Cooper, Heron, & Heward, 1987; Miltenberger, 1997), included in some systems for assessing the function of behavior problems (Groden, 1989; O'Neill, Horner, Albin, Storey, & Sprague, 1990), and perhaps widely used in clinical practice, the actual data obtained from such analyses are not included or summarized in published research (see Arndorfer, Miltenberger, Woster, Rortvedt, & Gaffaney, 1994; Durand & Kishi, 1987; Kennedy & Itkonen, 1993). Therefore, the utility of narrative recording in identifying behavioral function is unknown. As a means of gathering preliminary data, it is likely to be superior to indirect methods of assessment (see next section) merely because it involves direct observation. However, there are several potential problems associated with narrative recording beyond those common to all descriptive analysis methods. The first problem is reliability. Given the open-ended nature of typical ABC recording, it is possible that observers may record subjective interpretations or suspected motives rather than actual observed events. For example, in a large-scale study of over 400 individuals living in three Canadian institutions who engaged in SIB, Maurice and Trudel (1982) reported that staff, when asked about the circumstances under which SIB occurred, most often indicated that "frustration" was the immediate antecedent event. To the extent this and other inferred states (e.g., agitation, anger) are reported during ABC recording, reliability will be compromised, as will the ability to identify observable features of the environment that may occasion behavior. Second, it is unclear how compilations of ABC data should be summarized and interpreted. For example, although Arndorfer et al. presented the conclusions they reached based on the collection of ABC data, they did not indicate the basis for those conclusions, nor did they present any of the data. Finally, because antecedent and consequent events are recorded only when the target behavior is observed, it is unclear that these events are correlated with the target behavior because they could occur just as often in the absence of problem behavior. For these reasons, narrative recording seems best

		Antecedent-Behavior-Consequence (ABC) Analysis		
	Client:_____ Observer:_____			
	Target Behavior: _____ Date:_____			
Time	Location	Antecedents	Behavior	Consequences

Figure 3. Example of a data sheet used for ABC narrative recording

suited for the purpose originally suggested by Bijou et al. (1968); that is, to aid in the development of more formal observation methods.

The Scatter Plot

Another approximation to continuous observation is called the "scatter plot" and was first described by Touchette, MacDonald, and Langer (1985). Rather than recording behavior or even its antecedents and consequences as these events occur, the observer merely records the extent to which behavior occurred (none, a few occurrences, or many occurrences) at the end of predetermined (usually half-hour) intervals of time throughout the day and across successive days on a data grid (see example in Figure 4). If a recurring response pattern is observed and if there is some regularity to the individual's schedule, temporal distributions in behavior may be related to specific activities or the presence of particular individuals. Based on this information, it may be possible to reduce the frequency of problem behavior by altering the individual's daily routine.

Touchette et al. (1985) presented scatter plot data for three individuals who engaged in SIB. Results showed clear temporal patterns of responding associated with specific environmental events for two to the three individuals (a work activity for one individual; the presence of a staff member for the other). Subsequent changes in these events were associated with reductions in SIB. The authors concluded that, although the scatter plot does not identify specific behavioral antecedents or consequences, it may be useful in identifying more global "stimulus control" over a wide range of problem behavior and that, as a result, it may serve as both an efficient and adequate assessment tool under certain conditions.

The scatter plot has become a common assessment procedure in clinical practice (Desrochers, Hile, & Williams-Mosely, 1997), and references to its use can be found in several studies (e.g., Ardnorfer et al., 1994; Durand & Kishi, 1987;

Kennedy & Itkonen, 1993). However, the utility of the scatter plot remains unclear because the actual data have not been presented in these studies and no replications of the Touchette et al. (1985) study have appeared in the literature. Kahng et al. (1998) recently conducted such a replication by collecting scatter plot data over a 30-day period for each of 20 individuals who engaged in a variety of problem behaviors. Five sets of data were withdrawn from further analysis due to low interobserver agreement, and no temporal distributions in behavior were observed in any of the 15 remaining scatter plots when examined visually by a group of behavior analysts. These results indicate that, although it may be possible to identify recurring temporal patterns of behavior via the scatter plot (Touchette et al.), such patterns are unlikely to be encountered routinely. Kahng et al. also noted that the amount of time required to complete a scatter plot greatly exceeded that typically required to conduct a functional analysis.

Indirect (Anecdotal) Methods

These methods derive their name from the fact that direct observation of behavior is not conducted during assessment. Instead, the clinician attempts to identify environmental correlates of behavior by soliciting anecdotal reports from significant others such as parents, teachers, or caregivers. As extensions of the traditional clinical interview, these assessments provide a more consistent format for gathering verbal report data through the use of checklists, rating scales, or questionnaires.

The Motivation Analysis Rating Scale (MARS; Wieseler, Hanson, Chamberlain, & Thompson, 1985) and the Motivation Assessment Scale (MAS; Durand & Crimmins, 1988) are similar in design. They consist of statements (MARS) or questions (MAS) describing conditions under which behavior may or may not occur. Each item is scored by the respondent on a Likert scale (4-point range for the MARS, 7-point range for the MAS) to indicate the extent to which behavior occurs under the conditions described (e.g., never,

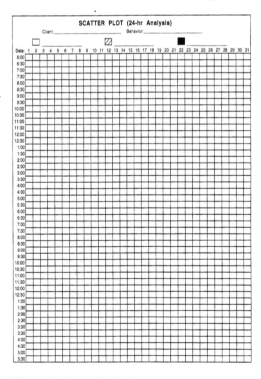

Figure 4. Example of a data sheet used for collecting scatter plot data.

seldom, etc.). The MARS contains 6 items, 2 each focusing on three potential functions: social-positive reinforcement, social-negative reinforcement, and automatic-positive reinforcement. The MAS contains 16 items addressing the same three functions as those addressed by the MARS; however, social-positive reinforcement is further delineated by its source (access to attention versus access to tangible reinforcers). Results are summarized by adding (or averaging) the point values for groups of questions pertaining to the same function, and it is assumed that the highest category total reflects the function of the target behavior.

The Behavioral Diagnosis and Treatment Information Form (BDTIF; Bailey & Pyles, 1989) and the Stimulus Control Checklist (SCC; Rolider & Van Houten, 1993) are designed as questionnaires and contain items similar to those found on the MARS and MAS. In addition, both the BDTIF and SCC include several questions that examine the influence of physiological variables on behavior. Unlike the MARS and the BDTIF, the BDTIF and the SCC do not yield numerical summary scores. Instead, the clinician considers and interprets information in the same manner as might be done following an interview.

Finally, the Functional Analysis Interview Form (FAIF; O'Neill et al., 1990) provides a format for conducting an extended clinical interview. The FAIF is an 11-part instrument containing sections on topographical descriptions, general factors that may influence behavior (medical conditions, diet, schedule, staffing patterns), antecedents and consequences, communication skills, reinforcers, and history of treatment.

Aside from the fact that indirect approaches to assessment lend structure to the interview process, their principal advantage is ease of use. With the exception of the FAIF, the instruments can be completed in a few minutes and require relatively little expertise to administer. As a result, these instruments are commonly used in practice and have been reported in a small proportion of studies as the primary bases for designing treatment procedures.

The major disadvantage of indirect assessments is that the verbal reports on which conclusions are based may be unreliable and therefore invalid. Very little research has been conducted on either the reliability or validity of the instruments described above. The MARS, BDTIF, SCC, and FAIF have not been evaluated adequately by independent investigators; however, several characteristics of the MAS have been examined in a series of studies.

In the original report on the MAS, Durand and Crimmins (1988) administered the scale to pairs of classroom teachers and aides for 50 students with developmental disabilities who engaged in SIB. Comparisons of mean category scores (four categories, each consisting of summed scores from four items) between raters yielded correlations ranging from .89 to .98. The authors also compared MAS scores with results obtained from functional analyses conducted with 8 of the students. In every case, the highest category score on the MAS matched the assessment condition containing the highest level of SIB. Furthermore, rank-order correlations between MAS category scores and levels of SIB across assessment conditions produced an overall coefficient of .99 (This finding is especially significant because it means that raters were able to predict not only the functional analysis condition showing the highest level of SIB, but also the relative distribution of SIB across the other assessment conditions). These results indicated that the MAS had a high degree of interrater reliability and almost perfect validity when compared with results obtained from a functional analysis.

In an attempt to replicate these findings, Zarcone, Rodgers, Iwata, Rourke, and Dorsey (1991) administered the MAS to pairs of caregivers and/or teachers of 55 individuals who engaged in SIB. To allow comparison with the data reported by Durand and Crimmins (1988), the authors calculated correlations between raters for category scores and obtained a mean coefficient of .41 (range, -.80 to .99). They also calculated item-by-item, percentage agreement scores and obtained a mean of 20% (range, 0% to 63%). Considering the fact that MAS scores are based on a rating scale with a large number of anchor points (seven) and that the numeric ratings represent nothing more than estimations, Zarcone et al. reanalyzed the data and counted an agreement if one rater's score was within plus or minus 1 of the other rater's score. Mean reliability based on these "adjacent" agreements was 48% (range, 0% to 88%). Finally, the authors calculated agreement based solely on whether pairs of raters yielded the highest total for the same category (irrespective of scores for individual items within that category and of the relative ranks for other categories) and found that raters agreed on the primary function of the behavior problem in only 29.1 % of the cases. In light of these results, indicating that the MAS was unreliable, the authors did not undertake a validity analysis.

Results from subsequent studies examining various aspects of the MAS have been similar to those reported by Zarcone et al. (1991). Interrater agreement, regardless of the method used for calculation, has been consistently low (Arndorfer et al., 1994; Conroy, Fox, Bucklin, & Good, 1996; Crawford, Brockel, Schauss, & Miltenberger, 1992; Kearney, 1994, Newton & Sturmey, 1991; Sigafoos, Kerr, & Roberts, 1994; Spreat & Connelly, 1996), and intrarater agreement—correspondence between repeated scoring by the same rater—has averaged only about 50% (Arndorfer et al.; Conroy et al.).

Rather than assessing the reliability of an already existing instrument, Sigafoos, Kerr, Roberts, and Couzens (1993) selectively combined items from the FAIF, SCC, and BDTIF into an 18-item composite. They administered this scale to pairs of caregivers for 18 individuals with developmental disabilities who engaged in frequent and intense episodes of aggression, and obtained a mean interrater agreement score of 43.32% (range, 20% to 86.66%).

Although future research may produce findings different than those reported to date, current results, especially those obtained for the MAS, indicate that indirect assessment of behavioral function is highly unreliable. This is not surprising, given the nature of the task and the conditions under which data are collected. Typical questions found in rating scales ask not only whether the informant has observed something in the past, but also the *degree* to which certain events are correlated with behavior, whether the behavior occurs under conditions difficult to observe, and/ or if the behavior is accompanied by affective states (e.g., Question # 9 from the

MAS: "Does it appear to you that he or she enjoys performing this behavior, and would continue even if no one was around?"). Responses to such questions require a history of observing the behavior under numerous conditions, accurate recall, and the ability to transform these recollections into rough estimates of conditional probability that conform to the questions being posed.

One suggested solution to the reliability problem has been to synthesize the ratings obtained from multiple informants (Kearney, 1994). This practice is analogous to that followed when individuals examine behavioral data and reach a consensus about the presence or absence of change. However, there is a high degree of correspondence between behavioral data and the events they portray. In the case of subjective ratings, pooling may have the effect of obscuring legitimate differences among informants, such that the more accurate scores of one informant are outweighed by the less accurate scores of others (Spreat & Connelly, 1996). Other suggestions have included using rating scales only with behaviors that occur at relatively high frequencies (Kearny) and soliciting ratings only from well-trained staff (Spreat & Connelly; Zarcone et al., 1991). However, given the anecdotal nature of the data being collected, it is doubtful that any of these strategies would yield results as reliable as those obtained through direct observation.

In summary, indirect assessment of behavioral function via rating scales has not been shown to be a reliable practice. Nevertheless, instruments such as the MAS may helpful as structured methods for gathering information during a clinical interview, assuming that results obtained are later verified using more objective measurement.

Areas for Future Research

As noted earlier in this chapter, the functional analysis of behavior disorders is one of the most intense areas of investigation in our field. The fact that much of this growth has occurred during the past decade can be readily seen in patterns of publication. For example, the cumulative index for Volume 20 of the *Journal of Applied Behavior Analysis* contained one key-word reference to functional analysis; the cumulative index for Volume 30 contained 96 references. With the research base expanding at this rate and in a number of different directions, it is difficult to limit suggestions for future investigations. Nevertheless, there are several broad areas of inquiry in which additional work is needed.

The first area involves continued refinement in methodology. It is apparent that the full functional analysis is comprehensive and that the brief version is efficient. Further improvements in both may yield a methodology (or several methodologies) that produce a high proportion of positive outcomes yet require little time, and the hierarchical approach described by Vollmer et al. (1995) represents a nice beginning. Additional refinements may result from a consideration of factors that maximize immediate control over behavior under test conditions. For example, the extent to which contingent attention (the maintaining reinforcer) increases the rate of a behavior during an assessment session may be a function of several factors, including: (a) the presence of salient discriminative stimuli (i.e., the same therapist associated paired with that condition) and (b) EOs (how much attention was received immediately prior to the session), qualitative or quantitative characteristics of reinforcers, and so forth. Each of these variables may be evaluated separately, and then the most effective elements may be combined. It is also possible that preliminary data from other sources, such as descriptive analyses, may eliminate the need to test for sensitivity to improbable functions. This shifts the burden of refinement. At the present time, there are no guidelines for selecting the "naturalistic" conditions in which descriptive data will be taken. In many investigations, it is common to obtain representative samples by collecting data during a variety of activities. However, it is possible that clearer results might be obtained by conducting observations during relatively few but highly disparate activities. For example, escape behavior is most likely to occur in a demand context, attention-maintained behavior is most likely to occur in a social (non-demand) context, and behavior maintained by automatic reinforcement is most likely to be maintained in a relatively barren environment. Thus, these three types of situations might serve as the primary contexts for collecting descriptive data.

A second area that remains a challenge is the assessment of extremely high-risk, low-frequency, or cyclical behaviors. These types of behavior either cannot be tolerated or usually are not seen, yet effective treatment may require identification of their controlling variables. Research efforts in this area may be guided by analyses of response classes (i.e., other behaviors that are correlated with but that are either more tolerable or more frequent than the target behavior), by repeated functional analyses conducted under varying environmental conditions (times, settings, etc.), or through the combined use of descriptive and functional analyses.

Finally, the major focus of functional analysis methodology has been on behavior disorders exhibited by children and those with disabling conditions such as mental retardation. Although the prevalence of behavior problems among these groups is high, it is dwarfed by the sheer numbers of behavior problems found in other populations. For example, eating disorders (anorexia, binge eating, etc.) are commonly observed in young adult females, and it is likely that these behaviors have a social component. Although the stimuli that are functionally related to these disorders may be so ubiquitous as to defy attempts to control them, functional analyses may identify important social contingencies whose alteration may have immense therapeutic benefit. As another example, there will be greater concern over the design of environments for older adults as the age distribution of the population shifts upward. Changes in lifestyle or physical functioning maybe associated with the onset of a number of behavior problems (e.g., noncompliance, skill loss, social isolation) whose maintenance is a function of current features of the environment. Thus, a functional analysis of problems associated with aging may ultimately prevent needless institutionalization. Finally, many behavior analysts who currently work in traditional areas of clinical practice can immediately contribute to efforts aimed and identifying the functional characteristics of common psychiatric disorders. By illustrating the use of functional analysis methodology with these very different problems, we hope that readers will be encouraged to make further extensions.

Reading Objectives

1. What is meant by the term "functional analysis," and how does its application differ with respect to behavioral acquisition and reduction?
2. Describe and give examples of the contingencies that maintain behavior problems.
3. What are the defining features of functional analyses, descriptive analyses, and indirect approaches to behavioral assessment?
4. In the general model for conducting a functional analysis, what are the basic test and control conditions and what are their key elements?
5. What experimental designs are commonly used in conducting functional analyses, and what are their strengths and limitations?
6. What are the advantages/limitations of functional analysis methodology?
7. What is meant by an analysis of "conditional probabilities" and why is such an analysis important in interpreting data from a descriptive analysis?
8. What are the major limitations of ABC recording and the scatter plot?
9. What is the major advantage and the major limitation of indirect approaches to assessment?
10. Based on your reading, suggest one method (not mentioned in the chapter) for improving functional analysis methodology.

References

Arndorfer, R. E., Miltenberger, R. G., Woster, S. H., Rortvedt, A. K., & Gaffaney, T. (1994). Home-based descriptive and experimental analysis of problem behaviors in children. *Topics in Early Childhood Special Education, 14,* 64-87.

Baer, D. M., Wolf, M. M., & Risley, T. R. (1968). Some current dimensions of applied behavior analysis. *Journal of Applied Behavior Analysis, 1,* 91-97.

Bailey, J. S., & Pyles, D. A. M. (1989). Behavioral Diagnostics. In E. Cipani (Ed.), *The treatment of severe behavior disorders: Behavior analysis approach* (pp. 85-107). Washington, D.C.: American Association on Mental Retardation.

Barrett, R. P., McGonigle, J. J., Ackles, P. K., & Brukhart, J. E. (1987). Behavioral treatment of chronic aerophagia. *American Journal of Mental Deficiency, 91,* 620-625.

Baumeister, A. A., & Forehand, R. L. (1973). Stereotyped acts. In N. R. Ellis (Ed.), *International review of research in mental retardation,* (pp. 55-93). New York: Academic Press.

Baumeister, A. A., MacLean, W. E., Kelly, J., & Kasari, C. (1980). Observational studies of retarded children with multiple stereotyed movements. *Journal of Abnormal Child Psychology, 8,* 501-521.

Berkson, G., & Mason, W. A. (1963). Stereotyped movements of mental defectives: 3. Situational effects. *American Journal of Mental Deficiency, 68,* 409-412.

Berkson, G., & Mason, W. A. (1965). Stereotyped movements of mental defectives: 4. The effects of toys and the character of the acts. *American Journal of Mental Deficiency, 70,* 511-524.

Bijou, S. W., Peterson, R. F., & Ault, M. H. (1968). A method to integrate descriptive and experimental field studies at the level of data and empirical concepts. *Journal of Applied Behavior Analysis, 1,* 175-191.

Carr, E. G., & Durand, V. M. (1985). Reducing behavior problems through functional communication training. *Journal of Applied Behavior Analysis, 18,* 111-126.

Carr, E. G., Newsom, C. D., & Binkoff, J. A. (1976). Stimulus control of self-destructive behavior in a psychotic child. *Journal of Abnormal Child Psychology, 4,* 139-153.

Carr, E. G., Newsom, C. D., & Binkoff, J. A. (1980). Escape as a factor in the aggressive behavior of two retarded children. *Journal of Applied Behavior Analysis, 13,* 101-117.

Carr, J. E., Taylor, C. C., Wallander, R. J., & Reiss, M. L. (1996). A functional-analytic approach to the diagnosis of a transient tic disorder. *Journal of Behavior Therapy and Experimental Psychiatry, 27,* 291-297.

Cataldo, M. F., & Harris, J. (1982). The biological basis for self-injury in the mentally retarded. *Analysis and Intervention in Developmental Disabilities, 2,* 21-39.

Conroy, M. A., Fox, J. J., Bucklin, A., & Good, W. (1996). An analysis of the reliability and stability of the Motivation Assessment Scale in assessing the challenging behaviors of persons with developmental disabilities. *Education and Training in Mental Retardation and Developmental Disabilities, 31,* 243-250.

Cooper, J. O., Heron, T. E., & Heward, W. L. (1987.) *Applied behavior analysis.* Columbus, OH: Merrill.

Cooper, L. J., Wacker, D. P., Sasso, G. M., Reimers, T. M., & Donn, L. K. (1990). Using parents as therapists to evaluate appropriate behavior of their children: Application to a tertiary diagnostic clinic. *Journal of Applied Behavior Analysis, 23,* 285-296.

Cowdery, G. E., Iwata, B. A., & Pace, G. M. (1990). Effects and side effects of DRO as treatment for self-injurious behavior. *Journal of Applied Behavior Analysis, 23,* 497-506.

Crawford, J., Brockel, B., Schauss, S., & Miltenberger, R. G. (1992). A comparison of methods for the functional assessment of stereotypic behavior. *Journal of the Association for Persons with Severe Handicaps, 17,* 77-86.

DeLissovoy, V. (1963). Head banging in early childhood: A suggested cause. *Journal of Genetic Psychology, 102,* 109-114.

Derby, K. M., Wacker, D. P., Sasso, G., Steege, M., Northup, J., Cigrand, K., & Asmus, J. (1992). Brief functional assessment techniques to evaluate aberrant behavior in an outpatient setting: A summary of 79 cases. *Journal of Applied Behavior Analysis, 25,* 713-721.

Desrochers, M. N., Hile, M. G., & Williams-Mosely, T. L. (1997). Survey of functional assessment procedures used with individuals who display mental retardation and severe problem behaviors. *American Journal on Mental Retardation, 101,* 535-546.

Durand, V. M., & Carr, E. G. (1987). Social influences on "self-stimulatory" behavior: Analysis and treatment application. *Journal of Applied Behavior Analysis, 20*, 119-132.

Durand, V. M., & Carr, E. G. (1991). Functional communication training to reduce challenging behavior: Maintenance and application in new settings. *Journal of Applied Behavior Analysis, 24*, 251-264.

Durand, V. M., & Carr, E. G. (1992). An analysis of maintenance following functional communication training. *Journal of Applied Behavior Analysis, 25*, 777-794.

Durand, V. M., & Crimmins, D. B. (1988). Identifying the variables maintaining self-injurious behavior. *Journal of Autism and Developmental Disorders, 18*, 99-117.

Durand, V. M., & Kishi, G. (1987). Reducing severe behavior problems among persons with dual sensory impairments: An evaluation of a technical assistance model. *Journal of the Association for Persons with Severe Handicaps, 12*, 2-10.

Emerson, E., Reeves, D., Thompson, S., Henderson, D., Robertson, J., & Howard, D. (1996). Time-based lag sequential analysis and the functional assessment of challenging behavior. *Journal of Intellectual Disability Research, 40*, 260-274.

Epstein, L. H., Parker, L., McCoy, J. F., & McGee, G. (1976). Descriptive analysis of eating regulation in obese and nonobese children. *Journal of Applied Behavior Analysis, 9*, 407-415.

Fisher, W. W., Ninness, H. A. C., Piazza, C. C., & Owen-DeSchryver, J. S. (1996). On the reinforcing effects of the content of verbal attention. *Journal of Applied Behavior Analysis*, 235-238.

Fisher, W. W., Piazza, C. C., & Chiang, C. L. (1996). Effects of equal and unequal reinforcer duration during functional analysis. *Journal of Applied Behavior Analysis, 29*, 117-120.

Groden, G. (1989). A guide for conducting a comprehensive behavioral analysis of a target behavior. *Journal of Behavior Therapy and Experimental Psychiatry, 20*, 163-169.

Hagopian, L. P., Fisher, W. W., Thompson, R. H., Owen-DeSchryver, J., Iwata, B. A., & Wacker, D. P. (1997). Toward the development of structured criteria for interpretation of functional analysis data. *Journal of Applied Behavior Analysis, 30*, 313-326.

Heller, R. F., & Strang, H. R. (1973). Controlling bruxism through automated aversive conditioning. *Behavior Research and Therapy, 11*, 327-329.

Horner, R. H., & Day, H. M. (1991). The effects of response efficiency on functionally equivalent competing behaviors. *Journal of Applied Behavior Analysis, 24*, 719-732.

Iwata, B. A. (1987). Negative reinforcement in applied behavior analysis: An emerging technology. *Journal of Applied Behavior Analysis, 20*, 361-378.

Iwata, B. A., Dorsey, M. F., Slifer, K. J., Bauman, K. E., & Richman, G. S. (1994). Toward a functional analysis of self-injury. *Journal of Applied Behavior Analysis, 27*, 197-209. (Reprinted from *Analysis and Intervention in Developmental Disabilities, 2*, 3-20, 1982).

Iwata, B. A., Duncan, B. A., Zarcone, J. R., Lerman, D. C., & Shore, B. A. (1994). A sequential, test-control methodology for conducting functional analyses of self-injurious behavior. *Behavior Modification, 18*, 289-306.

Iwata, B. A., Pace, G. M., Cowdery, G. E., & Miltenberger, R. G. (1994). What makes extinction work: An analysis of procedural form and function. *Journal of Applied Behavior Analysis, 27*, 131-144.

Iwata, B. A., Pace, G. M., Dorsey, M. F., Zarcone, J. R., Vollmer, T. R., Smith, R. G., Rodgers, T. A., Lerman, D. C., Shore, B. A., Mazaleski, J. L., Goh, H., Cowdery, G. E., Kalsher, M. J., & Willis, K. D. (1994). The functions of self-injurious behavior: An experimental-epidemiological analysis. *Journal of Applied Behavior Analysis, 27*, 215-240.

Iwata, B. A., Pace, G. M., Kalsher, M. J., Cowdery, G. E., & Cataldo, M. F. (1990). Experimental analysis and extinction of self-injurious escape behavior. *Journal of Applied Behavior Analysis, 23*, 11-27.

Iwata, B. A., Vollmer, T. R., & Zarcone, J. R. (1990). The experimental (functional) analysis of behavior disorders: Methodology, applications, and limitations. In A. C. Repp & N. N. Singh (Eds.), *Perspectives on the use of nonaversive and aversive interventions for persons with developmental disabilities* (pp. 301-330). Sycamore, IL: Sycamore Publishing Co.

Iwata, B. A., Vollmer, T. R., Zarcone, J. R., & Rodgers, T. A. (1993). Treatment classification and selection based on behavioral function. In R. Van Houten & S. Axelrod (Eds.), *Behavior analysis and treatment* (pp. 101-125). New York: Plenum.

Johnston, J. M., Greene, K. S., Rawal, A., Vazin, T., & Winston, M. (1991). Effects of caloric level on ruminating. *Journal of Applied Behavior Analysis, 24*, 597-603.

Kahng, S., Iwata, B. A., Fischer, S. M., Page, T. J., Treadwell, K. R. H., Williams, D. E., & Smith R. G. (1998). Temporal distributions of problem behavior based on scatter plot analysis. *Journal of Applied Behavior Analysis, 31*, 593-604.

Kearney, C. A. (1994). Interrater reliability of the Motivation Assessment Scale: Another, closer look. *Journal of the Association for Persons with Severe Handicaps, 19*, 139-142.

Kennedy, C. H., & Itkonen, T. (1993). Effects of setting events on the problem behavior of students with severe disabilities. *Journal of Applied Behavior Analysis, 26*, 321-327.

Lalli, J. S., Casey, S., & Kates, K. (1995). Reducing escape behavior and increasing task completion with functional communication training, extinction, and response chaining. *Journal of Applied Behavior Analysis, 28*, 261-268.

Lerman, D. C., & Iwata, B. A. (1993). Descriptive and experimental analyses of variables maintaining self-injurious behavior. *Journal of Applied Behavior Analysis, 26*, 293-319.

Lovaas, O. I., Freitag, G., Gold, V. J., & Kassorla, I. C. (1965). Experimental studies in childhood schizophrenia: Analysis of self-destructive behavior. *Journal of Experimental Child Psychology, 2*, 67-84.

Lovaas, O. I., Newsom, C., & Hickman, C. (1987). Self-stimulatory behavior and perceptual reinforcement. *Journal of Applied Behavior Analysis, 20,* 45-68.

Lovaas, O. I., & Simmons, J. Q. (1969). Manipulation of self-destruction in three retarded children. *Journal of Applied Behavior Analysis, 2,* 143-157.

Mace, F. C., & Belfiore, P. (1990). Behavioral momentum in the treatment of escape-motivated stereotypy. *Journal of Applied Behavior Analysis, 23,* 507-514.

Mace, F. C., Browder, D. M., & Lin, Y. (1987). Analysis of demand conditions associated with stereotypy. *Journal of Behavior Therapy and Experimental Psychiatry, 18,* 25-31.

Mace, F. C., & Lalli, J. S. (1991). Linking descriptive and experimental analyses in the treatment of bizarre speech. *Journal of Applied Behavior Analysis, 24,* 553-562.

Mace, F. C., Page, T. J., Ivancic, M. T., & O'Brien, S. (1986). Analysis of environmental determinants of aggression and disruption in mentally retarded children. *Applied Research in Mental Retardation, 7,* 203-221.

Mace, F. C., Webb, M. E., Sharkey, R. W., Mattson, D. M., & Rosen, H. S. (1988). Functional analysis and treatment of bizarre speech. *Journal of Behavior Therapy & Experimental Psychiatry, 19,* 289-296.

Maurice, P., & Trudel, G. (1982). Self-injurious behavior: Prevalence and relationships to environmental events. In J. H. Hollis & C. E. Meyers (Eds.), *Life-threatening behavior: Analysis and intervention* (pp. 81-103). Washington DC: American Association on Mental Deficiency.

Michael, J. L. (1982). Distinguishing between discriminative and motivational functions of stimuli. *Journal of the Experimental Analysis of Behavior, 37,* 149-155.

Michael, J. L. (1993). Establishing operations. *The Behavior Analyst, 16,* 191-206.

Miltenberger, R. G. (1997). *Behavior modification: Principles and procedures.* Pacific Grove, CA: Brooks/Cole.

Newton, J. T., & Sturmey, P. (1991). The Motivation Assessment Scale; inter-rater reliability and internal consistency in a British sample. *Journal of Mental Deficiency Research, 35,* 472-474.

Ninness, H. A. C., Fuerst, J., & Rutherford, R. (1995). A descriptive analysis of disruptive behavior during pre-and post-unsupervised self-management by students with serious emotional disturbance: A within-study replication. *Journal of Emotional and Behavioral Disorders, 3,* 230-240.

Northup, J., Wacker, D., Sasso, G., Steege, M., Cigrand, K., Cook, J., & DeRaad, A. (1991). A brief functional analysis of aggressive and alternative behavior in an outclinic setting. *Journal of Applied Behavior Analysis, 24,* 509-522.

O'Neill, R. E., Horner, R. H., Albin, R. W., Storey, K., & Sprague, J. R. (1990). *Functional analysis: A practical assessment guide.* Sycamore, IL: Sycamore, Publishing Co.

Peck, S. M., Wacker, D. P., Berg, W. K., Cooper, L. J., Brown, K. A., Richman, D., McComas, J. J., Frischmeyer, P., & Millard, T. (1996). Choice-making treatment of young children's severe behavior problems. *Journal of Applied Behavior Analysis, 29,* 263-290.

Piazza, C. C., Hanley, G. P., & Fisher, W. W. (1996). Functional analysis and treatment of cigarette pica. *Journal of Applied Behavior Analysis, 29*, 437-450.

Reimers, T. M., Wacker, D. P., Cooper, L. J., Sasso, G. M., Berg, W. K., & Steege, M. W. (1993). Assessing the functional properties of noncompliant behavior in an outpatient setting. *Child and Family Behavior Therapy, 15*, 1-15.

Repp, A. C., & Karsh, K. G. (1994). Hypothesis-based interventions for tantrum behaviors of persons with developmental disabilities in school settings. *Journal of Applied Behavior Analysis, 27*, 21-31.

Rolider, A., & Van Houten, R. (1993). The interpersonal treatment model. In R. Van Houten & S. Axelrod (Eds.), *Behavior analysis and treatment* (pp. 127-168). New York: Plenum.

Rortvedt, A. K., & Miltenberger, R. G. (1994). Analysis of a high-probability instructional sequence and time-out in the treatment of child noncompliance. *Journal of Applied Behavior Analysis, 27*, 327-330.

Sasso, G. M., Reimers, T. M., Cooper, L. J., Wacker, D., Berg, W., Steege, M., Kelly, L., & Allaire, A. (1992). Use of descriptive and experimental analyses to identify the functional properties of aberrant behavior in school settings. *Journal of Applied Behavior Analysis, 25*, 809-822.

Schroeder, S. R., Kanoy, R. C., Millick, J. A., Rojahn, J., Thios, S. J., & Stephens, M. (Eds.). (1982). Enviornmental antecedents which affect management and maintenance of programs for self-injurious behavior. In J. H. Hollis & C. E. Meyers (Eds.), *Life threatening behavior: Analysis and modification* (pp. 81-159). Washington, D.C.: American Association on Mental Deficiency.

Shirley, M. J., Iwata, B. A., Kahng, S., Mazaleski, J. L., & Lerman, D. C. (1997). Does functional communication training compete with ongoing contingencies of reinforcement? An analysis during response acquisition and maintenance. *Journal of Applied Behavior Analysis, 30*, 93-104.

Sigafoos, J., Kerr, M., Roberts, D., & Couzens, D. (1993). Reliability of structured interviews for the assessment of challenging behaviour. *Behaviour Change, 10*, 47-50.

Sigafoos, J., Kerr, M., & Roberts, D. (1994). Interrater reliability of the Motivation Assessment Scale: Failure to replicate with aggressive behavior. *Research in Developmental Disabilities, 15*, 333-342.

Skinner, B. F. (1953). *Science and human behavior.* New York: MacMillan.

Skinner, B. F. (1969). *Contingencies of reinforcement: A theoretical analysis.* Englewood Cliffs, NJ: Prentice-Hall.

Smith, R. G., Iwata, B. G., Goh, H., & Shore, B. A. (1995). Analysis of establishing operations for self-injury maintained by escape. *Journal of Applied Behavior Analysis, 28*, 515-535.

Solnick, J. V., Rincover, A., & Peterson, C. R. (1977). Some determinants of the reinforcing and punishing effects of timeout. *Journal of Applied Behavior Analysis, 10*, 415-424.

Spreat, S., & Connelly, L. (1996). Reliability analysis of the Motivation Assessment Scale. *American Journal on Mental Retardation, 100*, 528-532.

Touchette, P. E., MacDonald, R. F., & Langer, S. N. (1985). A scatter plot for identifying stimulus control of problem behavior. *Journal of Applied Behavior Analysis, 18*, 343-351.

Vaughan, M. E., & Michael, J. (1982). Automatic reinforcement: An important but ignored concept. *Behaviorism, 10*, 217-227.

Vollmer, T. R., Iwata, B. A., Duncan, B. A., & Lerman, D. C. (1993). Extensions of multielement functional analysis using reversal-type designs. *Journal of Developmental and Physical Disabilities, 5*, 311-325.

Vollmer, T. R., Iwata, B. A., Smith, R. G., & Rodgers, T. A. (1992). Reduction of multiple aberrant behaviors and concurrent development of self-care skills with differential reinforcement. *Research in Developmental Disabilities, 13*(3), 287-299.

Vollmer, T. R., Iwata, B. A., Zarcone, J. R., Smith, R. G., & Mazaleski, J. L. (1993a). The role of attention in the treatment of attention-maintained self-injurious behavior: Noncontingent reinforcement and differential reinforcement of other behavior. *Journal of Applied Behavior Analysis, 26*, 9-21.

Vollmer, T. R., Iwata, B. A., Zarcone, J. R., Smith, R. G., & Mazaleski, J. L. (1993b). Within-session patterns of self-injury as indicators of behavioral function. *Research in Developmental Disabilities, 14*, 479-492.

Vollmer, T. R., Marcus, B. A., Ringdahl, J. E., & Roane, H. S. (1995). Progressing from brief assessments to extended experimental analyses in the evaluation of aberrant behavior. *Journal of Applied Behavior Analysis, 28*, 561-576.

Vollmer, T. R., Northup, J., Ringdahl, J. E., LeBlanc, L. A., & Chauvin, T. M. (1996). Functional analysis of severe tantrums displayed by children with language delays: An outclinic assessment. *Behavior Modification, 20*, 97-115.

Wacker, D., Steege, M., Northup, J., Reimers, T., Berg, W., & Sasso, G. (1990). Use of functional analysis and acceptability measures to assess and treat severe behavior problems: An outpatient clinic model. In A. C. Repp & N. N. Singh (Eds.), *Perspectives on the use of nonaversive and aversive interventions for persons with developmental disabilities* (pp. 349-359). Sycamore, IL: Sycamore Publishing Co.

Wahler, R. G. (1975). Some structural aspects of deviant child behavior. *Journal of Applied Behavior Analysis, 8*, 27-42.

Wehby, J. H., Symons, F. J., & Shores, R. E. (1995). A descriptive analysis of aggressive behavior in classrooms for children with emotional and behavioral disorders. *Behavioral Disorders, 20*, 87-105.

Wehmeyer, M., Bourland, G., & Ingram, D. (1993). An analogue assessment of hand stereotypies in two cases of Rett syndrome. *Journal of Intellectual Disability Research, 37*, 95-102.

Wieseler, N. A., Hanson, R. H., Chamberlain, T. P., & Thompson, T. (1985). Functional taxonomy of stereotypic and self-injurious behavior. *Mental Retardation, 23*, 230-234.

Zarcone, J. R., Rodgers, T. A., Iwata, B. A., Rourke, D., & Dorsey, M. F. (1991). Reliability analysis of the Motivation Assessment Scale: A failure to replicate. *Research in Developmental Disabilities, 12*, 349-360.

Chapter 4

Current Issues in the Function-Based Treatment of Aberrant Behavior in Individuals with Developmental Disabilities

James E. Carr, Sean Coriaty, and Claudia L. Dozier
University of Nevada

Perhaps one of the biggest "paradigm shifts" in applied behavior analysis has been the change in the way decelerative interventions are prescribed for the aberrant behavior of individuals with developmental disabilities. This shift has also affected assessment and treatment practices with other populations; however, the most commonly studied clinical population in the behavior-analytic literature remains individuals diagnosed with mental retardation and related disabilities. Historically, the modal prescription method was to match an intervention to a specific behavioral topography. This led to the development of the Least Restrictive Alternative (LRA) philosophy of treatment selection, by which more intrusive interventions were only implemented after less intrusive interventions proved ineffective. Although the LRA philosophy was designed to minimize the application of punishment-based proce-dures, it often led to their prescription. Carr, Robinson, and Palumbo (1990) illustrated the possibility that without knowledge of behavioral function, the effectiveness of reinforcement-based procedures would be compromised. Conse-quently, interventions that were more intrusive would be implemented, possibly leading to the implementation of punishment-based procedures.

In the last two decades, the LRA model was altered so that interventions were increasingly matched to behavioral function rather than topography (Iwata, Vollmer, Zarcone, & Rodgers, 1993). This philosophical change has led to the development of functional assessment methods (for a review, see Iwata, Kahng, Wallace, & Lindberg, this volume), as well as function-based interventions. Many contempo-rary, function-based decelerative interventions are similar to those that were used before (e.g., extinction). However, our increased knowledge of behavioral function allows more confident treatment prescription. In addition, new interventions (e.g., noncontingent reinforcement) have been developed as a result of the functional approach. As a class of interventions, function-based procedures are clinically beneficial because they address (eliminate) the response-reinforcer contingency, instead of overpowering it. In addition, knowledge of behavioral function allows for the expansion of an aberrant behavior's functional response class to include more appropriate responses (e.g., via functional communication training).

Function-based interventions can still be incorporated into an LRA framework. Perhaps function-based interventions would be implemented as the first line of treatment. After they have failed and the functional assessment protocol is re-addressed, non-functional reinforcement-based procedures could be implemented. Finally, procedures that are more intrusive could be employed. The development of function-based strategies simply provides more "distance" between the initial treatment plan and "last-resort" aversive procedures.

The purpose of this chapter is not to provide a comprehensive review of all of the function-based decelerative procedures in the research literature; that could easily fill this entire volume. Instead, we offer a perspective for interpreting the research literature and highlight some important interventions and issues in the area. As mentioned above, most of the research conducted in this area has been with individuals diagnosed with developmental disabilities. However, we challenge the reader to conceptualize these advances in terms of the behavioral principles involved, so that their application can be envisioned with different populations. This chapter is divided into four primary sections. First, we present an alternative framework with which to conceptualize much of the current decelerative-intervention research. Next, we review two recent meta-analyses of the decelerative-intervention literature. Third, we review the four primary intervention strategies that have recently been reported in the research literature. Finally, six promising areas for future research are briefly discussed.

Conceptualizing Decelerative-Intervention Research Along the Basic-Applied Continuum

Behavior analysts have debated the merits of the basic-applied distinction of our science for years (e.g., Epling & Pierce, 1986). Recently, Wacker (1996) proposed a new classification that he termed "bridge" research. Essentially, a bridge study is one in which basic behavioral principles are studied, often using basic response preparations (Fisher & Mazur, 1997). In addition, there are clinical or applied features involved, such as a patient on a hospital ward. The result is a basic research study that provides data that are relevant to the target population. In essence, the basic preparation combined with clinical features *bridges* the basic-applied distinction. One recent example of a bridge study was reported by Carr, Bailey, Ecott, Lucker, and Weil (1998). The authors investigated a variation of noncontingent reinforcement (NCR) using an arbitrary manual response that was performed by adults diagnosed with mental retardation. The authors were able to demonstrate the effects of stimulus magnitude within NCR schedules. The study's successful outcome illustrates the beneficial features of bridge research. First, bridge studies are useful when the experimental manipulation is one that is necessary for the advancement of science, but is not immediately beneficial for the participant. Similarly, a study that requires many sessions that might result in ethical concerns over clinically relevant target behaviors (e.g., self-injury) could be conducted using the bridge-study model. In addition, bridge studies are useful for demonstrating the degree of correspondence of basic research findings between animal and human participants. Overall, this research conceptualization research has been useful and we expect to see many studies that fit this model in the future.

We propose that the majority of decelerative-intervention studies published in the applied literature are actually bridge studies. Consider the following example. Carr and Britton (1999) recently reported a study in which the attention-maintained problematic vocalizations of an adult male diagnosed with mental retardation were treated with an NCR procedure. Fifteen-minute sessions were conducted in which the effects of NCR were evaluated. The results showed the intervention effective across two different therapists in a multiple-baseline design. However, we do not conceptualize this study as *applied* behavior-analytic research. The intervention was only applied to the participant within sessions. His life outside of session was no different than before the study began. Although we used the information obtained from the study to develop a subsequent treatment plan for the participant, in our opinion, the research that was reported does not meet the definitions of applied behavior analysis (ABA). One of the primary tenets of ABA is that the treatment of socially significant behavior using systematic methods results in *meaningful* behavior change. The study reported by Carr and Britton, while contributory to the research literature, did not directly result in meaningful behavior change for the participant. In fact, the vast majority of decelerative-intervention research that is published today does not directly result in meaningful change to the participants within the context of the studies. Because of this, we conceptualize this type of research as bridge research, in addition to the studies that utilize basic response apparatuses. Although the target behavior in the Carr and Britton study was a clinically problematic behavior, it might as well have been an arbitrary manual response because the immediate outcome for the participant would probably have been the same.

Our conceptualization of the above research should not be viewed as criticism. In fact, we suspect that the majority of the criticism of current research as "non-applied" would be eliminated by conceptualizing the work as bridge studies. Our analysis is as follows. Traditional basic research is typically conducted with animals in controlled settings. Traditional applied research is typically conducted with humans in relatively uncontrolled settings. However, there have been many instances of basic animal findings failing to correspond to related work with humans (Branch & Hackenberg, 1998). The logical result of this would be to demonstrate the effectiveness of behavioral procedures directly with human participants. However, such technology demonstration and development would be difficult in naturalistic and often uncontrolled settings. For example, Vollmer, Iwata, Zarcone, Smith, and Mazaleski (1993) compared the effects of NCR with differential reinforcement of zero rates of responding (DRO) as treatment for attention-maintained self-injurious behavior (SIB) using a "session" approach. That is, SIB was only treated within sessions. This type of treatment comparison study would have been virtually impossible to conduct in a naturalistic setting with naturalistic change agents. Therefore, we deem this kind of treatment-development research necessary and conceptualize it as bridge research. As we see it, one of the problems with the current literature is that there is an abundance of basic and bridge/applied studies being reported; however, there exists few truly applied studies. Therefore, the response to the abundance of well-controlled clinical research that is primarily conducted within sessions is not to decry the work as non-applied. The solution is to produce more demonstrations of the findings from basic and bridge studies in naturalistic settings.

Recent Meta-Analyses of the Decelerative-Intervention Literature

Scotti, Ujcich, Weigle, Holland, and Kirk (1996) reviewed 179 studies published between 1988 and 1992 that focused on the treatment of the aberrant behavior of individuals diagnosed with developmental disabilities. The authors reported that the modal target behavior in these studies was SIB, with aggression, destructive/ disruptive behavior, and stereotypic behavior also being frequently reported. Unfortunately, the authors only found that 48% of the studies included some form of functional assessment prior to intervention. The most common interventions were reinforcement-based procedures (e.g., functional communication training), skill training, and environmental modification. The authors also reported that less than 6% of the studies used punishment-based procedures, and the majority of those were combined with other procedures. Overall, Scotti et al. found that since the publication of an earlier literature review (Scotti, Evans, Meyer, & Walker, 1991), there were increases in the use of nonaversive procedures and active programming, presumably resulting from the increased use of functional assessment methods.

More recently, Didden, Duker, and Korzilius (1997) published a meta-analysis of the treatment literature that included 482 empirical studies published between 1968 and 1994. To measure the treatment effectiveness of each reported procedure, the authors assessed the percentage of nonoverlapping data between baseline and treatment phases. Similar to what was reported by Scotti et al. (1996), the authors reported the most common aberrant behaviors as SIB, stereotypy, disruption, and aggression. Differential reinforcement interventions were the most commonly prescribed reinforcement-based procedures. The authors reported a greater abundance of punishment-based procedures than did Scotti et al. (1996). However, this is to be expected as Scotti et al. (1996) reviewed more recent research than did Didden et al. The authors used inferential statistics to determine the overall effectiveness of intervention classes. Response-contingent procedures were found more effective than antecedent strategies. However, these data must be interpreted with caution given that only 21% of the studies reported any type of functional assessment. Not surprising was the finding that the inclusion of a functional assessment made a statistically significant improvement in response reduction compared to studies without a functional assessment.

Overall, both of the above meta-analyses revealed that the decelerative-intervention research has increasingly incorporated "best-practice" strategies, become more function-based, and reduced its focus on punishment-based procedures. We believe it is important to note that both of these studies were reported in non-behavioral journals. As a field, ABA has not been very successful in the dissemination of its practices. We commend the authors of the above meta-analyses for sharing such expansive information with non-behavioral audiences. Although methodological problems do exist in the meta-analysis of single-subject research (Salzberg, Strain, & Baer, 1987), we believe the results of such efforts can still be critically analyzed for their contributions.

Four Important Decelerative Interventions for Aberrant Behavior

In the next section of the chapter, we discuss four important decelerative-intervention strategies for aberrant behavior: extinction, noncontingent reinforcement, functional communication training, and curricular revision. These are the most commonly researched intervention areas in the recent literature. Within our review of each intervention we discuss procedural details, recent findings, relevant behavioral principles, and considerations for future research.

Extinction

Extinction, one of the basic behavioral principles, has long been successfully implemented as a decelerative intervention. As treatment, extinction involves the systematic interruption of a response-reinforcer contingency by withholding the reinforcer maintaining an aberrant behavior contingent on its occurrence (Ducharme & Van Houten, 1994). Therefore, extinction technically cannot be implemented unless a functional assessment is first conducted to identify behavioral function. Extinction can exist in many procedural forms, each one being dependent on the function of the aberrant behavior. Too often, however, the term extinction is used synonymously with "planned ignoring" in applied settings, even though planned ignoring is only extinction for attention-maintained behaviors.

Iwata, Pace, Cowdery, and Miltenberger (1994) elegantly demonstrated the importance in distinguishing between procedural and functional variations of extinction. Three children diagnosed with mental retardation exhibited identical topographies of SIB (i.e., head hitting). Functional analyses revealed that each of the behaviors was maintained by a different reinforcer (i.e., attention, escape from instructional demands, sensory stimulation). Each child was provided both relevant and irrelevant forms of extinction. In all three cases, only the relevant or function-based extinction procedure was effective in reducing SIB. Similar findings were recently reported by Richman, Wacker, Asmus, and Casey (1998).

One of the most common procedural variations of extinction is "escape extinction" for behavior maintained by social negative reinforcement. For cases in which aberrant behavior functions to remove an individual from instructional demands, preventing such removal will function as extinction (e.g., Cooper et al., 1995; Iwata, Pace, Kalsher, Cowdery, & Cataldo, 1990; Lalli, Casey, Goh, & Merlino, 1994). As further illustration of the importance of linking extinction procedures to behavioral function, contraindicated treatment effects can result from applications of escape extinction to behaviors maintained by attention. Similarly, attention extinction (i.e., planned ignoring) is contraindicated for behaviors maintained by social negative reinforcement. In both of the above cases, well-intentioned, but contraindicated extinction procedures could result in reinforcement of the aberrant behavior.

Extinction for behavior maintained by automatic reinforcement has been termed "sensory extinction" (Rincover, 1978). Procedurally, sensory extinction involves the elimination or reduction of the sensory consequences (e.g., visual stimulation) produced by an aberrant behavior. Protective equipment (e.g., helmets, gloves, padding) is often employed to accomplish this goal. The primary limitation of sensory extinction is the difficulty associated with the identification of the maintaining reinforcers prior to treatment. If is often difficult to diagnose a behavior as automatically reinforced, even without identifying the specific sensory reinforcer. Even so, several studies have reported successful response reductions using sensory extinction procedures (e.g., Kennedy & Souza, 1995; Rincover, Cook, Peoples, & Packard, 1979). However, recent research suggests that sensory extinction procedures might achieve their reductions via a punishment mechanism instead of extinction (e.g., Mazaleski, Iwata, Rodgers, Vollmer, & Zarcone, 1994). Consequently, the classification of sensory extinction as a function-based intervention, or even as an extinction procedure, is tentative.

At least two preliminary factors must be considered for extinction interventions to be successful. First, extinction is particularly susceptible to treatment integrity failures. Unless extinction can be rigorously implemented across an individual's environment(s), intermittent reinforcement of the aberrant behavior might result. Second, extinction "eliminates" a response from an individual's repertoire. Unless that response was a member of a functional response class, the individual might then be deprived of an important reinforcer. Thus, extinction is often combined with adjunct response-acquisition strategies (e.g., differential reinforcement of alternative behavior) to provide the individual with another way to access the reinforcer.

Undesirable "side effects" resulting from extinction have long been reported in the research literature. These side effects include (a) slow treatment progress (e.g., Jones, Simmons, & Frankel, 1974), (b) an initial, temporary increase or "burst" in response rate (e.g., Neisworth & Moore, 1972), (c) emotional responding (e.g., Baumeister & Forehand, 1971), and (d) aggression (e.g., Goh & Iwata, 1994). However, much of the evidence for extinction side effects was collected before the widespread use of functional assessment. Consequently, whether those extinction procedures were correctly matched to behavioral function is largely unknown.

Unfortunately, there is an inordinate amount of clinical "lore" surrounding the use of extinction as a decelerative intervention. For example, Lerman and Iwata (1995) reviewed 113 extinction data sets from the research literature to assess the prevalence of the extinction burst. The authors reported a surprising finding – the extinction burst was evident in only 36% of the data sets. The authors also reported that the extinction burst only appeared in 12% of the data sets that included extinction combined with other operant procedures. The results from this study suggest much that we know about extinction might be suspect.

Another commonly reported finding related to the use of extinction as a decelerative intervention is the "partial reinforcement extinction effect" (PREE).

Previous research on the PREE has found that behaviors maintained by continuous reinforcement were less resistant to extinction than behaviors maintained by intermittent reinforcement. However, as recently reported by Lerman and Iwata (1996), many of the early extinction-research findings, with both animals and humans, have not been replicated with humans in clinically relevant environments. Lerman, Iwata, Shore, and Kahng (1996) reported a study in which the SIB of three individuals diagnosed with mental retardation was treated with extinction following periods of continuous or intermittent reinforcement. The authors found that 2 of the 3 individuals did not exhibit the PREE, again contradicting "established" findings from the research literature on extinction.

Apart from the clinical benefits associated with extinction, it is important that further research be conducted on extinction as a basic behavioral process for at least two reasons. As mentioned above, much of what we know about extinction and its associated effects is suspect. However, the widespread adoption of functional assessment methods has allowed for more valid examinations of extinction in applied settings, though more are clearly needed. Second, researchers are increasingly finding that extinction is an active behavior-change mechanism in the reductions observed in other interventions such as demand fading (e.g., Zarcone, Iwata, Smith, Mazaleski, & Lerman, 1994) and functional communication training (e.g., Shirley, Iwata, Kahng, Mazaleski, & Lerman, 1997). Extinction is a vital behavioral principle (and procedure) in the successful treatment of aberrant behavior. Future research is still needed on the specific effects, and side effects, of extinction across behavioral functions following various reinforcement schedules.

Noncontingent Reinforcement

One of the most frequently reported decelerative interventions in the recent research literature is NCR. The use of NCR as a therapeutic intervention emerged from the basic literature on response-independent schedules (e.g., Zeiler, 1968) and the early applied literature in which NCR was used as a control procedure (e.g., Hart, Reynolds, Baer, Brawley, & Harris, 1968). Although NCR refers to a *set of procedures*, the defining feature of each of them is that an aberrant behavior's maintaining reinforcer is delivered on a response-independent basis. NCR includes procedures in which reinforcing stimuli are delivered on fixed-time (FT), variable-time (VT), random-time (RT), and continuous-delivery schedules. NCR is most often initially administered in dense schedules, followed by a schedule-thinning process that is linked to the maintenance of response reductions. In addition, NCR is frequently accompanied by an extinction procedure. Recently, however, studies reporting successful applications of NCR without extinction have been reported (e.g., Lalli, Casey, & Kates, 1997).

The recent literature has identified several benefits of implementing NCR as treatment for aberrant behavior. First, NCR is typically a function-based procedure that addresses the response-reinforcer relationship, instead of overpowering it. Second, NCR has been shown to produce greater, or at least comparable behavior reductions compared to DRO (Vollmer et al., 1993), differential reinforcement of alternative behavior (DRA; Kahng, Iwata, DeLeon, & Worsdell, 1997), and extinction (Vollmer et al., 1998). Third, NCR has been shown to result in a higher rate of reinforcer delivery compared to other comparable procedures (e.g., DRO; Britton, Carr, Kellum, Dozier, & Weil, in press; Vollmer et al., 1993). Fourth, FT schedules have been reported as relatively easy to implement compared to other procedures. Although the delivery of stimuli at fixed times intuitively seems easier than implementing, for example, a DRO procedure, no social validity assessments have been reported to support this claim. Fifth, NCR has been shown to produce less extinction-induced behavior (e.g., aggression, response bursts) compared to other treatments (Vollmer et al., 1993; Vollmer et al., 1998).

In addition to the above benefits associated with NCR, recent treatment studies have demonstrated the generality of NCR across behavioral topography and function. NCR has been used to effectively treatment aberrant behavior maintained by attention (e.g., Hagopian, Fisher, & Legacy, 1994; Mace & Lalli, 1991; Vollmer et al., 1993), access to materials (e.g., Lalli et al., 1997; Marcus & Vollmer, 1996; Smith, Lerman, & Iwata, 1996), escape and/or avoidance of instructional demands (e.g., Kahng et al., 1997; Vollmer, Marcus, & Ringdahl, 1995), and automatic reinforcement (e.g., Roscoe, Iwata, & Goh, 1998; Sprague, Holland, & Thomas, 1997). Additionally, recent studies have reported that NCR can be implemented with "arbitrary" stimuli identified from preference assessments (Fischer, Iwata, & Mazaleski, 1997; Hanley, Piazza, & Fisher, 1997. This is useful for cases in which behavioral function cannot be determined or the maintaining reinforcer cannot be withheld (e.g., with some automatically reinforced behaviors). NCR has also been shown an effective treatment with a variety of aberrant behaviors, including aggression (e.g., Vollmer, Ringdahl, Roane, & Marcus, 1997; disruption (e.g., Fisher, Ninness, Piazza, & Owen-DeSchryver, 1996), inappropriate speech (e.g., Carr & Britton, 1999), pica (e.g., Piazza et al., 1998), rumination (e.g., Wilder, Draper, Williams, & Higbee, 1997), SIB (e.g., Fischer et al.), and stereotypy (e.g., Sprague et al.).

The current understanding in the literature is that NCR procedures can achieve their effects via three behavior-change mechanisms: (a) attenuation of the reinforcer's establishing operation, (b) extinction or disruption of the response-reinforcer relationship, and (c) reinforcement of other responses that temporally displace the target behavior (Carr, 1996). To date, there is greatest empirical support for the first two possibilities. The extinction hypothesis states that, through NCR, the response-reinforcer contingency is eliminated or interrupted, subsequently reducing the aberrant behavior. The success of lean NCR schedules to reduce responding supports this position (Hagopian et al., 1994). The EO (or satiation) hypothesis states that the noncontingent delivery of the behavior's reinforcer eliminates the "motivation" to engage in the behavior. The decelerative abilities of dense NCR schedules (e.g., Hagopian et al.) and NCR schedules with high-magnitude reinforcers (e.g., Carr et al., 1998) support this position.

There are least two limitations associated with the use of NCR procedures. First, NCR does not include an explicit behavioral acquisition component. However,

Marcus and Vollmer (1996) have demonstrated that NCR can be successfully combined with DRA procedures to accomplish this goal. A second potential limitation associated with NCR is the risk of adventitious, or accidental, reinforcement of the aberrant behavior. One would surmise that aberrant behavior that occurs at a high frequency would be more susceptible to adventitious reinforcement than a lower-frequency behavior. Using the same logic, a denser NCR schedule would be more likely to produce adventitious reinforcement than a leaner schedule. Surprisingly, a review of the NCR treatment literature reveals many instances of successful reduction with dense schedules and high-rate behaviors. To date, the variables that produce adventitious reinforcement have not yet been delineated. However, Vollmer et al. (1997) demonstrated the successful use of an omission contingency (i.e., fixed-time, non-resetting, momentary DRO) to reduce aberrant behavior that had been adventitiously reinforced using NCR.

As reviewed above, it is clear that NCR is an extremely promising technology for the treatment of aberrant behavior. However, the NCR treatment literature is still in its infancy, leaving many research questions unanswered. As mentioned above, the exact behavior-change mechanism(s) by which NCR achieves its effects are not well delineated. Future studies are necessary to determine the conditions under which the different mechanisms are involved. Second, adventitious reinforcement remains a potential side effect of NCR. A direct comparison of NCR with behaviors occurring at different frequencies would determine whether response frequency is a predictor variable for future adventitious reinforcement of the aberrant behavior. Third, although Lalli et al. (1997) provided an effective method for calculating initial NCR schedules, there still is not an agreed upon method for schedule thinning. We expect that this will occur as an ancillary finding in upcoming treatment studies. Fourth, several authors have reported bridge studies that allow NCR to be studied with individuals diagnosed with developmental disabilities using basic-operant preparations (e.g., Carr et al., 1998; Carr, Dozier, & Williams, 1999; Ringdahl & Vollmer, 1998). This practice has thus far proved successful. Future researchers could use this approach to study topics that are important for the literature, but perhaps not directly so for research participants who exhibit aberrant behavior.

A procedure that is related to NCR is environmental enrichment (EE), which consists of the noncontingent delivery of varied stimuli into an individual's environment (e.g., Horner, 1980). EE procedures are primarily used with behaviors maintained by automatic reinforcement and presumably produce their effects through stimulus competition and/or stimulus substitution. With stimulus competition, stimuli that are delivered are more reinforcing than the behavior's maintaining variable, resulting in an increase of alternative responses that temporally displace the target behavior. With stimulus substitution, the stimuli that are delivered are members of the same functional stimulus class as the behavior's maintaining reinforcer, resulting in an NCR-like effect. One of the limitations of the EE literature is that stimuli have sometimes been selected in an arbitrary manner. However, researchers have recently begun to explore the use of stimulus preference assessments to select stimuli for use in EE procedures (e.g., Ringdahl, Vollmer, Marcus, & Roane,

1997; Vollmer, Marcus, & LeBlanc, 1994). The refinement of EE procedures remains an important area for future study given the inherent difficulty in treating behaviors maintained by automatic reinforcement.

Functional Communication Training
(Differential Reinforcement of Alternative Behavior)

Differential reinforcement procedures have been extensively investigated in the behavioral literature for over three decades. During much of that time, DRO was one of the most common decelerative interventions reported in the literature (Lennox, Miltenberger, Spengler, & Erfanian, 1988). Another procedure in this category of intervention, DRA, has particular clinical appeal because it includes a behavioral acquisition component, unlike DRO. In 1985, Carr and Durand reported one of the first studies examining DRA procedures directly linked to the results of functional assessments. The authors chose the term "functional communication training" (FCT) to refer to this new function-based DRA. In FCT, the reinforcer responsible for maintaining the aberrant behavior is delivered to the individual contingent on an alternative or "communicative" response. Ideally, the following features should be also considered: (a) the aberrant behavior should be placed on extinction (Shirley et al., 1997), (b) the alternative response should require less effort to perform than the aberrant behavior (Horner & Day, 1991), and (c) the alternative response should be specifically tailored to the individual and his/her caregivers (Durand & Carr, 1992). Too often, paraprofessionals have interpreted FCT as merely teaching new forms of communication, without considering the above additional programming strategies. The resulting interventions are rarely successful.

FCT is most often prescribed for aberrant behavior maintained by social reinforcement (e.g., attention, access to materials, escape from instructional de-mands). In a recent article that summarized 21 inpatient FCT data sets, Hagopian, Fisher, Sullivan, Acquisto, and LeBlanc (1998) reported the modal behavioral function as attention, with escape a close second. The authors also reported successful applications of FCT with multiply controlled behavior (see also Day, Horner, & O'Neill, 1994). The article by Hagopian et al. (1998) is of particular importance because it is the first large-n summary of FCT. This type of analysis offers the advantage, not available with small-n studies, of addressing the external validity of FCT. For example, the authors reported that FCT combined with adjunct procedures (e.g., extinction, punishment) was successful in treating a wide range of behavior problems (e.g., SIB, aggression, disruption, pica, elopement). The authors also that reported FCT (without extinction or punishment) was always ineffective (see also Shirley et al., 1997). In addition, FCT with punishment was the most effective treatment variation, followed by FCT with extinction. These aggregated results are of utmost importance, because small-n treatment failures are unlikely to be published; therefore, this information would otherwise be unavailable.

FCT has received much attention in the recent literature; consequently, our understanding of the procedure is rapidly expanding. For example, studies reported by both Kahng et al. (1997) and Hanley, Piazza, Fisher, Contrucci, and Maglieri

(1997) found that FCT with extinction was equally effective as NCR in the treatment of socially maintained aberrant behavior. Shukla and Albin (1996) reported that FCT with extinction was effective in reducing all of the members of an individual's aberrant response class, whereas extinction was only effective in reducing the less severe responses and actually increased some of the more severe topographies. Both Durand and Carr (1992) and Derby et al. (1997) demonstrated long-term treatment gains resulting from FCT.

Recently, Fisher, Kuhn, and Thompson (1998) demonstrated the effective application of a stimulus control procedure to FCT. The advantage of this adjunct procedure is that often in the early stages of FCT implementation, the individual receives the reinforcer on an FR-1 schedule. However, this is rarely a practical strategy for long-term implementation. Some researchers have instead used schedule-thinning procedures to increase the probability of successful maintenance of FCT effects (e.g., Hagopian et al., 1998). The findings by Fisher et al. illustrate yet another procedure, discrimination training, that is capable of producing the same outcome. Ideally, schedule thinning could be combined with discrimination training so that the discriminative stimuli (S^Ds) would signal the availability of reinforcers at specific times.

The frequency at which FCT studies have been reported in the research literature, combined with the innovation and exceptional rigor of the majority of those studies, has been impressive. We have no doubt that FCT will continue to be further examined in the years to come. One area of research we believe is particularly important, and has not received much attention in the literature, is the selection of the alternative or communicative response. These responses are often manual signs or short verbal phrases, and the method by which they are selected for particular individuals is largely unknown. However, the field of augmentative and alternative communication has addressed these issues in great detail for years. This field has the information that can help us select appropriate communicative responses, while considering the physical limitations of our clients and the characteristics of their environments and caregivers to program for maximum generality. Hopefully, future behavioral researchers will incorporate some of these methods to further enhance the external validity of FCT.

Curricular Revision

Curricular revision is a treatment strategy for aberrant behavior maintained by escape from and/or avoidance of instructional demands (i.e., social negative reinforcement). Such behaviors could be functionally treated using escape extinction, noncontingent escape, or by teaching a functionally equivalent response (i.e., FCT/DRA). However, those procedures presuppose a relevant and interesting curriculum. Unfortunately, this is not often the case. The problems associated with a curriculum could be conceptualized as an operation that establishes escape from demands as a reinforcer. Thus, curricular revision that eliminates these problems could function to neutralize the establishing operation, thus reducing associated aberrant behavior.

Dunlap and his colleagues have published an interesting body of research demonstrating the use of curricular-revision procedures to reduce aberrant behavior and increase compliance in the classroom (e.g., Dunlap, Foster-Johnson, Clarke, Kern, & Childs, 1995; Dunlap & Kern, 1996; Dunlap, Kern-Dunlap, Clarke, & Robbins, 1991; Dyer, Dunlap, & Winterling, 1990; Ferro, Foster-Johnson, & Dunlap, 1996; Foster-Johnson, Ferro, & Dunlap, 1994; Kern, Childs, Dunlap, Clarke, & Falk, 1994). One of the limitations of some of the research in this area is a lack of functional assessment before intervention. For example, Dyer et al. reduced the aberrant behavior of three children diagnosed with autism by adding a task-choice feature to the curriculum. (We refer the reader to Kern et al. (1998) for an excellent review of choice-based procedures for the treatment of aberrant behavior.) Although the curricular revisions reported by Dyer et al. resulted in reductions in aberrant behavior, it is unknown how the interventions achieved their effects. Without information from a systematic functional assessment, behavioral function cannot be inferred from successful treatment. Alternatively, Dunlap et al. (1991) conducted a functional assessment in which hypotheses relating specific curricular situations to a student's aberrant behavior were tested. The results of the functional assessment indicated that fine-motor tasks, irrelevant tasks, lengthy tasks, and the inability to choose tasks were all related to increased frequencies of aberrant behavior. A subsequent revised curriculum resulted in successful reduction of the aberrant behavior across the school day.

Smith, Iwata, Goh, and Shore (1995) reported an assessment study that identified three specific curricular establishing operations that were associated with high rates of escape-maintained SIB. Adults diagnosed with mental retardation were given various instructional demands, during which they were allowed a brief escape for engaging in SIB. By including this negative reinforcement contingency concurrently with manipulations of the instructional variables, the authors were able to identify three specific establishing operations: novel tasks, long sessions, and high-rate instructions. This type of curriculum assessment, following an initial functional assessment, is ideal for designing a curricular-revision intervention. More assessments such as this one, and that reported by Dunlap et al. (1991) are clearly needed to advance the curricular revision literature.

A decelerative intervention that is related to curricular revision is demand fading (also known as stimulus or instructional fading). In demand fading, instructional requests are initially eliminated within teaching sessions. Once the escape-maintained aberrant behavior is reduced, the requests are systematically faded back to baseline levels. In one of the first studies of demand fading, Pace, Iwata, Cowdery, Andree, and McIntyre (1993) examined the effects of extinction with and without demand fading. The authors found that extinction combined with demand fading produced "large and immediate" decreases in SIB that were maintained as instructional demands were increased over time. When extinction was presented alone, SIB was variable with a "slight decreasing trend." Zarcone, Iwata, Hughes, and Vollmer (1993) successfully replicated these results with two additional findings. Extinction without demand fading produced an extinction burst, which did not occur when extinction was combined with demand fading. In addition, extinction reduced behavior to final criterion levels in fewer sessions than did extinction combined with demand fading. Zarcone, Iwata, Mazaleski, and Smith (1994) reported successful effects with demand fading alone, but required extinction to maintain the reductions. In an effort to extend the research on demand fading, Pace, Ivancic, and Jefferson (1994) successfully used demand fading to treat the excessive obscenity of a brain-injured adult. Similarly, Piazza, Moes, and Fisher (1996) combined demand fading with extinction and DRA to treat the escape-maintained destructive behavior of a boy diagnosed with autism.

In summation, demand fading, and to some degree extinction, has been demonstrated an effective intervention for aberrant behavior maintained by escape from demands. Presumably, individuals for whom this treatment was prescribed found the rate of task presentation, or some other feature of the task, aversive. The elimination and gradual reintroduction of the demands possibly resulted in habituation to the aversive feature(s) of the task.

Future research in the areas of curricular revision and demand fading is needed to further assess the situations in which these interventions are warranted. For example, an individual who emits escape-maintained aberrant behavior in the context of an appropriate curriculum might be a more appropriate candidate for escape extinction or noncontingent escape. What we need most are more rigorous curricular assessments so that (a) specific, problematic curriculum features can be neutralized, and (b) individuals can be selected for more appropriate interventions for escape-maintained behavior.

Promising Areas for Future Research

While attempting to organize future directions for decelerative-intervention research, we realized there were myriad possibilities. In an effort to simplify the possibilities, we chose areas in which there were already promising research findings. The first of six areas we will briefly discuss is the search for the underlying mechanisms responsible for decelerative-intervention effects. One of the benefits of a function-based approach to treatment is a clearer understanding of how interventions achieve their effects. Carr et al. (1998) recently reported a study that was designed to further illuminate the basic processes operating in NCR procedures. Similarly, Mazaleski, Iwata, Vollmer, Zarcone, and Smith (1993) reported a study that was designed, in part, to examine the role of extinction within DRO procedures. Our understanding of the basic behavioral principles that operate within decelerative interventions is vital to our comprehensive understanding of the procedures to program for maximal treatment gains.

The second area of research that clearly needs further study is the assessment and treatment of aberrant behavior using establishing operation modifications. Horner, Day, and Day (1997) recently reported a study in which temporally distal establishing operations were analyzed and successfully "neutralized" as treatment for aberrant behavior. Similarly, O'Reilly (1995) illustrated a relationship between sleep deprivation and subsequent escape-maintained aggression. Aberrant behavior, as well as adaptive behavior, is frequently affected by distal establishing operations. Future studies are needed to better assess these operations so that relevant interventions can then be prescribed.

Much of the research described in this chapter has focused on aberrant behavior maintained by single variables. However, any clinician will tell you that many aberrant behaviors are multiply controlled, or are affected by a number of factors. Although we have the ability to functionally analyze multiple controlled behaviors, little research has been reported related to the treatment of such behavior (e.g., Day, Horner, & O'Neill, 1994; Lalli & Casey, 1996; Smith, Iwata, Vollmer, & Zarcone, 1993). Further research is needed on the hierarchical assessment of multiple reinforcers and the subsequent treatment of multiply controlled aberrant behavior. In other words, we need to be able to determine if a primary behavioral function exists so that a single intervention might be applied. However, if we find that there are two or more functions of similar strength, a more complicated treatment package might result.

An intriguing series of studies has examined the effects of signaling clients about impending and unpleasant procedures. Derrickson, Neef, and Cataldo (1993) demonstrated that signaling to infants that invasive procedures were imminent resulted in reduced negative affective behaviors. Mace, Shapiro, and Mace (1998) used a similar procedure combined with NCR to signal reinforcer withdrawal and task onset in the treatment of SIB. More studies are needed to establish the generality of these findings and to elucidate how the interventions achieve their effects.

Many of the participants of the research studies reviewed in this chapter had rudimentary language skills or could at least respond to simple instructions. However, there have been virtually no studies examining the effects of rules or instructions on decelerative interventions. For example, what would the effect be on an NCR procedure if an individual were told that a reinforcer was going to be delivered independent of his/her behavior? Rule-governed behavior has been extensively studied in the basic literature, which has found that most of the behavior of verbal humans is affected by rules (Hayes & Ju, 1998). It is time to apply these basic findings on rule governance to the treatment of aberrant behavior in verbal individuals diagnosed with developmental disabilities.

The final area that we believe requires further research is an old one: the social validation of intervention effects (Wolf, 1978). The majority of treatment studies do not report measures of social validity (Carr, Austin, Britton, Kellum, & Bailey, 1999). We believe this is a result of the abundance of bridge studies in the decelerative-intervention literature. However, well-controlled "session" studies could still report measures of treatment acceptability and treatment outcome. One excellent example of a recent decelerative-intervention study that did include a social validity assessment was conducted by Hanley, Piazza, Fisher, Contrucci, and Maglieri (1997). The authors used a concurrent chain procedure to allow participants to choose between NCR and FCT interventions for aberrant behavior. The authors' consideration of the importance of social validity led to an amazing outcome: clients were allowed to select their own decelerative interventions. We consider the study by Hanley,

Piazza, Fisher, Contrucci, and Maglieri (1997) to be exemplary and hope that future authors take their lead and consider how the assessment of social validity could be incorporated into their own studies.

Reading Objectives

1. Why was the shift from non-functional to function-based interventions important?
2. Briefly describe how contemporary decelerative-intervention research can be classified as "bridge" research.
3. Briefly summarize the findings of two recent meta-analyses of decelerative-intervention research.
4. Briefly describe the issues relating to the contraindication of extinction procedures.
5. What is the extinction burst? What do the data on its prevalence indicate?
6. What are the procedural variations of NCR?
7. What are the three proposed behavior-change mechanisms underlying NCR effects?
8. How should FCT be programmed for maximum effectiveness?
9. How are demand fading and curricular revision related?
10. Consider the ethical concerns associated with the use of an escape extinction procedure in the context of a dysfunctional curriculum.

References

Baumeister, A. A., & Forehand, R. (1971). Effects of extinction of an instrumental response on stereotyped body rocking in severe retardates. *Psychological Record, 21,* 235-240.

Branch, M. N., & Hackenberg, T. D. (1998). Humans are animals, too: Connecting animal research to human behavior and cognition. In W. O'Donohue (Ed.), *Learning and behavior therapy* (pp. 15-35). Boston: Allyn and Bacon.

Britton, L. N., Carr, J. E., Kellum, K. K., Dozier, C. L., & Weil, T. M. (in press). A variation of noncontingent reinforcement in the treatment of aberrant behavior. *Research in Developmental Disabilities.*

Carr, E. G., & Durand, V. M. (1985). Reducing behavior problems through functional communication training. *Journal of Applied Behavior Analysis, 18,* 111-126.

Carr, E. G., Robinson, S., & Palumbo, L. W. (1990). The wrong issue: Aversive versus nonaversive treatment. The right issue: Functional versus nonfunctional treatment. In A. C. Repp & N. N. Singh (Eds.), *Perspectives on the use of nonaversive and aversive interventions for persons with developmental disabilities* (pp. 361-379). Sycamore, IL: Sycamore.

Carr, J. E. (1996). On the use of the term "noncontingent reinforcement." *Journal of Behavior Analysis and Therapy, 1,* 33-37.

Carr, J. E., Austin, J. L., Britton, L. N., Kellum, K. K., & Bailey, J. S. (1999). An assessment of social validity trends in applied behavior analysis. *Behavioral Interventions, 14,* 223-231.

Carr, J. E., Bailey, J. S., Ecott, C. L., Lucker, K. D., & Weil, T. M. (1998). On the effects of noncontingent delivery of differing magnitudes of reinforcement. *Journal of Applied Behavior Analysis, 31,* 313-321.

Carr, J. E., & Britton, L. N. (1999). Idiosyncratic effects of noncontingent reinforcement on problematic speech. *Behavioral Interventions, 14,* 37-43.

Carr, J. E., Dozier, C. L., & Williams, W. L. (1999). *Combining schedule density and stimulus magnitude in the programming of fixed-time schedules: A preliminary investigation.* Unpublished manuscript.

Cooper, L. J., Wacker, D. P., McComas, J. J., Brown, K., Peck, S. M., Richman, D., Drew, J., Frischmeyer, P., & Millard, T. (1995). Use of component analyses to identify active variables in treatment packages for children with feeding disorders. *Journal of Applied Behavior Analysis, 28,* 139-153.

Day, H. M., Horner, R. H., & O'Neill, R. E. (1994). Multiple functions of problem behaviors: Assessment and intervention. *Journal of Applied Behavior Analysis, 27,* 279-289.

Derby, K. M., Wacker, D. P., Berg, W., DeRaad, A., Ulrich, S., Asmus, J., Harding, J., Prouty, A., Laffey, P., & Stoner, E. A. (1997). The long-term effects of functional communication training in home settings. *Journal of Applied Behavior Analysis, 30,* 507-531.

Derrickson, J. G., Neef, N. A., & Cataldo, M. F. (1993). Effects of signaling invasive procedures on a hospitalized infant's affective behaviors. *Journal of Applied Behavior Analysis, 26,* 133-134.

Didden, R., Duker, P. C., & Korzilius, H. (1997). Meta-analytic study on treatment effectiveness for problem behaviors with individuals who have mental retardation. *American Journal on Mental Retardation, 101,* 387-399.

Ducharme, J. M., & Van Houten, R. (1994). Operant extinction in the treatment of severe maladaptive behavior. *Behavior Modification, 18,* 139-170.

Dunlap, G., Foster-Johnson, L., Clarke, S., Kern, L., & Childs, K. E. (1995). Modifying activities to produce functional outcomes: Effects on the problem behaviors of students with disabilities. *Journal of the Association for Persons with Severe Handicaps, 20,* 248-258.

Dunlap, G., & Kern, L. (1996). Modifying instructional activities to promote desirable behavior: A conceptual and practical framework. *School Psychology Quarterly, 11,* 297-312.

Dunlap, G., Kern-Dunlap, L., Clarke, S., & Robbins, F. F. (1991). Functional assessment, curricular revision, and severe behavior problems. *Journal of Applied Behavior Analysis, 24,* 387-397.

Durand, V. M., & Carr, E. G. (1992). An analysis of maintenance following functional communication training. *Journal of Applied Behavior Analysis, 25,* 777-794.

Dyer, K., Dunlap, G., & Winterling, V. (1990). The effects of choice-making on the problem behaviors of students with severe handicaps. *Journal of Applied Behavior Analysis, 23,* 515-524.

Epling, W. F., & Pierce, W. D. (1986). The basic importance of applied behavior analysis. *The Behavior Analyst, 9,* 89-99.

Ferro, J., Foster-Johnson, L., & Dunlap, G. (1996). Relation between curricular activities and problem behaviors of students with mental retardation. *American Journal on Mental Retardation, 101,* 184-194.

Fischer, S. M., Iwata, B. A., & Mazaleski, J. L. (1997). Noncontingent delivery of arbitrary reinforcers as treatment for self-injurious behavior. *Journal of Applied Behavior Analysis, 30,* 239-249.

Fisher, W. W., Kuhn, D. E., & Thompson, R. H. (1998). Establishing discriminative control of responding using functional and alternative reinforcers during functional communication training. *Journal of Applied Behavior Analysis, 31,* 543-560.

Fisher, W. W., & Mazur, J. E. (1997). Basic and applied research on choice responding. *Journal of Applied Behavior Analysis, 30,* 387-410.

Fisher, W. W., Ninness, H. A. C., Piazza, C. C., & Owen-DeSchryver, J. S. (1996). On the reinforcing effects of the content of verbal attention. *Journal of Applied Behavior Analysis, 29,* 235-238.

Foster-Johnson, L., Ferro, J., & Dunlap, G. (1994). Preferred curricular activities and reduced problem behaviors in students with intellectual disabilities. *Journal of Applied Behavior Analysis, 27,* 493-504.

Goh, H., & Iwata, B. A. (1994). Behavioral persistence and variability during extinction of self-injury maintained by escape. *Journal of Applied Behavior Analysis, 27,* 173-174.

Hagopian, L. P., Fisher, W. W., & Legacy, S. M. (1994). Schedule effects of noncontingent reinforcement on attention-maintained destructive behavior in identical quadruplets. *Journal of Applied Behavior Analysis, 27,* 317-325.

Hagopian, L. P., Fisher, W. W., Sullivan, M. T., Acquisto, J., & LeBlanc, L. A. (1998). Effectiveness of functional communication training with and without extinction and punishment: A summary of 21 inpatient cases. *Journal of Applied Behavior Analysis, 31,* 211-235.

Hanley, G. P., Piazza, C. C., & Fisher, W. W. (1997). Noncontingent presentation of attention and alternative stimuli in the treatment of attention-maintained destructive behavior. *Journal of Applied Behavior Analysis, 30,* 229-237.

Hanley, G. P., Piazza, C. C., Fisher, W. W., Contrucci, S. A., & Maglieri, K. A. (1997). Evaluation of client preference for function-based treatment packages. *Journal of Applied Behavior Analysis, 30,* 459-473.

Hart, B. M., Reynolds, N. J., Baer, D. M., Brawley, E. R., & Harris, F. R. (1968). Effects of contingent and noncontingent social reinforcement on the cooperative behavior of a preschool child. *Journal of Applied Behavior Analysis, 1,* 73-76.

Hayes, S. C., & Ju, W. (1998). Rule-governed behavior. In W. O'Donohue (Ed.), *Learning and behavior therapy* (pp. 374-391). Boston: Allyn and Bacon.

Horner, R. H., & Day, H. M. (1991). The effects of response efficiency on functionally equivalent competing behaviors. *Journal of Applied Behavior Analysis, 24,* 719-732.

Horner, R. H., Day, H. M., & Day, J. R. (1997). Using neutralizing routines to reduce problem behaviors. *Journal of Applied Behavior Analysis, 30,* 601-614.

Horner, R. D. (1980). The effects of an environmental "enrichment" program on the behavior of institutionalized profoundly retarded children. *Journal of Applied Behavior Analysis, 13,* 473-491.

Iwata, B. A., Pace, G. M., Cowdery, G. E., & Miltenberger, R. G. (1994). What makes extinction work: An analysis of procedural form and function. *Journal of Applied Behavior Analysis, 27,* 131-144.

Iwata, B. A., Pace, G. M., Kalsher, M. J., Cowdery, G. E., & Cataldo, M. F. (1990). Experimental analysis and extinction of self-injurious escape behavior. *Journal of Applied Behavior Analysis, 23,* 11-27.

Iwata, B. A., Vollmer, T. R., Zarcone, J. R., & Rodgers, T. A. (1993). Treatment classification and selection based on behavioral function. In R. Van Houten & S. Axelrod (Eds.), *Behavior analysis and treatment* (pp. 101-125). New York: Plenum.

Jones, F. H., Simmons, J. Q., & Frankel, F. (1974). An extinction procedure for eliminating self-destructive behavior in a 9-year-old autistic girl. *Journal of Autism and Childhood Schizophrenia, 4,* 241-250.

Kahng, S., Iwata, B. A., DeLeon, I. G., & Worsdell, A. S. (1997). Evaluation of the "control over reinforcement" component in functional communication training. *Journal of Applied Behavior Analysis, 30,* 267-277.

Kennedy, C. H., & Souza, G. (1995). Functional analysis and treatment of eye poking. *Journal of Applied Behavior Analysis, 28,* 27-37.

Kern, L., Childs, K. E., Dunlap, G., Clarke, S., & Falk, G. D. (1994). Using assessment-based curricular intervention to improve the classroom behavior of a student with emotional and behavioral challenges. *Journal of Applied Behavior Analysis, 27,* 7-19.

Kern, L., Vorndran, C. M., Hilt, A., Ringdahl, J. E., Adelman, B. E., & Dunlap, G. (1998). Choice as an intervention to improve behavior: A review of the literature. *Journal of Behavioral Education, 8,* 151-169.

Lalli, J. S., & Casey, S. D. (1996). Treatment of multiply controlled problem behavior. *Journal of Applied Behavior Analysis, 29,* 391-396.

Lalli, J. S., Casey, S., Goh, H., & Merlino, J. (1994). Treatment of escape-maintained aberrant behavior with escape extinction and predictable routines. *Journal of Applied Behavior Analysis, 27,* 705-714.

Lalli, J. S., Casey, S. D., & Kates, K. (1997). Noncontingent reinforcement as treatment for severe problem behavior: Some procedural variations. *Journal of Applied Behavior Analysis, 30,* 127-137.

Lennox, D. B., Miltenberger, R. G., Spengler, P., & Erfanian, N. (1988). Decelerative treatment practices with persons who have mental retardation: A review of five years of the literature. *American Journal of Mental Retardation, 92,* 492-501.

Lerman, D. C., & Iwata, B. A. (1995). Prevalence of the extinction burst and its attenuation during treatment. *Journal of Applied Behavior Analysis, 28,* 93-94.

Lerman, D. C., & Iwata, B. A. (1996). Developing a technology for the use of operant extinction in clinical settings: An examination of basic and applied research. *Journal of Applied Behavior Analysis, 29,* 345-382.

Lerman, D. C., Iwata, B. A., Shore, B. A., & Kahng, S. (1996). Responding maintained by intermittent reinforcement: Implications for the use of extinction with problem behavior in clinical settings. *Journal of Applied Behavior Analysis, 29,* 153-171.

Mace, A. B., Shapiro, E. S., & Mace, F. C. (1998). Effects of warning stimuli for reinforcer withdrawal and task onset on self-injury. *Journal of Applied Behavior Analysis, 31,* 679-682.

Mace, F. C., & Lalli, J. S. (1991). Linking descriptive and experimental analysis in the treatment of bizarre speech. *Journal of Applied Behavior Analysis, 24,* 553-562.

Marcus, B. A., & Vollmer, T. R. (1996). Combining noncontingent reinforcement and differential reinforcement schedules as treatment for aberrant behavior. *Journal of Applied Behavior Analysis, 29,* 43-51.

Mazaleski, J. L., Iwata, B. A., Rodgers, T. A., Vollmer, T. R., & Zarcone, J. R. (1994). Protective equipment as treatment for stereotypic hand mouthing: Sensory extinction or punishment effects? *Journal of Applied Behavior Analysis, 27,* 345-355.

Mazaleski, J. L., Iwata, B. A., Vollmer, T. R., Zarcone, J. R., & Smith, R. G. (1993). Analysis of the reinforcement and extinction components in DRO contingencies with self-injury. *Journal of Applied Behavior Analysis, 26,* 143-156.

Neisworth, J. T., & Moore, F. (1972). Operant treatment of asthmatic responding with the parent as therapist. *Behavior Therapy, 3,* 95-99.

O'Reilly, M. F. (1995). Functional analysis and treatment of escape-maintained aggression correlated with sleep deprivation. *Journal of Applied Behavior Analysis, 28,* 225-226.

Pace, G. M., Ivancic, M. T., & Jefferson, G. (1994). Stimulus fading as treatment for obscenity in a brain-injured adult. *Journal of Applied Behavior Analysis, 27,* 301-305.

Pace, G. M., Iwata, B. A., Cowdery, G. E., Adree, P. J., & McIntyre, T. (1993). Stimulus (instructional) fading during extinction of self-injurious escape behavior. *Journal of Applied Behavior Analysis, 26,* 205-212.

Piazza, C. C., Fisher, W. W., Hanley, G. P., LeBlanc, L. A., Worsdell, A. S., Lindauer, S. E., & Keeney, K. M. (1998). Treatment of pica through multiple analyses of its reinforcing functions. *Journal of Applied Behavior Analysis, 31,* 165-189.

Piazza, C. C., Moes, D. R., & Fisher, W. W. (1996). Differential reinforcement of alternative behavior and demand fading in the treatment of escape-maintained destructive behavior. *Journal of Applied Behavior Analysis, 29,* 569-572.

Richman, D. M., Wacker, D. P., Asmus, J. M., & Casey, S. D. (1998). Functional analysis and extinction of different behavior problems exhibited by the same individual. *Journal of Applied Behavior Analysis, 31,* 475-478.

Rincover, A. (1978). Sensory extinction: A procedure for eliminating self-stimulatory behavior in developmentally disabled children. *Journal of Abnormal Child Psychology, 6,* 299-310.

Rincover, A., Cook, R., Peoples, A., & Packard, D. (1979). Sensory extinction and sensory reinforcement principles for programming multiple adaptive behavior change. *Journal of Applied Behavior Analysis, 12,* 221-233.

Ringdahl, J. E., & Vollmer, T. R. (1998, May). An evaluation of noncontingent reinforcement effects as a function of baseline reinforcement schedules. In J. J. McComas (Chair), *Applications of basic behavioral principles.* Symposium conducted at the 24th Annual Convention of the Association for Behavior Analysis, Orlando, FL.

Ringdahl, J. E., Vollmer, T. R., Marcus, B. A., & Roane, H. S. (1997). An analogue evaluation of environmental enrichment: The role of stimulus preference. *Journal of Applied Behavior Analysis, 30,* 203-216.

Roscoe, E. M., Iwata, B. A., & Goh, H. (1998). A comparison of noncontingent reinforcement and sensory extinction as treatments for self-injurious behavior. *Journal of Applied Behavior Analysis, 31,* 635-646.

Salzberg, C. L., Strain, P. S., & Baer, D. M. (1987). Meta-analysis for single-subject research: When does it clarify, when does it obscure? *RASE: Remedial and Special Education, 8,* 43-48.

Scotti, J. R., Evans, I. M., Meyer, L. H., & Walker, P. (1991). A meta-analysis of intervention research with problem behavior: Treatment validity and standards of practice. *American Journal on Mental Retardation, 96,* 233-256.

Scotti, J. R., Ujcich, K. J., Weigle, K. L., Holland, C. M., & Kirk, K. S. (1996). Interventions with challenging behavior of persons with developmental disabilities: A review of current research practices. *Journal of the Association for Persons with Severe Handicaps, 21,* 123-134.

Shirley, M. J., Iwata, B. A., Kahng, S., Mazaleski, J. L., & Lerman, D. C. (1997). Does functional communication training compete with ongoing contingencies of reinforcement? An analysis during response acquisition and maintenance. *Journal of Applied Behavior Analysis, 30,* 93-104.

Shukla, S., & Albin, R. W. (1996). Effects of extinction alone and extinction plus functional communication training on covariation of problem behaviors. *Journal of Applied Behavior Analysis, 29,* 565-568.

Smith, R. G., Iwata, B. A., Goh, H., & Shore, B. A. (1995). Analysis of establishing operations for self-injury maintained by escape. *Journal of Applied Behavior Analysis, 28,* 515-535.

Smith, R. G., Iwata, B. A., Vollmer, T. R., & Zarcone, J. R. (1993). Experimental analysis and treatment of multiply controlled self-injury. *Journal of Applied Behavior Analysis, 26,* 183-196.

Smith, R. G., Lerman, D. C., & Iwata, B. A. (1996). Self-restraint as positive reinforcement for self-injurious behavior. *Journal of Applied Behavior Analysis, 29,* 99-102.

Sprague, J., Holland, K., & Thomas, K. (1997). The effect of noncontingent sensory reinforcement, contingent sensory reinforcement, and response interruption on stereotypical and self-injurious behavior. *Research in Developmental Disabilities, 18,* 61-77.

Vollmer, T. R., Iwata, B. A., Zarcone, J. R., Smith, R. G., & Mazaleski, J. L. (1993). The role of attention in the treatment of attention-maintained self-injurious behavior: Noncontingent reinforcement and differential reinforcement of other behavior. *Journal of Applied Behavior Analysis, 26,* 9-21.

Vollmer, T. R., Marcus, B. A., & LeBlanc, L. (1994). Treatment of self-injury and hand mouthing following inconclusive functional analyses. *Journal of Applied Behavior Analysis, 27,* 331-344.

Vollmer, T. R., Marcus, B. A., & Ringdahl, J. E. (1995). Noncontingent escape as treatment for self-injurious behavior maintained by negative reinforcement. *Journal of Applied Behavior Analysis, 28,* 15-26.

Vollmer, T. R., Progar, P. R., Lalli, J. S., Van Camp, C. M., Sierp, B. J., Wright, C. S., Nastasi, J., & Eisenschink, K. J. (1998). Fixed-time schedules attenuate extinction- induced phenomena in the treatment of severe aberrant behavior. *Journal of Applied Behavior Analysis, 31,* 529-542.

Vollmer, T. R., Ringdahl, J. E., Roane, H. S., & Marcus, B. A. (1997). Negative side effects of noncontingent reinforcement. *Journal of Applied Behavior Analysis, 30,* 161-164.

Wacker, D. P. (1996). Behavior analysis research in *JABA*: A need for studies that bridge basic and applied research. *Experimental Analysis of Human Behavior Bulletin, 14,* 11-14.

Wilder, D. A., Draper, R., Williams, W. L., & Higbee, T. S. (1997). A comparison of noncontingent reinforcement, other competing stimulation, and liquid rescheduling for the treatment of rumination. *Behavioral Interventions, 12,* 55-64.

Wolf, M. M. (1978). Social validity: The case for subjective measurement or How applied behavior analysis is finding its heart. *Journal of Applied Behavior Analysis, 11,* 203-214.

Zarcone, J. R., Iwata, B. A., Hughes, C. E., & Vollmer, T. R. (1993). Momentum versus extinction effects in the treatment of self-injurious escape behavior. *Journal of Applied Behavior Analysis, 26,* 135-136.

Zarcone, J. R., Iwata, B. A., Mazaleski, J. L., & Smith, R. G. (1994). Momentum and extinction effects on self-injurious escape behavior and noncompliance. *Journal of Applied Behavior Analysis, 27,* 649-658.

Zarcone, J. R., Iwata, B. A., Smith, R. G., Mazaleski, J. L., & Lerman, D. C. (1994). Reemergence and extinction of self-injurious escape behavior during stimulus (instructional) fading. *Journal of Applied Behavior Analysis, 27,* 307-316.

Zeiler, M. D. (1968). Fixed and variable schedules of response-independent reinforcement. *Journal of the Experimental Analysis of Behavior, 11,* 405-414.

Chapter 5

Behavior Analysis and School Psychology

Ruth A. Ervin and Kristal E. Ehrhardt
Western Michigan University

What is a School Psychologist? According to Fagan and Wise (1994), "a school psychologist is a professional psychological practitioner whose general purpose is to bring a psychological perspective to bear on the problems of educators and the clients educators serve. This perspective is derived from a broad base training in educational and psychological foundations as well as specialty preparation, resulting in the provision of comprehensive psychological services of a direct and indirect nature" (p. 3). This definition is broad, but it suggests the unique aspects of school psychology training and practice. That is, school psychologists are practitioners with specialty training in psychology *and* education that provide comprehensive psychoeducational services to clients. How needed services should be determined and the specific services that should be provided have been debated throughout the history of the field.

The primary purpose of this chapter is to explore the contribution of behavior analysis to the general services that school psychologists provide, including consultation, assessment, intervention (direct and indirect), supervision, research, and program evaluation. Each of these services has been identified as a critical component of school psychological practice by the National Association of School Psychologists (NASP, 1997). The chapter concludes with a discussion of research areas with important implications for the practice of school psychology.

Professional Practice in School Psychology

A fundamental way in which behavior analysis has influenced school psychology is by providing a general model for the discipline (e.g., Baer & Bushell, 1981). As Baer and Bushell note, from a behavioral perspective, the field can be "conceptualized as a system of service provision designed to help remediate school-based problems of children [that is] preventative [and] incorporates explicit efforts to resolve problems before child placement in special education is required" (p. 192). School psychology so construed has much in common with applied behavior analysis (Lentz & Shapiro, 1985).

Consistent with their behavior-analytic orientation, behavioral school psychologists assume that a child's "failure to profit from regular education is relatively common and results to some extent from idiosyncratic, inappropriately arranged environmental events" (Lentz & Shapiro, 1985, p. 199), rather than from some deficit within the child. The proper remedy for behavioral difficulties, therefore, is to ensure that environmental events are appropriately arranged. Determining the kinds of arrangements that are "appropriate" requires careful assessment of the child in her or his natural environment. So, too, does determining whether or not a proposed intervention is effective. Behavioral school psychologists are empiricists and, as Lentz and Shapiro emphasize, constantly "relate assessment to treatment and evaluation" (p. 200).

The behavioral model of school psychology differs fundamentally from the traditional model, which is "best conceptualized as the psychometric model which views the school psychologist's primary function to be that of diagnostician" (Lentz & Shapiro, 1985, p. 192). Behavioral school psychologists are much more than diagnosticians. Many of them are involved in consultation, assessment, intervention, research, supervision, and evaluation. Training in, and commitment to, behavior analysis strongly affects their activities in each of these areas.

Consultation

One aspect of school psychological service delivery that has been greatly influenced by behavior analysis is consultation or, more specifically, school-based behavioral consultation (Bergan, 1977; Kratochwill & Bergan, 1990). In general, "consultation is a fundamental form of interaction between a professional and an individual who wants to help a third party or a system change" (Zins, Kratochwill, & Elliott, 1993, p. 1). For example, a teacher may seek consultation with a school psychologist in order to address the learning needs of a particular student or to assist with a general classroom management problem.

This form of service delivery is of long-standing importance in school psychology (Reschly & Wilson, 1995). In fact, consultation is the "bread and butter" of practice for many behaviorally oriented school psychologists. To emphasize this point, Gresham and Kendall (1987) contended that, "in many ways, consultation is to the school psychologist as therapy/counseling is to the clinical/counseling psychologist" (p. 306).

The development of child-focused psychological consultation in this country may have emerged as early as the 1880s in Lightner Witmer's child psychology clinic at the University of Pennsylvania - the same clinic credited with the founding of school psychology (Brown, Pryzwansky, & Shulte, 1995; Henning-Stout, 1993; Noell & Witt, 1996). However, although consultation was widely practiced by physicians and mental health workers in the 1920s (Brown et al., 1995), it did not gain widespread attention until it was formalized by Caplan (1970) as a form of mental health service delivery.

Not long after Caplan (1970) formalized a mental health model of consultation, Bergan (1970; 1977) developed a formalized consultation process grounded in behavioral theory and principles. Later, Bergan's comprehensive model was refined by Kratochwill and Bergan (1990) and presented as a guide to the delivery of behavioral consultation in applied settings, including schools. The authors defined consultation as an indirect, problem-solving process involving a collegial relation-ship between the consultant (e.g., school psychologist) and the consultee (e.g., teacher, parent) in order to help a client (e.g., student, class) change in a desired direction (e.g., increase on-task behavior during math class). Through a series of three standard interviews, the consultant focuses on helping the consultee: a) specify the problem and validate the problem through baseline data collection, b) analyze the problem to determine whether it is a skill or a performance deficit and to identify relevant controlling variables (i.e., antecedents, consequences, settings events), c) develop an intervention plan based on problem analysis information, and d) implement and evaluate the intervention plan. This model recently has been adapted to include more than one care provider or professional in the process (e.g., Sheridan & Kratochwill, 1992) and to focus on problem-solving for the development of systems-level and organizational change (e.g., Curtis & Stollar, 1995; 1996; Knoff & Curtis, 1996).

Since its inception over 35 years ago, behavioral consultation has become the most widely adopted consultation practice in school settings (Gutkin & Curtis, 1990). With the influence of behavior analysis and its emphasis on empirical evaluation of applied practice, behavioral consultation has also become the most extensively researched model, accounting for over 75% of the research in consulta-tion (Martens, 1993). According to Martens, the popularity of training and research in behavioral consultation is primarily due to two factors: a) the procedures are grounded in behavior analysis and, thus, ongoing measurement and analysis are essential characteristics of the model, and b) the procedures are "sufficiently operationalized" (p. 65) with standardized protocols for interviewing and compe-tency-based training programs for consultants (e.g., Kratochwill & Bergan, 1990).

Research on behavioral consultation has been extensive (see Martens, 1993), yet, there is a need for continued inquiry. For example, Noell and Witt (1996) proposed that we should go so far as to reevaluate the following five assumptions of behavioral consultation: a) the indirect nature of consultation is a superior use of resources when compared to direct intervention, b) collaborative consultation is the most effective form of consultation, c) talking is sufficient to change the behavior of others (i.e., teachers, parents, other professionals), d) consultees (i.e., teachers, parents, other professionals) will generalize problem-solving skills developed in consultation to new problem situations, and e) direct contact between the consultant and client is unnecessary.

Traditionally, and evident in the five assumptions listed above, behavioral consultation has relied heavily on verbal exchanges between the consultant and the consultee. This focus on what is said during consultation and how what is said translates into successful intervention implementation has been a topic of recent concern in the field (e.g., Watson & Robinson, 1996; Witt, 1997). According to Witt:

> [If we want to assume that] talk (e.g., consultation, collaboration, teaming, problem-solving, etc.) is effective, then it is necessary to establish a functional relation between three key variables: a) what is said to someone

(e.g., during consultation), b) whether what is said translates into a change in behavior for the person we are talking to (e.g., the teacher implements an intervention as planned during our collaborative session), and c) whether the behavior change of the listener is correlated with some outcome such as a change in social behavior in children. (p. 289)

Unfortunately, recent studies indicate that with traditional behavioral consultation, teachers generally do not implement interventions as planned (i.e., intervention integrity is lacking), even when observed (e.g., Jones, Wickstrom, & Friman, 1997; Noell, Witt, Gilbertson, Ranier, & Freeland, 1997; Robbins & Gutkin, 1994; Wickstrom, Jones, LaFleur, & Witt, in press; Witt, Noell, LaFleur, & Mortenson, 1997). One strategy to deal with this problem is providing teachers with performance feedback on the degree to which they implement interventions with integrity (e.g., Cossairt, Hall, & Hopkins, 1973). This strategy has been shown to enhance the integrity with which teachers implement classroom interventions suggested during behavioral consultation (e.g., Jones et al., 1997; Noell et al., 1997; Witt et al., 1997). Furthermore, and importantly, improvements in intervention integrity following performance feedback have been demonstrated to result in improvements in student performance (e.g., Jones et al., 1997; Noell et al., 1997).

Despite the shortcomings of traditional behavioral consultation procedures, in schools where there is an ever-growing diversity of student needs and where limited time and resources are available for the delivery of direct services (e.g., assessment, direct intervention, counseling) - and this includes most schools - it is likely that school psychologists will continue to utilize consultation. In other words, rather than meeting directly with each student who experiences academic, social, or behavioral difficulties - a process that would require extensive time and resources beyond those currently available - school psychologists will probably continue to consult with teachers and parents to influence student functioning indirectly.

However, the manner in which consultation is conducted may change in light of recent findings regarding the lack of integrity with interventions implemented during traditional behavioral consultation and the importance of performance feedback (for recent commentary see Watson & Robinson, 1996 or Witt, 1997). In addition, with the growing need for systemic school reform and collaborative efforts to better meet student needs, it is likely that conjoint behavioral consultation (Sheridan, Kratochwill, & Bergan, 1996) and systems-level consultation (Curtis & Stollar, 1995; 1996; Knoff & Curtis, 1996) will play a larger role for behavioral school psychologists.

Psychological and Psychoeducational Assessment

A second area of focus for practice in school psychology is that of assessment. Within the field of school psychology, assessment has consistently been an area of great controversy. As mentioned previously, the traditional role of the school psychologist has been that of "diagnostician or sorter, in which the most visible function has been the psychoeducational assessment of children for placement in special education programs" (Fagan, 1995, p. 64). Federal, state, and local policies, regulations, and guidelines frequently mandate a "labeling" approach to assessment, and the primary function of much traditional academic and psychological assessment is to assign students to categories.

Many school psychologists spend most of their time categorizing students. For example, recent surveys reveal that school psychologists report spending about two-thirds of their time in activities related to classification for special education and placement purposes (Reschly & Wilson, 1995). Over half of this time is spent conducting individualized assessment activities with frequent use of standardized measures of children's aptitudes (i.e., intelligence tests) and achievement. Such tests characteristically categorize students based on their performance relative to that of some normative group.

Behavioral assessment serves a very different function. In essence, it involves "the identification of meaningful response units and their controlling variables for the purpose of understanding and of altering behavior" (Hayes, Nelson, & Jarrett, 1986, p. 464). In behavioral assessment, one selects target behaviors, devises an intervention, and evaluates the outcome of that intervention (Lentz & Shapiro, 1985).

To illustrate the differences between traditional and behavioral approaches to assessment, we will briefly describe how a school psychologist might tackle the assessment of Mark, an 11-year-old boy referred for concerns about his behavior and academic performance, primarily during reading. A school psychologist who subscribes to a traditional psychometric approach to assessment would likely focus efforts on determining whether or not Mark met criteria for classification under a special education disability category (e.g., learning disability). In order to accomplish this task, the psychologist would probably administer to Mark a battery of standardized tests, including: a) an intelligence test such as the Weschler Intelligence Scale for Children- Third Edition (WISC-III; Weschler, 1991), and b) a norm-referenced achievement test such as the Woodcock-Johnson Tests of Achievement (Woodcock & Johnson, 1990) or perhaps the Wide Range Achievement Test-Third Edition (WRAT-III; Wilkinson, 1993).

The WISC-III would provide information concerning Mark's general verbal and performance abilities relative to that of his same-aged peers. Results of norm-referenced achievement tests would provide information concerning Mark's academic performance (i.e., math, reading, spelling, etc.) relative to his peers. In addition, the school psychologist might administer a test of visual-motor perception or integration (e.g., Bender-Gestalt) or projective tests (e.g., Draw-A-Person: A quantitative scoring system; Naglieri, 1988).

Based on the information gathered, a determination of Mark's eligibility for special education services might be made through a multidisciplinary team meeting. The team would use the assessment data to determine whether Mark qualifies for special educational services and, if so, under which classification category (e.g., learning disabled, emotionally impaired) he would be served. Regardless of whether or not Mark met criteria for services, the next step in this process would be to determine intervention strategies and to explore the extent to which his needs could be met in the general education setting.

In contrast, a school psychologist who approached Mark's referral from a behavioral perspective would probably proceed by following a problem-solving process involving a) identifying specific problem behaviors in objective terms, b) analyzing the problem and forming hypotheses about potential controlling variables, c) devising an intervention plan based on preliminary assessment information, and d) conducting ongoing progress monitoring to ensure treatment integrity, outcome, and acceptability. Further, it would behoove the school psychologist to determine what resources would be required to solve the problem and to evaluate whether these resources were available. If not, an alternative intervention would probably be considered.

The types of assessment procedures that a behaviorally oriented school psychologist might use would include: a) informant assessments such as semi-structured interviews (e.g., teacher, students, parent), b) rating scales (e.g., Child-Behavior Checklist; Achenbach & Edelbrock, 1991), c) direct observations of the learning environment and student behavior in the classroom setting (e.g., descriptive functional assessment observations), d) direct assessment of mastery of academic skills through criterion-referenced instruments (e.g., Curriculum-Based Assessment; see Shapiro, 1996), and e) ongoing assessment (e.g., Curriculum-Based Measurement; Shinn, 1989; 1995) of the child's acquisition and retention of academic skills with the implementation of intervention strategies.

These assessment techniques yield information that is directly relevant to the student's behavior problems, not information that supposedly quantifies a hypothetical entity (e.g., learning disability) that allegedly causes those problems. Moreover, these techniques provide direct evidence of whether or not any intervention that is implemented is effective in remedying the problems that caused Mark's initial referral. Clearly, if one is interested in quantifying the behaviors that cause problems for students, and in determining whether treatments are useful in changing those behaviors, the techniques of behavioral assessment are of unparalleled value. Behavior analysts have written at length about techniques for quantifying behavior (e.g., Bellack & Hersen, 1988; Johnston & Pennypacker, 1993; Poling, Methot, & LeSage, 1995), and it may suffice here to note that assessment inside schools poses no unique problems.

Intervention

Developing interventions to help students with learning or conduct problems has become a major function of behavioral school psychologists. As Tilly and Flugum (1995) noted, in recent years there has been a push by professional organizations (such as NASP) toward the provision of intervention services to students, families, and schools. This trend is reflected in policy statements and publications (e.g., Christenson & Conoley, 1992; Graden, Zins, & Curtis, 1988; Stoner, Shinn, & Walker, 1991; Thomas & Grimes, 1995). Furthermore, after comparing the results of national surveys in 1986 and 1991-92, Reschly and Wilson

(1995) reported that school psychologists have indicated shifts in role preferences, with reduced emphasis on traditional psychoeducational assessment and more emphasis on interventions and behavioral consultation.

The term "intervention" has been used in many ways in behavior analysis and education. For this chapter, an educational intervention may be defined as "a planned modification of the environment made for the purpose of altering the environment in a prespecified way" (Tilly & Flugum, 1995, p. 485). As Tilly and Flugum discuss, three elements of this definition are of particular importance. First, interventions are "planned" - they are strategies that are carefully chosen and completely described. Second, they focus on environmental modifications. This means that rather than focusing narrowly on child-related variables, a host of environmental targets (e.g., teacher behaviors or elements of the physical classroom environment) are considered for change. Third, interventions are "goal directed" in that, they seek to modify behavior in a prespecified way.

It is common in school psychology to distinguish between direct and indirect interventions. Direct interventions are those in which a school psychologist interacts directly with the person whose behavior is targeted for change, and includes strategies to improve academic performance or to resolve behavior problems for individuals (e.g., a third-grade student with reading comprehension difficulties) or groups (e.g., second- and third-graders exhibiting conduct problems in the lunchroom). Counseling with individuals or groups is an example of a direct intervention. Indirect interventions are defined as those that are developed by a school psychologist and a consultee (e.g., a teacher) to benefit a client (e.g., a child). An essential element of indirect interventions is that they are carried out by the consultee or another interested party rather than by the school psychologist; hence, the "indirect" nature of the intervention. As with direct interventions, indirect interventions may be addressed at an individual or a group level (e.g., systems and organizational change). Also, indirect interventions may be self-managed, peer-mediated, or teacher-directed.

In most cases, school psychologists help to design interventions that are implemented by other people, such as teachers, aides, and parents, who consult with the school psychologist. This strategy is optimal, in that it allows a single psychologist to provide intervention services to the largest possible number of people. Occasionally, school psychologists have "hands-on" involvement in intervention, although such involvement may be limited to an initial demonstration of techniques. As discussed in the previous section, behavioral school psychologists rely upon techniques (e.g., functional assessment or curriculum-based assessment) that link assessment to intervention. Not only do the assessment tools provide information critical to intervention design; they also provide a mechanism for evaluating the success of a strategy.

An incredible variety of direct and indirect interventions is available and at least occasionally useful in school settings (NASP, 1997). Behavior analysts have developed many different techniques, based generally on principles of operant conditioning, for accelerating, decelerating, and establishing stimulus control over human behavior (e.g., Cooper, Heward, & Heron, 1987; Miltenberger, 1997). Many of these techniques have been used extensively in school settings. Thus, a school psychologist who is also a competent applied behavior analyst will possess a wealth of knowledge to assist in dealing with most of the behavioral problems presented by students in school settings. However, it should be noted that a major challenge in the area of direct intervention lies in appropriately matching interventions to individual students, ensuring proper implementation, and monitoring intervention outcomes.

Supervision

School psychologists may be involved with supervision in several ways. First, all school psychology students must be supervised. According to NASP training standards (NASP, 1997), school psychology trainees must receive highly structured and frequent guidance by a qualified school psychologist. At minimum, trainees obtain supervised experience in both practica and internship settings. As school psychology students develop more independence during internship, supervision typically is reduced. Nevertheless, even after graduation, supervision continues, because practicing school psychologists receive both administrative and professional supervision by the relevant educational or psychological professional. According to Fagan and Wise (1994), "administrative supervision refers to supervision regarding specific interpretation and implementation of district policies and regulations to school psychologists in their capacity as employees. Professional supervision refers to specific interpretation and implementation of actions taken by school psychologists in their capacity as professional psychologists" (p. 82).

Regardless of whom they are supervising, behaviorally oriented school psychologists recognize the importance of formulating accurate job descriptions, carefully monitoring supervisees' performances, and, if necessary, developing interventions to improve those performances. The same behavior-analytic strategies that are effective in assessing and altering behavior in school-age students can be used to good advantage in supervising graduate students and professional school psychologists. Specific suggestions for providing optimal supervision of interns are provided by Conoley and Bahns (1995). In addition to the strategies that they describe, management techniques borrowed from organizational behavior management are potentially useful in systems that provide supervision for a substantial number of people.

Research in School Psychology

Training in school psychology is often based on the scientist-practitioner model (Edwards, 1987; Phillips, 1993), which proposes that effective psychologists are able to integrate research and practice in their area (see Barlow, Hayes, & Nelson, 1984). According to Keith (1995), there are three hierarchical research roles that school psychologists might play as scientist-practitioners: a) consumer, b) distributor (i.e., synthesizers or disseminator), and c) conductor. The first role, that of consumer of research, is founded on the assumption that in order to "apply research to practice, school psychologists must read research and evaluate critically the research they read" (Keith, 1988, p. 502). In addition, because school psychologists are often called upon to consult with teachers, parents, administrators, and other professionals on the needs of students, they must be prepared to function as a distributor of research and to provide guidance regarding appropriate methods of assessment and intervention. Finally, school psychologists may actually conduct research.

Although many scholars agree that school psychology practitioners should integrate science into their applied practice, many apparently do not (McKee, Witt, Elliott, Pardue, & Judycki, 1987; Phillips, 1993). Surveys suggest that the role of scientist is ranked relatively low by school psychology practitioners (e.g., McKee et al.), and they reportedly spend less than 5% of their time in this role (Stoner & Green, 1992). According to McKee et al., even the role of consumer of research (e.g., reading the research literature), deemed an essential best practice role for school psychologists (Keith, 1995), is not widely practiced. Perhaps the availability of more user-friendly journals, publishing research articles that suggest practical strategies for improving behavior in the classroom, would increase the likelihood of practitioners contacting the research literature. In this regard, it is noteworthy that a journal with such an orientation, *Proven Practice: Prevention and Remediation Solutions for Schools*, has recently appeared.

Of course, several school psychologists are eminent scientists. Those who are behaviorally oriented characteristically make use of the tactics and strategies of research characteristic of applied behavior analysis, and they have shown repeatedly the value of single-subject designs and visual data analyses in school settings. It is, however, the case that practical exigencies frequently prevent school-based research from having the extreme methodological rigor of, for instance, a typical article published in the *Journal of Applied Behavior Analysis*.

Hawkins and Hursh (1992) have delineated three levels of research that vary in their function as well as their level of experimental rigor. For practicing school psychologists, the majority of research time would likely be spent conducting what Hawkins and Hursh (1992) referred to as Level 1 research, or accountable service delivery. Ideally school psychologists employ empirically validated intervention methods, conduct ongoing progress monitoring, and evaluate the outcome of interventions (Reschly & Ysseldyke, 1995). These activities are consistent with Level 1 research.

In contrast, practicing school psychologists would spend relatively little time conducting Level 3 (scientific-quality) research, which includes appropriate methodological safeguards (e.g., procedural integrity measures, interobserver agreement, experimental control) to "verify the credibility of the data and to assure that what appear to be positive effects are actually a result of the intervention and not some other variables" (Hawkins & Hursh, 1992, p. 68). Instead, Level 3 research would likely be conducted by graduate trainers who would then disseminate their findings for the benefit of practicing school psychologists and educators who are consumers of research. Like all research in applied behavior analysis, Level 3 school-based intervention research should be evaluated on the basis of treatment effectiveness, treatment integrity, social validity, and treatment acceptability (Shapiro, 1987).

Level 2 research falls somewhere in between the practical emphasis of Level 1 research and the experimental rigor associated with Level 3 research. Level 2 research might be conducted in order to "gather more convincing data about the effectiveness of your procedures or of a service (Hawkins & Hursh, 1992, p. 66)" or to convince the general public of the merit of your procedures so that continued research might be supported. Level 2 research may yield findings of sufficient believability to merit sharing in practice-oriented journals (i.e., *Proven Practice: Prevention and Remediation Solutions for Schools*), although they will rarely merit publication in a major research journal (i.e., *Journal of Applied Behavior Analysis*).

Program Planning and Evaluation

A final role that a school psychologist may fulfill is that of program planning and evaluation. Program planning and evaluation is a leadership role in which school psychology practitioners aid in planning, developing, and monitoring educational services and programs (Illback, Zins, Maher, & Greenburg, 1990). Examples of projects that school psychologists might help to develop include: (a) establishing a comprehensive model of inclusion for preschool children with disabilities in a preschool center for typically developing children, (b) implementing curriculum-based measurement system in an elementary school, and (c) training school-based teams in functional assessment and the development of effective behavioral support plans.

Planning, implementing, and evaluating a broad-spectrum program is not different in principle from planning, implementing, and evaluating a specific behavior-change intervention. The scale is, however, substantially different, as are the problems likely to be encountered. Broad-spectrum programs in schools rarely can be evaluated with methodological rigor; research in the area characteristically is Level 1 as defined by Hawkins and Hursh (1992), and occasionally Level 2. Systems analysis as practiced by organizational behavior analysts appears to be eminently well suited for program development and evaluation in schools, and is sometimes recommended for this purpose (e.g., Curtis & Stollar, 1995).

Translating Research into Practice: Future Inquiry for Behavioral School Psychologists

The field of behavior analysis or more specifically applied behavior analysis, has accumulated a wealth of empirical knowledge that is quite useful to school psychologists. For example, to help students attain their full potential, school psychologists need to know: a) how to utilize assessment strategies to match interventions to the needs of individual students, b) how to arrange educational environments to provide sufficient learning opportunities and contingencies to support the development of academic, pro-social, and behavioral skills, and c) how to monitor progress and evaluate outcomes so that appropriate modifications of interventions can be made in a systematic and timely fashion. An empirically sound technology for addressing each of these areas has been demonstrated in the behavior analysis literature, yet there is a continued need to translate this *research* into *effective practice*. School psychologists who are also skilled behavior analysts are in a unique position to assist in bridging this existing science-to-practice gap. In this section of the chapter, we will highlight the three aforementioned areas (i.e., linking assessment to intervention design, ensuring proper implementation, and evaluating outcomes) of importance and opportunity for future inquiry through the example of school-based functional assessment research.

Linking assessment to intervention. Matching interventions to behavior problems is especially difficult, and further research evaluating procedures for doing so is needed (Reschly, 1988; Reschly & Ysseldyke, 1995). In recent years, a particular form of behavioral assessment, termed functional assessment, has garnered considerable attention as a method for selecting interventions (e.g., Batsche & Knoff, 1995; Martens, 1993; Shapiro, 1996). Not only is this implied within the literature, but also through endorsements by national organizations (e.g., NASP, 1997; National Association of State Directors of Education, 1994; National Institutes of Health, 1989) and recent federal legislation (IDEA: Section 615 (k)(1)(B)).

In general, functional assessment is a process through which a broad range of information is gathered to identify environmental variables related to the occurrence and nonoccurrence of a target behavior (O'Neill et al., 1997). It is a structured problem-solving process that can guide the selection of interventions based upon the function of the problem behavior, thus linking assessment to intervention and increasing the likelihood of treatment effectiveness (Dunlap & Kern, 1996; Vollmer & Northup, 1996). More specifically, information obtained through a variety of sources (e.g., teacher interviews, direct observations, rating scales) is examined to develop hypotheses regarding the relationship between environmental variables and the occurrence of problem behaviors (e.g., O'Neill et al.). Next, these hypotheses are tested through brief experimental analyses with the result yielding information useful in generating individualized intervention strategies.

In school settings, where resources are limited, there is a need for an efficacious intervention selection process that closely links assessment to the selection of interventions. Several authors have argued that functional assessment is an approach superior to traditional psychiatric or school-based diagnostics because of the manner in which interventions are more closely linked to preliminary assessments (DuPaul & Ervin, 1996; Kratochwill & McGivern, 1996; Zentall & Javorsky, 1995).

Typically, interventions employed in school settings are based upon traditional methods of classroom management and focus on the topographies of behaviors rather than their functions (Kern, Childs, Dunlap, Clarke, & Falk, 1994). In addition, traditional discipline approaches may be punitive (e.g., office referrals) and limit opportunities for positive social and learning experiences (Kern et al.). In other words, in school settings we have typically tried to match interventions to what behaviors look like or to hierarchies of predetermined discipline procedures, with little attention toward trying to determine "why" problem behaviors occur.

Recent studies have shown that interventions implemented without consideration of behavioral function can become counter-therapeutic despite high intervention integrity (Broussard & Northup, 1995; Taylor & Miller, 1997). When interventions fail to be effective in altering target behaviors in a desired direction, behaviors may then become more resistant to new or modified interventions (Iwata, Dorsey, Slifer, Bauman, & Richman, 1982/1994). Interventions based upon preliminary functional assessment information are likely to be more effective than treatments not based on such data (Taylor & Miller, 1997). Thus, one advantage of determining the function of symptomatic behavior (functional assessment) is that the process can lead to tighter connections between diagnosis and treatment, thus, enhancing the likelihood of intervention success for multiple classroom problems (Repp, 1994).

Despite the fact that the process of linking assessment to intervention design through the identification of variables that set the occasion for and/or maintain problem behaviors is not a new concept in education (e.g., Bijou, Peterson, & Ault, 1968; Cone, 1997), relatively few *school-based* applications of this process have appeared in the literature (Blakeslee, Sugai, & Gruba, 1994 ; Ervin, Radford et al., 1998). It is, however, clear that functional assessment is possible in school settings (e.g., Dunlap et al., 1993; Lalli, Browder, Mace, & Brown, 1993; Repp & Karsh, 1994; Sasso et al., 1992). For example, some studies have examined the utility of functional assessment in identifying classroom variables related to the occurrence of low intensity behaviors (e.g., noncompliance, off-task behaviors) for students with average intellectual functioning in general education settings (e.g., Broussard & Northup, 1995; 1997; Dunlap et al., 1993; Kern et al., 1994; Lewis & Sugai, 1996; Umbreit, 1995).

Across the array of school-based empirical studies, investigators have noted the utility of functional assessment as a method for: a) examining pre-referral interventions in inclusive settings (e.g., Broussard & Northup, 1995), b) testing the utility of peer interventions (e.g., Broussard & Northup, 1997), c) determining the utility of time out procedures (Taylor & Miller, 1997), d) examining the role of classroom variables on the maintenance of problem behaviors associated with young children (e.g., Lewis & Sugai, 1996; Northup et al., 1995; Umbreit, 1995) and adolescents diagnosed with Attention-Deficit/Hyperactivity Disorder (ADHD; e.g., Ervin, DuPaul, Kern, & Friman, 1998), e) identifying interventions for students with severe emotional and/or behavioral disorders (e.g., Dunlap, Kern-Dunlap, Charle, & Robbins, 1991; Dunlap et al., 1993), and f) identifying interventions for adolescents with a multitude of emotional/behavioral disorders (e.g., Ervin, Kern et al., 1998).

Two general lines of inquiry are evident in the school-based research on functional analysis for linking assessment to intervention design, and both merit further attention. One line of inquiry is focused on the manipulation of maintaining variables for the primary purpose of determining behavioral function. For example, some school-based research (e.g., Northup et al., 1995) has focused on the manipulation of consequences or antecedent variables in analog conditions for the primary purpose of determining the function of behavior problems (e.g., self-injurious behavior, aggression). In school settings, the importance of such basic research is that it furthers our understanding of behavior and the role of environmental variables in the development and maintenance of problem behaviors exhibited in school settings.

A second line of inquiry in school-based functional assessment research has focused on the utility of functional assessment primarily as a process for linking assessment to intervention design. For example, traditional functional assessment procedures have been adapted to include manipulations of curricular variables (e.g., Dunlap et al., 1993) as well as adjunctive procedures (e.g., Ervin, DuPaul et al., 1998) for the primary purpose of intervention selection. When the purpose is intervention selection, school-based functional assessment typically involves identifying functional relationships between curricular variables and desirable/undesirable student behavior (for a recent review see Dunlap & Kern, 1996). Once specific curricular variables are identified, curricular modifications can be made to decrease or eliminate problem behaviors. This process has been demonstrated to yield favorable results with students with various disabilities including emotional/behavioral disorders (e.g., Dunlap et al., 1993; Ervin, Kern et al., 1998; Kern et al., 1994).

These two lines of inquiry can be illustrated through the example of school-based functional assessment research for students with ADHD. In pursuit of answers to basic research questions, Northup and colleagues (1995) conducted brief functional analyses of the problem behaviors exhibited in an analog classroom setting by three young children diagnosed with ADHD. Results of the functional analyses indicated that the peer attention condition was associated with the highest frequency of problem behaviors. In addition, for one student, problem behaviors were more clearly associated with environmental classroom variables when the student was taking stimulant medication. On a basic level, this line of inquiry has contributed to the field of school psychology by furthering our understanding of the role of classroom variables in the maintenance or exacerbation of problem behaviors exhibited by students with a disorder with a presumed biological basis (i.e., ADHD).

The work of Northup et al. (1995) has been extended to include case examples of the utility of functional assessment for younger students with ADHD in integrated school settings (e.g., Broussard & Northup, 1995; 1997; Lewis & Sugai, 1996; Umbreit, 1995) and for older students with ADHD and comorbid emotional/behavioral disorders (e.g., Ervin, DuPaul et al., 1998; Ervin, Kern et al., 1998). For example, Ervin, DuPaul et al. (1998) examined the utility of functional assessment in the development of interventions for two adolescents diagnosed with ADHD and Oppositional Defiant Disorder. Information obtained through descriptive assessments (i.e., interviews, observations) led to the development of several intervention strategies that were subsequently tested and confirmed through teacher manipulations of classroom variables. For both students, interventions evaluated from this process proved effective, practical, and acceptable by teachers and participants. In contrast to previous studies, Ervin, DuPaul et al. (1998) included adjunctive interventions strategies (i.e., setting up contingencies around an incompatible behavior) when the reduction of hypothesized controlling variables was difficult to achieve (i.e., reducing peer attention).

Ensuring proper intervention implementation. Once appropriate interventions have been identified, it is then important to ensure they are implemented with integrity (Witt, 1997). Within the functional assessment literature, as applications have moved from basic (e.g., clinic-analog) to more applied (e.g., school general education) settings, issues centering around the practicality, acceptability, and "teachability" of functional assessment procedures and outcomes have become of increasing importance. These issues may impede the degree to which traditional functional assessment procedures are feasible in school settings. For example, teachers may be reluctant or unable to manipulate certain events contingent on the occurrence of problem behavior (Ervin, DuPaul et al., 1998) despite the fact that they may inadvertently or unintentionally reinforce problem behaviors (e.g., responding to a student's call outs when they are maintained by teacher attention). Furthermore, when direct control over a presumed maintaining variable is difficult to achieve in the natural classroom setting (e.g., reducing peer attention for disruptive behavior), it may be necessary to default to the manipulation of antecedents or adjunctive procedures that set up reinforcing contingencies around an incompatible behavior (e.g., self-management of on-task behavior; Ervin, DuPaul et al., 1998; Ervin, Kern et al., 1998).

School psychologists have begun addressing the need to ensure proper intervention implementation by considering the selection of "keystone variables" (e.g., pivotal behaviors) to target for change that have the greatest likelihood of widespread change for the client (Barnett, Bauer, Ehrhardt, Lentz, & Stollar, 1996, p. 95). In addition to carefully selecting what to target for change, it is important to select interventions that are "ecological in nature, naturalistic in scope, contain elements from the research base that are predictive for success, and incorporate the constructs of social validity in a practical manner" (Lentz, Allen, & Ehrhardt, 1996, p. 118).

Once strong intervention strategies are selected, careful measures must be taken to ensure proper implementation. Ehrhardt, Barnett, Lentz, Stollar, and Reifin (1996), for example, developed intervention scripts collaboratively with parents and teachers to promote treatment integrity and acceptability of intervention strategies designed to reduce problem behaviors exhibited by preschool children. Results indicated that teachers and parents found the scripts acceptable and effective.

Progress monitoring and evaluating outcomes. Although functional assessment has received support in the literature, there is a need for continued monitoring and evaluation of its utility as an intervention selection process. In short, we have yet to determine the variables that influence whether teachers, school psychology practitioners, and other personnel are willing and able to use functional assessment and, if they are, the specific procedures that best lead to proactive and effective intervention selection in school settings. It is, however, clear that making procedures as simple and easy as possible is likely to increase their utility in school settings. Thus, what is needed is a form of functional assessment that does not require extensive time or effort to implement, yet still allows for enough precision to be effective in linking assessment to intervention (R. Detrich, personal communication, January 30, 1998).

Researchers have examined functional assessment based on semi-structured teacher interviews (Dunlap et al., 1991; O'Neill et al., 1997), student interviews (e.g., Kern et al., 1994; Reed Thomas, Sprague, & Horner, 1997), and teacher (Lewis & Sugai, 1996) or student (Kwak, Ervin, Anderson, & Austin, 1998) rating scales. These informant scales and interviews were developed in recognition of the fact that functional assessment can be a time-consuming and expensive process, often requiring expert support from external consultants (Lewis & Sugai). Similarly, teacher-friendly functional assessment training packages (e.g., Spectrum Center for Educational and Behavioral Development, 1996), texts (e.g., O'Neill et al., 1997), and state guidelines (e.g., Pennsylvania Department of Education, 1995) have been developed for the same purpose. Despite these endeavors to improve the utility of functional assessment procedures, the majority of research, thus far, has been conducted in a case study format, has included the extensive involvement of experts in behavior analysis (Lewis & Sugai), and generally has failed to include measures of feasibility and acceptability (Ervin, Radford et al., 1998).

In an invited essay on functional assessment, Cone (1997) argued that more "research is needed on the teachability of functional assessment approaches," and specifically, "the extent to which...teachers, parents,...can learn to conduct functional assessment/analyses" (p. 273). Although few studies (e.g., Piper, Ervin, Austin, & Whitten, 1997; Taylor, O'Reilly, & Lancioni, 1996) have examined the teachability of functional assessment procedures, we can draw from the school-based consultation training literature to guide this line of research. For example, we know that if consultation training is to be effective, it must be provided in conjunction with longitudinal on-site assistance (e.g., Bailey, 1989). Further, if there is no planning to provide training system-wide, research suggests that schools may become reliant on external consultants and procedures will not be implemented without their support (Fuchs, Fuchs, Harris, & Roberts, 1996). Generalizing from these findings, it appears that system-wide training in functional assessment is necessary if reliance on external consultants is to be minimized. Ongoing performance feedback is also likely to increase the use and value of functional assessment, as it does with respect to consultation (Watson & Kramer, 1995).

To summarize, if we expect school practitioners to incorporate functional assessment into their assessment repertoires, one important next step in this line of inquiry is to examine how to best incorporate functional assessment in school settings with specific attention to: a) the practicality of functional assessment in school settings (Ervin, DuPaul et al., 1998; Lewis & Sugai, 1996), b) the utility of student and teacher involvement in the process (Kwak et al. , 1998; Reed et al., 1997), c) the "teachability" of functional assessment procedures to teachers and school-based intervention assistance teams (Cone, 1997; Piper et al., 1997; Taylor et al., 1996), d) the time needed to conduct functional assessment in schools (Lewis & Sugai), e) the extent to which components of the functional assessment process are feasible in classroom settings and acceptable to teachers and students (Broussard & Northup, 1995; 1997; Ervin, DuPaul et al., 1998; Lalli et al., 1993; Radford & Ervin, 1997), and f) the resources and support needed from external consultants to ensure effective application in school settings

(Lewis & Sugai). Further research in each of these areas is merited. School psychologists with a behavior-analytic focus are in a unique position to provide training in functional assessment, and to participate in research designed to evaluate the effectiveness, integrity, and acceptability of functional assessment in schools.

Concluding Comments

Behavior analysis has played an important role in school psychology since the founding of the NASP in 1969. It continues to do so, as evidenced by the recent founding of the Behavioral School Psychology Special Interest Group of NASP in 1996 (Shriver, 1996). The primary mission of that group is to "promote the understanding and utilization of the science of behavior analysis in school psychology training and practice" (Shriver, p. 4). We believe, and have suggested in this chapter, that this is a worthy mission, insofar as behavior analysis provides a sound foundation for all of the activities characteristic of school psychology, including consultation, assessment, intervention, research, supervision, and evaluation. Effective school psychologists are apt to be good behavior analysts.

Reading Objectives

1. What is a school psychologist?
2. Briefly describe the five major roles and functions that a school psychologist might play. How has behavior analysis influenced each of these roles and functions?
3. What is consultation? How do school psychologists use consultation in their day-to-day practice?
4. Briefly describe the stages of a behavioral problem-solving approach to consultation.
5. What are some of the recent criticisms of traditional behavioral consultation? How might these concerns be addressed?
6. A behavioral school psychologist will likely approach assessment from a different perspective than a traditional school psychologist? Describe how these two approaches might differ in terms of their *purpose, procedures*, and *outcomes*.
7. In what ways do *indirect* and *direct* approaches to intervention differ? What are the potential advantages and disadvantages to using direct and indirect interventions in school settings?
8. School psychologists are generally trained to be *scientist-practitioners* (i.e., practitioners who integrate research into their school-based practice). In what ways might a school psychologist integrate research into practice? Is this a preferred role? Why or why not?
9. What is functional assessment? How is this process useful to school psychologists?
10. What are some barriers to the implementation of functional assessment procedures in school settings? In what ways can behavioral school psychologists and researchers assist in bridging the gap between *research* and *practice* in school-based functional assessment?

References

Achenbach, T. M., & Edelbrock, C. S. (1991). *Manual for the cross-informant program for the child behavior checklist.* Burlington: University of Vermont, Department of Psychiatry.

Baer, D. M., & Bushell, D. (1981). The future of behavior analysis in the schools? Consider its recent past, and then ask a different question. *School Psychology Review, 10,* 259-270.

Bailey, D. (1989). Issues and directions for preparing professionals to work with young handicapped children and their families. In J. J. Gallagher, P. Trahonis, and R. Clifford (Eds.), *Policy implementation and P.L. 99-457: Planning for young children with special needs* (pp. 97-132). Baltimore, MD: Brookes.

Barlow, D. H., Hayes, S. C., & Nelson, R. O. (1984). *The scientist-practitioner: Research and accountability in clinical and educational settings.* Elmsford, NY: Pergamon Press.

Barnett, D. W., Bauer, A. M., Ehrhardt, K. E., Lentz, F. E., & Stollar, S. A. (1996). Keystone targets for change: Planning for widespread positive consequences. *School Psychology Quarterly, 11,* 95-117.

Batsche, G. M., & Knoff, H. M. (1995). Best practices in linking assessment to intervention. In A. Thomas & J. Grimes (Eds.), *Best practices in school psychology III* (pp. 569-585). Washington, DC: National Association of School Psychologists.

Bellack, A. S., & Hersen, M. (1988). *Behavioral assessment.* New York: Pergamon Press.

Bergan, J. R. (1970). A systems approach to psychological services. *Psychology in the Schools, 8,* 315-319.

Bergan, J. R. (1977). *Behavioral consultation.* Columbus, OH: Merrill.

Bijou, S. W., Peterson, R. F., & Ault, M. H. (1968). A method to integrate descriptive and experimental field studies at the level of data and empirical concepts. *Journal of Applied Behavior Analysis, 1,* 175-191.

Blakeslee, T., Sugai, G., & Gruba, J. (1994). A review of functional assessment use in data-based intervention studies. *Journal of Behavioral Education, 4,* 397-413.

Broussard, C. D., & Northup, J. (1995). An approach to functional assessment and analysis of disruptive behavior in regular education classrooms. *School Psychology Quarterly, 10,* 151-164.

Broussard, C., & Northup, J. (1997). The use of functional analysis to develop peer interventions for disruptive classroom behavior. *School Psychology Quarterly, 12,* 65-76.

Brown, D., Pryzwansky, W. B., & Schulte, A. C. (1995). *Psychological consultation* (3rd ed.). Needham Heights, MA: Allyn & Bacon.

Campbell, D. T. (1988). The experimenting society. In S. Overman (Ed.), *Methodology and epistemology for social science* (pp. 299-314). Chicago: University of Chicago Press.

Caplan, G. (1970). *The theory and practice of mental health consultation.* New York: Basic Books.

Christenson, S. L., & Conoley, J. C. (Eds.). (1992). *Home-school collaboration: Enhancing children's academic and social competence.* Silver Spring, MD: National Association of School Psychologists.

Cone, J. D. (1997). Issues in functional analysis in behavioral assessment. *Behaviour Research and Therapy, 35,* 259-275.

Conoley, J. C., & Bahns, T. (1995). Supervision of interns. In A. Thomas & J. Grimes (Eds.), *Best practices in school psychology III* (pp. 111-122). Washington, DC: National Association of School Psychologists.

Cooper, J. O., Heron, T. E., & Heward, W. L. (1987). *Applied behavior analysis.* Columbus, OH: Merrill.

Cossairt, A., Hall, R. V., & Hopkins, B. L. (1973). The effects of experimenter's instructions, feedback, and praise on teacher praise and student attending behavior. *Journal of Applied Behavior Analysis, 6,* 89-100.

Curtis, M. J., & Stollar, S. A. (1995). Systems level consultation and organizational change. In A. Thomas & J. Grimes (Eds.), *Best practices in school psychology III* (pp. 51-58). Washington, DC: National Association of School Psychologists.

Curtis, M. J., & Stollar, S. A. (1996). Applying principles and practices of organizational change to school reform. *School Psychology Review, 25,* 409-417.

Dunlap, G., & Kern, L. (1996). Modifying instructional activities to promote desirable behavior: A conceptual and practical framework. *School Psychology Quarterly, 11,* 297-312.

Dunlap, G., Kern, L., deParczel, M., Clarke, S., Wilson, D., Childs, K. E., White, R., & Falk, G. D. (1993). Functional analysis of classroom variables for students with emotional and behavioral disorders. *Behavioral Disorders, 18,* 275-291.

Dunlap, G., Kern-Dunlap, L., Clarke, S., & Robbins, F. R. (1991). Functional assessment, curricular revision, and severe behavior problems. *Journal of Applied Behavior Analysis, 24,* 387-397.

DuPaul, G. J., & Ervin, R. A. (1996). Functional assessment of behaviors related to attention-deficit/hyperactivity disorder: Linking assessment to intervention design. *Behavior Therapy, 27,* 601-622.

Edwards, R. (1987). Implementing the scientist-practitioner model: The school psychologist as a data-based problem solver. *Professional School Psychology, 2,* 155-161.

Ehrhardt, K. E., Barnett, D. W., Lentz, F. E., Stollar, S. A., & Reifin, L. H. (1996). Innovative methodology in ecological consultation: Use of scripts to promote treatment acceptability and integrity. *School Psychology Quarterly, 11,* 149-168.

Ervin, R. A., DuPaul, G. J., Kern, L., & Friman, P. C. (1998). Classroom-based functional and adjunctive assessments: Proactive approaches to intervention selection for adolescents with attention-deficit/hyperactivity disorder. *Journal of Applied Behavior Analysis, 31,* 65-78.

Ervin, R. A., Kern, L., Clarke, S., DuPaul, G. J., Dunlap, G., & Friman, P. C. (1998). *Evaluating functional assessment-based intervention strategies for students with ADHD and comorbid disorders within the natural classroom context.* Manuscript submitted for publication.

Ervin, R. A., Radford, P. M., Kwak, M., Piper, A., Bertsch, K. Patrizio, M., & Ehrhardt, K. E. (1998). [A data-based descriptive analysis of the research on school-based functional assessment]. Unpublished raw data.

Fagan, T. K. (1995). Trends in the history of school psychology in the United States. In A. Thomas & J. Grimes (Eds.), *Best practices in school psychology III* (pp. 59-67). Washington, DC: National Association of School Psychologists.

Fagan, T. K, & Wise, P. S. (1994.) *School psychology: Past, present, and future.* White Plains, NY: Longman.

Fuchs, D., Fuchs, L. S., Harris, A. H., & Roberts, P. H. (1996). Bridging the research-to-practice gap with mainstream assistance teams: A cautionary tale. *School Psychology Quarterly, 11,* 244-266.

Graden, J. L., Zins, J. E., & Curtis, M. J. (Eds.). (1988). *Alternative educational delivery systems: Enhancing instructional options for all students.* Washington, DC: National Association of School Psychologists.

Gresham, F. M., & Kendall, G. K. (1987). School consultation research: Methodological critique and future research directions. *School Psychology Review, 3,* 301-308.

Gutkin, T. B., & Curtis, M. J. (1990). School-based consultation: Theory, techniques, and research. In T. B. Gutkin (Ed.), *Handbook of school psychology* (pp. 796-828). New York: John Wiley & Sons.

Hawkins, R. P., & Hursh, D. E. (1992). Levels of research for clinical practice: It isn't as hard as you think. *The West Virginia Journal of Psychological Research and Practice, 1,* 61-71.

Hayes, S. C., Nelson, R. O., & Jarrett, R. B. (1986). Evaluating the quality of behavioral assessment. In R. O. Nelson & S. C. Hayes (Eds.), *Conceptual foundations of behavioral assessment* (pp. 463-503). New York: Guilford Press.

Henning-Stout, M. (1993). Theoretical and empirical basis of consultation. In J. E. Zins, T. R. Kratochwill, & S. N. Elliott (Eds.), *Handbook of consultation services for children: Applications in educational and clinical settings* (pp. 15-45). San Francisco, CA: Jossey Bass.

Illback, R. J., Zins, J. E., Maher, C. A., & Greenburg, R. (1990). An overview of principles and procedures of program planning and evaluation. In T. B. Gutkin & C. R. Reynolds (Eds.), *Handbook of School Psychology (2nd ed.)* (pp. 799-280). New York, NY: John Wiley & Sons.

Individuals with Disabilities Education Act of 1997, Pub. L. No. 105-17, § 615.

Iwata, B., Dorsey, M., Slifer, K., Bauman, K., & Richman, G. (1994). Toward a functional analysis of self-injury. *Journal of Applied Behavior Analysis, 27,* 1997-209. (Reprinted from *Analysis and Intervention in Developmental Disabilities, 2,* 3-20, 1982).

Johnston, J. M., & Pennypacker, H. S. (1993). *Strategies and tactics of behavioral research.* Hillsdale, NJ: Erlbaum.

Jones, K. M., Wickstrom, K. F., & Friman, P. C. (1997). The effects of observational feedback on treatment integrity in school-based behavioral consultation. *School Psychology Quarterly, 12,* 316-326.

Keith, T. Z. (1988). Research methods in school psychology: An overview. *School Psychology Review, 17,* 502-520.

Keith, T. Z. (1995). Best practices in applied research. In A. Thomas & J. Grimes (Eds.), *Best practices in school psychology III* (pp. 135-143). Washington, DC: National Association of School Psychologists.

Kern, L., Childs, K. E., Dunlap, G., Clarke, S., & Falk, G. D. (1994). Using assessment-based curricular intervention to improve the classroom behavior of a student with emotional and behavioral challenges. *Journal of Applied Behavior Analysis, 27,* 7-19.

Knoff, H. M., & Curtis, M. J. (1996). Introduction to mini-series: Organizational change and school reform: School psychology at a professional crossroad. *School Psychology Review, 25,* 406-408.

Kratochwill, T. R., & Bergan, J. R. (1990). *Behavioral consulation in applied settings.* New York: Plenum Press.

Kratochwill, T. R., & McGivern, J. E. (1996). Clinical diagnosis, behavioral assessment, and functional analysis: Examining the connection between assessment and intervention. *School Psychology Review, 25,* 342-355.

Kwak, M. M., Ervin, R. A., Anderson, M., & Austin, J. (1997). *The correlation between student self-reported function of problem behavior and other measures of function: A pilot investigation.* Unpublished manuscript, Western Michigan University, Kalamazoo, MI.

Lalli, J. S., Browder, D. M., Mace, F. C., & Brown, D. K. (1993). Teacher use of descriptive analysis data to implement interventions to decrease students' problem behaviors. *Journal of Applied Behavior Analysis, 26,* 227-238.

Lentz, F. E., Allen, S. J., & Ehrhardt, K. E. (1996). The conceptual elements of strong interventions in school settings. *School Psychology Quarterly, 11,* 118-136.

Lentz, F. E., & Shapiro, E. S. (1985). Behavioral school psychology: A conceptual model for the delivery of psychological services. In T. Kratochwill (Ed.), *Advances in school psychology, vol. V* (pp. 191-221). Hillsdale, NJ: Lawrence Erlbaum Associates, Inc.

Lewis, T. J., & Sugai, G. (1996). Functional assessment of problem behavior: A pilot investigation of the comparative and interactive effects of teacher and peer social attention on students in general education settings. *School Psychology Quarterly, 11,* 1-19.

Martens, B. K. (1993). A behavioral approach to consultation. In J. E. Zins, T. R. Kratochwill, & S. N. Elliott (Eds.), *Handbook of consultation services for children: Applications in educational and clinical settings* (pp. 65-86). San Francisco, CA: Jossey Bass.

McKee, W. T., Witt, J. C., Elliott, S. N., Pardue, M., & Judycki, A. (1987). Practice informing research: A survey of research dissemination and knowledge utilization. *School Psychology Review, 16,* 338-347.

Miltenberger, R. G. (1997). *Behavior modification: Principles and procedures.* Pacific Grove, CA: Brooks/Cole.

Naglieri, J. A. (1988). *Draw A Person: A quantitative scoring system.* San Antonio: The Psychological Corporation.

National Association of School Psychologists (1997). *Principles for Professional Ethics.* Bethesda, MD: Author.

National Association of State Directors of Special Education (1994). *Assessment and eligibility in special education: An examination of policy and practice with proposals for change.* Alexandria, VA: National Association of School Psychologists.

National Institutes of Health (1989). *NIH consensus development conference on the treatment of destructive behaviors in persons with developmental disabilities.* Bethesda, MD: Author.

Noell, G. H., & Witt, J. C. (1996). A critical evaluation of five fundamental assumptions underlying behavioral consultation. *School Psychology Quarterly, 11,* 189-203.

Noell, G. H., Witt, J. C., Gilbertson, D. N., Ranier, D. D., & Freeland, J. T. (1997). Increasing teacher intervention implementation in general education settings through consultation and performance feedback. *School Psychology Quarterly, 12,* 77-88.

Northup, J., Broussard, C., Jones, K., George, T., Vollmer, T. R., & Herring, M. (1995). The differential effects of teacher and peer attention on the disruptive classroom behavior of three children with a diagnosis of attention deficit hyperactivity disorder. *Journal of Applied Behavior Analysis, 28,* 227-228.

O'Neill, R. E., Horner, R. H., Albin, R. W., Sprague, J. R., Storey, K., & Newton, J. S. (1997). *Functional assessment and program development for problem behavior: A practical handbook* (2nd ed.). Pacific Grove, CA: Brooks/Cole Publishing Company.

Pennsylvania Department of Education (1995). *Guidelines for effective behavioral support.* Harrisburg, PA: Author.

Phillips, B. N. (1993). Challenging the stultifying bonds of tradition: Some philosophical, conceptual, and methodological issues in applying the scientist-practitioner model. *School Psychology Quarterly, 8,* 27-37.

Piper, A., Ervin, R. A., Austin, J., & Whitten, E. (1997). [Assessing the impact of training teachers in problem-analysis skills through examination of verbal interactions.] Unpublished raw data.

Poling, A., Methot, L. L., & LeSage, M. G. (1995). *Fundamentals of behavior analytic research.* New York: Plenum Press.

Radford, P. M., & Ervin, R. A. (1997). [Student involvement in school-based functional assessment: Issues of integrity and acceptability]. Unpublished raw data.

Reed, H., Thomas, E., Sprague, J. R. & Horner, R. H. (1997). The student guided functional assessment interview: an analysis of student and teacher agreement. *Journal of Behavioral Education, 7,* 33-49.

Repp, A. (1994). Comments on functional analysis procedures for school-based behavior problems. *Journal of Applied Behavior Analysis, 27,* 409-411.

Repp, A. C., & Karsh, K. G. (1994). Hypothesis-based interventions for tantrum behaviors of persons with developmental disabilities in school settings. *Journal of Applied Behavior Analysis, 27,* 21-31.

Reschly, D. J. (1988). Special education reform: School psychology revolution. *School Psychology Review, 17,* 459-475.

Reschly, D. J., & Wilson, M. S. (1995). School psychology faculty and practitioners: 1986 to 1991 trends in demographic characteristics. *School Psychology Review, 24,* 62-80.

Reschly, D. J., & Ysseldyke, J. E. (1995). School psychology paradigm shift. In A. Thomas & J. Grimes (Eds.), *Best practices in school psychology III* (pp. 17-31). Washington, DC: National Association of School Psychologists.

Robbins, J. R., & Gutkin, J. R. (1994). Consultee and client and preventative outcomes following consultation: Some mixed empirical results and directions for future researchers. *Educational and Psychological Consultation, 5,* 147-167.

Sasso, G. M., Reimers, T. M., Cooper, L., Wacker, D. Berg, W., Steege, M., Kelly, L., & Allaire, A. (1992). Use of descriptive and experimental analyses to identify the functional properties of aberrant behavior in school settings. *Journal of Applied Behavior Analysis, 25,* 809-821.

Shapiro, E. S. (1987). Intervention research methodology in school psychology. *School Psychology Review, 16,* 290-305.

Shapiro, E. S. (1996). Academic skills problems: Direct assessment and intervention (2nd ed.). New York: The Guilford Press.

Sheridan, S. M., & Kratochwill, T. R. (1992). Behavioral parent-teacher consultation: Conceptual and research considerations. *Journal of School Psychology, 30,* 117-139.

Sheridan, S. M., Kratochwill, T. R., & Bergan, J. R. (1996). *Conjoint behavioral consultation.* New York: Plenum Press.

Shinn, M. R. (1989). *Curriculum-based measurement: Assessing special children.* New York, NY: The Guilford Press.

Shinn, M. R. (1995). Best practices in curriculum-based measurement and its use in a problem-solving model. In A. Thomas & J. Grimes (Eds.), *Best practices in school psychology III* (pp. 547-567). Washington, DC: National Association of School Psychologists.

Shriver, M. (1996). The founding of a special interest group for behavior analysis in school psychology: Minutes of the first meeting of the BSPIG. *Behavioral School Psychology Digest, 1,* 4-6.

Spectrum Center for Educational and Behavioral Development. (1996). *The focused classroom: Decoding student behavior grades K-6.* Berkeley, CA: Author.

Stoner, G., & Green, S. K. (1992). Reconsidering the scientist-practitioner model for school psychology practice. *School Psychology Review, 21,* 155-166.

Stoner, G., Shinn, M. R., & Walker, H. M. (Eds.). (1991). *Interventions for achievement and behavior problems*. Silver Spring, MD: National Association of School Psychologists.

Taylor, J., & Miller, M. (1997). When timeout works some of the time: The importance of treatment integrity and functional assessment. *School Psychology Quarterly, 12,* 4-22.

Taylor, I., O'Reilly, M., & Lancioni, G. (1996). An evaluation of an ongoing consultation model to train teachers to treat challenging behaviour. *International Journal of Disability, Development & Education, 43,* 203-218.

Thomas, A., & Grimes, J. (Eds.). (1995). Best practices in school psychology III. Washington, DC: National Association of School Psychologists.

Tilly, D. W., III, & Flugum, K. R. (1995). Ensuring quality interventions. In A. Thomas & J. Grimes (Eds.), *Best practices in school psychology III* (pp. 485-500). Washington, DC: National Association of School Psychologists.

Umbreit, J. (1995). Functional assessment and intervention in a regular classroom setting for the disruptive behavior of a student with attention deficit hyperactivity disorder. *Behavioral Disorders, 20,* 267-278.

Vollmer, T. R., & Northup, J. (1996). Some implications of functional analysis for school psychology. *School Psychology Quarterly, 11,* 76-92.

Watson, T. S., & Kramer, J. J. (1995). Teaching problem solving skills to teachers-in-training: An analogue experimental analysis of three methods. *Journal of Behavioral Education, 5,* 281-294.

Watson, T. S., & Robinson, S. L. (1996). Direct behavioral consultation: An alternative to traditional behavioral consultation. *School Psychology Quarterly, 11,* 267-278.

Weschler, D. (1991). *Manual for the Weschler Intelligence test for children* (3rd ed.). San Antonio: Psychological Corporation.

Wickstrom, K. F., Jones, K. M., LaFleur, L., & Witt, J. C. (in press). An analysis of treatment integrity in school-based consultation. *School Psychology Quarterly.*

Wilkinson, G. S. (1993). *Wide range achievement test 3* (3rd ed). Wilmington, DE: Wide Range.

Witt, J. C. (1997). Talk is not cheap. *School Psychology Quarterly, 12,* 281-292.

Witt, J. C., Noell, G. H., LaFleur, L. H., & Mortenson, B. P. (1997). Teacher use of interventions in general education settings: Measurement and analysis of the independent variable. *Journal of Applied Behavior Analysis, 30,* 693-696.

Woodcock, R. W., & Johnson, M. (1990). *Woodcock-Johnson test of achievement*. Allen, TX: Riverside.

Zentall, S. S., & Javorsky, J. (1995). Functional and clinical assessment of ADHD: Implications of DSM-IV in the schools. *Journal of Psychoeducational Assessment* (Monograph Series: Special ADHD Issue), 22-41.

Zins, J. E., Kratochwill, T. R., & Elliott, S. N. (Eds.). (1993). *Handbook of consultation services for children: Applications in educational and clinical settings*. San Francisco: Jossey-Bass.

Chapter 6

Assessment and Treatment of Habit Disorders

Raymond G. Miltenberger
North Dakota State University
Douglas W. Woods
University of Wisconsin, Milwaukee

Habit behaviors are repetitive or stereotyped responses that serve no apparent social function yet appear to be maintained by operant contingencies (Adesso, 1990; Hansen, Tishelman, Hawkins, & Doepke, 1990; Woods & Miltenberger, 1995). When such behaviors result in direct (i.e., physical damage) or indirect (i.e., poor social acceptability by others) harm to a person, they are considered habit disorders. Although habit disorders are thought to be maintained by automatic reinforcement in the form of self-stimulation or arousal reduction, they are typically defined topographically rather than functionally (Woods, Miltenberger, & Flach, 1996). Although many types of habit disorders can require treatment, in this chapter we only review the four that are likely to be encountered in a clinical setting: tic disorders, trichotillomania, thumb sucking, and nail biting.

Definition, Description, and Prevalence

Tic Disorders

There are three types of tic behavior patterns. Motor tics are rapid, repetitive, and often jerking muscle movements that are not caused by spasms, chorea, or tremors (Woods & Miltenberger, 1995). Examples include excessive or forceful eye-blinking, facial grimacing, and arm or neck jerking. Research suggests that approximately 1% of the population has a motor tic disorder (Ollendick, 1981). Vocal tics are "sudden, rapid, recurrent, nonrhythmic vocalizations" (American Psychiatric Association, 1994, p. 104; APA). Examples include barking sounds, coughing and throat clearing (unrelated to illness), snorting, and coprolalia (i.e., swearing; Woods & Miltenberger, 1995). The prevalence of vocal tics is unclear. However, Woods, Miltenberger, and Flach (1996) reported that as many as 6.5% of college students engage in throat clearing at least 5 times per day and identify it as a habit. Tourette's syndrome (TS) is diagnosed when a person exhibits motor and vocal tics (APA). The prevalence of TS is approximately .04-.05% and is more common in males (APA).

Individuals with tic disorders (especially TS) sometimes have concurrent problems such as obsessive-compulsive behaviors, attention deficit/hyperactive behavior, aggression management problems, and sleep problems. In some cases the tic itself causes physical damage such as cuts, burns, and bruises (Shimberg, 1995). Research has also demonstrated that adults who exhibit tics are viewed more negatively than those who do not (Woods, Long, Fuqua, Miltenberger, & Outman, 1998). These results extend to children (Friedrich, Morgan, & Devine, 1996) and developmentally disabled adults (Long, Woods, Miltenberger, Fuqua, & Boudjouk, in press). In addition, Long, Woods et al. demonstrated that individuals who exhibit tic behaviors are less likely to be hired for jobs than individuals who do not exhibit tics.

Trichotillomania

Trichotillomania refers to chronic hair pulling which results in noticeable hair loss (APA, 1994). Hair pulling (usually from the head) is sometimes followed by rubbing, chewing, or eating the pulled hair (Graber & Arndt, 1993). Individuals exhibiting trichotillomania often experience a feeling of tension/anxiety that is relieved after pulling the hair (APA). Approximately 1-4% of the population is diagnosed with trichotillomania, and adult females are 3 times more likely to receive the diagnosis than males (Graber & Arndt). Chronic hair pulling can result in hair-follicle damage (Muller & Winkelmann, 1972) or severe gastrointestinal difficulties when the hair is ingested (Mouton & Stanley, 1996). In addition, individuals who engage in chronic hair pulling are at greater risk for negative social evaluation (Long, Woods et al., in press).

Thumb Sucking

Thumb sucking occurs in up to 46% of children under the age of 4 (Traisman & Traisman, 1958) and continues in 19% of children over the age of 5 (Infante, 1976). Thumb or finger mouthing occurs in approximately 2.8% of college-age adults (Woods, Miltenberger, & Flach, 1996). Females are more likely to engage in thumb sucking, although the exact sex ratio is unclear (Friman, Larzelere, & Finney, 1994).

Although typically harmless, chronic thumb sucking can cause physical damage such as dental malocclusion, atypical root resorption, and increased risk of accidental poisoning (Friman & Schmitt, 1989). In addition, children who continue to suck their thumbs are perceived more negatively by their peers (Friman, McPherson, Warzak, & Evans, 1993). Frequent thumb sucking is common in children under 4 years, and except in unusual cases, does not require clinical attention. However, a child who engages in chronic thumb sucking after the age of 4 is at greater risk of developing the problems mentioned above and should be considered for treatment (Friman & Schmitt).

Nail Biting

Nail biting includes placing any digit into the mouth and biting either the nails or the skin around the nails. Despite being a very common habit among children (41.6%; Massler & Malone, 1950) and adults (10%; Woods, Miltenberger, & Flach, 1996), chronic nail biting can result in damage or inflammation of the tissue around the nail, possible infection, and shortening of the roots of the teeth (Silber & Haynes,

1992). There is also preliminary evidence that individuals who bite their nails are viewed as less socially acceptable than those who do not bite their nails (Long, Woods et al., in press).

Development and Current Etiological Theories of Habit Disorders.

In this section, we trace the history and describe the biological and behavioral explanations for the etiology of each of the common habit disorders.

Tic Disorders

TS and other tic disorders are believed to have occurred for a number of centuries, although TS was not classified until 1885 when Georges Gilles de la Tourette described similar behaviors in nine individuals (Shimberg, 1995). According to the biological perspective, tic disorders result from both genetic and neurological variables. Genetic research has shown a 77% concordance rate among monozygotic twins as compared to a rate of 23% for dizygotic twins. Neurologically, an excess of the neurotransmitter dopamine may be responsible for tics, although this has not yet been clearly demonstrated (Bruun & Bruun, 1994). It appears that the etiology of tic disorders has some biological basis, despite the preliminary nature of the research database.

Behavioral theorists combine biological and learning explanations to suggest that some individuals with tic disorders are biologically predisposed for the occurrence of tics to be reinforced via tension reduction in the tic musculature. This view suggests that individuals experience heightened tension in specific muscle groups and that tics may be maintained by tension reduction in those muscles. In such a case, the muscles are tense prior to the occurrence of the tic, and this tension is temporarily reduced following an occurrence of the tic (Evers & van de Wetering, 1994). Although there is little evidence in support of, or opposing this theory, studies have shown that tics can be increased by positive and negative reinforcement (Carr, Taylor, Wallander & Reiss, 1996; Scotti, Schulman, & Hojnacki, 1994) and the presence of an anxiety provoking person (Malatesta, 1990).

Trichotillomania

Trichotillomania was first described in 1889 by the French dermatologist Hallopeau (Franzini & Grossberg, 1995). Etiological explanations of the behavior began to be presented in the 1940s (Franzini & Grossberg). Biological theories have not established a causal link between neurological activity and trichotillomania. However, the limited success of some psychoactive drugs such as fluoxetine and clomiprimine have led some theorists to posit that trichotillomania may be related to a seratonin deficiency (Iancu, Weizman, Kindler, Sasson, & Zohar, 1996). In addition, some studies suggest that differences in brain function are responsible for some hair pulling (e.g., Swedo et al., 1991).

The behavioral explanation of trichotillomania suggests that hair pulling produces automatic reinforcing consequences such as tactile stimulation resulting from stroking or manipulating the hair, or tension/anxiety reduction (Franzini &

Grossberg, 1995). In addition, the behavior may be maintained through social consequences. Indeed, many people engaging in trichotillomania report a feeling of tension that is relieved following an episode of hair pulling (APA, 1994), and at least one study has shown that hair manipulation increases when individuals are anxious (Woods & Miltenberger, 1996b).

Thumb Sucking

Biological theorists offer virtually no explanation for the etiology of thumb sucking. However, behavioral theorists have suggested that the behavior is learned (Friman, Finney, & Christophersen, 1984). Behavioral theorists suggest that thumb sucking begins in infancy as it modulates arousal (i.e., comforts the anxious child or arouses the bored child). As the child's verbal repertoire and other functional skills develop, more adaptive behaviors replace the functions of thumb sucking in most children, and thumb sucking gradually ceases (Friman & Schmitt, 1989). In cases where thumb sucking continues, the behavior seems to be maintained by an arousal modulation function (Rapp, Miltenberger, Galensky, Roberts, & Ellingson, in press).

Nail Biting

Biological theorists have not been quick to address nail biting, although some studies suggest that there is a familial link among nail biters (e.g., Leonard, Lenane, Swedo, Rettew, & Rapoport, 1991). Additionally, Leonard et al. suggested that nail biting was maintained by the same biological processes affected by clomipramine. The behavioral theory suggests that nail biting functions to reduce tension/anxiety or increase arousal in under-stimulating situations (Woods & Miltenberger, 1996b). Although there are little empirical data to support this hypothesis, a study by Hansen et al. (1990) found that nail biters reported being more likely to bite when alone and engaging in a passive activity (e.g., reading). These data seem to support the arousal increasing effect purported by Woods and Miltenberger (1996b).

Assessment of Habit Behaviors

In this section, different strategies for assessing habit disorders will be discussed. We start with a section on methods of data collection, discuss the importance of social validation, and conclude with a section on functional assessment of habit disorders.

Measuring Habit Behaviors

The type of data collection procedures employed by the behavior analyst depends partly on the topography of the target behavior. Certain topographies lend themselves to certain types of measurement strategies.

Direct observation. Regardless of the habit behavior being measured, it is preferable to have direct (live or videotaped) observations of the habit behavior. The use of direct observation circumvents the possible methodological concerns encountered when using self- or parental-report (Kazdin, 1992). The most desired method of scoring data during direct observations however, depends on the type of behavior you are measuring. For behaviors with a relatively short duration (i.e., tic disorders), frequency or partial interval recording are best. The short duration of each tic occurrence and lack of a physical trace makes alternative scoring procedures difficult.

In assessing longer duration behaviors (such as thumb sucking, nail biting, and hair pulling), it may be best to use a duration measure. Duration scoring procedures have been utilized with thumb sucking (Knight & McKenzie, 1974; Long, Miltenberger, Ellingson, & Ott, in press; Rapp, Miltenberger, Galensky, et al., in press; Skiba, Pettigrew, & Alden, 1971) and trichotillomania (Long, Miltenberger, & Rapp, in press; Miltenberger, Long, Rapp, Lumley, & Elliott, 1998; Rapp, Miltenberger, Long, Elliott, & Lumley, 1998). Recently, Miltenberger, Rapp, and Long (1999) reported the use of real-time recording to assess the duration of hairpulling. Real time recording assesses the exact timing of each instance of the behavior within the observation period and results in a measure of the frequency and duration of the behavior.

Indirect observation procedures. Nail biting may be measured using physical trace procedures. Most often, nail biting is assessed by measuring the length of the fingernails (from cuticle to tip) on each digit (Davidson, Denney, & Elliott, 1980; Long, Miltenberger, Ellingson, & Ott, in press; Vargas & Adesso, 1976). Physical trace measures have also been used to measure thumb sucking by placing a piece of litmus paper on the thumb which changes colors when the thumb is sucked (Hughes, Hughes, & Dial, 1979). Physical trace measures used in assessing trichotillomania include counting hairs removed from the head (Altman, Grahs, & Friman, 1982) and measuring areas of baldness in the participant (Tarnowski, Rosen, McGrath, & Drabman, 1987). Although the physical trace measure appears to be a useful way to measure some habits, the occurrence of the behavior and the physical trace might not always correspond highly (e.g., a small amount of the behavior might produce a substantial amount of damage).

Perhaps the most popular (yet least desirable) data collection methods have been the use of self-report, self-monitoring, and parental report procedures. These procedures have been used to assess tic disorders, trichotillomania, nail biting, and thumb sucking (Woods & Miltenberger, 1996a). Despite their widespread use, these procedures have been criticized for methodological problems such as proneness to bias and distortion, lack of specificity, and relatively poor correspondence with more objective assessment strategies (Barlow & Hersen, 1984). In addition to these concerns, the act of self-monitoring may decrease the frequency of some habits (Woods & Miltenberger, 1996a). Because of these problems, we recommend using self-recording procedures only when direct observation or physical trace procedures are not possible.

Assessing the Social Validity of Habit Disorder Treatments and Outcome

Assessing the actual occurrence of habit disorders is an important element of a good research or clinical evaluation. However, it is equally important to assess the social validity of the treatment procedures and results. Procedures that are not acceptable or decreases that are not noticed by individuals in the client's natural environment are of little practical use.

The assessment of treatment acceptability using standardized measures has only been conducted extensively in evaluating the habit reversal procedure. Using the Treatment Evaluation Inventory-Short Form (Kelley, Heffer, Gresham, & Elliott, 1989), researchers have shown that parents or guardians find the simplified habit reversal procedures to be acceptable to treat motor tics (Woods, Miltenberger, & Lumley, 1996b), object chewing (Woods, Miltenberger, & Lumley, 1996a), stuttering (Elliott, Miltenberger, Rapp, Long, & McDonald, 1998; Wagaman, Miltenberger, & Arndorfer, 1993); thumb sucking (Rapp et al., in press), and other oral-digital habits (Long, Miltenberger, Ellingson, & Ott, in press).

Social validity of treatment outcome is typically assessed by taking randomly sampled videotaped segments from baseline and treatment conditions and showing them to independent raters (Wagaman et al., 1993; Woods, Miltenberger, & Lumley, 1996a, 1996b). The rater rates each sample using an instrument such as the Social Validity Scale (Woods, Miltenberger, & Lumley, 1996b). Baseline and treatment ratings are then compared to determine whether the behavior change is socially valid. The use of interventions that do not produce socially valid results is, therefore, questionable.

A Functional Approach to the Assessment of Habit Disorders.

Traditionally, the assessment of habit disorders (perhaps driven by the diagnostic model) has been topographical. However, researchers have started assessing the function of habit behaviors. Functional assessment may provide two key pieces of information for those working with habit disorders. First, the information could provide data needed to modify etiological theories of the various habit disorders. Second, and perhaps more relevant to the clinician, the information could be used to alter treatment plans in an effort to maximize their effectiveness.

Malatesta (1990) used an alternating treatments design to demonstrate that the occurrence of a tic was increased by the mere presence of another person (a child's father). Despite this effect, the author did not offer a possible operant function for the tic. In another evaluation of antecedent conditions, Woods and Miltenberger (1996b) showed that hair and face manipulation occurred more frequently when participants were made anxious while object manipulation occurred more frequently when participants were in an non-stimulating environment. The authors hypothesized that habits involving the hair and face functioned to decrease arousal while object manipulation may have functioned to increase arousal.

Although these two studies identified possible antecedents, a number of studies evaluated the effects of manipulating the consequences of habits. Carr, Taylor et al.

(1996) conducted a functional analysis of vocal tics. Exposing the participant to five conditions (alone, free play with a peer, tic-contingent social disapproval, tic-contingent escape from math, and high sensory stimulation), the experimenters found that tics were most likely to occur in the disapproval and escape conditions, suggesting that tics were maintained by attention and escape. Despite the increased occurrence of the tic in these conditions, it is unlikely that these were the only variables responsible for the behavior as the tic occurred frequently in all conditions. Similar procedures were conducted by Scotti et al. (1994) who found that the motor and vocal tics of an adult male were exacerbated by escape from demand situations.

In another study that manipulated the consequences of habits, Rapp et al. (in press) exposed a thumb-sucking child to 4 conditions (alone, social disapproval, free play, and demand). Results showed that the behaviors were most likely to occur when in the alone and free-play conditions, suggesting a self-stimulation function. In addition, Miltenberger et al. (1998) exposed two participants who pulled their hair to alone, demand, and social disapproval conditions. Results showed that hair pulling and hair manipulation for one participant and hair pulling and thumb sucking for the other were most likely to occur in the alone condition (see Figure 1). These results suggest that both hair pulling and thumb sucking were maintained by some type of self-stimulation.

Although these studies have been an important start, two challenging questions remain. First, how can we conduct a functional analysis that manipulates the consequences purported to maintain habits when they might be automatic consequences of the behavior itself (i.e., tension reduction, relief from boredom, and self-stimulation)? Second, does the functional analysis provide useful information that cannot be obtained from a less time consuming, functional assessment interview?

Rapp, Miltenberger, Ellingson, Galensky, and Long (in press) addressed this first question in their functional analysis of hair pulling exhibited by a young woman with moderate mental retardation. The woman pulled her hair and then manipulated the pulled hair between her fingers. After conducting a functional analysis similar to Miltenberger et al. (1998), the authors found that the hair pulling occurred predominantly in the alone condition and hypothesized a self-stimulatory function. To identify the specific source of sensory stimulation, the authors conducted further experimental manipulations and determined that the maintaining variable was the tactile stimulation produced by manipulating the hair once it was pulled. Further research of this nature is important to help us better understand the variables maintaining hair pulling and other habit disorders.

Within the constraints of the typical clinical setting, we recommend that the clinician conduct a functional assessment before a functional analysis (Iwata, Dorsey, Slifer, Bauman, & Richman, 1994/1982). Using behavioral interviews and naturalistic observation, the clinician can usually establish hypotheses about the function of the habit behavior (Miltenberger, 1997). A functional analysis should be conducted if confusion remains about the function of the behavior after conducting the functional assessment.

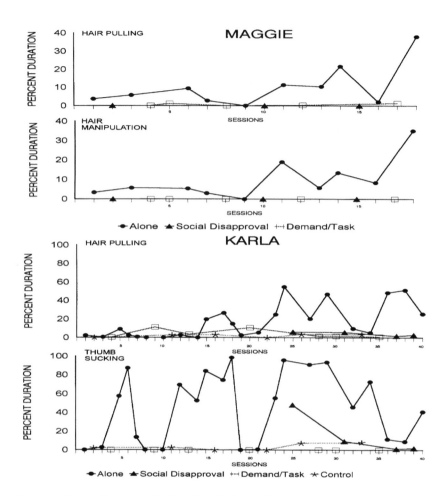

Figure 1. Percent duration of hair pulling, hair manipulation and thumb sucking across time for two participants who were repeatedly exposed to four different functional analysis conditions (alone, social disapproval, demand/task, and control). From Miltenberger, Long et al. (in press). Copyright 1998 by the Association for Advancement of Behavior Therapy. Reprinted by permission of the publisher.

The course of any good assessment, whether it be for data collection, social validation, or to determine the function of the behavior, is to provide information that will evaluate or enhance the treatment procedure. A wide array of treatments has been used with habit disorders. In the next section, we briefly review the medical treatments (if any) used to treat each habit disorder, followed by the most common and effective behavioral treatments.

Treatment of Habit Disorders

Tic Disorders

Medical treatments. The three most common medications used to treat tic disorders are haloperidol, clonidine, and pimozide (Shimberg, 1995). In a review of pharmacological treatments for tic disorders, Peterson, Campise, and Azrin (1994) found that pimozide and haloperidol decreased tic frequencies by 50-60%. Clonidine did not appear to be effective. Despite their relative efficacy, drugs used to treat tics may have side effects such as dry mouth, constipation, sedation, and possible risk of developing permanent movement disorders such as tardive dyskinesia (Maxmen & Ward, 1995). Because of the limited efficacy and possibility of unwanted side effects, it would behoove researchers to seek alternatives to pharmacotherapy.

Behavioral treatments. A number of behavioral treatments have been applied to tic disorders. In this section, we review two common treatments; massed (negative) practice (MP) and habit reversal.

In MP, the participant intentionally engages in the target behavior rapidly and with great effort for a specified frequency or length of time (Peterson & Azrin, 1993). Despite its widespread occurrence in the literature, the efficacy of MP is questionable. Most studies evaluating MP have been case studies, thus limiting their interpretability (Peterson & Azrin, 1993). In studies using adequate methodology, 28.5% of the participants experienced tic decreases, 28.5% experienced no change, and 43% experienced increases in tic frequency. This suggests that MP may not be an effective treatment for tic disorders.

The second major treatment used in managing tic disorders is habit reversal (HR); a multi-component procedure originally developed to treat nervous habit and motor tics (Azrin & Nunn, 1973). In recent years, HR has received the majority of attention from researchers (Woods & Miltenberger, 1995).

The HR procedure consists of a number of components. To increase the awareness of the habit behavior, four techniques are used. With *response description*, the client gives a detailed description of the habit behavior (usually while in front of a mirror). The purpose is to describe the chain of behaviors that constitutes the habit. *Response detection* is implemented to teach the client to identify each occurrence of the behavior. The clinician praises the client for correctly identifying an occurrence of the behavior, and provides corrective feedback if the client fails to identify an occurrence. This is continued until the client correctly identifies most of the habit behaviors. *Early warning* is used to identify physical cues experienced by the client prior to the occurrence of the habit, such as a growing feeling of muscle tension in the area that is involved in the tic. The final awareness technique, *situation awareness training*, requires participants to identify the circumstances in which the habit behavior occurs most frequently.

After awareness is established, *competing response* (CR) training is implemented. Contingent on the occurrence of the target behavior, the client engages in a behavior (for approximately 1-3 minutes) that is incompatible with the target habit behavior. Behaviors chosen for CRs typically involve isometric tensing of muscles that oppose the habit behavior. CRs are socially inconspicuous and do not interfere with ongoing activities (Azrin & Nunn, 1973).

After the CR is established, three techniques are used to increase motivation. With *habit inconvenience review*, the client reviews all the difficulties (social, occupational, physical) that result from the habit behavior. With *public display*, the client demonstrates control of the habit behavior in the presence of others. In the *social support* procedure, significant others in the client's life remind the client to use the CR when they see him or her engage in the target habit but fail to engage in the CR, and praise the client for correct implementation of the CR. The final technique, *symbolic rehearsal*, is used to promote generalization by asking the clients to imagine themselves controlling the habit behavior (by engaging in the CR) in the habit-prone situations.

The entire HR package was initially implemented by Azrin and Nunn (1973) in one, 2-hour session, but has since been implemented in varying amounts of time (Woods & Miltenberger, 1996a). In their initial evaluation of this procedure, Azrin and Nunn (1973) demonstrated a 99% reduction in self-reported tic and habit frequency at a 7-month follow-up in 10 of 12 clients. These procedures were also evaluated by Azrin, Nunn, and Frantz (1980c) who found similar results. Although impressive, the results of these studies should be interpreted with caution due to the self-report method of data collection and the lack of an adequate research design. Finney, Rapoff, Hall, and Christophersen (1983) conducted a more internally valid evaluation of the HR procedures. In this study, the authors added relaxation training to the standard HR package, and with direct observation, demonstrated significant, socially valid decreases in the tic behavior of two children.

Azrin and Peterson (1988) further evaluated HR procedures to treat TS. Results showed that, at 6-8 months post-treatment, tic frequency was reduced by 93-95%. In a follow-up study by Azrin and Peterson (1990), a group of 5 participants with TS who received the same HR package were compared to a group of five TS patients on a waiting list. Tic frequency decreased significantly for the treatment group while the control group did not change until treatment was implemented for them.

Although the HR procedures of Azrin and Nunn (1973) had proven to be effective, the implementation of such a large number of techniques was seen by some as time consuming and of questionable clinical utility due to the increased response effort on both the part of the client and clinician (Miltenberger, Fuqua, & McKinley, 1985; Woods & Miltenberger, 1995; Woods, Miltenberger, & Lumley, 1996b). Because of these concerns, studies were conducted to determine the active components of HR. Miltenberger, Fuqua, and McKinley (1985) evaluated the standard HR package (Finney et al., 1983) and a package consisting of only awareness training and CR training. Results showed that both packages were effective and produced socially valid results. The authors concluded that awareness training and the CR were the most important HR components.

Peterson and Azrin (1992) evaluated a number of behavioral treatments for TS in an alternating treatments approach. In a comparison of the differential effectiveness of relaxation training, self-monitoring, and CR training, the authors found that

CR training produced the greatest decrease in tic frequency, although the three treatments did not differ statistically.

In another attempt to simplify the procedures, Woods, Miltenberger, and Lumley (1996b) sequentially implemented the components of awareness training, self-monitoring, social support, and CR in children with tics in a multiple baseline design (see Figure 2). Results showed that awareness training eliminated tics in one child and reduced them in another. Self-monitoring further reduced the tics in that child and eliminated them in another. The simplified package of awareness training, CR, and social support greatly reduced tics in one child and further decreased tics in the child for whom awareness training and self-monitoring had produced

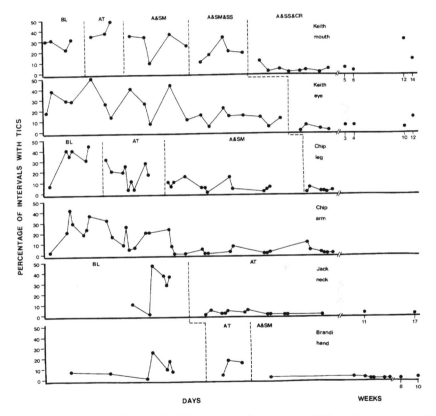

Figure 2. Percentage of intervals with tics across time for four children who were exposed to a sequential implementation of habit reversal treatment components in a multiple baseline across participants and behaviors design. The treatment components included baseline (BL), awareness training (AT), awareness training and self-monitoring (AT&SM), awareness training, self-monitoring, and social support (AT&SM&SS), and awareness training, social support, and competing response training (AT&SS&CR). From Woods, Miltenberger, and Lumley (1996b), p. 489. Copyright 1996 by the Society for the Experimental Analysis of Behavior, Inc. Reprinted by permission of the author.

moderate tic decreases. The improvements in the tics were seen as socially valid and the treatment was favorably evaluated by the participants' parents.

As is suggested by studies evaluating simplified versions of HR, the effects of awareness training or self-monitoring seem to play a large role in the effectiveness of HR. A number of studies have shown awareness training (Wright & Miltenberger, 1987) and self-monitoring (Billings, 1978; Hutzell, Platzek, & Logue, 1974; Ollendick, 1981; Thomas, Abrams, & Johnson, 1971) to be effective in reducing tic frequency. Although it may appear that increasing the awareness of the behavior (as is done in awareness training or self-monitoring) is responsible for the behavior change, this is unlikely for two reasons. First, there is evidence that some tic decreases reportedly caused by awareness training were actually produced by participants developing and using a CR without explicit training (Woods, Miltenberger, & Lumley, 1996b). Second, Sharenow, Fuqua, and Miltenberger (1989) showed that a CR involving muscles not involved in the tic (a dissimilar CR) was as effective as a physically incompatible CR in reducing motor tics. This suggests that self-monitoring (e.g., making a checkmark on a card) may function as a dissimilar CR. Combined, these findings cast doubt on the beneficial effects of increased awareness as a sole treatment for tics. From the research on simplified HR treatment of tic disorders, it appears that awareness training and consistent application of a CR (Carr, Bailey, Carr, & Coggin, 1996) are the necessary components, although more research needs to be done to investigate the necessity of awareness training and social support procedures.

Habit reversal has been the primary behavioral treatment for tic disorders, however a number of other behavioral interventions have met with some success. In one study, biofeedback reduced tics by at least 40% (O'Connor, Gareau, & Borgeat, 1995). Tics have been eliminated using differential reinforcement of other behavior (DRO) procedures (Alexander et al., 1973; Wagaman, Miltenberger, & Williams, 1995), assertiveness training (Mansdorf, 1986), and various contingency management procedures (for a complete review, see Peterson & Azrin, 1993).

Trichotillomania

Medical treatments. Attempts to reduce trichotillomania with medications have varied widely with respect to medication type and effectiveness. Medications used to treat trichotillomania include fluoxetine, clomipramine, imipramine, haloperidol, and lithium (Peterson et al., 1994). Despite a number of case reports, there are few randomized, double-blind studies conducted to evaluate medication treatments of trichotillomania (Peterson et al., 1994). Swedo et al. (1989) used self- and physician-report data to show that clomipramine was more effective than desipramine, reducing hair pulling by 50% in two-thirds of the participants. Two studies (Christenson, Mackenzie, Mitchell, & Callies, 1991; Streichenwein, & Thornby, 1995) found that fluoxetine was no more effective than a placebo condition. Although the research is limited, it appears that medications have not been proven effective in treating trichotillomania.

Behavioral treatments. Behavioral treatments have produced better results than medical treatments. Habit reversal has been the most extensively evaluated

(Friman et al., 1984). Studies show that HR is more effective than MP (Azrin, Nunn, & Frantz, 1980b) and is effective in 60% of the cases when presented in a group format (Mouton & Stanley, 1996). Rapp et al. (1998) found that simplified HR procedures involving awareness and CR training with parental social support were effective and produced socially valid results when evaluated in a multiple baseline across participants design for three children. In addition to these well-controlled studies, a number of case studies have demonstrated the effectiveness of the original HR procedures (Fleming, 1984; Rosenbaum, & Ayllon, 1981; Tarnowski et al., 1987) as well as the simplified procedures (Rosenbaum, 1982).

Although HR is an effective treatment for hair pulling, some research has suggested limitations. Long, Miltenberger, and Rapp (in press) and Rapp, Miltenberger and Long (1998) found that simplified HR alone did not reduce hair pulling in two participants. For one 7-year-old girl, additional contingencies (differential reinforcement and response cost) had to be placed on the hair pulling to eliminate the behavior (Long, Miltenberger and Rapp, in press). In the second participant (who was diagnosed with a developmental disability) the simplified HR was not effective until a device created by the authors was used to enhance awareness. The device (a modified hearing aid) was placed on the participant so that when her hand came within 6 inches of her head, a tone was produced, prompting her to engage in the CR. The use of this device following simplified HR procedures greatly decreased the hair pulling (Rapp, Miltenberger and Long, 1998).

In addition to HR, a number of other behavioral treatments have been utilized for hair pulling. In one case study, Anthony (1978) found that self-monitoring was effective in reducing trichotillomania. In another case study, Bayer (1972) did not show an effect of self-monitoring until an aversive condition (saving pulled hairs and bringing them to the therapist) was added. Ristvedt and Christenson (1996) applied capsaicin (a local pain enhancer) to the scalp of a 38-year-old female after implementing simplified HR with her. The authors reported an immediate decrease in hair pulling behavior. Other studies have decreased trichotillomania by eliminating a covarying habit behavior such as thumb sucking (Altman et al., 1982; Friman & Hove, 1987; Watson & Allen, 1993), or using various reinforcement and punishment procedures (Peterson et al., 1994).

Thumb sucking

Behavioral treatments. No medications have been used to treat chronic thumb sucking. However, one of the most popular and effective treatments has been the use of a bitter substance applied to the thumb. When the substance is on the thumb, the act of placing the thumb in the mouth produces an unpleasant taste. The bitter substance alone or in conjunction with a reinforcement program usually results in a reduction, if not complete elimination, of thumb sucking (Altman et al., 1982; Friman, 1990; Friman, Barone, & Christophersen, 1986; Friman & Hove, 1987; Friman & Leibowitz, 1990).

The second most popular behavioral treatment for thumb sucking is habit reversal. Azrin, Nunn, and Frantz-Renshaw (1980) compared a group of children receiving HR procedures to a group of children using a bitter substance. Results based on parental reports showed that HR procedures were more effective than the bitter substance though the results of statistical tests were not presented to support these conclusions.

Rapp et al. (in press) found that a simplified package of awareness training, CR, and social support nearly eliminated thumb sucking in one child, while the package plus a "remote detection" procedure eliminated the behavior in a second child. In the remote detection procedure, the child was observed via video while alone in a room, and prompts to use the CR were delivered when thumb sucking was observed. Christensen and Sanders (1987) compared HR, DRO, and wait-list control groups consisting of children who sucked their thumbs. Both procedures decreased thumb sucking to the same degree and the results were maintained over time.

Other successful contingency management procedures for reducing thumb sucking include a program using social praise to reinforce behaviors incompatible with thumb sucking (Skiba et al., 1971), DRO with edible reinforcers (Hughes et al., 1979), and a negative punishment procedure in which reading to a child was stopped contingent on thumb sucking (Knight & McKenzie, 1974). Other treatments include using a splint on the thumb to treat nocturnal thumb sucking (Lewis, Shilton, & Fuqua, 1981; Watson & Allen, 1993) and preventing a covarying response (i.e., holding a doll; Friman, 1988). It appears that the two most common and effective treatments for thumb sucking are HR and aversive treatments although both may be supplemented by contingency management procedures.

Nail biting

Medical treatments. Only one medical intervention has been attempted with nail biting. Leonard et al. (1991) compared a group of nail biters who received clomiprimine to a group receiving desiprimine. Following a two-week placebo period where no change was evidenced, the drugs were administered and results showed clomiprimine was more effective than desiprimine. However, there was a 50% dropout rate and the clinical validity of the procedures is questionable.

Behavioral treatments. In contrast to the paucity of research on medical interventions, successful behavioral interventions for nail biting have been reported in the literature quite frequently. The three most common types of behavioral treatments are HR, aversive treatments (e.g., electric shock, bitter substance applied to the fingers, or MP), and self-monitoring.

Bucher (1968) eliminated nail biting in 65% of participants using a portable self-administered shock device. However, the data were self-reported for both nail-biting episodes and use of the shock device. Vargas and Adesso (1976) compared groups of participants randomly assigned to MP, bitter substance, and control groups. Using nail length as the dependent variable, results showed that the three aversive conditions were more effective than no treatment, but the interventions did not differ from each other. Vargas and Adesso (1976) also had one-half of the participants self-monitor while the other half did not. Results showed that self-monitoring resulted in increased nail length. A number of other studies have demonstrated the effectiveness of self-monitoring as a treatment for nail biting (Adesso, Vargas, & Siddall, 1979; McNamara, 1972).

Ladouceur (1979) compared the effects of four treatments in a group format. Fifty people received HR, HR plus self-monitoring, self-monitoring, self-monitoring plus daily charting of progress, or no treatment. Results showed that all of the treatment groups improved over the control group, but that the groups did not differ from each other. The author concluded that the CR was an unnecessary component. However, as discussed earlier, self-monitoring could have simply been functioning as a dissimilar CR, thus producing the same results in all groups.

Habit reversal procedures have been evaluated in a number of studies. DeLuca and Holborn (1984) found that the CR alone was more effective than a relaxation technique in reducing nail biting. Frankel and Merbaum (1982) found that a HR self-help manual (Azrin & Nunn, 1977) was more effective in reducing nail biting than a wait-list control condition. Glasgow, Swaney, and Schafer (1981) found the HR manual and a self-help manual describing a self-monitoring/contingency management program to be equally effective. Nunn and Azrin (1976) demonstrated that HR was more effective than a wait-list control, though the data were self-reported, and the results of statistical tests were not reported. De La Horne and Wilkinson (1980) found that HR produced more long-term gains than a standard information treatment.

In a study evaluating simplified HR procedures for individuals with developmental disabilities who bit their nails, Long, Miltenberger, Ellingson, and Ott (in press) found that the HR package failed to produce clinically acceptable results in any of the participants until additional procedures (i.e., remote prompting, differential reinforcement) were added to increase treatment compliance. Miltenberger and Fuqua (1985) also found that HR was effective in treating nail biting based on the participants' self-monitoring. In addition, the authors evaluated the CR used contingently and noncontingently (scheduled daily practice) and concluded that a contingent CR was more effective than a noncontingent CR.

In a study comparing MP to HR, Azrin, Nunn, and Frantz (1980a) demonstrated that self-reports of nail biting were decreased 99% in the CR group compared to 60% in the MP group. Silber and Haynes (1992) compared three common techniques (bitter substances, self-monitoring, and HR) used to treat nail biting. Participants were randomly assigned to one of the three treatment groups. Using nail length as the dependent variable, results showed that while self-monitoring was ineffective, both the CR and the bitter substance produced significant improvements. The CR training proved to be more clinically valid. Allen (1996) replicated these three procedures, but demonstrated that the bitter substance was the only treatment to produce significant improvements.

Other treatments used for managing nail biting include the threat of response cost (Stephen & Koenig, 1970), contingency contracting (Ross, 1974), and covert sensitization (Daniels, 1974; Davidson, & Denney, 1976; Paquin, 1977). Although these treatments were demonstrated to be effective, there is little reason to believe they would be more effective than the HR or aversive procedures.

Conclusions

A number of different behaviors are included under the label of habit disorders. Habit disorders are repetitive behaviors that have negative physical consequences (e.g., nail damage or hair loss) and/or negative social consequences for the individual (e.g., stigma or decreased social acceptance) and thus warrant treatment in many cases. Because the negative social consequences for the individual exhibiting a habit disorder have received little attention from researchers, further study of these potential negative effects is warranted (e.g., Woods et al., 1998).

In this chapter, we described the possible behavioral explanations for habit disorders, as well as assessment and treatment procedures commonly used with them. Although it is speculated that habit behaviors are maintained by automatically reinforcing consequences involving self-stimulation, tension reduction, or modulation of arousal (e.g., Woods & Miltenberger, 1996b), socially reinforcing consequences may also play a role in some cases. Future research is needed to understand the variables responsible for the etiology and maintenance of habit disorders.

A variety of techniques is available for the assessment of habit disorders. Direct observation is preferred when possible, although the private nature of some habits (e.g., trichotillomania) makes direct observation difficult. Videotape recording provides a way to obtain direct observation of habits that occur in private (Long, Miltenberger, & Rapp, in press; Miltenberger et al., 1998; Rapp et al., 1998). Physical trace methods such as recording bald areas of hair pullers and nail length of nail biters are valuable for recording the outcomes of some habit disorders. Finally, social validation of treatment procedures and outcome is important.

In this chapter, we described functional analysis and functional assessment as an emerging area of habit disorder research. Due to the time intensive nature of a functional analysis, we recommended that a functional assessment be conducted in lieu of a functional analysis prior to clinical treatment of habit disorders when possible. Future research should compare the utility of both approaches in the assessment variables maintaining habit disorders. From assessment, our attention turned to the treatments of habit disorders. In comparing medical and behavioral treatments for habit disorders, it appears that behavioral treatments have been better researched and have produced better results than medical treatments. A possible area of future research would be to directly compare the effectiveness of medical treatments to behavioral treatments for various habit disorders.

Of the behavioral treatments, it appears that HR, in either the original or the simplified form, is the most effective treatment across the spectrum of habit disorders. Although we only discussed the effectiveness of HR with four habit disorders in this chapter, the procedure has been shown to be effective with other behaviors such as stuttering (Miltenberger, Wagaman, & Arndorfer, 1996; Miltenberger & Woods, 1998; Wagaman et al., 1993; Wagaman, Miltenberger, & Woods, 1995), object chewing (Woods, Miltenberger, & Lumlay, 1996b), and other "nervous habits" (Woods & Miltenberger, 1995; 1996a). As specified throughout the chapter, studies comparing different behavioral techniques to habit reversal would be useful. Specifically, we need to determine the differential effectiveness of aversive treatments and habit reversal in the treatment of thumb sucking and nail biting.

In summary, applied behavior analysis has provided an excellent solution to the sometimes-puzzling area of habit disorders. The assessment methodology, research design, and treatments developed in the field of applied behavior analysis have proven most successful in addressing habit disorders. Though a number of questions remain, continued diligence by researchers using the tools of applied behavior analysis will result in empirically sound answers.

Reading Objectives

1. Define habit disorders and identify four different types.
2. Describe behavioral theories for each of the four habit disorders discussed in the chapter. Discuss the adequacy of support for these theories.
3. Know for which habit disorders event recording and duration recording are most appropriate. Also, know the advantage of real-time recording offers.
4. Describe the use of physical-trace data collection procedures with trichotillomania.
5. For each habit disorder described in the chapter, discuss the problems that develop as a result of the behavior (physical and social).
6. Describe the habit reversal procedure for any habit disorder (original as well as simplified version).
7. For each habit disorder discussed in the chapter, name the most effective procedure (behavioral or biological) along with other procedures investigated in the literature.
8. Know what evidence exists suggesting that self-monitoring may not involve an active awareness component.
9. Know the methods that have been used to measure treatment acceptability and social acceptability of habit disorder treatments.
10. Given a habit disorder, describe how to conduct a functional assessment/analysis of the behavior by incorporating methods discussed in the chapter.

References

Adesso, V. J. (1990). Habit Disorders. In A. Bellack, M. Hersen, & A. Kazdin (Eds), *International handbook of behavior modification and therapy* (2nd ed.). New York: Plenum Press.

Adesso, V. J., Vargas, J. M., & Siddall, J. W. (1979). The role of awareness in reducing nail-biting behavior. *Behavior Therapy, 10,* 148-154.

Alexander, A. B., Chai, H., Creer, T. L., Miklich, D. R., Renne, C. M., & Cardoso, R. (1973). The elimination of chronic cough by response suppression shaping. *Journal of Behavior Therapy and Experimental Psychiatry, 4,* 75-80.

Allen, K. W. (1996). Chronic nailbiting: A comparison of competing response and mild aversion treatments. *Behaviour Research and Therapy, 34,* 269-272.

Altman, K., Grahs, C., & Friman, P. (1982). Treatment of unobserved trichotillomania by attention-reflection and punishment of an apparent covariant. *Journal of Behavior Therapy and Experimental Psychiatry, 13,* 337-340.

American Psychiatric Association (1994). *Diagnostic and statistical manual of mental disorders* (4th ed.). Washington, D.C.: Author.

Anthony, W. Z. (1978). Brief intervention in a case of childhood trichotillomania by self-monitoring. *Journal of Behavior Therapy and Experimental Psychiatry, 9,* 173-175.

Azrin, N. H., & Nunn, R. G. (1973). Habit reversal: A method of eliminating nervous habits and tics. *Behaviour Research and Therapy, 11,* 619-628.

Azrin, N. H., & Nunn, R. G. (1977). *Habit control in a day.* New York: Simon & Schuster.

Azrin, N. H., Nunn, R. G., & Frantz, S. E. (1980a). Habit reversal versus negative practice treatment of nailbiting. *Behaviour Research and Therapy, 18,* 281-285.

Azrin, N. H., Nunn, R. G., & Frantz, S. E. (1980b). Treatment of hairpulling (trichotillomania): A comparative study of habit reversal and negative practice training. *Journal of Behavior Therapy and Experimental Psychiatry, 11,* 13-20.

Azrin, N. H., Nunn, R. G., & Frantz, S. E. (1980c). Habit reversal vs. negative practice treatment of nervous tics. *Behavior Therapy, 11,* 169-178.

Azrin, N. H., Nunn, R. G., & Frantz-Renshaw, S. E. (1980). Habit reversal treatment of thumb sucking. *Behaviour Research and Therapy, 18,* 395-399.

Azrin, N. H., & Peterson, A. L., (1988). Habit reversal for the treatment of tourette syndrome. *Behaviour Research and Therapy, 26,* 347-351.

Azrin, N. H., & Peterson, A. L. (1990). Treatment of tourette syndrome by habit reversal: A waiting-list control group comparison. *Behavior Therapy, 21,* 305-318.

Barlow, D. H., & Hersen, M. (1984). *Single case experimental designs.* New York: Pergamon.

Bayer, C. A. (1972). Self-monitoring and mild aversion treatment of trichotillomania. *Journal of Behavior Therapy and Experimental Psychiatry, 3,* 139-141.

Billings, A. (1978). Self-monitoring in the treatment of tics: A single-subject analysis. *Journal of Behavior Therapy and Experimental Psychiatry, 9,* 339-342.

Bruun, R. D., & Bruun, B. (1994). *A mind of its own.* New York: Oxford University Press.

Bucher, B. D. (1968). A pocket-portable shock device with application to nailbiting. *Behaviour Research and Therapy, 6,* 389-392.

Carr, J. E., Bailey, J. S., Carr, C. A., & Coggin, A. M. (1996). The role of independent variable integrity in the behavioral management of Tourette Syndrome. *Behavioral Interventions, 11,* 35-45.

Carr, J. E., Taylor, C. C., Wallander, R. J., & Reiss, M. L. (1996). A functional-analytic approach to the diagnosis of a transient tic disorder. *Journal of Behavior Therapy and Experimental Psychiatry, 27,* 291-297.

Christenson, G. A., Mackenzie, T. B., Mitchell, J. E., & Callies, A. L. (1991). A placebo-controlled, double blind crossover study of fluoxetine in trichotillomania. *American Journal of Psychiatry, 148*, 1566-1571.

Christensen, A. P., & Sanders, M. R. (1987). Habit reversal and differential reinforcement of other behavior in the treatment of thumb sucking: An analysis of generalization and side effects. *Journal of Child Psychology and Psychiatry, 28*, 281-295.

Daniels, L. K. (1974). Rapid extinction of nail biting by covert sensitization: A case study. *Journal of Behavior Therapy and Experimental Psychiatry, 5*, 91-92.

Davdison, A. M., & Denney, D. R. (1976). Covert sensitization and information in the reduction of nailbiting. *Behavior Therapy, 7*, 512-518.

Davidson, A. M., Denney, D. R., & Elliott, C. H. (1980). Suppression and substitution in the treatment of nailbiting. *Behaviour Research and Therapy, 18*, 1-9.

De La Horne, D. J., & Wilkinson, J. (1980). Habit reversal treatment for fingernail biting. *Behaviour Research and Therapy*, 18, 287-291.

DeLuca, R. V., & Holborn, S. W. (1984). A comparison of relaxation training and competing response training to eliminate hair pulling and nail biting. *Journal of Behavior Therapy and Experimental Psychiatry, 15*, 67-70.

Elliott, A. J., Miltenberger, R. G., Rapp, J. T., Long, E. S., & McDonald, R. (1998). Brief application of simplified habit reversal to stuttering in children. *Journal of Behavior Therapy and Experimental Psychiatry, 29*, 289-302.

Evers, R. A. F., & van de Wetering, B. J. M. (1994). A treatment model for motor tics based on a specific tension-reduction technique. *Journal of Behavior Therapy and Experimental Psychiatry, 25*, 255-260.

Finney, J. W., Rapoff, M. A., Hall, C. L., & Christophersen, E. R. (1983). Replication and social validation of habit reversal treatment for tics. *Behavior Therapy, 14*, 116-126.

Fleming, I. (1984). Habit reversal treatment for trichotillomania: A case study. *Behavioural Psychotherapy, 12*, 73-80.

Frankel, M. J., & Merbaum, M. (1982). Effects of therapist contact and a self-control manual on nailbiting reduction. *Behavior Therapy, 13*, 125-129.

Franzini, L. R., & Grossberg, J. M. (1995). *Eccentric and bizarre behaviors.* New York: John Wiley & Sons.

Friedrich, S. Morgan, S. B., & Devine, C. (1996). Children's attitudes and behavioral intentions toward a peer with tourette syndrome. *Journal of Pediatric Psychology, 21*, 307-319.

Friman, P. C. (1990). Concurrent habits: What would Linus do with his blanket if his thumb-sucking were treated? *American Journal of Diseases of Children, 144*, 1316-1318.

Friman, P. C. (1988). Eliminating chronic thumb sucking by preventing a covarying response. *Journal of Behavior Therapy and Experimental Psychiatry, 19*, 301-304.

Friman, P. C., & Barone, V. J., & Christophersen, E. R. (1986). Aversive taste treatment of finger and thumb sucking. *Pediatrics, 78*, 174-176.

Friman, P. C., Finney, J. W., & Christophersen, E. R. (1984). Behavioral treatment of trichotillomania: An evaluative review. *Behavior Therapy, 15*, 249-265.

Friman, P. C., & Hove, G. (1987). Apparent covariation between child habit disorders: Effects of successful treatment for thumbsucking on untargeted chronic hair pulling. *Journal of Applied Behavior Analysis, 20*, 421-425.

Friman, P. C., Larzelere, R., & Finney, J. W. (1994). Exploring the relationship between thumb-sucking and psychopathology. *Journal of Pediatric Psychology, 19*, 431-441.

Friman, P. C., & Leibowitz, J. M. (1990). An effective and acceptable treatment alternative for chronic thumb and finger sucking. *Journal of Pediatric Psychology, 15*, 57-65.

Friman, P. C., McPherson, K. M., Warzak, W. J., & Evans, J. (1993). Influence of thumb-sucking on peer social acceptance in first-grade children. *Pediatrics, 91*, 784-786.

Friman, P. C., & Schmitt, B. D. (1989). Thumb sucking: Pediatrician's guidelines. *Clinical Pediatrics, 28*, 438-440.

Glasgow, R. E., Swaney, K., & Schafer, L. (1981). Self-help manuals for the control of nervous habits: A comparative investigation. *Behavior Therapy, 12*, 177-184.

Graber, J., & Arndt, W. B. (1993). Trichotillomania. *Comprehensive Psychiatry, 34*, 340-346.

Hansen, D. J., Tishelman, A. C., Hawkins, R. P., & Doepke, K. J. (1990). Habits with potential as disorders: Prevalence, severity, and other characteristics among college students. *Behavior Modification, 14*, 66-80.

Hughes, H., Hughes, A., & Dial, H. (1979). Home-based treatment of thumb sucking. *Behavior Modification, 3*, 179-186.

Hutzell, R. R., Platzek, D., & Logue, P. E. (1974). Control of symptoms of gilles de la tourette's syndrome by self-monitoring. *Journal of Behavior Therapy and Experimental Psychiatry, 5*, 71-76.

Iancu, I., Weizman, A., Kindler, S., Sasson, Y., & Zohar, J. (1996). Serotonergic drugs in trichotillomania: Treatment results in 12 patients. *Journal of Nervous and Mental Disease, 184*, 641-644.

Infante, P. F. (1976). An epidemiologic study of finger habits in pre-school children, as related to malocclusion, socioeconomic status, race, sex, and size of community. *Journal of Dentistry in Children, 43*, 33-38.

Iwata, B. A., Dorsey, M. F., Slifer, K. J., Bauman, K. E., & Richman, G. S. (1994). Toward a functional analysis of self-injury. *Journal of Applied Behavior Analysis, 27*, 197-209. (Reprinted from *Analysis and Intervention in Developmental Disabilities, 2*, 3-20, 1982).

Kazdin, A. E. (1992). *Research design in clinical psychology*. Boston: Allyn & Bacon.

Kelley, M. L., Heffer, R. W., Gresham, F. M., & Elliott, S. N. (1989). Development of a modified treatment evaluation inventory. *Journal of Psychopathology and Behavioral Assessment, 11*, 235-247.

Knight, M. F., & McKenzie, H. S. (1974). Elimination of bedtime thumb sucking in home settings through contingent reading. *Journal of Applied Behavior Analysis, 7*, 33-38.

Ladouceur, R. (1979). Habit reversal treatment: Learning an incompatible response or increasing the subject's awareness? *Behaviour Research and Therapy, 17*, 313-316.

Leonard, H. L., Lenane, M. C., Swedo, S. E., Rettew, D. C., & Rapoport, J. L. (1991). A double-blind comparison of clomipramine and desipramine treatment of severe onychphagia (nail-biting). *Archives of General Psychiatry, 48*, 821-827.

Lewis, M., Shilton, P., & Fuqua, R. W. (1981). Parental control of nocturnal thumbsucking. *Journal of Behavior Therapy and Experimental Psychiatry, 12*, 87-90.

Long, E. S., Miltenberger, R. G., Ellingson, S., & Ott, S. (in press). Simplified habit reversal treatment for fingernail biting and related oral-digital habits exhibited by individuals with mental retardation. *Journal of Applied Behavior Analysis.*

Long, E. S., Miltenberger, R. G., & Rapp, J. T. (in press). Simplified habit reversal plus adjunct contingencies in the treatment of thumb sucking and hair pulling in a young girl. *Child and Family Behavior Therapy.*

Long, E. S., Woods, D. W., Miltenberger, R. G., Fuqua, R. W., & Boudjouk, P. (in press). Examining the social effects of habit behaviors exhibited by individuals with mental retardation. *Journal of Developmental and Physical Disabilities.*

Malatesta, V. J. (1990). Behavioral case formulation: An experimental assessment study of transient tic disorder. *Journal of Psychopathology and Behavioral Assessment, 12*, 219-232.

Mansdorf, I. J. (1986). Assertiveness training in the treatment of a child's tics. *Journal of Behavior Therapy and Experimental Psychiatry, 17*, 29-32.

Massler, M., & Malone, A. J. (1950). Nailbiting: A review. *Journal of Pediatrics, 36*, 523-531.

Maxmen, J. S., & Ward, N. G. (1995). *Psychotropic drugs: Fast facts.* New York: W. W. Norton & Company.

McNamara, J. R. (1972). The use of self-monitoring techniques to treat nailbiting. *Behaviour Research and Therapy, 10*, 193-194.

Miltenberger, R. G. (1997). *Behavior modification: Principles and procedures.* Pacific Grove, CA: Brooks/Cole.

Miltenberger, R. G., & Fuqua, R. W. (1985). A comparison of contingent vs. non-contingent competing response practice in the treatment of nervous habits. *Journal of Behavior Therapy and Experimental Psychiatry, 16*, 195-200.

Miltenberger, R. G., Fuqua, R. W., & McKinley, T. (1985). Habit reversal with muscle tics: Replication and component analysis. *Behavior Therapy, 16*, 39-50.

Miltenberger, R. G., Long, E. S., Rapp, J. T., Lumley, V. A., & Elliott, A. J. (1998). Evaluating the function of hair pulling: A preliminary investigation. *Behavior Therapy, 29*, 211-219.

Miltenberger, R. G., Rapp, J. T., & Long, E. S. (1999). A low tech method for conducting real time recording. *Journal of Applied Behavior Analysis, 32*, 119-120.

Miltenberger, R. G., Wagaman, J. R., & Arndorfer, R. E. (1996). Simplified treatment and long-term follow-up for stuttering in adults: A study of two cases. *Journal of Behavior Therapy and Experimental Psychiatry, 27,* 181-188.

Miltenberger, R. G., & Woods, D. W. (1998). Speech disfluencies. In T. S. Watson & F. Gresham (Eds.), *Handbook of child behavior therapy* (pp. 127-142). New York: Plenum.

Mouton, S. G., & Stanley, M. A. (1996). Habit reversal training for trichotillomania: A group approach. *Cognitive and Behavioral Practice, 3,* 159-182.

Muller, S. A., & Winkelmann, R. K. (1972). Trichotillomania: A clinicopathological study of 24 cases. *Archives of Dermatology, 105,* 535-540.

Nunn, R. G., & Azrin, N. H. (1976). Eliminating nailbiting by the habit reversal procedure. *Behaviour Research and Therapy, 14,* 65-67.

O'Connor, K., Gareau, D., & Borgeat, F. (1995). Muscle control in chronic tic disorders. *Biofeedback and Self-Regulation, 20,* 111-122.

Ollendick, T. H. (1981). Self-monitoring and self-administered overcorrection: The modification of nervous tics in children. *Behavior Modification, 5,* 75-84.

Paquin, M. J. (1977). The treatment of a nail-biting compulsion by covert sensitization in a poorly motivated client. *Journal of Behavior Therapy and Experimental Psychiatry, 8,* 181-183.

Peterson, A. L., & Azrin, N. H. (1992). An evaluation of behavioral treatments for tourette syndrome. *Behaviour Research and Therapy, 30,* 167-174.

Peterson, A. L., & Azrin, N. H. (1993). Behavioral and pharmacological treatments for tourette syndrome: A review. *Applied and Preventive Psychology, 2,* 231-242.

Peterson, A. L., Campise, R. L., & Azrin, N. H. (1994). Behavioral and pharmacological treatments for tic and habit disorders: A review. *Developmental and Behavioral Pediatrics, 15,* 430-441.

Rapp, J. T., Miltenberger, R. G., Ellingson, S., Galensky, T. L., & Long, E. S. (in press). Extending applied behavior analysis with basic applied research: A functional analysis of hair pulling. *Journal of Applied Behavior Analysis.*

Rapp, J. T., Miltenberger, R. G., Galensky, T. L., Roberts, J., & Ellingson, S. A. (in press). Functional analysis and simplified habit reversal treatment of thumbsucking. *Child and Family Behavior Therapy.*

Rapp, J. T., Miltenberger, R. G., Long, E. S., Elliott, A. J., & Lumley, V. A. (1998). Simplified habit reversal treatment for chronic hairpulling in three adolescents: A clinical replication with direct observation. *Journal of Applied Behavior Analysis, 31, 299-302.*

Rapp, J. T., Miltenberger, R. G., & Long, E. S. (1998). Augmenting simplified habit reversal with an awareness enhancement device: preliminary findings. *Journal of Applied Behavior Analysis, 31,* 665-668

Ristvedt, S. L., & Christenson, G. A. (1996). The use of pharmacologic pain sensitization in the treatment of repetitive hairpulling. *Behaviour Research and Therapy, 34,* 647-648.

Rosenbaum, M. S., & Ayllon, T. (1981). The habit-reversal technique in treating trichotillomania. *Behavior Therapy, 12,* 473-481.

Rosenbaum, M. S. (1982). Treating hair pulling in a 7 year old male: Modified habit reversal for use in pediatric settings. *Developmental and Behavioral Pediatrics, 3,* 241-243.

Ross, J. A. (1974). The use of contingency contracting in controlling adult nailbiting. *Journal of Behavior Therapy and Experimental Psychiatry, 5,* 105-106.

Scotti, J. R., Schulman, D. E., & Hojnacki, R. M. (1994). Functional analysis and unsuccessful treatment of tourette's syndrome in a man with mental retardation. *Behavior Therapy, 25,* 721-738.

Sharenow, E. L., Fuqua, R. W., & Miltenberger, R. G. (1989). The treatment of muscle tics with dissimilar competing response practice. *Journal of Applied Behavior Analysis, 22,* 35-42.

Shimberg, E. F. (1995). *Living with tourette syndrome.* New York: Simon & Schuster.

Silber, K. P., & Haynes, C. E. (1992). Treating nailbiting: A comparative analysis of mild aversion and competing response therapies. *Behaviour Research and Therapy, 30,* 15-22.

Skiba, E. A., Pettigrew, L. E., & Alden, S. E. (1971). A behavioral approach to the control of thumb sucking in the classroom. *Journal of Applied Behavior Analysis, 4,* 121-125.

Stephen, L. S., & Koenig, K. P. (1970). Habit modification through threatened loss of money. *Behaviour Research and Therapy, 8,* 211-212.

Streichenwein, S. M., & Thornby, J. I. (1995). A long-term, double blind, placebo controlled crossover trial of the efficacy of fluoxetine for trichotillomania. *American Journal of Psychiatry, 152,* 1192-1196.

Swedo, S. E., Leonard, H. L., Rapoport, J. L., Lenane, M. C., Goldberger, B. A., & Cheslow, B. A. (1989). A double blind comparison of clomipramine and desipramine in the treatment of trichotillomania. *New England Journal of Medicine, 321,* 497-501.

Swedo, S. E., Rapoport, J. L., Leonard, H. L., Schapiro, M. B., Rapoport, S. I., & Grady, C. L. (1991). Regional cerebral glucose metabolism of women with trichotillomania. *Archives of General Psychiatry, 48,* 828-833.

Tarnowski, K. J., Rosen, L. A., McGrath, M. L., & Drabman, R. S. (1987). A modified habit reversal procedure in a recalcitrant case of trichotillomania. *Journal of Behavior Therapy and Experimental Psychiatry, 18,* 157-163.

Thomas, E. J., Abrams, K. S., & Johnson, J. B. (1971). Self-monitoring and reciprocal inhibition in the modification of multiple tics on gilles de la tourette syndrome. *Journal of Behavior Therapy and Experimental Psychiatry, 2,* 159-171.

Traisman, A. S., & Traisman, H. S. (1958). Thumb and finger sucking: A study of 2,650 infants and children. *Journal of Pediatrics, 52,* 566-572.

Vargas, J. M., & Adesso, V. J. (1976). A comparison of aversion therapies for nailbiting behavior. *Behavior Therapy, 7,* 322-329.

Wagaman, J. R., Miltenberger, R. G., & Arndorfer, R. E. (1993). Analysis of a simplified treatment for stuttering in children. *Journal of Applied Behavior Analysis, 26,* 53-61.

Wagaman, J. R., Miltenberger, R. G., & Williams, D. E. (1995). Treatment of a vocal tic by differential reinforcement. *Journal of Behavior Therapy and Experimental Psychiatry, 26,* 35-39.

Wagaman, J. R., Miltenberger, R. G., & Woods, D. W. (1995). Long term follow-up of a behavioral treatment for stuttering in children. *Journal of Applied Behavior Analysis, 28,* 233-234.

Watson, T. S., & Allen, K. D. (1993). Elimination of thumb sucking as a treatment for severe trichotillomania. *Journal of the American Academy of Child & Adolescent Psychiatry, 32,* 830-834.

Woods, D. W., Long, E. S., Fuqua, R. W., Miltenberger, R. G., & Outman, R. C. (1998). *Evaluating the social acceptability of persons with tic disorders.* Unpublished Manuscript.

Woods, D. W., & Miltenberger, R. G. (1995). Habit reversal: A review of applications and variations. *Journal of Behavior Therapy and Experimental Psychiatry, 26,* 123-131.

Woods, D. W., & Miltenberger, R. G. (1996a). A review of habit reversal with childhood habit disorders. *Education and Treatment of Children, 19,* 197-214.

Woods, D. W., & Miltenberger, R. G. (1996b). Are persons with nervous habits nervous? A preliminary examination of habit function in a nonreferred population. *Journal of Applied Behavior Analysis, 29,* 259-261.

Woods, D. W., Miltenberger, R. G., & Flach, A. D. (1996). Habits, tics, and stuttering: Prevalence and relation to anxiety and somatic awareness. *Behavior Modification, 20,* 216-225.

Woods, D. W., Miltenberger, R. G., & Lumley, V. A. (1996a). A simplified habit reversal treatment for pica-related chewing. *Journal of Behavior Therapy and Experimental Psychiatry, 27,* 257-262.

Woods, D. W., Miltenberger, R. G., & Lumley, V. A. (1996b). Sequential application of major habit-reversal components to treat motor tics in children. *Journal of Applied Behavior Analysis, 29,* 483-493.

Wright, K. M., & Miltenberger, R. G. (1987). Awareness training in the treatment of head and facial tics. *Journal of Behavior Therapy and Experimental Psychiatry, 18,* 269-274.

Chapter 7

Behavioral Pediatrics: The Confluence of Applied Behavior Analysis and Pediatric Medicine

Nathan J. Blum
Children's Seashore House of Children's Hospital of Philadelphia,
University of Pennsylvania School of Medicine
Patrick C. Friman
University of Nevada

Behavioral pediatrics is the branch of pediatrics that focuses on the relationship between behavior and pediatric health care. The scope of the field is quite broad and includes the study of: 1) the evaluation and treatment of behavior problems in primary care settings; 2) the influence of biologic variables on behavior; 3) the effects of behaviors or emotions on biologic variables; and 4) the interaction between biologic and behavioral factors in the evaluation, treatment, and outcome of medical problems. Increased understanding of the reciprocal nature of interactions between biology and behavior and the high prevalence of behavioral concerns in pediatric settings has led to dramatic growth in behavioral pediatrics over the past 30 years. Behavior analysts have made significant contributions to behavioral pediatrics during this time and the continuing growth of behavioral pediatrics provides multiple opportunities for behavior analysts interested in working in health care settings.

Further progress in behavioral pediatrics will be dependent on data-based analysis of the relationships between biologic and behavioral variables. In addition, physicians and other behavioral health professionals are being asked increasingly to develop efficient and cost-effective interventions with data-based outcome measures. Collection of observational data on problems of importance, precisely defined interventions for those problems, and data-based evaluation of outcomes are hallmarks of both behavior analysis and pediatric science. This similarity of hallmarks creates a unique opportunity for collaboration between behavior analysts and pediatric care providers to address the important questions in behavioral pediatrics.

In this chapter, we provide an overview of some of the types of problems evaluated in behavioral pediatrics. We discuss important contributions of behavior analysis to the management of some common behavior problems and use the discussion of these problems to illustrate the impact of biologic variables on behavior and behavioral variables on biology. We will discuss more briefly some areas of behavioral pediatrics that could provide new opportunities for behavior-analytic research. Overall, we emphasize that there are multiple clinical behavior problems and research questions that may be best addressed through collaboration between behavioral pediatricians and behavior analysts.

Relationship Between Pediatrics and Behavior Analysis

Primary care providers are the professionals who are most likely to provide initial recommendations to families regarding behavioral or emotional concerns. The types of interventions that are most likely to be utilized are supportive counseling, behavioral counseling, or referral. Research by behavior analysts has been a major contributor to both developing and evaluating interventions for many of the common behavior problems in primary care (Cataldo, 1982; Christophersen, 1994; Christophersen & Rapoff, 1979). The principle behind many of these interventions, that behaviors are altered by their consequences, is familiar to most primary care providers. Thus, many of these interventions have been incorporated into the practice of primary care. Indeed, reviews on discipline in the pediatric literature discuss mostly behavioral interventions such as increasing parental attention for appropriate behaviors and the use of time-out from positive reinforcement for inappropriate behaviors (Howard, 1991). Reviews on the management of sleep problems discuss interventions for bedtime resistance and night waking that are based largely on social learning theory (Blum & Carey, 1996).

Despite the acceptance of behavioral interventions into primary care practice, behavior analysis is yet to be widely accepted in the medical community. Lack of familiarity with the scientific basis of the field and the lack of understanding of the methodologies, especially the use of single-subject experimental designs, contribute to the lack of acceptance. Although the basic principles of social learning theory are appealing to physicians, the terminology used by behavior analysts is often not familiar to physicians, decreasing their understanding of the interventions and interest in collaboration (Allen, Barone, & Kuhn, 1993). Finally behavior analysts may be viewed as not accepting or attending to emotional factors such as anxiety or depression and family dynamic factors that are widely accepted as contributing to behavior problems within both the medical and the psychologic community. Incorporating these constructs into behavior-analytic theories, assessments, and interventions are likely to advance the field and increase its acceptance (e.g., Friman, Hayes, & Wilson, 1998). At a local level, behavior analysts interested in collaborating with physicians should consider attending and presenting at medical conferences and lectures. They may attend case management discussions and offer to help physicians implement behavioral assessments or interventions (Allen et al., 1993). When patients are referred to them, prompt data-based feedback on the interventions will be impressive to the physician, and in today's managed care environment, may be needed to justify on-going treatment to the child's insurance company. Behavior analysts can become more involved in medical professional organizations, providing a community resource for questions related to behavior. Increased collaboration between physicians and behavior analysts strengthens both fields and thereby improves outcomes for pediatric patients.

Behavior Problems in Primary Care Settings

Twenty to thirty percent of children seen in primary care have symptoms that meet criteria for a behavioral or emotional disorder (Costello et al., 1988; Horowitz, Leaf, Leventhal, Forsyth, & Speechley, 1992), and another 40% or more may exhibit behaviors or emotions that cause their parents concern and/or cause some functional impairment for the child, but do not meet criteria for a disorder (Costello & Shugart, 1992). The types of concerns commonly seen in primary care settings vary with the age of the child. With infants, parents are often concerned about excessive crying and sleep problems. In preschool children, concerns about oppositional behaviors, toileting, attentional problems, selective eating, and fears or worries predominate (Earls, 1980; Lavigne et al., 1993). Concerns about these behaviors frequently persist into the school age years, when academic and school behavior problems are also common (Kanoy & Schroeder, 1985).

Minor behavior problems will often remit without the direct intervention of a professional. Thus pediatric advice about behavior problems is frequently limited to recommending that parents let their child "grow out of it." However, this approach ignores the significant stress that the behaviors can place on a family at the time that they are occurring, a fact that is highlighted by the increased risk of child abuse that occurs in association with many problem behaviors (Kempe, Helfer, & Krugman, 1987; Schmitt, 1987). Furthermore, children do not always "grow out of" their behavior problems and in most cases it is not possible to distinguish those who will "grow out of it" from those that will not. Poorly managed oppositional behaviors can evolve into much more serious problem behaviors that require extraordinary therapeutic interventions for remission (Caspi & Moffitt, 1995). Unresolved toileting problems can lead to serious medical problems such as megacolon, urinary tract infection, and the unstable bladder of childhood (Friman, 1986, 1995; Friman & Jones, 1998; Friman & Christophersen, 1986). Untreated sleep problems can lead to habitually disrupted sleep patterns, family discord, and child maltreatment (Blampied & France, 1993; Blum & Carey, 1996; Edwards & Christophersen, 1994; Ferber, 1985). Lastly, unsolved school problems can lead to incomplete education and school failure which are in turn instrumental in the development of delinquency, drug use, and ultimately criminal behaviors (Daly et al., 1998). Thus, children, families, and pediatric providers would all benefit from the availability of brief, problem specific, effective advice for parents complaining of these common behavior problems in their children.

The three descriptors in the previous sentence may be the biggest obstacles to routine provision of such advice. Physicians have little time to spend with their patients and thus, if the technology available to them is not brief, specific, and routinely effective, they are unlikely to provide it to their patients. Depending on the problem, of course, they are likely to wait for the child to "grow out of it" or to refer the family for a psychiatric consult. Applying brief, problem specific, effective advice is clearly a preferable option, but such options may not be readily available. Referring the family to a behavior interventionist who specializes in providing such advice to families would be another option, but again, such individuals are not readily available. Thus, the obstacles to provision of treatment for routine child behavior problems in primary care are actually rich opportunities for applied behavior analysts. For those behavior analysts whose primary interest is research and development, defining, describing, and testing brief problem specific procedures that can be used by pediatricians is a much needed service. For those behavior analysts whose primary interest is clinical practice, applying brief, problem specific, and effective interventions for children and families referred by pediatricians for routine behavioral concerns is also a much-needed service. Reinforcers for engaging in behavior related to these services are readily available in diverse pediatric settings ranging from private practice to university medical school settings. The changes in the health care environment instigated by managed care in recent years have made those reinforcers even more available.

It is beyond the scope of this chapter to discuss the behavioral management of all of the common problem behaviors discussed above. Instead, in this section we will illustrate the kind of approach we are recommending by reviewing a very common pediatric complaint, sleep disturbance, and four interventions derived from behavioral theory. In subsequent sections we will discuss subsets of toileting problems (i.e., enuresis and encopresis) in order to fortify some theoretical points.

Sleep Problems

Teaching children to go to bed, go to sleep, and stay asleep throughout the night is difficult for many families in this culture (Blampied & France, 1993; Blum & Carey, 1996; Edwards & Christophersen, 1994; Ferber, 1985). A representative survey indicated that at least 30% of families contend with this problem three or more nights a week (Lozoff, Wolf, & Davis, 1985). The difficulties reported by parents include bedtime struggles such as resistance to going to bed, fussing and crying while in bed, and night wakes with fussing, crying, and unauthorized departures from the bedroom. These problems are important because they disrupt both the parents' and child's sleep, increasing the chance of the child exhibiting irritable behaviors during the day and increasing the parents' fatigue which decreases their ability to manage these behaviors (Teitelbaum, 1977). Although behavioral pediatric advice about sleep is appropriate from three months on, its importance is much amplified if bedtime struggles continue after six months of age. One intervention for child sleep problems employed by many pediatric providers (and often parents acting on their own) involves medication. Because our concern here is with behaviorally oriented advice, we refer interested readers to reviews of sleep problems that include information on medication (e.g., Edwards & Christophersen, 1994).

The cardinal component of the most effective behavioral interventions for sleep problems involves extinction. As children develop sleep habits, they often learn to associate specific environmental factors with self-quieting and the induction of sleep. Misinformed parental efforts to help their child sleep often result in problematic sleep associations that mitigate the process of falling asleep. For example, for most children sleep induction is enhanced with the presence of a parent to soothe and cuddle them and thereby ease the transition from wakefulness to sleep. These parental activities can contribute to a constellation of stimuli that control children's responses while in bed. With the parent present, rapid sleep induction typically occurs. Unfortunately, when this parent is absent at bedtime, the child is left without the stimulus that is most powerfully associated with sleep. Children's response to the typically present parent's absence resembles an extinction burst. Intense and prolonged crying is typical (Blampied & France, 1993; Edwards & Christophersen, 1994; Ferber, 1985). Because of the primordial nature of parental response to child upset, parents often directly intervene by either soothing or disciplining their child. For reasons that rest solidly on behavioral principles, these interventions often make the situation worse. The soothing parent reinforces the crying that preceded it. The disciplining parent provokes further crying, decreasing the chance of the child calming on his or her own. Many parents will then shift their tactic from disciplining to soothing which is effective in the short term, but over the long term predictably makes the problem worse. The situation presents no evident effective intervention for the parent. Soothing the child reinforces crying, discipline compounds the crying, and ignoring the crying increases its intensity and duration (Blampied & France, 1994; Edwards & Christophersen, 1994; Ferber, 1985; Lozoff et al., 1985). Not surprisingly, parents faced with sleep disturbance in their children often ask their pediatrician for advice. Three of the most commonly recommended procedures, extinction, scheduled extinction, and positive routines, are discussed below along with a fourth, self-quieting, that is newer and thus less common but has a compelling theoretical basis.

Extinction. This approach to bedtime problems involves no visits by the parent to the child's bedroom after the child has gone to bed. In effect, the child is left to "cry it out." Generally, extinction works more rapidly than other approaches but it presents problems that mitigate its overall effectiveness (Adams & Rickert, 1989; Edwards & Christophersen, 1994; Rickert & Johnson, 1988). For example, the child's crying can be highly aversive during the first nights of implementation. If the family lives in an apartment complex, or the treatment is implemented during a season when windows are open, the crying and screaming can draw the attention of neighbors with predictably problematic consequences. Additionally, extended crying and screaming differentially affects parents. Discord is possible (probable) when crying is substantially more aversive for one parent than the other (Adams & Rickert; Ferber, 1985). Thus extinction is a straightforward behavioral approach to sleep problems in children but it has a fragile social validity. In an attempt to improve social validity, sleep researchers have developed other methods that employ extinction but decrease its aversiveness for parents with scheduling and positive routines.

Graduated extinction. This procedure involves advising parents to ignore bedtime problem behavior for specific time intervals that gradually increase. The optimal length of the intervals has not been established empirically, but expert advice (Ferber, 1985) and some scientific study (Adams & Rickert, 1989) recommends beginning with a 5-minute interval on the first episode, 10 at the second, and 15 minutes for subsequent episodes on night one. These intervals increase over the course of a week ending with 35 minutes for the first episode on night seven, 40 for the second, and 45 minutes for all subsequent episodes and nights. Although children can tantrum for longer than 45 minutes at night, the data and a large amount of clinical experience described by Ferber suggests that very few do.

A pressing question about graduated extinction is why it works. At first glance, it would seem to be the perfect procedure for teaching children to gradually cry longer and longer, culminating in a reliable 45-minute bout reproducible throughout the night. No empirically derived analysis is available, so the following is speculation. The procedure is perhaps more appropriately labeled a differential reinforcement schedule than scheduled extinction. The parents only visit the room if their child is crying and thus visits are contingent. However, increasing the response requirement to 45 minutes of crying may lean the schedule so much that the reinforcing effects of sleep supersede the reinforcing effects of parental visitation. Additional speculation can be accessed on an Internet list serve called BEHAV-AN (http://listserv.nodak.edu/archives/behav-an.html with the subject line of "mad about you"). On December 16, 1997, the popular television show by that name aired an episode devoted to the married stars employing graduated extinction to teach their six-month-old infant to sleep. The show resulted in an extended string on the BEHAV-AN list serve.

Positive routines. This procedure involves a hybrid of extinction and a reinforcing bedtime ritual. Parents determine a bedtime they prefer for their child and the time their child typically falls asleep. Beginning shortly before the time the child typically falls asleep, parents engage the child in four to seven quiet activities lasting no longer than 20 minutes total. During the activities, the parents issue easily followed instructions and richly supply reinforcement for compliance. Although not so indicated in the original report, the instructional component is reminiscent of the high probability instructional sequence used in behavioral momentum research (Mace et al., 1988). In positive routines, as in behavioral momentum, the children follow a series of instructions with a high probability of compliance with a terminal instruction whose probability of compliance is low. With positive routines, the terminal instruction is "now stay in bed and go to sleep" or something equivalent. If at any time after the completion of the routines and the terminal instruction the child leaves the bed, the parent places them back in bed, telling them that the routine is over and it is time for bed. Crying or verbalizations are ignored. At specified intervals (e.g., one week) the parents move the positive routine back in time five to ten minutes. They continue this backward movement until they arrive at the parent preferred bedtime. For example, the child may typically fall asleep at 9:15 and the parents' preferred bedtime might be 8:15. Thus, it could take between six and eight weeks for the parents to arrive at the bedtime they prefer for their child. Experimental comparison of the positive routines procedure with scheduled extinction showed that both produced substantially improved bedtime behavior for children, but that the parents using positive routines reported significantly improved marital relations, suggesting a more socially valid procedure (Adams & Rickert, 1989).

Self-quieting skills. In this novel procedure, the skills necessary for a child to manage bedtime upset are taught during the day. These skills involve an operant class referred to as "self-quieting" (Christophersen, 1994; Edwards, 1993; Edwards & Christophersen, 1993, 1994). Briefly, the procedure involves establishing instructional control and improved discipline through use of time-out (Christophersen, 1988) and high density nurturing or "time-in" during the day. The time-in sets the occasion for effective time-out by increasing the contrast between the two conditions (Christophersen, 1988; Solnick, Rincover, & Peterson, 1977). When children are placed in time-out for discipline infractions or ignored instructions, the exit criteria involves "self-quieting" (i.e., stopping crying and manding departure). Self-quieting is also the skill needed to establish problem-free sleep induction. The theory is that "self-quieting" is more easily learned by the child and taught by the parents during the day when they are at ease and rested than at night when they are fatigued and irritable. Once a readily produced operant class of self-quieting responses are established during the day, the parent sets the occasion for their use at night using a method similar to that used during the day. Specifically, parents provide an extended period of "time-in" at bed time (20-30 minutes of stories, hugs, etc.), say "good night," and ignore what follows. A fundamental difference between night and day procedures is in the terminal reinforcer. During the day, it is departure from time-out. At night, it is sleep. Obviously, research is needed to determine whether the compelling logic of the procedure is supported by empirical findings. Preliminary outcome evidence indicates the procedure is effective at establishing problem free bedtimes and, perhaps more importantly, it is highly acceptable to parents (Christophersen, 1994; Edwards, 1993; Edwards & Christophersen, 1993, 1994).

This brief discussion of child sleep problems and their treatment is by no means complete. It includes three of the most commonly recommended approaches to the resolution of sleep problems and a relatively new procedure with much promise. The thrust of the presentation is that infant and child sleep disturbance is a very important, and common presenting complaint in Pediatrics but its treatment is unlikely to be part of conventional medical training. Behavior-analytic research has made a significant contribution to current interventions for sleep problems and provides an excellent opportunity for further behavior-analytic contributions to Pediatrics. The sleep problems discussed appear to have a fundamentally operant basis and, not surprisingly, they respond well to operant-based treatment. Please note that although our discussion suggests a relatively large amount of research has been conducted, the actual amount is small when compared with the extent of the problem in this culture - much more remains to be done. The successes obtained thus far notwithstanding, functional assessment (a hallmark of behavior analysis) has been employed very little in study of sleep problems and it is plausible that treatment failures are the result of a mismatch between treatment and problem function. Additionally, although the clinically oriented behavior analyst may feel confident in including all four of the procedures described above in their armamentarium, new procedures, especially those with high social validity, are needed.

Influence of Biologic Variables on Behavior

Few conflicts in behavioral science have been as enduring or as acrimonious as the debate between those who see human development and behavior as determined by internal biologic forces (nature) and those who view human development and behavior as determined by environmental forces (nurture). Although most recognize that both nature and nurture contribute to human development and behavior, the complexity involved in delineating the contributions of environmental and biologic variables to human development and behavior has allowed the debate on the relative importance of nature versus nurture to continue. The complexity involved in measuring environmental influences on human behavior is familiar to behavior analysts and will not be discussed here. Instead, we will discuss a common toileting problem, encopresis (soiling underwear), in which a medical condition (constipation) has been shown to contribute to the behavior. In addition, we will discuss one current area of research aimed at better delineating the influence of genetic factors on human behavior and possible roles for behavior analysts in this research.

Functional encopresis.

Definition. Functional encopresis, a common presenting complaint in pediatrics (3-5% of all referrals), is a disorder in which children either voluntarily or involuntarily pass feces into or onto an inappropriate location, usually their clothing (Friman & Jones, 1998; Wright, 1973; Wright, Schaefer, & Solomon, 1979). Encopresis is not diagnosed if the problem is exclusively due to an anatomic or neurologic abnormality that prevents continence. The current criteria from DSM-IV (American Psychiatric Association, 1994) are: (a) inappropriate passage of feces at least once a month for at least three months; (b) chronological or developmentally equivalent age of four years; and (c) not due exclusively to the direct physiological effects of a substance (e.g., laxatives) or a general medical condition except through a mechanism involving constipation.

Physiology of bowel. The large intestine or colon is the distal end of the alimentary tract that is sequentially composed of the esophagus, stomach, small intestines, and colon. A thorough review of the colonic system is beyond the scope of this chapter (for more thorough reviews see Weinstock & Clouse, 1987 or Whitehead & Schuster, 1985). Some rudimentary description of the system, however, is necessary to understand the biology that supplies the logic of effective treatment. The colon is a tubular shaped organ with a muscular wall. It connects the small intestine to the rectum and anus. It has three primary functions, fluid absorption, storage, and evacuation. Extended storage and planned evacuation are the defining features of fecal continence. Movement of waste through the colon is achieved through muscular contractions called peristalsis, which produce a wave-like motion of the colon walls. As the waste moves through the colon, water is absorbed creating semi-solid feces. Movement through the colon is potentiated by a variety of external events that instigate muscular contractions in the colonic wall. For example eating a meal increases colonic contractions (referred to as the gastrocolonic reflex) and moving about will have a similar affect (referred to as the orthocolonic reflex).

Most of the time the rectum, the distal end of the large colon, contains little or no feces, but prior to defecation, muscular contractions in the colonic wall propel feces into the rectum. This results in distension of the rectum, which stimulates sensory receptors in the rectal mucosa, and in the muscles of the pelvic floor, resulting in relaxation of the internal sphincter which facilitates defecation. This process is involuntary, but the child can inhibit defecation by contracting the external sphincter. The child can manipulate the external sphincter and use the same three muscle groups (diaphragm, abdominal musculature, levator ani) that instigate or forestall urination to instigate or forestall defecation. The push used to complete most bowel movements is called a Valsalva Maneuver and it is physiologically and phenomenologically similar to the push needed to inflate a balloon or deliver a baby.

Etiology. Between 80% and 95% of encopresis cases can be traced to a primary causal variable, constipation (Levine, 1975; Wright et al., 1979). DSM-IV distinguishes between encopresis with and without constipation (retention). Consistent with the theme of this section, we will focus only on those cases that include constipation. Although definitions for constipation vary, children who frequently go two or more days without a bowel movement are probably prone to constipation. A common complaint by the parents of encopretic children is that the children deliberately soil their clothing (Wright et al., 1979), but this type of accusation is usually false (Levine, 1982). The primary cause of the soiling is fecal retention (constipation). In most cases, retention is not caused by characterological or psychopathological problems (Friman, Mathews, Finney, & Christophersen, 1988; Gabel, Hegedus, Wald, Chandra, & Chaponis, 1986). Retention is usually the result of a constellation of factors, many of which are beyond a child's immediate control (Levine, 1982). These factors include a constitutional predisposition (i.e., slow gastrointestinal transit time), diet, insufficient leverage for passage of hard stools, and occasional or frequent painful passage of hard stools resulting in negative reinforcement for holding stools (Christophersen & Rapoff, 1983). Rarely, retention may be related to sexual abuse. For some children, especially those with extreme constipation and/or treatment failure, there is an increased threshold of awareness of rectal distension, a possibly weak internal sphincter, and/or a tendency to contract the external sphincter during the act of defecation (Meunier, Marechal, & De Beaujeu, 1979; Wald, Chandra, Chiponis, & Gabel, 1986). The combined effect of all these factors is a lowered probability of voluntary stool passage and a heightened probability of fecal retention.

Chronic fecal retention results in fecal impaction, which results in enlargement of the colon. Colon enlargement results in decreased motility of the bowel system and occasionally, involuntary passage of large stools and frequent soiling due to seepage of soft fecal matter. The seepage is often referred to as paradoxical diarrhea because the children retain large masses of stool and thus are functionally constipated, but their colon allows passage of soft stool around the mass which results in diarrhea (Christophersen & Rapoff, 1983; Levine, 1982).

That fecal impaction is related to encopresis has been established by several investigators, primary among which are Davidson (1958), Levine (1975), and Wright (1975). All independently reported that 80% of their patients had fecal impaction accompanying fecal incontinence at the first clinic visit. After his 1975 report, Levine and his colleagues developed a simple clinical procedure to identify fecal impaction from a x-ray of the lower abdomen (Barr, Levine, Wilkinson, & Mulvihill, 1979). Because of the improved diagnostic method, Levine revised his initial 80% estimate of fecal impaction's coexistence with fecal incontinence to 90% (Christophersen & Rapoff, 1979).

Differential diagnosis. There are rare anatomic and neurologic problems that can lead to fecal retention and soiling. Anatomic problems include a variety of eccentric formations in locations of the anus which are detectable on physical exam and require medical management (Hatch, 1988). Hirschsprung's disease or congenital aganglionosis is a disorder in which the nerves that control the muscles in the wall of part or all of the colon are absent causing severe constipation. Its incidence is approximately 1 in 25,000 and it usually causes severe symptoms in infancy (Levine, 1975). Thus, the clinical presentation itself should prevent the astute clinician from mistaking one for the other. The possible exception is ultra short segment Hirschsprung's disease, which has a subtler clinical picture. However, the existence of this condition is controversial and, even if it does exist, proper collaboration between pediatrician and behavior analyst should ensure timely diagnosis.

Evaluation. As with all behavioral pediatric conditions with a medical presentation, the initial encounter contains a "go no further" maxim - following the history, or if possible, prior to the initial visit, the behavior analyst should refer the child to a physician (preferably a pediatrician) for a medical examination. The encopresis exam should include a routine check of history and abdominal palpation, rectal examination, and sometimes a x-ray of the abdomen to determine the extent of fecal impaction. A barium enema is rarely necessary unless features of the exam suggest Hirschsprung's disease.

In addition to routine behavior and psychological assessments, the behavioral interview for encopresis should include questions related to constipation. These include asking whether: 1) there is ever a long period between bowel movements; 2) bowel movements are atypically large (stop up the toilet); 3) fecal matter ever has an unusually foul odor; 4) fecal matter is ever hard, difficult, or painful to pass; and 5) whether the child ever complains of not being able to feel the movement or make it to the toilet on time. An additional question that pertains more to treatment history than to pathogenesis is whether the child ever hides soiled underwear.

Affirmative answers to any or all of these questions are highly suggestive of retentive encopresis and hiding underwear indicates a history that includes some form of punishment.

The encopresis evaluation is the first step in treatment. Encopresis is not well understood outside of the medical community and the child's parents are likely to be under the influence of the characterological and psychopathological interpretations that are prevalent in western culture. The parent's interpretation of the condition is also likely to influence how the children view their problem. Thus, the encopresis evaluation can actually begin treatment by providing accurate information that "demystifies" the problem. Lastly, the evaluation should include questions about diet and timing of meals. Low fiber diets and irregular meals can be contributing factors in encopresis.

Treatment. During the past 15 years, several descriptive and controlled experimental studies have supported a multi-component approach to treatment of chronic retentive encopresis, partly derived from the pioneering work of Davidson (1958), Christophersen and Rainey (1976), Levine (1975), and Wright (1975). As indicated above, the first component can be addressed within the evaluation. Specifically, the entire elimination process including its disordered manifestations should be "demystified" (Christophersen & Rapoff, 1983; Levine, 1982). Generally this means providing information about bowel dynamics and the relationship of the problem to constipation (Levine, 1982). Second, if there is a fecal impaction it should be removed with enemas and/or laxatives (Christophersen & Rapoff, 1983; Levine, 1982; O'Brien, Ross, & Christophersen, 1986). Third, the child should sit on the toilet for about five minutes, one or two times a day (O'Brien et al.; Wright, 1975). Fourth, the parents should promote proper toileting with encouragement and not with coercion. Additionally, they should not reserve all their praise and affection for proper elimination; a child should be praised just for sitting on the toilet (Christophersen & Rapoff, 1983; Levine, 1982; Wright, 1975). Fifth, a stool softener such as mineral oil (Davidson, 1958) or glycerin suppositories (O'Brien et al.; Wright & Walker, 1977) should be used in order to ease the passage of hard stools. Sixth, dietary fiber should be increased in the child's diet (Houts, Mellon, & Whelan, 1988; O'Brien et al.). Seventh, in order to increase and maintain motility in the child's colon, the child's activity levels and fluid intake should be increased (Levine, 1982). Eighth, during toileting episodes the child's feet should be on a flat surface. Foot placement is crucial to the Valsalva maneuver (grunting push necessary to produce a bowel movement) (Levine, 1982; O'Brien et al.). Ninth, the child should be rewarded for all bowel movements in the toilet (Christophersen & Rainey; Levine, 1982; O'Brien et al.; Wright & Walker).

The literature on this approach (or variations thereof) has progressed sufficiently to lead to group trials. For example, in a study of 58 children with encopresis, 60% were completely continent after five months and those that did not achieve full continence averaged a 90% decrease in accidents (Lowery, Srour, Whitehead, & Schuster, 1985). There are other examples (e.g., Stark et al., 1997).

However, not all children succeed with the conventional approach and for these children augmentative methods have been developed. In a manner typical of behavior analysis, preparation for developing the methods began with study of behaviors associated with treatment failure (Stark, Spirito, Lewis, & Hart, 1990). Incorporating behavior management methods relevant to the behaviors, teaching parents to use them, and delivering treatment in a group format resulted in an 83% decrease in accidents in 18 treatment resistant children with encopresis with treatment gains maintained or even improved at six months follow up (Stark, Owens-Stively, Spirito, Lewis, & Guevremont, 1990).

Behavioral Phenotypes

The collection of genes within an individual are referred to as that individual's genotype. With the exception of identical twins, all individuals will have a different genotype. The phenotype refers to the observable characteristics of an individual determined by genetic variations or gene-environment interactions. Typically, genetic studies focus on detailed physical features that compose an individual's phenotype such as the spacing of eyes, location, form, and size of the ears, pattern of the finger print, and many other features. A large number of genetic disorders that produce characteristic physical features in an individual have been identified (e.g., individuals with Down syndrome have a characteristic physical appearance). In these cases, the common genetic anomaly creates increased homogeneity in the physical appearance of individuals with the genetic disorder relative to peers without the disorder (Dykens, 1995). However, individuals with the disorder do not appear identical as other genetic factors and environmental factors influence appearance (e.g., nutrition).

Recently it has been demonstrated that, in addition to physical features, individuals with genetic disorders may have phenotypical behavioral features as well. Perhaps the most thoroughly studied behavioral phenotype is that of Lesch-Nyhan Syndrome. This genetic disorder is associated with abnormal movements, mental retardation, and the nearly universal occurrence of self-biting of the lips and/or fingers (Anderson & Ernst, 1994). Although self-biting has long been recognized as a phenotypic feature of Lesch-Nyhan syndrome, only more recently has it been recognized that individual's with Lesch-Nyhan syndrome have abnormalities in a specific brain neurotransmitter, dopamine (Breese et al., 1995). The combination of recognition of this behavioral phenotype, along with improved understanding of the brain abnormalities in Lesch-Nyhan syndrome has led to the development of an animal model of Lesch-Nyhan syndrome that also demonstrates self-mutilating behavior. The self-mutilating behaviors in this animal model respond to pharmacologic intervention in a manner similar to the self-mutilating behaviors of individuals with Lesch-Nyhan Syndrome (Breese et al., 1995). Clearly, the recognition of this behavioral phenotype has the potential to play an important role, not just in treating Lesch-Nyhan syndrome, but also in increasing our understanding of the relationship between brain neurochemistry and at least one type of self-injurious behavior.

Prader-Willi syndrome provides another example of a fairly well described behavioral phenotype. Individuals with Prader-Willi syndrome, a genetic disorder involving a deletion of part of chromosome 15, have growth impairments, mental retardation, and a voracious appetite leading to intense food-seeking behaviors (i.e., hyperphagia), and obesity by the time the child is of school age (Donaldson et al., 1994). Although it is not currently known how the genetic disorder produces hyperphagia, further investigation of this genotype-behavioral phenotype relationship has the potential to greatly increase our understanding of the some of the relationships between biology and the environment that cause obesity.

The Role For Behavior Analysis

The above examples are two of the most clear demonstrations of behavioral phenotypes in that they involve dramatic aberrant behaviors which occur in nearly all individuals with a known genetic disorder. However, just as a particular physical feature of a phenotype may not be present in all individuals with a genetic disorder, characteristics of a behavioral phenotype will not necessarily be present in all individuals with a particular genetic disorder (Dykens, 1995). Furthermore, the behaviors that make up a phenotype may be subtler than those described above. Thus, the identification of behavioral phenotypes requires complex genetic, epidemiologic, and behavioral analysis. Frequently, claims of an association between a behavioral phenotype and a genetic disorder have later been demonstrated to be better explained by confounding variables (Einfeld & Hall, 1994). Even when behavioral phenotypes do exist, the constituent behaviors are still influenced by environmental variables. For example, individuals with Fragile-X syndrome, the most common inherited cause of mental retardation in males, have been demonstrated to exhibit gaze aversion when greeting others (e.g., when an arm is extended towards them for a handshake, they accept and shake the hand, but turn their gaze and entire upper body away from the person whose hand they are shaking; Wolff, Gardner, Paccia, & Lappen, 1989). In the Wolff et al. investigation, the gaze aversion occurred in 78% to 89% of adolescents and adults with Fragile-X syndrome, but in only 6% of individuals with other causes of mental retardation. However, when individuals with Fragile-X syndrome are followed longitudinally, the behavior is rarely seen prior to 8 years of age, but is usually present by 12 years of age (Wolff et al., 1989). Thus, gaze aversion could be viewed as a behavioral phenotype or as a behavior typically learned between 8 and 12 years of age due to an interaction between some other aspect of Fragile-X syndrome and environment influence. Alternatively, it could be related to a gene that is only expressed with ongoing development.

These types of questions about the relationship of developmental and environmental variables to the expression of putative behavioral phenotypes are well suited to behavior-analytic research and they are not rare. For example, in Prader Willi syndrome, the hyperphagia often does not seem to begin until between 2 and 6 years of age (Donaldson et al., 1994). Children with Williams Syndrome have been demonstrated to have prominent smiles and well-developed social and verbal skills

(Wang & Bellugi, 1993), all of which are likely to be reinforced by the environment, but it is not clear to what extent these are learned behaviors. Advances in genetics are offering new opportunities to increase understanding of the biologic influences on behavior, but behavior-analytic research will be necessary to clearly define the relationships between genotype and behavioral phenotypes. Unfortunately, at the current time, collaboration between geneticists and behavior analysts is rare.

Influence of Behavior on Biologic Variables

In the previous section we have discussed situations where biologic variables influence behavior. In this section, we consider the influence of behavior on biology. A large number of behaviors increase or decrease the risk of disease and behavior analysts have engaged in a variety of studies aimed at promoting healthy behaviors (Finney, Miller, & Adler, 1993; Friman & Christophersen, 1986; Irwin, Cataldo, Matheny, & Peterson, 1992; Stark et al., 1993; Winett et al., 1991). It is beyond the scope of this chapter to review this research, but it is worth noting that the large number of behaviors that contribute to morbidity and mortality provide vast opportunities for behavior-analytic research and intervention.

In addition to promoting healthy behaviors, behavioral pediatricians are interested in the ability of behaviors to directly alter physiologic processes within the individual for the purpose of treatment. The most direct application of these strategies is in the use of biofeedback. Biofeedback involves the use of electrical or electro-mechanical equipment to measure and increase the salience of stimuli associated with pertinent physiologic processes and training patients to discriminate them. The penultimate goal of biofeedback is to train individuals to alter the physiologic processes in healthful directions and the ultimate goal is to train them to do so without biofeedback (Culbert, Kajander, & Reaney, 1996). One of the earliest and most common uses of biofeedback is the urine alarm for the treatment of enuresis. We will review some aspects of the treatment of this common problem and briefly mention other areas where biofeedback is being used.

Enuresis. Enuresis is estimated to occur in as high as 20% of first-grade children (Friman, 1986; 1995; Friman & Jones, 1998). Functional enuresis involves incontinence past the age of five years without an anatomic or neurologic cause. The cause of enuresis is not known. Although most historical and still some current accounts of enuresis link it to causal psychopathology, recent reviews (Friman, 1986; 1995; Friman & Jones, 1998) and one current scientific study (Friman, Handwerk, Swearer, McGinnis, & Warzak, in press) suggest that most enuretic children do not exhibit clinically significant psychopathology. Studies of some children with enuresis suggest that they may have difficulty concentrating their urine during the night and thus produce more urine nocturnally than their non-enuretic peers (Lackgren, Neveus, & Stenberg, 1997; Rittig, Knudsen, Norgaard, Pedersen, & Djurhuus, 1989), but the overall importance of urinary concentration difficulties is controversial because the prevalence of children with the problem may be quite low (Eggert & Kuhn, 1995). Finally, nocturnal enuresis may be viewed as merely a deficit in the skills necessary to prevent urination while asleep (Houts, 1991). In order to understand the latter view and the role of the urine alarm, it is necessary to briefly review some of the physiology of the systems that govern urination.

The bladder (detrusor) is an elastic hollow organ with a muscular wall. It's shape resembles an upside down balloon with a long narrow neck; it has two primarily mechanical functions, storage and release of urine (Vincent, 1974). Extended storage and volitional release are the defining properties of urinary continence. In infancy, distension of the bladder leads to contraction of the bladder and automatic (nonvolitional) evacuation of urine. As children mature, the capacity of the central nervous system to inhibit bladder contraction increases, typically coinciding with the development of continence in early childhood (Berk & Friman, 1990; Koff, 1995).

The components of the urogenital system that are under volitional control to establish continence are the muscles of the pelvic floor. Except during imminent or actual urination, these muscles remain in a state of tonus or involuntary partial contraction which maintains the bladder neck in an elevated and closed position (Vincent, 1974). Even after initiation of urination has begun, contraction of the pelvic floor muscles can abruptly raise the bladder neck and terminate urination. However, for children with nocturnal enuresis, these urinary inhibitory responses are either not present or are sporadic during sleep (Friman, 1995; Friman & Jones, 1998; Houts, 1991).

The two most common treatments for nocturnal enuresis are medications and the enuresis alarm. Medications such as Desmopressin and Imipramine can provide symptomatic treatment - approximately 25-40% will be dry most nights on these medications, however when the medications are stopped the enuresis usually returns (Moffatt, 1997). The enuresis alarm is a moisture-sensitive switching system, the closing of which (when the child wets the bed) rings the alarm. Repeated pairing of awakening by the alarm with episodes of wetting is consistently described in the literature as the single most effective treatment for enuresis (Friman, 1986; 1995; Friman & Jones, 1998). Its success rate is higher (approximately 75%) and its relapse rate lower (approximately 41%) than any other drug or skill-based treatment.

The urine alarm is a biofeedback system in that it increases the salience of urination during sleep in order to help individuals stop bed wetting, but the mechanism by which the alarm improves enuresis is unknown. Changes in secretion of hormones that affect the ability to concentrate urine (Friman, 1995; Friman & Jones, 1998; Houts, 1991) or alterations in the brain's inhibition of bladder contraction are at least theoretically possible, but have not been investigated. Behavioral explanations initially described the mechanism as classical conditioning with the alarm as the unconditioned stimulus, bladder distention the conditioned stimulus, and waking as the conditioned response. However, most individuals successfully treated with the alarm learn to sleep through the night without wetting (or waking). Subsequent literature emphasized a negative reinforcement paradigm in which the children repeatedly awakened by the alarm avoided it by urinating in the toilet (initially) and (ultimately) holding their urine until a more convenient time. The current prevailing account involves a combination of the two previous accounts with classical conditioning of pelvic floor muscles and operant condition-ing of volitional behaviors related to continence (Houts). The key distinguishing feature of the current account is that children are not necessarily trained to awaken to the alarm, merely to engage their urinary inhibition system while asleep - a skill that would be difficult to teach without the biofeedback system.

The enuresis alarm produces cures slowly and during the first few weeks of alarm use, the child often awakens only after voiding completely. The aversive properties of the alarm, however, inexorably strengthen the skills necessary to avoid it. These skills include sensory awareness of urinary need and waking to urinate or contraction of the pelvic floor muscles that offset urination.

In another application suggestive of biofeedback, the urine alarm has also been used to treat diurnal enuresis (Friman & Vollmer, 1995). Only two studies are available and the first used a much simpler conceptualization (Halliday, Meadow, & Berg, 1987). Specifically, this early study merely suggested the alarm served as a reminder for urination. The Friman and Vollmer study, however, was conducted with a young girl who was initially unresponsive to urinary urge and onset, but who rapidly became responsive with use of the alarm. The decreasing latency between alarm onset and appropriate response was characteristic of learning curves resulting from biofeedback treatment.

Biofeedback devices much more sophisticated than the enuresis alarm are now available. Physiologic processes that can be monitored include muscle tension, skin temperature, respiratory rate, blood pressure, and skin moisture (sweating). These devices have been used in treatment of a wide variety of disorders including headaches, anxiety disorders, sleep disorders, and dysfunction of the autonomic nervous system (Culbert et al., 1996). The ability of human behaviors to alter physiologic processes such as skin temperature and blood pressure that have not been thought to be under volitional control is being increasingly demonstrated. Other behaviors capable of altering physiologic processes are being researched. For example, awareness enhancement techniques (hypnosis) have been used to alter the level of mediators of the immune system in saliva (Olness, Culbert, & Uden, 1989), and to decrease the recurrence rate of mouth ulcers (Andrews & Hall, 1990). These types of findings highlight the need for further research into the complex relation-ship between behavior and biology.

Interaction Between Biology and Behavior

Biology and behavior do not represent separate processes within individuals, but interacting systems that could no more function independently than the heart and the brain. As the reciprocal capacity of biologic and behavioral variables to influence each other becomes increasingly clear, decisions about selecting appropri-ate treatments become more complex. One reason for the complexity is that there are a rapidly growing number of medical and behavioral problems for which there are both clearly effective behavioral and clearly effective medical treatments. How the behavioral pediatric provider is to proceed (whether pediatrician or behavior analyst) is a question that is complicated by the existence of effective treatments from entirely different domains. The question can be addressed, on a problem by problem basis, by behavior analysis. We will demonstrate this by briefly discussing two exemplar problems (although there are many others): pharmacologic and behavioral treatments for enuresis (discussed above) and for Attention-Deficit/Hyperactivity Disorder (ADHD). The question at issue in these discussions involves whether a combination of pharmacologic and behavioral treatment is superior to either alone.

Enuresis. That learning is the basis for the effects of the urine alarm (as argued above) suggests that medications (e.g., desmopressin) that decrease the frequency of wet nights (i.e., learning trials) would decrease the effectiveness of the alarm. However, the one study that has examined desmopressin and the urine alarm found that the combination was more effective than the alarm alone (Bradbury & Meadow, 1995). Further research is needed to confirm this finding but it, nonetheless, underscores the importance of research on combined behavioral and pharmacologic interventions.

ADHD. Stimulant medications such as methylphenidate (Ritalin) have been demonstrated to decrease disruptive behaviors and improve on-task behavior for children diagnosed with ADHD (Spencer et al., 1996). A variety of behavioral interventions utilizing differential reinforcement procedures, often in combination with extinction or punishment procedures, have also been demonstrated to decrease disruptive behavior and improve on-task behavior. Therefore, most recommendations about treatment for ADHD advocate multi-modal treatment combining behavioral and pharmacologic interventions.

A recent study by the first author examined the validity of recommending combined treatments. The study targeted disruptive behavior in three children with mental retardation and hyperactivity using a design that allowed comparison of a behavioral treatment alone, medication alone, and the combination of the two (Blum, Mauk, McComas, & Mace, 1996). The behavioral treatment was a differential reinforcement of alternative behavior procedure in combination with guided compliance, which was compared with a no behavioral treatment (baseline) condition using a multi-element design across all medication conditions. The pharmacologic treatment, methylphenidate, was alternated with placebo using a reversal design (see Figure). Two different doses of methylphenidate were assessed (i.e., 0.3 mg/kg and 0.6 mg/kg).

As shown in the Figure, the behavioral treatment was effective in decreasing disruptive behavior in all 3 participants. The high dose of methylphenidate was effective for Bill and Art, but Ted suffered side effects on the higher dose and did not show any beneficial effect on the lower dose. For Bill the behavioral treatment and methylphenidate produced similar effects. For Art the medication was more effective than the behavioral treatment alone. The combination of pharmacologic treatment and behavioral treatment was not more effective than either treatment alone, but the high efficacy of each treatment would have made it difficult to demonstrate interactive effects. Nevertheless, if the primary goal of treatment were to decrease disruptive behavior it would be difficult to recommend combined pharmacologic and behavioral treatment for any of the participants in this study.

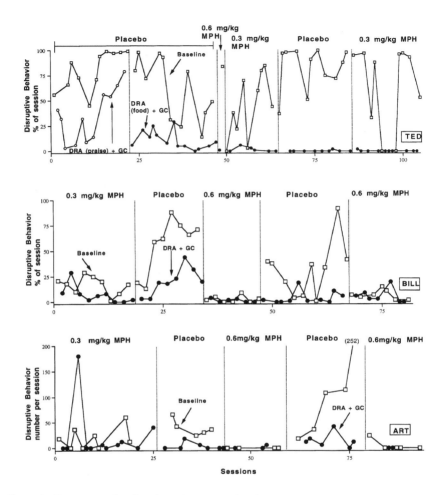

Figure 1. Percentage of each task session engaged in disruptive behaviors (Ted, Bill) or number of disruptive behaviors per hour during each session (Art). Baseline conditions (open squares) were counterbalanced with a differential-reinforcement-of-alternative-behavior and guided compliance (DRA + GC) intervention across all methylphenidate (MPH) and placebo phases. The open circles indicate praise and attention were the reinforcers, and the filled circles indicate that verbal praise and an edible item were the reinforcers. From Blum et al. (1996), p. 311.

Other studies that have used single-subject analyses have come to similar conclusions regarding the treatment of disruptive behaviors. Schell et al. (1986) found that both methylphenidate alone and a behavioral intervention alone (i.e., reinforcement for correct responses on an academic task) decreased defiant behavior in a 5-year-old with mild mental retardation and ADHD. However, the combined treatment was not more effective than methylphenidate alone. Johnson, Handen,

Lubetsky, and Sacco (1994) found that a combination of methylphenidate and a token economy with an accuracy contingency was only slightly more effective than either intervention alone in increasing on-task behavior. However, decreasing disruptive behavior or improving on-task behavior is only one goal of treatment for children with ADHD. Both of the above studies found that when work accuracy was the dependent measure, the behavioral treatment did have additive affects with medication in some subjects, while in others the combined treatment was not more effective than the behavioral treatment alone. These studies suggest that behaviors composing ADHD are members of different response classes and thus may respond differently to various combinations of treatments. Better understanding of how these types of treatments interact and of their relative efficacy for different behaviors should allow better targeting of both pharmacologic and behavioral treatments in developing treatment plans for ADHD and other problem behaviors.

Summary

Behavioral pediatrics is a diverse field, which includes the study of common behavior problems and the study of complex interactions between biology and behavior that affect health. We have provided a limited review of some the aspects of behavioral pediatrics, but it must be acknowledged that there are many aspects of the area that we have not addressed (e.g., infant colic, oppositional behaviors, habit disorders, chronic illness, and pain). We have highlighted some of the significant contributions to behavioral pediatrics that behavior analysts have made. Most importantly, we hope we have conveyed that there are multiple clinical and research opportunities for behavior analysis in health care settings. Increased collaboration between physicians and behavior analysts will greatly increase our understanding of the interactions between biology and behavior and improve the health of children.

Reading Objectives

1. Describe the breadth of questions addressed in behavioral pediatrics.
2. Describe the aspects of primary care which provide opportunities for behavior analysts interested in common pediatric behavior problems.
3. Identify at least 5 steps behavior analysts can utilize to increase collaboration with physicians.
4. Describe the behavioral principles utilized in the management of bedtime struggles and night waking.
5. Describe the relationship between constipation and encopresis.
6. Describe a multi-component treatment program for encopresis.
7. Describe the treatment of enuresis using a urine alarm.
8. Describe at least three possible contributions of behavior analysis to the study of behavioral phenotypes.
9. Discuss ways in which behavior analysis may contribute to the investigation of the efficacy of behavioral, pharmacologic, and combined interventions.
10. Discuss ways that behavioral and pharmacologic interventions may augment or interfere with each other.

References

Adams, L. A., & Rickert, V. I. (1989). Reducing bedtime tantrums: Comparison between positive routines and graduated extinction. *Pediatrics, 84,* 756-761.

Allen, K. D., Barone, V. J., & Kuhn, B. R. (1993). A behavioral prescription for promoting applied behavior analysis within pediatrics. *Journal of Applied Behavior Analysis, 26,* 493-502.

American Psychiatric Association (1994). *Diagnostic and statistical manual of mental disorders* (4th ed.). Washington, D. C.: Author.

Anderson, L. T., & Ernst, M. (1994). Self-injury in Lesch-Nyhan Disease. *Journal of Autism and Developmental Disorders, 24,* 67-81.

Andrews, V. H., & Hall, H. R. (1990). The effects of relaxation/imagery training on recurrent aphthous stomatitis: A preliminary study. *Psychosomatic Medicine, 52,* 526-535.

Barr, R. G., Levine, M. D., Wilkinson, R. H., & Mulvihill, D. (1979). Chronic and occult stool retention: A clinical tool for its evaluation in school aged children. *Clinical Pediatrics, 18,* 674-686.

Berk, L. B., & Friman, P. C. (1990). Epidemiologic aspects of toilet training. *Clinical Pediatrics, 29,* 278-282.

Blampied, N. M., & France, K. G. (1993). A behavioral model of sleep disturbance. *Journal of Applied Behavior Analysis, 26,* 477-492.

Blum, N. J., & Carey, W. B. (1996). Sleep problems among infants and young children. *Pediatrics in Review, 17,* 87-93.

Blum, N. J., Mauk, J. E., McComas, J. J., & Mace, F. C. (1996). Separate and combined effects of methylphenidate and a behavioral intervention on disruptive behavior in children with mental retardation. *Journal of Applied Behavior Analysis, 29,* 305-319.

Bradbury, M. G., & Meadow, S. R. (1995). Combined treatment with the enuresis alarm and desmopressin for nocturnal enuresis. *Acta Paediatrica, 84,* 1014-1018.

Breese, G. R., Criswell, H. E., Duncan, G. E., Moy, S. S., Johnson, K. B., Wong, D. F., & Mueller, R. A. (1995). Model for reduced brain dopamine in Lesch-Nyhan syndrome and the mentally retarded: Neurobiology of neonatal-6-hydroxy dopamine lesioned rats. *Mental Retardation and Developmental Disabilities Research Reviews, 1,* 111-119.

Caspi, A., & Moffitt, T. (1995). The continuity of maladaptive behavior: From description to understanding in the study of antisocial behavior. In D. Cicchetti & D. Cohen (Eds.), *Developmental Psychopathology* (Vol. 2, pp. 472-511). New York: Wiley.

Cataldo, M. F. (1982). The scientific basis for a behavioral approach to pediatrics. *Pediatric Clinics of North America, 29,* 415-423.

Christophersen, E. R. (1988). *Little people.* Kansas City, MO: Westport Press.

Christophersen E. R. (1994). *Pediatric compliance: A guide for the primary care physician.* New York: Plenum.

Christophersen, E. R., & Rainey, S. (1976). Management of encopresis through a pediatric outpatient clinic. *Journal of Pediatric Psychology, 1,* 38-41.

Christophersen, E. R., & Rapoff, M. A. (1979). Behavioral pediatrics. In O. F. Pomerleau & J. P. Brady (Eds.), *Behavioral medicine: Theory and practice* (pp. 99-123). Baltimore: Williams & Wilkins.

Christophersen, E. R., & Rapoff, M. A. (1983). Toileting problems of children. In C. E. Walker & M. C. Roberts (Eds.), *Handbook of clinical child psychology* (pp. 583-605). New York: Wiley.

Costello, E. J., Edelbrock, C., Costello, A. J., Dulcan, M., Burns, B. J., & Brent, D. (1988). Psychopathology in pediatric primary care: The new hidden morbidity. *Pediatrics, 82*, 415-424.

Costello, E. J., & Shugart, M. A. (1992). Above and below the threshold: Severity of psychiatric symptoms and functional impairment in a pediatric sample. *Pediatrics, 90*, 359-368.

Culbert, T. P., Kajander, R. L., & Reaney, J. B. (1996). Biofeedback with children and adolescents: Clinical observations and patient perspectives. *Journal of Developmental and Behavioral Pediatrics, 17*, 342-350.

Daly, D. L., Friman, P. C., Larzelere, R. E., Smith, G., Osgood, D. W., & Thompson, R. W. (1998). Educating out-of-home adolescents: A longitudinal analysis of length of stay in residential care. Manuscript submitted for publication.

Davidson, M. (1958). Constipation and fecal incontinence. *Pediatric Clinics of North America, 5*, 749-757.

Donaldson, M. D. C., Chu, C. E., Cooke, A., Wilson, A., Greene, S. A., & Stephenson, J. B. P. (1994). The Prader-Willi syndrome. *Archives of Disease in Childhood, 70*, 58-63.

Dykens, E. M. (1995). Measuring behavioral phenotypes: Provocations from the "new genetics". *American Journal on Mental Retardation, 99*, 522-532.

Earls, F. (1980). Prevalence of behavior problems in 3-year-old children: A cross national replication. *Archives of General Psychiatry, 37*, 1153-1157.

Edwards, K. J. (1993). The use of brief time outs during the day to reduce bedtime struggles. *Dissertation Abstracts International, 54*, 2181.

Edwards, K. J., & Christophersen, E. R. (1993). Automated data acquisition through time-lapse videotape recording. *Journal of Applied Behavioral Analysis, 26*, 503-504.

Edwards, K. J., & Christophersen, E. R. (1994). Treating common sleep problems of young children. *Journal of Developmental and Behavioral Pediatrics, 15*, 207-213.

Eggert, P., & Kuhn, B. (1995). Antidiuretic hormone regulation in patients with primary nocturnal enuresis. *Archives of Diseases in Childhood, 73*, 508-511.

Einfeld, S. L., & Hall, W. (1994). When is a behavioral phenotype not a phenotype? *Developmental Medicine and Child Neurology, 36*, 467-70.

Ferber, R. (1985) *Solve your child's sleep problems.* New York: Simon & Schuster.

Finney, J. W., Miller, K. M., & Adler, S. P. (1993). Changing protective and risky behaviors to prevent child-to-parent transmission of cytomegalovirus. *Journal of Applied Behavior Analysis, 26*, 471-472.

Friman, P. C. (1986). A preventive context for enuresis. *Pediatric Clinics of North America, 33*, 871-886.

Friman, P. C. (1995). Nocturnal enuresis in the child. In R. Ferber & M. H. Kryger (Eds.), *Principles and practice of sleep medicine in the child* (pp. 107-114). Philadelphia: Saunders.

Friman, P. C., & Christophersen, E. R. (1986). Biobehavioral prevention in primary care. In N. Krasnegor, J. D. Arasteh, & M. F. Cataldo (Eds.), *Child health behavior: A behavioral pediatrics perspective* (pp. 254-280). New York: John Wiley & Sons.

Friman, P. C., Handwerk, M. L., Swearer, S. M., McGinnis, C., & Warzak, W. J. (in press). Do children with primary nocturnal enuresis have clinically significant behavior problems? *Archives of Pediatrics and Adolescent Medicine.*

Friman, P. C., Hayes, S. C., & Wilson, K. (1998). Why behavior analysts should study emotion: The example of anxiety. *Journal of Applied Behavior Analysis, 31,* 137-156.

Friman, P. C., & Jones, K. M. (1998). Elimination disorders in children. In S. Watson, & F. Gresham (Eds.), *Handbook of child behavior therapy* (pp. 239-260). New York: Plenum.

Friman, P. C., Mathews, J. R., Finney, J. W., & Christophersen, E. R. (1988). Do children with encopresis have clinically significant behavior problems? *Pediatrics, 82,* 407-409.

Friman, P. C., & Vollmer, D. (1995). Successful use of the nocturnal urine alarm for diurnal enuresis. *Journal of Applied Behavior Analysis, 28,* 89-90.

Gabel, S., Hegedus, A. M., Wald, A., Chandra, R., & Chaponis, D. (1986). Prevalence of behavior problems and mental health utilization among encopretic children. *Journal of Developmental and Behavioral Pediatrics, 7,* 293-297.

Hatch, T. F. (1988). Encopresis and constipation in children. *Pediatric Clinics of North America, 35,* 257-281.

Halliday, S., Meadow, S. R., & Berg, I. (1987). Successful management of daytime enuresis using alarm procedures: A randomly controlled trial. *Archives of Disease in Children, 62,* 132-137.

Horwitz, S. M., Leaf, P. J., Leventhal, J. M., Forsyth, B., & Speechley, K. N. (1992). Identification and management of psychosocial and developmental problems in community-based, primary care pediatric practices. *Pediatrics, 89,* 480-485

Houts, A. C. (1991). Nocturnal enuresis as a biobehavioral problem. *Behavior Therapy, 22,* 133-151.

Houts, A. C., Mellon, M. W., & Whelan, J. P. (1988). Use of dietary fiber and stimulus control to treat retentive encopresis: A multiple baseline investigation. *Journal of Pediatric Psychology, 13,* 435-445.

Howard, B. J. (1991). Discipline in early childhood. *Pediatric Clinics of North America, 38,* 1351- 1369.

Irwin, C. E., Cataldo, M. F., Matheny, A. P., Peterson, L. (1992). Health consequences of behaviors: Injury as a model. *Pediatrics, 90,* 798-807.

Johnson, C. R., Handen, B. L., Lubetsky, M. J., & Sacco, K. A. (1994). Efficacy of methylphenidate and behavioral intervention on classroom behavior in children with ADHD and mental retardation. *Behavior Modification, 18,* 470-487.

Kanoy, K. W., & Schroeder, C. S. (1985). Suggestions to parents about common behavior problems in a pediatric primary care office: Five years of follow-up. *Journal of Pediatric Psychology, 10,* 15-30.

Kempe, C. H., & Helfer, R. E., & Krugman, R. D. (1987). *The battered child* (5th ed.). Chicago: University of Chicago Press.

Koff, S. A. (1995). Why is desmopressin sometimes ineffective at curing bedwetting? *Scandinavian Journal of Urology & Nephrology. Supplementum, 173,* 103-108.

Lackgren, G., Neveus, T., & Stenberg, A. (1997). Diurnal plasma vasopressin and urinary output in adolescents with monosymptomatic nocturnal enuresis. *Acta Paediatrica, 86,* 385-390.

Lavigne, J. V., Binns, H. J., Christoffel, K. K., Rosenbaum, D., Arend, R., Smith, K., Hayford, J. R., McGuire, P. A., & Pediatric Practice Research Group. (1993). Behavioral and emotional problems among preschool children in pediatric primary care: Prevalence and pediatrician's recognition. *Pediatrics, 91,* 649-655.

Levine, M. D. (1975). Children with encopresis: A descriptive analysis. *Pediatrics, 56,* 407-409.

Levine, M. D. (1982). Encopresis: Its potentiation, evaluation, and alleviation. *Pediatric Clinics of North America, 29,* 315-330.

Lowery, S., Srour, J., Whitehead, W. E., & Schuster, M. M. (1985). Habit training as treatment of encopresis secondary to chronic constipation. *Journal of Pediatric Gastroenterology and Nutrition, 4,* 397-401.

Lozoff, B., Wolf, A. W., & Davis, N. S. (1985). Sleep problems seen in pediatric practice. *Pediatrics, 75,* 477- 483.

Mace, F., Hock, M. L., Lalli, J. S., West, B. J., Belfiore, P., Pinter, E., & Brown, D. K. (1988). Behavioral momentum in the treatment of noncompliance. *Journal of Applied Behavioral Analysis, 21,* 123-142.

Meunier, P., Marechal, J. M., & De Beaujeu, M. J. (1979). Rectoanal pressures and rectal sensitivity in chronic childhood constipation. *Gastroenterology, 77,* 330-336.

Moffatt, M. E. (1997). Nocturnal enuresis: A review of the efficacy of treatments and practical advice for clinicians. *Journal of Developmental and Behavioral Pediatrics, 18,* 49-56.

O'Brien, S., Ross, L. V., & Christophersen, E. R. (1986). Primary encopresis: Evaluation and treatment. *Journal of Applied Behavior Analysis, 19,* 137-145.

Olness, K., Culbert, T., & Uden, D. (1989). Self-regulation of salivary immunoglobulin A by children. *Pediatrics, 83,* 66-71.

Rickert, V. I., & Johnson, M. (1988). Reducing nocturnal awaking and crying episodes in infants and young children: A comparison between scheduled awakings and systematic ignoring. *Pediatrics, 81,* 203-212.

Rittig, S., Knudsen, U. B., Norgaard, J. P., Pedersen, E. B., & Djurhuus, J. C. (1989). Abnormal diurnal rhythm of plasma vasopressin and urinary output in patients with enuresis. *American Journal of Physiology, 256,* 644-671.

Schell, R. M., Pelham, W. E., Bender, M. E., Andree, J. A., Law, T., & Robbins, F. R. (1986). The concurrent assessment of behavioral and psychostimulant interventions: A controlled case study. *Behavioral Assessment, 8*, 373-384.

Schmitt, B. D. (1987). Seven deadly sins of childhood: Advising parents about difficult developmental phases. *Child Abuse and Neglect, 11*, 421-432.

Solnick, J. V., Rincover, A., & Peterson, C. R. (1977). Some determinants of the reinforcing and punishing effects of timeouts. *Journal of Applied Behavior Analysis, 10*, 415-424.

Spencer, T., Biederman, J., Wilens, T., Harding, M., O'Donnell, D., & Griffin, S. (1996). Pharmacotherapy of Attention-Deficit Hyperactivity Disorder across the life cycle. *Journal of the American Academy of Child and Adolescent Psychiatry, 35*, 409-432.

Stark, L. J., Knapp, L. G., Bowen, A. M., Powers, S. W., Jelalian, E., Evans, S., Passero, M. A., Mulvihille, M. M., & Hovell, M. (1993). Increasing caloric consumption in children with cystic fibrosis: Replication with 2-year follow-up. *Journal of Applied Behavior Analysis, 26*, 435-450.

Stark, L. J., Opipari, L. C., Donaldson, D. L., Danovsky, D. A., Rasile, D. A., & Del Santo, A. F. (1997). Evaluation of a standard protocol for rententive encopresis: A replication. *Journal of Pediatric Psychology, 22*, 619-633.

Stark, L. J., Owens-Stively, J., Spirito, A., Lewis, A., & Guevremont, D. C. (1990). Group behavioral treatment of retentive encopresis. *Journal of Pediatric Psychology, 15*, 659-671.

Stark, L. J., Spirito, A., Lewis, A. V., & Hart, K. J. (1990). Encopresis: Behavioral parameters associated with children who fail medical management. *Child Psychiatry and Human Development, 20*, 169-179.

Teitelbaum, P. (1977). Levels of integration of the operant. In W. K. Honig & J. E. R. Staddon (Eds.), *Handbook of operant behavior* (pp. 7-27). Englewood Cliffs, NJ: Prentice Hall.

Vincent, S. A. (1974). Mechanical, electrical and other aspects of enuresis. In J. H. Johnston & W. Goodwin (Eds.), *Reviews in Pediatric Urology* (pp. 280-313). New York: Elsevier.

Wald, A., Chandra, R., Chiponis, D., & Gabel, S. (1986). Anorectal function and continence mechanisms in childhood encopresis. *Journal of Pediatric Gastroenterology and Nutrition, 5*, 346-351.

Wang, P. P., & Bellugi, U. (1993). Williams syndrome, Down syndrome and cognitive neuroscience. *American Journal of Diseases of Children, 147*, 1246-1251.

Weinstock, L. B., & Clouse, R. E. (1987). A focused overview of gastrointestinal physiology. *Annals of Behavioral Medicine, 9*, 3-6.

Whitehead, W. E., & Schuster, M. M. (1985). *Gastrointestinal disorders: Behavioral and physiological basis for treatment*. New York: Academic Press.

Winett, R. A., Moore, R. F., Wagner, J. L., Hite, L. A., Leahy, M., Neubauer, T. E., Walberg, J. L, Walker, W. B., Lombard, D., Geller, E. S., & Mundy, L. L. (1991). Altering shoppers' supermarket purchases to fit nutritional guidelines: An interactive information system. *Journal of Applied Behavior Analysis, 24*, 95-105.

Wolff. P. H., Gardner, J., Paccia, J., & Lappen, J. (1989). The greeting behavior of fragile-X males. *American Journal on Mental Retardation, 93*, 406-411.

Wright, L. (1973). Handling the encopretic child. *Professional Psychology, 3*, 137-144.

Wright, L. (1975). Outcome of a standardized program for treating psychogenic encopresis. *Professional Psychology, 6*, 453-456.

Wright, L., Schaefer, A. B., & Solomons, G. (1979). *Encyclopedia of pediatric psychology*. Baltimore: University Park Press.

Wright, L., & Walker, E. (1977). Treatment of the child with psychogenic encopresis. *Clinical Pediatrics, 16*, 1042-1045.

Chapter 8

Behavioral, Family-Style Residential Care for Troubled Out-of-Home Adolescents: Recent Findings

Patrick C. Friman
University of Nevada

Introduction

More than one-half million children are in out-of-home placement in this country and their number increases daily. Residential placement is an expanding mode of care for these children, especially when they are adolescent, emotionally disturbed and/or delinquent (Chamberlain & Friman, 1997; Friman, 1996; Friman, Osgood et al., 1996). Evaluating this mode of care is difficult, however, because residential care is a fuzzy concept. Its concrete particulars are sometimes so divergent that the only similarity sufficient to establish their conceptual relationship is out-of-home placement, and yet there are many other types of out-of-home options (Friman, Evans, Larzelere, Williams, & Daly, 1993; Handwerk, Friman, Mott, & Stairs, 1998). Unfortunately, early particulars included big, institutional-style programs with many children, few staff, and multiple threats (often "made good") to child health and well being. Equally unfortunate is the stigma, derived from these harmful programs, that now adheres to the entire concept of residential care (Chamberlain & Friman; Friman; Friman, Osgood et al., 1996). Writing an article favorable to a current version of residential care runs the risk of being dismissed or ignored by readers (justifiably) opposed to other earlier versions unless the current version is clearly defined and distinguished from the problematic others. Favorable research findings obtained in any version of care are also at risk for being dismissed or ignored because they can be interpreted as an endorsement of the full fuzzy concept. Clearly residential care needs a conceptual reconstruction, but that is beyond the scope of this chapter.

The topic of this chapter is devoted to a contemporary segment of residential care that involves a behaviorally oriented, family-style program for youth whose own families are untenable and who are either unsuitable for foster care or have no foster care options. By behaviorally oriented I mean emphasis on overt performance in domains that are critical to social assimilation (e.g., school work, social interactions, vocational activities, peer relations) and ongoing evaluation, not just of the youth but of those whose job it is to care for the youth (cf., Daly & Dowd, 1992). The core concept involves operationalizing target performances for the youth and providing direct teaching – instruction and consequences for relevant performance. Most typically, this is done with a token economy or a point system. By "family style," I mean that youth live with married couples who may or may not have children of their own and who are specially trained to provide surrogate care and to conduct treatment in the manner specified above. By "untenable or unavailable (biological) families," I mean those that do not exist, cannot be contacted, or that cannot be relied upon to guarantee a reasonable amount of care, health and, safety for the child. By "unsuitable for foster care," I mean youth whose threat to themselves or others is sufficiently plausible to require the increased supervision available in residential care.

Few programs fit all of these criteria. Many programs are behaviorally oriented, but few of these are family style. Many programs are family style, but few of these are behaviorally oriented. There are a number of programs that fit several of the criteria above (e.g., family style, emphasis on overt performance, consequence based treatment), but that do not collect sufficient research data to be included in an empirically derived review. One that does is the Teaching Family Model (TFM), which has been described extensively in the literature (e.g., Braukman & Wolf, 1987; Phillips, Phillips, Fixsen, & Wolf, 1974). Briefly, in TFM a married couple lives in a large domestic home with six to eight adolescents. Some of the major features of the program are: a) a token economy motivational system wherein youth earn points and exchange them for privileges; b) a self-government system that allows youth to participate in development of the rules and structure of their daily lives; c) a focus on teaching social skills from a standardized social skills curriculum; d) an emphasis on normalization; and e) a continuous evaluation system, part of which involves the youth evaluating the teaching family couple. At least 22 programs across the country use a certified version of the TFM, and as many as 100 programs use a modified version.

The original research for the TFM was conducted at Achievement Place, the alpha site for the TFM. Achievement Place research was described and reviewed extensively during the 1970s and 1980s (e.g., Braukman & Wolf, 1987; James et al., 1983). Doing so here would be redundant. Currently, the largest TFM program is the Boys Town Family Home Program (FHP; Coughlin & Shanahan, 1991). In recent years, it has become very active in research, generating several lines of inquiry. However, this research has never been reviewed. Therefore, a review of FHP research will occupy the core of this chapter, although other lines of research will sometimes be integrated to develop theoretical points. Please note that some of the findings described are not only new for residential care, but for psychology in general.

The chapter is divided into three primary sections. The first section describes a variety of data that provide empirically derived profiles of youth in care. Of special interest in this first section is a report on the biological children of the couples who provide care, as no data have ever been published on these children. The second section describes a variety of experimentally derived outcomes of care. Of special interest in this section is educational data from one of the largest longitudinal studies ever conducted on residential care. The third section provides a synthesis of all the findings, a behavioral interpretation, and a concluding statement. Of special interest in this section is a brief behavioral critique of the common criticism that within-program effects of behavioral residential care do not maintain at long-term follow-up.

Before proceeding, the behaviorally oriented reader should beware that the first and second sections of the chapter include some language, methods, and analyses that are more typical of mainstream psychology than of behavior analysis. Reasons for this peculiar format are fully detailed in the final section of the chapter.

Profiles of Youth in Care

Demographics. An analysis of files on 1,236 youth residing at FHP between 1993 and 1997 indicates 64% were boys, 36% girls, and 41% were minorities. The largest minority was African American (25%), with Hispanic, Oriental, and American Indian youth comprising the remainder. At admission, the average youth was 14.4 years of age, had completed 8 years of education, had at least one out-of-home placement, and qualified for at least one psychiatric diagnosis according to referral sources. The average length of stay was 22 months.

Daily Incident Report (DIR). One of the least inferential methods of assessing the psychological makeup of youth in care is direct observation of their behavior. The DIR consists of 65 codes of distinct classes of behavior, which supervisors code on a daily basis. Although these observations involve preferred and nonpreferred behaviors, nonpreferred behaviors will be emphasized here. Administrators complete the DIR on all youth under their care during the previous 24 hours by specifying any codes representing important behaviors occurring during that interval and accompanying it with a descriptive narrative (e.g., code 24, Physical Assault-Peer, accompanied by a narrative describing an inter-peer assault). The DIR codes and narratives are entered into a computerized database and are retrievable for clinical and research purposes. For research purposes, factor analyses and intercoder reliabilities for the DIR have been established (Larzelere, 1991, 1996). The factor analyses involved codes from all youth appearing on the DIR during 1988 and 1989 (N = 989). Rotated factor pattern matrices indicate four scientifically useful factors: Aggression, Sexual Acting Out, Suicidal Behaviors, and Avoidance. Reliability analyses were conducted by randomly selecting two months of codes and narratives from all codes and narratives from 1988 to 1991. The narratives for these codes (with their accompanying code numbers blacked out) were then supplied to a reliability coder who recoded each using the code catalogue. Kappa coefficients obtained from the comparisons ranged from .66 to .97, which indicated that codes from the DIR met high standards of intercoder agreement.

Suicide risk. At admission, all youth complete the Suicide Probability Scale (SPS), a measure of suicide risk consisting of 36 items from a larger pool based on their ability to distinguish adults who had attempted suicide from those who had not. It has a Total Weighted Score and four sub-scales based on factor analysis: Hopelessness, Suicide Ideation, Negative Self-Evaluation, and Hostility (Cull & Gill,

1988). The SPS manual identifies t-scores of 70 or more on the Total Weighted Score as clinically significant and recommends that precautions be taken. In a major study of suicide risk and the predictive validity of the SPS, scores from all youth entering the FHP between 1988 and 1991 (N = 836) were analyzed for their ability to predict suicide attempts. The observational interval was the length of stay for the 836 youth (M=20.4 months; range, 7 days to 69 months). The criterion variables were the suicide codes (i.e., suicide statements and attempts, and self-destructive behavior) from the DIR. Results indicated a mean total weighted SPS score of 66.2 for those who attempted suicide and 57.1 for those who did not; the difference was significant. More importantly, the SPS did demonstrate statistically significant validity in predicting suicide attempts as well as suicidal statements and self-destructive behaviors. The results are the first known demonstration of predictive validity of any measure of suicide risk in adolescents (Larzelere, Smith, Batenhorst, & Kelly, 1996; see also Shaffer, 1996). Thus, the SPS (and other instruments with similar constructs) may be an important part of a comprehensive plan to prevent suicide in adolescents in residential care. A very important caveat needs emphasis, however. Although no suicides occurred during the 6-year interval, the SPS predicted fewer than half of the 29 attempts, indicating it is insufficient as a primary predictor of adolescent suicide.

A follow-up study provided another important clue to accurate prediction: the relationship between suicide communications and attempts. Some type of suicide communication precedes 80% of attempted and completed adolescent suicides (Berman & Jobes, 1990). During a 9-year interval, the DIR documented 46 suicide attempts by FHP youth. None were completed, but degree of lethality of attempt was highly variable, ranging from ingestion of a small number of over-the-counter analgesic tablets to hanging. Analysis of the DIR indicated an inverse relationship between lethality of attempt and number of prior suicide communications (Handwerk, Larzelere, Friman, & Mitchell, 1998). These findings suggest that youth in residential care who are serious about suicide may not be directly communicative about their intentions. Collectively, the findings from both FHP suicide studies reveal a large gap in knowledge about suicide prediction. This gap underscores the value of high indices of suspicion, high levels of vigilance, and intensive response prevention. Until more is known, any suicidal communication issued in care, direct or indirect, should be met with a major preventive effort.

Behavior problems assessment. The primary instruments used to assess youth behavior problems at admission to the FHP are the Child Behavior Checklist (CBCL; Achenbach, 1991a) and the Youth Self Report (YSR; Achenbach, 1991b). The CBCL is a structured rating scale that asks parents or caretakers to rate the occurrence of 118 behavior and emotional problems. The scale is designed for use with youth between the ages of four and 18 years. The CBCL yields scores on eight syndrome scales: Withdrawn, Somatic Complaints, Anxious/Depressed, Social Problems, Thought Problems, Attention Problems, and Delinquent and Aggressive Behavior. It also has three broad-band scales, Internalizing Problems, Externalizing Problems, and Total Problems. The YSR is the self-report version of the CBCL. The

YSR yields scores on the same scales as the CBCL and raw scores from both can be converted into t-scores based on normative data.

An important issue is the comparative value of the CBCL versus the YSR. Eight years of administering both has yielded an obdurate finding: the youth describe themselves as normal and their caretakers describe them as abnormal. Other information strongly supports the caretaker description. For example, a comparison of CBCL and YSR scores from youth in three out-of-home settings (FHP, an emergency shelter, and a psychiatric hospital) all showed normal YSR scores and significantly elevated CBCL scores (Handwerk, Larzelere, Soper, & Friman, 1999). Fifty percent of girls in FHP had confirmed histories of sexual abuse and informal reports by the girls and their caretakers put this figure much higher. The chances these girls, as a group, would not exhibit elevated clinical problems is very small. Virtually all youth entering the program have at least one diagnosis provided by a licensed provider and at least 35% enter with prescriptions for behavior and mood altering medications. Data obtained from other instruments (e.g., SPS; see below) is also more consistent with the CBCL. Data from longitudinal outcome studies show FHP youth with substantially suppressed performance across a number of important areas of psychological functioning (e.g., Friman, Osgood et al., 1996). In short, the YSR does not appear to be a useful instrument for residential care.

Psychodiagnosis. Diagnostic information on FHP youth is obtained from the Diagnostic Interview Schedule for Children (DISC; Shaffer et al., 1993). The DISC is a highly structured interview used by lay interviewers to obtain diagnostic criteria for common psychiatric disorders of childhood and adolescence. The DISC comes in multiple forms including paper and pencil (DISC), a user friendly computerized version (C-DISC), and child and parent informant versions. All versions have been used with FHP youth but most research findings are from the youth informant C-DISC. The C-DISC provides a comprehensive symptomatic and diagnostic report and is useful not only for assessing program needs at admission, but also for assessing outcomes at six month intervals (Friman, Almquist, Soper, & Lucas, 1995; 1996). The C-DISC can also detect subtle comorbidites, the ignorance of which can thwart effective treatment planning (e.g., Friman & Lucas, 1996). For these reasons, the C-DISC is administered to FHP youth at admissions, six months, and one year. Only admissions data will be reviewed in this section.

An analysis of DISC results for 463 FHP youth (163 girls, 300 boys), ranging in age from 11 to 18 years ($M = 14.4$), showed the average youth met criteria for 2.5 DSM-IV diagnoses (Diagnostic and Statistical Manual of Mental Disorders, 4th ed.; American Psychiatric Association, 1994), 3 for girls and 2 for boys. Both of these findings are important. Previously, outside of information from referral sources (which is highly variable in quality), little was known about the psychiatric makeup of FHP youth. Historically, these youth have been described as either predelinquent or delinquent and their problems defined in terms of aberrant conduct rather than psychological makeup. This perspective more readily leads to interventions that involve juvenile detention and justice than evaluation and treatment. The CBCL data showing high levels of psychiatric concerns for FHP youth partially broadened the treatment perspective, but it was limited in two ways. First, the data were partially offset by the contradictory findings from the YSR. Second, CBCL data are not readily convertible into observable behaviors or psychiatric diagnoses. The DISC does both.

The DISC data on girls were also important. Predelinquent and delinquent girls have been studied very little until recently and thus, little is known of their psychiatric makeup. Additionally, the limited extant literature may not be relevant—it reports, for example, that boys in residential care have more behavior problems than girls (Wurtele, Wilson, & Prentice-Dunn, 1983). As indicated, the DISC data at FHP show the opposite is true and it is supported by several other sources. The girls have a much higher rate of confirmed sexual abuse than do the boys. The girls are placed in out-of-home settings at an earlier age and their prior placements are greater in number and level of restrictiveness (Turk et al., 1997). Although there are no significant differences on their SPS and YSR scores (the limitations of each have been addressed above) the girls' CBCL scores are significantly higher.

DISC data also provide information on the kinds of psychological problems exhibited by youth entering the program. As indicated above, historically these have been assumed to be problems of conduct. This assumption is supported by DISC results showing that Conduct Disorder is the most frequently occurring diagnosis, with 40% of youth testing positive and little difference between boys and girls. A surprise finding, however, was the extent of internalizing disorders. Forty-four percent of girls and 22% of boys tested positive for an anxiety disorder and 22% of girls and 8% of boys tested positive for Major Depression. These findings underscore two points made previously: FHP youth have substantial psychiatric problems and the girls exhibit considerably more of these than the boys.

The value of this information is most apparent in treatment planning. For example, study of the FHP youth has yielded a previously unreported comorbidity, social phobia and disruptive behavior disorder (Friman & Lucas, 1996). A core component of social phobia is avoidance of perceived or real criticism (Friman, Hayes, & Wilson, 1998). A typical intervention for disruptive behavior is an adult approach that substantially elevates the possibility of criticism. Thus, adult approach to disruption may instigate intensive avoidant and escape responses. In fact, the principal function of disruptive behavior in youth that also suffer social phobia may be avoidance and escape (Friman & Lucas). Thus, the DISC findings on this comorbid pattern underscore the value of a functional analysis of disruptive behavior prior to treatment planning. Other examples include the reactive effect extended verbal teaching interactions can have on anxious youth, the deleterious effect extended loss of privileges can have on depressed youth, and the exacerbating effect anxiety and depression can have on anger, hostility, and aggression. Current research projects at FHP are addressing these issues.

Biological Children of Family Teachers (Birth Children)

Risk of behavior problems. A very important question for Family Teachers is whether living among delinquent adolescents will adversely affect the behavior of their own children. As indicated above, the FHP youth exhibit a variety of clinically significant behaviors. Thus, they present at least three behavioral risk factors for birth children. The first involves the modeling of inappropriate behavior. The second involves direct attempts by FHP youth to manipulate, manage, or otherwise alter the behavior of the birth children. The third involves diminishment of parental social and emotional resources. Despite the importance of the birth-child risk issues (for residential and foster care), there is virtually no published relevant research.

We have recently conducted three pertinent studies; two to be described here and one to be described in the Program Outcomes section. The first study involved administering the CBCL to three groups of children: a birth children group (all birth children over the age of four; $n = 55$, 27 boys, 28 girls, ages 4 to 18, $M = 9.3$), a clinically referred group (children at an outpatient child psychology clinic; $n = 119$, 76 boys, 43 girls, ages 4 to18, $M = 8.3$ years), and a non-referred group (children seen for pediatric well child care; $n = 154$, 90 boys, 64 girls, ages 4 to 18, $M = 8.2$ years).

The results of study one indicated the scores of the birth children were significantly lower than the scores of the other two groups, and also than the standardization sample for the CBCL itself (i.e., mean Total Problem Score of 44). Correlational analyses between length of time in the group home and CBCL scores were also nonsignificant (Friman, Panther, Larzelere, Shanahan, & Daly, 1993). These results are positive, but possibly suspect because the informant for the birth child sample was the child's mother who may have had an overly optimistic view of her child's behaviors. Study two addressed this issue using a similar format two years later (i.e., birth child, referred, and nonreferred groups) with one important difference. Four informants were used for the birth children: both parents, an in-home assistant, and the children's school teacher (who completed the Teacher Report Form [TRF; Achenbach, 1991c] a teacher oriented version of the CBCL). Results across all four informants in the second study directly replicated results from the first study (Friman, Schmidt, Miller, & Shanahan, 1995). Collectively, the results from both studies suggest living among the residents of the FHP is not a behavioral risk for birth children of family teachers. The results can also be interpreted as an indirect indication of the safe and therapeutic environment of the FHP (Daly & Dowd, 1992).

Program Outcomes

One of the most important concerns about residential care is its effect on the youth in care. In this section of the chapter I will describe a variety of program outcomes that include results from repeat administrations of the CBCL and DISC, measures of quality of life, educational achievements, and results from behavior analysis and treatment of a variety of special clinical problems.

CBCL. The CBCL outcome study involved all youth who were admitted to FHP after April 1, 1991 and who departed anytime during 1993 or 1994 (N = 258). In the study, we compared the admissions CBCL, completed by a parent or caretaker with the departure CBCL, completed by youth Family Teachers. Results indicated both boys and girls improved significantly. The mean scores for Internalizing

Disorders moved from the bottom of the clinical range at admission to the normal range at departure. The mean scores on Externalizing Disorders and Total Problems moved from the middle of the clinical range at admission to the bottom at departure. The size of the effect was a quarter of a standard deviation for boys and three quarters of a standard deviation for girls.

One possible criticism of the CBCL outcomes is that they reflect measurement variance and not behavioral change. That different caretakers complete the admission and departure CBCLs makes the criticism particularly salient. There are multiple other sources of information that are consistent with the CBCL outcomes, however, and I will describe some of them below.

DISC. As indicated above, FHP youth complete the DISC at admissions, six months, and one year. Inspection of their scores shows a sharp decline in number of diagnoses and positive symptoms from admissions to one year. Not only does the number of diagnoses reduce from an average of 2.5 per youth at admission to 0.5 at one year, a rate typical of a normal population, but also the discrepancy between boys and girls vanishes.

Of interest are which diagnoses respond most favorably to a 1-year stay. Not surprisingly, these appear to be the disorders of conduct. For example, the percentage of youth testing positive for Conduct Disorder reduces from 40% at admission to less than 5% at one year. Declines from admission to one year for other disorders of conduct include 19% to near 0% for Substance Dependence, 15% to 2% for Oppositional Defiant Disorder, and 10% to 4% for attention-deficit/hyperactivity disorder (ADHD). Some of the Internalizing Disorders also decline to less than 5%, including Major Depression and Dysthymia. The anxiety disorders are an exception. The percentage of youth that test positive does decline substantially, from 33% at admission to 13% at one year. But the 13% figure represents the most frequently occurring positive diagnosis at one year (Friman, Almquist et al., 1996).

Thus the DISC data suggest something of clinical interest about youth in residential care; they may be a highly anxious group. Their fears and worries do substantially decline after a year in the program but remain elevated compared to levels in a normal population. To a behavioral audience, however, this should not be a surprise. Anxiety is a disorder of avoidance and escape (cf., Friman, Hayes, & Wilson, 1998). Youth life before placement at the FHP is highly unpredictable and unpleasant. Under those conditions, avoidance and escape responding is much more likely to generate reinforcement than approach and pursuit. Thus, the pre-FHP environment may shape durable avoidant response patterns (and their emotional covariates) that typify anxiety disorders. And a year in the program is sufficient for reduction of these, but not for elimination.

Whether the change in scores represents actual behavior change or merely measurement variance is just as valid a concern with the DISC as it is with the CBCL. A recent study directly addresses this issue for three disruptive behavior disorders: Oppositional Defiant Disorder (ODD), Conduct Disorder (CD), and ADHD (Friman, Handwerk et al., 1999). Although findings were similar across all three diagnostic groupings, to save space I will discuss only ODD. The study involved four groups of youth (N=370) who had completed a DISC at admissions and at one year. Group one included youth testing positive for ODD at time-point 1 and not at time-point 2. Group two tested negative at time-point 1 and positive at time-point 2. Group three tested positive at times 1 and 2. Group 4 tested negative at times 1 and 2. The analysis used hierarchical linear modeling (HLM) which is fundamentally a regression of regressions using within- and between-subjects factors (cf., Friman, Osgood et al., 1996; Osgood & Smith, 1995). In this study, the within-subjects factor was group and the between-subjects factor was aggression tracked by the DIR. The results indicate a significant relationship between changes on the DISC and changes in aggression on the DIR. Youth with ODD at time-point 1 and not at time-point 2 had correspondingly high and low levels of aggression at times 1 and 2. Youth who did not have ODD at time-point 1 but did at time-point 2 had correspondingly low and high levels of aggression at times 1 and 2. Youth with ODD at both points had correspondingly high levels of aggression at both points and youth who did not have ODD at times 1 and 2 had correspondingly low levels of aggression at both time points. Collectively, the results represent the first study to provide external validation for the disruptive behavior scales on the DISC. More pertinent to this chapter is that declining DISC scores were accompanied by directly observed changes in youth behavior as indicated on the DIR. Thus, the changing scores appear to involve something other than measurement variance.

Quality of life. A major concern by critics of residential care involves the quality of life for youth in care. To address this issue the FHP conducted one of the largest longitudinal evaluations in the history of residential care. Briefly, the longitudinal study was a comparison of a treatment group of youths (N=497) who were residents in the program and a comparison group of youths (N=84) that were referred to and accepted into the program but did not attend. Both groups of youths were matched on a number of demographic variables. During the 8-year study, the youth in the comparison group received a variety of alternative services and are thus more accurately described as a treatment-as-usual group than a control group. The dependent measures in the study were obtained during interviews conducted with youth in both groups every three months for up to eight years. The study examined outcome in a number of different areas (some to be discussed subsequently) one of which was quality of life (cf., Daly et al., 1998; Friman, Daly, Handwerk, Smith, & Larzelere, 1997; Friman, Osgood et al., 1996; Osgood & Smith, 1995; Thompson et al., 1996)

Three often-cited quality-of-life variables that are reflective of problems in residential care are sense of isolation from family and friends, and relationship with supervising adults. A prevailing belief about residential care is that it produces an inexorable sense of isolation from family and friends and that relationships with supervising adults are adversarial, servile, or collusional. These beliefs have at least two sources. The first is in the logical conclusion that the all-encompassing nature of residential life and the presence of institutional barriers to outside contact can cause a sense of isolation. The second source is from case descriptions and first-hand accounts of life in residential settings that emphasize isolation and disconnection from family and friends and the emergence of manipulative and/or predatory behavior (Friman, 1996; Friman, Osgood et al., 1996; Chamberlain & Friman, 1997). The results from the FHP study contradict these prevailing beliefs. There was no difference between groups on any of these quality of life variables at time-point 1 but, at time-point 2, a significant decrease in sense of isolation and a significant improvement in relationships with supervising adults emerged and maintained throughout the study (Friman, Osgood et al.). The average length of stay was 22 months, yet the results maintained for up to 8 years (i.e., long after the youth left the study). Thus the study group learned effective ways to stay closer to friends, family, and authoritative adults while in the program and continued to employ them after they departed. Additionally, length-of-stay data showed that youth at all levels, ranging from 6 to more than 50 months, had significantly closer and better relationships than youth in the comparison group and that the longer youth remained in the program, the greater that difference was (Friman, Daly et al., 1997).

Extrinsic versus intrinsic motivation. A contemporary and influential criticism of behavioral residential care is that its reliance on external motivational systems (cf, point cards, token economies) undermines the intrinsic motivation or "self control" of youth in care (cf., Deci & Ryan, 1985; Kohn, 1993; Lepper & Greene, 1978; Levine & Fasnacht, 1974; VanderVen, 1995). Three FHP experimental outcomes counter this criticism. The first outcome involves the FHP longitudinal study that included assessments of sense-of-control. Both groups reported a gradually increasing sense of control with a significantly greater increase for the FHP group (Friman, Osgood et al., 1996). The second outcome also involves findings from the longitudinal study that showed significantly greater success on educational outcomes for the FHP group (Thompson et al., 1996). Fortifying this second outcome are the results showing that increased length of stay in the program increased the successes of the FHP youth on these educational tasks (Daly et al., 1998).

The third outcome is from a direct test of the FHP point system. The study was a multielement, within-subjects assessment of two FHP youth with variable scholastic interests (McGinnis, Friman & Carlyon, in press). Each was given a choice between three tasks, one of which was a series of math problems. Behavior during math activities was reinforced with the typical point award method used in FHP school programs with one exception; it was faded and subsequently withdrawn altogether. Multiple effects of the program and its withdrawal were ongoingly assessed. Results showed point awards substantially increased the amount and accuracy of math problems completed with greater increases for those youth with initially low interest. Some reductions followed withdrawal but performance remained above baseline levels for both youth. Following the study, regard for math also remained high for both youth.

Collectively, the three outcomes counter the popular theoretical position that external rewards produce artificial or ephemeral behavior change and excessive reliance on others for direction. Whether these outcomes are pertinent for youth not in residential care cannot be determined from available FHP research, but some generalizations can be made for youth that are. The motivation system may seem artificial when compared against the more "naturally occurring" systems in the lives of nonclinical youth at home in their intact families. However, for a fair test, the FHP system must be compared to the actual alternatives in the lives of troubled youth from fractured or nonexistent homes rather than an abstract ideal. An abundance of research shows relationships between troubled adolescents and their parents are often typified by unproductive, unpredictable, and unpleasant patterns of negative and coercive interactions (Patterson, 1982; Patterson, Reid, & Dishion, 1992). By comparison, FHP youth may have experienced the system of external rewards as clearer, more consistent, and as enhancing a sense of control over their lives and increasing their opportunities to noncoercively evoke positive responses from adults who care for them.

Birth children. Twenty-five children (12 boys, 13 girls, ages 4 to 17, $M = 8.8$ years) from the first birth-child study (Friman, Panther et al., 1993) were still living on campus during the second study (Friman, Schmidt et al., 1995) two years later. Thus a small measure of outcome was obtainable for these children through comparison of their CBCL scores at those two time points (Friman, Shanahan, Larzelere, & Daly, 1996). The first two studies indicated that birth children did not exhibit increased behavior problems at the time of their assessments by parents, teachers, and in-home assistants. Correlational analyses between length of time in the group home and scores on the CBCL for both studies were nonsignificant. The findings from the outcome study extend the earlier findings by showing that at time-point 2, scores trended lower on every scale and subscale of the CBCL except one, with a nearly significant reduction on Total Problems. Collectively, the three studies suggest birth children at FHP are not at risk for increased behavior problems. Results from the outcome study further suggest birth children's behavior may actually improve from extended stays in the program.

Educational Outcomes

Conventional outcomes. The importance of effective education for youth in residential care was emphasized in several early influential publications (e.g., Hobbs, 1982; Weinstein, 1974) and current critics of care argue its future is dependent on delivery of education (e.g., Eisikovits & Schwartz, 1991). Despite these emphatic messages and dire warnings, effects of care on the provision of education have been studied very little. To address this gap in the literature, the FHP longitudinal study included a cluster of conventional educational outcomes.

The results showed that the FHP youth accomplished significantly more on several educational variables than the youth in the matched-comparison group (Thompson et al., 1996). Although initially not different from the comparison group, at every measurement point during and following their placement, the treatment group reported significantly more help with homework, higher grades, more years of school completed, higher graduation rates, and more positive attitudes toward postsecondary education. Most importantly, the results show that the superior performance of the treatment group was mediated by length of stay (LOS). That is, the FHP group with the shortest LOS ($M = 6$ months or less) also had the lowest performance on the five variables and, conversely, the group with the longest LOS ($M = 50$ months or more) had the highest performance (Daly et al., 1998).

Reading. The FHP schools have incorporated a specialized reading program. The average youth entering the program is more than two years behind grade level in reading ability (Curtis & Longo, 1997). Employing the developmental framework for reading instruction developed at the Harvard Reading laboratory by Jeanne Chall (1996), the program routinely reverses the trend in reading failure exhibited by youth entering FHP. The average youth who takes all components of the reading program exhibits gains on individually administered tests of basic reading and vocabulary, indicating improvement from below fourth grade levels to the eighth-grade level and above within a 2-year instructional period.

Highly Disruptive Behavior and the Influence of Ratios

Youth-to-staff ratios. The influence of population density and staff allocation on program outcome has been studied very little, despite the increasing out-of-home population of youth and limited evidence of placement success. To address this issue, an exploratory study at the FHP assessed the influence of home population increases on the number of behavior problems exhibited by youth in the home. The dependent measure was the Parent Daily Report (PDR, Chamberlain & Reid, 1991), a 31-item checklist of child problem behavior. The family teachers in the study completed it daily, reflecting each youth's behavior problems for the previous 24 hours. The outcome of interest was the change in number of reported behavior problems occurring as a function of change in population density. The results indicated that increasing home population by one youth resulted in an average increase of one behavior problem per youth living in the home (Moore, Osgood, Larzelere, & Chamberlain, 1994). The results supported the common notion that lower youth-to-staff ratios result in better program outcomes.

To further test this assumption, we placed 23 of the most troublesome youth at FHP in Reduced-Ratio Homes (RRH), wherein the ratio of youth to staff was 4:1 instead of 8:1. All of the youth in the study were failing in the program and were at risk for program termination and referral to a more restrictive facility. The RRHs protected these youth's placements, resulting in an additional mean length of stay of 950 days with no increase in program restrictiveness. Additionally, placement in the RRHs increased the rate of program success to a level equivalent to that of average youth in regular homes (Friman, Toner, Soper, Sinclair, & Shanahan, 1996).

Negative-to-positive interactional ratios. Adult relationships (e.g., marriage) are strongly influenced by the ratio between positive (e.g., favors, affection) and negative exchanges (e.g., criticism, insults). In fact, a robust finding in marital interactional research is that when a positive exchange ratio of 5:1 is reached, regardless of interactional style and marriage type, marriages tend to be stable and successful (Gottman, 1994). We derived an intervention from the marital research and applied it to six of the most troublesome youth at the FHP. The dependent measure again involved the PDR. The intervention required family teachers to double the youths' daily ratio of point awards to point fines. Baseline ratios averaged

3:1 and intervention ratios averaged 8:1. Results indicated the increase in ratio was an effective means of decreasing problem behavior. Viewed from a multiple-baseline perspective, clear evidence of experimental control emerged in data from 3 of the 6 participants with a suggestion of control in a fourth. Viewed from a quantitative-analytic perspective, pooled time series indicated a mean reduction of one behavior problem per youth per day which was statistically significant (Friman, Jones, Smith, Daly, & Larzelere, 1997).

Within-Subject Outcomes for Special Problems

As I have shown, the FHP population is afflicted with a variety of behavioral and psychological problems. Most of these improve as a function of being in the program in general, although modifications can help (e.g., ratio reductions). Some specific clinical problems maintain despite the general beneficial effect of the program, however, and individualized treatments are required and provided. These specific problems present some of the best opportunities for behavior analysis and intervention in residential care. Below I will discuss several examples.

Social rejection. Early problems with social interactions can adversely affect subsequent social desirability, distance, and development. In turn, these social problems can adversely affect other aspects of child life including home, school, and recreation. The result is a psychologically unhealthy montage that can ultimately impel an out-of-home placement (cf., Dishion, Andrews, & Crosby, 1995; Dishion, Patterson, Stoolmiller, & Skinner, 1991; Parker & Ascher, 1987; Strain, Guralnick, & Walker, 1986). Without corrective action for youth that are placed, the social problems maintain or worsen (Gold & Osgood, 1992). Although no data on social rejection within residential placement are available, informal FHP staff observations and baseline data (e.g., time-point 1 from the FHP longitudinal study) suggest many placed youth have problems with social acceptance. A primary emphasis of the FHP is social skills and thus it is not surprising that social problems improve as a function of time in placement (Friman et al., 1996; Friman, Daly et al., 1998). Still, informal reports from FHP staff indicate approximately one youth per class in the FHP school programs and one per home in the main program is highly socially rejected, despite the extensive social skills training.

To address this problem we developed positive peer reporting (PPR), an intervention for improving the social interactions and acceptability of these highly rejected youth. PPR involves rewarding children for publicly reporting positive features of a rejected peer's behavior. In the initial study, PPR improved the classroom-based social interactions and social acceptance of a highly rejected 13-year-old girl (Ervin, Miller, & Friman, 1996). There have been three systematic replications. The first substantially improved the social interactions and acceptance of four rejected boys in the group home rather than the classroom (Bowers, 1997). The second showed that PPR not only dramatically improved positive social interactions, but it also decreased a variety of behavior problems in the group home setting (Bowers, McGinnis, Ervin & Friman, in press). The third improved social interaction and acceptance with three rejected youth and showed the effects occurred as a function of an increase in cooperative behavior by the rejected youth (Jones, Young, & Friman, 1999). Collectively these studies suggest PPR is an effective method for improving the social life of rejected youth in residential care.

In addition to their practical value, the results have some theoretical importance. For example, the potential prosocial influence of peer attention was established decades ago (e.g., Patterson & Anderson, 1964), but the research in recent years has emphasized its role in the development and maintenance of disruptive or antisocial behavior instead (e.g., Chamberlain & Friman, 1997; Dishion et al., 1991;1995; Patterson et al., 1992). The PPR research reverses this trend somewhat by showing peer approval, even when mediated by delinquent youth in residential care, can be a powerful prosocial influence. This general result suggests it is the contingencies of reinforcement that determine the direction of peer attention and not the kind of children who mediate it. Said slightly differently, structuring a social environment to reinforce positive peer influence by delinquent adolescents is not just possible in principle, but also in practice.

Diurnal enuresis. Enuresis is a common problem in children, and especially in clinical populations. The most typical cases are nocturnal, but diurnal enuresis is not rare. It is also important because of the adverse effect it can have on social relationships and physical health (Friman & Jones, 1998). Perhaps because of higher rates, most of the treatment literature is devoted to nocturnal enuresis. In a preliminary study, we evaluated the use of the most common nocturnal intervention, the urine alarm, for diurnal use. The 15-year-old girl participant agreed to this treatment providing it occurred only in her group home. After two positive alarm episodes, and the second with a very short duration, the enuresis ceased altogether (Friman & Vollmer, 1995). This case is one the few empirical evaluations of diurnal treatment and the only one using the alarm.

Anxiety disorders. As shown in the DISC analyses, FHP youth have a high level of anxiety problems (Friman, Almquist, et al., 1995; 1996) and occasionally they are so extreme, special clinical interventions are needed. For example, one 14-year-old youth was so fearful of insects, mere classmate taunts about their presence instigated extraordinary disruption (e.g., overturned desks, screams). A functional analysis led to an intervention focused on reinforcing completion of written problem solving with gradually increasing proximity to live insects. At the study's end, the youth could complete a high rate of math problems with live crickets on his desk. Additionally, his teacher witnessed him kill a spider with a tissue, place it in a waste receptacle, and return to his seat without a comment (Jones, Swearer, & Friman, 1999). Another example involves a 15-year-old boy who habitually bit himself so severely when tense or nervous his mouth would fill with blood. Treatment involved relaxation training and replacement activities such as gum chewing and tongue-lip tracing. Behavioral observations, blood samples, self-reports, and two medical evaluations all indicated complete resolution of the problem following treatment and complete healing of all damaged gum tissue (Jones, Swearer, & Friman, 1997).

A final example involved a 14-year-old old boy whose disruptive behavior was so severe that his referral involved more of a discharge summary than a request for treatment. A functional assessment revealed his disruptive conduct had an avoidance function, especially with adults. Prior to referral, it was assumed to have attention seeking and manipulative functions. An intervention based on the avoidance hypothesis (modified adult approach to conduct problems) eliminated the disruptive behavior (Friman & Lucas, 1996).

Synthesis and Behavior-Analytic Exegesis

The research summarized above was conducted in a behavioral residential program (FHP), but not all of it is behaviorally oriented research. Many of the assessments and analytic methods described are not typical of behavior analysis. The reasons for inclusion of such diverse research are largely political and economical. Although behavioral programs are typically designed using traditional behavioral methods, they cannot be fully evaluated with them. Evaluation of large programs requires some use of actuarial methods to determine how many youth improve over time in one program versus another. These evaluations are at least as important for program survival as those that determine whether behaviors of specific youth respond to specified contingencies. For example, in the study on interactional ratios (Friman, Jones, et al., 1997), the data from two of the six youth did not indicate behavioral control. However, data from the entire group indicated a mean reduction in behavior problems of one per youth per day. There are 560 youths in FHP. If the intervention were applied to the entire program and similar results were obtained, it could mean a reduction of 204,400 behavior problems (560 X 365 days) in one year. The value of experimental control notwithstanding, these quantified data would surely be more persuasive for administrators faced with the question of whether to adopt ratio-based program changes than data from the multiple-baseline designs.

This is not to say behavior-analytic methods are not useful – they are critical, and results from them were described several places in the manuscript (e.g., sections on social rejection, extrinsic motivation, interactional ratios, special problems). However, funding agencies, referral sources, accreditation boards, and oversight committees are as (probably more) interested in evaluations of large groups of youth than they are in highly controlled single-subject investigations. Additionally, these interested parties are often trained to understand the importance of evaluation findings only if they are derived from instruments with standardized scores loading on conventional mental health constructs (e.g., DSM-IV, developmental psychopathology). Quite simply, some of the contingencies that govern the health, vitality, and ultimate influence of a residential program often involve the use of non-behavioral methods.

For example, the Achievement Place Program produced hundreds of single-subject design studies, all indicating the positive influence of various aspects of its technology (e.g., Braukmann & Wolf, 1987; James et al., 1983). The program was generously supported by large and continuing grants from several agencies. Yet its funding was cut and its national influence diminished by a single (and not particularly well-conducted) program evaluation suggesting its strong within-program changes did not maintain at long-term follow-up (Jones, Weinrott, & Howard, 1981). The logic of the conclusion of the study will be critiqued below. But the overall effect of the study serves a larger point being made now. Behavior analysts can win many battles in residential care and still lose wars if they do not become knowledgeable in the methods of program evaluation. To adequately serve large behavioral residential programs for troubled adolescents in this country, researchers need to be ready, willing, and able to conduct studies that use language, methods, and analyses that are more consistent with mainstream psychology than with behavior analysis.

Having said all that, I will briefly reiterate what we have learned from the various evaluations summarized above. Youth come to FHP with many psychological problems as measured by conventional psychological methods (e.g., CBCL, DISC, SPS). Even if youth stay in the program for less than six months their problems improve and the longer they stay, the more improvement is seen. They are significantly more likely to obtain a formal education than matched youth in other programs and this likelihood is positively correlated with length of stay. A variety of special programs for problems ranging from reading deficiencies to simple phobias are remarkably effective. In sum, the evaluation results suggest that the FHP is a safe, therapeutic environment that reduces clinical problems, induces a sense of self-control, promotes family and peer relationships and fosters educational achievement for its resident youth.

The therapeutic elements in the special programs (e.g., reading, simple phobia) were reasonably well defined, but the elements of the FHP in general may not be as clear. The philosophy of the FHP is relatively simple; place youth with nonpreferred behaviors in an environment that is rigorously programmed to promote preferred alternatives. Implicit in the philosophy is that pre-placement problem behaviors occur as a function of contingencies resulting in reinforcement of the behaviors or punishment of their preferred alternatives. In other words, the puzzle of youth misbehavior resolves when their pre-placement environments are examined. Prior to placement, they emitted prosocial, conventionally adaptive behaviors, but these were not selected by prevailing contingencies. They also emitted antisocial, conventionally maladaptive behaviors, and these were selected instead.

When youth enter the FHP, however, the contingencies change. From day one, behaviors from their conventionally antisocial, unacceptable repertoires are targeted for nonpreferred consequences and even small approximations of prosocial behavior are richly reinforced. This process inexorably shapes larger and larger repertoires of preferred behavior during their stay and thus, from a behavioral perspective, it should not be surprising that the kinds of results described above are seen.

Please note that although this behavioral exegesis seems compellingly logical, it is not widely accepted. In fact a large group of childcare authorities seem convinced that the FHP cannot work. For example, authorities in the area of child motivation argue that gains produced by external motivation systems are artificial and that most of their results are harmful (Deci & Ryan, 1985; Kohn, 1993; Lepper & Greene, 1978; Levine & Fasnacht, 1974; VanderVen, 1995). Authorities on peer relations argue that placing deviant peers together only produces more deviant behavior and limits the possibility of prosocial development (Chamberlain & Friman, 1997; Dishion et al., 1991; 1995; Patterson et al., 1992). Authorities on out-of-home care argue that residential care inexorably creates an environment that selects adversarial, collusional, and generally manipulative behaviors in resident youth (Chamberlain & Friman; Friman, 1996; Friman, Osgood et al., 1996). Authorities on other kinds of residential care (e.g., positive peer culture) argue that failure to use youth as "therapists" and supervisors limits the possibility of youth success (Brendtro & Ness, 1983; see also, Gold & Osgood, 1992). Authorities on education argue that direct instruction, a hallmark of the FHP, produces weak, transitory learning and disrespect for the learning process (e.g., King & Goodman, 1994). Authorities on emotional development in residential settings argue that direct intervention is harmful (Bettleheim, 1974). There are many other examples. Obviously, given the breadth and influence of the many authorities doubtful about the possibility of benefit or concerned about the probability of harm, persuasion is difficult at best. I hope, however, that viewing a few of the FHP research results will persuade at least some to view behavioral residential care more favorably.

A troubling issue for residential care researchers is maintenance of effects (cf., Jones, et al., 1981). The FHP addresses this issue in part by including formal education as part of the program. Skills learned can be lost, but grades earned, school years passed, and graduation achieved cannot be taken away. Additionally, the FHP longitudinal study produced results indicating improvements in areas of functioning that lasted for the duration of the 8-year study (i.e., years after youth left the program; Daly, et al., 1998; Friman, Daly et al., 1997; Friman, Osgood et al., 1996; Thompson et al., 1996). But perhaps the question of maintenance itself should be examined from a behavioral perspective.

At first glance, the maintenance issue appears to be rooted in a medical orientation to residential care. That is, the youth have a mental illness - the job of care is to cure the illness - once cured, the youth go on to live relatively symptom-free lives outside of care. These kinds of effects are often expected for medicine. For example, patients with appendicitis are treated by having their appendix surgically removed and following recovery from surgery, they are never bothered by appendicitis again. Criticisms that the effects of residential care do not maintain after placement seem to be predicated on an expectation of similar outcomes. But is illness the best metaphor for the problems of youth in care? As indicated above, many assessments conducted in residential care employ the language of illness (e.g., DISC), but as also indicated, these are often used in response to political and economic contingencies. Although the assessments provide information on the nature of youth problems (albeit indirect at best) and can also aid treatment planning (e.g., Friman & Lucas, 1996), there is no compelling evidence to indicate they are measuring disease or illness. Attempts to define mental illness in nonbiological terms (e.g., Wakefield, 1992) have not recruited a consensus (e.g., Follette & Houts, 1996; Sarbin, 1997). The gold standard of psychiatric diagnosis remains a biological marker, and no sensitive and specific biological markers for the types of psychological problems by youth at FHP have been identified (cf., Friman et al., 1998; Hoes, 1986). Thus, there is no cogent basis for thinking of these youth's problems in terms of illness.

A behavioral conceptualization is that the problems of youth in residential care involve learned patterns and skill deficiencies and that serious delinquency may productively be thought of as a learning-based, handicapping condition requiring social prosthetics after program departure (e.g., Wolf, Braukmann, & Ramp, 1987). The notion that youth are either in a program or not in a program is artificial from a behavioral perspective. The behavioral view is that the environment programs behavior and, of course, youth are always in an environment. The distinction between structured program versus unstructured program may also be artificial. The program of the streets (e.g., gang entry, mobility, succession) may be just as structured as any residential program. One major difference, however, is in the types of contingencies both kinds of programs (street versus residential) employ. The reinforcers mediated by the street program will frequently be much more powerful (e.g., sex, drugs) than those mediated in residential care (e.g., points, after-school privileges, adult approval). Additionally, the punishers employed in the streets are much more severe (e.g., banishment, beatings) than those employed in care (e.g., point fines, level changes, loss of privileges). Also, the programs of the streets do not have the same sort of oversight committees (e.g., none) as residential programs (e.g., human rights review committees, certification boards, layers of supervision, etc.). Given the enormous power and limited restraint of street programs compared to residential programs, it should surprise no one that many youth, absent social prosthetics, would revert to preplacement behaviors.

Conclusion

Residential care is a fuzzy concept. Behavioralizing a component of it as family-style care was an important break with the institutionalized past and a step towards a healthier, safer, more therapeutic future. Although not all (perhaps not many) have converted to this view, research results such as those described above could aid the conversion process. Additionally, the population of out-of-home youth is large and growing in this country and so to is the need for placement alternatives. These alternatives should be safe and provide behavioral, psychological, and educational benefits for resident youth. The fundamental point of this chapter is not that all behavioral residential programs provide these benefits, but rather that it is possible to design programs that do. This task seems ideally suited for a new generation of applied behavior analysts.

Reading Objectives

1. Define behavioral family-style residential care.
2. Provide a brief description of the Teaching Family Model.
3. Describe the relationship between daily behavioral incidents and validation of suicide assessment.
4. Discuss the limitations of the Youth Self Report for evaluating youth entering residential care.

5. Discuss the relative risk of behavior problems for the birth children of married couples working in residential care.
6. Describe three important psychological outcomes of residential care determined by the evaluation research described in the chapter.
7. Describe three experimental outcomes that counter the popular theoretical position that using extrinsic rewards to motivate behavior is harmful.
8. Describe at least two educational outcomes from behavioral family-style residential care.
9. Describe at least one empirically demonstrated way youth-to-staff ratios influences youth behavior.
10. Describe at least one empirically demonstrated way negative to positive interactional ratios influences youth behavior.

I gratefully acknowledge Michael Handwerk and Robert Larzelere for assistance on preparation of this manuscript and the Carmel Hill Foundation for partial financial support.

References

Achenbach, T. M. (1991a). *Manual for the Child Behavior Checklist/4-18 and 1991 Profile*. Burlington, VT: University of Vermont Department of Psychiatry.

Achenbach, T. M. (1991b). *Manual for the Youth Self-Report and Profile*. Burlington, VT: University of Vermont Department of Psychiatry.

Achenbach, T. M. (1991c). *Manual for the Teacher Report Form and Profile*. Burlington, VT: University of Vermont Department of Psychiatry.

American Psychiatric Association (1994). *Diagnostic and statistical manual of mental disorders* (4th ed.). Washington, DC: Author.

Berman, A. L., & Jobes, D. A. (1990). *Adolescent suicide assessment and intervention*. Washington DC: American Psychological Association.

Bettleheim, B. (1974). *A home for the heart*. New York: Knopf.

Bowers, F. E., McGinnis, C., Ervin, R. A., & Friman, P. C. (in press). Merging research and practice: The example of positive peer reporting applied to social rejection. *Education and Treatment of Children*.

Bowers, F. E., (1997). *Improving the social interactions and acceptance of socially rejected adolescents in the residential group home setting*. Unpublished doctoral dissertation. University of Southern Mississippi, Hattiesburg.

Braukman, C., & Wolf, M. (1987). Behaviorally-based group homes for juvenile offenders. In E. K. Morris & C. J. Braukman (Eds.), *Behavioral approaches to crime and delinquency: A handbook of application, research, and concepts* (pp. 135-160). New York: Plenum.

Brendtro, L. K., & Ness, A. E. (1983). *Re-educating troubled youth*. Hawthorn, NY: Aldine.

Chall, J. S. (1996). *Stages of reading*. New York: Harcourt Brace.

Chamberlain, P., & Friman, P. C. (1997). Residential programs for antisocial children and adolescents. In D. M. Stoff, J. Breiling, & J. D. Maser (Eds.), *Handbook of antisocial behavior* (pp. 416-424). New York: John Wiley & Sons.

Chamberlain, P., & Reid, J. (1991). Parent observation and report of child symptoms. *Behavioral Assessment, 9,* 97-109.

Coughlin, D., & Shanahan, D. (1991). *Boys Town family home program: Training manual.* Boys Town, NE: Boys Town Press.

Cull, J. G., & Gill, W. S. (1988). *Suicide Probability Scale.* Los Angeles: Western Psychological Services.

Curtis, M. E., & Longo, A. M. (1997). Reversing reading failure in young adults. *Focus on Basics, 1,* 18-21.

Daly, D. L., & Dowd, T. P. (1992). Characteristics of effective, harm-free environments for children in out-of-home care. *Child Welfare, 71,* 487496.

Daly, D. L., Friman, P. C., Larzelere, R., Smith, W., Osgood, W., & Thompson, R. W. (1998). *Educating out-of-home adolescents: A longitudinal analysis of length of stay in residential care.* Manuscript submitted for publication.

Deci, E. L., & Ryan, R. M. (1985). *Intrinsic motivation and self-determination in human behavior.* New York: Plenum Press.

Dishion, T. J., Andrews, D. W.; & Crosby, L. (1995). Antisocial boys and their friends in early adolescence: Relationship characteristics, quality, and interactional process. *Child Development, 66,* 139-151.

Dishion, T. J., Patterson, G. R., Stoolmiller, M., & Skinner, M. L. (1991). Family, school, and behavioral antecedents to early adolescent involvement with antisocial peers. *Developmental Psychology, 27,* 172-180.

Eisikovits, Z., & Schwartz, I. M. (1991). The future of residential education and care. *Residential Treatment for Children and Youth, 8,* 5-19.

Ervin, R., Miller, P., & Friman, P. C. (1996). Feed the hungry bee: Using positive peer reports to improve the social interactions and acceptance of a socially rejected girl in residential placement. *Journal of Applied Behavior Analysis, 29,* 251-253.

Follette, W. C., & Houts, A. C. (1996). Models of scientific progress and the role of theory in taxonomy development: A case study of the DSM. *Journal of Consulting and Clinical Psychology, 64,* 1120-1132.

Friman, P. C. (1996). Let research inform our design for youth in residential care. *The Brown Child and Adolescent Behavior Letter, 12,* 1-3.

Friman, P. C., Almquist, J., Soper, S., & Lucas, C. P. (1995, November). *Using the computerized diagnostic interview schedule for children to assess adolescents entering residential care.* Paper presented at the Annual Convention of the Association for Advancement of Behavior Therapy, Washington, D.C.

Friman, P. C., Almquist, J., Soper, S., & Lucas, C. P. (1996, November). *Using the computerized diagnostic interview schedule for children (DISC) to assess the clinical effects of residential care.* Paper presented at the Annual Convention of the Association for Advancement of Behavior Therapy, New York.

Friman, P. C., Daly, D., Handwerk, M., Smith, G., & Larzelere, R. (1997). *Quality of life and length of stay in residential care: A longitudinal evaluation.* Manuscript in preparation.

Friman, P. C., Evans, J., Larzelere, Williams, G., & Daly, D. L. (1993). Correspondence between child dysfunction and program intensiveness: Evidence of a continuum of care across five child mental health programs. *The Journal of Community Psychology, 21,* 227-233.

Friman, P. C., Handwerk, M., Larzelere, R., Smith, G., Lucas, C., & Shaffer, D. (1999). *Do DISCIII disruptive behavior diagnoses predict aggression?* Manuscript submitted for publication

Friman, P. C., Hayes, S. C., & Wilson, K. G. (1998). Why behavior analysts should study emotion: The example of anxiety. *Journal of Applied Behavior Analysis, 31,* 137-156.

Friman, P. C., & Jones, K. M. (1998). Elimination disorders in children. In T. S. Watson, & F. M. Gresham (Eds.), *Handbook of child behavior therapy* (pp. 239-260). New York: Plenum.

Friman, P. C., Jones, M., Smith, G., Daly, D., & Larzelere, R. (1997). Decreasing disruptive behavior by adolescents in residential placement by increasing their positive to negative interactional ratios. *Behavior Modification, 21,* 470-486.

Friman, P. C., & Lucas, C. (1996). Social phobia obscured by disruptive behavior disorder: A case study. *Clinical Child Psychology and Psychiatry, 1,* 401-409.

Friman, P. C., Osgood, D. W., Shanahan, D., Thompson, R. W., Larzelere, R., & Daly, D. L. (1996). A longitudinal evaluation of prevalent negative beliefs about residential placement for troubled adolescents. *Journal of Abnormal Child Psychology, 24,* 299-324.

Friman, P. C., Panther, L., Larzelere, R., Shanahan, D., & Daly, D. L. (1993, November). *Assessing behavior problems in birth children of group home parents caring for disturbed adolescents.* Paper presented at the Annual Convention of the Association for Advancement of Behavior Therapy, Atlanta, GA.

Friman, P. C., Schmidt, D., Miller, P., & Shanahan, D. (1995, November). *Assessing behavior problems in birth children of group home parents of disturbed adolescents II: Results from four informants.* Paper presented at the Annual Convention of the Association for Advancement of Behavior Therapy, Washington, D.C.

Friman, P. C., Shanahan, D., Larzelere, R., & Daly, D. (1996, November). *Assessing behavior problems in birth children of group home parents for troubled adolescents III: Effects over time.* Paper presented at the Annual Convention of the Association for Advancement of Behavior Therapy, New York.

Friman, P. C., Toner, C., Soper, S., Sinclair, S., & Shanahan, D. (1996). Maintaining placement for troubled and disruptive adolescents in voluntary residential care: The role of reduced youth-to-staff ratio. *Journal of Child and Family Studies, 5,* 335-345.

Friman, P. C., & Vollmer, D. (1995). Successful use of the nocturnal urine alarm for diurnal enuresis. *Journal of Applied Behavior Analysis, 28,* 89-91.

Gold, M., & Osgood, D. W. (1992). *Personality and peer influence in juvenile corrections.* Westport, CT: Greenwood.

Gottman, J. (1994). *Why marriages succeed or fail.* New York: Simon & Schuster.

Handwerk, M. L., Friman, P. C., Mott, M. A., & Stairs, J. M. (1998). The relationship between program restrictiveness and youth behavior problems. *Journal of Emotional and Behavioral Disorders, 6,* 170-179.

Handwerk, M. L., Larzelere, R. E., Friman, P. C., & Mitchell, A. (1998). The relationship between lethality of attempted suicide and prior suicidal communications in a sample of residential youth. *Journal of Adolescence, 21,* 407-414.

Handwerk, M. L., Larzelere, R. E., Soper, S. H., & Friman, P. C. (1999). Parent and child discrepancies in reporting severity of problem behaviors in three out-of-home settings. *Psychological Assessment, 11,* 14-23.

Hobbs, N. (1982). *The troubled and troubling child.* San Francisco: Jossey-Bass.

Hoes, M. J. A. J. M. (1986). Biological markers in psychiatry. *Acta Psychiatrica Belgica, 86,* 220-241.

James, I. L., Maloney, D. M., Thompson, L., Watson, E. W., Brooks, L. E., Blase, K. A., & Collins, L. B. (1983). *Teaching family bibliography.* Boys Town, NE: Boys Town Press.

Jones, K. M., Swearer, S. M., & Friman, P. C. (1999). A case study of behavior assessment and treatment of insect phobia. *Journal of Applied Behavior Analysis, 32,* 95-98.

Jones, K. M., Swearer, S. M., & Friman, P. C. (1997). Relax and try this instead: Abbreviated habit-reversal for maladaptive oral self-biting. *Journal of Applied Behavior Analysis, 30,* 697-699.

Jones, K. M., Young, M. M., & Friman, P. C. (1999). Increasing peer praise of socially rejected delinquent youth: Effects on cooperation and acceptance. Manuscript submitted for publication.

Jones, R. R., Weinrott, M. R., & Howard, J. R. (1981). *The national evaluation of the teaching family model.* (Final Rep., Grants MH25631 & MH31018). Eugene, OR: Evaluation Research Group.

King, D. F., & Goodman, K. S. (1994). Whole language: Cherishing learners and their language. *Language, Speech, & Hearing Services in the Schools, 21,* 221-227.

Kohn, A. (1993). *Punished by rewards: The trouble with gold stars, incentive plans, A's, praise, and other bribes.* New York: Houghton Mifflin.

Larzelere, R. E. (1991). *Factor analysis of morning report data* (Residential Research Technical Rep. No. 91-3). Boys Town, NE: Father Flanagan's Boys Home.

Larzelere, R. E. (1996). *Intercoder reliabilities and construct groupings for important codes on the Daily Incident Report* (Residential Research Technical Rep. No. 96-1). Boys Town, NE: Father Flanagan's Boys Home.

Larzelere, R. E., Smith, G. L., Batenhorst, L. M., & Kelly, D. B. (1996). Predictive validity of the Suicide Probability Scale among adolescents in group home treatment. *Journal of American Academy of Child and Adolescent Psychiatry, 35,* 166-172.

Lepper, M. R., & Greene, D. (1978). *The hidden costs of reward.* Hillsdale, NJ: Lawrence Erlbaum.

Levine, F. M., & Fasnacht, G. (1974). Token rewards may lead to token learning. *American Psychologist, 29,* 817-820.

McGinnis, C., Friman, P. C., & Carlyon, W. (in press). The effect of token rewards on "intrinsic" motivation for doing math. *Journal of Applied Behavior Analysis.*

Moore, K. J., Osgood, D. W., Larzelere, R. E., & Chamberlain, P. (1994). Use of pooled time series in the study of naturally occurring clinical events and problem behavior in a foster care setting. *Journal of Consulting and Clinical Psychology, 62,* 718-728.

Osgood, D. W., & Smith, G. L. (1995). Applying hierarchical linear modeling to extended longitudinal evaluations. *Evaluation Review, 19,* 3-38.

Parker, J. G., & Asher, S. R. (1987). Peer relations and later personal adjustment: Are low-accepted children at risk? *Psychological Bulletin, 102,* 357-389.

Patterson, G. R. (1982). *Coercive family processes.* Eugene, OR: Castalia.

Patterson, G. R., & Anderson, D. (1964). Peers as social reinforcers. *Child Development, 35,* 961-960.

Patterson, G. R., Reid, J. B., & Dishion, T. J. (1992). *Antisocial boys.* Eugene, OR: Castalia.

Phillips, E. L., Phillips, E. A., Fixsen, D. L., & Wolf, M. M. (1974). *The teaching-family handbook.* Lawrence, KS: University of Kansas Press.

Sarbin, T. R. (1997). On the futility of psychiatric diagnostic manuals (DSMs) and the return of personal agency. *Applied and Preventive Psychology, 6,* 233-243.

Shaffer, D. (1996). Discussion of a predictive validity of the Suicide Probability Scale among adolescents in group home treatment. *Journal of American Academy of Child and Adolescent Psychiatry, 35,* 172-174.

Shaffer, D., Schwab-Stone, M., Fisher, P., Cohen, P., Piacentini, J., Davies, M., Conners, K., & Regier, D. (1993). The diagnostic interview schedule for children-revised version (DISC-R): I. Preparation, field testing, interrater reliability, and acceptability. *Journal of the American Academy of Child and Adolescent Psychiatry, 32,* 643-650.

Strain, P. S., Guralnick, M. J., & Walker, H. M. (1986). *Children's social behavior.* Orlando, FL: Academic Press.

Thompson, R. W., Smith, G. L., Osgood, D. W., Dowd, T. P., Friman, P. C., & Daly, D. (1996). Residential care: A study of short and long-term effects. *Children and Youth Services Review, 18,* 139-162.

Turk, K., Friman, P. C., Handwerk, M. L., Robinson, S., Hoff, K., & Gagnon, W. (1997). *Gender differences in youth in residential care.* Paper presented at the Association for Advancement of Behavior Therapy, Miami, FL.

VanderVen, K. (1995). "Point and level systems": Another way to fail children and youth. *Child and Youth Care Forum, 24,* 345-367.

Wakefield, J. C. (1992). The concept of mental disorder: On the boundary between biological facts and social values. *American Psychologist, 47,* 373-388.

Weinstein, L. (1974, December). *Evaluation of a program for re-educating disturbed children: A followup comparison with untreated children.* Washington, DC: HEW, Bureau for the Education of the Handicapped.

Wolf, M. M., Braukmann, C. J., & Ramp, K. A. (1987). Serious delinquent behavior as part of a significantly handicapping condition: Cures and supportive environments. *Journal of Applied Behavior Analysis, 20,* 347-359.

Wurtele, S. K., Wilson, D. D., & Prentice-Dunn, S. (1983). Characteristics of children in residential treatment programs. *Journal of Clinical Child Psychology, 12,* 137-144.

Chapter 9

Behavioral Contributions to Brain-Injury Rehabilitation

Harvey E. Jacobs
Cumberland, A Brown Schools Hospital
for Children and Adolescents

What is Acquired Brain Injury?

Acquired brain injury (ABI) is the leading cause of death and disability for people 45 years of age and younger. A brain injury occurs every 10 seconds in the United States and every four minutes, one person dies of their injury and another person becomes severely disabled for life. To place these statistics in another perspective, consider that every day two jetliners collide. All of the passengers in the first jet die while all of the passengers in the second jet become moderately to severely disabled for life. Treating these injuries costs this country over 80 billion dollars annually. Yet, this is only the tip of the iceberg when one considers the wages and productivity that are also lost to our society each year.

Contrary to popular assumption, brain injury is not an old-age disease. Most people who sustain traumatic brain injury are young at the time of their injury; an average of 22 years of age and just beginning their independent adult lives, careers, and families. A large proportion of people who sustain brain injury from strokes, tumors, and other non-traumatic sources are also relatively young and almost all who survive the initial medical consequences of their injuries have normal life-span expectations. However, due to long term impairments from their injuries, up to 200,000 people per year may now face decades, and in some cases up to a half century, of severe disability and dependency upon others.

For the purposes of this chapter, it is probably best to distinguish ABI, which may originate from traumatic and non-traumatic sources, from other forms of brain impairment that may occur such as genetic disorders (e.g., Huntington's Chorea), viral insults (e.g., Jacob-Cruzfeld disease), progressive dementias (e.g., Alzheimer's Disease, Pick's Disease), developmental disorders (e.g., Cerebral Palsy, Down's Syndrome), and birth-related trauma.

We can further classify ABI according to traumatic or non-traumatic etiologies. Traumatic brain injury (TBI) is defined as brain damage from a blow, or other externally inflicted trauma, to the head that results in significant impairment to the individual's physical, psychosocial, and/or cognitive functional abilities. It is characterized by altered consciousness (coma and/or post-traumatic amnesia) during the acute phase after injury, the duration of which varies greatly between individuals and with the severity of the injury (Corthell & Tooman, 1985). According to data from the Brain Injury Association (1995), TBI is most commonly the result of a car or motorcycle crash (50%), fall (21%), gunshot wound (12%), sports/recreation accident (10%), or other causes (7%).

Non-traumatic brain injuries involve non-degenerative and non-congenital events that result in brain damage. These include anoxia (loss of oxygen to the brain secondary to stroke, near drowning, partial suffocation, etc.), toxemia (brain damage secondary to poisoning from drugs or toxins), CVA (stroke), space-occupying bodies (e.g., tumors), encephalitis, viral and bacterial infections, and surgically induced damage, all of which can adversely affect cognitive, physical and social function.

Although it is commonly accepted that no two brain injuries are alike, the form and manner in which brain injury occurs can help to identify some of the challenges a person may be likely to face. Focal brain injuries such as stroke and gunshot wounds (from a small caliber bullet) usually involve relatively defined areas of the brain and may result in specific challenges, with sparing of functions attributed to other areas of the brain. For example, a person who experiences a stroke along their left motor cortex may exhibit right-sided paralysis, but retain other abilities. A single gunshot wound to the occipital lobes at the back of the brain may result in blindness. Similar outcomes may be noted for people who sustain local brain injury from tumors, surgeries, or other discrete localized damage.

Alternatively, diffuse brain injuries involve damage to many different parts of the brain. For example, in a TBI caused by an automobile crash, the driver's head may first strike the windshield causing damage to the frontal lobes of the brain. He/she may then strike the back or side of the head as he/she is thrown back against the seat, causing associated physical damage to the temporal, parietal, occipital lobes, and so on. In addition, the massive energy passing through the brain from the impact can cause it to shift and twist, increasing the areas of damage as a result of the violent shaking and reverberation that occurs.

Blood vessels and tissue within the brain may be torn apart by these combined forces, causing additional intracranial bleeds and tissue damage. The extra blood and trapped cerebral spinal fluid may increase the pressure within the cranial vault, especially in the case of a closed head injury, which can cause further damage by pressing soft brain tissue against the hard and uneven surfaces inside the skull. The increased intracranial pressure also makes it difficult for oxygen-rich arterial blood to circulate, thereby causing starvation to other cells.

The effect of a TBI can be much like placing a pumpkin in a box and rolling the box down a flight of stairs. Much like the pumpkin rattling around in the box and being bruised each time it hits a stair, the brain, which has the consistency of half-set Jell-O, is bounced about within the cranial vault of the skull, thereby distributing cellular damage. The result is a broader distribution of impairments involving discrete, as well as integrated abilities. Most frequently, the frontal and temporal lobes, areas ascribed to memory, judgment, self-control, speech, and analysis of non-verbal and spatial relationships are likely to be injured.

A person who experiences brain injury due to anoxia may also have diffuse injury since cells in many different areas of the brain become injured or die from oxygen starvation. Many such cases are notable for severe learning and memory dysfunction, in part because memory is regarded as a distributive process that involves many parts of the brain. In addition, the hippocampus, considered an important system in memory management, is highly sensitive to oxygen loss and one of the first areas to be affected. Similarly, different toxins may affect different parts of the brain in cases of toxemia.

The bottom line is that the brain is a complex organ that clearly regulates almost all aspects of an organism's life and behavior. It can be discretely and drastically affected by a wide range of insults that each may result in its own specialized effect on behavior.

Development of Brain-Injury Rehabilitation Services

Rehabilitation treatment following most forms of brain injury made few evolutionary advances until the 1970s. Until that time, many people did not survive the initial medical consequences of severe brain injury, and most brain-injury rehabilitation services focused on helping older people recover from strokes and other cerebral-vascular disorders. Patients were typically housed on a general rehabilitation ward and provided with basic training in self-care skills or were prepared for convalescent care. A then commonly accepted perception was that people with severe brain injury were not able to learn effectively and could become emotionally labile (i.e., overly emotional, easily agitated). The most frequent course of treatment at the time was to return surviving patients home, where most people became housebound, or place them in a nursing home if their care needs were too great for family members.

By the mid-1970s, however, advances in emergency medicine and neurosurgical techniques were helping more people survive the initial consequences of their injuries. People also began to recognize that this new group of patients failed to fit in with other patients with disability due to brain injury. First, these new patients were generally younger than most other survivors were. Whereas common treatment convention for older survivors of stroke may have been to help them comfortably live out the rest of their years, most people with traumatic brain injury were just beginning their adult lives. Young, typically single, having recently left home, this group rarely had the resources or extended family that most people rely on when they retire. In addition, people in this group did not want to retire. Their lives were just beginning. Second, family members often reported significant changes in the abilities, emotions, and behaviors of survivors when they returned home. Spouses sometimes reported that the returning spouse looked the same as before the injury, but acted differently, sometimes in subtle or not so subtle ways. Increases in emotional lability, especially as it related to issues of frustration, depression, withdrawal, hypo- or hyper-sexuality, stamina, judgment, reasoning problem solv-ing, and other abilities were frequently noted. Existing rehabilitative services were simply not adept in addressing these challenges. Third, the widely held assumptions regarding inability to learn following brain injury were quickly shattering. Research by Ben-Yishay and colleagues (e.g., Ben-Yishay, Diller, Gerstman, & Gordon, 1970) clearly demonstrated that people continued to learn, both instrumentally and verbally after injury, albeit sometimes in different ways. Finally, health insurance companies who had historically paid for medical treatment and rehabilitation began to recognize the unique needs and newly developing services for this population.

Thus, with increased recognition, promising treatments, and identified sources of funding, specialized brain-injury rehabilitation units began to develop, first on inpatient hospital units and then in outpatient, nursing home, and community venues. Unlike more traditional rehabilitation units, these specialized services focused on the particular needs of this younger population. Therapies were integrated from individual disciplines (e.g., speech, occupational therapy, physical therapy, psychology, nursing, medicine) into inter- and trans-disciplinary teams. Hence, rather than providing a patient with three individual hours of therapy with goals determined by three individual therapists, the focus of treatment shifted to using the combined knowledge of each professional as a team to help address the integrated challenges of life and learning following brain injury.

Family members also became more involved with many phases of treatment and training to help them adapt to new roles as both caretakers and facilitators. New challenges were quickly recognized as the chronological order of adult care taking was reversed. Rather than the adult child taking care of aged parents, aged parents were once again taking care of their now adult offspring, especially when this person was unmarried or did not have a family with which to return. This quickly fostered concerns about what would happen once the parents died or required later-life care taking of their own.

Programs developed quickly. Whereas there were less than six recognized brain injury rehabilitation centers operating in the United States in the late 1970s, over 500 programs were in operation by the late 1980s (National Head Injury Foundation, 1988). Continuum-of-care services were rapidly established to address a wide range of presenting challenges. Emergency evacuation and neuro-trauma services more effectively replaced emergency rooms to better respond to critical treatment issues in the first hours following brain injury. Inpatient rehabilitation services helped people establish basic self-care skills and return home. A cadre of comprehensive outpatient programs assisted with issues of independent living and community integration. Vocational rehabilitation services began to help capable people attain compensated employment. Residential and transitional living programs supported those who were unable to return to their pre-injury living settings. Specialized neurobehavioral programming was established to help individuals address severe behavior dysfunction. Family and caregiver support groups flourished nationwide through the National Head Injury Foundation and subsequent Brain Injury Association. Other services were developed for various other medical and restorative issues that individuals faced.

Since most services were reimbursed through health insurance policies, it was natural for most programming to develop inside hospitals and other medical service-delivery systems. In many situations, these funding sources were either willing or obligated to provide reimbursement, as long as a service could be defined as medically necessary or of medical origin. However, many medically based programs were expensive, in part because of the cultures and operational requirements of such systems. Hospitals rarely took advantage of available community resources, choosing to create their own systems and use their own staff. This approach was often more expensive and less effective than other available options. However, financial contingencies actually supported the process. In addition, most models were predicated (or at least marketed) on the concept of neurological cure and restoration, rather than developing supports for long-term impairments, even though the medical technology to appropriate such outcomes was not (and is still not) available. This emphasis was partially based on the cultural orientation of hospital systems - that they cure people – and, in part, by the fact that a funding source would be willing to pay for expensive services over a short-term period if it eliminated the "problem" and ended their obligation for future payments and services. On the other hand, funding sources were reluctant to pay for a service, no matter how inexpensive it might be, if there was no predictable end in sight.

However, people were not "cured" of their brain injuries, and services became increasingly expensive. Not all programs were able to document the efficacy of their services, and in some cases, there were concerns of insurance fraud. Without consistent and documented outcomes, funding sources also began to question to previously supported medically based services and denied payment. With the advent of managed care, fewer services were being paid for, and many programs began to close.

Unfortunately, time has marched backwards, and today most people who require services following brain injury have only limited options. Those requiring inpatient hospitalization may experience only very short stays and be discharged when they are no longer at risk of dying, rather than when they are able to develop sufficient skills to be independent within a less restrictive setting. Subsequent outpatient services have also become very time limited, sometimes 30 days or less, with services once again being provided by individual therapists without the benefit of team process that was shown to be so crucial in the 1980s.

Funding philosophies have also dramatically changed. Defined benefits now represent the maximum services available rather than financial guidelines to be considered along with each individual's clinical process when determining length of treatment. Many people are not even able to get the maximum benefits of their insurance contract, and return to their homes and families with incomplete results and negligible opportunities. People with mild and moderate brain injury often receive no services at all, although the effects of their impairments may be equally debilitating. New models and approaches to address the challenges of disability following brain injury are needed. This is an exceptionally fertile area for behavior analysts.

So, What Is a Behavior Analyst to Do?

Behavior analysis may be able to address a number of the challenges and questions that people who experience disability following brain injury face. Our field has long focused on functional outcomes, operational definitions, practical implementation strategies, empirical clinical management, consumer-directed programming, and use of the natural environment, especially as it relates to community and home-based intervention. In addition, behavior analysis has a unique understanding and perspective of environmental-organism relationships. At the same time, many training programs for behavior analysts tend to minimize or discount training in the neurosciences. Part of this may be based on an earlier period of the field's development when behavior analysts were working to establish their own identity and distinguish their particular brand science from more *mentalistic* concepts. The quote cited by Skinner (1957) in his book *Verbal Behavior* ("What is mind? Never matter. What is Matter? Never mind.") is illustrative of this concern, but fails to distinguish between mentalistic and neurological constructs of behavior. Mind and brain remain synonymous for too many behavior analysts. They are not, and substantial advancements have occurred in the neurosciences over the past 40 years, especially in areas of imaging and understanding some of the cellular organization of the brain. Although some neuroscience disciplines tend to over-promote the role of the brain in learning and behavior, it is important to recognize the delicate balance between organism and environment in order to develop effective services.

For behavior analysts, this means understanding some of the neurological correlates to behavior and learning. Again, this does not require one to accept a mentalistic orientation of behavior, but only to acknowledge that what is between the ears is no longer simply a "black box". New technologies developed over the past 30 years can help us empirically image and evaluate selected aspects of neurologic function. Such technologies allow us to expand our functional investigation of the world and develop more innovative and precise intervention strategies that involve both the environment and the organism.

Perhaps the most important issue for a behavior analyst to understand is how dramatically brain injury can change the manner in which a person interacts with his or her daily world. Damage to different parts of the brain can directly affect the manner in which a person hears, sees, feels, tastes, and otherwise senses his or her world. It is not unusual for people to have changes in body temperature regulation, level of fatigue, balance, coordination, or other conditions that most of us take for granted. Hence, the ability to analyze information (stimuli) and solve problems can be dramatically compromised.

Changes in learning can occur from many factors, including a reduction in the ability to remember, decreased ability to attend to task, problems recognizing words or objects, inability to carry out instructions, difficulties solving problems and reasoning, and a host of other challenges. Some people experience global language difficulties, either understanding the vocal or written language of others (receptive aphasia) or in producing their own language (expressive aphasia). There is also a wide range of discrete language impairments that can have devastating effects. To even begin to understand how all of these changes can so drastically affect daily life and behavior, just imagine the last time you felt "under the weather," and how it affected your ability to perform your daily activities. Now, multiply that deficit by a factor of 1,000 and extend it over the rest of your life. You can now begin to understand how changes in such processes can easily affect a person's life following brain injury.

Challenges in social behavior may include increased impulsivity or lethargy, decreased frustration tolerance, depression, anxiety, social obtuseness, poor awareness of one's surroundings, agitation, and other socially admonished repertoires (Jacobs, 1987; 1988). Some of these challenges may be caused by direct neurologic impairment to the frontal or temporal lobes of the brain. It is not surprising to hear family members complain that a once-mature adult is again acting like an adolescent. The frontal lobes, which help mediate self-monitoring, are one of the last areas of the brain to develop; something that is evident to anybody who has ever had a teenager. Other challenges may occur as a reaction to treatment services (environmental iatrogenics) and still others due to changes in social roles and functions. Most frequently, however, it is the interaction of all of these different factors that produce the noted change.

Perhaps the most salient question to consider when developing rehabilitation programming for people who experience disability following brain injury is as follows: *What are the mechanisms of perception and learning after injury (compared to before injury) and how can these be optimized?* Behavior analysis is uniquely positioned to understand the critical interface between the organism and environment and to help people adjust and adapt to very different lives following brain injury. To help put this in perspective, consider what it would be like to move to a foreign country where many of the things you naturally do have different meanings. In addition, you cannot understand other people because they are speaking a foreign language. In many cases, people with brain injury have to re-learn old skills, but in new ways because of changes in the manner that they perceive, learn, remember, and interact with their daily world. Since science and medicine offer few breakthroughs that can directly repair a damaged brain, we must rely on helping people learn new strategies to meet the demands of daily living, or teach them (or others who may care for people with severe disabilities) how to manipulate the environment to provide the necessary supports to assure the greatest possible success within each person's abilities and available resources.

A second important area of contribution by behavior analysts may involve team building and service-system development. Since the early days of our field, we have sought to work with consumers, preferably in their own natural environments and with other people who may be appropriate facilitators. This requires the ability to understand the orientation and focus of other people and combine diverse talents and contributions towards unified goals. Supplementary and consistent with this task is the ability to objectively define goals and outcomes, the means to evaluate progress toward such goals, and the ability to operationalize a course of action. Too few rehabilitation programs have the ability to functionally evaluate outcomes and overall course of treatment.

A third critical area for contribution is in helping people de-phenomenalize the concept of behavior or attribute it only to actions that are not desired by others. Too often, rehabilitation settings only consider behavior as a salient force when the client is not complying with a therapist's request, is agitated, is having difficulty with the task, or is making life difficult for others. In a similar vein, behavior is often regarded as its own entity rather than an instantaneous product of interaction of a person with his or her environment. Consequently, similar to other settings in which behavior analysts first worked, initial requests for assistance by others usually first focus on reducing problematic behavior. There is a further expectation that such service can be rendered immediately, and there is minimal recognition that successful intervention needs to focus on positive skill development, continual support or training, and maintenance of effect.

While behavior analysts have much to offer the field and individuals that experience disability following brain injury, there are also several areas of caution that are intrinsic to our field. The first is the topic of dubious disciplinary distinctions. Many other professionals in brain-injury rehabilitation have been trained under other theoretical models and may not appreciate or be fully aware of the scope and orientation of behavior analysis. Therefore, "in fighting" can sometimes occur when people do not understand the principles or focus of behavior analysis. Addressing this issue takes patience, understanding, and excellent teaching skills.

Second, few training programs in behavior analysis offer students formal practica in brain-injury rehabilitation. Most behavior-analytic practica involve educational settings or programs serving people with developmental disabilities. It should come as no surprise that the principles of behavior that so adroitly operate in such settings also operate in settings serving people that experience disability following brain injury. However, programming structure and emphasis can be very different for people with different origins of impairment. Many people with disability following brain injury have unique patterns of learning with notable strengths and weaknesses. Successful programming involves careful assessment of these patterns and optimizing intervention accordingly. Too many behavior analysts also make the mistake of emphasizing consequences over antecedents when developing programs for this population. The vast majority of presenting challenges involves difficulties with information processing compared to lack of motivation. Without careful assessment, however, it is too easy to assume that a person *will not*, rather than, *cannot* do something due to a lack of salient discriminative stimuli to guide their behavior.

In addition, most people who develop disability following brain injury lived *normal lives* prior to their injury. Hence, many people have complex experiences and behavioral repertoires that they may not now be able to successfully access, along with expectations of what they still cannot do. It becomes extremely frustrating for a person to be unable to accomplish what he or she once took for granted. Consequently, it often takes substantial time, effort, patience, and experience to sort out one's abilities from one's challenges and accommodate to new ways of living.

Consider how you would feel if, because of a significant memory impairment, you could no longer remember when you had eaten your last meal or what you were supposed to do next.

Key Behavioral Contributions to Brain-Injury Rehabilitation

There are clearly many areas in which behavioral technologies can be of significant benefit to people who experience disability following brain injury. One very challenging area relates to our field's distinction between verbal and nonverbal behavior. Verbal mediation is our culture's preferred means of teaching and disseminating information. However, many people develop deficiencies in these abilities following brain injury. Whereas most other disciplines equate verbal mediation with vocal-verbal behavior, behavior analysis uniquely recognizes a broader definition of verbal behavior, as behavior that is reinforced by the mediation of the listener (Skinner, 1957). This allows consideration of a number of non-vocal verbal communication strategies. Hence, people who fail vocal-verbal training in traditional rehabilitation treatment may be successful with other forms of verbal skills training. Additionally, Skinner's taxonomy of verbal behavior allows consideration of training specific components of verbal behavior such as mands, tacts, echoics, intraverbals, and other discrete categories when broader spectrum training is not possible.

There is also a wide range of other instrumental training techniques that may be of benefit to verbally challenged individuals. For example, Jacobs, Lynch, Cornick, and Slifer (1986) modified a systematic desensitization procedure (see Wolpe, 1969) for an adolescent who was globally aphasic and could not understand the vocal-verbal instructions that are usually used to help the client relax and proceed through the stimulus hierarchy of this procedure. Although the client was unable to follow vocal-verbal instructions, he appeared to be relaxed in the presence of a television. As a result, the television was used to help the client relax in each step of the stimulus hierarchy that was successively presented. Each time the client became anxious, the previous step of the hierarchy was reintroduced in the presence of the television until he became calm and the procedure could continue. The technique allowed the client to master several hospital settings that were critical to his treatment.

Slifer et al. (1996) demonstrated how different procedures had unique effects relative to a client's level of post-traumatic amnesia. Children who were conscious, but still demonstrating significant amnesia, responded poorly to vocal-verbal direction and responded well to contingency management techniques and differential reinforcement of other behavior (DRO). Once their amnesia cleared, vocal-verbal language instruction proved superior to these basic operant procedures.

Other behavioral principles can also be highly effective in helping people who experience disability following brain injury. For example, Zencius, Wesolowski, Burke, and Hough (1990) demonstrated how a variety of simple, common, and most importantly, client-relevant antecedents (e.g., instructions, maps, strategically placed signs) significantly reduced noncompliance in a very short period of time in clients who exhibited aberrant behavior.

Helping people break down complex tasks through well-operationalized task analyses can also be highly effective. Too often, instructions designed to help people master such tasks are based on assumptions of usability by the therapist rather than actual effect for the client. For example, O'Reilly, Green, and Braunling-McMorrow (1990) modified in-home checklists to promote home accident prevention. Existing checklists already identified potential home hazards, but did not specify what clients were to do in each situation. Consequently, the clients were at risk of losing their opportunity to live in their own apartments. Each client's accident prevention skills were first assessed. Task analyses of requisite skills were then developed and incorporated into their checklist. Training was then provided, as necessary, to assure skill proficiency, and checklists were modified until they had their desired effect. Subsequent analysis revealed that the revised checklists alone were sufficient to sustain home safety intervention skills by the end of training and in the subsequent follow-up evaluation.

Giles and colleagues (Giles & Clark-Wilsho, 1988; Giles & Shore, 1989) taught severely impaired individuals who had been chronically dependent on others for morning care activities such as washing and dressing. Interventions were adapted to each client's morning routine and involved breaking complex tasks down into simple elements, establishing chains of behavior, teaching clients to follow the skill sequences, and reinforcement for completing steps of the task.

Task analyses are also highly effective in helping clients sustain motivation through goal-setting procedures. Jacobs, et al (1996) documented how an individual who was having trouble developing standing tolerance, a key requirement for ambulation training, was able to succeed when he and his therapist worked together to establish the intermittent steps required to achieve this goal. In a separate setting, the authors involved a highly amnesic patient in the design of a training hierarchy to help her re-establish swallowing. The client had not been previously involved in programming because of assumptions that her amnesia would frustrate her partici-pation. Client involvement in both program design and ongoing review of data helped to further improve the overall efficacy of each intervention.

Contingency management techniques can be very effective when properly implemented. However, too often program designers either assume that the problem is one of ineffective consequences for behavior, or fail to conduct a functional analysis of the situation before intervention. For example, Haley (1983) reported the case of a woman in a nursing home who frequently got into arguments with staff and was considered an "agitated patient." In order to induce her compliance, the staff were using access to cigarettes as a reinforcer. A careful analysis of the situation (principally by talking to the woman) revealed that this plan was having the opposite effect. She clearly stated that she did not trust the staff because she felt that they were stealing her cigarettes. By sitting down with both the client and staff, it was possible to unambiguously define the situation for all parties and resolve the situation. In fact, within one week the woman had made such substantial progress that she was transferred to a rehabilitation program and eventually home.

Silver, Boake, and Cavazos (1994) added a monetary reinforcement system to the daily self-care regimen of a 12-year-old child with anoxic brain injury to reduce the level of staff assistance required in daily dressing, toileting, and undressing. The steps in the child's daily protocol had already been established through a careful task analysis. Intervention consisted of paying the client a penny for each step she successfully completed. Pennies were empirically selected as a potential reinforcer because of their observed effect in previous situations and not because of assumed value. Treatment gains were maintained at the client's home at six-month follow-up.

A highly favored technique in cognitive rehabilitation is errorless learning (Glisky, Schacter, & Tulving, 1986; Wilson, Baddley, & Cockburn, 1989), which has its roots in the experimental analysis of behavior from the work of Terrace (1966). Much like Terrace' s early work in errorless discrimination, these procedures begin at the basal level of the individual and gradually guide development of the skill through a series of successive and successful approximations and stimulus fading. Perhaps one of the most critical issues in rehabilitation involves the maintenance and generalization of treatment effect. Too often, rehabilitation techniques that demonstrate promise within a facility fail to generalize to or maintain in a client's natural environment. This is especially critical when working with people with severe behavior dysfunction, as lack of enduring effect may result in their unnecessary long-term placement in residential programming or other incarceration. Unfortunately, few such studies have reported enduring generalization or maintenance effects. Godfrey and Knight (1988) used functional skills training to assist a 33-year-old male who had failed to return to the community following an intensive memory-training program. That program helped improve the client's concentration and reduce his aggression in group therapy sessions, but not on his home unit. Skills training first focused on self-medication and participating in a community-based sheltered workshop. Skills were dissected via task analyses and sequentially trained through verbal prompting and social reinforcement. These supports were faded as skills improved. The client was subsequently taught to live in a community-based lodge and use public transportation. Twelve-month follow-up indicated stable community placement.

Silver and Stelly-Seitz (1992) addressed adipsia in a child with a hypothalamic injury following a gunshot wound. The child's refusal to drink, despite encouragement by his mother and hospital staff, resulted in a gastrostomy-tube placement. A multi-component program was established in which intervention occurred in an isolated area to reduce distraction. Social approval and preferred foods were first provided during each meal following any sip of liquid, and social interaction was removed for 30 seconds each time the child refused the liquid. Shaping procedures also made access to preferred food contingent on progressively larger sips of water. Once preliminary effects were established by one staff member, other staff and the child's mother were also trained in the technique. Intervention continued for 17 days as oral consumption of liquid increased to the point at which there was no clinical evidence of dehydration. Ten days later, the gastrostomy tube was removed and the child returned home. His mother reported that normal patterns of drinking gradually returned and were sustained over time.

Single-subject evaluation designs, a staple of behavior analysis, can be important tools in rehabilitation programming (Jacobs, 1993). It is widely recognized that no two brain injuries are alike, and a treatment procedure that may work for one person may be ineffective for another. Hence, careful assessment and empirical documentation of effects should be standard protocols during treatment, but often are not. At a minimum, A-B designs should be used to help assess if ongoing intervention is better than preceding conditions. However, many therapists feel that they do not have enough time to conduct such evaluations. Furthermore, it is often difficult to establish a stable baseline before implementing intervention because of the continually decreasing number of sessions most funding sources will allow for treatment. Still, there is good evidence that such rigor ultimately makes treatment more cost-effective, rather than expensive.

For example, Pace and Colbert (1996) documented how the use of single-subject methodology helped to manage the cost of treatment. Specific treatment goals that were required for the client to complete multidisciplinary home-based rehabilitation and live at home were first established between the client, staff, the treatment team, and the insurance company before intervention was initiated. Individual therapists then assumed particular goals for their treatment, followed prescribed protocols, and recorded each session's progress using objective data that were reviewed by a case coordinator. This allowed procedures to be modified as needed during the course of treatment and made continuous information on treatment progress available to all parties. The tenure of individual therapies was also determined by client progress and terminated when prescribed goals were attained. As a result, over the course of in-home treatment, therapy costs were reduced from over $1,700 per week at the start of treatment to $550 per week during the last week of treatment.

Zencius, Wesolowski, Burke, and McQuade (1989) used an additive design to evaluate which of several different techniques was most effective to encourage a client to use her prosthetic device. Staff originally thought that social attention was the primary motivating factor for the client to use the device, but, they actually learned that simple placement of the equipment in the client's path as she left her room each morning was sufficient to facilitate its use. Using a multi-element design, Jacobs et al. (1996) determined that the popular procedure of placing headphones on a client with his favorite music was actually ineffective in managing his shouting. The authors found that an alternative (and more appropriate) technique of engaging him with staff was subsequently developed.

Turner, Greene, and Braunling-McMorrow (1990) helped reduce the dysfunctional social behaviors of a client using a changing-criterion design and token reinforcement. Initial periods free of dysfunctional social behaviors were relatively short in order to give the client a chance to succeed in the task. Over a 15-week period, criterion intervals were gradually lengthened until the behavior was no longer considered a problem.

A variety of techniques has been reported to help clients improve social skills in home, group, and community settings. In some cases, the use of consequences to reduce aberrant behavior has been sufficient. Burke and Lewis (1986) implemented a point system for a 21-year-old male with anoxic injury who was noted to shout, interrupt others, and engage in nonsensical talk. Points, which could be exchanged for a variety of reinforcers, were awarded for the absence of such behaviors during mealtimes. Results indicated a substantial reduction in all three behaviors, both in the residential treatment dining room, as well as in community restaurants, even after treatment had been terminated. Unfortunately, the authors did not indicate what pro-social behaviors replaced the behaviors that were reduced by this procedure.

Gajar, Schloss, Schloss, and Thompson (1984) used feedback to teach on-topic conversational skills to young adults with head injury. The authors evaluated effects according to norm-referenced criteria, another demonstration of the importance of the consumer and their community when determining effect. Notable speaking-skill deficits by participants included confabulation (making up tales about events that may or may not have happened), perseverative responding (excessive repetition of the same response), inability to stay on topic, excessive self-disclosures, interruptions, and inappropriate laughter. Baseline assessment, compared to other adults of their age and without injury, revealed that the two participants were at least one standard deviation below their peers in responding appropriately to conversational topics. The clients were first asked to talk about selected topics while observers in another room flashed a green light when their conversation was on topic, and a red light when their conversation was off topic. In a subsequent self-monitoring condition, each participant was trained to flash either the green or red light based on the appropriateness or inappropriateness of their conversation. Conversational skills improved to peer-equivalent levels during the therapist feedback intervention and during the self-monitoring condition, but deteriorated below referential skill levels when baseline conditions were reinstated. Skills improved with the re-implementation of treatment. These same procedures were subsequently used to teach heterosexual conversational skills to head-injured youth (Schloss, Thompson, Gajar, & Schloss, 1985).

Foxx and colleagues (Foxx, Marchand-Martella, Martella, & Braunling-McMorrow, 1988; Foxx, Martella, & Marchand-Martella, 1989) used a composite program to teach community problem-solving skills. Four general community areas were targeted: (a) community awareness and transportation, (b) medication, alcohol, and drugs, (c) stating one's rights, and (d) emergencies, injuries, and safety. The trainer first modeled effective skills in selected community situations and then presented a cue card that listed criterion components for solving problems. Participants were then required to use these criteria to formulate their own solutions, with the trainer subsequently providing feedback, prompting, and coaching to each participant through each problem-solving component. Later, the criterion cue cards were dropped from training and participants were required to formulate their solutions. In both studies, participants quickly responded to training and demonstrated between 55% and 200% improvement in post-test generalization probes over baseline scores. A contrast group that participated in pre- and post-test assessments, but not training, failed to demonstrate any improvement over a similar period.

Many successful interventions have utilized combinations of procedures. Lane, Wesolowski, and Burke (1989) combined stimulus control, a token economy, and brief time-out to reduce trash hoarding. Previous interventions including counseling, fines, a different token economy system, differential reinforcement of incompatible behavior (DRI), overcorrection, and time-out had all been ineffective. The revised program was conducted in two phases. First, the client was given baseball cards throughout the day when he did not hoard trash in his clothing. Within a week, the cards were established as conditioned reinforcers that could also be exchanged for hats, posters, and other items. Next, the authors established stimulus conditions for picking up trash, namely when wearing an apron and gloves and while cleaning up in the dining room after meals. The client earned baseball cards when he collected trash at these times and disposed of it properly. He was verbally reprimanded when he was seen picking up trash at other times and then escorted away from the area for a brief time-out of 10 to 15 seconds. Trash hoarding was eliminated within 15 days and the effect was sustained one year later.

Burke and Wesolowski (1988) used a multi-component program to reduce memory failure, increase work-site attendance, and reduce the assaultive behavior of a male client. A careful analysis of the situation indicated that these behaviors were inter-related. Failure to remember a task was usually followed by increased staff attention and prompting, both of which can be powerful social reinforcers. The client sometimes became disoriented and disruptive once off task, which resulted in containment by male staff. This usually escalated the client's agitation to levels of personal and property destruction, with subsequent removal from treatment. Ultimately, the client would miss work and receive significant attention by female nursing staff who would attend his wounds. To address these issues, the client's environment was rearranged with cues and mnemonic devices that he could effectively use to participate in daily tasks. A token economy was established to promote attendance and work participation, and he was taught relaxation techniques to use when he started to become tense. Finally, time to interact with female staff was made available each day he participated in his program. Within two months, disruptive episodes ceased, the client consistently used his memory aids, and he was participating regularly at work.

The multiple sources that can effect aggressive behavior in this population have been noted in a number of studies. Feeney and Ylvisaker (1995) focused on consumer involvement and antecedent intervention to help aggressive high school students become more successful in class. The program included concrete-task organizers to help each student compensate for cognitive impairments, daily routines to compensate for problems of behavioral self-regulation, student involvement in the development of their programs, and programming for frequent success as a means of maintaining the momentum of tasks. Aggression decreased and compliance to school tasks increased under training conditions, but returned to baseline when the intervention was removed. The intervention was re-established with good effect. The study recognized that the aggression was a response to other variables (e.g., student inability to be academically successful) and emphasized the use of antecedents over consequences to mediate these challenges.

Treadwell and Page (1996) and Pace, Ivancic, and Jefferson (1994) have used functional analysis procedures to isolate the relative effects of environmental factors on aggressive behavior. Client behavior was first recorded across a variety of specific stimulus conditions using single-subject methods to identify which situations were more and less likely to evoke the unsanctioned response. For example, one client may have demonstrated higher agitation under demand conditions but be cooperative in distracting environments with lower task demands. Another client may have decompensated in situations with high stimulus loads, but not when receiving profuse attention. Each client's environment and treatment program was subsequently modified to take advantage of settings that optimized their abilities. The resulting behavior change was dramatic. In some cases, a chronic and severe behavior dysfunction that had existed for over a year was successfully addressed within a matter of weeks.

Similarly, Zencius et al. (1990) used a variety of techniques across clients to manage hypersexual disorders. Verbal feedback for appropriate and inappropriate social interaction with males was sufficient to redirect a female client who was promiscuous with males. The exhibitionism by a male client was first addressed through a detailed interview of the client's urges, feelings, and fantasies before and during acts of exhibitionism. The client was also provided with a self-monitoring notebook in which he was asked to record his urges and feelings when he had the desire to expose himself. He could then masturbate in a secluded area to fantasies of situations presented to him in a dating-skills training class. These combined procedures reduced exhibitionism from two episodes during the first week of his admission to one episode during 15 weeks of treatment, and one episode over the next four weeks of follow-up data. Finally, the inappropriate touching and kissing of hands by a male client was reduced through redirection and stimulus specificity. The client was allowed to give back rubs during a daily scheduled relaxation class, but not at other times. Inappropriate touching was decreased by over 300%.

Finally, there have been few studies that investigated the effect of managing staff behavior as a means of increasing client gains in brain-injury rehabilitation. Among the most notable, Mozzoni and Bailey (1996) first assessed the teaching techniques of staff who worked with clients but were not making expected progress on an inpatient rehabilitation unit. Skills were rated by a checklist that focused on 14 basic teaching techniques. Therapists were then provided with specific feedback, along with brief training if needed to incorporate suggested teaching skills into their daily practice. These changes produced dramatic improvement in therapeutic progress and goal attainment for all clients, yet required minimum therapist time to learn the suggested teaching skills.

Future Directions

The 1990s have been officially recognized as the *Decade of the Brain* and significant advances have been realized in (a) the medical management of brain injury, (b) neuro-imaging, (c) better understanding of the functional structures and organization of brain tissue, (d) new supportive and assistive technologies that help moderate disability and ameliorate handicap, and (e) new technologies that allow functional and empirical analysis of scientific relations.

Changes in society's perception about rights to health-care and changes in funding guidelines challenge the service delivery systems that have been developed over the past two decades. There are increasing demands for accountability and cost-effectiveness of services, with demonstration of enduring effect in natural environments. People who experience disability following brain injury are beginning to better understand their rights and responsibilities, making them more assertive consumers and partners in programming. It is, perhaps, one the most challenging and exciting times to be involved in this field. It is also a time when there is likely to be a paradigmatic shift in the manner in which treatments are designed and services are delivered. This offers important opportunities for people involved in both clinical and behavioral systems analysis.

Perhaps one of the most provocative and fruitful research areas for behavior analysis is in the development of environmental prostheses to help people with cognitive deficits following brain injury. Putting aside the debate over how cognition is defined for the moment, it is clear that many people respond, recall, and learn differently following brain injury than before. The challenge is to help people develop the ability to again mediate complex forms of behavior. In this manner, there is a rich repository of information in *Journal of the Experimental Analysis of Behavior*. Since the late 1950s significant research focusing on environmental models of "cognition training" in both humans and non-humans has been published in this journal and other affiliated sources. As previously noted, some of the work in the area of the errorless discrimination (Terrace, 1966) has are ready been adopted. However, we have only begun to scratch the surface in this area and there is clearly more data from studies in areas such as generalization, stimulus equivalency training, habituation, self-monitoring, and self-awareness that can offer equally potent procedures.

Another exciting opportunity rests in the adaptation of applied service delivery systems and programs developed for people with disability due to other forms of impairment to assist people with disability following brain injury. A significant amount of work adapting supported employment models initially developed for people with developmental disabilities has already been reported by Wehman and colleagues (Wehman, Kreutzer, Stonnington, & Wood, 1988; Wehman et al., 1990). Jacobs and colleagues (Jacobs, 1997; Jacobs & DeMello, 1996) have also reported significant effects adapting consumer-directed and community based Clubhouse programs that were originally developed by, and for, people who experience disability due to psychiatric impairment. The need for innovative long-term, supportive programming has long been recognized, but lags behind many of the other challenges of post-injury life.

Approximately 30 years ago, the noted neuropsychologist Muriel Lezak observed that although brain injury may start out as a medical challenge, over time it is transformed into a social challenge. To date, much of the work has been directed towards services during the first two years following injury. Hence, a good deal of time has been directed towards early intervention efforts that focus on preventing death from initial injury and moderating impairment. Initial rehabilitation services today principally focus on moderating disability and restoring basic function. However, as people who experience disability following brain injury return to home and community environments, the principal challenge becomes one of minimizing the social barriers that may be created by disability. Perhaps the most important, but least successful, area to date has been in injury prevention. As noted by the Brain Injury Association, the only cure for brain injury is in its prevention.

These are all areas in which behavior analysts excel and may be of service, working in partnership with other disciplines and technologies, and in ultimate service to people who experience disability following brain injury who may choose to access our support.

Reading Objectives

1. Describe the incidence of ABI in this country and its affiliated treatment and social costs.
2. Provide a basic definition of ABI and its delineation from other forms of brain-related impairment.
3. Compare and contrast traumatic brain injury from non-traumatic brain injury. List at least three etiologies (causes) for each.
4. Describe the evolution of brain injury rehabilitation services over the past three decades and four key factors that promoted this development.
5. Distinguish between mentalistic and neurological constructs of behavior.
6. Explain how neurological and social factors can individually and conjointly contribute to handicap following brain injury.
7. What is the most salient question to consider when developing rehabilitation programming for people who experience disability following brain injury?
8. Describe three critical challenges in brain injury rehabilitation programming that behavior analysis is uniquely positioned to address.
9. Describe two areas of caution for behavior analysts to consider when becoming involved in brain injury rehabilitation programming.
10. List eight key contributions to treatment, assessment, and evaluation where behavior analysis has demonstrated promising effect. Cite examples for each contribution listed.

References

Ben-Yishay, Y., Diller, L., Gerstman, L., & Gordon, W. (1970). Relationship between initial competence and ability to profit from cues in brain-damaged individuals. *Journal of Abnormal Psychology, 75,* 248-259.

Brain Injury Association, Inc. (1995). *The costs and causes of traumatic brain injury.* Alexandria, VA: Author.

Burke, W. H., & Lewis, F. D. (1986). Management of maladaptive social behavior of a brain injured adult. *International Journal of Rehabilitation Research, 9,* 335-342.

Burke, W. H., & Wesolowski, M. D. (1988). Applied behavior analysis in head injury rehabilitation. *Rehabilitation Nursing, 13,* 186-188.

Corthell, D., & Tooman, M. (Eds.). (1985). *Rehabilitation of TBI (traumatic brain injury). Twelfth Institute on Rehabilitation Issues, University of Wisconsin-Stout.* Menomonie, WI: Stout Vocational Rehabilitation Institute, Research and Training Center.

Feeney, T. J., & Ylvisaker, M. (1995). Choice and routine: Antecedent behavioral interventions for adolescents with severe traumatic brain injury. *Journal of Head Trauma Rehabilitation, 10,* 67-86.

Foxx, R. M., Marchand-Martella, N. E., Martella, R. C., & Braunling-McMorrow, D. (1988). Teaching a problem solving strategy to closed head injured adults. *Behavioral Residential Treatment, 3,* 193-210.

Foxx, R. M., Martella, R. C., & Marchand-Martella, N. E. (1989). The acquisition, maintenance, and generalization of problem-solving skills by closed head injured adults. *Behavior Therapy, 20,* 61-76.

Gajar, A., Schloss, P. J., Schloss, C. N., & Thompson, C. K. (1984). Effects of feedback and self-monitoring on head trauma youths' conversation skills. *Journal of Applied Behavior Analysis, 17,* 353-358.

Giles, G. M., & Clark-Wilsho, J. (1988). The use of behavioral techniques in functional skills training after severe brain injury. *American Journal of Occupational Therapy, 42,* 658-665.

Giles, G. M., & Shore, M. (1989). A rapid method for teaching severely brain injured adults how to wash and dress. *Archives of Physical Medicine and Rehabilitation, 70,* 156-158.

Glisky, E. L., Schacter, D. L., & Tulving, E. (1986). Learning and retention of computer-related vocabulary in memory-impaired patients: Method of vanishing cues. *Journal of Clinical and Experimental Neuropsychology, 8,* 292-312.

Godfrey, H. D. P., & Knight, R. G. (1988). Memory training and behavioral rehabilitation of a severely head injured adult. *Archives of Physical Medicine and Rehabilitation, 69,* 458-460.

Haley, W. E. (1983). Behavioral management of the brain damaged patient: A case study. *Rehabilitation Nursing, 8,* 26-28.

Jacobs, H. E. (1987). The Los Angeles Head Injury survey: Project rationale and design implications. *Journal of Head Trauma Rehabilitation, 2,* 37-50.

Jacobs, H. E. (1988). The Los Angeles Head Injury survey: Procedures and preliminary findings. *Archives of Physical Medicine and Rehabilitation, 69,* 425-431.

Jacobs, H. E. (1993). *Behavior analysis guidelines and brain injury rehabilitation: People, principles and programs.* Gaithersburg, MD: Aspen. (Now available from the Brain Injury Association).

Jacobs, H. E. (1997). The Clubhouse: Addressing work-related behavioral challenges through a supportive social community. *Journal of Head Trauma Rehabilitation, 12,* 14-27.

Jacobs, H. E., & DeMello, C. (1996). The Clubhouse model and employment following brain injury. *Journal of Vocational Rehabilitation, 7,* 169-179.

Jacobs, H. E., Lynch, M., Cornick, J., & Slifer, K. (1986). Behavior management of aggressive sequelae in Reyes' Syndrome. *Archives of Physical Medicine and Rehabilitation, 67,* 558-563.

Jacobs, H. E., Hart, T., Mory, K. D., Griffin, C., Martin, B. A., & Probst, J. (1996). Single subject evaluation designs in rehabilitation: Case studies on inpatient units. *Journal of Head Trauma Rehabilitation, 11,* 86-94.

Lane, I. M., Wesolowski, M. D., & Burke, W. H. (1989). Teaching socially appropriate behavior to eliminate hoarding in a brain injured client. *Journal of Behavior Therapy and Experimental Psychiatry, 20,* 79-82.

Mozzoni, M. P., & Bailey, J. S. (1996). Improving training methods in brain injury rehabilitation. *Journal of Head Trauma Rehabilitation, 11,* 1-17.

National Head Injury Foundation. (1988). *Resource directory.* Washington, DC: Author.

O'Reilly, M. F., Green, G., & Braunling-McMorrow, D. (1990). Self-administered written prompts to teach home accident prevention skills to adults with brain injuries. *Journal of Applied Behavior Analysis, 23,* 431-446.

Pace, G. M., Ivancic, M. T., & Jefferson, G. (1994). Stimulus fading as treatment for obscenity in a brain-injured adult. *Journal of Applied Behavior Analysis, 27,* 301-305.

Pace, G. M., & Colbert, B. (1996). Role of behavior analysis in home and community based neurological rehabilitation. *Journal of Head Trauma Rehabilitation, 11,* 18-26

Schloss, P. J., Thompson, C. K., Gajar, A. H., & Schloss, C. N. (1985). Influence of self-monitoring on heterosexual conversational behaviors of head trauma youth. *Applied Research in Mental Retardation, 6,* 269-282.

Silver, B. V., & Stelly-Seitz, C. (1992). Behavioral treatment for adipsia in a child with hypothalamic injury. *Developmental Medicine and Child Neurology, 34,* 539-542.

Silver, B. V., Boake, C., & Cavazos, D. (1994). Improving functional skills using behavioral procedures in a child with anoxic brain injury. *Archives of Physical Medicine and Rehabilitation, 75,* 742-745.

Skinner, B. F. (1957). *Verbal behavior.* New York: Appleton-Century-Crofts.

Slifer, K. J., Tucker, C. L., Gerson, A. C., Cataldo, M. D., Sevier, R. C., Suter, A. H., & Kane, A. C. (1996). Operant conditioning for behavior management during posttraumatic amnesia in children and adolescents with brain injury. *Journal of Head Trauma Rehabilitation, 11,* 39-50.

Terrace, H. C. (1966). Stimulus control. In W. C. Honig (Ed.), *Operant behavior: Areas of research and application.* New York: Appleton-Century-Crofts.

Treadwell, K., & Page, T. J. (1996). Functional analysis: Identifying the environmental determinants of severe behavior disorders. *Journal of Head Trauma Rehabilitation, 11,* 62-74.

Turner, J. M., Greene, G., & Braunling-McMorrow, D. (1990). Differential reinforcement of low rates of responding (DRL) to reduce dysfunctional social behaviors of a head injured man. *Behavioral Residential Treatment, 5,* 15-27.

Wehman P., Kreutzer, J. S., Stonnington, H. H., & Wood, W. (1988). Supported employment for persons with traumatic brain injury: A preliminary report. *Journal of Head Trauma Rehabilitation, 3,* 82-93.

Wehman, P. H., Kreutzer, J. S., West, M. D., Sherron, P. D., Zasler, N. D., Groah, C. H., Stonnington, H. H., Burns, C. T., & Sale, P. R. (1990). Return to work for persons with traumatic brain injury: A supportive employment approach. *Archives of Physical Medicine and Rehabilitation, 71,* 1047-1052.

Wilson, B. A., Baddley, A. D., & Cockburn, J. M. (1989). How do old dogs learn new tricks: Teaching a technological skill to brain injured people. *Cortex, 25,* 115-119.

Wolpe, J. (1969). *The practice of behavior therapy.* New York: Pergamon.

Zencius, A. H., Wesolowski, M. D., Burke, W. H., & Hough, S. (1990). Managing hypersexual disorders in brain injured clients. *Brain Injury, 4,* 175-181.

Zencius, A. H., Wesolowski, M. D., Burke, W. H., & McQuade, P. (1989). Antecedent control in the treatment of brain injured clients. *Brain Injury, 3,* 199-205.

Chapter 10

Behavioral Psychotherapy and the Rise of Clinical Behavior Analysis

Steven C. Hayes and Richard T. Bissett
University of Nevada

Many of the best established procedures in applied empirical clinical work have emerged from within behavior analysis. These include in particular the many types of contingency management procedures (e.g., time-out or token economies). While the successes have been substantial, early human applications targeted fairly discrete overt behavior and usually involved children or institutionalized populations. The rationale for this narrow focus was that these populations provided a greater opportunity to achieve stimulus control and to directly manipulate environmental contingencies (e.g., Ayllon & Azrin, 1969; Risley & Wolf, 1967). Until fairly recently, the applied behavior analytic tradition had largely ignored verbal psychotherapy.

Behavior analysts' have long held a general skepticism about the value of "talking cures." In part this was a counter reaction against the empirical weaknesses of early psychotherapies – but the larger part was that the client-therapist relationship and the complexities of language were not easily described in behavioral terms, and when they were so described, there seemed to be few reasons to focus energies there instead of in other places. Skinner's approach to verbal behavior (Skinner, 1957), essentially treated it as a mere discriminated operant. Indeed, Skinner considered the behavior of a rat in a normal animal operant experiment to be a limited form of "verbal behavior" (Skinner, 1957, footnote 11, p. 108). If direct contingencies are the primary issue, even for verbal behavior itself, there are few reasons to look to the psychotherapy session for powerful approaches to human behavior change. Thus, what conceptual interest there was in psychotherapy (e.g., Ferster, 1972), did not lead to new psychotherapy approaches.

All of that has changed. There now are several robust behavior analytic psychotherapies. A new sub-field, clinical behavior analysis, has emerged (see Dougher, 2000, for a book length review). Clinical behavior analysis can be defined as (Dougher & Hayes, 2000):

a) that part of applied behavior that applies the assumptions, principles and methods of modern functional contextual behavior analysis to the range of problems, settings, and issues typically confronted by clinical psychologists working in outpatient settings

b) including the identification of the variables and processes that play a role in the development, maintenance, and treatment of clinical disorders,

c) paying special attention to the role and use of verbal events in disorders and their treatment, and as a result,

d) emphasizing modern behavioral interpretations of the processes and principles involved in language and cognition.

So defined, the rise of clinical behavior analysis is a story of the rise of an intellectual area of behavior analysis, and a set of practical applications of that area within applied behavior analysis.

Rule-Governed behavior

The simple behavior analytic distinction between contingency-shaped and rule-governed behavior is the initial domino in a series of changes that have lead both to a post-Skinnerian analysis of language and to the development of several innovative behavioral psychotherapies. The link between rule-governed behavior and psychotherapy is natural, since both concern how verbal stimuli can change how humans interact with their environment.

Skinner defined rule-governed behavior as behavior controlled by contingency-specifying stimuli (1966). He never defined what he meant by "specifying" a contingency, however – relying instead on common sense examples. The seed planted by the rule-governed behavior concept for clinical behavior analysis thus ironically comes from two sources: empirical attention paid to this concept and its conceptual inadequacy.

Empirically, it was quickly learned that, in contrast with behavior that has been directly shaped or established by minimal instructions (Hayes, Brownstein, Zettle, Rosenfarb, & Korn, 1986; Matthews, Shimoff, Catania, & Sagvolden, 1977; see Catania, Shimoff, & Matthews, 1989, and Hayes, Zettle, & Rosenfarb, 1989 for reviews) rule-governed behavior is relatively insensitive to changes in contingencies that are not described by the rule itself (e.g., Hayes et al., 1986;). At least two major sources of the insensitivity effect were identified: rules can preclude contact with other important environmental features (Joyce & Chase, 1990), and rules add social standards for performance (Rosenfarb & Hayes, 1984; see Hayes et al., 1989 for a review).

The insensitivity effect was exciting because it seemed to parallel certain forms of psychopathological behavior. Indeed, all contemporary behavior analytic psychotherapies avoid a mindless reliance on rules as a result.

The conceptual inadequacy comes because of certain inconsistencies between Skinner's views on rule-governed behavior and verbal behavior (Parrott, 1987). Rules may "specify" contingencies, but they cannot do so verbally in Skinner's system. For Skinner, a "verbal stimulus" is merely the stimulus product of verbal behavior (Skinner, 1957, p. 34), and the behavior of the listener is not verbal. It is generally agreed that "rules are powerful events. They permit a remarkably indirect, conventional, and specific form of stimulus control. Rules allow the establishment of remote social contingencies and a rapid modification of the range of behaviors available to make contact with the environment. They can also make other important sources of control over behavior ineffective" (p. 378, Hayes & Ju, 1998). Without a coherent technical account of the nature of verbal stimuli and of "specification," however, Skinner's account was unable to carry the water that behavior analysts wished the concept to carry.

This change in thinking can be seen in the rise and fall of research on rule-governance within behavior analysis. A hot topic in the mid-1980s, rule-governed behavior was cold as ice by the early-1990s. Instead, another topic had become red hot, and for the same reason: it seemingly provided an avenue for the analysis of human language and cognition.

Derived Stimulus Relations

In stimulus equivalence studies, a matching-to-sample format (i.e., given a sample, pick one of several comparisons) is often used to teach a series of conditioned discriminations (e.g., given A1 pick B1, given A2 pick B2, etc.). This kind of direct training corresponds roughly to the kind of training imagined in the concept of the tact: in the presence of an actual dog, the speaker is reinforced for saying "dog". Imagine that a child is taught that given the written word D-O-G, he or she should say "dog". Suppose the child is also taught that in the presence of the written word D-O-G, he or she should point to an actual dog. The child will now probably be able to say "dog" upon seeing an actual dog. Yet, this latter instance of behavior has not been directly taught in a fashion such as that imagined by Skinner's analysis of the tact.

Much of the interest in stimulus equivalence was due to its obvious similarity to verbal processes. Even the earliest studies (e.g., Sidman, 1971) made the connection, and it was confirmed by subsequent research. For example, the emergence of derived relations was shown with human infants (Devany, Hayes, & Nelson, 1986; Lipkens, Hayes, & Hayes, 1993), but not if they did not possess some spontaneous productive or receptive use of symbols (Devany et al., 1986). Further, it did not seem to be shown with non-humans (D'Amato, Salmon, Loukas, & Tomie, 1985; Dugdale & Lowe, 2000; Kendall, 1983; Lipkens, Kop, & Matthijs, 1988).

These derived stimulus relations, furthermore, could easily be shown to make a practical behavioral difference. If words participate in equivalence relations with situations that occasion them, some of the stimulus functions acquired by the words transfer to related events, and conversely some of the stimulus functions of the related events inhere in the words. Several demonstrations of transfer are available and include conditioned reinforcing functions (Hayes, Brownstein, Devany, Kohlenberg, & Shelby, 1987; Hayes, Kohlenberg, & Hayes, 1991), discriminative functions of public (Hayes et al., 1987) and private (DeGrandpre, Bickel, & Higgins, 1992) stimuli, elicited conditioned emotional responses (Dougher, Auguston, Markham, Greenway, & Wulfert, 1994), extinction functions (Dougher et al., 1994), and sexual responses (Roche & Barnes, 1997).

As the literature on derived stimulus relations has expanded, a number of studies have shown that it is possible to produce a wide variety of derived stimulus relations such as same, different, opposite, or more-than/less-than (e.g., Dymond & Barnes, 1995; Steele & Hayes, 1991). If relational cues are pretrained so as to select for non-arbitrary stimulus relations of a given kind (e.g., opposites: given a short line pick a long line) then these same cues will produce the same kind of relational pattern even in arbitrary situations. For example, via such relational cues subjects in the Steele and Hayes (1991) experiment learned that A1 was the opposite of B3 and C3 and the same as B1 and C1. Testing showed that the subjects then derived that B3 and C3 were the same, and that each of these were the opposite of B1 and C1. When they later learned that the arbitrary stimulus D1 was opposite to C3, during a test phase they then treated D1 as the opposite and not the same as B3.

Derived multiple stimulus relations lead to behavioral functions that are extremely indirect in the sense that they have not been established directly through training. The psychological functions of an event in a relational network can alter, under some contextual conditions, the functions of other events in such a network. While the *transfer* of stimulus function correctly describes the process of one member of a class coming to have one or more functions of another member of an equivalence class, the term *transfer* is too narrow when the primary relations involved move beyond the relation of equivalence. Consider, for example, the relation of oppositeness. If a training history established A as the opposite of B, and A is given a punishing function, it would be expected that B may have a reinforcing function. In this example, it would actually be misleading to say that the stimulus functions of B transferred from A to B because the trained and derived functions are different. Rather, the stimulus functions of B are *transformed* based on its derived relation to A. Demonstrations of transformed stimulus functions are becoming increasingly common (Dymond & Barnes, 1995; Roche & Barnes, 1997).

At the present time there is only one well-developed behavioral theory in this area, relational frame theory (Hayes, Barnes-Holmes, & Roche, in press), but even without theoretical agreement about the etiological processes involved, derived stimulus relations begin to offer a more comprehensive analysis of verbal stimuli. It is increasingly common for behavior analysts to think of verbal stimuli and stimuli that have functions based on derived stimulus relations and the transformation of stimulus functions. If so, one can think of rule-governance as involving the transformation of psychological functions among networks of derived stimulus relations (Hayes & Hayes, 1989, 1992).

The Clinical Impact of Modern Behavioral Approaches to Language

Thinking of human language and cognition in terms of derived stimulus relations has many important impacts on the identification of the variables and processes that play a role in the development, maintenance, and treatment of clinical disorders. We will briefly point to a few examples.

Emotions

While Skinner argued that an analysis of private events such as emotions was scientifically legitimate (Skinner, 1945), he also argued that emotions were co-occurring phenomena of the same contingencies that precipitate overt motor behaviors and that they have "no functional significance, either in a theoretical analysis or the practical control of behavior" (p. 181; Skinner, 1953). However, to the extent that emotional labels are bidirectionally reactive (negative experiences adhere to words and vice versa), it is not necessarily true that "the change in feeling and the change in behavior have a common cause" (p. 62; Skinner, 1974) because both nonverbal and verbal contingencies are mixed in the control of the overt and emotional behavior (Friman, Hayes, & Wilson, 1998). For example, many fears and phobias seem to be indirect and verbally entangled. Oftentimes, even careful clinical interviews can reveal no direct history to account for a client's fear. The transformation of derived stimulus relations provides a working model for such indirectly acquired functions.

Experiential Avoidance

If the core of human language is derived stimulus relations, then experiential avoidance is built into human language. A derived stimulus relation based view of language suggests that the event and the description of the event interact bidirectionally with one another. If so, verbal self-awareness will be painful when what is known is painful. For example, a trauma survivor may avoid thinking or talking about the trauma, because the very process of contacting it verbally will bring some of the stimulus functions of the original experience to bear in the description (Hayes & Gifford, 1997).

This simple insight has profound implications for clinical behavior analysis, because it suggests that when humans construct private events verbally, they promptly tend to avoid or escape those that they do not like: a process termed "experiential avoidance" (Hayes, Wilson, Gifford, Follette, & Strosahl, 1996). There is substantial evidence that experiential avoidance can be harmful (Hayes et al., 1996). Perhaps for that reason, clinical behavior analysis has been foremost among areas that have attempted to find ways to undermine these avoidance processes.

Plausibility of Indirect Cause and Indirect Interventions

Indirectness refers the degree to which behavioral interactions can be regulated by historical features that are remote in terms of formal similarity, contiguity, or direct contingencies. If derived stimulus relations are at the core of human language, then verbal stimuli can acquire functions very indirectly. This indirectness makes the analysis of clinical problems difficult, but it also makes the use of verbal interactions to change these problems plausibly useful. For that reason, modern behavioral accounts of human language make sense of the special attention clinical behavior analysts pay the role and use of verbal events both in the analysis of clinical disorders and their treatment.

There are many other examples of how thinking of human language and cognition in terms of derived stimulus relations has guided the development of clinical behavior analysis. We will return to this topic after first describing some examples of clinical behavior analysis.

Examples of Modern Behavioral Psychotherapy

Dialectical Behavior Therapy (DBT)

Dialectical Behavior Therapy (DBT; Linehan, 1993) was designed to treat the parasuicidal behavior of individuals diagnosed with borderline personality disorder (BPD). The treatment is dialectical in its conceptualization of the process of change as an ongoing synthesis between alternative and even contradictory positions. Perhaps the primary dialectical principle within DBT is that between acceptance and change. Acceptance strategies are closely aligned with the notion of unconditional positive regard in client-centered therapy, while change strategies are very similar to those of traditional cognitive or behavioral therapies in which the therapeutic objective is direct change of thoughts or overt behavior. Neither strategy is viewed as superior; each alone can be problematic. For example, change-based initiatives may come to be viewed as invalidating. The underlying message may be interpreted by the client as "I am not good enough. I have to change to be good enough." Alternatively, acceptance initiatives may also prove to be equally invalidating. Here the underlying message may be "You need to learn to accept that your life will continue to be painful." Therapy is viewed as an ever finer balancing of acceptance and change themes.

DBT defines three broad stages of therapy. In Stage 1 the objective is for the client to obtain basic capabilities, such as decreasing suicidal and other dysfunctional behaviors, and increasing behavioral skills, such as core mindfulness skills, interpersonal effectiveness, emotional regulation, distress tolerance, and self-management. Stage 2 focuses on reducing any post-traumatic stress through exposure. Finally, in Stage 3, the therapeutic focus moves to increasing self respect and the achieving individual goals. At this stage DBT focuses on the interpersonal client behaviors within the therapy session, and how the evolving client-therapist relationship can be generalized to relations with other important people in the client's environment.

The acceptance strategies utilized in DBT seek to foster within clients an awareness of their private emotions and thoughts and the workings of the real physical world through both an inward and outward focusing of attention. Mindfulness training may be conceptualized as a behavioral translation of meditation, and includes exercises in "just observing" one's private events, focused awareness, and distancing from the content of personal experiences (i.e., the content of various thoughts, the reactions to various emotions, etc.). Distress tolerance training applies mindfulness skills to personal experience. The intention of distress tolerance is for the client to view their experience (thoughts, emotions, behaviors) as they are, beyond any evaluative component or attempt to change, avoid, or control them. The change strategies that DBT utilizes include skills training, contingency management, cognitive modification, and exposure. Direct cognitive modification along the lines of those advocated by Ellis (1962, 1973) or Beck (Beck, Rush, Shaw, & Emery, 1979; Beck & Freeman, 1990) are utilized, although to a far lesser degree than contingency clarification.

Integrative Couple's Therapy

Integrative Couple's Therapy (ICT; Jacobson & Christensen, 1996) conceptualizes couple distress behaviorally as primarily due to a decrease in the value of reinforcement received from the relationship. ICT utilizes a combination of change and acceptance strategies. Change strategies include behavior exchange (BE) and communication/problem-solving training (CPT). BE consists of identifying individual behaviors of one partner that the other partner will find reinforcing, and then increasing the frequencies of those behaviors. Communication training consists of teaching couples how to listen actively, maintain good eye contact, paraphrase and summarize what is heard, and reflect and validate the speaker. Problem-solving consists of training in problem definition and solution. While these rule-based strategies are often effective, there are other areas that do not lend themselves to rule control. For example, many problems reflect deep-seated individual differences that are likely to be highly resistant to change. In other areas, a couple may have the ability to change, but may remain unwilling. Finally, the pressure to change is often itself a major barrier to change (Lawrence, Eldridge, Christensen, 1998). For these situations, especially, ICT promotes acceptance-based strategies.

Strategies to augment the acceptance of one's emotional responding include 1) empathic joining, 2) viewing the problematic pattern as an "it", 3) building tolerance for a partner's aversive behavior, and 4) fostering self-care. These acceptance strategies are believed to achieve their effect through contingency-shaped, rather than rule-governed, processes. For example, in behavior exchange, the couple is not given a clearly stated rule. Rather, they are given a rather open-ended directive to choose to give their partners something favorable sometime during the week and to also choose whether to acknowledge any behavioral gifts they may receive from their partner. A partner may speculate that there is an underlying rule (such as "if I can do more nice things for my partner, things will get better"), but the power of behavioral exchange really comes from the couple getting in touch directly with the contingencies of giving and receiving (e.g., it may be nice to be the recipient of a back rub, and it may be also nice to receive appreciation for giving a partner a back rub, and these positive results may generalize to other contexts).

Functional Analytic Psychotherapy

Functional Analytic Psychotherapy (FAP; Kohlenberg & Tsai, 1987) is based on a behavioral analysis of the therapeutic relationship. FAP is meant to be used either in conjunction with traditional behavioral approaches or when the client's presenting issues are such that the interpersonal aspects of the client's ability to relate are the collective problem that needs to be treated. These interpersonal difficulties may be due to discrimination deficits or a deficient, excessive, or aversive behavioral repertoire. FAP consciously attempts to avoid certain kinds of rule-governed behavior, since many rules may keep clients from contacting important feedback in the form of real-world contingencies. Instead, FAP assumes that new and more useful behavior can be shaped during the process of psychotherapy by the contingent responding of the therapist to client problems that occur in session, as well as to improvements in those behaviors. The underlying therapeutic assumption is that it is easier to deal with actual relevant behavior within session than with a mere description of the behavior. Essentially, the core therapeutic behavioral intention within FAP is to have the clients come under the control of rules that are effective – rules that produce valuable contingencies.

The FAP therapist is asked to a) notice instances of problematic client behaviors; b) structure the therapy environment to increase the likelihood of observing these behaviors; c) be aware of occasioning these behaviors; d) contingently respond to instances of client improvement in these behaviors; and e) describe and train the client to describe his or her problematic behavior in functional terms – e.g., what is the relationship between behaviors (e.g., thoughts and feelings), the conditions that give rise to the behavior, and the consequences following the behavior.

Acceptance and Commitment Therapy

This approach derives from the philosophy of functional contextualism (Biglan & Hayes, 1996; Hayes, 1993) and contemporary behavior analysis (Hayes & Wilson, 1993). The core idea in Acceptance and Commitment Therapy (ACT; Hayes, Strosahl, & Wilson, 1999; Hayes & Wilson, 1994) is that the relation between private events (e.g., thoughts, emotions, physical sensations, memories) and overt behavior is contextually established and maintained. Rather than try to change the content of these private events, the context that relates them to undesirable overt behavior is challenged.

ACT argues that humans are unique to the degree they substitute cognitions for direct experience ('cognitive fusion') and work to avoid negatively evaluated private experiences ('experiential avoidance'). Many forms of psychopathology can be conceptualized as unhealthy efforts to escape or avoid or control or suppress emotions, thoughts, memories, and other private experiences (Hayes et al., 1996), based on the domination of derived stimulus relations over other forms of behavioral regulation. The general goal of ACT is to encourage a client to contact private events without needless defense ('psychological acceptance'), and to reduce the needless domination of language ("deliteralization") while at the same time setting concrete goals based on overall values and behaving in a way that moves toward these goals ("commitment"). Thus, ACT seek to redirect direct change efforts toward more readily changeable domains, such as overt behavior or life situations, rather than personal history or automatic thoughts and feelings (see Hayes, Jacobson, Follette, & Dougher, 1994 for a book length review of acceptance methods) by altering the context in which such efforts occur. More specifically, ACT is designed to: a) lessen the degree to which thoughts are taken literally and to promote the evaluation of thoughts on the basis of the degree to which they lead to valued life changes, b) undermine reason giving and believability of reasons in areas where these efforts have been used to justify and excuse ineffective behavior, c) foster the experience of private events, rather than engage in counterproductive avoidance behavior, d) clarify life values and identify barriers to implementation of life goals, and e) foster commitments to actions linked to life values. ACT shares common ground with experiential therapies in that experiencing and feeling are accepted and valued, not controlled out of existence. While some of the techniques used in ACT are borrowed from experiential approaches, the core conceptualization remains thoroughly behavioral.

Common Characteristics of Modern Behavioral Psychotherapy

All four of these approaches have been shown to produce significant behavior change, but we will not review those data here. Our focus, instead, is conceptual. In what sense are these four examples of innovative psychotherapies also examples of "clinical behavior analysis?" There are several notable commonalties, but we will describe only two here in any detail.

Contextualism and Radical Functionalism

Behavior analysis is based on a pragmatic philosophy: what is true is what works. Behavior is understood in terms of its function, not its form, and function is always understood in relation to a context.

Not all of these therapies are self-consciously cast in terms of contextual and pragmatic philosophy, but even a superficial analysis of each show them to be both contextual and radically functional. They all display a notable and quite unusual disinterest in changes in formally defined behaviors until the larger function of those behaviors are understood. There is little interest in pathologizing either the client, or certain formal behavioral events. Importantly, the contextual features of these approaches often deal explicitly with the referential nature of language, showing some sensitivity to the philosophical and theoretical developments in the behavioral analysis of human verbal events.

For example, ACT challenges the context of literality and control that is thought to bring together private behaviors (e.g., thoughts and emotions) and public overt behaviors, and attempts to refocus client energies from changing dysfunctional thoughts or avoiding feelings to contacting real-world contingencies. DBT accomplishes employs mindfulness exercises to change the functions of various thoughts and emotions. FAP attempts to increase the proportion of the client's experience that is contingency-shaped, rather than rule-governed, by providing a new social/verbal context, namely the therapeutic relationship itself. ICP encourages a focus on the function and utility of behavior so as to allow the client to contact contingencies that may have always been available but which were never contacted because of holding on to a posture of the need to change one's partner.

Another indication of the contextual and radically functional nature of these treatments, is their focus on both acceptance and change. When problematic behavior is defined solely in structural terms, direct change efforts are seemingly the only option available. To a structuralist, acceptance is a kind of admission of failure. In all of these therapies, a given behavior may or may not be targeted for direct change efforts, and the distinction between the two is no topographical but functional.

ICT explicitly includes both acceptance and change strategies, distinguishing acceptance strategies as being contingency-shaped and change strategies as being rule-governed. Both are viewed as fundamental change processes, however, as moving to an acceptance posture is itself a change from equilibrium. For ICT, the acceptance/change distinction also reflects the differing effects of verbal behavior on private versus public behavior (Cordova & Jacobson, 1993). Specifically, acceptance strategies have as their objective an acceptance of private thoughts, memories, emotions, etc., while change strategies have as their objective a change in publicly observable behaviors. This distinction is similar to ACT's distinction between rule-based control efforts applied to private versus public events. For example, there is evidence that attempts to control private thoughts or avoid emotions can paradoxically lead to the opposite effect of increasing those very thoughts or emotional reactions (e.g., Wegner, Schneider, Carter, & White, 1987; Wegner, Schneider, Knutson, & McMahon, 1991). These findings suggest that rules of control and change, while often effective in the overt behavioral domain, may not work as well in the world of private events.

For DBT the chief therapy focus is the acceptance and change dialectic. Basically, the therapeutic initiative is one of both accepting/validating the client and, within this context, introducing the possibility of change. DBT encourages clients to experience distressful thoughts and emotions as they are, without changing or avoiding them, and also to attempt to titrate or otherwise control (i.e., change) the experience.

FAP pays the least attention to acceptance, except in the area of client acceptance. The therapeutic relationship is built both on positive regard and on contingent reinforcement of change (i.e., shaping). Thus, the tension between acceptance and change exists in this treatment approach as well.

Caution About Rule-Based Insensitivity

One of the biggest distinctions between traditional behavior therapy or cognitive therapy and clinical behavior analysis is the caution the latter show about the use of direct instructions and rules. In the 1980's, the basic behavior analytic literature provided ample evidence of the need for this caution, and due to the link between these approaches and behavior analysis, all of them have attended to this concern.

FAP is very aware that rules can make people insensitive to contingencies, even when the contingencies are contacted (e.g., Hayes et al., 1986). Accordingly, FAP has been designed to avoid most therapist-generated rules altogether, although FAP encourages clients to verbalize rules that work. FAP achieves this intention by its great emphasis on shaping, in which instructions are minimized and contingent responding maximized. DBT is also explicitly cautious about the negative consequences that sometimes attend rule-based interventions and concerned that therapist suggestions (rules) may be perceived by the client as invalidating. The dialectical nature of DBT is expressed in its conceptualization of reality as containing natural contradictions or polarities. Clients may have a history of rather rigidly following rules, and they may become confused in a context in which it is not easy to identify or describe the underlying regularity (e.g., in a situation in which there are many exceptions). DBT therapists often respond to this confusion through means other than logical advice, which is not effective in accounting for the (apparently) illogical. Instead, metaphor, narrative, mythology, and paradox are offered as less literal means to somehow make sense of and accept ambiguity. Clients are encouraged to become comfortable with holding inconsistent or contradictory thoughts (rules) and to work toward finding a balance or integration.

ICT explicitly added acceptance strategies to help overcome the problems that can surround rule-based insensitivity. ICT conceptualizes these acceptance strategies as contingency-shaped, as opposed to more rule-governed change strategies. The underlying ICT assumption appears to be similar to ACT, in which, once freed from ineffective change efforts, clients may begin responding to newly perceived contingencies.

ACT is keenly aware that rules and other verbal behavior can desensitize the listener to the effects of environmental contingencies. ACT targets this phenomenon directly through cognitive deliteralization techniques and by emphasizing that clients trust their own direct experience. In some of these approaches (e.g., DBT and ACT) derived stimulus relations and the functions produced by them are weakened by deliberate deliteralization procedures such as mediation, repeating a word over and over, deliberate use of paradox or confusion, and use of metaphors (Hayes & Wilson, 1994). In others (e.g., FAP) dysfunctional verbal behaviors may simply be ignored.

This does not mean that rules are not used. Rather, all four psychotherapy models work to increase the influence of rules in the areas in which they are effective (e.g., values; noticing natural contingencies) and reduce the influence of rules in those areas in which they are a hindrance (e.g., self-avoidance). For example, FAP attempts to augment effective forms of verbal control by having clients tact in detail relevant controlling stimuli and contingencies. DBT therapists, like FAP therapists, spend a great deal of time just stating the contingent relationships that are currently in force. ACT augments rules and verbal control in the form of values clarification, overt commitments, and the statement of contact with meaningful contingencies as "rules of effective living."

Other Dimensions

There are several other dimensions that could be analyzed in much the same way including the avoidance of arbitrary contingencies and attention to natural contingencies, the use of the therapeutic relationship, and the importance of values and purposes. In each of these areas, among others, these four therapies show that they are "fellow travelers."

Conclusion

We have defined clinical behavior analysis as that part of applied behavior analysis that applies the assumptions, principles and methods of modern functional contextual behavior analysis to the range of problems, settings, and issues typically confronted by clinical psychologists working in outpatient settings including the identification of the variables and processes that play a role in the development, maintenance, and treatment of clinical disorders. If nothing else was added to the definition, clinical behavior analysis is a small but recognizable aspect of applied behavior analysis since its inception. What is new, however, is the special attention clinical behavior analysts have paid to the role and use of verbal events in disorders and their treatment, based on a modern behavioral interpretation of the processes and principles involved in language and cognition.

We have tried to show that this new emphasis has removed the barriers that previously existed to the development of clinical behavior analysis, namely, the treatment of private events as epiphenomena and extreme skepticism about indirect verbal methods of behavior change. A view of language based on derived stimulus relations changes both of these attributes. Thus, it is no surprise that several new behavioral psychotherapies have emerged in the last ten years, very much in parallel to the rise of interest in rule governance and derived stimulus relations. As we have tried to show, the four major examples of systems of treatment in clinical behavior analysis, are recognizably related to the assumptions of modern contextual behavioral thinking. That does not make these approaches good, but it does make our more general point: something quite new has arrived in the world of applied behavior analysis.

References

Ayllon, T., & Azrin, N. (1969). *The token economy: A motivational system for therapy and rehabilitation.* New York: Appleton-Century-Crofts.

Beck, A. T., & Freeman, A. (1990). *Cognitive therapy of personality disorders.* New York: Guilford Press.

Beck, A. T., Rush, A. J., Shaw, B. T., & Emery, G. (1979). *Cognitive therapy of depression.* New York: Guilford Press.

Biglan, A., & Hayes, S. C. (1996). Should the behavioral sciences become more pragmatic? The case for functional contextualism in research on human behavior. *Applied and Preventive Psychology, 5,* 47-57.

Catania, C., Shimoff, E., & Matthews, B. A. (1989). An experimental analysis of rule-governed behavior. In S. C. Hayes (Ed.), *Rule-governed behavior: Cognition, contingencies, and instructional control* (pp. 119-152). New York: Plenum.

Cordova, J. V., & Jacobson, N. S. (1993). Couple distress. In D. H. Barlow (Ed.), *Clinical handbook of psychological disorders: A step-by-step treatment manual* (pp. 481-512). New York, NY: Guilford Press.

D'Amato, M. R., Salmon, D. P., Loukas, E., & Tomie, A. (1985). Symmetry and transitivity of conditional relations in monkeys (Cebus apella) and pigeons (Columba livia). *Journal of the Experimental Analysis of Behavior, 44*, 35-47.

DeGrandpre, R. J., Bickel, W. K., & Higgins, S. T. (1992). Emergent equivalence relations between interoceptive (drug) and exteroceptive (visual) stimuli. *Journal of the Experimental Analysis of Behavior, 58*, 9-18.

Devany, J. M., Hayes, S. C., & Nelson, R. O. (1986). Equivalence class formation in language-able and language-disabled children. *Journal of the Experimental Analysis of Behavior, 46*, 243-257.

Dougher, M. J. (Ed.). (2000). *Clinical behavior analysis*. Reno, NV: Context Press.

Dougher, M. J., & Hayes, S. C. (2000). Clinical behavior analysis. In M. J. Dougher (Ed.), *Clinical behavior analysis* (pp. 11-26). Reno, NV: Context Press.

Dougher, M. J., Auguston, E. M. , Markham, M. R., Greenway, D. E., & Wulfert, E. (1994). The transfer of respondent eliciting and extinction functions through stimulus equivalence classes. *Journal of the Experimental Analysis of Behavior, 62*, 331-351.

Dugdale, N., & Lowe, C. F. (2000). Testing for symmetry in the conditional discriminations of language-trained chimpanzees. *Journal of the Experimental Analysis of Behavior, 73*, 5-22.

Dymond, S., & Barnes, D. (1995). A transformation of self-discrimination response functions through the arbitrarily applicable relations of sameness, more than, and less than. *Journal of the Experimental Analysis of Behavior, 64*, 163-184.

Ellis, A. (1962). *Reason and emotion in psychotherapy*. New York: Lyle Stuart.

Ellis, A. (1973). My philosophy of psychotherapy. *Journal of Contemporary Psychotherapy, 6*, 13-18.

Ferster, C. B. (1972). An experimental analysis of clinical phenomena. *The Psychological Record, 22*, 1-16.

Friman, P. C., Hayes, S. C., & Wilson, K. G. (1998). Why behavior analysts should study emotion: The example of anxiety. *Journal of Applied Behavior Analysis, 31*, 137-156.

Hayes, S. C. (1993). Analytic goals and the varieties of scientific contextualism. In S. C. Hayes, L. J. Hayes, H. W. Reese, & T. R. Sarbin (Eds.), *Varieties of scientific contextualism* (pp. 11-27). Reno, NV: Context Press.

Hayes, S. C., Barnes-Holmes, D., & Roche, B. (Eds.). (in press). *Relational Frame Theory: A Post-Skinnerian account of human language and cognition*. Reno, NV: Context Press.

Hayes, S. C., Brownstein, A. J., Devany, J. M., Kohlenberg, B. S., & Shelby, J. (1987). Stimulus equivalence and the symbolic control of behavior. *Mexican Journal of Behavior Analysis, 13*, 361-374.

Hayes, S. C., Brownstein, A. J., Zettle, R. D., Rosenfarb, I., & Korn, Z. (1986). Rule-governed behavior and sensitivity to changing consequences of responding. *Journal of the Experimental Analysis of Behavior, 45*, 237-256.

Hayes, S. C., & Gifford, E. V. (1997). The trouble with language: Experiential avoidance, rules, and the nature of verbal events. *Psychological Science, 8*, 170-173.

Hayes, S. C., & Hayes, L. J. (1989). The verbal action of the listener as a basis for rule-governance. In S. C. Hayes (Ed.), *Rule-governed behavior: Cognition, contingencies, and instructional control* (pp. 153-190). New York: Plenum.

Hayes, S. C., & Hayes, L. J. (1992). Verbal relations and the evolution of behavior analysis. *American Psychologist, 47*, 1383-1395.

Hayes, S. C., Jacobson, N. S., Follette, V. M., & Dougher, M. J. (Eds.). (1994). *Acceptance and change: Content and context in psychotherapy*. Reno, NV: Context Press.

Hayes, S. C., & Ju, W. (1998). The applied implications of rule-governed behavior. In W. T. O'Donohue (Ed.), *Learning and behavior therapy* (pp. 374-391). Boston, MA: Allyn & Bacon, Inc.

Hayes, S. C., Kohlenberg, B. S., & Hayes, L. J. (1991). The transfer of specific and general consequential functions through simple and conditional equivalence classes. *Journal of the Experimental Analysis of Behavior, 56*, 119-137.

Hayes, S. C., Strosahl, K., & Wilson, K. (1999). *Acceptance and Commitment Therapy: An experiential approach to behavior change*. New York: Guilford Press.

Hayes, S. C., & Wilson, K. G. (1993). Some applied implications of a contemporary behavior analytic account of verbal behavior. *The Behavior Analyst, 16*, 283-301.

Hayes, S. C., & Wilson, K. G. (1994). Acceptance and Commitment Therapy: Altering the verbal support for experiential avoidance. *The Behavior Analyst, 17*, 289-303.

Hayes, S. C., Wilson, K. W., Gifford, E. V., Follette, V. M., & Strosahl, K. (1996). Emotional avoidance and behavioral disorders: A functional dimensional approach to diagnosis and treatment. *Journal of Consulting and Clinical Psychology, 64*, 1152-1168.

Hayes, S. C., Zettle, R. D., & Rosenfarb, I. (1989). Rule following. In S. C. Hayes (Ed.), *Rule-governed behavior: Cognition, contingencies, and instructional control* (pp. 191-220). New York: Plenum.

Joyce, J. H., & Chase, P. N. (1990). Effects of response variability on the sensitivity of rule-governed behavior. *Journal of the Experimental Analysis of Behavior, 54*, 251-262.

Kendall, S. B. (1983). Tests for mediated transfer in pigeons. *The Psychological Record, 33*, 245-256.

Kohlenberg, R. J., & Tsai, M. (1987). Functional analytic psychotherapy. In N. Jacobson (Ed.), *Psychotherapists in clinical practice: Cognitive and behavioral perspectives* (pp. 388-443). New York: Guilford.

Lawrence, E., Eldridge, K. A., & Christensen, A. (1998). The enhancement of traditional behavioral couples therapy: Consideration of individual factors and dyadic development. *Clinical Psychology Review, 18*, 745-764.

Linehan, M. M. (1993). *Cognitive-behavioral treatment of borderline personality disorder*. New York: Guilford.

Lipkens, G., Hayes, S. C., & Hayes, L. J. (1993). Longitudinal study of derived stimulus relations in an infant. *Journal of Experimental Child Psychology, 56,* 201-239.

Lipkens, R., Kop, P. F. M., & Matthijs, W. (1988). A test of symmetry and transitivity in the conditional discrimination performances of pigeons. *Journal of the Experimental Analysis of Behavior, 49,* 395-409.

Matthews, B.A., Shimoff, E., Catania, C., & Sagvolden, T. (1977). Uninstructed human responding: Sensitivity to ratio and interval contingencies. *Journal of the Experimental Analysis of Behavior, 27,* 453-467.

Parrott, L. J. (1987). Rule governed behavior: An implicit analysis of reference. In S. Modgil & C. Modgil (Eds.), *B. F. Skinner: Consensus and controversy.* Barcombe, England: Falmer Press.

Risley, T. R., & Wolf, M. M. (1967). Establishing functional speech in echolalic children. *Behaviour Research and Therapy, 5,* 73-88.

Roche, B., & Barnes, D. (1997). A transformation of respondently conditioned stimulus function in accordance with arbitrarily applicable relations. *Journal of the Experimental Analysis of Behavior, 67,* 275-301.

Rosenfarb, I., & Hayes, S. C. (1984). Social standard setting: The Achilles' heel of informational accounts of therapeutic change. *Behavior Therapy, 15,* 515-528.

Sidman, M. (1971). Reading and auditory-visual equivalence. *Journal of Speech and Hearing Research, 14,* 5-13.

Skinner, B. F. (1945). The operational analysis of psychological terms. *Psychological Review, 52,* 270-276.

Skinner, B. F. (1953). *Science and human behavior.* New York: Free Press.

Skinner, B. F. (1957). *Verbal behavior.* New York: Appleton-Century-Crofts.

Skinner, B. F. (1966). An operant analysis of problem solving. In B. Kleinmuntz (Ed.), *Problem-solving: Research, method, and theory* (pp. 225-257). New York: Wiley.

Skinner, B. F. (1974). *About behaviorism.* New York: Knopf.

Steele, D. L., & Hayes, S. C. (1991). Stimulus equivalence and arbitrarily applicable relational responding. *Journal of the Experimental Analysis of Behavior, 56,* 519-555.

Wegner, D. M., Schneider, D. J., Carter, S. R., III, & White, T. L. (1987). Paradoxical effects of thought suppression. *Journal of Personality and Social Psychology, 53,* 5-13.

Wegner, D. M., Schneider, D. J., Knutson, B., & McMahon, S. R. (1991). Polluting the stream of consciousness: The effect of thought suppression on the mind's environment. *Cognitive Therapy and Research, 15,* 141-152.

Chapter 11

Behavioral Interventions for Children With Autism

William D. Frea and Glenda L. Vittimberga
California State University, Los Angeles

Autistic disorder is a pervasive developmental disorder (PDD) that affects nearly 1 in every 1,000 births (Bryson, Clark, & Smith, 1988; Honda, Shimizu, Misumi, & Niimi, 1996; Sugiyama & Abe, 1989). The essential features of the disorder are (1) qualitative impairments in social interaction, (2) abnormal and impaired communication development, and (3) restrictive, repetitive, and stereotyped patterns of behavior, interests, and activities (American Psychiatric Association, 1994). Applied behavior analysis has played the leading role in discovering and evaluating treatments for autistic disorder. In the early 1960s, behavioral researchers began to explore approaches to teaching children with autism that proved to be effective (Ferster, 1961; Ferster & DeMyer, 1961, 1962; Lovaas, Berberich, Perloff, & Schaeffer, 1966; Lovaas, Freitag, Gold, & Kassorla, 1965). These approaches led to a stream of validated interventions in the areas of language development, play acquisition, functional skills training, and increased social responding that continue to be built upon today. Whereas the challenges of the 1960s and 1970s were in demonstrating that children with autism could benefit from teaching, the challenges that applied behavior analysts face going into the twenty-first century are focused more on the development of assessments and interventions that are both functional and well suited for application in children's homes, schools, and community settings (Koegel, Koegel, Frea, & Smith, 1995).

This chapter will review current research and issues in the field of autism across four areas: (1) disruptive and destructive behaviors, (2) self-stimulatory behavior, (3) language development, and (4) social skills. We also present several directions for future research. Our goal is to provide an understanding of the role of applied behavior analysis in the treatment of the comprehensive needs of children with autism and their families.

Disruptive and Destructive Behaviors

Problematic behaviors in autism, such as tantrums, self-injury, and aggression, are typically thought of as the most significant obstacles to providing effective intervention. Early treatment approaches included punishment procedures such as contingent electric shock, which provided immediate decreases in self-injurious behaviors (Lovaas & Simmons, 1969). Other forms of punishment included thigh slaps, harsh verbal reprimands, and time-out procedures (Bostow & Bailey, 1969; White, Nielsen, & Johnson, 1972). While effective in producing immediate reductions in problematic behaviors, these procedures tended to show limited generalization and maintenance. Applied behavior analysts have long known that punished behaviors sometimes recur when the punisher is no longer provided contingent on the behavior. In the past decade, there has been significant discussion in the behavioral literature about whether there is a need for the use of aversive procedures in the treatment of severe behavior problems (Horner et al., 1990; Meyer & Evans, 1989). The following section discusses current trends within two of the most pivotal areas of the literature on treating disruptive and destructive behaviors: functional assessment and antecedent manipulation strategies.

Functional Assessment and Functional Communication Training

A focus toward a more individualized approach to treatment selection occurred in the field of applied behavior analysis when researchers began to examine the different reasons that individuals were engaging in problematic behaviors. Individuals with autism were a primary focus in the evolution of functional assessment procedures (Carr, 1977). Iwata, Dorsey, Slifer, Bauman, and Richman (1994/1982) examined the functional nature of self-injury, finding that even in the most profound cases there was often a social function involved. This landmark study led to a flood of research, particularly in the *Journal of Applied Behavior Analysis*, into the relationship between the acquisition of alternative forms of communication and dramatic decreases in problematic behaviors (e.g., Carr & Durand, 1985; Frea & Hughes, 1997; Horner & Day, 1991; Sasso et al., 1992; Wacker et al., 1990). For a more extensive review of the functional assessment literature, we refer the reader to the chapter by Iwata, Kahng, Wallace, and Lindberg (this volume; 1999).

Although the term "functional analysis" has typically referred to analog (experimental) assessments with tightly controlled manipulations of discriminative and reinforcing stimuli, approaches to performing functional assessments vary. There are several resources available for structuring descriptive assessments. For example, O'Neill et al. (1997) created a handbook that provides a discussion of assessment approaches, as well as interview and observation forms. Frea, Koegel, and Koegel (1993) created a similar resource that provides a checklist for parents to use in assessing problem behaviors of children with autism in the home. Carr et al. (1994) published a guide to functional assessment that relies on user-friendly index cards. All of these approaches have been useful in providing relatively simple options to teachers, families, and interventionists for collecting antecedent, consequence, and other environmental information surrounding problematic behavior.

The need for parents to become involved in the functional assessment process has also been addressed (Frea & Hepburn, in press; Koegel, Koegel, Kellegrew, & Mullen, 1996; Lucyshyn, Albin, & Nixon, 1997; Mullen & Frea, 1995; Wacker et al., 1998). Parent involvement in functional analysis has been largely limited to providing data to clinicians. Since it is widely recognized that parent involvement in developing and implementing behavioral interventions is a crucial component in promoting adaptive behavior in children with autism, it seems reasonable to teach parents to conduct independent functional assessments of behavior. Teaching parents to assess the functions of interfering behaviors and to teach appropriate, functional responses to their children may help to increase appropriate behavior, promote generalization, and provide parents with the tools to manage the continually changing behaviors of their children with autism (Frea & Hepburn, 1999).

Family participation in intervention planning and implementation is seen as a critical issue in the area of behavior problems (Koegel, Steibel, & Koegel, 1998; Lucyshyn et al., 1997; Vaughn, Clarke, & Dunlap, 1997). While most would agree that input from parents is pivotal in planning effective support strategies, the question of parents' ability to learn independent assessment approaches to help guide their teaching efforts is often overlooked. The issue of continued and repeated dependence on professionals to organize assessment efforts is one of incredible importance to families of children with autism. While effective and widely accepted instruments for gathering assessment information for severe problem behaviors exist, efforts are still needed to examine the abilities of parents in planning interventions independently based on their own structured observations and knowledge of their child and home.

Functional assessment information primarily informs teaching goals, as well as efforts to provide environmental supports. Carr and Durand (1985) examined functional analyses in the classroom, and developed a technology for functional communication training to provide children with autism alternative responses to gain the types of reinforcers for which they were engaging in problematic behaviors. This study was critical in orienting the field toward exploring a better understanding of the need to establish communication goals targeted at critical social functions. Although there has been a multitude of articles that have examined functional communication training as an intervention for disruptive and destructive behaviors, most view the process in its simplest terms; that is, the relationship between functional communication and decreased behavior problems. More recently articles that underscore the importance of viewing communication goals in a broader family and community context have appeared (e.g., Albin, Lucyshyn, Horner, & Flannery, 1996; Frea & Hepburn, in press; Lucyshyn et al., 1997). This represents an important area of research if our emerging behavioral technology is going to be successfully applied in natural settings.

Antecedent Approaches

The field of autism, as well as the related field of positive behavior support, has become increasingly aware of the need to assess stimulus variables in managing problematic behavior (Carr, Yarbrough, & Langdon, 1997). Similarly, as more is learned about assessing and accommodating stimuli contributing to behavior problems, broader antecedent strategies to behavioral support for autism are being researched (Sweeney & LeBlanc, 1995). Recently antecedent approaches have been better defined by applied behavior analysts, who continue to enhance technologies for assessing environmental and biological variables that impact problematic behaviors (Baer, 1997; Luiselli & Cameron, 1998). By evaluating and manipulating antecedent stimuli, problematic behaviors are preempted and functional skills better acquired. While antecedent strategies are typically one factor in a multicomponent approach to positive behavior support (Bambara, Mitchell-Kvacky, & Iacobelli, 1994), this section describes two specific antecedent strategies that have been well researched in the area of autism.

Preference assessments and choice making strategies have lent much to the antecedent literature for creating behavior change (Bambara, Ager, & Koger, 1994; Bambara, Koger, Katzer, & Davenport, 1995; Datillo & Rusch, 1985; Peck, 1985). The study of the influence of child-preferred activities on the behavior of children with autism has found that preferred activities generate more positive social behavior (Koegel, Dyer, & Bell, 1987). Allowing children with autism to choose rewards (Dyer, 1987) and tasks (Dyer, Dunlap, & Winterling, 1990) results in decreases in problematic behaviors that may occur during instruction. Interest in the area of choice-making has grown recently as researchers discover more about its applicability for decreasing problematic behavior (cf., Kern et al., 1998). It is clear at this time that, as students learn to assert preferences and gain more control over their environments, problematic behaviors decrease (Ip, Szymanski, Johnston-Rodriguez, & Karls, 1994; Seybert, Dunlap, & Ferro, 1996). This has important implications for improving the quality of teaching efforts for children with autism. For example, one recent study found that performance (i.e., accuracy, production, child affect, problematic behaviors) during academic tasks improved in children with autism when choices pertaining to the order of task and materials necessary for task completion were provided (Moes, in press).

Another set of antecedent strategies that represent a growing trend in the intervention literature is behavioral momentum (Mace et al., 1988). Access to reinforcement prior to being prompted to perform difficult tasks creates a higher probability for success. One approach to providing such access is the presentation of tasks that have been previously demonstrated to be readily completed by the student. By interspersing requests that have a high-probability of compliance into instructional activities, teachers and clinicians are more likely to see increased compliance to more challenging requests (Davis, Brady, Williams, & Hamilton, 1992; Horner, Day, Sprague, O'Brien, & Heathfield, 1991; Mace & Belfiore, 1990; Singer, Singer, & Horner, 1987; Zarcone, Iwata, Hughes, & Vollmer, 1993; Zarcone, Iwata, Mazaleski, & Smith, 1994). This typically involves the presentation of a series of requests that have a high likelihood for compliance just prior to a more difficult request. These strategies allow the child to experience more frequent reinforcement, and thus increase the child's motivation to respond more frequently (Koegel & Koegel, 1986). It is also possible that other reinforcing antecedents such as social comments prior to requests result in a higher probability for compliance (Kennedy, Itkonen, & Lindquist, 1995).

Physical exercise has also been a well-researched antecedent strategy for problematic behavior. However, since most of the research in this area has focused on self-stimulatory behavior, it will be discussed in the following section.

Self-Stimulatory Behaviors

Stereotypic behavior that is maintained independent of the social environment is clearly one of the most serious obstacles for individuals with autism. Often referred to as self-stimulation, these behaviors involve repeated and persistent body movements such as rocking or hand flapping. Behavioral interventions have been successful in reducing the frequency and duration of self-stimulatory behaviors (Keuthen & O'Sullivan, 1998), and in fact tend to be more successful than medication in many cases (Scotti, Evans, Meyer, & Walker, 1991; Singh, Landrum, Ellis, & Donatelli, 1993). There is still much uncertainty about the etiology of stereotypic movements. It is assumed that for most individuals this behavior serves no other function than sensory or kinesthetic feedback (Crawford, Brockel, Schauss, & Miltenberger, 1992; Schreibman, 1988). What is certain is that these behaviors severely limit interactions with learning environments and social models for children with autism.

Increasing Environmental Responding

Early research found that children with autism did not engage in appropriate play when self-stimulation was occurring (Koegel, Firestone, Kramme, & Dunlap, 1974). When the self-stimulation was suppressed through punishment, however, play increased. Other research also demonstrated that suppressing self-stimulatory behavior resulted in an increased ability to attend to learning materials (Koegel & Covert, 1972; Romanczyk, 1977). This apparent inverse relationship between stereotypic responding and attention to the environment has led to research that focuses on prompting attention or acknowledgment of environmental stimuli as a means to naturally suppress self-stimulation. In a study by Frea (1997), an auditory prompt was provided with a common digital wristwatch that was set to chime at gradually increasing intervals. This prompt served to evoke orienting responses (e.g., "He's mowing the lawn.") that varied depending on the abilities of each participant. The result of this intervention was an increase in the children's orienting and commenting on environmental stimuli, and a decrease in stereotypic responding.

Physical Exercise

Applied behavior analysis has been used to explore exercise as an antecedent intervention (Bachman & Fuqua, 1983). Such studies have provided participants with varying levels of exercise immediately prior to specific activities or tasks. The use of physical exercise has been found to decrease stereotypic behavior in individuals with autism (Elliott, Dobbin, Rose, & Soper, 1994; Kern, Koegel, & Dunlap, 1984; Powers, Thibadeau, & Rose, 1992; Watters & Watters, 1980). These studies have generally found that the antecedent exercise must be vigorous aerobic exercise (e.g., jogging vs. walking) for the benefits to be meaningful (Celiberti, Bobo, Kelly, & Harris, 1997). It has been reported that decreases in self-stimulation typically last for less than an hour.

Self-Management

Self-management has been successful as a treatment approach for self-stimulation for students who can successfully discriminate between the presence and absence of a behavior (Koegel & Koegel, 1990). This procedure typically provides reinforcement for successful self-monitoring of the behavior or discriminative stimuli that evoke the behavior (Koegel, Frea, & Surratt, 1994). When monitoring, the individual typically records (e.g., with a checklist) appropriate behavior when prompted by a common digital watch alarm. When criteria are reached (i.e., the number of checked boxes) the individual recruits a reward which may function as a reinforcer. It has generally been found that self-monitoring the absence of stereotypic behavior has been more successful than monitoring the presence of self-stimulation.

Overcorrection

Overcorrection procedures, which have been particularly successful with toilet training, have also been researched as interventions for self-stimulation. Azrin, Kaplan, and Foxx (1973) referred to this technique as "autism reversal," which involved developing postures and exercises that were essentially the opposite of the stereotypy. These techniques have been well researched for aggression and toileting, but have seldom been explored for treating self-stimulation (Foxx & Azrin, 1972, 1973). For a more extensive review of the overcorrection literature, see Cooper, Heron, and Heward (1987).

Using Self-Stimulatory Behavior as a Reinforcer

Researchers have explored the use of contingent problematic behaviors as reinforcers. Similar to Premack's (1959) exploration of highly probable responses as reinforcers for less probable responses, this research has explored the use of stereotypic behavior as a reinforcer for academic and imitative tasks. Across three experiments, it was found that performance on difficult tasks improved during conditions in which self-stimulation, delayed echolalia, or perseverative behavior were provided as reinforcers (Charlop, Kurtz, & Casey, 1990). In fact, self-stimulatory behavior proved to be a more effective reinforcer than edible consequences. This study built on previous research examining the possible reinforcing and sensory properties of stereotypic behavior (Lovaas, Newsom, & Hickman, 1987; Rincover & Newsom, 1985). Similar research has evaluated objects of obsession as reinforcers in the reduction of problematic behaviors including self-stimulation (Charlop & Haymes, 1996; Charlop-Christy & Haymes, 1998).

Speech and Language

One of the most significant contributions of applied behavior analysis to the field of autism research is in the area of interventions for speech and language disorders. Communication deficits represent one of the three primary diagnostic features of PDD, and are often the first to be noticed by parents. Language is often reported as the developmental area of most concern to parents. This is a reasonable concern since nearly half of all individuals with autism struggle to acquire any meaningful use of language (Bryson et al., 1988; Lord & Paul, 1997; Rimland, 1964). Even for children with autism who do develop spoken language, there is a constant struggle with issues of functional communication, pragmatics, and the social implications that are the direct results of communication deficits. These children are at risk for developing problematic behaviors if their ability to access basic wants and needs with meaningful systems of communication are left undeveloped. The field of applied behavior analysis has addressed the issue of communication deficits with two major lines of intervention methodology; those based on discrete-trial strategies, and milieu-based therapy.

"Discrete-Trial" Intervention

The earliest published intervention attempts from the field of applied behavior analysis used operant procedures to systematically shape vocal qualities and other various aspects of language (Lovaas, 1966; Lovaas et al., 1966; Risley & Wolf, 1967). These interventions typically targeted a single aspect of spoken language (e.g., production of specific phonemes), and were reliant on discrete-trial methods to prompt and reinforce the autistic child's imitation of a spoken model. Stimuli were presented to the child, along with prompts to label the objects (e.g., "say ball"). Correct responses were then reinforced with food, praise, and affection, while incorrect responses, self-stimulation, or disruptions were punished (Lovaas, 1977). It should be noted, however, that punishment procedures have been mostly discontinued within these treatment programs. The focus of these early interventions was typically the form and structure of language production, rather than the functional or social aspects of language. These studies produced the earliest evidence that systematic prompting and reinforcement associated with operant procedures could be used to shape verbal utterances in children with serious communication disorders.

Today, such discrete-trial methods have been largely refined and expanded. More recent studies have focused on such behaviors as spontaneous language use and play, and have even incorporated social validation measures (e.g., Matson, Sevin, Box, Francis, & Sevin, 1993). Attempts have been made to better plan for future classroom integration, and the classroom format has been incorporated into some training models. The quintessential model is that of Dr. Ivar Lovaas' Young Autism Project at University of California, Los Angeles (UCLA). This program is perhaps the largest and most comprehensive of its kind. The basic structure of UCLA's program has been described primarily in *The Me Book* (Lovaas, 1981), and in a subsequent outcome study (Lovaas, 1987). An essential feature of the UCLA Young Autism Project is that it provides intensive discrete-trial based early intervention for children with autism. The program targets children under the age of four, and includes a 40-hour weekly curriculum for three years. The curriculum emphasizes speech and language, initially targeting imitation skills and the reduction of interfering behaviors, and expanding to include receptive and expressive language, and more complex interactional and pre-academic skills. The teaching modality in the UCLA project is based primarily on discrete trials. Basic skills are presented in massed trials and continue until mastery is achieved. When basic skills are mastered, new sets of drills involving more complex skills are introduced. Subsequent maintenance checks are incorporated to ensure that learned skills are not forgotten.

To date, Lovaas and his colleagues have published two outcome studies reporting on a group of 19 children who received intensive services (an average of 40 hours per week) for a period of two or more years (Lovaas, 1987; McEachin, Smith, & Lovaas, 1993). These children were compared to a control group of children with autism enrolled in various special education programs and minimal weekly behavioral services (approximately 10 hours). Measures were taken on children's pre- and post-treatment IQ scores, and educational placement. Overall, it was reported that approximately 90% of the experimental group achieved significant improvements in IQ and educational placements, as compared to minimal changes in the IQ and educational placement for children in the control groups. Specifically, the authors reported that 47% of the experimental group achieved IQs in the "normal" range after treatment, compared to a pre-treatment mean IQ of 63. In 1993, a follow-up study was published (McEachin et al., 1993) that re-evaluated the children from the experimental group to see if gains in IQ and educational placement were maintained since the previous evaluation. The results of this investigation indicated that children in the experimental group were found to have higher IQ scores, less restrictive educational placements, and more adaptive behavior compared to the children in the control group at follow-up, indicating that the gains from the Young Autism Project were maintained over time. In addition, the authors described several of the children from the experimental group, previously diagnosed with autism, as achieving "normal functioning."

Obviously, claims such as these have a tremendous impact on researchers, practitioners, educators, and particularly, parents of children with autism. In several school districts around the country, parents unhappy with their children's lack of progress in school and feeling that a critical window for early intervention was closing, have successfully sued the public school systems, forcing them to provide intensive, discrete-trial programs (Alternatives to Lovaas therapy, 1996; Gresham & MacMillan, 1998). Not everyone, however, has been unilaterally encouraging of widespread adaptation of this approach. There have been several responses to the published data from the UCLA project. Although most who have commented on the Young Autism Project agree that the results are important and promising, there has been a widespread call to view the outcomes as preliminary until the results have been independently replicated (Foxx, 1993; Kazdin, 1993). Of concern are several methodological issues that threaten the validity of these studies, such as (1) non-random assignment of children to experimental and control groups, (2) the use of different measures of intelligence for different children, and (3) the use of different measures of intelligence before and after treatment. Others have criticized the use of the term "normal functioning." Mundy (1993) suggested that the outcome measures used in this study were not sensitive to the complex pragmatic and relational problems that can co-occur with a normal IQ, but which still result in significant impairment for children with autism. Additionally, there is some concern that the children selected for UCLA's experimental group were of higher intellectual functioning than might be evidenced in a random, representative sample of children with autism. This suggests a need to acknowledge that the promising results reported in the Lovaas (1987) and McEachin, Smith, and Lovaas (1993) studies may apply only to a select group of children. Future replications should attempt to incorporate children with heterogeneous features in an attempt to delineate if certain children benefit less than others and the characteristics of the children who benefit most.

What is not subject for debate is that the work from UCLA's Young Autism Project is landmark and extremely important in the field of autism and language development, and that children can and do learn skills within the confines of a strict paradigm. The work of Ivar Lovaas was pivotal in demonstrating to the world that children with autism could learn.

Milieu-Based Language Approaches

Many clinicians, teachers, parents, and researchers question the appropriateness of using highly structured conditions to teach language and communication. Language must be functional across settings. When teaching language under maximum stimulus control, prompt dependency is often the result, with little or no use of spontaneous language occurring in other environments (Charlop, Schreibman, & Thibodeau, 1985; Schreibman, 1988). As principles of generalization would dictate, removing language development from its natural social context will result in limits to its functional use in non-treatment environments (Stokes & Osnes, 1988).

Milieu teaching strategies address issues of generalization and spontaneous speech production. If discrete-trial methodologies represent therapist-guided, highly structured learning environments for language, milieu-based training represents its philosophical opposite. The essential features of the collection of interventions based on milieu-style learning are that they occur in natural contexts (e.g., play and social routines in classroom or home), use reinforcement that would occur naturally in social contexts, and are guided by the child's choices.

Hart and Risley (1968, 1975) first outlined an incidental teaching approach that included teaching strategies such as modeling, manding and modeling, time delay, and incidental teaching within the classroom setting. Researchers have examined these strategies and further developed milieu teaching strategies to assist caregivers in supporting language development across functional routines in the home and school (e.g., Cavallaro & Bambara, 1982; Charlop & Walsh, 1986; Halle, Marshall, & Spradlin, 1979; Warren & Kaiser, 1986; Warren, McQuarters, & Rogers-Warren, 1983).

Examples of such strategies include teaching the parent to "bait" the environment with items that are highly desirable to the child (e.g., favorite toys, activities, snacks). Ideally, these objects are placed within sight, but out of reach, creating a "need" for the child to communicate to the adult in order to gain access or assistance obtaining the item. The parent will prompt a request by asking, "What do you want?"

If the child does not respond, the request is modeled, "I want phone." The child's imitation of the verbal model is reinforced through access to the preferred item.

This methodology provides a modeling procedure that begins with establishing attention and a model to the child. If the child does not respond correctly, he or she is given a corrective model or feedback. Once the child acquires words, generalization is programmed through the mand-model procedure (Rogers-Warren & Warren, 1980). This requires the child to respond to questions such as, "What do you want?". Initiations are programmed using time-delay procedures (Halle, Baer, & Spradlin, 1981). With this procedure, situations are present or arranged where the child will need assistance. A delay is used as a prompt for the child to request assistance.

The Natural Language Paradigm (Koegel, O'Dell, & Koegel, 1987) is a similar set of procedures that provides for the manipulation of variables within natural language teaching conditions. This manualized approach is represented by the following components: (1) child's choice of stimulus items, (2) variation in target stimuli, (3) verbal prompts from caregiver or clinician, (4) play-based interaction, (5) reinforcement of child's attempts, and (6) reinforcers that are natural to the interaction (Koegel, 1995; Koegel et al., 1989). Grounded in the philosophy of earlier incidental teaching approaches, this paradigm is intended to be taught to parents and teachers, and to be conducted in the child's natural environments from the beginning of the intervention (Laski, Charlop, & Schreibman, 1988). Thus, generalization and maintenance of language gains are immediately promoted.

Alternative and Augmentative Communication Systems

The field of applied behavior analysis has also made progress in increasing communication interventions for children who are nonverbal, and not making gains with speech based programs. Aided, augmentative, and/or alternative systems have proven quite effective in building communication for children with autism (Mirenda & Schuler, 1988; Prizant & Wetherby, 1989). Applied behavior analysts have taught alternative or augmentative systems very effectively to children with autism. At this time, the earlier focus on strategies such as sign language for children with autism (e.g., Carr, 1979; Carr, Binkoff, Kologinsky, & Eddy, 1978) has given way to an emphasis on the use of picture symbols. There are several logical reasons for this shift. Whereas signing is difficult to understand by those not taught or told what the signs mean, picture symbols are easier for all to understand. In addition, picture symbol use appears to be easier to teach, and lends itself more to early reciprocal interactions (Mirenda & Schuler, 1986). One example is the Picture Exchange Communication System (PECS; Bondy & Frost, 1994; Frost & Bondy, 1994). With this system, the child exchanges picture cards for desired items. Children are first taught (through physical guidance and reinforcement), that the act of handing a picture card to an adult produces a reinforcing social response (access to a preferred stimulus). Children are then taught to discriminate between cards and to become independent in identifying their communication board and the person with whom to communicate.

The above format for picture exchange is an excellent example of a discrete-trial based methodology that considers issues of generalization, avoiding prompt dependency, and functionality throughout the stages of intervention. After the initial stage of teaching the exchange skills using physical guidance of the response and immediate reinforcement, children are immediately taught independent and spontaneous communicative responding. Similar to the milieu-based strategies, PECS can utilize natural reinforcers and activities that are motivating to the child. These factors make picture exchange systems a potentially effective approach for children who continue to struggle with communication development, and who are displaying problematic behaviors in the classroom as a result of communication needs. As noted above, increases in functional communication typically result in decreases in problematic behaviors. Preliminary research indicates that picture exchanges can be an important component within positive behavior support planning (Frea & Arnold, 1999).

Play and Social Skills

Impaired social interaction is central to the autistic spectrum. For children with autism, these deficits are severe, and interact with impairments of language and behavior. These children typically display poor social relatedness, low social initiation, atypical toy play, inappropriate affect, and interfering disruptive and aggressive behaviors. Targets of these interventions have included teaching social initiations to peers, social responsiveness to peer statements, ongoing reciprocal social exchanges, and symbolic play behavior. The following section discusses several categories of social interaction interventions represented in the applied behavior analysis treatment literature, including peer prompting, affection or socialization activities, self-management, and pivotal response training.

Peer-Based Strategies

It is widely accepted that children with autism can benefit from exposure to typically developing peers in integrated settings (Frea, 1995; Strain, 1983). Integrated settings provide children with developmental disabilities needed models of appropriate behavior, and increased opportunity to engage in reinforcing social activity in natural contexts. The challenge of successful social integration has been documented through studies of the social patterns of integrated groups of children with and without disabilities, where data indicate that typical peers initiate infrequently with children with developmental disabilities (Guralnick & Groom, 1987, 1988). There is no question that additional structure is required to promote interaction between peers and children with disabilities in order for these children to benefit fully from integrated settings.

One of the first major lines of social intervention research involved teaching peers to socially initiate to children with autism, and to prompt and provide reinforcement for appropriate social responding and play behaviors (Odom & Strain, 1986). Peers were a logical choice of change agent. They participate in the natural contingencies and therefore can promote generalization, maintenance, and independence from more artificial prompting systems. Peer-mediated interventions begin with careful selection of peer trainers, as the social skills of the peers involved significantly impact the outcome of the intervention (Odom & Strain). Ideally, peers with a relatively high social status in the classroom, as measured by peer rankings or other sociometrics, may be considered initially. Odom and Brown (1993) suggested that peer trainers should demonstrate age appropriate play and social skills, good verbal communication skills, no history of negative peer interactions, compliance to teacher directives, attention to task for up to 10 minutes, and a willingness to participate in peer training. Peers chosen for training can then be supported in learning how to facilitate social interaction with students with autism. During a variety of training activities, peers can learn specific interactional skills that facilitate the social behavior of target peers with autism. Such skills may include simple prompting and reinforcement of social behaviors (Coe, Matson, Craigie, & Gossen, 1991), sharing, playing, and assisting children with autism (Brady, Shores, McEvoy, Ellis, & Fox, 1987), incidental teaching strategies to prompt labeling and turn taking (McGee, Almeida, Sulzer-Azaroff, & Feldman, 1992), and attending to and commenting on the behavior and communicative attempts of target peers (Goldstein, Kaczmarek, Pennington, & Shafer, 1992). These strategies have been successful in increasing social responding, reciprocal social interaction, and verbal and nonverbal play behaviors for young children.

The intent of peer-based strategies is that the peer provides all of the support for social interaction within the classroom environment. However, it is reasonable to assume that some peer tutors need additional support, such as teacher prompting and reinforcement, to effectively implement the social facilitation strategies. Peer-mediated interventions have typically relied on a high level of prompting from teachers or assistants to produce correct prompting behavior from peers. One option for creating more independence by peers is the use of self-management. Self-regulatory interventions have proven effective in increasing the independence of peer interactions (Sainato, Goldstein, & Strain, 1992). These approaches, which are useful in helping peers to independently increase their use of facilitative strategies in peer-based interventions, can also be used by children with autism, and will be discussed in a later section.

Group Affection or Socialization Activities

Group socialization activities, or group affection activities, serve to increase playful and intimate peer interactions within integrated classroom environments (Brown, Ragland, & Foxx, 1988). This approach to group activities targets "affectionate" play and socialization-related behaviors of young children, such as hugs, tickles, and social games, that occur in natural play contexts and are likely to be mutually reinforcing (Twardosz, Nordquist, Simon, & Botkin, 1983). These activities can be conducted during classroom-wide naturally occurring social activities, or in the context of integrated small-group play routines. Increased social responding and length of interactions between children with autism and their peers has been achieved by using teacher-lead small group activities that target hugs, pats "high-fives," and social games such as "duck-duck-goose" (McEvoy et al., 1988). This strategy serves to increase the probability that peers will interact with children with disabilities during play periods when affection activities are not in place (Frea, Craig, Odom, & Johnson, in press).

Self-Management

A challenge of all interventions for children with autism is the ability to program independent responding. One of the strengths of self-management is its expectation that the individual will become his or her own therapist (Koegel et al., 1994). Self-management interventions involve teaching the child to discriminate between appropriate and inappropriate social behavior, record appropriate responses, and self-administer reinforcement. This style of intervention has been successfully used with children with autism to increase social-communicative and play behaviors. Self-management procedures have been effective in treating verbal responsivity, topic shifting, vocal volume, eye gaze, affect, and facial expression (Frea & Hughes, 1997; Koegel & Frea, 1993; Koegel, Koegel, Hurley, & Frea, 1992). Self-management has also been useful in teaching appropriate play in unsupervised contexts by shaping increasingly longer intervals of play (Stahmer & Schreibman, 1992).

While self-management has proven to be successful for increasing appropriate social skills and programming for generalization, it is still important to assess for the appropriate skills to self manage. Specifically, it is important to remember that inappropriate social behavior often serves a communicative function, and alternative behaviors need to be functionally equivalent (Frea & Hughes, 1997). When planning to use self-management of social behavior, a functional assessment should be considered first, to ensure that increasing social skills will have a more powerful effect on decreasing inappropriate social behaviors.

Pivotal Response Training.

Pivotal Response Training (PRT) has been used as an intervention for language development for over 10 years, and has recently been applied with success in the areas of symbolic and sociodramatic play (Schreibman, Stahmer, & Pierce, 1996). Pivotal responses are those responses that, when targeted during intervention, have broad effects on other positive behaviors. PRT outlines criteria for addressing these area of deficit (Koegel et al., 1989), including providing clear instructions and questions, interspersing maintenance tasks with acquisition tasks, following child choice, providing direct, immediate, and contextually relevant reinforcement, reinforcing approximations of targeted behavior, teaching turn taking, and addressing responsivity to multiple cues through direct intervention (Koegel, 1995).

Symbolic play has always been difficult for children with autism to learn. It requires a level of social understanding that would typically be seen as far more advanced than can be expected for children with autism. Recent research has found that children with autism can make substantial gains in participating in symbolic play activities. Stahmer (1995) increased the complex and creative symbolic play of young children with autism, using PRT-based symbolic play training. Data were taken on the following behaviors: (1) using one object as if it were another, (2) attributing properties to an object which it did not have, and (3) referring to absent objects as if they were present. Of particular interest is the successful generalization to new play settings and new toys that was accomplished within this study.

While any type of typical play is a challenge for children with autism, sociodramatic play represents a particularly tough challenge. Sociodramatic play refers to play that follows a specific pretend theme, usually centered on familiar routines (e.g., "playing house"). In its truest form, it requires an understanding of social norms, and an ability to engage in pretend play to model behaviors that mimic those norms. Thorp, Stahmer, and Schreibman (1995) used PRT strategies to teach sociodramatic play to three children with autism, 5 to 9 years of age. All three children were able to learn sociodramatic play, as well as display increases in positive social behaviors, after PRT. As with the previous play study, participants in this study also were able to generalize play behaviors to other settings and toys. One of the hindrances to generalization to other play partners has been that PRT has often been performed by adults. Recent studies, however, have reported success with teaching peers to perform PRT (Pierce & Schreibman, 1995, 1997). In this study, 10-year-old peers were able to teach complex social behavior to their peers with autism. This suggests a promising future for research in this intervention area.

Directions for Future Research

Non-Aversive Approaches to Treatment

While the debates surrounding the movement in support of nonaversive behavior management are hardly new (Evans & Meyer, 1985; Gast & Wolery, 1986; Horner et al., 1990; LaVigna & Donnellan, 1986; McGee, Menolascino, Hobbs, & Monousek, 1987; Thompson, 1990), there remains a minority who continue to find value in the use of painful stimuli or stigmatizing procedures to treat problematic behaviors such as self-injury in school (Jacob-Timm, 1996), residential (Williams, Kirkpatrick-Sanchez, & Crocker, 1994), and community settings (Linscheid, Pejeau, Cohen, & Footo-Lenz, 1994). The argument continues to be made for consumers' right to effective treatment options and thus, the need for access to punishment procedures. While the allure of an immediate suppression of self-injury with punishment is understandable, the field now has ample evidence that nonaversive approaches can be equally effective and enduring. At this time, the technology of positive behavior support has successfully documented effective approaches to decreasing the most problematic behaviors. The new journal, *Journal of Positive Behavior Interventions*, is one example of the popularity and success of this technology. The goal for the future is to provide caregivers with an understanding of this technology, and to focus on providing information to schools, community agencies, and organizations that promotes this understanding more broadly. Once technologies such as functional assessment, antecedent manipulations, and a focus on teaching adaptive communication and behavior begin to be articulated regularly by teachers, psychologists, speech and language pathologists, and paraprofessionals, we can begin to expect less reliance on aversive procedures.

Systematic Selection of Appropriate Interventions

Autism has been discussed as a spectrum disorder (along with PDD and Asperger's Syndrome), as well as a disorder of clusters representing different styles of social interaction (Wing, 1997; Wing & Gould, 1979). No one is certain how to begin classifying the different "types of autism" represented by this growing population of individuals. This is an incredibly heterogeneous population, with significant variability in responding to different language, behavioral, and social skills interventions. Each child presents with different symptoms and different successes and challenges across school, home, and community environments. These facts, along with a necessary respect for family differences, present interventionists with a formidable challenge each time a new child with autism is identified.

Currently, the field is a long way from packaging interventions to meet the needs of specific subtypes of children. However, there have been important contributions toward this goal. Discrete-trial methods are clearly beneficial for some children (Lovaas, 1987). While currently mired in controversy regarding exaggerated claims (cf., Foxx, 1993; Gresham & MacMillan, 1997, 1998; Smith & Lovaas, 1997), more research is needed to address where this methodology fits into the larger picture of independent, broad, and generalized functioning for children with autism. Self-management is another approach that continues to receive attention for its successes in increasing independent responding. However, little research has looked at its use with younger children or its application within broader treatment packages.

Our knowledge of how children with autism learn continues to grow, along with our technologies for assessment and intervention. Unfortunately, applied behavior analysis appears to be hindered in its attempts to approach more comprehensive treatment packages by several factors. One of those factors is the ability to reach the classroom and homes where our approaches must be tested. Researchers often express frustration with the time it takes our interventions to reach their targeted populations (Schreibman, 1997). It is a reasonable assumption that broader dissemination, and increased meaningful feedback from other professionals and families, would facilitate our understanding of the potential benefits and impact of our treatment packages

Contextualized Approaches to Assessment and Treatment Planning

The full benefits of any intervention rely on the family's or school's ability to integrate the strategies into the typical interactions and routines that occur naturally every day. The issue of improving the "goodness of fit" of behavioral interventions applied in natural settings (e.g., homes, classrooms, job sites, shopping malls) has become an increasingly important area of investigation. The needs, means, and values of families must be assessed prior to intervention if there is going to be any expectation that generalization and maintenance will take place without the family ascribing to an artificial home or community atmosphere. The issue of contextual or ecological fit has been addressed by a number of researchers (Albin et al., 1996; Bailey et al., 1990; Bernheimer & Keogh, 1995; Lucyshyn et al., 1997; Moes & Frea, 1999; Peck, 1993; Robbins, Dunlap, & Plienis, 1991). This growing literature suggests that families and educators are unlikely to subscribe to and implement intervention strategies over time that are incompatible with their ongoing practices and goals.

Careful assessment of the family context has been recognized as a valuable component in facilitating the success of intervention efforts. One unit of analysis that has proven useful in guiding assessment and intervention efforts is the daily routines of the family (Lucyshyn et al., 1997; Vaughn et al., 1997). Daily routines represent the specific contexts in which difficulties present themselves and interventions will be applied. Other important parameters when assessing family context include the social interactions within and beyond the family environment, the caregiving demands experienced, and the workload of the caregivers. (Bernheimer & Keogh, 1995; Costigan, Floyd, Harter, & McClintock, 1997; Moes, 1995; Moes & Frea, 1999). It is necessary to consider such aspects of daily family life in order to ensure that families can incorporate teaching opportunities into necessary daily routines. This is particularly important, considering the history of behavioral interventions that have been taught to families in a highly rigid and structured manner, potentially creating additional and incompatible routines. The goal of these emerging approaches that attempt to achieve contextual fit is to ensure that interventions integrate, rather than compete, with the daily activities that individual families value and upon which they depend.

Reading Objectives

1. What are the primary characteristics of autistic disorder?
2. Briefly describe two antecedent strategies for managing problematic behavior.
3. How has self-stimulatory behavior been used as a reinforcer? Consider this approach from a social validity perspective.
4. Briefly describe the primary features of "discrete-trial" intervention as proposed in this chapter.
5. Briefly describe the primary features of milieu-based therapy as proposed in this chapter.
6. Are "discrete-trial" and milieu-based approaches mutually exclusive? Briefly describe how these two approaches could be combined to maximize the benefits of each.
7. How is the Picture Exchange Communication System used to teach language?
8. How have peers been utilized in therapy for children with autism?
9. How have self-management procedures been utilized with children with autism? Consider *when* this approach might be problematic.
10. Briefly describe the controversy relating to the use of aversive reductive procedures. How do these issues integrate with a functional approach to treatment?

References

Albin, R. W., Lucyshyn, J. M., Horner, R. H., & Flannery, K. B. (1996). Contextual fit for behavioral support plans: A model for "goodness of fit". In R. L. Koegel, L. K.

Koegel, & G. Dunlap (Eds.), *Positive behavioral support: Including children with difficult behavior in community settings* (pp. 81-98). Baltimore: Paul H. Brookes.

Alternatives to Lovaas therapy. (1996, October). *Early Childhood Reports-Bonus Report*, 1-4.

American Psychiatric Association. (1994). *Diagnostic and statistical manual* (4th ed.). Washington, DC: Author.

Azrin, N. H., Kaplan, S. J., & Foxx, R. M. (1973). Autism reversal: Eliminating stereotyped self-stimulation of retarded individuals. *American Journal of Mental Deficiency, 78*, 241-248.

Bachman, J. E., & Fuqua, R. W (1983). Management of inappropriate behaviors of trainable mentally impaired students using antecedent exercise. *Journal of Applied Behavior Analysis, 16*, 477-484.

Baer, D. M . (1997). *Environment and behavior*. Boulder, CO: Westview.

Bailey, D. B., Simeonsson, R. J., Winton, P. J., Huntington, G. S., Comfort, M., Isbell, P., O'Donnell, K. J., & Helm, J. M. (1990). Family-focused intervention: A functional model for planning, implementing, and evaluating individualized family services in early intervention. *Journal of the Division for Early Childhood, 10*, 156-171.

Bambara, L. M., Ager, C., & Koger, F. (1994). The effects of choice and task preference on the work performance of adults with severe disabilities. *Journal of Applied Behavior Analysis, 27*, 555-556.

Bambara, L. M., Koger, F., Katzer, T., & Davenport, T. A. (1995). Embedding choices in the context of daily routines: An experimental case study. *Journal of the Association for Persons with Severe Handicaps, 20*, 185-195.

Bambara, L. M., Mitchell-Kvacky, N. A., & Iacobelli, S. (1994). Positive behavioral support for students with severe disabilities: An emerging multicomponent approach for addressing challenging behaviors. *School Psychology Review, 23*, 263-278.

Bernheimer, L. P., & Keogh, B. K. (1995). Weaving intervention into the fabric of everyday life: An approach to family assessment. *Topics in Early Childhood Special Education, 15*, 415-433.

Bondy, A. S., & Frost, L. A. (1994). The picture-exchange communication system. *Focus on Autistic Behavior, 9*, 1-19.

Bostow, D. E., & Bailey, J. W. (1969). Modification of severe disruptive and aggressive behavior using brief timeout and reinforcement procedures. *Journal of Applied Behavior Analysis, 2*, 31-38.

Brady, M. P., Shores, R. E., McEvoy, M. A., Ellis, D., & Fox, J. J. (1987). Increasing social interactions of severely handicapped autistic children. *Journal of Autism and Developmental Disorders, 17*, 375-390.

Brown, W. H., Ragland, E. U., & Foxx, J. J. (1988). Effects of group socialization procedures on the social interactions of preschool children. *Research in Developmental Disabilities, 9*, 359-376.

Bryson, S. E., Clark, B. S., & Smith, T. M. (1988). First report of a Canadian epidemiological study of autistic syndromes. *Journal of Child Psychology and Psychiatry, 29*, 433-445.

Carr, E. G. (1977). The motivation of self-injurious behavior: A review of some hypotheses. *Psychological Bulletin, 84*, 800-816.

Carr, E. G. (1979). Teaching autistic children to use sign language: Some research issues. *Journal of Autism and Developmental Disorders, 9*, 345-359.

Carr, E. G., Binkoff, J. A., Kologinsky, E., & Eddy, E. (1978). Acquisition of sign language by autistic children. I. Expressive labeling. *Journal of Applied Behavior Analysis, 11*, 489-501.

Carr, E. G., & Durand, V. M. (1985). Reducing behavior problems through functional communication training. *Journal of Applied Behavior Analysis, 18*, 111-126.

Carr, E. G., Levin, L., McConnachie, G., Carlson, J. I., Kemp, D. C., & Smith, C. E. (1994). *Communication-based intervention for problem behavior: A user's guide for producing positive change.* Baltimore: Paul H. Brookes.

Carr, E. G., Yarbrough, S. C., & Langdon, N. A. (1997). Effects of idiosyncratic stimulus variables on functional analysis outcomes. *Journal of Applied Behavior Analysis, 30*, 673-686.

Cavallaro, C. C., & Bambara, L. (1982). Two strategies for teaching language during free play. *Journal of the Association for Persons with Severe Handicaps, 7*, 80-93.

Celiberti, D. A., Bobo, H. E., Kelly, K. S., & Harris, S. L. (1997). The differential and temporal effects of antecedent exercise on the self-stimulatory behavior of a child with autism. *Research in Developmental Disabilities, 18*, 139-150.

Charlop, M. H., & Haymes, L. K. (1996). Using obsessions as reinforcers with and without mild reductive procedures to decrease autistic children's inappropriate behaviors. *Journal of Autism and Developmental Disorders, 26*, 527-546.

Charlop, M. H., Kurtz, P. F., & Casey, F. G. (1990). Using aberrant behaviors as reinforcers for autistic children. *Journal of Applied Behavior Analysis, 23*, 163-181.

Charlop, M. H., Schreibman, L., & Thibodeau, M. G. (1985). Increasing spontaneous verbal responding in autistic children using a time delay procedure. *Journal of Applied Behavior Analysis, 18*, 155-166.

Charlop, M. H., & Walsh, M. E. (1986). Increasing autistic children's spontaneous verbalizations of affection: An assessment of time delay and peer modeling procedures. *Journal of Applied Behavior Analysis, 19*, 307-314.

Charlop-Christy, M. H., & Haymes, L. K. (1998). Using objects of obsession as token reinforcers for children with autism. *Journal of Autism and Developmental Disorders, 28*, 189-198.

Coe, D. A., Matson, J. L., Craigie, C. J., & Gossen, M. A. (1991). Play skills of autistic children: Assessment and instruction. *Child and Family Behavior Therapy, 3*, 13-40.

Cooper, J. O., Heron, T. E., & Heward, W. L. (1987). *Applied behavior analysis.* Columbus, OH: Merrill.

Costigan, C. L., Floyd, F. J., Harter, K. S. M., & McClintock, J. C. (1997). Family processes and adaptation to children with mental retardation: Disruption and resilience in family problem–solving interactions. *Journal of Family Psychology, 11*, 515-529.

Crawford, J., Brockel, B., Schauss, S., & Miltenberger, R. G. (1992). A comparison of methods for the functional assessment of stereotypic behavior. *Journal of the Association for Persons with Severe Handicaps, 17*, 77-86.

Datillo, J., & Rusch, F. (1985). Effects of choice on leisure participation for persons with severe handicaps. *Journal of the Association for Persons with Severe Handicaps, 10*, 194-199.

Davis, C. A., Brady, M. P., Williams, R. E., & Hamilton, R. (1992). Effects of high-probability requests on the acquisition and generalization of responses to requests in young children with behavior disorders. *Journal of Applied Behavior Analysis, 25*, 905-916.

Dyer, K. (1987). The competition of autistic stereotyped behavior with usual and specially assessed reinforcers. *Research in Developmental Disabilities, 8*, 607-626.

Dyer, K., Dunlap, G., & Winterling, V. (1990). Effects of choice making on the serious problem behavior of students with severe handicaps. *Journal of Applied Behavior Analysis, 23*, 515-524.

Elliot, R. O., Dobin, A. R., Rose, G. D., & Soper, H. V. (1994). Vigorous, aerobic exercise versus general motor training activities: Effects on maladaptive behavior and stereotypic behaviors of adults with both autism and mental retardation. *Journal of Autism and Developmental Disorders, 24*, 565-576.

Evans, I. M., & Meyer, L. H. (1985). *An educative approach to behavior problems: A practical decision model for interventions with severely handicapped learners*. Baltimore: Paul H. Brookes.

Ferster, C. B. (1961). Positive reinforcement and behavioral deficits of autistic children. *Child Development, 32*, 437-456.

Ferster, C. B., & DeMyer, M. K. (1961). The development of performance in autistic children in an automatically controlled environment. *Journal of Chronic Diseases, 13*, 312-345.

Ferster, C. B., & DeMyer, M. K. (1962). A method for the experimental analysis of the behavior of autistic children. *American Journal of Orthopsychiatry, 32*, 89-98.

Foxx, R. M. (1993). Sapid effects awaiting independent replication. *American Journal on Mental Retardation, 97*, 375-376.

Foxx, R. M., & Azrin, N. H. (1972). Restitution: A method of eliminating aggressive disruptive behavior of retarded and brain damaged patients. *Behaviour Research and Therapy, 10*, 15-27.

Foxx, R. M., & Azrin, N. H. (1973). The elimination of autistic self-stimulatory behavior by overcorrection. *Journal of Applied Behavior Analysis, 6*, 1-14.

Frea, W. D. (1995). Social-communicative skills in high-functioning children with autism. In R. L. Koegel & L. K. Koegel (Eds.), *Teaching children with autism: Strategies for initiating positive interactions and improving learning opportunities* (pp. 53-66). Baltimore: Paul H. Brookes.

Frea, W. D. (1997). Reducing stereotypic behavior by teaching orienting responses to environmental stimuli. *Journal of the Association for Persons with Severe Handicaps, 22,* 28-35.

Frea, W. D., & Arnold, C. L. (1999). *The effects of a picture exchange program on the disruptive behavior of preschoolers with autism.* Manuscript submitted for publication.

Frea, W. D., Craig, L. A., Odom, S. L., & Johnson, D. (in press). Differential effects of structured social integration and group friendship activities for promoting social interaction with peers. *Journal of Early Intervention.*

Frea, W. D., & Hepburn, S. L. (1999). A demonstration of teaching parents of children with autism how to perform functional assessments to plan interventions for extremely disruptive behaviors. *Journal of Positive Behavioral Interventions, 1,* 112-116

Frea, W. D., & Hughes, C. (1997). Functional analysis and treatment of social-communicative behavior of adolescents with developmental delays. *Journal of Applied Behavioral Analysis, 30,* 701-704.

Frea, W. D., Koegel, L. K., & Koegel, R. L. (1993). *Understanding why problem behaviors occur: A guide for assisting parents to analyze causes of behavior and design treatment plans.* University of California, Santa Barbara.

Frost, L .A., & Bondy, A. S. (1994). The Picture Exchange Communication .System (PECS): Training manual. Cherry Hill, NJ: Pyramid Educational Consultants, Inc.

Gast, D. L., & Wolery, M. (1986). Severe maladaptive behaviors. In M. E. Snell (Ed.), *Systematic instruction of persons with severe handicaps* (3rd ed.) (pp. 300-332). Columbus, OH: Merrill Publishing.

Goldstein, H., Kaczmarek, L., Pennington, R., & Shafer, K. (1992). Peer-mediated intervention: Attending to, commenting on, and acknowledging the behavior of preschoolers with autism. *Journal of Applied Behavior Analysis, 25,* 289-305.

Gresham, F. M., & MacMillan, D. L. (1997). Autistic recovery? An analysis and critique of the empirical evidence on the early intervention project. *Behavioral Disorders, 22,* 185-201.

Gresham, F. M., & MacMillan, D. L. (1998). Early intervention project: Can its claims be substantiated and its effects replicated? *Journal of Autism and Developmental Disorders, 28,* 5-13.

Guralnick, M. J., & Groom, J. M. (1987). The peer relations of mildly delayed and non-handicapped preschool children in main-streamed playgroups. *Child Development, 58,* 1556-1572.

Guralnick , M. J., & Groom, J. M. (1988). Friendships of preschool children in mainstreamed playgroups. *Developmental Psychology, 24,* 595-604.

Halle, J. W., Baer, D. M., & Spradlin, J. E. (1981). Teachers' generalized use of delay as a stimulus control procedure to increase language use in handicapped children. *Journal of Applied Behavior Analysis, 14,* 387-400.

Halle, J. W., Marshall, A. M., & Spradlin, J. E. (1979). Time delay: A technique to increase language use and facilitate generalization in retarded children. *Journal of Applied Behavior Analysis, 12,* 431-440.

Hart, B., & Risley, T. R. (1968). Establishing the use of descriptive adjectives in the spontaneous speech of disadvantaged preschool children. *Journal of Applied Behavior Analysis, 1*, 109-120.

Hart, B., & Risley, T. R. (1975). Incidental teaching of language in the preschool. *Journal of Applied Behavior Analysis, 8*, 411-420

Honda, H., Shimizu, Y., Misumi, K., & Niimi, M. (1996). Cumulative incidence and prevalence of childhood autism in children in Japan. *British Journal of Psychiatry, 169*, 228-235.

Horner, R. H., & Day, H. M. (1991). The effects of response efficiency on functionally equivalent competing behaviors. *Journal of Applied Behavior Analysis, 24*, 719-732.

Horner, R. H., Day, H. M., Sprague, J. R., O'Brien, M., & Heathfield, L. T. (1991). Interspersed requests: A non-aversive procedure for reducing aggression and self-injury during instruction. *Journal of Applied Behavior Analysis, 24*, 265-278.

Horner, R. H., Dunlap, G., Koegel, R. L., Carr, E. G., Sailor, W., Anderson, J., Albin, R. W., O'Neill, R. E. (1990). Toward a technology of "nonaversive" behavior support. *The Journal of the Association for Persons with Severe Handicaps, 15*, 125-132.

Ip, S. M. V., Szymanski, E. M., Johnston-Rodriguez, S., & Karls, S. F. (1994). Effects of staff implementation of a choice program on challenging behaviors in persons with developmental disabilities. *Rehabilitation Counseling Bulletin, 37*, 347-357.

Iwata, B. A., Dorsey, M. F., Slifer, K. J., Bauman, K. E., & Richman, G. S. (1994). Toward a functional analysis of self-injury. *Journal of Applied Behavior Analysis, 27*, 197-209. (Reprinted from *Analysis and Intervention in Developmental Disabilities, 2*, 3-20, 1982).

Jacob-Timm, S. (1996). Ethical and legal issues associated with the use of aversives in the public schools: The SIBIS controversy. *School Psychology Review, 25*, 184-199.

Kazdin, A. E. (1993). Replication and extension of behavioral treatment of autistic disorder. *American Journal of Mental Retardation, 97*, 377-379.

Kennedy, C. H., Itkonen, T., & Lindquist, K. (1995). Comparing interspersed requests and social comments as antecedents for increasing student compliance. *Journal of Applied Behavior Analysis, 28*, 97-98.

Kern, L., Koegel, R. L., & Dunlap, G. (1984). The influence of vigorous versus mild exercise on autistic stereotyped behaviors. *Journal of Autism and Developmental Disorders, 14*, 57-67.

Kern, L., Vorndran, C. M., Hilt, A., Ringdahl, J. E., Adelman, B. E., & Dunlap, G. (1998). Choice as an intervention to improve behavior: A review of the literature. *Journal of Behavioral Education, 8*, 151-169.

Keuthen, N. J., & O'Sullivan, R. L. (1998). Behavioral treatment of stereotypic movement disorders. *Psychiatric Annals, 28*, 335-340.

Koegel, L. K. (1995). Communication and language intervention. In R. L. Koegel & L. K. Koegel (Eds.), *Teaching children with autism: Strategies for initiating positive interactions and improving learning opportunities* (pp. 17-32). Baltimore: Paul H. Brookes.

Koegel, L. K., Koegel, R. L., Hurley, C., & Frea, W. D. (1992). Improving social skills and disruptive behavior in children with autism through self-management. *Journal of Applied Behavior Analysis, 25,* 341-353.

Koegel, L. K., Koegel, R. L., Kellegrew, D., & Mullen, K. (1996). Parent education for prevention and reduction of severe problem behavior. In L. K. Koegel, R. L. Koegel, & G. Dunlap (Eds.), *Positive behavior support: Including people with difficult behavior in the community.* Baltimore: Paul H. Brookes.

Koegel, L. K., Steibel, D., & Koegel, R. L. (1998). Reducing aggression in children with autism toward infant or toddler siblings. *Journal of the Association for Persons with Severe Handicaps, 23,* 111-118.

Koegel, R. L., & Covert, A. (1972). The relationship of self-stimulation to learning in autistic children. *Journal of Applied Behavior Analysis, 5,* 381-387.

Koegel, R. L., Dyer, K., & Bell, L. K. (1987). The influence of child preferred activities on autistic children's social behavior. *Journal of Applied Behavior Analysis, 20,* 243-252.

Koegel, R. L., Firestone, P. B., Kramme, K. W., & Dunlap, G. (1974). Increasing spontaneous play by suppressing self-stimulation in autistic children. *Journal of Applied Behavior Analysis, 7,* 521-528.

Koegel, R. L., & Frea, W. D. (1993). Treatment of social behavior in autism through the modification of pivotal pragmatic skills. *Journal of Applied Behavior Analysis, 26,* 369-377.

Koegel, R. L., Frea, W. D., & Surratt, A. V. (1994). Self-management of problematic social behavior. In E. Schopler & G. Mesibov (Eds.), *Behavioral issues in autism* (pp. 81-97). New York: Plenum.

Koegel, R. L., & Koegel, L. K. (1986). The effects of interspersed maintenance tasks on academic performance in a severe childhood stroke victim. *Journal of Applied Behavior Analysis, 19,* 425-430.

Koegel, R. L., & Koegel, L. K. (1990). Extended reductions in stereotypic behavior of students with autism through a self-management treatment package. *Journal of Applied Behavior Analysis, 23,* 119-127.

Koegel, R. L., Koegel, L. K., Frea, W. D., & Smith, A. E. (1995). Emerging interventions for children with autism: Longitudinal and lifestyle implications. In R. L. Koegel & L. K. Koegel (Eds.), *Teaching children with autism: Strategies for initiating positive interactions and improving learning opportunities* (pp. 1-16). Baltimore: Paul H. Brookes.

Koegel, R. L., O'Dell, M. C., & Koegel, L. K. (1987). A natural language paradigm for teaching nonverbal autistic children. *Journal of Autism and Developmental Disabilities, 17,* 187-199.

Koegel, R. L, Schreibman, L., Good, A., Cerniglia, L., Murphy, C., & Koegel, L. K. (1989). *How to teach pivotal behaviors to children with autism: A training manual.* Unpublished manuscript. University of California, Santa Barbara.

Laski, K. E., Charlop, M. H., & Schreibman, L. (1988). Training parents to use the natural language paradigm to increase their autistic children's speech. *Journal of Applied Behavior Analysis, 21,* 391-400

LaVigna, G. W., & Donnellan, A. M. (1986). *Alternatives to punishment: Solving behavior problems with non-aversive strategies.* New York: Irvington.

Linscheid, T. R., Pejeau, C., Cohen, S., & Footo-Lenz-M. (1994). Positive side effects in the treatment of SIB using the Self-Injurious Behavior Inhibiting System (SIBIS): Implications for operant and biochemical explanations of SIB. *Research in Developmental Disabilities, 15,* 81-90.

Lord, C., & Paul, R. (1997). Language and communication in autism. In D. J. Cohen & F. J. Volkmar (Eds.), *Handbook of autism and pervasive developmental disorders* (2nd ed) (pp. 195-225). New York: John Wiley and Sons.

Lovaas, O. I. (1966). A program for the establishment of speech in psychotic children. In J. K. Wing (Ed.), *Early childhood autism.* London: Pergamon.

Lovaas, O. I. (1977). *The autistic child: Language development through behavior modification.* New York: Irvington.

Lovaas, O. I. (1981). *Teaching developmentally disabled children: The me book.* Baltimore: University Park.

Lovaas, O. I. (1987). Behavioral treatment and normal educational and intellectual functioning in young autistic children. *Journal of Consulting and Clinical Psychology, 55,* 3-9.

Lovaas, O I., Berberich, J. P., Perloff, B. F., & Schaeffer, B. (1966). Acquisition of imitative speech in schizophrenic children. *Science, 151,* 705-707.

Lovaas, O. I., Freitag, G., Gold, V. J., & Kassorla, I. C. (1965). Experimental studies in childhood schizophrenia. I. Analysis of self-destructive behavior. *Journal of Experimental Child Psychology, 2,* 67-84.

Lovaas, O. I., Newsom, C., & Hickman, C. (1987). Self-stimulatory behavior and perceptual reinforcement. *Journal of Applied Behavior Analysis, 20,* 45-68.

Lovaas, O. I., & Simmons, J. Q. (1969). Manipulation of self-destruction in three retarded children. *Journal of Applied Behavior Analysis, 2,* 143-157.

Luiselli, J. K., & Cameron, M. J. (1998). *Antecedent control: Innovative approaches to behavioral support.* Baltimore: Paul H. Brookes.

Lucyshyn, J. M., Albin, R. W., & Nixon, C. D. (1997). Embedding comprehensive behavioral support in family ecology: An experimental, single-case analysis. *Journal of Consulting and Clinical Psychology, 65,* 241-251.

Mace, F. C., & Belfiore, P. (1990). Behavioral momentum in the treatment of escape-motivated stereotypy. *Journal of Applied Behavior Analysis, 23,* 507-514.

Mace, F. C., Hock, M. L., Lalli, J. S., West, B. J., Belfiore, P., Pinter, E., & Brown, D. K., (1988). Behavioral momentum in the treatment of noncompliance. *Journal of Applied Behavior Analysis, 21,* 123-141.

Matson, J. L., Sevin, J. A., Box, M. L., Francis, K. L., & Sevin, B. M. (1993). An evaluation of two methods for increasing self-initiated verbalizations in autistic children. *Journal of Applied Behavior Analysis, 26,* 389-398.

McEachin, J. J., Smith, T., & Lovaas, O. I. (1993). Long-term outcome for children with autism who received early intensive behavioral treatment. *American Journal on Mental Retardation, 97,* 359-372.

McEvoy, M. A., Nordquist, V. M., Twardosz, S., Heckman, K. A., Wehby, J. H., & Denny, R. K. (1988). Promoting autistic children's peer interaction in an integrated early childhood setting using affection activities. *Journal of Applied Behavior Analysis, 21,* 193

McGee, G. G., Almeida, M. C., Sulzer-Azaroff, B., & Feldman, R. (1992). Promoting reciprocal interactions via peer incidental teaching. *Journal of Applied Behavior Analysis, 25,* 117-126.

McGee, J. J., Menolascino, F. J., Hobbs, D. C., & Menousek, P. E. (1987). *Gentle teaching: A non-aversive approach to helping persons with mental retardation.* New York: Human Science.

Meyer, L. H., & Evans, I. M. (1989). *Nonaversive intervention for behavior problems: A manual for home and community.* Baltimore: Paul H. Brookes.

Mirenda, P., & Schuler, A. L. (1986). Teaching individuals with autism and related disorders to use visual symbols to communicate. In S. Blackstone (Ed.), *Augmentative communication: An introduction.* Rockville, MD: American Speech-Language-Hearing Association.

Mirenda, P., & Schuler, A. L. (1988). Augmenting communication for persons with autism: Issues and strategies. *Topics in Language Disorders, 9,* 24-43.

Moes, D. R. (1995). Parent education and parenting stress. In R. L. Koegel & L. K. Koegel (Eds.), *Teaching children with autism: Strategies for initiating positive interactions and improving learning opportunities* (pp. 79-93). Baltimore: Paul H. Brookes.

Moes, D. R. (in press). Integrating choice-making opportunities within teacher-assigned academic tasks to facilitate the performance of children with autism. *Journal of the Association of Persons with Severe Handicaps.*

Moes, D. R., & Frea, W. D. (1999). *A focus on family context in the treatment of challenging behavior of children with autism.* Manuscript submitted for publication.

Mullen, K. B., & Frea, W. D. (1995). A parent-professional consultation model for functional analysis. In R. L. Koegel & L. K. Koegel (Eds.), *Teaching children with autism: Strategies for initiating positive interactions and improving learning opportunities* (pp. 175-188). Baltimore: Paul H. Brookes.

Mundy, P. (1993). Normal versus high-functioning status in children with autism. *American Journal on Mental Retardation, 97,* 381-384.

Odom, S. L., & Brown, W. H. (1993). Social interaction skills interventions for young children with disabilities in integrated settings. In C. A. Peck, S. L. Odom, & D. D. Bricker (Eds.), *Integrating young children with disabilities into community programs* (pp. 39-64). Baltimore: Paul H. Brookes.

Odom, S. L., & Strain, P. S. (1986). A comparison of peer initiation and teacher-antecedent interventions for promoting reciprocal social interaction of autistic preschoolers. *Journal of Applied Behavior Analysis, 19,* 59-72,

O'Neill, R. E., Horner, R. H., Albin, R. W., Sprague, J. R., Storey, K., & Newton, J. S. (1997). *Functional assessment and program development for problem behavior* (2nd ed). Pacific Grove, CA: Brookes/Cole.

Peck, C. (1985). Increasing opportunities for social control by children with autism and severe handicaps: Effects of student behavior and perceived classroom climate. *Journal of the Association for Persons with Severe Handicaps, 10*, 183-194.

Peck, C. (1993). Ecological perspectives on the implementation of integrated early childhood programs. In C. A. Peck, S. L. Odom, & D. D. Bricker (Eds.), *Integrating young children with disabilities into community programs: Ecological perspectives on research and implementation* (pp. 3-15). Baltimore: Paul H. Brooks.

Pierce, K. L., & Schreibman, L. (1995). Increasing complex social behaviors in children with autism: Effects of peer-implemented pivotal response training. *Journal of Applied Behavior Analysis, 28*, 285-295.

Pierce, K. L., & Schreibman, L. (1997). Multiple peer use of pivotal response training to increase social behaviors of classmates with autism: Results from trained and untrained peers. *Journal of Applied Behavior Analysis, 30*, 157-160.

Powers, S., Thibadeau, S., & Rose, K. (1992). Antecedent exercise and its effects on self-stimulation. *Behavioral Residential Treatment, 7*, 15-22.

Premack, D. (1959). Toward empirical behavior laws: Positive reinforcement. *Psychological Review, 66*, 219-233.

Prizant, B. M., & Wetherby, A. M. (1989). Enhancing language and communication in autism: From theory to practice. In G. Dawson (Ed.), *Autism: Nature, diagnosis, and treatment* (pp. 282-309). New York: Guilford.

Rimland, B. (1964). *Infantile autism.* New York: Appleton-Century-Crofts.

Rincover, A., & Newsom, C. D. (1985). The relative motivational properties of sensory and edible reinforcers in teaching autistic children. *Journal of Applied Behavior Analysis, 18*, 237-248.

Risley, T. R., & Wolf, M. M. (1967). Establishing functional speech in echolalic children. *Behaviour Research and Therapy, 5*, 73-88.

Robbins, F. R., Dunlap, G., & Plienis, A. J. (1991). Family characteristics, family training, and the progress of young children with autism. *Journal of Early Intervention, 15*, 173-184.

Rogers-Warren, A. K., & Warren, S. F. (1980). Mand for verbalization: Facilitating the display of newly-taught language. *Behavior Modification, 4*, 361-382.

Romanczyk, R. G. (1977). Intermittent punishment of self-stimulation: Effectiveness during application and extinction. *Journal of Consulting and Clinical Psychology, 45*, 53-60.

Sainato, D. M., Goldstein, H., & Strain, P. S. (1992). Effects of self-evaluation on preschool children's use of social interaction strategies with their classmates with autism. *Journal of Applied Behavior Analysis, 25*, 127-141.

Sasso, G. M., Reimers, T. M., Cooper, L. J., Wacker, D., Berg, W., Steege, M., Kelly, L., & Allaire, A. (1992). Use of descriptive and experimental analyses to identify the functional properties of aberrant behavior in school settings. *Journal of Applied Behavior Analysis, 25*, 809-822.

Schreibman, L. (1988). *Autism.* Newbury Park, CA: Sage.

Schreibman, L. (1997). Theoretical perspectives on behavioral intervention for individuals with autism. In D. J. Cohen & F. R. Volkmar (Eds.), *Handbook of autism and pervasive developmental disorders* (pp. 920-933). New York: John Wiley and Sons.

Schreibman, L., Stahmer, A. C., & Pierce, K. L. (1996). Alternative applications of pivotal response training: Teaching symbolic play and social interaction skills. In L. K. Koegel, R. L. Koegel, & G. Dunlap (Eds.), *Positive behavior support: Including people with difficult behavior in the community*. Baltimore: Paul H. Brookes.

Scotti, J. R., Evans, I. M., Meyer, L. H., & Walker, P. (1991). A meta-analysis of intervention research with problem behavior: Treatment validity and standards of practice. *American Journal of Mental Retardation, 96*, 233-256.

Seybert, S., Dunlap, G., & Ferro, J. (1996). The effects of choice-making on the problem behavior of high school students with intellectual disabilities. *Journal of Behavioral Education, 6*, 49-65.

Singer, G. H. S., Singer, J., & Horner, R. H. (1987). Using pretask requests to increase the probability of compliance for students with severe disabilities. *Journal of the Association for Persons with Severe Handicaps, 12*, 287-291.

Singh, N. N., Landrum, T. J., Ellis, C. R., & Donatelli, L. S. (1993). Effects of thorazine and visual screening on stereotypy and social behavior in individuals with mental retardation. *Research in Developmental Disabilities, 14*, 163-177.

Smith, T., & Lovaas, O. I. (1997). The UCLA young autism project: A reply to Gresham and MacMillan. *Behavioral Disorders, 22*, 202-218.

Stahmer, A. C. (1995). Teaching symbolic play skills to children with autism using pivotal response training. *Journal of Autism and Developmental Disorders, 25*, 123-141.

Stahmer, A. C., Schreibman, L. (1992). Teaching children with autism appropriate play in unsupervised environments using a self-management treatment package. *Journal of Applied Behavior Analysis, 25*, 447-459.

Stokes, T. F., & Osnes, P. G. (1988). The developing applied technology of generalization and maintenance. In R. H. Horner, G. Dunlap, & R. L. Koegel (Eds.), *Generalization and maintenance: Life-style changes in applied settings* (pp. 5-20). Baltimore: Paul H. Brookes.

Strain, P. S. (1983). Generalization of autistic children's social behavior change: Effects of developmentally integrated and segregated settings. *Analysis and Intervention in Developmental Disabilities, 3*, 23-34.

Sugiyama, T., & Abe, T. (1989). The prevalence of autism in Nagoya, Japan: A total population study. *Journal of Autism and Developmental Disorders, 19*, 87-96.

Sweeney, H. M., & LeBlanc, J. M. (1995). Effects of task size on work-related and aberrant behaviors of youths with autism and mental retardation. *Research in Developmental Disabilities, 16*, 97-115.

Thompson, T. (1990). The Humpty Dumpty world of "aversive" interventions. *Journal of the Association for Persons with Severe Handicaps, 5*, 136-139.

Thorp, D. M., Stahmer, A. C., & Schreibman, L. (1995). Effects of sociodramatic play training on children with autism. *Journal of Autism and Developmental Disorders, 25*, 265-282.

Twardosz, S., Nordquist, V. M., Simon, R., & Botkin, D. (1983). The effects of group affection activities on the interaction of socially isolate children. *Analysis and Intervention in Developmental Disabilities, 13*, 311-338.

Vaughn, B. J., Clarke, S., & Dunlap, G. (1997). Assessment-based intervention of severe behavior problems in a natural family context. *Journal of Applied Behavior Analysis, 30*, 713-716.

Wacker, D. P., Berg, W. K., Harding, J. W., Derby, K. M., Asmus, J. M., & Healy, A. (1998). Evaluation and long-term treatment of aberrant behavior displayed by young children with disabilities. *Journal of Developmental and Behavioral Pediatrics, 19*, 260-266.

Wacker, D. P., Steege, M. W., Northrup, J., Sasso, G., Berg, W., Reimer, T., Cooper, L., Cigrand, K., & Donn, L. (1990). A component analysis of functional communication training across three topographies of severe behavior problems. *Journal of Applied Behavior Analysis, 23*, 417-429.

Warren, S. F., & Kaiser, A. P. (1986). Incidental language teaching: A critical review. *Journal of Speech and Hearing Disorders, 51*, 291-299.

Warren, S. F., McQuarters, R. J., & Rogers-Warren, A. K. (1983). The effects of teaching mands and models on the speech of unresponsive language-delayed children. *Journal of Speech and Hearing Research, 26*, 43-52.

Watters, R. G., & Watters, W. E. (1980). Decreasing self-stimulatory behavior with physical exercise in a group of autistic boys. *Journal of Autism and Developmental Disorders, 10*, 379-387.

White, G. D., Nielsen, G., & Johnson, S. M. (1972). Time-out duration and the suppression of deviant behavior in children. *Journal of Applied Behavior Analysis, 5*, 111-120.

Williams, D. E., Kirkpatrick-Sanchez, S., & Cocker, W. T. (1994). A long-term follow-up of treatment for severe self-injury. *Research in Developmental Disabilities, 15*, 487-501.

Wing, L. (1997). Syndromes of autism and atypical development. In D. J. Cohen & F. R. Volkmar (Eds.), *Handbook of autism and pervasive developmental disorders* (pp. 148-170). New York: John Wiley and Sons.

Wing, L., & Gould, J. (1979). Severe impairments of social interaction and associated abnormalities in children: Epidemiology and classification. *Journal of Autism and Developmental Disorders, 9*, 11-29.

Zarcone, J. R., Iwata, B. A., Hughes, C. E., & Vollmer, T. R. (1993). Momentum versus extinction effects in the treatment of self-injurious escape behavior. *Journal of Applied Behavior Analysis, 26*, 135-136.

Zarcone, J. R., Iwata, B. A., Mazaleski, J. L., & Smith, R. G. (1994). Momentum and extinction effects on self-injurious escape behavior and noncompliance. *Journal of Applied Behavior Analysis, 27*, 649-658.

Chapter 12

Organizational Behavior Management in Human Service Settings

Dennis H. Reid and Marsha B. Parsons
Louisiana State University Medical Center and Carolina Behavior Analysis and Support Center, Morganton, NC

An area of major impact of applied behavior analysis is the human services. Behavior analysis research and application have advanced the treatment capabilities of essentially every type of human service profession. The scope of the treatment technology developed through applied behavior analysis is well illustrated in the diverse and comprehensive topics reviewed in Chapters 1 - 12 of this text.

The availability of an effective treatment technology, such as that developed through applied behavior analysis, is a necessity if human service agencies are to successfully provide supports and services desired by the agencies' consumer clientele. However, such availability does not ensure the treatment success of respective agencies. Equally important as the availability of an effective treatment technology is the effective application of the technology. Agency staff must proficiently apply the available technology if agency clients are to benefit from respective treatment procedures.

The importance of effective application of behavioral treatment procedures is perhaps best illustrated in the field of developmental disabilities. Developmental disabilities arguably represents the area of most significant impact of applied behavior analysis (Reid, 1992). In most human service settings providing supports for individuals with developmental disabilities, the vast majority of treatment services are provided by personnel who do not have professional training in a clinical field. Most supports and services are provided by, for example, teacher assistants, group home staff, institutional direct support persons, and vocational support staff. These individuals typically enter their human service roles with little or no training in how to provide behavioral treatment services for persons with disabilities (Parsons, Reid, & Green, 1996). The lack of training presents serious obstacles to the successful application of effective treatment technologies in behavior analysis.

Recognition of the difficulties in applying behavioral treatment procedures in typical human service agencies occurred relatively early in the development of applied behavior analysis (Whitman, Scibak, & Reid, 1983). Such recognition led researchers to begin focusing on use of behavioral training programs to enhance the proficiency with which human service staff applied behavioral treatment procedures with their clientele. The early investigations on training and managing the treatment-related performance of human service personnel represented the beginning stages of a new specialty area of applied behavior analysis – Organizational Behavior Management (OBM) in the human services. The focus of OBM is the use of behavior analytic principles and procedures to enhance performance in the work place. From the point of view of applied behavior analysis and human services, OBM focuses on improving the operation of human service agencies by maximizing the quality of staff work performance.

Although OBM currently represents a relatively small specialty area within the general field of applied behavior analysis, there has been a very considerable amount of OBM research and application in the human services. To illustrate, in a 1995 bibliography of OBM in developmental and related disabilities, over 270 articles, chapters and books are cited (Reid & Parsons, 1995a). The purpose of this paper is to review the current status of OBM in the human services.

Organization of Review

In keeping with the general format of other text chapters, this review is organized into four main sections. In the first section, a summary is presented of the research that resulted in the development of OBM as a specialty area as well as its primary procedural technology. Because most of the research represented in the first section occurred in the 1970s and 80s, a brief overview of more recent OBM research is presented in the second section of this paper. In the third section, the relationship of OBM to other supervisory and management approaches that are common in the human services will be described. Finally, based on the summaries of existing research in OBM, areas will be discussed in the fourth section that warrant continued attention of OBM researchers and practitioners in order to further enhance OBM's contribution in the human services, as well as the field of applied behavior analysis in general.

The Research Foundation of Organizational Behavior Management

Organizational Behavior Management has focused on two aspects of staff work performance that represent the essence of successful provision of quality supports and services in human service agencies. The first aspect pertains to staff having the necessary skills to perform their duties in a competent manner. The second aspect relates to staff applying those skills proficiently during the day-to-day work routine. The focus of OBM on these two critical aspects of agency functioning has resulted in two major areas of OBM research and application: staff training and staff management.

Staff Training Research

As indicated previously, in the early stages of applied behavioral research, investigators recognized the need for human service staff to be skilled in applying behavioral procedures if many persons with disabilities were to benefit from the developing behavioral technology. It was likewise recognized that most human service staff responsible for providing hands-on services for agency consumers were not aware of, or skilled in, behavioral treatment procedures. Consequently, initial behavioral investigations involving the work performance of human service staff focused on training staff in basic behavioral procedures such as reinforcing desirable client behavior, prompting, shaping and extinction (see Frazier, 1972; Gardner, 1973, for reviews of the early staff training research).

Following successful demonstrations that basic behavioral treatment procedures could be taught to human service personnel who had no professional background, researchers began to investigate use of a wider variety of behavioral training procedures to train staff in more varied job responsibilities (see Demchak, 1987; Reid & Green, 1990, for reviews of the latter staff training investigations). The most prevalent of the behavioral approaches for training work skills to staff has been multifaceted training programs. Multifaceted approaches involve the use of a large number of behavior change procedures that are combined into one training program. However, there is also a basic set of training procedures that represents the core of most multifaceted staff training programs. The latter procedures include verbal instruction, written instruction, performance modeling, performance practice, and performance feedback.

Verbal or vocal instruction represents a rather traditionally accepted means of staff training. Verbal instruction involves a vocal presentation to staff of the rationale for certain job skills, related background information and a description of the specific job skills to be performed. Verbal instruction typically has been presented through direct person-to-person contact such as an interaction between a trainee and a staff trainer (Montegar, Reid, Madsen, & Ewell, 1977) and to a lessor degree, through audiovisual formats such as computer-assisted programs (Singer, Sowers, & Irvin, 1986) and slide-tape presentations (Edwards & Bergman, 1982). Written instruction has also been used in a variety of training programs, involving self-instructional manuals prepared by an agency specifically for training one type of job skill (Hundert, 1982), commercially available, published papers or books for training a variety of general work skills (Stumphauzer & Davis 1983), performance checklists (Inge & Snell, 1985) and pictorial presentation of work duties (Stoddard, McIlvane, McDonagh, & Kledaras, 1986).

Reviews of the research on vocal and written instruction (Reid, Parsons, & Green, 1989) have indicated these procedures are generally best suited for teaching verbal skills to staff (i.e., the ability to discuss the subject matter) in contrast to teaching performance skills (i.e., how to actually do a job). Job-related verbal skills are of course important, in that being able to articulate the requirements of a job task can enhance staffs' understanding of their job requirements. However, being able to discuss the requirements and other aspects of a job does not ensure that staff actually know how to perform the job proficiently. Typically, for training programs to be effective in teaching performance skills to staff, instructions must be combined with more performance-based staff training strategies such as performance modeling, practice and feedback.

Performance modeling entails the demonstration of a work task via live (Mansdorf & Burstein, 1986) or filmed (Kissel, Whitman, & Reid, 1983) models. Frequently, when modeling is used to train staff, the modeling is conducted in simulated work situations. Such situations often involve trainers and/or trainees role-playing consumer behavior (Jones & Eimers, 1975) according to a planned script in order to ensure that each skill targeted to be taught to staff is demonstrated. However, modeling has also been conducted in a less structured manner by a trainer in the trainee's actual work site, involving the consumers for whom the trainees are responsible (Templeman, Fredericks, Bunse, & Moses, 1983).

In most behavioral training programs, modeling as just described is usually followed by performance practice. Performance practice involves a trainee rehearsing the skill that is being trained, often in conjunction with verbal and/or written instructions. As with performance modeling, trainees may practice the targeted work activities in the environment in which they routinely work (Stoddard et al., 1986) or in simulated work settings (Delameter, Connors, & Wells, 1984). An important advantage of performance practice is that the process provides the trainer with clear information as to whether the trainee has acquired the targeted skill. That is, practice provides an opportunity for the trainer to directly observe the staff member perform the new work skill that is being trained, with a subsequent determination as to whether the staff person truly has mastered the skill of concern.

Probably the most critical procedure incorporated within multifaceted approaches to staff training is performance feedback. When used as a part of a staff training program, performance feedback refers to information provided to a staff trainee regarding the (non)proficiency with which the trainee has performed the skill being trained. The purpose of feedback provided in this manner is to shape future performance. Feedback has been provided in a variety of ways in staff training programs including vocal (Fabry & Reid, 1978), videotaped (Kissel et al., 1983), publicly posted (Greene, Willis, Levy, & Bailey, 1978) and privately written (Fitzgerald et al., 1984) formats.

Results of the rather extensive body of research on behavioral staff training procedures provide convincing support for the utility of these approaches for training important work skills to human service staff. In short, a well articulated, effective technology exists for training a very wide variety of job skills (see Reid & Parsons, 1995b, for a step-by-step review of applying the staff training technology). The research has also repeatedly indicated, however, that a qualification is warranted when considering the use of staff training procedures. Specifically, staff training should be considered as being frequently necessary for assisting human service staff in performing their work duties proficiently, but rarely sufficient in this regard. This feature of staff training represents one of the most important conclusions stemming from the staff training research. Consequently, staff training alone should not be relied on to ensure work duties are routinely performed in a quality manner. Rather, staff training should be used in conjunction with procedures designed to effectively manage staffs' routine application of their job skills in the day-to-day work environment.

Staff Management Research

Research in OBM has developed a large and varied number of strategies for managing, or supervising, the work performance of staff in human service agencies. Many of the developed procedures are very similar to procedural components in staff training. However, there has been more research on the efficacy of the individual procedural components involved in managing staff performance than those involved in staff training. Staff management research has received more attention among OBM researchers for two likely reasons. First, due to the well established technology for training work skills to human service staff, this area does not appear to be in as much need for research relative to staff management strategies. Second, the most frequently observed problems with staff work performance appear to occur not because of a lack of sufficient skills on the part of staff (i.e., representing a need for staff training), but because of a failure of the work place environment to ensure that the skills are used appropriately in the daily work routine.

For organizational and descriptive purposes, management procedures for changing and maintaining ongoing work performance generally have been grouped into four categories. The categories represent antecedent management strategies, consequence strategies, self-management procedures, and multifaceted programs.

Antecedent supervisory procedures. Antecedent supervisory procedures are strategies conducted before staff are expected to perform a given work duty with the intent that the strategies will increase the likelihood that staff will complete the work duty in a satisfactory manner. One of the most frequently researched antecedent procedures involves on-the-job instructions such as brief verbal directions, memoranda, and instructional meetings. Instructional strategies used as part of an ongoing staff management program are intended to prompt staffs' performance in regard to something the staff know how to do, in contrast to instructional procedures used in staff training in which the intent is to establish a work skill in a staff member's performance repertoire. Research on on-the-job instructional strategies indicates these types of procedures can be effective in changing staff performance if the desired performance does not represent a major or long-term alteration in staffs' routine work activities. In contrast, these procedures usually have little impact on changing staff performance that occurs frequently during the routine work day or week (Reid et al., 1989).

An antecedent management procedure similar to instructions involves increasing job structure. Increasing the structure of a staff person's job refers to a precise elaboration regarding what a staff person is expected to do, when and how often it should be done, where the job duty should occur, with whom it should be done and with what materials (Iwata, Bailey, Brown, Foshee, & Alpern, 1976). Increasing job structure differs from on-the-job instruction by providing considerably more direction to staff regarding the expected performance of a particular job duty. Methods for increasing job structure include staff activity schedules (Parsons, Cash, & Reid, 1989), performance checklists (Lattimore, Stephens, Favell, & Risley, 1984) and duty cards (Sneed & Bible, 1979). Increasing job structure is generally more effective than instructions for ensuring that staff perform their respective job duties, but also usually requires more effort on the part of supervisors relative to using on-the-job instructional strategies.

Another type of antecedent management procedure, performance modeling, involves providing a physical demonstration of the desired work behavior in a manner similar to that described with staff training. The intent of modeling as a management procedure is to provide an immediate prompt in staffs' work area for staff to perform a certain job duty. Although modeling was used successfully in several early OBM investigations to improve staff work performance (e.g., Gladstone & Spencer, 1977; Wallace, Davis, Liberman, & Baker, 1973), generally this antecedent procedure has not received very much research attention as a specific management strategy.

Consequence management procedures. From our perspective, the most important contribution of OBM in regard to managing the work performance of human service staff has been the demonstration of systematic use of performance consequences to improve day-to-day work performance. Of all potential procedures for changing or maintaining staff work performance from both a staff training and management perspective, consequence procedures have been the most frequently investigated and the most consistently effective. Most consequence procedures involve some type of feedback, through which information about staff work performance is presented to staff (see Balcazar, Hopkins, & Suarez, 1986; Ford, 1980, for reviews of feedback procedures in OBM). In addition to descriptive or factual information about a staff member's performance, most management applications of feedback in the research literature also provide evaluative judgements about the adequacy of staff performance. The evaluative information may be praise statements (Montegar et al., 1977) or comparison to some preestablished work goal (Burg, Reid, & Lattimore, 1979). Evaluative comments are generally included because the comments appear to improve the performance enhancement efficacy of descriptive feedback procedures (Brown, Willis, & Reid, 1981; Realon, Lewallen, & Wheeler, 1983).

A variety of formats for providing feedback to staff have been evaluated in OBM investigations, including spoken or verbal feedback (Montegar et al., 1977), privately written feedback (Shoemaker & Reid, 1980), and publicly posted feedback (Greene et al., 1978). Generally, each type of feedback has been effective in improving some aspect of staff work performance. Relative advantages and disadvantages of different types of feedback have not been thoroughly investigated to date, although some recent research has suggested there may be significant differences regarding how different types of feedback are received by staff (see comments on OBM acceptability later in this chapter).

Although essentially all consequence procedures involve feedback to some degree, there are certain types of consequences that are not designed to provide detailed, descriptive information about job performance per se. The latter procedures are intended to have a purely reinforcing effect on specific aspects of staff performance. A variety of consequences have been demonstrated through OBM research to have reinforcing effects on desired staff performance including, for example, money, free meals, commercial trading stamps, discount coupons, and special privileges or events such as preferred work schedules, relief from undesired work duties, trips away from the work site, and special recognition ceremonies (Reid et al., 1989). However, despite the reinforcing effects of these types of consequences and subsequent improvements in staff work performance, it is often difficult for practical, economic and labor-relations reasons to arrange to use such items and privileges in a contingent manner in typical human service settings. Hence, more recent research has tended to focus on consequence applications that rely on feedback procedures as a means of reinforcing desired staff work performances. From a general perspective, feedback represents a readily available means of improving work performance in essentially any human service setting with relatively minimal time investment and essentially no economic cost. Effective use of feedback procedures does require a certain set of skills among supervisors, and not all supervisors in human service agencies display those skills without appropriate training (Parsons & Reid, 1995).

Self-management procedures. The third type of management procedure, self-management strategies, involves many of the antecedent and consequence procedures just described. The primary difference with self-management procedures is that whereas the management approaches discussed earlier are dependent upon supervisors for implementation, with self-management strategies a supervisor systematically involves staff in managing their own performance. The most frequently investigated self-management procedure has been self-recording, in which staff maintain records of their performance (Burg et al., 1979). Other types of self-management procedures include goal setting, in which a staff member participates with a supervisor to establish a goal or standard for work performance (Burgio, Whitman, & Reid, 1983), and self-reinforcement, which refers to staff providing themselves with a positive consequence following some pre-specified work performance (Burgio et al., 1983). Generally, when self-management procedures have been evaluated in OBM, they have proven effective in changing designated aspects of staff work performance. Overall however, these management procedures in and of themselves have been evaluated considerably less frequently than other OBM management strategies, and warrant continued research to allow more definitive conclusions regarding their utility in staff management.

Multifaceted supervisory procedures. Multifaceted staff management approaches, like multifaceted staff training programs, incorporate a large number of antecedent, consequence and/or self-management strategies into one supervisory intervention. A prototypical multifaceted management intervention may involve, for example, verbal and written instructions, goal-setting, private verbal feedback, written feedback, and publicly-posted feedback (Parsons et al., 1989). The rationale behind the use of multifaceted management programs is basically an attempt to maximize the probability of resolving a staff performance problem. By combining a number of procedural components – each of which at times can singularly bring about behavior change – into one management program, the probability of resolving the problem of concern is enhanced relative to relying on one procedure alone. Multifaceted programs often represent the management approach of choice for resolving intractable staff performance problems because of the consistent effectiveness of such management approaches. Multifaceted management programs have been used to address a wide range of staff performance issues in human services including absenteeism, administrative performance, client teaching skills, health and safety routines, and therapeutic interactions with consumers (see Reid et al., 1989, for a review). However, one disadvantage of these types of management strategies is that due to the large number of procedural components involved, the approaches can be relatively effortful and time consuming for supervisors to use on a routine basis.

Recent Research in Organizational Behavior Management

As indicated earlier, the research in the 1970s and 80s just summarized essentially established OBM as a professional field within the human services. Since then, OBM research in human service settings generally can be categorized within three main areas. This section summarizes the areas in which the more recent OBM research has been reported.

Continuation of Early Research Focus

The largest area of OBM investigation in the 1990s is really a continuation of the focus of the preceding two decades of OBM research. Investigators have continued to apply various types of behavioral procedures to improve different aspects of human service staff performance. For the most part, the more recent investigations have focused on applying consequence (e.g., DeVries, Burnett, & Redmon, 1991; Wilson, Reid, & Korabek-Pinkowski, 1991) and multifaceted (Parsons, Harper, Jensen, & Reid, 1997; Parsons et al., 1996) procedures to improve a wider variety of staff performance areas than previously addressed. Relatively little attention has been directed in the more recent research to applying antecedent and self-management procedures. The relative lack of investigations on the latter procedures is probably due at least in part to results of the earlier research which indicated that antecedent and self-management strategies did not appear to be as consistently effective as consequence and multifaceted procedures for improving targeted aspects of staff work performance. Most current research includes antecedent and self-management procedures usually only as part of multifaceted programs (e.g., Gillat & Sulzer-Azaroff, 1994; Johnson, Welsh, Miller, & Altus, 1991) in contrast to singular applications of the respective procedures. In regard to use of consequence and multifaceted management programs, there have been a number of variations of the procedures in attempts to expand or refine the existing technology for improving and maintaining staff work performance (see Phillips, 1998; Schell, 1998, for detailed reviews of the recent OBM research in selected human services). Additionally, a novel category of OBM procedures has been reported in terms of peer management in the work place. Although the amount of research attention given to involving human service staff in the management of their co-workers' job performance has been limited to date, available results suggest that peer management may represent a useful addition to the OBM technology (Fleming & Sulzer-Azaroff, 1992).

Applications of Organizational Behavior Management in an Expanded Variety of Human Service Agencies

Related to the OBM research focus just noted, recent investigations have begun to expand the types of human service settings in which OBM procedures have been used successfully to improve staff work performance. Such expansion is most apparent in agencies serving individuals with developmental disabilities, which continue to represent the most common type of human service setting in which OBM research is conducted (i.e., relative to human service agencies serving other clinical populations such as preschools, nursing homes and psychiatric facilities). Expansion in the types of developmental disabilities agencies in which OBM applications have been investigated has paralleled changes in the developmental disabilities field in general. Prior to the mid 1980s, large institutional settings represented a major place of residence for many people with developmental disabilities, and also represented the most frequent type of setting in which OBM investigations were conducted. Since that general time period, there has been a consensus in the developmental disabilities field that the quality of life of individuals with these types of disabilities is improved by moving from, or never entering, institutional settings in lieu of smaller community-based living arrangements. Correspondingly, there has been a decrease in OBM research in institutional settings and an increase in research in community settings such as group homes (see Harchik & Campbell, 1998, for a recent review of the OBM research in community settings for individuals with developmental disabilities).

Increasing the Acceptability of Organizational Behavior Management

A third area in which recent OBM research has focused pertains to increasing the acceptability of OBM procedures among persons working in human service agencies. This body of research was initiated for two primary reasons. First, it has become well recognized that use of management strategies that staff find acceptable can have a beneficial impact on the quality of staffs' work life relative to management procedures that staff find unacceptable (Reid & Parsons, 1995b). Second, one means of increasing the use of OBM procedures among more human service agencies may be to enhance the degree to which agency personnel find the procedures desirable (Balcazar, Shupert, Daniels, Mawhinney, & Hopkins, 1989).

To date, there are several general findings that stem from the OBM research on acceptability. Primarily, among investigations in which staff acceptance of OBM management strategies has been evaluated, results have consistently indicated that such strategies tend to be more acceptable to staff relative to other types of management approaches with which staff are familiar (Parsons, 1998). Results of

OBM acceptability research have also indicated that there are likely to be distinct differences in the degree of staff acceptance among different OBM procedures. For example, in regard to the most frequently used OBM procedure, feedback, research suggests that feedback provided immediately to staff after staffs' work performance has been observed is more desirable to staff than feedback that is presented in a delayed format several days later (Reid & Parsons, 1996). For another frequently used OBM procedure, performance monitoring, research has indicated that staffs' acceptance of having their performance monitored can be enhanced if the staff are well familiarized with the rationale for the monitoring and the procedures constituting the monitoring process (Reid & Parsons, 1995c). A comprehensive review regarding research on the acceptability of OBM procedures is provided elsewhere (Parsons, 1998).

Relationship of Organizational Behavior Management to Other Common Management Approaches in the Human Services

Organizational Behavior Management represents only one of many approaches to management and supervision in the human services. Actually, referring to the management of respective human service agencies as an approach is somewhat of a misnomer. A common characteristic of human service management in many agencies is the lack of a consistent or organized means of attempting to ensure staff perform their duties in the expected manner. Relatedly, many agencies have attempted to adopt a particular management approach but the attempts have proven unsuccessful. Newly adopted management approaches are often quickly abandoned when key executive staff leave the agency or the novelty of the approach diminishes. In other cases, agency supervisors become disgruntled with the new approach due to lack of observed improvements in agency functioning or staff dislike of the management procedures. Such disgruntlement leads supervisors to forego the new management strategy.

In some ways, OBM has been more durable than most other approaches to human service staff management (see Reid & Parsons, 1995b, for a summary of management approaches in the human services that have been short lived). Two characteristics of OBM probably have played a major role in the continuation of OBM as a management option in the human services. First, the management procedures of OBM are well articulated in terms of what managers and supervisors should do to change or maintain specific areas of staff work performance (Babcock, Fleming, & Oliver, in press). A common problem of many management approaches that become popularized for application in the human services is that the approaches do not specify what should be done to affect staff work performance (Reid et al., 1989). In the latter situations, working managers become disillusioned with a management approach because of difficulty determining what they should do differently from their usual management strategies. Second, because OBM is based in large part on research that demonstrates the effectiveness of OBM procedures in actual human service settings, OBM has more visible support for its effectiveness relative to typical management approaches employed in the human services. The applied research basis of OBM increases the likelihood of its procedural effectiveness when used by managers, such that managers are likely to be reinforced for applying OBM strategies by observing improvements in staff work performance.

With the exception of two general characteristics of OBM as just noted, it is beyond the scope of this chapter to compare and contrast an OBM approach with other management approaches that have, at one time or another, been popular in the human services. However, for detailed comparisons with one of the most recently popularized management approaches in the human services – that involving quality management strategies such as Continuous Quality Improvement and Total Quality Management – interested readers are referred to other available sources (e.g., Babcock et al., 1998). It should also be recognized, however, that when considering the number of human service agencies in the United States, OBM does not represent a commonly used management approach. With several notable exceptions (e.g., Christian, 1983; Wolf, Kirigin, Fixsen, Blase, & Braukmann, 1995), very few human service agencies have adopted a comprehensive OBM approach for managing the agency's service delivery system. Most OBM applications have been with relatively circumscribed areas of an agency's overall operation. Essentially, use of OBM procedures in human service agencies has followed the format of the OBM research summarized earlier in which one specific area of staff job responsibilities was targeted for improvement with a behavioral management program. In short, OBM strategies have been used to improve specific areas of staff performance relatively frequently across different agencies, but have been used quite infrequently with major components of overall agency functioning (for an exception, see Williams, this volume).

Areas for Future Research in Organizational Behavior Management

Although OBM research conducted over the last three decades has resulted in an impressive technology for managing staff performance in the human services, the technology is not yet complete, nor is the available technology used to the degree it could be used to enhance the human services. There are three major areas in which additional research would be particularly useful to continue to build a comprehensive management technology and to expand application of the existing technology. These areas, which in many ways represent extensions of the research already initiated in the 1990s as just summarized, include: a) utilizing OBM strategies to address additional performance areas of concern in a wider variety of human service settings, b) large scale/long term OBM applications within organizations, and c) issues affecting the adoption of OBM as the management approach of choice across a larger number of human service organizations.

Extension of the Existing Technology to Additional Performance Areas and Types of Human Service Settings

As previously noted, the most common human service setting in which OBM research has occurred has been large residential centers for people with developmental disabilities. The second most common setting has been school systems, involving mainstream schools and schools for persons with special needs (see Phillips, 1998, for a recent review of OBM in schools and related settings). Organizational Behavior Management applications have occurred much less frequently in the many other types of organizations and agencies that constitute the field of human services, such as psychiatric centers, nursing homes, community group homes and child care centers.

Expanding the Scope of OBM Research in Human Service Settings

Additional research is needed to examine the extent to which components of the OBM technology evaluated in one type of setting can be generalized to staff performance in other types of service settings, each of which has unique concerns regarding staff performance and quality supports and services. To illustrate, as referred to earlier, community-based residential options for people with developmental and related disabilities have become available at a rapid rate since the mid 1980s. In these settings, staff often must work independently with only intermittent contact with supervisors relative to more frequent supervisory contact that usually occurs in larger residential settings in which most OBM research has occurred. Determining how OBM may enhance staff performance in work places where supervisors are infrequently present represents one of many important research questions for applying OBM to the increasing number of community living arrangements in which human service supports are currently offered (Harchik & Campbell, in press). Although OBM research has begun to target community residential settings recently, the number of investigations has not kept pace with the rapid increase in number and type of community organizational settings in which supports and services are provided for people with developmental and related disabilities.

In addition to expanding OBM research to address staff performance issues across a broader spectrum of the human services, one particular type of staff performance warrants research attention regardless of the service setting. The vast majority of OBM research conducted to date has targeted the performance of paraprofessional or direct support staff in human services. In contrast, the performance of professional staff (other than teachers) has been the focus of OBM investigations much less frequently. As used here, "professional staff" refers to personnel who have received formal, specialized training for performing a specific job. Professional staff in human services typically include nurses, doctors, case managers, social workers, vocational counselors, speech pathologists, psychologists, and occupational/ physical therapists, to name only a few. Examinations of professional staff performance in the OBM literature – while traditionally quite limited– currently do not appear to be growing in number. In a recent review of 244 OBM studies conducted since 1984 in settings serving people with developmental disabilities, only 2 investigations involving professional staff other than teachers were identified (Schell, 1998).

The performance areas of concern with professional staff that may be targeted for improvement with OBM applications can be quite varied (see Reid, 1987, for a selected overview). However, one area of professional staff performance is of particular relevance in regard to OBM research in human services. As previously mentioned, in many organizations, the majority of direct support services for consumers is provided by paraprofessional staff. Professional personnel often are expected to train paraprofessional staff to carry out the professionals' designated treatment procedures with agency clients, as well as to assist in ensuring paraprofessional staff routinely apply the procedures in a proficient manner. However, few professional clinicians in the human services are trained in methods of training or supervising the work performance of others. Research is needed to demonstrate effective strategies for teaching professional staff to transfer their specialized skills to the day-to-day performance repertoires of paraprofessional staff (see Schell, 1998, for a related discussion).

Long-Term/Large-Scale Applications of Organizational Behavior Management

A key direction for future research is to expand the scope of OBM within respective human service agencies by evaluating the efficacy of OBM procedures over extended periods of time, and to determine variables associated with long-term effectiveness. To be truly effective, a management approach must not only effectively prevent and resolve staff performance problems, but also maintain satisfactory performance over time. Most OBM investigations to date have demonstrated only short-term effectiveness in that relatively few investigations have included follow-up observations of staff performance for more than a few months following intervention. Among those studies that have evaluated the application of OBM procedures over extended time periods, encouragement exists for the durability of OBM procedures (see Babcock et al., 1998, for a summary). Durability of management procedures nevertheless remains a concern because long-term maintenance of staff performance may prove more difficult than initially affecting performance change given the many obstacles to maintenance in human service organizations such as staff turnover, reorganization and frequent budgetary alterations.

Related to the need for research on the durability of OBM applications is the need to evaluate applications within more comprehensive aspects of the overall operations of human service agencies (Hopkins, 1995). As referred to earlier, the vast majority of OBM applications have generally been restricted to relatively small-scale demonstration projects, addressing only a small portion of an agency's service provision. A primary reason for the lack of research on large-scale applications of OBM procedures in a given agency is the difficulty researchers face in obtaining sufficient control of an agency's operation in order to conduct systematic evaluations of interventions designed to impact major portions of the agency's service system (Babcock et al., 1998). Nevertheless, in order to more significantly impact human services, investigations are needed to demonstrate how OBM approaches can be effectively applied in a more comprehensive fashion across large domains of respective agencies' service responsibilities. The effective outcomes among the few reports noted earlier that have evaluated OBM interventions across major portions of an agency's operation (see also Dyer, Schwartz, & Luce, 1984; Parsons et al., 1989; Williams, this volume) suggests that continued research in this area is likely to result in substantial contributions to human service management.

One variable that seems especially relevant for determining how to expand the scope of OBM procedures within human service organizations is the development of a technology for training and managing supervisor performance. Supervisors cannot be expected to apply OBM effectively unless they are knowledgeable about OBM principles and skilled in OBM practices. Historically, relatively little OBM research has addressed supervisor performance as a dependent variable, although there are indications of increased research interest in interventions for training supervisors to utilize OBM procedures in the training and management of their staff (Gillat & Sulzer-Azaroff, 1994; Methot, Williams, Cummings, & Bradshaw, 1996; Parsons & Reid, 1995). It seems probable that many of the same strategies demonstrated to be effective with nonsupervisory personnel will also be effective when applied to important areas of supervisory performance. The exact extent to which variations in existing OBM procedures are warranted can only be determined through increased research attention on supervisory performance.

Another, and related, means of expanding the use of OBM procedures in the human services is to expose more management trainees to the OBM field. Currently there are very few undergraduate and graduate programs related to the human services that train potential managers and supervisors in OBM principles and practices. It would seem that being skilled in OBM procedures, and perhaps observing the effectiveness of such procedures through practicum experiences in respective human service agencies, would increase the likelihood new managers would apply OBM procedures relative to the more usual situation in which managers begin their managerial roles with no background in OBM.

Adoption of Organizational Behavior Management as the "Management Approach of Choice" in Human Services

Despite a considerable amount of research demonstrating that an OBM approach to supervision is quite effective when applied to specific areas of staff performance, as noted earlier OBM is not widely practiced in the human services. This lack of adoption by management personnel has led to calls for research to identify variables, in addition to effectiveness, that may influence the practice of OBM in human service organizations. In particular, there have been numerous calls to evaluate variables affecting consumer satisfaction with OBM procedures (Parsons, 1998). Consumer satisfaction generally refers to the extent to which supervisors and staff view a management practice as desirable in that the procedure appears fair, practical, and unlikely to have negative effects on agency personnel (Davis & Russell, 1990). In attempting to measure consumer satisfaction, OBM researchers have relied primarily on rating scales to reflect consumer satisfaction with a given management practice. As indicated previously, supervisors and staff have consistently rated OBM procedures highly acceptable. However, anecdotal reports do not always corroborate such ratings (see Davis & Russell, 1990, for a similar discussion). Recent research has also suggested that rating scales may not be the most sensitive means of measuring consumer satisfaction with management procedures. For example, when direct support staff in a residential facility for people with developmental disabilities were asked to complete a rating scale to reflect their satisfaction with two common formats for receiving feedback from their supervisor (immediate vs. delayed), both formats were rated equally satisfactory (Reid & Parsons, 1996). In contrast, when given a choice of which feedback format the staff would prefer to receive in the future, 73% chose to receive immediate feedback while none of the staff chose delayed feedback (27% expressed no preference). In light of the latter results, additional research seems needed to determine the most valid and reliable indicators of consumer satisfaction with OBM procedures. When such indicators have been more precisely determined, researchers can undertake the task of improving the acceptability of effective management procedures. The experimental manipulation of acceptability variables represents another broad and essentially untapped area for future OBM research.

One variable likely to influence the acceptability of management procedures is efficiency – that is, the time and resources required of managers to implement the procedures. In this regard, a concern with OBM approaches is that the procedures can be time-consuming and effortful to implement (Reid & Parsons, 1995b). Organizational Behavior Management investigations have not consistently reported information related to the amount of time or resources required to implement various management procedures. As more researchers include efficiency data, a better determination can be made regarding the most efficient management strategy required to gain satisfactory results. Efficiency can also be addressed in future research by conducting component analyses of multifaceted management approaches to determine which components are truly critical to the success of the management intervention, thereby eliminating certain components that are not necessary for affecting changes in staff performance.

Another variable related to the acceptability of OBM procedures is how the procedures are introduced within human service agencies. Although OBM consists of a technology that can be applied within essentially any type of human service agency, applications of the technology are likely to be better received, and therefore adopted, if applied in a manner commensurate with the idiosyncratic concerns, needs, and terminology of individual human service agencies (see Crow & Snyder, 1998, for an extended discussion of OBM application issues). At times, those of us who have promoted an OBM approach may have focused more on our own view regarding what would be important to change within a given human service agency through OBM applications. It would appear more advantageous, at least initially, to determine what an agency's consumers, staff, and management view as most important. Such determinations would include, for example, the most desired outcomes for agency consumers and the most valued service delivery processes among agency executives. Organizational Behavior Management applications should then focus on supporting those aspects of agency functioning, and the applications should be introduced in a manner that is clearly seen as supportive of the desired outcomes and processes. Considering the demonstrated effectiveness of OBM when applied to designated areas of staff performance, it would seem as more managers become aware of OBM as a means of obtaining outcomes that are highly valued in the managers' agencies, the contribution of OBM within the human services could be broadened significantly.

Reading Objectives

1. The availability of an effective treatment technology is a necessary condition for the successful provision of human services. What is a second necessary condition regarding the technology for successful human services?
2. Name and define the two aspects of work performance that have been the focus of OBM research and represent the essence of successful provision of quality supports and services in human services agencies.
3. Describe the basic set of OBM procedures that comprise the core of most multifaceted staff training programs.
4. What are the most important conclusions that can be drawn from OBM research conducted to date on staff training?
5. List and describe the four categories of management procedures for directly changing ongoing work performance.
6. What are two likely reasons why OBM procedural acceptability has been a focus of recent research?
7. Describe two general characteristics of OBM that may account for the continuation of OBM management approaches relative to other management approaches popularized within human services.
8. Explain why research examining OBM applications involving professional staff in human service settings seems warranted.
9. Why might applications involving supervisory performance be crucial to expanding the scope of OBM within human service agencies?
10. What is one of the principal criticisms of an OBM approach and how might future research address this criticism?

References

Babcock, R. A., Fleming, R. K., & Oliver, J. R. (1998). OBM and quality improvement systems. *Journal of Organizational Behavior Management, 18*, 33-59

Balcazar, F., Hopkins, B. L., & Suarez, Y. (1986). A critical, objective review of performance feedback. *Journal of Organizational Behavior Management, 7*, 65-89.

Balcazar, F. E., Shupert, M. K., Daniels, A. C., Mawhinney, T. C., & Hopkins, B. L. (1989). An objective review and analysis of ten years of publication in the

Journal of Organizational Behavior Management. *Journal of Organizational Behavior Management, 10,* 7-37.

Brown, K. M., Willis, B. S., & Reid, D. H. (1981). Differential effects of supervisor verbal feedback and feedback plus approval on institutional staff performance. *Journal of Organizational Behavior Management, 3,* 57-68.

Burg, M. M., Reid, D. H., & Lattimore, J. (1979). Use of a self-recording and supervision program to change institutional staff behavior. *Journal of Applied Behavior Analysis, 12,* 363-375.

Burgio, L. D., Whitman, T. L., & Reid, D. H. (1983). A participative management approach for improving direct-care staff performance in an institutional setting. *Journal of Applied Behavior Analysis, 16,* 37-53.

Christian, W. P. (1983). A case study in the programming and maintenance of institutional change. *Journal of Organizational Behavior Management, 5,* 99-153.

Crow, R. E., & Snyder, P. (1998). Organizational Behavior Management in early intervention: Status and implications for research and development. *Journal of Organizational Behavior Management, 18,* 131-156.

Davis, J. R., & Russell, R. H. (1990). Behavioral staff management: An analogue study of acceptability and its behavioral correlates. *Behavioral Residential Treatment, 5,* 259-270.

Delameter, A. M., Connors, C. K., & Wells, K. C. (1984). A comparison of staff training procedures: Behavioral applications in the child psychiatric inpatient setting. *Behavior Modification, 8,* 39-58.

Demchak, M. A. (1987). A review of behavioral staff training in special education settings. *Education and Training in Mental Retardation, 22,* 205-217.

DeVries, J. E., Burnett, M. M., & Redmon, W. K. (1991). AIDS prevention: Improving nurses' compliance with glove wearing through performance feedback. *Journal of Applied Behavior Analysis, 24,* 705-711.

Dyer, K., Schwartz, I. S., & Luce, S. C. (1984). A supervision program for increasing functional activities for severely handicapped students in a residential setting. *Journal of Applied Behavior Analysis, 17,* 249-259.

Edwards, G., & Bergman, J. S. (1982). Evaluation of a feeding training program for caregivers of individuals who are severely physically handicapped. *Journal of The Association for the Severely Handicapped, 7,* 93-100.

Fabry, P. L., & Reid, D. H. (1978). Teaching foster grandparents to train severely handicapped persons. *Journal of Applied Behavior Analysis, 11,* 111-123.

Fitzgerald, J. R., Reid, D. H., Schepis, M. M., Faw, G. D., Welty, P. A., & Pyfer, L. M. (1984). A rapid training procedure for teaching manual sign language skills to multidisciplinary institutional staff. *Applied Research in Mental Retardation, 5,* 451-469.

Fleming, R., & Sulzer-Azaroff, B. (1992). Reciprocal peer management: Improving staff instruction in a vocational training program. *Journal of Applied Behavior Analysis, 25,* 611-620.

Ford, J. E. (1980). A classification system for feedback procedures. *Journal of Organizational Behavior Management, 2,* 183-191.

Frazier, T. W. (1972). Training institutional staff in behavior modification principles and techniques. In R. D. Ruben, H. Fensterheim, J. D. Henderson, & L. P. Ullmann (Eds.), *Advances in behavior therapy: Proceedings of the Fourth Conference of the Association for Advancement of Behavior Therapy* (pp. 171 - 178). New York: Academic Press.

Gardner, J. M. (1973). Training the trainers. A review of research on teaching behavior modification. In R. D. Rubin, J. P. Brady, & J. D. Henderson (Eds.), *Advances in behavior therapy, Volume 4* (pp. 145 - 158). New York: Academic Press.

Gillat, A., & Sulzer-Azaroff, B. (1994). Promoting principals' managerial involvement in instructional improvement. *Journal of Applied Behavior Analysis, 27,* 115-129.

Gladstone, B. W., & Spencer, C. J. (1977). The effects of modeling on the contingent praise of mental retardation counselors. *Journal of Applied Behavior Analysis, 10,* 75-84.

Greene, B. F., Willis, B. S., Levy, R., & Bailey, J. S. (1978). Measuring client gains from staff-implemented programs. *Journal of Applied Behavior Analysis, 11,* 395-412.

Harchik, A. E., & Campbell, A. R. (1998). Supporting people with developmental disabilities in their homes in the community: The role of Organizational Behavior Management. *Journal of Organizational Behavior Management, 18,* 83-101.

Hopkins, B. L. (1995). An introduction to developing, maintaining, and improving large-scale, data-based programs. *Journal of Organizational Behavior Management, 15,* 7-10.

Hundert, J. (1982). Training teachers in generalized writing of behavior modification programs for multihandicapped deaf children. *Journal of Applied Behavior Analysis, 15,* 111-122.

Inge, K. J., & Snell, M. E. (1985). Teaching positioning and handling techniques to public school personnel through inservice training. *The Journal of The Association for Persons With Severe Handicaps, 10,* 105-110.

Iwata, B. A., Bailey, J. S., Brown, K. M., Foshee, T. J., & Alpern, M. (1976). A performance-based lottery to improve residential care and training by institutional staff. *Journal of Applied Behavior Analysis, 9,* 417-431.

Johnson, S. P., Welsh, T. M., Miller, L. K., & Altus, D. E. (1991). Participatory management: Maintaining staff performance in a university housing cooperative. *Journal of Applied Behavior Analysis, 24,* 119-127.

Jones, F. H., & Eimers, R. C. (1975). Role playing to train elementary teachers to use a classroom management "skill package". *Journal of Applied Behavior Analysis, 8,* 421-433.

Kissel, R. C., Whitman, T. L., & Reid, D. H. (1983). An institutional staff training and self-management program for developing multiple self-care skills in severely/ profoundly retarded individuals. *Journal of Applied Behavior Analysis, 16*, 395-415.

Lattimore, J., Stephens, T. E., Favell, J. E., & Risley, T. R. (1984). Increasing direct care staff compliance to individualized physical therapy body positioning prescriptions: Prescriptive checklists. *Mental Retardation, 22*, 79-84.

Mansdorf, I. J., & Burstein, Y. (1986). Case manager: A clinical tool for training residential treatment staff. *Behavioral Residential Treatment, 1*, 155-168.

Methot, L. L., Williams, W. L., Cummings, A., & Bradshaw, B. (1996). Measuring the effects of a manager-supervisor training program through the generalized performance of managers, supervisors, front-line staff and clients in a human service setting. *Journal of Organizational Behavior Management, 16*, 3-34.

Montegar, C. A., Reid, D. H., Madsen, C. H., & Ewell, M. D. (1977). Increasing institutional staff to resident interactions through in-service training and supervisor approval. *Behavior Therapy, 8*, 533-540.

Parsons, M. B. (1998). A review of procedural acceptability in Organizational Behavior Management. *Journal of Organizational Behavior Management, 18*, 173-190.

Parsons, M. B., Cash, V. B., & Reid, D. H. (1989). Improving residential treatment services: Implementation and norm-referenced evaluation of a comprehensive management system. *Journal of Applied Behavior Analysis, 22*, 143-156.

Parsons, M. B., Harper, V. N., Jensen, J. M., & Reid, D. H. (1997). Integrating choice into the leisure routines of older adults with severe disabilities. *The Journal of The Association for Persons With Severe Handicaps, 22*, 170-175.

Parsons, M. B., & Reid, D. H. (1995). Training residential supervisors to provide feedback for maintaining staff teaching skills with people who have severe disabilities. *Journal of Applied Behavior Analysis, 28*, 317-322.

Parsons, M. B., Reid, D. H., & Green, C. W. (1996). Training basic teaching skills to community and institutional support staff for people with severe disabilities: A one-day program. *Research in Developmental Disabilities, 17*, 467-485.

Phillips, J. F. (1998). Applications and contributions of Organizational Behavior Management in schools and day treatment settings. *Journal of Organizational Behavior Management, 18*, 103-129.

Realon, R. E., Lewallen, J. D., & Wheeler, A. J. (1983). Verbal feedback vs. verbal feedback plus praise: The effects on direct care staff's training behaviors. *Mental Retardation, 21*, 209-212.

Reid, D. H. (1987). *Developing a research program in human service agencies: A practitioner's guidebook.* Springfield, IL: Charles C Thomas.

Reid, D. H. (1992). The need to train more behavior analysts to be better applied researchers. *Journal of Applied Behavior Analysis, 25*, 97-99.

Reid, D. H., & Green, C. W. (1990). Staff training. In J. L. Matson (Ed.), *Handbook of behavior modification with the mentally retarded* (2nd Ed.) (71-90). New York: Plenum Press.

Reid, D. H., & Parsons, M. B. (1995a). *Staff training and management: Bibliography of Organizational Behavior Management reports in developmental disabilities and related human services.* Morganton, NC: Developmental Disabilities Services Managers, Inc.

Reid, D. H., & Parsons, M. B. (1995b). *Motivating human service staff: Supervisory strategies for maximizing work effort and work enjoyment.* Morganton, NC: Habilitative Management Consultants, Inc.

Reid, D. H., & Parsons, M. B. (1995c). Comparing choice and questionnaire measures of the acceptability of a staff training procedure. *Journal of Applied Behavior Analysis, 28,* 95-96.

Reid, D. H., & Parsons, M. B. (1996). A comparison of staff acceptability of immediate versus delayed verbal feedback in staff training. *Journal of Organizational Behavior Management, 16,* 35-47.

Reid, D. H., Parsons, M. B., & Green C. W. (1989). *Staff management in human services: Behavioral research and application.* Springfield, IL: Charles C Thomas.

Schell, R. M. (1998). Organizational Behavior Management: Applications with professional staff. *Journal of Organizational Behavior Management, 18,* 157-171.

Shoemaker, J., & Reid, D. H. (1980). Decreasing chronic absenteeism among institutional staff: Effects of a low-cost attendance program. *Journal of Organizational Behavior Management, 2,* 317-328.

Singer, G., Sowers, J., & Irvin, L. K. (1986). Computer-assisted video instruction for training paraprofessionals in rural special education. *Journal of Special Education Technology, 8,* 27-34.

Sneed, T. J., & Bible, G. H. (1979). An administrative procedure for improving staff performance in an institutional setting for retarded persons. *Mental Retardation, 17,* 92-94.

Stoddard, L. T., McIlvane, W. J., McDonagh, E. C., & Kledaras, J. B. (1986). The use of picture programs in teaching direct care staff. *Applied Research in Mental Retardation, 7,* 349-358.

Stumphauzer, J. S., & Davis, L. C. (1983). Training Mexican American mental health personnel in behavior therapy. *Journal of Behavior Therapy & Experimental Psychiatry, 14,* 215-217.

Templeman, T. P., Fredericks, H. D. B., Bunse, C., & Moses, C. (1983). Teaching research in-service training model. *Education and Training of the Mentally Retarded, 28,* 245-252.

Wallace, C. J., Davis, J. R., Liberman, R. P., & Baker, V. (1973). Modeling and staff behavior. *Journal of Consulting and Clinical Psychology, 41,* 422-425.

Whitman, T. L., Scibak, J. W., & Reid, D. H. (1983). *Behavior modification with the severely and profoundly retarded: Research and application.* New York: Academic Press.

Wilson, P. G., Reid, D. H., & Korabek-Pinkowski, C. A. (1991). Analysis of public verbal feedback as a staff management procedure. *Behavioral Residential Treatment, 6,* 263-277.

Wolf, M. M., Kirigin, K. A., Fixsen, D. L., Blase, K. A., & Braukmann, C. J. (1995). The teaching-family model: A case study in data-based program development and refinement (and dragon wrestling). *Journal of Organizational Behavior Management, 15,* 11-68.

Chapter 13

Basic Behavioral Research and Organizational Behavior Management

Alan Poling, Alyce M. Dickinson, John Austin, and Matt Normand
Western Michigan University

Nearly 50 years ago, Skinner (1953) predicted that behavioral principles derived from basic laboratory research would form the foundation of a useful, problem-solving science of human behavior. In the inaugural issue of the *Journal of Applied Behavior Analysis* (*JABA*), Baer, Wolf, and Risley (1968) announced the arrival of such a science, christened "applied behavior analysis." In the 30 years since that article appeared, applied behavior analysis has flourished. One of several areas evidencing remarkable growth is called organizational behavior management.

Organizational behavior management (OBM) (Frederiksen & Lovett, 1980) and performance management (PM) (Daniels, 1989) are terms used interchangeably to refer to the use of behavior analysis in business, industry, and government. OBM has proven useful for dealing with a wide range of behavioral problems in both the public (e.g., Brand, Staelin, O'Brien, & Dickinson, 1982) and the private (e.g., Merwin, Thomason, & Sanford, 1989) sectors. For example, OBM has improved the services provided by doctors and other staff at a medical facility (Gikalov, Baer, & Hannah, 1997); reduced machine set-up time in a rubber manufacturing company (Wittkopp, Rowan, & Poling, 1990); reduced application processing time in a university admissions department (Wilk & Redmon, 1990); facilitated the use of statistical process control in a machine shop (Henry & Redmon, 1990); increased innovation in a public utility company (Smith, Kaminski, & Wylie, 1990); enhanced the effectiveness of performance management training in city government (Nordstrum, Lorenzi, & Hall, 1991); increased functional sales behaviors in salespersons (Luthans, Paul, & Taylor, 1985); increased on-time project completions by engineers (McCuddy & Griggs, 1984); increased the safety and productivity of roofers (Austin, Kessler, Riccobono, & Bailey, 1996), and; increased the friendliness of police officers (Wilson, Boni, & Hogg, 1997).

Several different procedures were used in these examples, and in other OBM applications. For instance, behavior has been improved by altering its antecedents and consequences through a training procedure (Brown, Malott, Dillon, & Keeps, 1980; Komaki, Barwick, & Scott, 1978); by providing prompts and task-related information (Austin, Hatfield, Grindle, & Bailey, 1993; Carter, Hansson, Holmberg, & Melin, 1979; Engerman, Austin, & Bailey, 1997; Greene & Neistat, 1983;

Runnion, Watson, & McWhorter, 1978); by setting goals (Eldridge, Lemasters, & Szypot, 1978; Komaki, Barwick, & Scott, 1978); by providing written or verbal performance feedback (Henry & Redmon, 1990; Silva, Duncan, & Doudna, 1981; Wittkopp et al., 1990) or praise (Gaetani & Johnson, 1983; Komaki, Blood, & Holder, 1980); by contingent reinforcement (Foxx & Schaeffer, 1981; Newby & Robinson, 1983; Smith et al., 1990), and; by complex "package interventions" (Wilk & Redmon, 1990).

Performance feedback, which is information that is given to persons regarding the quantity or quality of their past performance (Prue & Fairbank, 1981), appears to be the OBM procedure used most often in published articles. In a review of all articles published in the *Journal of Organizational Behavior Management* (*JOBM*) from 1977-1986, Balcazar et al. (1989) reported that 50% of the studies used feedback, either alone or in combination with other procedures. Prue and Fairbank (1981) suggested that feedback is often the intervention of choice because of its low cost, simplicity, and flexibility. In addition, feedback has been demonstrated to be effective in a variety of applications (e.g., Johnson & Masotti, 1990; Ralis & O'Brien, 1986; Sulzer-Azaroff, Loafman, Merante, & Hlavacek, 1990).

Given how often and how effectively it has been used in OBM, it is rather ironic that the manner in which performance feedback affects behavior often is unknown. In 1982, Peterson contended that "feedback" is not a principle of behavior, but is instead an ambiguous term used to describe a wide range of manipulations (independent variables). Depending on how feedback is arranged, it might serve a reinforcing, punishing, or discriminative stimulus function. It might also act as an establishing operation, or engender new rule-governed behavior. Therefore, Peterson suggested that,

> In summary, procedures labeled feedback can be explained by operant principles and need a behavioral analysis to determine why they are effective. Such an analysis would also help design "feedback" to be maximally effective. Presumably various aspects of information about performance could be manipulated to have several behavioral effects, leading to more powerful changes in behavior. Indeed, rules could be developed telling behavioral technicians how to establish "feedback" as an effective conditioned reinforcer, or a discriminative stimulus, or an establishing stimulus. Much ambiguity would be eliminated if behavior analysts no longer used the term "feedback." It is not a new principle of behavior and does not refer to a specific procedure; it at best has simply become professional slang (p. 102).

Peterson's critical analysis of the concept of feedback did not lessen organizational behavior analysts' enthusiasm for the term, or foster careful empirical analyses of how feedback affects behavior. His criticism was, however, consistent with the spirit of the times, insofar as several of Peterson's colleagues noted that, as applied behavior analysis grew, it had moved progressively away from its basic research roots in the experimental analysis of behavior, becoming ever more technological and imprecise (e.g., Branch & Malagodi, 1980; Deitz, 1978; Epling & Pierce, 1983; Hayes, Rincover, & Solnick, 1980; Michael, 1980; Pierce & Epling, 1980; Poling, Picker, Grossett, Hall-Johnson, & Holbrook, 1981). Most authors were in some regard critical of the alleged schism between applied behavior analysis and the experimental analysis of behavior, but some were not (e.g., Baer, 1981). A common criticism was that basic research findings were being ignored by applied researchers and practitioners.

Basic and Applied Research

In general, "basic" and "applied" research are best viewed as endpoints on a continuum that scales the practical benefits of experimentation, not as clear and discrete categories. As we use the terms, basic behavioral research is designed to provide information about behavior and the variables that control it. A basic research study does not directly attempt to solve a problem, and need not benefit participants. Historically, research in this vein has been categorized as the experimental analysis of behavior (Skinner, 1953). Applied research, in contrast, is intended to remedy a behavioral problem, and usually benefits participants directly. Such research typically would be categorized as applied behavior analysis (Baer et al., 1968). Basic research can, of course, have significant implications for application, even though it was not designed to meet this end. For instance, as we discuss later, several scientists and practitioners have suggested that the matching equation, which is based on the experimental analysis of behavior, can be put to use in predicting and controlling problem behaviors in the workplace and elsewhere. Others disagree.

In some cases, basic research is intended specifically to provide information that suggests strategies for improving human behavior. An example that we consider later involves the laboratory studies of incentive pay conducted by Alyce Dickinson and her colleagues. The primary justification for conducting such studies is to garner information relevant to the selection of pay systems in the everyday world. As we shall see, however, making the leap from laboratory simulations to practical implications is fraught with difficulty.

Quantifying the Relation between Basic and Applied Areas

One problem in considering the relation between basic and applied behavior analysis is in quantifying the extent to which the fields interact. In an early attempt to generate relevant data, Poling et al. (1981) looked at cross-citation rates in the *Journal of the Experimental Analysis of Behavior* (*JEAB*) and the *Journal of Applied Behavior Analysis* (*JABA*). They also surveyed members of the editorial boards of *JEAB* and *JABA*. The former journal is probably the most prestigious outlet for basic behavior analytic research, the latter for applied behavioral research. Poling and colleagues found that, from 1968 through 1979, articles published in *JEAB* were cited increasingly infrequently in *JABA*. Moreover, a survey of editorial board members revealed that few read both journals, published in both journals, or found both journals useful in their research. Most editors of *JABA* reported that *JEAB* research had decreased in value to applied researchers across time, and the majority of editors of both journals felt that the basic and applied research areas were growing apart. They did not, however, agree as to whether this emerging schism was harmful.

In a follow-up to the Poling et al. study, Poling, Alling, and Fuqua (1994) determined cross-citation rates for *JABA* and *JEAB* during 1983-1992. Across years, 0.3 to 4.8% of *JABA* citations were *JEAB* articles, with a mean of 2.4%. For *JABA* citations in *JEAB*, the mean was 0.6% and the range across years was 0.1 to 1.7%. For both journals, there were no obvious trends in the percentage of cross-citations across time. The *JEAB* article most often cited in *JABA* was Herrnstein (1970), which was cited 12 times. That article deals with quantitative analysis of behavior and the matching equation (or law).

When the data for *JEAB* citations in *JABA* from 1983-1992 (Poling et al., 1994) are compared to findings from 1968 through 1979 (Poling et al., 1981), it is apparent that the downward trend evident in the first survey did not continue. In fact, the percentage of total references in *JABA* articles that came from *JEAB* was higher for each year from 1983 through 1992 than for any year during the late 1970s. Perhaps the oft-repeated suggestion that applied behavior analysts should attend more carefully to basic research findings (e.g., Epling & Pierce, 1983; Pierce & Epling, 1980) has exercised some behavioral control. Or it may be that basic researchers are attending increasingly to topics that potentially are of applied significance, a tack some authors have suggested to be gainful (e.g., Epling & Pierce, 1986; Poling et al., 1981). If they are, however, they are not commonly citing *JABA* articles for verification: From 1983 through 1992, very few references in *JEAB* were from *JABA* (Poling et al., 1994).

Although OBM articles are published in *JABA*, many of the articles come from other applied areas. Studies of *JEAB* citations in *JABA* have not reported data separately for OBM and other areas, thus, the extent to which basic research is cited in OBM articles is unknown.

Basic-research Citations in JOBM Articles: 1992-1997

As an initial step towards assessing the influence of basic behavioral research on OBM, we determined how frequently *JEAB* and other basic research sources were cited in articles published from 1992-1997 in *JOBM*, which is devoted entirely to OBM. To do so, a single observer rated each reference in every article as to whether the reference came from *JEAB* or another basic-research outlet (e.g., *Journal of Experimental Psychology, Learning and Motivation*).

Figure 1 shows for each year and for all years together the percentage of *JOBM* citations that came from basic-research sources. There were no trends across years, although considerable variability was evident. In total, 98 of 1269 references (7.7%) were rated as basic-research citations; 87 of those references (6.8%) came from *JEAB*. This value is substantially higher than that reported by Poling et al. (1994) for *JEAB* citations in *JABA* articles. Although analysis is complicated by the different time bases involved in the two surveys, comparing the present data to those reported by Poling et al. (1994) suggests that people active in OBM may be more inclined to cite

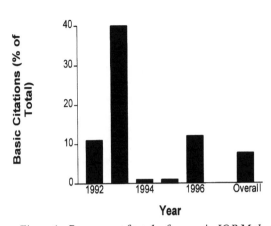

Figure 1. Percentage of total references in JOBM that were from basic-research sources.

basic-research sources than are those active in other areas of applied behavior analysis.

Figure 2 shows for each year and for all years together the percentage of *JOBM* articles that cited at least one basic-research reference. Here again, data were variable across years, but no trends were evident. Across the rated years, 40 of 72 *JOBM* publications (55%) contained one or more basic-research reference. We made no attempt to ascertain how those references were used, however, and the extent to which they contributed to developing and conceptualizing behavior-change procedures is unknown

In all, 72 different *JEAB* articles were cited in *JOBM* publications from 1992-1997. One article (Baum, 1973) was cited four times, one article was cited three times (Rao & Mawhinney, 1991), and 10 articles were cited twice. The most-cited article (Baum, 1973) is concerned with the quantitative analysis of behavior, specifically, the matching equation (law). As noted previously, matching was also the topic of the *JEAB* article most-often cited in *JABA* publications from 1983-1992, although the specific article was written by Herrnstein (1970). The third most-cited *JEAB* article also was written by Herrnstein (1961) and dealt with matching.

Given that basic research in the quantitative analysis of behavior appears to have had a considerable influence of applied behavior analysis in general, and OBM in particular, we address the topic at some length later in this chapter.

Basic Research Areas with Potential Applied Implications

Interest in real and ideal relations between basic and applied behavior analysis has not abated over time (e.g., Baer,

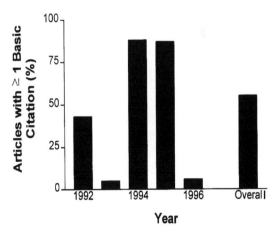

Figure 2. Percentage of total articles published in JOBM that cited at least one basic research reference.

1987; Davey, 1988; Epling & Pierce, 1986; Hayes, 1991; Perone, Galizio, & Baron, 1988). It fact, interest appears to have grown over the past few years, during which *JABA* has published special articles dealing with developments in basic research and their potential applications. Among the topics that have been considered are schedules of reinforcement (Lattal & Neef, 1996), stimulus class formation (Stromer, Mackay, & Remington, 1996), response effort (Friman & Poling, 1995), convergence (Hineline & Wacker, 1993), relational responding (Hayes & Hayes, 1993), language as behavior (Cataldo & Brady, 1994); matching (Pierce & Epling, 1995), behavioral pharmacology (Kirby & Bickel, 1995), discriminated operants (Nevin & Mace, 1994), collateral effects of behavioral interventions (Shull & Fuqua, 1993), and the nature of reinforcement (Iwata & Michael, 1994). In addition, abstracts from *JEAB* articles have appeared recently in *JABA*.

It is beyond our scope to examine the possible implications for OBM of the various areas of basic research discussed in *JABA*. Readers interested in the practical implications of basic research findings are well advised to read the articles cited in the preceding paragraph. Although coverage rarely deals specifically with OBM applications, the implications of basic research for OBM are not fundamentally different than for other areas of applied behavior analysis, and we recommend the articles highly. Most were written by two people, an expert in applied behavior analysis and a specialist in the experimental analysis of behavior, and they characteristically offer impressive arguments for the practical implications of basic research findings.

Unfortunately, it is difficult to evaluate the veracity of these arguments. We have argued elsewhere (e.g., Dickinson & Poling, 1996; Poling & Foster, 1993; Poling, Schlinger, Starin, & Blakely, 1990), and remain convinced, that humans are similar to other animals in their sensitivity to environmental arrangements. But we have also argued that it is unwise to extrapolate findings from basic research settings to very different applied settings. For example, Latham and Huber (1992) reviewed a series of eight articles that examined the effects of scheduling incentive pay in various ways. They used the results of those studies to support the contention that "the operant principles developed through basic research can be utilized in applied settings to design reinforcement schedules that evoke desired behavior from individual employees or employee groups" (Latham & Huber, 1992, p. 146).

Dickinson and Poling (1996) contended that, in fact, the studies reviewed by Latham and Huber (1992) did not involve manipulations of like-named reinforcement schedules from the basic laboratory, and that their results cannot be compared meaningfully to basic-research findings. For example, in the eight studies of concern, conditioned reinforcers were employed, complex response sequences (e.g., planting 1,000 trees) were arranged as operants, the possibility existed that instructions (or rules) affected sensitivity to programmed contingencies, and delays to reinforcement were substantial (hours or days). Moreover, an hourly pay schedule also was in effect in six of the eight studies. These conditions are very different than those characteristically arranged in basic research on schedules.

Nonetheless, Latham and Huber (1992) discussed these conditions as if they involved simple (e.g., fixed-ratio, variable-ratio) schedules of reinforcement, and attempted to relate workers' performance under these schedules to patterns characteristically observed in basic research involving like-named simple schedules. Dickinson and Poling (1996) acknowledged that the manipulations examined by Latham and Huber (1992) were in many cases effective in improving productivity. But, they claimed, these results cannot validly be explained in terms of alterations in simple reinforcement schedules. Although such an analysis appears to tie important applied findings to well established behavioral phenomena, the tie is a weak one, perhaps best viewed as a metaphorical extension, and with caution.

Of course, some will disagree with Dickinson and Poling (1996), and find Latham and Huber's analysis elegantly simple and utterly compelling. There is no gold standard for evaluating the validity, or practical value, of attempts to integrate basic and applied research findings. Mace (1994) has, however, made the case that the applied relevance of basic research is likely to be enhanced when a three-step approach is followed:

1. Animal models of important human problems are developed.
2. Findings generated by these models are replicated with humans in controlled settings.
3. Findings based on animal models and controlled human experiments are used to generate interventions that are tested with humans exhibiting the behavior problem of concern in the natural environment.

As Pierce and Epling (1995) point out, there are very few examples of the actual application of this model. One is their work concerning activity anorexia (Pierce & Epling, 1994). A second, they claim, is research involving the matching law. As indicated previously, the basic-research article most often cited in *JOBM* in recent years deals with this topic. Therefore, it merits consideration.

Matching and OBM[1]

In brief, the term "matching" refers to how organisms distribute their behavior (or time) between two (or more) concurrent schedules of reinforcement. Concurrent schedules operate simultaneously and independently for two or more response classes (Catania, 1991). If those schedules are variable-interval (VI) schedules arranging equal amounts of food delivery, the proportion of responses allocated to each alternative often is equal to (i.e., "matches") the proportion of reinforcers obtained under that alternative.

Matching was first demonstrated by Herrnstein (1961), who exposed pigeons to several different concurrent VI schedules of food delivery. Each VI schedule specified that food became available aperiodically and was delivered dependent on a keypeck, with the average time between successive food availabilities equal to the schedule value. Herrnstein recorded the number of pecks emitted and the number

1. A substantial portion of our discussion of matching is based on Poling and Foster (1993).

of food deliveries obtained under each alternative. He found that the relative proportion of responses emitted under a schedule matched the relative proportion of reinforcers (food deliveries) under that alternative, a relation that is expressed in equation 1, which is the first version of the matching equation, or "matching law."

$B_1/(B_1 + B_2) = R_1/(R_1 + R_2)$ (Equation 1)

where B_1 is behavior (i.e., total responses) allocated to alternative one, B_2 is behavior allocated to alternative two, R_1 is the number of reinforcers received under alternative one, and R_2 is the number of reinforcers received under alternative two.

Because Equation 1 did not always provide a good description of performance under concurrent schedules, other versions of the matching equation were developed. One, the generalized matching equation (Baum, 1974), is prominent in the basic research literature. It appears as Equation 2:

$\log (B_1/B_2) = a \log (r_1/r_2) + \log c$ (Equation 2)

where B is the measure of behavior (responses or time) under a component schedule, r is the obtained reinforcement rate under a component schedule, and the two alternative component schedules are designated by the subscripts. The slope of the line fitted to the data, a, is a measure of the degree to which behavior is influenced by differences in reinforcement rates (i.e., the sensitivity of behavior to reinforcement). Log c, the intercept, is an estimate of bias in behavior for one or the other schedule.

A third well-known version of the matching equation was developed by Herrnstein to describe behavior under what appear to be single-alternative situations, such as multiple schedules (Herrnstein, 1970). This equation is based on the premise that an organism always is faced with alternative responses, each reinforced under some schedule. It takes the form:

$B_1 = k(R_1)/(R_1 + R_o)$ (Equation 3)

where B_1 is behavior allocated to alternative one (the scheduled, or known, operant), R_1 is reinforcement received under alternative one, k is the asymptotic rate of B_1, and R_o is the sum of all reinforcement other than that produced under alternative one. If it is assumed that R_o and k are constant across conditions, Equation 3 predicts a hyperbolic relation between rate of responding and rate of reinforcement under a given simple (or multiple) schedule (Herrnstein, 1970; McDowell, 1988).

Many studies demonstrate that the generalized matching equation provides a good description of relations between behavioral outputs and environmental inputs under a range of conditions (e.g., Baum, 1979; Davison & McCarthy, 1988; Mazur, 1991; Williams, 1988), although there are limits (e.g., Elsmore & McBride, 1994; Sevastano & Fantino, 1994). Put simply, the relations codified by the matching equations are real behavioral phenomena.

They are not, however, phenomena revealed through research designed to develop an animal model of a human behavior problem. In fact, no mention is made of behavior problems in the early literature on matching. Thus, research in matching does not meet Mace's (1994) first criterion for a line of basic research most likely to have applied implications. That this is so, however, does not mean that the research has no implications. Certainly the second two steps in Mace's model can be taken absent the first.

With matching, the second step - which can be construed as showing that data produced with nonhumans in controlled settings holds with humans in controlled settings - has indeed been taken. Several studies have shown that the matching equation adequately describes humans' performance under conditions similar to those where it so describes nonhumans' performance, as indicated in reviews by Pierce and Epling (1983, 1995) and McDowell (1988). There is no doubt that matching can be demonstrated as readily in humans as in nonhumans tested under comparable, controlled conditions. Thus, the second step in Mace's model is sound with regard to matching analyses.

Although many authors have addressed the topic (e.g., Fuqua, 1984; Mace, McCurdy, & Quigley, 1990; McDowell, 1981, 1982, 1988; Myerson & Hale, 1984; Pierce & Epling, 1983, 1995; Rachlin, 1989), there is no agreement as to whether matching can be profitably used to develop useful interventions, or to explain behavior problems in everyday situations.. Over two decades ago, Mawhinney suggested that the matching law is relevant to organizational behavior management (Mawhinney, 1975; Mawhinney & Ford, 1977), and further arguments in favor of this position have appeared more recently (e.g., Mawhinney & Gowan, 1991; Redmon & Lockwood, 1987).

The natural sciences are fundamentally quantitative, and it is proper that anyone who favors a natural-science approach to the study of behavior finds matching analyses fascinating. But that is not to say that all who favor such an approach believe that matching analyses are of value in OBM. Among those who have argued that matching is largely irrelevant to OBM are Poling and Foster (1992). The details of their argument will not be repeated here, but their primary points are:

1. There are no demonstrations that the matching equation adequately describes organizational behavior, and there are no effective procedures based on the matching equation.

2. Behavior in organizations characteristically is controlled by multiple environmental variables that are difficult to isolate and quantify environments in which people live and work cannot accurately be described as concurrent schedules. Unless environmental inputs (environmental variables) can be quantified and related to behavioral outputs, matching analyses are impossible. Matching analyses are of value first and foremost because they are quantitative; qualitative extensions (e.g., Redmon & Lockwood, 1987) are of little or no value in predicting or controlling behavior.

3. Organizational settings differ substantially from the basic-research settings in which the matching equation adequately describe behavior. In particular, behavior in the workplace often appears to be, in part, rule-governed. No one has extended the application of matching analyses to rule-governed behavior.

4. Even if matching analyses could be applied to organizational behav-
    ior, no benefit would derive from the practice. In OBM, describing
    precisely the relation between environmental inputs and behavioral
    outputs is far less important than altering environmental inputs so that
    behavior changes in desired ways. OBM researchers and practitioners
    have developed a sizable number of rough-and-ready, but generally
    effective, strategies for behavior change. Analyzing these interventions
    in terms of matching is much like slicing bologna with a microtome.

In fairness, the points outlined above are open to debate, and time may well
prove Poling and Foster (1992) wrong. Even if it does not, applied researchers
certainly suffer no harm from learning about matching and trying to extend what
they learn to everyday human activities. There is, as discussed later, general value in
learning as much as possible about behavioral relations, of almost any sort. As Mace
(1994) suggested, however, the practical significance of basic research findings
should be easiest to see in those situations where the basic research was designed to
explicate a human behavior problem. One such line of basic research is discussed in
the following section.

Dickinson and Associates' Studies of Incentive Pay

As indicated earlier, Dickinson and her colleagues have undertaken basic
research to examine the effects of individual monetary incentives on worker
productivity. Although this research is indeed basic, it was generated by questions
that arose from the application of monetary incentive systems in business. In 1974,
with guidance from William Abernathy, a Memphis-based behavioral consultant,
Union National Bank in Little Rock, AR, began implementing behaviorally-based
monetary incentive systems. By the early 1980s, 75 individualized monetary
incentive programs had been installed, covering 70% of the bank's 485 employees
(Dierks & McNally, 1987). During that time, the bank hired Kathleen McNally, a
behaviorally-trained psychologist, to oversee and continue that work. In 1987,
Dierks, the Senior Vice President and Personnel Director, and McNally described
the success of their pay systems:

> In 1985, $1 million was paid in incentive payments on a $9 million annual
> payroll. But it's more than worth it. Using these principles, we have
> increased productivity 200-300 percent. Our net profit per employee is
> $11,000 per year while other Little Rock banks show $5,700 and $4,200 (p.
> 61).

In spite of this success, McNally wanted to refine the pay systems. While they
were certainly working well, several features lacked empirical justification. Dickinson
and her colleagues began investigating a number of questions posed by McNally.
Two of those have been the focus of much of this work: (1) Is there a functional
relationship between the percentage of total pay that is incentive-based and worker
productivity; and (2) Does the absolute amount of money earned in incentives
influence worker productivity? The broader utility of this research, along with its

rationale, have been discussed in detail elsewhere (Dickinson & Gillette, 1993; Frisch & Dickinson, 1990; LaMere, Dickinson, Henry, Henry, & Poling, 1996; Oah & Dickinson, 1992) and will not be considered here. Instead, the present focus will be on the relevance of such basic research to application, and on the difficulties of balancing controlled experimentation with the production of useful data.

Frisch and Dickinson (1990) conducted the first study in the series, examining the effects of five different percentages of incentive pay on worker performance. In a between-groups study, 75 college students were randomly assigned to one of five pay conditions. Subjects in the 0% incentive pay group received a guaranteed base pay but were not given the opportunity to earn incentives. Subjects in the remaining four groups also received a guaranteed base wage but in addition were able to earn 9, 23, 38, or 50% of their total pay in incentives. Each subject participated in 15 45-minute sessions. The task consisted of assembling parts made from bolts, nuts, and washers. The measure of work performance was the number of quality parts assembled. At the end of each session, an experimenter counted the number of

Table 1. Planned Versus Actual Percentages of Incentive Pay in the Study by Frisch and Dickinson (1990)

Planned Percentages	0%	9%	23%	38%	50%
Total Incentives Available per Session	0.00	0.37	0.93	1.50	2.00
Base Pay Available($)	4.00	3.63	3.07	2.50	2.00
Total Pay Available($)	4.00	4.00	4.00	4.00	4.00
Actual Percentages	0%	3%	11%	20%	35%
Average Incentives Earned per Session	0.00	0.11	0.39	0.63	1.08
Base Pay Earned($)	3.85	3.63	3.07	2.50	2.00
Total Pay Earned($)	3.85	3.74	3.46	3.13	3.08

quality parts assembled, plotted it on a graph in the presence of the subject, and paid the subject.

In order to simulate a work environment where employees must meet minimum performance standards or face termination, all subjects were required to assemble a minimum of 50 parts per session to receive their base pay. Incentive subjects then received a per piece incentive for each part in excess of 50. Because actual workers often engage in off-task activities, a number of competitive activities were made available to subjects, and subjects were able to take work breaks whenever they desired.

The initial parameters of the pay system were based on the maximum number of parts that pilot subjects assembled. Thus, for example, subjects in the 50% incentive group had to assemble 120 parts during the session in order to receive 50% of their total pay in incentives. Only rarely did subjects assemble that many parts. As a result, they did not earn as much in incentives as the researchers had anticipated. The actual percentages of incentives subjects earned were 3, 11, 20, or 35%. Table 1 displays the planned versus actual percentages, and the amount of money earned by subjects in each group.

The data were graphed and, in addition, the group means from the last five sessions were statistically compared. As can be seen in Figure 3, subjects who received incentives assembled significantly more parts than subjects who received only base pay, although higher percentages of incentives did not result in higher levels of performance. The power of incentives is especially clear for subjects who received only 3% of their total pay in incentives, yet performed significantly better than those

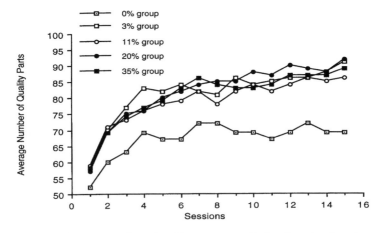

Figure 3. Average number of quality parts assembled each session by subjects in the five incentive groups studied by Frisch and Dickinson (1990). Percentages indicate the level of total pay earned as incentives.

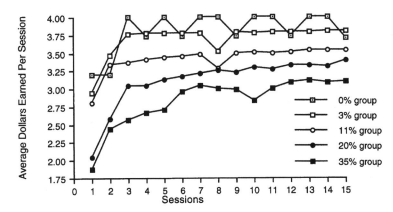

Figure 4. Average amount of money earned each session by subjects in the five incentive groups studied by Frisch and Dickinson (1990). Groups are labeled according to the percentage of total pay earned as incentives.

who received hourly pay, and about as well as those who received higher incentives. Particularly striking is the fact that subjects in the 3% incentive group earned an average of only $0.11 in incentives during the 45-minute sessions.

In order to determine whether the amount of money earned influenced performance, the average amount of money earned by subjects in each of the five groups was compared. As shown in Figure 4, the higher the percentage of incentives, the lower the total amount of money earned. When viewed in conjunction with the performance data, these data suggest that performance was not affected by the total amount of money earned.

The results of the Frisch and Dickinson (1990) study were interesting for three reasons. First, monetary incentives increased performance significantly when compared to hourly wages, even for subjects who earned only 3% of their total pay in incentives. Prior to this study, compensation experts had argued that individuals would not respond to incentive percentages that were less than 30% (Fein, 1970; Henderson, 1985). Second, performance was comparable regardless of the percentage of total pay that was incentive-based, suggesting that the contingency between pay and performance, rather than the percentage of incentives, was the critical determinant of performance. Third, performance was not affected by the total amount of money earned, the total amount earned in incentives, or the per piece incentive values. Thus, absolute monetary payoffs appear to be less important than the contingency between pay and performance.

Dickinson and Gillette (1993) replicated and extended the preceding study. Two issues, relevant to the generality of the results, were of concern to these researchers. First, Frisch and Dickinson's (1990) experimental sessions were short, spanning only 45 minutes. Given this, participating in alternative activities could easily be delayed until after the session, or simply foregone. Although off-task performance was not formally assessed, researchers noted that subjects rarely took breaks from work. In actual work settings, employees do take breaks. Moreover, monetary incentives may improve performance primarily by decreasing the time that workers spend performing attractive off-task activities. It may be that short experimental sessions preclude on-task performance differences that would be generated by incentive pay arrangements in more realistic settings. Dickinson and Gillette addressed this concern by lengthening experimental sessions to three and four hours.

Second, Frisch and Dickinson examined only a limited range of incentive percentages. Dickinson and Gillette (1993) reasoned that percentages of incentive pay higher than those arranged by Frisch and Dickinson might yield higher performances by providing a stronger link between pay and performance. Whereas the highest incentive percentage examined by Frisch and Dickinson was 35%, Dickinson and Gillette compared performance when subjects earned 30 or 100% of their total pay in incentives.

Two studies were conducted, with a total of 12 college students serving as subjects. A counterbalanced ABA design was used so that each subject was exposed to both pay systems. Experimental sessions were three or four hours in length, and subjects completed 8 to 14 sessions. The task consisted of a computerized simulation of a proof operator's job at a bank. Simulated bank checks with differing cash values were presented on a computer screen, and subjects entered the cash value of the checks using the computer keyboard. The measure of performance was the number of correctly entered checks. In the 30% pay condition, subjects received a base pay and earned a per check incentive when their performance exceeded a specified performance standard. The total amount of money that subjects could earn in incentives approximated 30% of their total pay. In the 100% incentive pay condition (a piece rate pay system), subjects received a per check incentive for each correctly completed check. No base pay was provided. As in the Frisch and Dickinson study (1990), subjects were free to take breaks whenever they wanted for as long as they wanted. Refreshments and alternative activities were available in a lounge area during these breaks.

In general, performance was not systematically affected by the percentage of total pay that was incentive-based, even though the link between performance and pay was stronger in the 100% condition than in the 30% condition. Furthermore, due to the way in which the pay systems were designed, subjects earned less money during the piece rate pay condition than during the 30% pay condition, yet performance was comparable. Both sets of results are consistent with those reported by Frisch and Dickinson.

Although the results of these laboratory studies are similar, there are many reasons why they might not generalize to the work setting. The sanitized laboratory contingencies simply differ from the complex, interwoven contingencies of an organization, and thus behavior controlled by the two may be quite different. Three differences will be noted here, although there certainly are others. First, in the laboratory studies, few subjects took breaks from their work even when sessions lasted three or four hours; the reality of the workplace, where people regularly take breaks, was not captured in the simulations. The presence of the experimenter, the knowledge of session length, or the absence of strongly rewarding alternative activities are among the variables that may have prevented subjects from taking breaks in the laboratory (Dickinson & Matthews, 1997).

Second, the amount of money paid in the studies was small in comparison to the wages most people actually earn. People's sensitivity to incentive pay may well differ as a function of absolute pay level. Third, in the simulation but not usually in the workplace, subjects worked alone, free from social contingencies. While eliminating the possibility of social interaction helps to isolate the effects of monetary incentives, doing so does not reflect actual characteristics of the workplace.

Recognizing the limitations of laboratory investigations, and at the same time trying to use the findings of such investigations to improve productivity, LaMere, Dickinson, Henry, Henry and Poling (1996) examined the effects of different percentages of incentives on the performance of 22 roll-off truck drivers. Roll-off drivers pick-up and deliver large waste disposal dumpsters (10-40 cubic yards in size) to commercial and construction sites. The drivers were divided into two groups, and a multiple-baseline design across groups was used for the initial implementation of the incentive system. Incentive pay was subsequently increased two times. These raises were introduced simultaneously to both groups due to a management decision to maintain pay equity. The performance of the drivers was measured for approximately four years.

For Group 1, the baseline and the initial incentive phases lasted 20 and 28 weeks, respectively; for Group 2, the baseline and initial incentive phases lasted 34 and 15 weeks, respectively. The two subsequent incentive phases lasted 39 weeks and 107 weeks for both groups of drivers. Drivers received a constant base pay throughout the study. In the initial phase, drivers received 3% of their total pay in incentives. In the two subsequent phases, drivers received 6% and 9% of their total pay in incentives. Incentive pay was dependent on above-average weekly performance, calculated according to a rather elaborate formula that took into account differences in the tasks drivers performed. The drivers received their incentive pay as part of their regular weekly paycheck, however, the amount of the incentives they earned and their actual hourly pay (base pay plus incentives/hours worked) were listed separately on their pay stubs. Group performance was graphed weekly.

Both groups of drivers increased their performance when the initial incentive system was introduced, and performance remained high for the duration of the study. Although there was an increasing trend across the three incentive phases, performance did not differ significantly as a function of incentive pay level. These results should, however, be interpreted with caution. A quasi-experimental design was used, performance improved throughout the study although the increases did not correspond with changes in the incentive values, and the range of incentive percentages was small. Nonetheless, results of this applied study support those reported in the laboratory investigations; that is, that small percentages of incentives can significantly affect behavior, but further increases do not necessarily produce incrementally higher performance.

The three studies just described illustrate the difficulties inherent in both laboratory and applied investigations. The well-controlled laboratory studies provided meaningful data about the effects of monetary incentives *within that context*. In the applied setting, the intervention was multi-faceted, as is often required in such settings. Moreover, due to practical constraints, a quasi-experimental design was adopted. For these two reasons, the effects of the changes in incentives cannot be easily isolated.

Dickinson and Matthews (1997) returned to the laboratory to continue working on incentive pay. One of their objectives was to develop an experimental procedure that would, in fact, evoke the types of off-task behavior seen in work settings. This was done in an attempt to increase the realism of the laboratory simulations, and consequently the ecological validity of findings. Work breaks were formally established as part of the experimental sessions, and subjects were reminded when it was time to take a break. Subjects were, however, able to continue working if they wished to do so. In addition, computer games were offered as alternative activities, in hopes that they would compete better with the experimental task than the alternative activities used in previous studies. A between-groups design was adopted, with subjects earning 0, 10, or 100% of their total pay in incentives. A quality inspection task was used.

Dickinson and Matthews' (1997) procedures consistently engendered off-task behavior, for the first time in studies of this sort. In addition, monetary incentives decreased the amount of time subjects engaged in off-task activities relative to levels in the 0% incentive condition, although actual task completions did not differ significantly across the 0, 10, and 100% incentive conditions. In an attempt to explain the absence of differences in task completion, Dickinson and Matthews (1997) noted that quality inspection tasks are notorious for generating between-subjects variability, and much variability was evident in their study, reducing the likelihood of detecting treatment effects. Given the problem of between-subjects variability, they suggested that within-subject designs should be used in future studies.

Mace's (1994) three-step analysis must be modified somewhat to be applied to the work of Dickinson and her associates, insofar as their work did not begin with studies of nonhumans. It did, however, begin with demonstrating a behavior relation in controlled settings (step 2), then using that relation to develop a behavior-change intervention proven to be effective in an applied setting (step 3). That similar results were obtained in two laboratory simulations (Frisch & Dickinson, 1990; Dickinson & Gillette, 1993) and in a single applied study (LaMere et al., 1996) suggests, but certainly does not prove, that the simulations are adequate. The fact that Dickinson and Matthews (1997), who attempted to use a more "naturalistic" arrangement, failed to replicate results from earlier simulations suggests that rather small differences in procedure may affect worker sensitivity to incentive arrangements. Moreover, the single applied study based on lab simulations was limited in design and scope, as discussed previously. Like almost all behavior analytic research, the studies of Dickinson and her associates provide limited, but potentially useful, information. Combining that information with information from other sources, including practical experience and the substantial literature on pay-for-performance interventions, helps practitioners to develop incentive-pay plans. But the success of those plans cannot be known *a priori*. Basic research findings may provide a starting point for intervening to change troublesome human behavior, but maximally effective treatments are developed only through continuous evaluation and refinement in the natural environment. Regardless of what is learned under controlled laboratory conditions, "revise and re-evaluate," will remain the mantra of OBM.

The Value of Understanding Basic Research

Understanding basic research findings is neither necessary nor sufficient for success as an OBM practitioner. But this is not to say that such understanding is of no value. Consider, for example, that people who understanding matching, in particular, Herrnstein's hyperbola, realize that there are limits to the rate-increasing effects of reinforcement. They are unlikely to be "sack of M & Ms" practitioners who believe that all behavioral problems can be solved, given a big enough sack. People conversant with matching also realize that women and men in organizations constantly make choices that are lawfully related to environmental variables. They know that behavioral repertoires are interdependent, therefore, the effects of particular interventions characteristically are not limited to particular target responses, but are also likely to affect other behaviors. Finally, they are potentially able to make more persuasive arguments for the exquisite sensitivity of behavior to its consequences, and for the fundamental orderliness of behavior.

As another example, people familiar with the work of Dickinson and her colleagues are unlikely to posit that performance increases directly with the proportion of workers' pay arranged as incentives. They are, however, apt to realize that linking pay to performance is likely to have positive effects, and to use interventions based on such linkage whenever possible. Those interventions may or may not work, but they are at least based on a logical, data-based assumption. This is a point in their favor, regardless of whether or not they prove effective.

Controlled investigations in laboratory settings are unparalleled for illustrating principles of behavior. One has only to read a classic (e.g., Honig, 1966; Honig & Staddon, 1977) or more recent (e.g., Catania, 1997) text dealing with the experimental analysis of behavior to see that chaining, extinction, fading, punishment, reinforcement, satiation, shaping, stimulus control, stimulus equivalence, and many other principles of behavior were developed from, or are most clearly demonstrated in, basic research studies. Although one certainly can understand these principles without contacting the basic-research literature, contacting it may well be of heuristic benefit. Moreover, having at least passing familiarity with basic as well as applied research increases the size of the audience with whom one can meaningfully interact, and may suggest novel interventions and analyses of behavior in organizations.

The downside is that mastering the basic-research literature is costly in terms of time and effort, effort perhaps better spent in learning other things. Some understanding can, of course, be attained by reading summaries, especially those (like the *JABA* articles mentioned previously) intended to point out the applied implications of basic-research findings. But a little knowledge is indeed a dangerous thing, and can tempt one to offer superficial explanations of complex behavioral phenomena. It is this sort of explanation to which we have previously objected (Dickinson & Poling, 1996; Poling & Foster, 1992), and against which we again caution.

Areas for Further Research

We do not, however, caution OBM practitioners against truly understanding basic-research findings, or using those findings in legitimate attempts to understand and change behavior in organizations. Nor do we discourage basic researchers from targeting behavioral phenomena with applied implications. Although it is impossible to predict with accuracy that a given line of basic research will have significant implications for OBM, there are certainly research areas that appear to merit further attention. For example, the work on incentive pay conducted by Dickinson and her associates could be extended to ever more realistic simulations of the workplace.

A second potentially fruitful line of research comprises studies designed to test models of human behavior developed to aid OBM practitioners. Although these models often are reasonable and have some degree of face validity, they rarely are supported by solid data. A case in point is Dick Malott's analysis of the role of rule-governed behavior in organizations (Malott, 1992; Malott, Malott, & Shimamune, 1992; Malott, Shimamune, & Malott, 1992). One of his contentions (e.g., Malott, 1992, p. 53) is that rules are easy to follow if they involve outcomes that are probable and sizable, regardless of whether those outcomes are delayed or immediate. In contrast, rules are hard to follow if their outcomes are improbable or small but cumulative. This surmise could be tested empirically, but this has not occurred. The same is true of several other components of Malott's model. Given the absence of compelling data, the validity and usefulness of Malott's model of behavior in organizations is difficult to ascertain, although attempts to do so have appeared (e.g., Baer, 1992; Baum, 1992; Rachlin, 1992). Clearly, basic research designed to test the fundamental premises of Malott's model would be of some value.

Attempts to provide compelling functional analyses of behavior in organizations also merit attention. Understanding the rules as well as the antecedent and postcedent stimuli that control a given behavior is prerequisite for the kind of precise analysis afforded by the matching equation, and is useful for designing successful behavior-change interventions. It appears, however, that the techniques commonly used for functional analysis (e.g., Cone, 1997; Iwata, this volume; *JABA*, 1994) will need considerable elaboration to be useful when applied to the complex actions of people in organizations. As Ervin and Ehrhardt (this volume) point out, a step in this direction has been taken in school settings - which are organizations - and some useful interventions have been based on assessment techniques that were first developed in basic research settings. John Austin (this volume) describes several informal approaches to assessing variables maintaining or hindering organizational behavior, however, these models are admittedly simplistic relative to the state-of-the-art functional analyses of applied behavior analysis.

In truth, most areas of basic research have no obvious implications for OBM, which has a set of established procedures for assessing and changing behavior. If interpreted with care, however, some lines of basic research may help OBM practitioners to understand the variables that control behavior in organizations and, therefore, to develop maximally effective interventions. If interpreted cavalierly, however, basic research findings can mislead practitioners into thinking that they know why people behave as they do and, therefore, to stop seeking further explanations. At that point, scientific progress stops, just as surely as if the faulty analysis arose from religion, common sense, cognitive psychology, or personal experience. Basic science alone, no matter how sound or innovative, does not produce a better world.

Author Notes

The authors would like to thank Coal Poling for his insightful suggestions during the formative stages of this chapter.

Reading Objectives

1. Describe some of the domains and job settings in which OBM has demonstrated its effectiveness.
2. What is the most widely used intervention in OBM? Why is it the most widely used intervention?
3. Explain the dichotomy between basic and applied research.
4. Describe Mace's (1994) three step approach to ensure the applied relevance of basic research.
5. What is the matching law? How is it quantified?
6. What are two of the research questions Dickinson and colleagues have been investigating regarding the effects of incentive pay?
7. Describe the basic preparation used by Dickinson and colleagues in their research on the effects of incentive pay.
8. What is a primary difference between lab studies and the actual workplace regarding productivity, and how did Dickinson and Matthews (1997) attempt to deal with this issue?
9. "Understanding basic research findings is neither necessary nor sufficient for success as an OBM practitioner" – discuss.
10. Describe three potential areas for future research as stated by the authors.

References

Austin, J., Hatfield, D. B., Grindle, A. C., & Bailey, J. S. (1993). Increasing recycling in office environments: The effects of specific, informative cues. *Journal of Applied Behavior Analysis, 26,* 247-253.

Austin, J., Kessler, M. L., Riccobono, J. E., & Bailey, J. S. (1996). Using feedback and reinforcement to improve the performance and safety of a roofing crew. *Journal of Organizational Behavior Management, 16,* 49-75.

Baer, D. M. (1981). A flight of behavior analysis. *The Behavior Analyst, 4*, 85-91.

Baer, D. M. (1987). The difference between basic and applied behavior analysis is one behavior. *The Behavior Analyst, 22*, 101-106.

Baer, D. M. (1992). Much ado about something: Comments on papers by Malott and Malott, Shimamune, and Malott. *Journal of Organizational Behavior Management, 12*, 77-84.

Baer, D. M., Wolf, M. M., & Risley, T. R. (1968). Some current dimensions of applied behavior analysis. *Journal of Applied Behavior Analysis, 1*, 91-97.

Balcazar, F. E., Shupert, M. K., Daniels, A. C., Mawhinney, T. C., & Hopkins, B. L. (1989). An objective review and analysis of ten years of publication in the *Journal of Organizational Behavior Management. Journal of Organizational Behavior Management, 10*, 7-38.

Baum, W. M. (1973). The correlation-based law of effect. *Journal of the Experimental Analysis of Behavior, 20*, 137-153.

Baum, W. M. (1974). On two types of deviation from the matching law: Bias and undermatching. *Journal of the Experimental Analysis of Behavior, 22*, 231-242.

Baum, W. M. (1979). Matching, undermatching, and overmatching in studies of choice. *Journal of the Experimental Analysis of Behavior, 32*, 269-281.

Baum, W. M. (1992). For parsimony's sake: Comments on Malott's "A theory of rule-governed behavior and organizational behavior management." *Journal of Organizational Behavior Management, 12*, 81-84.

Branch, M. N., & Malagodi, E. F. (1980). Where have all the behaviorists gone? *The Behavior Analyst, 3*, 31-38.

Brand, D. D., Staelin, J. R., O'Brien, R. M., & Dickinson, A. M. (1982). Improving white collar productivity at HUD. In R. M. O'Brien, A. M. Dickinson, & M. P. Rosow (Eds.), *Industrial behavior modification* (pp. 307-334). New York: Pergamon Press.

Brown, M. G., Malott, R. W., Dillon, M. J., & Keeps, E. J. (1980). Improving customer service in a large department store through the use of training and feedback. *Journal of Organizational Behavior Management, 2*, 251-265.

Carter, N., Hansson, L., Holmberg, B., & Melin, L. (1979). Shoplifting reduction through the use of specific signs. *Journal of Organizational Behavior Management, 2*, 73-84.

Cataldo, M. F., & Brady, J. V. (1994). Deriving relations from the experimental analysis of behavior. *Journal of Applied Behavior Analysis, 27*, 763-770.

Catania, A. C. (1991). Glossary. In I. H. Iversen & K. A. Lattal (Eds.), *Experimental analysis of behavior* (Part 2, pp. G1-G44). Amsterdam: Elsevier.

Catania, A. C. (1997). *Learning.* Englewood Cliffs, NJ: Prentice-Hall.

Cone, J. D. (1997). Issues in functional analysis in behavioral assessment. *Behaviour Research and Therapy, 35*, 259-275.

Daniels, A. C. (1989). *Performance management.* Tucker, GA: Performance Management Publications.

Davey, G. (1988). Trends in human operant theory. In G. Davey & C. Cullen (Eds.), *Human operant conditioning and behavior modification* (pp. 1-14). Chichester, UK: Wiley.

Davison, M. C., & McCarthy, D. (1988). *The matching law: A research review.* Hillsdale, NJ: Erlbaum.

Deitz, S. M. (1978). Current status of applied behavior analysis: Science versus technology. *American Psychologist, 33*, 805-814.

Dickinson, A. M., & Gillette, K. L. (1993). A comparison of the effects of two individual monetary incentive systems on productivity: Piece rate pay versus base pay plus incentives. *Journal of Organizational Behavior Management, 14*, 3-82.

Dickinson, A. M., & Matthews, G. A. (1997, January). *The effects of the percentage of incentive pay on productivity and quality.* Presented at the conference of the Florida Association for Behavior Analysis and the Organizational Behavior Management Network, Daytona Beach, FL.

Dickinson, A. M., & Poling, A. D. (1996). Schedules of monetary reinforcement in organizational behavior management: Latham and Huber (1992) revisited. *Journal of Organizational Behavior Management, 16*, 71-91.

Dierks, W., & McNally, K. (1987, March). Incentives you can bank on. *The Personnel Administrator, 32*, 61-65.

Eldridge, L., Lemasters, S., & Szypot, B. (1978). A performance feedback intervention to reduce waste: Performance data and participant responses. *Journal of Organizational Behavior Management, 1*, 258-266.

Elsmore, T. F., & McBride, S. A. (1994). An eight-alternative concurrent schedule: Foraging in a radial maze. *Journal of the Experimental Analysis of Behavior, 61*, 331-348.

Engerman, J. A., Austin, J., & Bailey, J. S. (1997). Prompting patron safety belt use at a supermarket. *Journal of Applied Behavior Analysis, 30*, 577-579.

Epling, W. F., & Pierce, W. D. (1983). Applied behavior analysis: New directions from the laboratory. *The Behavior Analyst, 3*, 1-9.

Epling, W. F., & Pierce, W. D. (1986). The basic importance of applied behavior analysis. *The Behavior Analyst, 9*, 89-99.

Fein, M. (1970). *Wage incentive plans.* Norcross, GA: American Institute of Industrial Engineers.

Foxx, R. M., & Schaeffer, M. H. (1981). A company-based lottery to reduce the personal driving of employees. *Journal of Applied Behavior Analysis, 14*, 273-285.

Frederiksen, L. W., & Lovett, S. B. (1980). Inside organizational behavior management: Perspectives on an emerging field. *Journal of Organizational Behavior Management, 2*, 193-203.

Friman, P. C., & Poling, A. (1995). Making life easier with effort: Basic findings and applied research on response effort. *Journal of Applied Behavior Analysis, 28*, 583-590.

Frisch, C. J., & Dickinson, A. M. (1990). Work productivity as a function of the percentage of monetary incentives to base pay. *Journal of Organizational Behavior Management, 11*, 13-33.

Fuqua, R. W. (1984). Comments on the applied relevance of the matching law. *Journal of Applied Behavior Analysis, 17*, 381-386.

Gaetani, J. J., & Johnson, C. M. (1983). The effect of data plotting, praise, and state lottery tickets on decreasing cash shortages in a retail beverage chain. *Journal of Organizational Behavior Management, 5,* 5-15.

Gikalov, A. A., Baer, D. M., & Hannah, G. T. (1997). The effects of work task manipulation and scheduling on patient load, revenue, eyewear turnover, and utilization of staff and doctor time. *Journal of Organizational Behavior Management, 17,* 3-35.

Greene, B. F., & Neistat, M. D. (1983). Behavior analysis in consumer affairs: Encouraging dental professionals to provide consumers with shielding from unnecessary x-ray exposure. *Journal of Applied Behavior Analysis, 16,* 13-27.

Hayes, S. C. (1991). The limits of technological talk. *Journal of Applied Behavior Analysis, 24,* 417-420.

Hayes, S. C., & Hayes, L. J. (1993). Applied implications of current *JEAB* research on derived relations and delayed reinforcement. *Journal of Applied Behavior Analysis, 26,* 507-511.

Hayes, S. C., Rincover, A., & Solnick, J. V. (1980). The technical drift of applied behavior analysis. *Journal of Applied Behavior Analysis, 13,* 275-285.

Henderson, R. I. (1985). *Compensation management: Rewarding performance.* Reston, VA: Reston.

Henry, G. O., & Redmon, W. K. (1990). The effects of performance feedback on the implementation of a statistical process control (SPC) program. *Journal of Organizational Behavior Management, 11,* 23-46.

Herrnstein, R. J. (1961). Relative and absolute strength of response as a function of frequency of reinforcement. *Journal of the Experimental Analysis of Behavior, 4,* 267-272.

Herrnstein, R. J. (1970). On the law of effect. *Journal of the Experimental Analysis of Behavior, 13,* 143-266.

Hineline, P. N., & Wacker, D. P. (1993). *JEAB,* November '92: What's in it for the *JABA* reader? *Journal of Applied Behavior Analysis, 26,* 269-274.

Honig, W. K. (1966). *Operant behavior: Areas of research and application.* New York: Appleton-Century-Crofts.

Honig, W. K., & Staddon, J. E. R. (1977). *Handbook of operant behavior.* Englewood Cliffs, NJ: Prentice-Hall.

Iwata, B. A., & Michael, J. L. (1994). Applied implications of theory and research on the nature of reinforcement. *Journal of Applied Behavior Analysis, 27,* 183-193.

Johnson, C. M., & Masotti, R. M. (1990). Suggestive selling by waitstaff in family-style restaurants: An experiment and multisetting observations. *Journal of Organizational Behavior Management, 11,* 35-54.

Kirby, K. C., & Bickel, W. K. (1995). Implications of behavioral pharmacology research for applied behavior analyses: *JEAB's* special issue celebrating the contributions of Joseph V. Brady (March 1994). *Journal of Applied Behavior Analysis, 28,* 105-112.

Komaki, J., Barwick, K. D., & Scott, L. R. (1978). A behavioral approach to occupational safety: Pinpointing and reinforcing safe performance in a food manufacturing plant. *Journal of Applied Psychology, 53,* 434-445.

Komaki, J., Blood, M. R., & Holder, D. (1980). Fostering friendliness in a fast food franchise. *Journal of Organizational Behavior Management, 2,* 151-164.

LaMere, J. M., Dickinson, A. M., Henry, M., Henry, G., & Poling, A. (1996). Effects of a multi-component monetary incentive program on the performance of truck drivers: A longitudinal study. *Behavior Modification, 20,* 385-406.

Latham, G. P., & Huber, V. L. (1992). Schedules of reinforcement: Lessons from the past and issues from the future. *Journal of Organizational Behavior Management, 12,* 125-149.

Lattal, K. A., & Neef, N. A. (1996). Recent reinforcement-schedule research and applied behavior analysis. *Journal of Applied Behavior Analysis, 29,* 213-230.

Luthans, F., Paul, R., & Taylor, L. (1985). The impact of contingent reinforcement on retail salespersons' performance behaviors: A replicated field experiment. *Journal of Organizational Behavior Management, 7,* 25-35.

Mace, F. C. (1994). Basic research needed for stimulating the development of behavioral technologies. *Journal of the Experimental Analysis of Behavior, 61,* 529-550.

Mace, F. C., McCurdy, B., & Quigley, E. A. (1990). A collateral effect of reward predicted by matching theory. *Journal of Applied Behavior Analysis, 23,* 197-205.

Malott, R. W. (1992). A theory of rule-governed behavior and organizational behavior management. *Journal of Organizational Behavior Management, 12,* 45-65.

Malott, R. W., Malott, M. E., & Shimamune, S. (1992). Comments on rule-governed behavior. *Journal of Organizational Behavior Management, 12,* 91-101.

Malott, R. W., Shimamune, S., & Malott, M. E. (1992) Rule-governed behavior and organizational behavior management: An analysis of interventions. *Journal of Organizational Behavior Management, 12,* 103-116.

Mawhinney, T. C. (1975). Operant terms and concepts in the description of individual work behavior: Some problems of interpretation, application, and evaluation. *Journal of Applied Psychology, 60,* 704-712.

Mawhinney, T. C., & Ford, J. D. (1977). The path goal theory of leader effectiveness: An operant interpretation. *Academy of Management Review, 2,* 398-411.

Mawhinney, T. C., & Gowen, C. R., III. (1991). Gainsharing and the law of effect as the matching law: A theoretical framework. *Journal of Organizational Behavior Management, 11,* 61-75.

Mazur, J. E. (1991). Choice. In I. H. Iversen & K. A. Lattal (Eds.), *Experimental analysis of behavior* (Part 1, pp. 219-250). Amsterdam: Elsevier.

McCuddy, M. K., & Griggs, M. H. (1984). Goal setting and feedback in the management of a professional department: A case study. *Journal of Organizational Behavior Management, 6,* 53-64.

McDowell, J. J. (1981). On the validity and utility of Herrnstein's hyperbola in applied behavior analysis. In C. M. Bradshaw, E. Szabadi, & C. F. Lowe (Eds.), *Quantification of steady-state operant behavior* (pp. 311-324). Amsterdam: Elsevier/North-Holland.

McDowell, J. J. (1982). The importance of Herrnstein's mathematical statement of the law of effect for behavior therapy. *American Psychologist, 37,* 771-779.

McDowell, J. J. (1988). Matching theory in natural human environments. *The Behavior Analyst, 11,* 95-109.

Merwin, G. A., Thomason, J. A., & Sanford, E. A. (1989). A methodology and content review of organizational behavior management in the private sector: 1978-1986. *Journal of Organizational Behavior Management, 10,* 39-56.

Michael, J. (1980). Flight from behavior analysis. *The Behavior Analyst, 3,* 1-22.

Michael, J. (1993). Behavioral effects of remote contingencies. *Concepts and principles of behavior analysis* (pp. 87-93). Kalamazoo, MI: Society for the Advancement of Behavior Analysis.

Myerson, J., & Hale, S. (1984). Practical implications of the matching law. *Journal of Applied Behavior Analysis, 17,* 377-380.

Neef, N. (1994). Functional analysis approaches to behavioral assessment and treatment [Special issue]. *Journal of Applied behavior Analysis, 27*(2).

Nevin, J. A., & Mace, F. C. (1994). The ABCs of JEAB, September 1993. *Journal of Applied Behavior Analysis, 27,* 561-565.

Newby, T. J., & Robinson, P. W. (1983). Effects of grouped and individual feedback and reinforcement on retail employee performances. *Journal of Organizational Behavior Management, 5,* 51-68.

Nordstrum, R. R., Lorenzi, P., & Hall, R. V. (1991). A behavioral training program for managers in city government. *Journal of Organizational Behavior Management, 11,* 189-213.

Oah, S., & Dickinson, A. M. (1992). A comparison of the effects of a linear and an exponential performance pay function on work productivity. *Journal of Organizational Behavior Management, 12,* 85-123.

Perone, M., Galizio, M., & Baron, A. (1988). The relevance of animal-based principles in the laboratory study of human operant conditioning. In G. Davey & C. Cullen (Eds.), *Human operant conditioning and behavior modification* (pp. 59-85). Chichester, UK: Wiley.

Peterson, N. (1982). Feedback is not a new principle of behavior. *The Behavior Analyst, 5,* 101-102.

Pierce, W. D., & Epling, W. F. (1980). What happened to analysis in applied behavior analysis? *The Behavior Analyst, 3,* 1-9.

Pierce, W. D., & Epling, W. F. (1983). Choice, matching, and human behavior: A review of the literature. *The Behavior Analyst, 6,* 57-76.

Pierce, W. D., & Epling, W. F. (1994). Activity anorexia: An interplay between basic and applied behavior analysis. *The Behavior Analyst, 17,* 7-24.

Pierce, W. D., & Epling, W. F., (1995). The applied importance of research on the matching law. *Journal of Applied Behavior Analysis, 28,* 237-241.

Poling, A., Alling, K., & Fuqua, R. W. (1994). Self- and cross-citations in the *Journal of Applied Behavior Analysis (JABA)* and the *Journal of the Experimental Analysis of Behavior (JEAB):* 1983-1992. *Journal of Applied Behavior Analysis, 27,* 729-731.

Poling, A., & Foster, T. M. (1993). The matching law and organization behavior management revisited. *Journal of Organizational Behavior Management, 14,* 83-97.

Poling, A., Picker, M., Grossett, D., Hall-Johnson, E., & Wittkopp, C. (1981). The schism between experimental and applied behavior analysis: Is it real and who cares? *The Behavior Analyst, 4*, 93-102.

Prue, D. M., & Fairbank, J. A. (1981). Performance feedback in organizational behavior management: A review. *Journal of Organizational Behavior Management, 3*, 1-16.

Rachlin, H. (1989). *Judgement, decision, and choice: A cognitive/behavioral synthesis.* New York: W. H. Freeman.

Rachlin, H. (1992). An important first step, but not the last word on rule-governed behavior and OBM: Comments on papers by Malott and Malott, Shimamune, and Malott. *Journal of Organizational Behavior Management, 12*, 85-89.

Ralis, M. T., & O'Brien, R. M. (1986). Prompts, goal setting, and feedback to increase suggestive selling. *Journal of Organizational Behavior Management, 8*, 5-18.

Rao, R. K., & Mawhinney, T. C. (1991). Superior-subordinate dyads: Dependence of leader effectiveness on mutual reinforcement contingencies. *Journal of the Experimental Analysis of Behavior, 56*, 105-118.

Redmon, W. K., & Lockwood, K. (1987). The matching law and organizational behavior. *Journal of Organizational Behavior Management, 8*, 57-72.

Runnion, A., Watson, J. O., & McWhorter, J. (1978). Energy savings in interstate transportation through feedback and reinforcement. *Journal of Organizational Behavior Management, 1*, 180-191.

Sevastano, H. L., & Fantino, E. (1994). Human choice in concurrent ratio-interval schedules of reinforcement. *Journal of the Experimental Analysis of Behavior, 61*, 453-463.

Shull, R. L., & Fuqua, R. W. (1993). The collateral effects of behavioral interventions: Applied implications from *JEAB*, January 1993. *Journal of Applied Behavior Analysis, 26*, 409-415.

Silva, D. B., Duncan, P. K., & Doudna, D. (1981). The effects of attendance-contingent feedback and praise on attendance and work efficiency. *Journal of Organizational Behavior Management, 3*, 59-69.

Skinner, B. F. (1953). *Science and human behavior.* New York: Macmillan.

Smith, J. M., Kaminski, B. J., & Wylie, R. G. (1990). May I make a suggestion? Corporate support for innovation. *Journal of Organizational Behavior Management, 11*, 125-146.

Stromer, R., Mackay, H. A., & Remington, B. (1996). Naming, the formation of stimulus classes, and applied behavior analysis. *Journal of Applied Behavior Analysis, 29*, 409-431.

Sulzer-Azaroff, B., Loafman, B., Merante, R. J., & Hlavacek, A. C. (1990). Improving occupational safety in a large industrial plant: A systematic replication. *Journal of Organizational Behavior Management, 11*, 99-120.

Wilk, L. A., & Redmon, W. K. (1990). A daily-adjusted goal-setting and feedback procedure for improving productivity in a university admissions department. *Journal of Organizational Behavior Management, 11*, 55-75.

Williams, B. A. (1988). Reinforcement, choice, and response strength. In R. C. Atkinson, R. J. Herrnstein, G. Lindzey, & R. D. Luce (Eds.), *Stevens' handbook of experimental psychology: Vol. 2: Learning and cognition* (pp. 167-244). New York: Wiley.

Wilson, C., Boni, N., & Hogg, A. (1997). The effectiveness of task clarification, positive reinforcement and corrective feedback in changing courtesy among police staff. *Journal of Organizational Behavior Management, 17,* 65-99.

Wittkopp, C. J., Rowan, J. F., & Poling, A. (1990). Use of a feedback package to reduce machine set-up time in a manufacturing setting. *Journal of Organizational Behavior Management, 11,* 7-22.

Chapter 14

Performance Analysis
and Performance Diagnostics

John Austin
Western Michigan University

Industrial and organizational psychology is a field with a short history relative to the physical and biological sciences, and even relative to psychology as whole. The first Ph.D. in Industrial Psychology was awarded to Bruce V. Moore in 1921 from the Carnegie Institute (now Carnegie-Mellon Institute) (Landy, 1989). Since that time, the field has rapidly grown to include broad areas of interest such as personnel psychology and human resource management, social-industrial psychology, and engineering psychology. Today, employers are advertising for individuals with knowledge and expertise in such specific areas as work motivation and incentive systems, job satisfaction and quality of work life, criterion development and validation, selection, training, behavior-based safety, systems analysis, and analysis of man-machine interactions.

Even within the study of work motivation and management however, there are distinct areas of specialization. One of these areas includes the analysis of performance, performance systems, and performance management of employees. *Performance analysis* is a process of problem solving based in part on behavioral and operant approaches to management, developed to assist managers and/or organizational consultants in assessing performance problems. From a performance analysis perspective, a consultant enters an organization and is presented with a general and often nondescript problem of employee, departmental, or plant-wide performance.

It is the analyst's job to then pinpoint (Daniels, 1989) the appropriate area of problem performance, analyze that performance through the use of some diagnostic or algorithmic procedure, and recommend a correction for the problem. This "correction" may entail some degree of training delivered by the performance analyst and the training itself may be designed to prepare the organization and its members to implement the recommended solution(s) to their performance problem(s). In the following pages, I will a) discuss the issue of levels of analysis in organizational behavior management; b) describe what ramifications this has for organizational diagnosis; c) review some procedures recognized to be effective in conducting a performance analysis at each of three levels of analysis, and; d) suggest three areas for future research in the area of performance analysis.

Levels of Analysis

One can see that when dealing with organizations, there are a seemingly infinite number of levels at which to analyze, depending on the tradition and perspective of the analyst. The traditions from which the current paper stems are twofold. First, there are the organizational behavior (Vecchio, 1988) and human resource management (Cascio, 1989) traditions in the discipline of business, in which the level of analysis is primarily focused on the cognitive aspects of managing the individual employee (or groups of employees) and solving problems associated with this level, as opposed to more large-scale approaches such as organization design, development, and cultural analysis (Beer, 1980). Second, there are the performance management and performance engineering traditions (Gilbert, 1978; Daniels, 1989) which focus applied psychological principles and research such as *organizational behavior management* (OBM) and environmental design issues on solving organizational problems with productivity, safety, quality, and other types of individual/group level processes.

The many levels of analysis within organizations present a real potential for confusion among the terms (and their implications) used for naming organizational analysis procedures. In addition, performance management (PM) and OBM are not exactly in the "mainstream" of organizational psychology. For these reasons, before reviewing performance analysis procedures used at the level of employee behavior, I must first discuss this issue in the context of larger-scale and more "mainstream" organizational diagnosis (Howard, 1994) and some of its associated procedures.

Organizational Diagnosis

Ann Howard (1994) presents a broadly applicable definition of organizational diagnosis as "a systematic method for gathering data about how organizations function as social systems and an analysis of the meaning of those data" (p. 8). She notes that it is also called problem identification, organizational analysis (Mills, Pace, & Peterson, 1988), and organizational assessment (Lawler, Nadler, & Cammann, 1980). Regardless of what it is called, organizational diagnosis is an activity of problem solving, directed at finding antecedents and consequences responsible for the current state of affairs in an organization (Howard, 1994). Writing in the area covers topics at various levels of vantage within any organization, such as organization-wide change and development (Burke, 1994), organization design (Walton & Nadler, 1994), staffing the organization (Walker & Bechet, 1994), assessing training needs (Zemke, 1994), realigning organization cultures (Rogers & Byham, 1994), assessing needs of teams (Fisher, 1994), and designing effective reward systems for departments or entire organizations (Lawler, 1994), among others. As a result of these differing levels of analysis, there are numerous beliefs as to exactly what activities comprise organizational diagnosis (Harrison, 1995; Howard, 1994).

Individuals in the area of organizational diagnosis, even when focused on just one level of the organization such as individual or group processes, argue that it is necessary to consider all factors in a broad scope of the areas under scrutiny. They would argue, as Howard (1994) did, that "a proper diagnosis should correctly identify core problems" (p. 9), and Porras (1987), that "with the several other layers of less fundamental changes obscuring the truly core issues the system needs to change, organizations wind up attacking problems that are symptoms and find that the problems keep popping back up, often in slightly different forms" (p. 13).

Therefore, regardless of the particulars in which an organizational diagnostician engages, he/she will always be interested in more than just employee performance. In many analyses (see for example, Harrison, 1995; Manzini, 1988) actual employee performance is downplayed, perhaps being viewed as a symptom of some deeper problem "within" the employee or culture rather than the problem itself. Questionnaires and interviews are heavily relied upon to provide insight into employee and management attitudes, feelings, quality of work life, and other perceptions of the work environment. Most analysts at this level stress the importance of considering the organizational part under scrutiny in the larger context of the organization as a whole functioning in its particular business environment and marketplace. In short, organizational diagnosis differs substantially from performance analysis along at least two distinct dimensions: a) unlike performance analysis, organizational diagnosis does not take observable behavior and the work environment as its focus and is therefore not behavior-analytic; and b) unlike performance analysis, organizational diagnosis is necessarily undertaken on a grand scale, in efforts to describe and analyze the *entire* organization.

Performance analysts have found many sets of procedures, based on principles of applied behavior analysis, that are effective in dealing with the problems that organizations encounter. Often this is accomplished through a method of successive approximations: through first piloting on a small scale and refining solutions to problems, and then rolling them out to a large scale for the entire organization. Perhaps we have not explored the attitudes, thoughts and feelings of entire organizations in analyzing problems precisely because we have found success in the more behavior-analytic approaches of performance analysis.

In some sense, the sheer size of such organizational diagnosis projects makes them idealistic. The fact that there are no data to support their comprehensive nature is not surprising: how would one conduct such a study and obtain reliable, valid results on such a broad scale? From a scientific standpoint, it seems to make sense that to conduct worthy research, one needs to first examine the processes from a more narrow level of analysis. Some organizational diagnostic models do in fact examine more basic processes but they do not extrapolate from more basic diagnostic research. Rather, they attempt to amalgamate research conducted on each of the processes that they contend influence organizations and therefore logically should be considered in a comprehensive analysis. For example, there is considerable research on leadership (Fiedler, 1967; House, 1971: Vroom & Yetton, 1973), communications (Dance, 1970; Rogers & Agarwala-Rogers, 1976), organization structure (Scott & Mitchell, 1976), job satisfaction (Locke, 1969; Porter, 1962; Schaffer, 1953), and individual outcomes such as responsibility, autonomy, and knowledge of results (Hackman & Oldham, 1976).

What many organizational diagnosis writers attempt to do is to extrapolate from this research conducted on a micro level up to the level of the entire organization and its external environment. A different approach, however, may be to conduct research on narrowly-based diagnostic endeavors (i.e., understanding how we should diagnose small-scale problems), and attempt to extrapolate up to the level of more complex and broadly-based diagnostic endeavors (i.e., understanding how we should diagnose large-scale problems). This is not to say that comprehensive diagnosis is not an appropriate goal, but rather that such analyses are indeed so important and complex that they must be well understood before they can be maximally applied.

Theory-Driven Approaches to Performance Analysis

In this section, I will review some of the more commonly used procedures in performance analysis. I call them "theory-driven" because none have explicit empirical support although most have been used as implicit paradigms for demonstration research. That is, whereas none of these has been scientifically evaluated for effectiveness, most have been used as guides by practitioners and applied scientists in solving organizational problems. First I will review the diagnostic *models* and then move on to the more focused and prescriptive diagnostic *algorithms*.

Diagnostic Models

Performance analysts have typically worked at three levels of analysis in organizations: the individual level, the process level, and the systems level. Although there have been other similar models proposed, the primary model used at the individual level is the ABC analysis (Daniels, 1989). The primary model used at the level of processes is process mapping (Rummler & Brache, 1995)[1]. The primary model used at the systems level is the total performance system, or TPS (Brethower, 1982). See figure 1 for a visual representation of the three models and the relationships between them.

ABC analysis. The ABC analysis is a performance diagnostic model made popular by Aubrey C. Daniels' (1989) work entitled *Performance Management*. Based originally on Skinner's (1938, 1953) and Ferster and Skinner's (1957) laboratory research examining animal behavior, the operant analysis was first extended to behavior therapy for phobias and anxiety (Wolpe, 1958) and other psychological disorders (see Kazdin, 1978 for a history), and then to helping individuals with developmental disabilities engage in appropriate behavior (Birnbrauer, Wolf, Kidder, & Tague, 1965) and social interaction (Allen, Hart, Buell, Harris, & Wolf, 1964). Later, the operant analysis was applied in community settings to encourage carpooling (Jacobs, Fairbanks, Poche, & Bailey, 1982), reductions in littering (Geller, Witmer, & Tuso, 1977; LaHart & Bailey, 1975), increasing recycling (Geller, 1975; Jacobs, Bailey, & Crews, 1984; Austin, Hatfield, Grindle, & Bailey, 1993), and safety belt usage (Engerman, Austin & Bailey, 1997; Rudd & Geller, 1985). It has since been the fundamental model of choice for many applied and basic researchers working in areas such as language (Chase & Parrot, 1986), behavioral pharmacology (Poling,

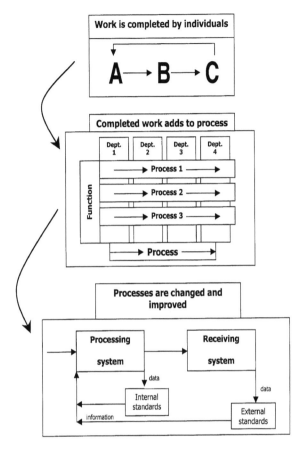

Figure 1. A visual representation of prevalent models at the individual (top), process (middle), and systems (bottom) levels of analysis.

1986) education (Gardner, 1994), cultural practices (Geller, 1994), psychotherapy (Hayes, Jacobson, Follette, & Dougher, 1994; Hayes, this volume), assessment and treatment of behavioral disorders (Ninness, Glenn, & Ellis, 1993), developmental psychology (Bijou, 1959; Gewirtz & Baer, 1958), and business management (Frederiksen, 1982; O'Brien, Dickinson, & Rosow, 1982).

The ABC analysis is a variant on Skinner's (1953) analysis which argues that the manipulable variables of which behavior is a function can be classified into two primary types: antecedents and consequences. Antecedents are stimuli which precede behavior and include prompts, reminders, instructions, and the broader environmental context or what Bandura (1977a) termed "situation", whereas consequences are stimuli which follow a behavior, including any results of behaving in a particular manner. Daniels' version of the operant analysis for work (i.e., the ABC analysis) does not use all of Skinner's analyses, but rather just the fundamental principles. In addition, Daniels' analysis is admittedly simplified for presentation to groups of clients with little or no background in psychology.

Daniels (1989) recommends an ABC analysis be conducted when: 1) some desired behavior is not occurring often enough, and when 2) some undesired behavior is occurring too often. The following seven-step process to be used in conducting an ABC analysis is described by Daniels (1989) in *Performance Management* (p. 43):

Step 1: Describe the performance you don't want and who is doing it (the problem).

Step 2: Describe what this person should be doing (correct or desired performance).

Step 3: Determine the severity of the problem. If the problem occurs frequently, complete steps 4-7.

Step 4: Complete an ABC analysis for the problem performance.
  a) write the person's name and problem performance on a form.
  b) list all possible antecedents and consequences.
  c) cross out any consequence not relevant to the performer.
  d) indicate whether each remaining consequence is P/N, I/F, C/U.

Step 5: Complete an ABC analysis for the correct performance.
  a) write the correct performance for the performer.
  b) complete as in step 4.

Step 6: The diagnosis: summarize the antecedents and consequences which are presently occurring.

Step 7: The solution: Add "positive, immediate, and certain" consequences and antecedents for the correct performance.

In his presentation of the seven-step process, Daniels elaborates on each of the steps, making their appropriate use clearer to the reader. Daniels describes how to operationalize performance problems in his explanation of step 1. When confronted with a vague problem such as "low morale", he recommends the analyst ask, "What did I see the person do (or hear that he did) that led me to conclude that he is lazy, has a bad attitude, or has poor morale?" (Daniels, 1989, p. 42). Asking questions such as this should lead the analyst to a more behavioral definition of the problem. In step 2 the analyst is asked to describe the desired performance in active terms. For example, if the problem is that an employee is making too many errors and the manager wants the person to commit fewer errors, the desired performance stated in active terms would be to "increase error-free work" – not "to commit no errors". The reason for this is that "making no errors" is an easy thing to do, and that in itself will not help the business. The employee actually needs to continue working and make fewer errors, translating into increased error-free work. Step 3 stresses that this analysis will not be useful for problems occurring only once or very infrequently, and which are not too severe. It should be used only for recurring problems of importance to the organization.

In Step 4, listing the antecedents and consequences is the "backbone" (p. 44) of the analysis, so listing every possibility is a necessity. Some antecedents listed for the problem behavior of not wearing safety glasses include: forgot to put them on, doesn't have them, left them somewhere, doesn't believe an accident will occur, sees others not wearing them, the glasses are a lot of trouble, and thinks he/she won't get caught. Some consequences for the same problem behavior include: sees better without them, less trouble, more comfortable, doesn't have to keep track of them, might have injury, boss may chew him/her out, and might get suspended or fired. The next part of step 4 includes crossing out the consequences that are not important for the employee. For example, many managers will list organizational consequences such as decreased profit, increased costs, decreased quality, etc., but these often do not have any importance to the employee. The final phase of step 4 is classifying each consequence across three categories. The analyst must ask, is the consequence, 1) positive or negative: is it something that the person wants or does not want?; 2) immediate or future: the longer the delay between the behavior and the consequence, the less effective the consequence; and 3) certain or uncertain: what is the probability that it will occur, given the occurrence of the behavior? The more certain a consequence, the more effective.

Step 5 directs the analyst or manager to complete an ABC analysis for the desired performance, using the same process as in step 4. The diagnosis (step 6) consists of a summary of the current contingencies occurring in the workplace. This summary of antecedents and consequences tells the analyst what is occurring and whether it is positive or negative, immediate or future, and certain or uncertain. Generally, the problem behavior will be maintained by several positive-immediate-certain (PIC's) consequences and/or negative-immediate-certain (NIC's) consequences. In step 7, Daniels explains that as a result of this analysis, the analyst now knows where he/she must add PIC's and antecedents for the correct behavior. The reader should note, however, that the **only** solution proposed by the ABC analysis is the addition of PIC's.

The ABC analysis provides a clear, step-by-step procedure for analyzing performance problems. Daniels' consulting firm, Aubrey Daniels and Associates (ADA), frequently trains managers to conduct such analyses and complete small PM projects within two weeks of instruction. This indicates that the procedure is quite easy to learn. On the other hand, however, the procedure is general and the result is always the same. Consultants and students could use such a procedure in solving problems, although there are no data to demonstrate whether even ADA's consultants make effective use of the procedure. The procedure says nothing about what consultants actually do on the job (i.e., do they routinely go through each of the seven steps?), rather it offers a procedure for analyzing performance problems, derived from Skinner's theory.

The misinterpretation of Skinner's (1957) work entitled *Verbal Behavior*, coupled with organizational applied behavior analysts' (Frederiksen, 1982; O'Brien, Dickinson, & Rosow, 1982) focus on noncognitive activity, however, has led to other models which "account for human cognition" (Bandura, 1977b; Luthans & Kreitner, 1985). Luthans and Kreitner provide a variant on the ABC analysis in which the role of cognition is also considered. Based on the research of Bandura (1977a) and his social learning approach, Luthans and Kreitner (1985) propose an SOBC model in which behavior (B) is a function of the (S) situation and external stimuli, the (O) organism's cognitions and attributions preceding the behavior, and the (C) consequences of behavior. The fundamental tenet remains that behavior is a function of its consequences, but the social learning approach "also takes into account cognitive

mediating processes (especially attributions which can be used to predict subsequent behavior) and covert (unobservable, nonenvironmentally-based events) [sic]
as well as overt environmental antecedents and consequences" (Luthans & Kreitner,
1985, p. 15). According to Bandura (1969, 1977a), social learning differs from
traditional operant analyses because it recognizes the role of vicarious processes
such as modeling, it recognizes the effects of covert cognitive processes, and it
recognizes the role of self-control processes.

An example at the individual level. As an example of the utility of an
individual level analysis, imagine that a plastics manufacturing firm is having trouble
with a higher than desired scrap rate. The manager looks at the behavior of the
machine operators, analyzing the antecedents, behaviors, and consequences involved in producing the current product and those in producing the desired quality
product. What they find is that when the parts are left in the pressing machine too
long, they become defects, adding to the scrap rate. Some antecedents involved in
this behavior include: there are many parts which pile up if the operator slows down;
there are many parts in need of attention by the operator, which takes time; there
are no clear standards for what constitutes good parts; etc. Some consequences of the
high scrap rate behavior include: occasional quality audits sometimes catch a bad
part; other bad parts, when detected by the operator, go into a recycling bin and are
fed back into the machine making it easier to pitch parts in the recycling bin when
the operator gets behind in production; and when the manager detects that scrap rate
is high, the operator is yelled at.

Such analysis yields some ideas to change the behavior of the operator, such as
adding a job aid to clarify what is good and bad about specific parts; adding a noise
from the pressing machine to prompt operators to remove the parts on time; and
adding regular feedback and praise from the manager when scrap rate is managed
effectively by the operator.

Process mapping. According to Rummler and Brache (1995), "a business
process is a series of steps designed to produce a product or service" (p. 45). Every
organization engages in a variety of processes on a daily basis. The key point at this
level of analysis is, "an organization is only as effective as its processes" (p. 45).
Indeed, no amount of individual level performance management will allow good
employees to be competitive when using a faulty process.

Process mapping is a technique used to elucidate the flaws in organizational
processes so that they may be designed to operate more efficiently. Figure 1 shows
how processes (horizontal rectangles) in organizations tend to work across departments or functions (vertical rectangles). Because processes move across the functional boundaries (i.e., from sales, to marketing, to management, to product design,
and so on), these functions are required to work together in completing the final
product. This act of working together to add value to a product is the process.

The first step in creating process maps, therefore, is to assemble a team
representative of each of the functions involved in a particular process. These
representatives then need to discuss each of the steps in the current process, so that
an "is" map can be constructed. In constructing the "is" map, each of the

departments are listed vertically on the left side of the paper, and as the process develops over time, each step of the process is listed next to the department responsible for its completion horizontally in order from left to right and connected by arrows to indicate the temporal order.

After examining the "is" map, there will often be obvious unnecessary duplication, inefficient steps, and steps that are necessary but not happening (termed "disconnects" by Rummler and Brache, 1995) in the process. When these are detected, the next step is to construct a "should" map, which is a diagram of the way processes should be working. This is completed in the same way as the "is" map, but all inefficiencies, duplication, and disconnects are corrected. Once both process maps are completed, the team can formulate a plan to redesign the work flow and improve the processes. This usually leads to an improved product, faster production or shipping time, and reduced costs due to less duplication.

An example at the process level. If we continued to use the manufacturing example from the individual level analysis above, we would see that there are actually several functions involved in producing the single part in question. Before each shift, an engineer arrives to adjust the machine settings so that when it operates properly, it is capable of producing high quality parts. As parts are produced, a quality inspector examines parts two times per shift. As boxes of parts are filled by the operator, a warehouse employee loads them to pallets and transports them to the warehouse floor, where the parts in each box are again counted. In the warehouse, the shipping coordinator takes inventory and arranges for them to be hauled to the customer. At that point, the parts are a product of the processing system.

From such an analysis, we may see some obvious shortcomings of the process. First, we see that the high scrap rate could be a function, in part, of the pressing machines. Assuming the operator can not be trained to make adjustments on-line, if the engineers adjusted the machines throughout the day instead of only in the morning, the scrap rate may be reduced. Second, the quality inspector only checks the product two times during an eight hour shift. If this were increased, feedback could be given to both the operator and the engineer so that appropriate adjustments could be made to reduce scrap rate during the shift. Finally, the parts are counted first by the operator, and then by the warehouse staff. This, being a time-intensive job, could be made more efficient through having a machine count the parts, creating a box that holds only a certain number of parts, or through some other means.

The total performance system. The bottom of figure 1 illustrates the total performance system (Brethower, 1982; 1997). Although this model can be applied at any level in the organization (from individual to system level), I prefer to use it to incorporate each of the previous levels into an adaptive system. The model begins with any input to the system, such as orders to be filled. As the orders are *processed* by the organization, they may pass through several difference stages and be added to by people across several different functions of the organization (as described above at the process level). The finished product is then compared to internal standards and any discrepancy is fed back to the organization (i.e., the processing system). The products are shipped to the receiving system, which in this case could be the customer or a vendor. The receiving system may also engage in processes designed to add value to the product or it may be the final destination for the product. Either way, the receiving system evaluates the product based on their external standards, and feeds back any discrepancy to the processing system. This model allows an analyst to look at the functioning of an entire organization on a single sheet of paper, and to easily identify areas potentially in need of improvement.

An example at the systems level. To continue with our plastics manufacturing example, at the systems level we see that the plant manufacturing represents the processing system, and perhaps their customer represents the receiving system. Since we have covered the processing system analysis above, a TPS would allow us to take a broader focus and examine the internal and external standards and the data fed back to the processing system. In this example, it turns out that not only is there a problem internally with scrap rate (perhaps in part because the internal standards are not fixed and applied), but there is an external problem with this as well. That is, when the customer picks up the parts, they inspect them with a representative of our manufacturing plant. However, when the parts are received at the receiver's plant, they are inspected again, but often with more rigorous standards. When rejects are detected at the receiver's plant, the entire shipment is returned at the expense of our manufacturing plant. The solution here is simple: to make sure that the internal standards (used by the manufacturing plant) are in agreement with the external standards (of the receiving plant). This can be accomplished through improving communication between the processing system and the receiving system, and may take the form of meetings, policies, and/or feedback sessions.

Diagnostic Algorithms

The difference between diagnostic models and algorithms is that the latter are more prescriptive, given a particular problem. That is, whereas the models broadly direct our attention to a level of analysis and perhaps to classes of stimuli within that level, algorithms give the analyst specific questions to ask, usually within several categories.

The approaches described in this section will include those of Mager and Pipe (1970), Gilbert (1978), Kent (1985), Bailey and Austin (1996), and Brethower (1997). The models were grouped together because each proposes a series of questions to be asked in a systematic order by an analyst or manager in solving performance problems. In addition, the questions and their order were not empirically determined, but logically by the writer through his experiences as a performance analyst.

Mager and Pipe (1970). Mager and Pipe (1970) provide a set of troubleshooting algorithms to be used when performance problems arise "...because someone isn't doing what he [sic] is supposed to be doing or what you would like him [sic] to be doing" (p. v, Preface). They suggest the manager or analyst begin by describing the performance discrepancy through examining the difference between what is being done and what is supposed to be done, asking why the performance is dissatisfying, and asking what exact event causes the feeling that things aren't right. Second, the manager should ask whether the performance discrepancy is important, and if it is, why it is important. Other questions regarding the importance of the problem include asking what would happen if the discrepancy were left alone, and if doing something to resolve the discrepancy could have any worthwhile result. If the problem is seen as important, it must be resolved, and attempts to resolve the problem could possibly have worthwhile results, the manager or analyst is instructed to ask whether the problem is an issue of skill deficiency or not.

To determine if it is a skill deficiency, the analyst or manager is to ask if the person could do the task if their life depended on it and whether their present skills are adequate to achieve the desired performance. At this point, the algorithm breaks into two areas of questioning: problems resulting from lack of skill and problems resulting from other management-related issues.

Once the manager determines that the problem is a result of a skill deficiency, he/she is instructed to ask if the person in question has ever performed to the desired level in the past (perhaps the individual has forgotten how to do the task), if the skill was used often (does he/she get regular feedback about performance on the task), if there is a simpler solution such as providing a job aid, checklist, or informal on-the-job training, and/or if the person has the capability of learning the job as desired. If the person could not do the task in the past (and can not do it in the present), then formal training is necessary. If the person could do it in the past, but is not performing as desired presently and the skill is not used often, one should arrange for the individual to practice the task in order to maintain his/her skills. If the skill is used often and the performance is not satisfactory, Mager and Pipe (1970) contend there may be a simpler solution such as providing a job aid or a checklist so the person does not have to remember a large amount of information. If none of the above seems to work, and the analyst or manager is sure that the problem is a skill deficiency, he/she should consider whether the individual has the physical and mental capacities to learn the job, or if the individual is somehow overqualified.

If the problem is not a result of a skill deficiency (i.e., the employee could do the task if his/her life depended on it), the performance analyst is instructed to consider if the desired performance is punishing to the employee by asking what the consequence of performing as desired is to the employee. If it is punishing, the analyst should remove the punishment. If there are rewards for performing differently than desired (the analyst may discover this through asking what the employee gets out of performing in his/her own way, or asking if the employee gets more attention for misbehavior than for appropriate behavior), then positive consequences for appropriate performance of the task must be designed. If the above do not apply, the analyst is to ask if the performance really matters to the performer.

Depending on exactly how it matters to the employee, the analyst then should change the consequences so that completing the task means that something will happen as a result. Finally, if none of the above questions lead to the solution of the problem, and the analyst is sure the problem is not a lack of skill or practice, the analyst should ask if there are obstacles to performing as desired. Obstacles can be identified through asking questions such as does the employee know what is expected of him/her, asking if there are conflicting demands on the employee's time, asking if there are policies or a lack of authority preventing the performance, and asking if the work environment (i.e., lighting, temperature, etc.) is somehow restricting the performance of the employee.

After the manager or analyst has considered all of the above issues and questions and possible solutions derived from them, he/she should then evaluate all of the possible solutions generated on the grounds of cost, time, effort, and biggest impact. At this point, the solution should be implemented and evaluated to decide if it has made a difference in the status of the performance problem. If there is some problem with its efficacy, the manager should try the next best solution, and so on, until one works. Mager and Pipe (1970) make it very clear that the analyst should not hesitate to re-analyze a problem, as there may be several correct answers for any one problem.

Mager and Pipe (1970) provide a very simple, yet elegant model for the analysis of performance problems. They claim the model could easily be used by managers or consultants, and it seems to require little knowledge of psychological principles. It does require knowledge of consequences and how to analyze them in the workplace, although Mager and Pipe (1970) gloss over this point by suggesting that the manager "arrange a consequence" (p. 70) when they see that the employee does not feel that his/her performance matters.

Their approach is obviously loosely based on the operant model of learning, as one can see from the recommendations to examine the consequences if there is no skill deficit. This is certainly a strength in that the algorithm at least has some theoretical grounding, even though only one small part of the model is based on the operant model and the overall efficacy of the algorithm has not been tested. The model appears relatively complete for an analysis of individual and/or group performances at the behavioral level (rather than attitudinal), however it seems that they suggest some higher cost or lower-probability solutions (e.g., training and con sequences) before other lower cost or higher-probability ones (e.g., job aids and prompts).

In solving performance problems, it makes sense that one should look for and test those solutions which are lowest in cost first. While Mager and Pipe (1970) allude to a strategy such as this, they only mention it briefly at the very end of the book – it is not built into their algorithm. For instance, they instruct the analyst to consider training as a solution before considering adding a checklist to the work environment to help the employee remember information and ordering of steps for complex tasks.

Gilbert (1978). Gilbert (1978) assumes that when analyzing performance, most consultants and managers are in the same situation as the "crack mechanic" (p. 144) who knows everything about a machine but still takes hours to find and correct the problem. He/she takes so long because there is no set of algorithms to effectively guide their search behavior. While he/she may know volumes about how the engine works, the mechanic does not know all of the important questions to ask, nor the correct order in which to ask them.

Once the problem area is identified, Gilbert recommends asking three questions before even attempting to "engineer" behavior (p. 164-165):

1) Have I clearly described the goal, missions, and responsibilities of the performance system? Am I entirely satisfied with them and with my description of them? Are they described as measurable accomplishments[2] and not as behaviors?

2) Do I have sensible requirements and standards of performance that are based on exemplary possibilities? And do I have a reasonably reliable and accurate way of measuring these standards?

3) Have I found where the greatest opportunity for improving performance lies? The greatest PIPs (performance improvement potentials) [my addition] with the biggest stakes?

When the analyst has answered "yes" to all three questions, he/she may then proceed to the next phase of question asking. In this phase, there are six levels of information the analyst collects, and they progress in the following order: 1) information issues; 2) instruments and equipment issues; 3) motivation and incentives issues; 4) knowledge issues; 5) capacity issues; and 6) motivation and motives issues.

To begin with assessing the information issues, Gilbert has three primary questions which the analyst must ask (p. 165):

1) Do people know what accomplishments are expected of them and what the standards are?

2) Are people informed as quickly as possible—and with high frequency—about how well they are performing? Are they truly informed, and not just given data that are difficult to understand? Are the data accurate? Are the data tied to performance, so that they measure only the performance over which people have real control? And do the data tell the people in what respect they are not performing well? Is there an enforcement system that ensures that the information will be dispersed as it should be?

If any of these questions prompts a "no" response, then adequate feedback systems must be designed. If the analyst can not do this, then he/she should seek the help of someone who can. And the final question (p. 166):

3) Does the incoming information efficiently guide performance? Is it free from confusion and a model of clarity? Are there adequate guides as to how to perform a job so that memory isn't critical? Are these guides models of simplicity and clarity?

If these questions prompt a "no" response, the work setting must be engineered at the point of the performance problem so as to create clear and simple antecedents for appropriate performance. Gilbert has something to say about who should and should not be consulted (i.e., to avoid subject matter experts, because they will tend to aim for completeness and detail rather than simplicity) in such design issues, but he does not describe in detail exactly how to create such antecedents.

When performance problems involve instruments issues, the solutions, according to Gilbert (1978), are often first a matter of common sense and then a matter of return on the investment of appropriate resources and equipment. He suggests the following questions in analyzing instrument-related problems (p. 166):

Are the tools and materials people have to work with designed mechanically to fit human beings? Are better tools available? Are they optimally arranged and made available for use?

When a "no" response is prompted by these questions, the solution becomes rather obvious, but then the analyst is faced with the problem of actually solving design problems. Gilbert (1978) notes that these are often best solved by industrial engineers and human factors specialists.

The motivation and incentives issues that Gilbert (1978) proposes raising are prompted by the following questions (p. 167):

Is there something in it for people who perform well? Are the incentives made contingent upon good performance? Do people know that? Are there competing incentives to perform poorly; and, if so, is the balance of consequences in favor of positive performance? Are the incentives scheduled well enough to protect against discouragement and extinction of performance? Are all the available incentives being used?

Gilbert (1978) contends that a "good, hard, unbiased look at the incentives available" (p. 167) to people should provide the diagnostic evidence needed for the analyst or manager to pinpoint problems and develop solutions.

Gilbert's (1978) fourth stage of troubleshooting questions is directed at determining whether the employees have the knowledge required to complete their jobs (p. 167):

Would people fail to perform to exemplary standards even if their lives depended on it–even when they have adequate information, instruments, and incentives to do so? Does the exemplary performer seem to know something that other people don't?

If the manager or analyst answers "yes" to these questions, Gilbert (1978) argues that training is the intervention of choice, as the problem has been identified as knowledge-based.

If knowledge (or a lack thereof) is not the root of the performance problem, Gilbert (1978) suggests the analyst or manager look toward issues of the capacity required to perform the job, by asking questions such as (p. 168):

Is it certain and proven that one must have special aptitudes, intelligence scores, verbal skills, manual dexterities, and so on [sic], in order to perform in an acceptable, if not exemplary, manner? Is the proof so sound that there are virtually no exceptions to it?

Even when it is the case that special abilities or aptitudes are necessary to perform well, Gilbert (1978) argues that such a condition is usually the result of poorly designed performance systems. Therefore, answers and analysis in this phase could lead the manager or analysts back to the design phases of information and instruments. Only if the answer to these questions is a overwhelming "yes" should the analyst or manager consider selection of individuals to be the problem.

The final phase in the performance troubleshooting model is the consideration of motivation and motives issues. Gilbert (1978) proposes the following question in analyzing these issues (p. 168):

Is the performance inherently so dull, unrewarding, or punishing that people must have special motives to succeed in it, even when the incentives provided are excellent?

If the answer to this question is "yes", then performance engineering is not the remedy. Gilbert (1978) implies that this will rarely be the case, that most cases will indeed fall into systems design issues (knowledge, information, instruments) or performance engineering issues (incentives and motivation), however when all else has been analyzed and performance remains at a low level, managers can attempt to select individuals on the basis of their motives. Gilbert (1978) concedes that when all else fails, perhaps the manager can find people willing to work in specifically monotonous jobs.

Gilbert's (1978) approach to solving performance problems is similar to the organizational diagnosis literature in that he first logically lists the possible areas in which performance problems can occur (i.e., information, knowledge, capacity, incentives, etc.). His approach then becomes algorithmic however, as he lists the questions to be asked within each of the potential problem areas. Gilbert never really addresses the issue of how one identifies current and potential performance problems. He presents no evidence for the efficacy of his approach, and although it seems obvious that the approach is largely based on operant principles, he provides no indication of this.

Kent (1986), Bailey and Austin (1996), and Brethower (1997). The last algorithms I will review in this section of the chapter include those of Kent (1986), Bailey and Austin (1996), and Brethower (1997). Kent's (1986) book presents his "Problem Diagnosis Algorithm". It involves 25 questions which the analyst should ask. The first few of these seem to be the least intrusive, such as asking if the employee is aware of their job duties, and if they are not, to tell them what to do; asking if they are aware of their performance, and if they are not, to arrange for performance feedback; and asking if they are aware of the performance standards, and if they are not, letting them know the standards. The next questions include asking if the employee recognizes the importance of the task and if not, if the employee's priorities and values are appropriate; asking if the job is too simple; asking if there are any distractions to performance; asking if the job is appropriately designed; and asking if the job is too big or complex for the average employee.

Asking if the job is too complex before assessing the employee's training needs is an improvement over Mager and Pipe's (1970) model. If the job does not appear too complex, the analyst should decide if the employee possesses the needed skills by asking if the employee has been trained in the skills, if the training program used is generally successful, and if it is, if the employee has a learning disability. Much like

Mager and Pipe's (1970) version, if the employee does not lack the skill needed, the analyst is to ask if the employee needs practice.

Kent (1986) addresses the issue of employee perceptions by suggesting that the analyst ask if the employee thinks there is a lack of time to complete the task, and if the employee perceives there to be a lack of equipment, materials, funds, tools, support, or other resources. The lack of support or resources assessed here is quite similar to Mager and Pipe's (1970) handling of the issue of obstacles to successful performance.

Kent (1986) also adds a part, similar to Mager and Pipe (1970) and based on the operant model of learning, asking if the employee's poor performance is being rewarded, if the employee's good work is being punished, if there is pressure against good work, and if the employee's good work is being extinguished. If the poor work is being rewarded, the analyst is instructed to eliminate the inappropriate reinforcers and reinforce the good behavior. If the good work is being punished or if there is pressure against good work, the analyst is to eliminate the source of punishment and reinforce the good behaviors; and if the employee's good work is being extinguished (meaning there is no reinforcement for it), the analyst is supposed to start an appropriate reinforcement schedule for the employee's good behaviors (Kent, 1986).

The latter half of the model contains items which seem more nebulous: did the employee forget the directions or forget to do the job; was the poor work simply a matter of human error; does the employee have personal problems; is the employee insecure or lacking self-esteem; is there a personality conflict; does the employee distrust the company or management about receiving rewards; and is the employee apathetic or unconcerned with the work.

The model proposed by Kent (1986) has problems similar to those of Mager and Pipe (1970). The algorithm suggests asking some higher cost or lower probability questions before the lower cost or higher probability questions. For example, it is not until question number 17 that Kent's analyst asks if the employee misunderstood the directions or not! This is after the analyst has considered how to restructure the incentives given to the employee for appropriate performance, and whether or not to re-train the employee! Any model which is to take into account the intrusiveness of the intervention must attend to issues such as these.

Finally, although Kent (1986) mentions Herbert Simon, Ed Lawler, and Victor Vroom (renown researchers and theoreticians) in the acknowledgments, he does not cite any research in the book. Therefore, there is no cited precedent for the questions to be asked, or their ordering (except for Kent's explanation in the foreword that these have developed over a decade of helping solve performance problems in a large number of businesses in Canada).

Bailey and Austin (1996) suggested a brief algorithm intended to incorporate much of the ones proposed by Mager and Pipe (1970), Gilbert (1978), and Kent (1986). The order in which the questions are to be asked is based on the intrusiveness of interventions suggested for that cause. Intrusiveness is defined in two primary ways: through the probability of the point of intervention being the actual cause of the problem, and through the cost associated with finding out if that point is the actual cause of the problem (i.e., the monetary costs and other resources such as managerial time and effort associated with the intervention and its evaluation). The questions are as follows:

1) Does the employee have a personal problem that requires counseling or other assistance?
2) Does the person understand what behavior is expected? Do they have the skill?
3) Does the equipment work? Is it in good repair? Is the environment conducive to top performance?
4) Are there any disincentives for performing the task?
5) Is a competing behavior being reinforced?
6) Does the person get any feedback?
7) Does the behavior produce any important positive consequence?

Brethower's (1997) book entitled "Improving the value of performance: Case studies" contains several models and many algorithms for analyzing performance problems (including the TPS described in an above section). Only two of these will be discussed below: the productive work group checklist, and the performance system analysis worksheet.

The productive work group checklist is a series of questions an analyst may ask when examining the effectiveness of teams. The questions cover three areas of analysis:

1) Production
   Outputs: Are there specific standards for timeliness, quality, and cost?
   Are there useful measures for standards?
   Are standards and measures known by members of the work group?
   Are standards regularly met?
   Is the work group designed to make use of the best knowledge and skill of members?

2) Group processes
   Is it really a group? Can the group make significant decisions to direct its work?
   Are there group norms supporting cooperation? For resolving con-flicts? For reaching agreements? For working productively?
   Are group norms consistent with organizational practices?

3) Group support
   Are individual long term interests aligned with group interests? Organizational interests?
   Are individual short term interests aligned with group interest? Organizational interests?
   Are there group norms supporting individual interests? For assuring individual participation?

Each of the above algorithms can be easily used by someone trained in applied behavior analysis to arrive at reasonable diagnoses for organizational problems. One efficient aspect of these is that when the diagnosis is reached, it is usually directly suggestive of the intervention required to fix the problem.

The performance system analysis worksheet is an more specific version of Gilbert's (1978) troubleshooting algorithm discussed above, with an important addition. I will not restate Gilbert's algorithm here, but Brethower's additions include an analysis of the perceptions of:

1) The stakeholders

Who perceives there to be a problem or opportunity? What are their interests? What data exist to document the extent of the problem?

2) The current deficiencies

What should happen that does not? What happens that should not? What are the good and bad results of these deficiencies? What performance gaps exist? What are the current levels and trends?

3) The current strengths

What is going well? What strengths are there to build on? What are the current levels and trends?

The worksheet then instructs the analyst to go on to an analysis of goals by examining:

1) The desired state

What would the organization be like if the problem were solved? What organizational results would be achieved? How would that benefit the performers?

2) The importance

What is the economic, social and/or strategic value of the results?

3) The outputs

What outputs or accomplishments are needed to make the changes?

The final phase of the worksheet is to ask specific questions in the six categories suggested by Gilbert (1978): information and direction; tools and materials; goals and incentives; knowledge, skills and attitudes; abilities; and motives and values. The reader should see Brethower's (1997) book for a list of questions under each specific category, as these differ somewhat from Gilbert's (1978) list.

Toward an Empirical Approach to Understanding Performance Analysis

Whereas the field of OBM has provided neither empirical demonstrations nor evaluations of performance analysis techniques[3], the field of organizational behavior (OB) has generated a great deal of research on managerial problem solving, and although performance analysis is not all that managers do, it can be argued that they engage in some forms of performance analysis and problem identification. By far the most frequently used method for studying managerial problem solving (which, for now, is the closest group of empirical studies to a field of performance analysis) are outcome measures (Payne, Braunstein, & Carroll, 1978). Outcome measures such as correctness of final solutions, choice proportions, rankings, or ratings are useful in many respects, but they are not informative of the **process** by which problems are solved.

I contend that in order to write about and teach others how one is to successfully analyze performance problems, we must first know something about what makes some analysts successful and others unsuccessful. However, to reliably acquire such knowledge, researchers must be able to accurately describe the process (or at least one of many possible processes) by which successful analysts arrive at appropriate solutions. Unfortunately, such process-tracing methods are rare (Russo, Johnson, & Stephens, 1989), especially for complex tasks such as performance analysis and other tasks related to management (see Schweiger, 1983 for an exception), and verbal protocol analysis (Ericsson & Simon, 1993) is the most widely used process tracing method today (see also Hayes, 1986; and Austin & Delaney, in press, for behavior-analytic accounts of protocol analysis).

Think aloud procedures have been used to understand verbal behavioral problem solving processes in management-related areas such as accounting (Bouwman, 1984); job choice (Barber & Roeling, 1993; Soelberg, 1965); supervisor evaluations (Martin & Klimoski, 1990); strategic decision making (Schweiger, Anderson, & Locke, 1985); consumer choice (Bettman & Zins, 1977); design of management information systems (Vitalari, 1980); and aircraft accident investigations (Braunstein & Coleman, 1967).

Austin (1996) conducted a study designed to examine the process of question asking in which experts and managers engage when solving performance problems. Each of 10 expert management consultants (average experience was approximately 17 years) and 10 experienced managers (average experience was approximately 15 years) were first provided three practice trials and then asked to think out loud while solving three performance problems. Subjects were given a one sentence presenting problem, such as, "Are we paying our employees correctly in order to get the best performance out of them?" They were then asked to develop a workable set of recommendations for the manager to implement. They were allowed to ask the experimenter any question to gain additional information or they could provide an implementation plan immediately. When asked questions, the experimenter answered from a script developed through extensive piloting. If subjects asked a question to which there was no scripted answer, the experimenter answered, "I do not have that information".

Analyses of the data revealed several findings relevant to performance analysis and managerial problem solving (all data are reported in Austin, 1996, and more focused analyses are presented in Austin, 1998a & 1998b). The findings most relevant to this chapter were that the subjects who consistently had the best solutions each asked questions in four primary areas: antecedents, equipment and process, knowledge and skills, and consequences. It is these four (empirically derived) areas around which I have attempted to begin constructing a more empirical approach to

Performance Diagnostic Checklist

Answer each of the following questions, providing data in support of your answer if possible.

Antecedents and Information
Yes No

O O Is there a written job description telling exactly what is expected of the employee?

O O Has the employee received adequate instruction about what to do?
(not training - explicit instructions like "I want you to do this, this, and this before we leave today...")

O O Are employees aware of the mission of the department/organization?
Can they tell you what it is?

O O Are there job or task aids in the employees' immediate environment?
Visible while completing the task in question? Reminders to prompt the task at the correct time/duration?

O O Is the supervisor present during task completion?

O O Are there frequently updated, challenging, and attainable goals set that employees are comfortable with/feel are fair?

Equipment and Processes
Yes No

O O If equipment is required, is it reliable? In good working order? Ergonomically correct?

O O Is the equipment & environment optimally arranged in a physical sense?

O O Are larger processes suffering from certain incomplete tasks along the way (process disconnects)?

O O Are these processes arranged in a logical manner, without unnecessary repetition? Are they maximally efficient?

O O Are there any other obstacles that are keeping the employee from completing the task?

Knowledge and Skills
Yes No

O O Can the employee tell you he/she is supposed to be doing and how to do it?
Have they mastered the task? If fluency is necessary, are they fluent?

O O Can the employee physically demonstrate completion of the task? Have they mastered the task? If fluency is necessary, are they fluent?

O O Does the employee have the capacity to learn how to complete the job?

Consequences
Yes No

O O Are there consequences delivered contingent on the task?
-frequency? (list)_____
-immediacy? (list)_____
-consistency/probability? (list)_____
-positive or negative? (circle one)
-Are there premack reinforcers?

O O Do employees see the effects of performance? (How? Natural /arranged)

O O Do supervisors deliver feedback? (How? Written / verbal; direct /indirect)

O O Is there performance monitoring? (Self / supervisor direct / supervisor indirect)

O O Is there a response effort associated with performing?

O O Are there other behaviors competing with the desired performance?

Figure 2. A sample of a performance diagnostic checklist, currently used by the author in teaching Performance Management at Western Michigan University.

performance analysis. The strength of an empirical approach in this area is that is can be continually improved upon through additional research and testing.

Figure 2 is a worksheet used in an undergraduate performance management course I currently teach at Western Michigan University. At this point in time, there is limited empirical support for the broad areas (antecedents, equipment and processes, knowledge and skills, and consequences) and not necessarily the specific questions beneath each area listed in the figure. Additional research is needed to

Table 1. Summary of Behavior-Analytic Approaches to Performance Analysis.

Name of Analysis	Representative Citation	Focus and Features
Diagnostic Models		
ABC analysis	Daniels (1989)	Individual level analyses
Process mapping	Rummler & Brache (1995)	Process level analyses
Total performance system (TPS)	Brethower (1972)	Individual, process and systems-level analyses
Diagnostic Algorithms		
Performance analysis flowchart	Mager & Pipe (1970)	Discriminates training from consequence problems
Troubleshooting	Gilbert (1978)	Questions in 6 areas
Problem diagnosis algorithm	Kent (1986)	25 questions across many areas
Least intrusive treatment analysis	Bailey & Austin (1996)	Questions from least to most intrusive
Productive groups worksheet	Brethower (1997)	Questions in 3 areas of group performance
Performance system analysis worksheet	Brethower (1997)	Adds preliminary questions in 3 areas to Gilbert's (1978) algorithm
Performance diagnostics	Austin, Carr & Agnew (1999)	Questions in 4 areas developed from expert/novice studies

pinpoint exactly which questions tend to be most useful when addressing specific problems.

Areas for Future Research

If our goals as *organizational* applied behavior analysts include producing techniques (as mentioned in Williams, this volume) that are useful in solving socially important problems in an empirical, analytical, technological, conceptually systematic, and effective manner, that demonstrates generality (Baer, Wolf, & Risley, 1968), then we need to begin collecting data on approaches to performance analysis. One potential procedure for studying performance analysis is to first conduct controlled examinations of how people (i.e., experts) actually solve problems, in efforts to extrapolate key skills that can then be taught to novices.

Using Protocol Analysis

An immediate problem in pursuing such a research goal, however, is how we should obtain reliable and valid data about problem solving. Ericsson and Simon (1993), although cognitive scientists, have laid a foundation for collecting verbal reports as behavioral data. Hayes' (1986) review of their initial work contained some criticism, but was largely supportive. Kent Johnson has for years been reported to utilize a think aloud problem solving (TAPS) procedure to help learners at his Morningside Academy (reported in Lindsley, 1996).

Other behavior analysts have since used the procedures, known as protocol analysis, to study problem solving. For instance, Wulfert, Dougher, and Greenway (1991) used verbal reports to examine verbal components of equivalence class formation. In addition, in the study described above, Austin (1996; 1998a; 1998b) used protocol analysis to study the problem solving of expert management consultants, and using information gathered in those initial studies, is presently developing a computer-based training program to teach undergraduate and graduate students to solve performance problems more effectively.

Measuring Maintaining Variables

A second area that future research could contribute to the understanding of performance analysis is in developing experimental and descriptive procedures to actually measure the maintaining variables involved in work performance (Austin, Carr, & Agnew, 1999). If we can reconceptualize the algorithms and models presented in this chapter as an approach to functional assessment in organizations, we can work to develop ways to measure the maintaining and/or hindering variables at work. It seems clear that the functional analysis that has become best practice (Mace, 1994) for applied behavior analysts working in developmental disabilities will not simply directly map onto an organizational analysis. However, it also seems clear that the laws of behavior are just as valid in organizations as in any other applied setting. The challenge is to discover better ways of measuring and manipulating the contingencies in this complex setting.

Conducting Relevant Demonstrations

A third and final area for future research in the area of performance analysis is in conducting demonstrations using some of the algorithms and models discussed above. It can be argued that most of the organizational applied behavior analysis studies published in the *Journal of Applied Behavior Analysis* and the *Journal of Organizational Behavior Management* have used the operant model (i.e., the ABC framework) as their implicit paradigm of choice. However, just as applied behavior analysis (ABA) in developmental disabilities has used the functional analysis to make great scientific strides, so should OBM. That is, applied behavior analysts should, when working in any setting, measure the variables maintaining behavior **before** changing the behavior.

Austin, Carr and Agnew (1999) discuss several reasons why OBM practitioners have not measured maintaining variables, but one obvious reason is that organizations are extremely complex and there may be an overwhelming number of variables to measure. To add to the confusion, some variables, such as equipment failure, may be hindering variables as opposed to the facilitative variables of praise and attention.

This should not entirely deter researchers, for we can use approximations to reach our goal. For instance, Austin and LaFleur (1998) used a combination of Gilbert's troubleshooting algorithm and Austin's performance diagnostic model to improve the performance of a small business in the chimney service industry. This was an approximation because not all, but rather only some, of the important variables were measured before intervening. Another study used an interview-based informant assessment to determine the least-intrusive intervention for improving timeliness in a restaurant setting (Austin & Warden, 1998). Other studies such as these can be conducted across industries, and after time, could lead to a more systematic method for measuring the important variables at work.

Notes

1.   In all fairness, Rummler and Brache (1995) describe a similar three-level view of organizations in which analyses occur at the performer level, the process level, and the organizational level. I have presented analyses at the three levels using techniques utilized by other behavior analysts (i.e., Daniels, 1989; and Brethower, 1982) because I find them to be more easily understood than those of Rummler and Brache at the individual and organizational levels.

2.   Gilbert (1978) distinguishes between measurable accomplishments and behavior because managers and analysts will sometimes attempt to measure numerous behaviors, not all of which affect the bottom-line. Accomplishments, by definition, are those behaviors and/or chains of behavior which have some impact on the functioning of the organization.

3. With the possible exceptions of LaFleur and Hyten (1995), who reported using Gilbert's algorithm, and Smith and Chase (1990), who reported using Gilbert's vantage analysis to solve organizational problems. Neither study reported reliable data collection in utilizing the diagnostic methods.

Reading Objectives

1. Define performance analysis.
2. What is organizational diagnosis and how does it differ from performance analysis?
3. What are the three levels of analysis at which performance analysts have typically worked in organizations?
4. Describe a diagnostic method for each level of analysis.
5. According to the author, what is the difference between diagnostic "models" and "algorithms"?
6. Be able to describe each of the diagnostic algorithms (i.e., Mager and Pipe, 1970; Gilbert, 1978; Kent, 1985; Bailey & Austin, 1996; and Brethower, 1997) in enough detail so that you could tell a manager how to do each.
7. Explain the talk aloud (i.e., protocol analysis) techniques used by Austin (1996). How does this preparation get at process rather than outcome of problem solving?
8. Make up one possible study in the area of performance analysis in which it would be appropriate to use protocol analysis.
9. Make up one possible study in the area of performance analysis in which it would be possible to systematically examine the variables maintaining and/or hindering performance.
10. Make up one possible study in the area of performance analysis in which it would be possible to examine the relative effects of the algorithms described in this chapter.

References

Allen, K. E., Hart, B., Buell, J. S., Harris, F. R., & Wolf, M. M. (1964). Effects of social reinforcement on isolate behavior of a nursery school child. *Child Development, 35*, 511-518.

Austin, J., Hatfield, D. B., Grindle, A. C., & Bailey, J. S. (1993). Increasing recycling in office environments: The effects of specific, informative cues. *Journal of Applied Behavior Analysis, 26*, 247-253.

Austin, J. (1996). *Organizational troubleshooting in expert management consultants and experienced managers.* Unpublished doctoral dissertation, Florida State University, Tallahassee, FL.

Austin, J. (1998a). *Using concurrent verbal reports to study solution of employee performance problems*. Manuscript in preparation.

Austin, J. (1998b). *A behavioral approach to the study of performance analysis*. Manuscript in preparation.

Austin, J., Carr, J. E., & Agnew, J. (1999). The need for assessment of maintaining variables in OBM. *Journal of Organizational Behavior Management, 19,* 59-87.

Austin, J., & Delaney, P. F. (1999). Protocol analysis as a tool for behavior analysis. *The Analysis of Verbal Behavior, 15,* 41-56.

Austin, J., & LaFleur, D. (1998, May). *Functional assessment in organizations: A case study*. Paper presented at the 24th Annual convention of the Association for Behavior Analysis, International, Orlando, FL.

Austin, J., & Warden, K. A. (1998). *Using a function-based least-intrusive intervention to improve timeliness in a restaurant*. Manuscript in preparation.

Baer, D. M., Wolf, M. M., & Risley, T. R. (1968). Some current dimensions of applied behavior analysis. *Journal of Applied Behavior Analysis, 1,* 91-97.

Bailey, J. S., & Austin, J. (1996). Evaluating and improving productivity in the workplace. In B. Thyer & M. Mattaini (Eds.), *Behavior analysis and social work* (pp. 179-200). Washington, DC: APA.

Bandura, A. (1969). *Principles of behavior modification*. New York: Holt, Rinehart, and Winston.

Bandura, A. (1977a). *Social learning theory*. Englewood Cliffs, NJ: Prentice Hall.

Bandura, A. (1977b). Self-efficacy: Toward a unifying theory of behavioral change. *Psychological Review, 84,* 191-215.

Barber, A. E., & Roehling, M. V. (1993). Job postings and the decision to interview: A verbal protocol analysis. *Journal of Applied Psychology, 78,* 845-856.

Beer, M. (1980). *Organization change and development: A systems view*. Glenview, IL: Scott, Foresman.

Bettman, J. R., & Zins, M. A. (1977). Constructive processes in consumer choice. *Journal of Consumer Research, 4,* 72-85.

Bijou, S. W. (1959). Learning in children. *Monographs of the Society for Research in Child Development, 24*(5), Serial No. 74.

Birnbrauer, J. S., Wolf, M. M. Kidder, J. D., & Tague, C. E. (1965). Modifying the classroom behavior of pupils with token reinforcement. *Journal of Experimental Child Psychology, 2,* 219-235.

Bouwman, M. (1984). Expert vs. novice decision making in accounting: A summary. *Accounting, Organizations, and Society, 9,* 325-327.

Braunstein, M. L., & Coleman, O. F. (1967). An information processing model of the aircraft accident investigator. *Human Factors, 9,* 61-70.

Brethower, D. M. (1982). The total performance system. In R. M. O'Brien, A. M. Dickinson, & M. P. Rosow (Eds.), *Industrial behavior modification* (350-369). New York: Pergamon Press.

Brethower, D. M. (1997). *Improving the value of performance: Case studies*. Ada, MI: Author.

Burke, W. W. (1994). Diagnostic models for organization development. In A. Howard & Associates (Eds.), *Diagnosis for organizational change: Methods and models* (pp. 53-84). New York, NY: Guilford Press.

Cascio, W. F. (1989). *Managing human resources: Productivity, quality of work life, profits.* (2nd ed.). New York: McGraw-Hill.

Chase, P. N., & Parrot, L. J. (1986). *Psychological aspects of language: The West Virginia lectures.* Springfield, IL: Thomas.

Dance, F. E. (1970). The "concept" of communication. *Journal of Communication, 20,* 201-210.

Daniels, A. C. (1989). *Performance management.* Tucker, GA: Performance Management Publications.

Engerman, J. A., Austin, J., & Bailey, J. S. (1997). Prompting patron safety belt use at a supermarket. *Journal of Applied Behavior Analysis, 30,* 577-579.

Ericsson, K. A., & Simon, H. A. (1993). *Protocol analysis: Verbal reports as data* (Revised edition), Cambridge, MA: The MIT Press.

Ferster, C. B., & Skinner, B. F. (1957). *Schedules of reinforcement.* New York: Appleton-Century-Crofts.

Fiedler, F. E. (1967). *A theory of leadership effectiveness.* New York: McGraw-Hill.

Fisher, K. (1994). Diagnostic issues for work teams. In A. Howard & Associates (Eds.), *Diagnosis for organizational change: Methods and models* (pp. 239-265). New York, NY: Guilford Press.

Frederiksen, L. W. (Ed.) (1982). *Handbook of organizational behavior management.* New York: Wiley.

Gardner, R, III (1994). *Behavior analysis in education: Focus on measurably superior instruction.* Pacific Grove, CA: Brooks-Cole.

Geller, E. S. (1975). Increasing desired waste disposals with instructions. *Man-Environment Systems, 5,* 125-128.

Geller, E. S. (1994). 10 principles for achieving a total safety culture. *Professional Safety, 39,* 18-24.

Geller, E. S., Witmer, J. F., & Tuso, M. A. (1977). Environmental interventions for litter control. *Journal of Applied Psychology, 62,* 344-351.

Gewirtz, J. L., & Baer, D. M. (1958). The effect of brief social deprivation on behaviors for a social reinforcer. *Journal of Abnormal and Social Psychology, 56,* 49-56.

Gilbert, T. F. (1978). *Human competence.* New York: McGraw-Hill.

Hackman, J. R., & Oldham, G. R. (1976). Motivation through the design of work: Test of a theory. *Organizational Behavior and Human Performance, 16,* 250-279.

Harrison, M. D. (1995). *Diagnosing organizations: Methods, models, and processes* (2nd ed.). Newbury Park, CA: Sage.

Hayes, S. C. (1986). The case of the silent dog—verbal reports and the analysis of rules: A review of Ericsson and Simon's protocol analysis: Verbal reports as data. *Journal of the Experimental Analysis of Behavior, 45,* 351-363.

Hayes, S. C., Jacobson, N. S., Follette, V. M., & Dougher, M. J. (Eds.). (1994). *Acceptance and change: Content and context in psychotherapy.* Reno, NV: Context Press.

House, R. J. (1971). A path-goal theory of leader effectiveness. *Administrative Science Quarterly, 16,* 321-338.

Howard, A. (1994). Diagnostic perspectives in an era of change. In A. Howard & Associates (Eds.), *Diagnosis for organizational change: Methods and models* (pp. 3-25). New York, NY: Guilford Press.

Jacobs, H. E., Bailey, J. S., & Crews, J. I. (1984). Development and analysis of a community-based resource recovery program. *Journal of Applied Behavior Analysis, 17,* 127-145.

Jacobs, H. E., Fairbanks, D., Poche, C., & Bailey, J. S. (1982). Behavioral community psychology: Encouraging carpool formation on a university campus. *Journal of Applied Behavior Analysis, 15,* 141-149.

Kazdin, A. E. (1978). *History of behavior modification: Experimental foundations of contemporary research.* Baltimore, MD: University Park Press.

Kent, R. S. (1986). *25 steps to getting performance problems off your desk...and out of your life!.* New York: Dodd, Mead, and Company.

LaFleur, T., & Hyten, C. (1995). Improving the quality of hotel banquet staff performance. *Journal of Organizational Behavior Management, 15,* 69-93

LaHart, D., & Bailey, J. S. (1975). Reducing children's littering on a nature trail. *Journal of Environmental Education, 7,* 37-45.

Landy, F. J. (1989). *Psychology of work behavior.* Belmont, CA: Wadsworth.

Lawler, E. E., III (1994). Effective reward systems: Strategy, diagnosis, and design. In A. Howard & Associates (Eds.), *Diagnosis for organizational change: Methods and models* (pp. 210-238). New York, NY: Guilford Press.

Lawler, E. E., III, Nadler, D. A., & Cammann, C. (1980). *Organizational assessment: Perspectives on the measurement of organizational behavior and the quality of work life.* New York: Wiley.

Lindsley, O. R. (1996). Is fluency free-operant response-response chaining? *The Behavior Analyst, 19,* 211-224.

Locke, E. A. (1969). What is job satisfaction? *Organizational Behavior and Human Performance, 4,* 309-336.

Luthans, F., & Kreitner, R. (1985). *Organizational behavior modification and beyond: An operant and social learning approach.* Glenview, IL: Scott, Foresman, and Company.

Mace, F. C. (1994). The significance and future of functional analysis methodologies. *Journal of Applied Behavior Analysis, 27,* 385-392.

Mager, R. F., & Pipe, P. (1970). *Analyzing performance problems.* Belmont, CA: Fearon Publishers.

Manzini, A. O. (1988). *Organizational diagnosis: A practical approach to company problem solving and growth.* New York: Amacom.

Martin, S. L., & Klimoski, R. J. (1990). Use of verbal protocols to trace cognitions associated with self- and supervisor evaluations of performance. *Organizational Behavior and Human Decision Processes, 46,* 135-154.

Mills, G. E., Pace, R. W., & Peterson, B. D. (1988). *Analysis in human resource training and organization development.* Reading, MA: Addison-Wesley.

Ninness, H. A. C., Glenn, S. S., & Ellis, J. (1993). *Assessment and treatment of emotional or behavioral disorders.* Westport, CT: Praeger.

O'Brien, R., Dickinson, A. M., & Rosow, M. P. (Eds.). (1982). *Industrial behavior modification.* New York: Pergamon.

Payne, J. W., Braunstein, M. L., & Carroll, J. S. (1978). Exploring predecisional behavior: An alternative approach to decision research. *Organizational Behavior and Human Performance, 16,* 17-44.

Poling, A. D. (1986). *A primer of human behavioral pharmacology.* New York: Plenum.

Porras, J. I. (1987). *Stream analysis: A powerful way to diagnose and manage organizational change.* Reading, MA: Addison-Wesley.

Porter, L. W. (1962). Job attitudes in management: I. Perceived deficiencies in need fulfillment as a function of job level. *Journal of Applied Psychology, 46,* 375-384.

Rogers, E. M., & Agarwala-Rogers, R. (1976). *Communication in organizations.* New York: Free Press.

Rogers, R. W., & Byham, W. C. (1994). Diagnosing organization cultures for realignment. In A. Howard & Associates (Eds.), *Diagnosis for organizational change: Methods and models* (pp. 179-209). New York, NY: Guilford Press.

Rudd, J. R., & Geller, E. S. (1985). A university-based incentive program to increase safety belt use: Toward cost-effective institutionalization. *Journal of Applied Behavior Analysis, 18,* 215-226.

Rummler G., & Brache, A. (1995). *Improving performance: Managing the white space on the organizational chart.* San Francisco, CA: Jossey-Bass.

Russo, J. E., Johnson, E. J., & Stephens, D. L. (1989). The validity of verbal protocols. *Memory and Cognition, 17,* 759-769.

Schaffer, R. H. (1953). Job satisfaction as related to need satisfaction in work. *Psychological Monographs, 67,* (304).

Schweiger, D. M. (1983). Is the simultaneous verbal protocol a viable method for studying managerial problem solving and decision making? *Academy of Management Journal, 26,* 185-192.

Schweiger, D. M., Anderson, C. R., & Locke, E. A. (1985). Complex decision making: A longitudinal study of process and performance. *Organizational Behavior and Human Decision Processes, 36,* 245-272.

Scott, W. G., & Mitchell, T. R (1976). *Organizational theory: A structural and behavioral approach.* Homewood, IL: Richard D. Irwin.

Skinner, B. F. (1938). *Behavior of organisms.* New York: Appleton-Century.

Skinner, B. F. (1953). *Science and human behavior.* New York: Macmillan.

Skinner, B. F. (1957). *Verbal behavior.* New York: Appleton-Century-Crofts.

Smith, J. M., & Chase, P. N. (1990). Using the Vantage Analysis Chart to solve organization-wide problems. Special Issue: Promoting excellence through performance management. *Journal of Organizational Behavior Management, 11*, 127-148.

Soelberg, P. A. (1965). *A study of decision making: Job choice*. Unpublished doctoral dissertation, Carnegie Institute of Technology, Pittsburg, PA.

Vecchio, R. P. (1988). *Organizational behavior*. Hinsdale, IL: The Dryden Press.

Vitalari, N. P. (1980). *A study of business systems analysis problem solving behavior in the requirements determination task for computer-based information systems*. Unpublished doctoral dissertation, University of Minnesota.

Vroom, V. H., & Yetton, P. W. (1973). *Leadership and decision making*. Pittsburgh: University of Pittsburgh Press.

Walker, J. W., & Bechet, T. P. (1994). Addressing future staffing needs. In A. Howard & Associates (Eds.), *Diagnosis for organizational change: Methods and models* (pp. 113-138). New York, NY: Guilford Press.

Walton, E., & Nadler, D. A. (1994). Diagnosis for organizational design. In A. Howard & Associates (Eds.), *Diagnosis for organizational change: Methods and models* (pp. 84-111). New York, NY: Guilford Press.

Wolpe, J. (1958). *Psychotherapy by reciprocal inhibition*. Palo Alto, CA: Stanford University Press.

Wulfert, E., Dougher, M. J., & Greenway, D. E. (1991). Protocol analysis of the correspondence of verbal behavior and equivalence class formation. *Journal of the Experimental Analysis of Behavior, 56*, 489-504.

Zemke, R. E. (1994). Training needs assessment: The broadened focus of a simple concept. In A. Howard & Associates (Eds.), *Diagnosis for organizational change: Methods and models* (pp. 139-151). New York, NY: Guilford Press.

Chapter 15

Behavioral Approaches to Organizational Safety

Mark P. Alavosius, Augustus E. Adams,
David K. Ahern, and Michael J. Follick
Behavior Safety Advantage,
Abacus Risk Management Technologies

Overview

Work-related injuries/illnesses and associated pain and disability continue at unacceptably high levels despite decades of effort to improve work place safety. Behavior-based safety arose as behavior analysts examined the application of principles of behavior to the improvement of work safety. Today, behavior-based safety programs are often included in efforts to develop safety systems for work environments. Safety professionals increasingly recognize that significant improvements in work safety could be realized if behavioral systems to establish and maintain work safety practices were part of safety management systems. Academic training programs producing safety professionals include little material on behavior analysis and at present the safety profession is ill-equipped to apply behavior analysis as part of their safety services and consultation. This chapter reviews the prevalence of work-related injuries and illnesses, considers behavioral safety as an emerging technology for large-scale improvements in work safety, presents an ongoing project that illustrates the potential contributions of behavior analysis to occupational safety, and concludes with recommendations for future research and practice.

Work-related Injuries and Illnesses

According to the Bureau of Labor Statistics (BLS, 1995) there are 8.4 work-related injuries per 100 workers in America. This translates to approximately 6.3 million injuries in 1995 alone. The financial cost of occupational injuries is soaring and upwards of 57 billion dollars are spent annually to pay lost wages, medical expenses, insurance costs, legal fees, and other costs of work injuries (Burton, 1995). It is estimated that these cases result in 2.25 million lost work days per year. The societal costs of work-related injuries and illnesses is truly staggering when one considers the human suffering, disability, and lost productivity represented by these data.

It is instructive to note that the highest incidence rates of work-related injuries and illnesses occurs in small employers. Organizations that employ between 50 and 249 employees are plagued with the highest rates of work-related injuries (BLS, 1995). We might speculate that smaller businesses have the highest incidence rates because they are least able to afford to integrate effective safety technologies into their operations. In our experience managing the workers' compensation programs for hundreds of small and mid-sized employers (e.g., ranging from 20 to 1,500 employees) we find that small employers (< than 20 employees) usually have closely supervised work forces with owners who are actively engaged in day-to-day operations. These businesses are often quite safe and many experience years of injury/illness-free operation. As businesses grow, however, management systems often fail to keep pace with the increasing complexity of expanding operations and larger work forces. Compromises are often needed to balance production/service pressures, the desires to further grow the business, and work safety. Companies experiencing growth that has outpaced development of their management systems and facing pressures to remain competitive in the market place are perhaps least able to afford effective safety technologies. The safety industry is fraught with fads, gimmicks, and untested safety programs that find purchase by managers seeking a quick, inexpensive, but visible response to their safety problems. For example, advertisements for safety posters with catchy slogans, pre-packaged safety committee agenda programs, and an assortment of safety videos fill the safety journals and promise improvements in safety with relatively low cost and effort.

Reviewing the Bureau of Labor Statistics' injury/illness data reveals some of the range of opportunities that exist for workers to be injured or made ill by their work. Sprains and strains occur across a wide range of occupations that require workers to lift, pull, push, carry, reach, bend, and twist. Nursing personnel are at particular risk for these injuries due to the physical demands of caring for patients. Construction workers, warehouse workers, material handlers, and numerous other jobs expose workers to injuries from handling heavy loads. Office workers, assemblers on production lines, cashiers, phone operators, painters, and data entry personnel are among those with high incidence of repetitive motion disorders. Many workers are victims of work-place violence in settings such as law enforcement, human service organizations, schools, and convenience stores. Motor-vehicle accidents injure truck drivers, delivery service personnel, sales people and others whose jobs require driving. Workers required to handle chemicals (refiners, platers, lab technicians, mechanics, painters, etc.) are exposed to toxic materials that pose potential for injury and illness from chronic exposure. Workers in dusty environments (mines, construction, demolition) suffer respiratory disorders. Agricultural workers suffer machine injuries and chemical exposures. Working children and youth experience high rates of injury perhaps due to excessive risk-taking, inexperience, and poor orientation to the hazards of their work. This list could proceed for many pages but this short account prompts consideration of the diversity of work injuries and illnesses, the complexity of work and work environments, and the range of behaviors that are involved in accidents and their prevention.

Behavioral Safety

Behavioral scientists have examined accidents as the result of the interaction of work behavior and the physical environment (Sulzer-Azaroff, 1978). This conceptualization leads to the analysis of work environments and how workers perform tasks. From this view, unsafe work behaviors may result from faulty or incomplete learning. People engage in unsafe conduct because they have not acquired the competencies required to act safely. In other cases, people may have acquired the competency but the work environment fails to select and maintain the requisite safety performance. Safety performance management is an emerging technology based on experimentally derived principles of behavior. Behavior is influenced by the antecedents and consequences of behavior and these conditions can be managed to shape performance (Skinner, 1953). Considerable research shows that safety and health performance management can be accomplished in a variety of work settings such as mining (Rhoton, 1980, Fox, Hopkins, & Anger, 1987), plastics manufacturing (Hopkins, Conrad, & Smith, 1986), nursing (Alavosius & Sulzer-Azaroff, 1986), food processing (Komaki, Barwick, & Scott, 1978), manufacturing (Chokar & Wallin, 1984), electronics manufacturing (Sulzer-Azaroff & de Santamaria, 1980), apparel manufacturing (Harshbarger & Rose, 1991), and human service organizations (van den Pol, Reid, & Fuqua, 1983). A number of texts (e.g., Geller, 1988; Krause, Hidley, & Hodson, 1990; McSween, 1995) are available describing behavioral procedures for improving safety performance. A variety of behavior change procedures incorporating reinforcement, punishment, and stimulus control have been found effective in improving work safety. An impressive research base spanning over twenty years supports the merit of applying behavior analysis to improve work safety.

Practicing safety performance management effectively requires not only competence in behavior analysis but skill in analyzing and managing the complex contingencies operative in work environments. Successful application is accomplished by arranging work contingencies (the relationships among antecedents, behaviors, consequences) to primarily strengthen safe behaviors and secondarily discourage unsafe ones. Practically, this entails development of the structure and functions of management and development of a culture that supports safety. Typically, the development process begins with data analyses guiding identification of desired safety practices. Reviewing an organization's accident log is often a starting point in the search for behavioral safety targets. Incident reports describing both work injuries and illnesses and "near-misses" can reveal characteristics of risky work behaviors and their context. Analyses of these behaviors identify those variables that expose workers to the greatest risk for injury and help specify safety practices that should replace risky alternatives.

Specifying optimally safe technique is usually the most challenging activity in developing a behavioral safety program. In many cases, the safest way to perform a job is not easily determined. Consider repetitive motion tasks such as packing products for shipment. The movements of a packer that exposes her to cumulative trauma include repetitive reaching, grasping, twisting, and other manipulations of materials. The rotation of the fingers, wrist, arms, and shoulders, the force of the pinch grip to grasp products, the length of the reach, and the frequency of the motions all play a part in cumulative trauma. Specifying the safest topography and rate of these movements is a challenging assignment that probably exceeds the expertise of most safety and production managers.

One objective of the task specification process is to identify the task components in sufficient detail to permit development of an observational system that detects meaningful variation in how workers actually perform the work. Additional information can be obtained by interviewing workers and supervisors about their observations of work and recommendations regarding safe performance. Ergonomic guidelines can inform decisions as to how to best conduct these tasks. Often, consultation with content-area experts (e.g., ergonomists, industrial hygienists, industrial engineers, etc.) is needed to articulate optimal work practices.

Typically we find that workers' own behavior (i.e., those behaviors proximate to the injury) are most frequently identified as the primary contributor to work accidents. Less frequently identified are the behaviors of supervisors, managers and executives as contributing to work-related injuries. As one examines the proximate behaviors leading to injuries and illnesses more distal behaviors are found that set the stage for their occurrence. A comprehensive assessment of an organization's safety program should reveal a lattice-work of behaviors from those of the top executives through management levels to front-line workers that operate to assess and control risks for work accidents. An even broader assessment would consider the culture of work and explore how marketplace contingencies, industry traditions, and cultural practices influence self-protective behaviors and safety practices. Much research in behavioral safety has tended to focus on the behaviors of workers that are proximate to the injury or illness (e.g., examine lifting technique in efforts to prevent back injuries) and have not examined the complexity of organizational behaviors (e.g., setting work schedules, production goals, staffing patterns, etc.) and cultural practices (e.g., risk-taking) that are the context for work-related injury. Table 1 outlines general classes of behavior across broad levels of an organization.

These classes of behavior influence safety often in unplanned ways. For example, consider a nurse's aide caring for nonambulatory patients in a residential care facility (note: A job leading to high rates of back injuries and often targeted for safety interventions). The technique this person uses to lift, carry, and transfer patients is crucial to the success and safety of the patient handling assignments. Using sloppy, uncoordinated or otherwise faulty lifting technique can lead to injury to both the caregiver and the patient. One approach to improve the safety of patient handling is to improve caregivers' transfer technique. This can be accomplished by task analyzing transfer procedures, arranging for on-the-job observation of work practices, and providing performance feedback to caregivers on the safety of their work (Alavosius & Sulzer-Azaroff, 1985, 1986, 1990). Whereas this has proven to be an effective method to establish work safety practices, it is an approach that requires commitment from management and allocation of supervisory time to sustain its operation. Lacking these support systems, feedback systems tend to falter. Accuracy

Table 1. Organizational Behaviors Affecting Work Safety

Executive	Manager	Employee
Organizational Behaviors	Operational Behaviors	Work Behaviors
Goals Policies Priorities Budgets Oversight	Objectives Procedures Staffing Purchases Data Analyses	Jobs Assignments Techniques

of observations may deteriorate, feedback becomes less objective, and performance drifts. Although we have seen the emergence of peer-operated feedback systems, maximally effective ones probably require the resources and oversight provided by formal support of management systems dedicated to improving safety performance. A nurse aide's safety is also affected by other behaviors occurring within the care facility. The clinical decisions regarding patient care, the selection of wheelchairs and adaptive equipment, the training and certification of nurse aides, the setting of staffing patterns, planning work schedules, and a host of other events foster or impede safety performance. A comprehensive behavioral safety program needs to assess and organize these behaviors, evaluate their interactions, and incorporate contingencies that coordinate their performance to produce the desired outcomes.

Once safety practices are analyzed yielding descriptions of optimal safety technique, workers can be trained using mastery learning, shaping, rehearsal, goal-setting, and positive reinforcement to establish desired safety practices. Once mastery levels are obtained, behavioral observations and data-driven reinforcement and feedback maintain those behaviors and progressive discipline corrects persistent unsafe work behaviors. In some cases stimulus control procedures can be used to occasion safety performance. For example, a photograph of a bench worker might be taken when that person's work posture is adjusted to an optimal ergonomic configuration. This photo might be established as a prompt to encourage the worker to make postural adjustments as work continues. A wide variety of behavior change interventions can be applied effectively to improve safety practices. Engineering work environments that maintain managers' commitment to safety systems is imperative, however, for these interventions to have lasting benefit.

Behavioral safety requires that managers and workers adopt organized procedures to monitor their work habits and perhaps interact in new ways that ultimately change the safety culture of work. There are well-established techniques to improve workers' health and safety behaviors (see McAfee & Winn, 1989 and Sulzer-Azaroff, Harris, & McCann, 1994 for reviews) demonstrated to be effective in a variety of replications across many industries and work settings. The challenge to practitioners is to develop cost-effective methods that apply behavioral principles establishing safe work habits and to integrate these methods into the management systems and culture of work. One interesting solution finding wide application in the transportation industry is using telecommunications to orchestrate feedback to drivers on their driving safety. A number of vehicles now carry signs showing toll free phone numbers to call to report on the drivers' performance. This system captures observations from the driving public and channels data to the managers of the fleets. These managers can then provide feedback to the drivers often immediately via contact using mobile phones. A majority of the feedback in these systems is negative; the public usually reports violations of traffic rules and drivers' discourtesy. In about 10% of cases, however, the feedback is positive (e.g., the driver is reported to aid lost motorists, help those with breakdowns, etc.)[1]. These systems are reported to be effective for identifying unsafe drivers, curtailing serious traffic violations, and reducing motor vehicle accidents. The systems are ingenious in their use of technology to provide performance feedback to performers acting in remote locations and their integration with driver management systems.

Interdisciplinary approaches to work safety (e.g., those involving safety engineering, biomechanical analyses, ergonomic interventions, interactive safety training, occupational medicine, industrial hygiene, etc.) are increasing in sophistication and application, however, work injuries continue despite these advances. Behavior analysis offers a truly powerful technology for enhancing the effectiveness of safety initiatives by improving the performance of organizational members. Behavior analysis with its focus on objective, measurable changes in behavior and a well-established foundation of effective behavior change strategies is well poised to make significant impact on the huge social problem of work-related injuries. Below is a description of an ongoing project conducted by the Abacus Group illustrating a behavioral safety application provided to many companies that collectively employ thousands of workers.

A Case Example: Analysis of COST© - Comprehensive Occupational Safety Training

Background

Abacus (The Abacus Service Company, Inc.) presently provides management services to both insured and self-insured workers compensation programs within New England. It developed and now manages several workers' compensation "trusts" in Rhode Island, representing almost 350 small employers. Additionally, Abacus manages a workers' compensation indemnity program for a New England-based insurer. AbacusTechnologies, an affiliate of Abacus Service Company, researches, develops, and provides management technologies and decision support tools to improve occupational health and safety.

In the management of workers' compensation programs Abacus is responsible for the development and implementation of accident/injury prevention programs and claims management services. As part of Abacus' management of workers' compensation programs, Abacus has developed and tested behavioral safety programs to establish and maintain the safety management expertise of managers in hundreds of small to mid-sized companies. The National Institute for Occupational Safety and Health (NIOSH) has funded several Abacus projects to evaluate and refine programs via the Small Business Innovation Research (SBIR) Program. Data are presented below on the loss experience of a sample of 50 Rhode Island companies (from manufacturing, sales, and service) selected from among 350 members of three group self-insurance programs that completed the behaviorally-based *COST*© *program*.

Context and Contingencies

Before describing this research, an explanation of the context of the operations enabling the studies is necessary. Understanding the context of this work (i.e., the business community and market contingencies) permits appreciation of the some of the complexities of this large-scale applied research program. This research program is made possible by Abacus' role as manager of workers' compensation programs for hundreds of employers. Workers' compensation assists employers to manage the costs of work-related injuries and illnesses and is required for all but the smallest employers. Workers' compensation systems *finance* risk for work-related incidents by collecting premiums from numerous companies to cover expected losses and dispersing the risk across multiple employers. Essentially it collects sufficient premium to build reserves that will cover the expenses incurred from even the most catastrophic claim. Workers' compensation programs *manage* risk by supporting managed care activities that constrain the costs of care for work-related injuries and supporting employers' efforts to prevent injuries and illnesses through health and safety programs.

Self-insurance is a mechanism of workers' compensation insurance that finds broad appeal particularly by employers seeking direct control of the costs of their work-related injuries and illnesses. In self-insurance an employer finances and manages risk by relying primarily on internal resources. This requires that the employer have financial reserves to cover the expected costs of work-related injuries and illnesses and some confidence that catastrophic events will not overwhelm the organization's ability to bear the costs. For this reason, self-insurance is beyond the reach of most smaller employers. In a self-insured group (hereafter referred to as a SIG), individual employers who may lack the resources to self-insure independently band together to form a cooperative that collectively pools its resources to finance and manage its risks for occupational injuries. This is an alternative to traditional workers' compensation insurance in which employers individually purchase insurance coverage for their operations from an insurance company. With self-insurance, employers bear their own risks for expenses incurred as a consequence of work injuries. The company pays for its losses; if these are excessive, the company bears the expense, if the losses are low, the company retains the savings. With traditional insurance, the employer pays an annual premium based on the size of their operation, the risks of the work, their company's loss history and other factors. The insurance company bears the risk for the losses and essentially insulates the employer from excessive financial loss. Companies that enjoy low losses still pay a premium (the surplus is profit to the insurance company), although they may benefit from lower future premiums.

In the late 1980's the cost of workers' compensation insurance had grown unbearably high for many Rhode Island employers and self-insurance offered a viable alternative. Many joined Abacus-managed SIG's to take control of the risk financing and risk management activities required to insure themselves against losses. Pooling the resources of hundreds of employers and spreading the risk across multiple companies permits accumulation of reserves sufficient to cover potential losses and dispersion of risk across many companies. It also creates powerful social contingencies within the business community that act to educate company owners about work-related injuries and illnesses and promote investment in safety management systems.

Abacus formed and managed three SIG's that grew to include over 350 Rhode Island companies (one group for companies involved in the manufacture and distribution of jewelry; a second group for automobile dealers, parts suppliers, service shops, and related companies; and a third group for small miscellaneous manufacturers - boat builders, textiles, printers, etc.). Each group is governed by a Board of Directors made up of executives and owners of member companies. These Boards assumed fiduciary responsibility for the well-being of the SIG's and provide oversight of Abacus' management of the workers' compensation program. Details of the management systems for these groups extends well beyond the scope of this chapter. It is important to understand that for the individual employers, the membership contingencies were designed such that it was beneficial to be a member in good standing within the SIG. Recall that the individual employers pool their resources and jointly bear the risks of all members. If the SIG's losses are less than the annual contributions of each member to the reserve pool a surplus accumulates that is returned proportionally to group members. Thus a financial incentive exists that rewards prevention of injuries and illnesses in all members. If the SIG's losses exceed the pool, the member companies are collectively liable for the losses. Thus a financial penalty exists for poor safety performance.

In management of the SIG's, Abacus developed various surveillance systems to measure the performance of all member companies and identify those companies in need of assistance with their safety programs. These surveillance systems permit timely targeting of companies with emerging safety problems and objective feedback to executives on their companies' status relative to their peers in the business community. Thus a social contingency is in operation that benchmarks each company's safety performance relative to its neighbors in the business community. It is upon this platform of financial and social contingencies that companies participate in safety development programs that include behavioral interventions to improve executive, manager, and employee utilization of safety practices. These contingencies support owners' commitment to safety and drive active involvement of management in their companies' safety process. One indication of the power of these contingencies for promoting safety is the long-term cooperation of employers with the Abacus safety programs.

Loss Control

Activities for controlling losses in a workers' compensation program can be broadly divided into two functional categories. One functional area is to manage the treatment and rehabilitation of injured workers and thereby limit the severity, time out of work, and costs of injuries. Abacus developed a managed care model that is provided to all members to help injured workers navigate the health-care system and return to work in a timely manner. The second area is management of work safety to prevent the occurrence of injuries and illnesses. Both management areas provide numerous opportunities for behavioral interventions to enhance organizations' effectiveness in managing and preventing work-related injuries. For this chapter, the second area is of interest as illustration of the application of behavior analysis to large-scale safety interventions.

SIG Operations

Abacus SIG member companies range in size from as small as 20 or fewer employees to over 400 employees. All SIG members are located in Rhode Island and are in relatively close geographic distance to one another. Approximately 30% of the SIG's workforce is minority or disadvantaged workers and many managers supervise a diverse, multi-cultural work force. Each company is required to assign manager(s) to coordinate the company's managed care and safety programs. These managers are trained to complete activities to assist injured workers to report their injuries, receive appropriate treatment and ultimately return to work. Additionally, each company designates safety managers who are trained by Abacus to set up ongoing safety programs that involve audit, inspection, and observation systems, procedures for accident investigations, and safety training and supervision systems. Each company reports to Abacus all injuries as they occur and Abacus case and claims managers assist the injured workers from onset of their injury/illness through resolution of their claim. Documentation of companies' safety management activities (e.g., self-inspection reports, safety team minutes, accident investigations) are also sent to Abacus. Abacus safety personnel visit sites routinely and inspect operations for risks, train company personnel, and consult on safety initiatives. Periodically (quarterly at present) each employer receives a performance report showing key performance measures on the activities of their safety and managed care programs and outcome measures quantifying their progress in controlling the frequency, severity, and costs of work-related injuries.

Measures of companies' losses (incidence rates of injuries, financial losses, and lost work days) were used to identify 50 high risk companies within the groups; collectively, these 50 employ approximately 2,500 workers. These 50 companies completed a behaviorally-based safety training program (COST© - Comprehensive Occupational Safety Training) in addition to the interventions described above to further develop their safety management. The COST© program is a behaviorally-based training procedure that guides company safety personnel through a systematic process of analyzing existent safety management and developing a comprehensive, positive strategy to control hazards and establish safe work habits. The COST© program includes multi-media instruction and materials for training managers to assemble safety teams, conduct data-based selection of safety targets, investigate accidents, analyze risky work practices, train co-workers to establish safety practices, organize positive reinforcement systems to promote maintenance, and consistently apply corrective discipline to alter unsafe habits. Additionally, safety professionals visited each organization to consult on engineering and administrative controls and assist with implementation of the COST© procedures.

COST© Elements

1. *A company safety coordinator* is identified and charged with responsibilities for developing the structure and operations of a safety team. Guidance is provided to insure formation of a safety team with representatives from labor, management, and executives, to structure job duties and responsibilities, and guide operation of this team.

2. *Data collection and analysis procedures* include:

   Site inspections and hazard identification by a safety professional who reviews the company's accident records, interviews management, and tours the facility. Inspectors thoroughly review the risks inherent in the operation and the extent of current safety controls. Engineering controls, administrative controls and personal protective equipment are evaluated for adequacy. The inspection provides an overview of the work environment and current safety management. Initial recommendations for improvements are identified.

   Accident investigation by safety team personnel to identify factors contributing to work injuries and illnesses and plan corrections to prevent recurrence.

   Loss analyses by safety team personnel to review and analyze accident records, identify trends, and select safety targets. These analyses guide goal setting.

   Insurance loss run analysis and review to evaluate the costs of work-related injuries and illnesses.

   Company self-inspections used by safety team members and others to periodically audit the workplace monitoring the presence or absence of hazards. Corrective actions are initiated and tracked by the self-inspection process.

   Job safety analyses by safety team personnel to evaluate critical work safety behaviors. Tasks are analyzed into their components and critical features are identified. Both safe and unsafe elements are noted. Observation of actual work techniques establishes baselines of current work habits.

3. *Safety Improvement Process*
Goal setting to identify company targets and set objectives for improvement.
Safety interventions including engineering, administrative controls and personal protective equipment.
Follow-up and review to plot progress and prompt continued problem-solving.

4. *Behavior Change and Maintenance Techniques*
Training procedures are presented so safety team personnel can provide effective training when workers' performance is poor due to lack of skill. Procedures to train workers to mastery are presented to insure that workers acquire the skills required for safety.
Reinforcement procedures are presented so that managers insure that workers' safety behaviors are strengthened and maintained.
Feedback procedures assist managers to refine workers' safety habits and promote their endurance.
Progressive discipline is recommended to correct unsafe activities. Guidelines for appropriate discipline are provided to assist managers in curtailing repeated violations of safety practices.

COST© Materials

1. *An instructor's manual* guides the COST© trainer through the activities required to develop competence in the company safety coordinator. It includes session objectives, training outlines, demonstrations, and assignments.

2. *A slide presentation* accompanies the instructor's manual and illustrates key concepts and procedures.

3. *A user's manual* explains to managers the procedures needed for safety performance management and the rationale for their use. It is geared to the small business manager and includes forms and outlines to organize implementation. These manuals serve as training tools to assist the COST© manager to train others to complete activities required by the program.

4. *Video demonstrations* are used to promote adoption of the management strategies. Safety committee meeting format and procedures, accident investigations, self-inspections, behavioral observations, on-the-job training and feedback, and corrective discipline techniques are topics of demonstration video exercises and video examples. Continued development of the content and organization of the video presentations are part of session evaluations. Focus groups are used to evaluate these materials and indicate refinements.

5. *Forms* are provided to structure safety team meetings and minutes, develop self-inspection protocols, complete loss analyses, investigate

accidents and record findings, document improvement planning, and complete observations and analyses of work safety behaviors.

Early in development, we recognized the need to provide small companies with easy to use materials to guide the formation and operation of safety programs. Our materials are geared towards the small business manager with little or no formal training in occupational safety.

Aims of the NIOSH Funded Phase I Evaluation of the

COST© Project.

Incidence rates of occupational injury and illness and incurred costs are the primary outcome measures used to assess the program's effectiveness. The results from ongoing management evaluation indicated that behavioral safety technologies can have an immediate and substantial impact on work-related injuries/illnesses and their costs. The COST© program was examined in rigorous detail with NIOSH (National Institute of Occupational Safety and Health) grant support to further develop the technologies.

Repeated measures analysis of covariates was conducted on pre- and post-treatment measures of participating companies' losses to assess if occupational health and safety within small businesses are substantially improved when managers adopt systematic, data-based loss control strategies. The specific aims of the Phase I COST© evaluation were:

1. To analyze existing data on frequency and type of work-related injuries, medical and indemnity costs, lost work days, and employer/ employee satisfaction collected from the first 50 small companies (mean = 45 employees) in Rhode Island to receive the behaviorally-based, prototype safety training program (COST©).

2. To develop a survey instrument to assess the added expenses and barriers for small business associated with implementing COST© and administer it to the 50 companies.

3. To arrange for selected employers/employees from the 50 companies to review the COST© prototype materials and suggest refinements. To then revise the materials informed by customer feedback and the data analyses noted above.

4. To prepare for a large scale randomized trial of COST© in Phase II to include small businesses from a wide range of industries, varying in size (5 - 500 employees) and with different risk financing mechanisms, (e.g., insured vs. self-insured).

Specific aim #1: Evaluate key outcome measures. Analysis of existing data was performed on a total of fifty (50) companies that underwent COST© training from 1993 to 1995. Each of the fifty companies was followed for at least six months post COST©, 40 (80%) were followed for 12 months post COST© training, and 31 (62%) for 18 months. These companies were selected for COST© because of their high injury rates and associated costs relative to comparable SIG member companies.

Measures obtained and/or derived associated with work-related injuries for each company included (1) total incurred costs[2], (2) lost time case incidence rate[3], (3) loss ratio[4], (4) compensable accident and injury incidence rates[5], and (5) employer/employee satisfaction with and obstacles to implementing COST©. Figure 1 shows the change in total incurred costs (i.e., payments and reserves for indemnity, medical, legal, and other expenses) by COST© phase.

The two primary outcome measures that were analyzed statistically are: (1) lost time case incidence rate, and (2) loss ratio. These variables were chosen as the most

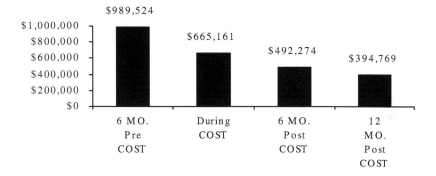

Figure 1: Incurred losses for 50 COST© companies at major milestones

sensitive measures of injury rates and costs. Preliminary to statistical hypothesis testing about the effects of COST©, an analysis was performed to determine whether the time of COST© training (e.g., January 1993 vs. January 1995) was a significant factor since COST© sessions covered a 2.5-year period. There were no statistically significant differences among COST© sessions on lost time incidence rates or loss ratios as a function of time of the COST© training (p > .05).

Lost time case incidence rate and loss ratios derived for COST© companies were analyzed in a Repeated Measures Analysis of Covariance (ANCOVA) design, statistically controlling for number of employees. The amount of time that a manager was not significantly related to the two primary outcome measures (p's > .05). Hence, that variable was not included as a covariate in the analysis. Figures 2 and 3 present the results from separate ANCOVA's for lost time case incidence rate and loss ratio, respectively for 6 months pre COST© training, during COST©, and 6 and 12 months post COST©. Figure 2 indicates that a statistically significant mean reduction was observed in the lost time case incidence rates for the 50 companies from 6 months pre COST© to 6 months post. This effect is maintained at 12 months $(F(3,116) = 13.91$, p <.0001). Similarly, Figure 3 shows a statistically significant reduction in loss ratios for companies undergoing COST© from 6 months pre to 6 months post, with maintenance at 12 months $(F(3,116) = 7.64$, p < .0001). The

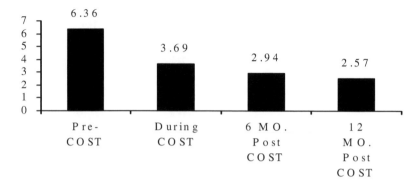

Figure 2: Number of Lost Time Cases per 100 EE's (50 companies)

power estimates derived from the analysis of lost time case incidence rates was .86 and for loss ratios was .98.

Since companies were defined as COST©-eligible based on higher than average incidence rates, the observed decrease over time may represent a statistical artifact of regression to the mean. This possible explanation for the findings are unlikely for two reasons. First, the average lost time case incidence rate and loss ratio for the self-insured groups as a whole were 4.3 and 34, respectively, which is higher than the

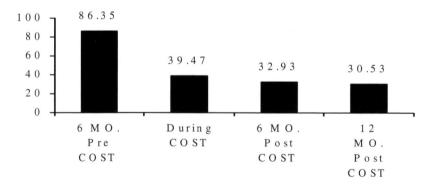

Figure 3: Loss Ratio for 50 COST© Companies

observed values at 6 months post COST©. Second, the observation of a further decline at 12 months is contrary to what would be the expected reversal in the trend based on regression to the mean. Moreover, the declining trend continues at 18 months post COST© for the companies for which data are currently available (lost time case incidence rate: 18 month post = 2.00, loss ratio: 18 month post = 20.00).

Table 2 presents mean lost day incidence rates by COST© Phase. Results indicate that the mean lost days incidence rate declines across COST© phases.

Tables 3 and 4 present the cross tabulation of the top 5 accident and injury incidence rates by COST© phase, e.g., 6 months pre COST©. Results indicate that *Struck By* accidents and *Sprain/Strain* injuries are the most frequent. The data show reductions in these accidents and injuries at the six month post COST© phase consistent with overall reductions in lost cases. At the 12 month post COST© phase there was an increase in *Contact* and *Slip/Fall* accidents relative to the 6 month post COST© phase although still below the pre COST© phase.

Table 2. Data Show the Lost Work Days per 100 Employees by COST© Phase.

COST© Phase	6 Months Pre	During	6 Months Post	12 Months Post
lost days incident rate	184	111	84	58

All of the top five injury rates decrease at the 6 month post COST© phase relative to the pre COST© period. At the 12 month post COST© phase, *sprain/strain* and *laceration/puncture* injuries continue to decline. At the 12 month juncture, *bruise/inflammation* and *fracture/dislocation* stabilized or showed slight increase relative to the 6 month post COST© period.

Specific aim #2: Survey obstacles to implementation. An assessment of the session evaluations (15 question survey using a 5 point scale; 1 = completely dissatisfied, 5 = completely satisfied) completed by all COST© participants at the conclusion of each session was done to evaluate consumer satisfaction. Overall satisfaction with COST© ranged from 4.5 to 4.65 where 5 equals completely satisfied. High satisfaction was expressed for the quality of the COST© program (4.6 - 4.8) and program content (4.4 - 4.5). To assess long-term satisfaction with COST© and obstacles encountered in implementation we surveyed employers about the additional expenses of implementing the COST© Program such as personnel costs associated with formation of the safety committee, additional clerical support, and costs of bi-weekly or monthly self-inspection activities. Identification of expense categories associated with modifications and work site re-design as recommended by COST© were also requested. To the extent possible, estimates of actual expenditures for the aforementioned categories were collected. Barriers to successful implementation were also surveyed.

The follow-up survey was mailed to a target group of past participants. The survey was mailed to those alumni of the training program who had demonstrated a high level of interest and participation. By selecting the members of the target group in this way we sought to receive back a high percentage of the surveys mailed, but also to acquire more useful survey information (such as 'additional comments') in addition to the basic-level survey responses. In all, thirty-eight (38) surveys were sent to past COST© participants. Eight of these past participants were unfortunately

Table 3. Data Show the Incidence Rates by COST© Phase for Significant Accident Types.

| Accident Type | | COST© Phase | | | |
		6 Months Pre	During	6 Months Post	12 Months Post
	Struck By	1.25	.95	1.15	1.04
	Handling	1.20	.56	.79	.65
	Contact	.80	.79	.54	.76
	Slip/Fall	.91	.62	.42	.76
	Bodily Motion	.48	.41	.25	.07

Table 4. Data Show the Incidence Rates by COST© Phase for Significant InjuryTypes.

| Injury Type | | COST© Phase | | | |
		6 Months Pre	During	6 Months Post	12 Months Post
	Sprain/ Strain	2.17	1.55	1.49	1.26
	Laceration/ Puncture	1.17	.43	.82	.79
	Bruise	.60	.60	.34	.43
	Inflammation	.74	.35	.34	.36
	Fracture/ Dislocation	.37	.35	.17	.25

no longer with the company where his/her survey was sent, so these eight surveys were eliminated from the pool. Of the thirty (30) remaining surveys, twenty-three (23) were received back, resulting in a 76.7 % return rate.

The survey instrument was a four-page document posing sixty-two (62) survey items, forty-four (44) were forced-response questions, and eighteen (18) required the respondent to write in his/her individual comments. Survey items fell under seven section headings: Program Cost/Benefit, Program Quality, Program Content, Program Format, Training Methods, Obstacles to Implementation, and Program Follow-up. All sections were used to assess customer satisfaction with the training program, but, one section, Obstacles to Implementation, was also used to assess Program success and to suggest warranted improvements to the training program.

The results of this section are of particular interest in developing and refining safety training programs, since the responses are those of the people trying to implement safety programs in their companies. Participants were first asked what general obstacles they encountered implementing the overall Program, and then what specific obstacles related to the individual elements of the Program (Safety Committee, Accident Investigation, Self-Inspection, Safety Targeting, and Safety Improvement Plan). Each of these six survey items included a representative listing of possible obstacles, compiled by the Abacus safety staff based on their experience. Respondents were instructed to check all obstacles that they had encountered. The results were analyzed and plotted in bar graph form to better illuminate trends. Selected bar graphs are included here as Figures 4 and 5 to illustrate the results.

The survey results showed that time management was the most significant problem faced by the small employer, in implementing the COST© Program. Time management (and related obstacles, such as 'maintaining a regular schedule' [Safety Committee], 'responding immediately' [Accident Investigation], and 'scheduling' [Self-inspections and Observations]) was by far the problem selected most often by survey respondents (82.6 % of survey respondents selected at least one of these

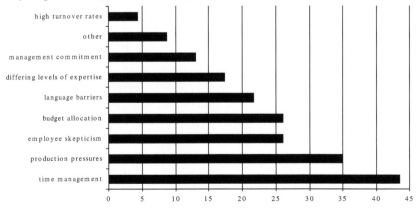

_ure *Figure 4. Obstacles to COST© implementation (% of respondents)*

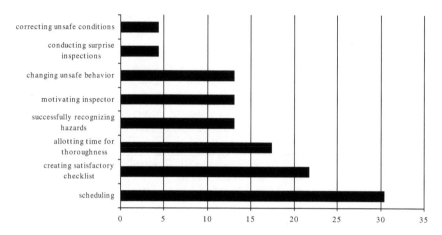

Figure 5. Obstacles to self-inspections (% of respondents)

problems). Another significant insight gained from the survey results regards the Safety Improvement Plan. Garnering employee cooperation and enthusiasm for the safety program is a problem faced by most, if not all, small employers. Fifty-two percent of survey respondents selected at least one of these three related problems: 'motivating employees', 'sustaining motivation', and 'employees see safety measures as impractical'. Other significant problems faced by small employers include production pressures, focusing on fact-finding as opposed to finding fault during accident investigations, and creating a satisfactory checklist to use for observations. Refinements in the Program and materials to increase efficiency are indicated by these surveys. Procedures to reinforce employees' participation in the Program are also indicated.

Estimates of monetary costs and benefits associated with the implementation of the COST© Program were more difficult to extract from the survey respondents. Responses to questions regarding costs resulting from Program implementation and benefits gained from Program implementation ranged from qualitative responses to exact estimates. Disregarding those surveys who did not answer (i.e., left blank) or who responded 'unknown', the majority of survey respondents (84.6 %) indicated that implementing the COST© Program cost them $1000 or less. One survey respondent indicated that implementation cost his/her company more than $10,000. This company incurred these costs by re-designing press guarding and provision of a safety incentive system.

Specific aim #3: Refine materials. Based upon review of training evaluations and instructors' input, the training materials were revised to improve their content, organization, readability, and utility. The graphic design of the COST© manual was changed to improve its presentation. Given that time management constraints were identified as a key obstacle to implementing the COST© procedures, the manual included checklists and forms to help managers implement and evaluate the system.

These were also made available to consumers on computer disk to permit their customization for particular applications. For example, the inspection audit forms and behavioral observation checklists can be edited to tailor their content to specific applications.

The interactive elements of the training materials were further developed by additional workshop activities and videotape sequences that illustrate key behavioral safety practices. Videos were shot in actual work environments to accurately depict the application of procedures by managers. One video, for example, presents a manager's dilemma in balancing safety with production pressures. The video is interactive; vignettes offer the viewer choices as to how the manager might communicate with employees and provide feedback on safety techniques. The video and prototype CD ROM were evaluated in five test sessions. Forty-six managers and safety professionals critiqued the materials during safety training sessions (at Abacus offices and an ASSE sponsored safety forum). Using a 5-point Likert scale where 5 indicated strong agreement, reviewers agreed that the video would assist them in training supervisors to use positive feedback (4.06), was realistic (4.16), was believable (4.15), and was clear and understandable (4.47). These sessions confirmed that the video and exercises enhanced the instructional power of materials. More development work is underway; additional videos supplement the written materials and provide practice in observing and scoring safety behaviors, conducting functional analyses of safety practices, and shaping desired performance.

Specific aim #4: Comparative trial. The empirical evidence presented above suggests that COST© significantly reduces workplace injuries and associated costs when provided to small businesses in the context of self-insured groups. However, COST© has yet to be field-tested in a traditional insured indemnity model. Also, COST© has not been compared to a general safety training approach commonly available in the marketplace to small employers. We are conducting, with Phase II funding from NIOSH, a randomized, controlled, comparative trial with COST© versus a general safety training approach within a large insured indemnity program to continue the development and testing process.

Summary and Future Directions

Examination of the outcomes of behavioral safety programs and consumer satisfaction with these programs indicate that behavioral safety interventions can be highly effective in reducing occupational injuries and illnesses and their associated costs. Direct savings in terms of reduced incurred costs and lost work time significantly can exceed the costs of implementation making these technologies commercially viable. It is instructive to consider the barriers to large-scale dissemination of our technologies and proceed to systematically develop and test strategies to move forward. The research tradition that has brought behavioral safety to its current levels will continue to be fruitful, however, large-scale studies of behavioral safety interventions will likely require behavior analysts become skillful with research and program evaluation methodologies that include strategies other than single-subject designs that have been the preferred design in most of the ground-breaking research in this area. This is not to diminish the value of these designs, but to acknowledge the importance of randomized clinical trials in evaluating the outcomes of behavioral safety systems. Generally lacking in our published studies of behavioral safety are cost-benefit analyses that examine the value of our interventions. Decisions to install or not install safety technologies are often driven by both economic and humanitarian motives; decisions as to which technology to install probably hinge on effectiveness and economics.

Clearly, a large obstacle to broad-scale application is limitations in our understanding of the technology transfer process. Insufficient models exist in behavior analysis to show the course of truly large-scale application. Further refinements in behavioral technologies and materials to heighten their impact and ease their use are underway and will continue. In behavioral safety, multi-media instruction, distance learning, technologies for safety behavior analyses, and computer-based feedback technologies will enable wider distribution of behavioral safety systems to larger audiences. Safety incentive systems are poorly understood and discussions of them among safety managers is better characterized by dogma than data. Additional testing of these technologies in diverse work environments with diverse populations is needed for more broad-scale applications. How behavioral safety systems operate within different organizational systems needs to be better understood. Our published reports of behavioral safety interventions usually give only cursory descriptions of the organizational variables that operate to enable or impede program effectiveness. It is evident that behavioral safety applications at their current level of development provide a viable technology for producing demonstrable improvements in work safety within employers from a variety of industries and services. More limiting to large-scale applications are under-developed distribution systems that have yet to successfully penetrate the vast market for behavioral safety. Unfortunately, this is both good and bad for those seeking to rigorously develop, test, and transfer behavioral safety technologies to those who will benefit. Opportunities exist for researchers, teachers, managers, and systems analysts to apply their competencies to an important social problem. The risk is that the ill-trained, incompetent, and poseurs will proclaim themselves behavioral safety experts and proceed to exhaust interest in behavioral safety as has happened to many management fads marketed to the public by pop psychologists and management consultants (O'Shea & Madigan, 1997).

At present, the safety profession is ill prepared to provide quality behavioral safety services. Lischeid, Sulzer-Azaroff, and Alavosius (1997) surveyed the college and university safety programs in America recognized by the ASSE (American Society of Safety Engineers) to determine how extensive is the presentation of behavioral safety in their curricula. The results indicated that the topic is marginally presented in these programs at best. Currently their are about 10,000 certified safety professionals (CSP's). This profession provides safety services, consultation, and safety management to numerous work organizations. Practicing CSP's increasingly recognize the value of behavioral-approaches to safety and are calling for inclusion of this topic in college/university safety curricula and post-graduate professional training. This provides an opportunity for academic behavior analysts to venture beyond psychology programs and teach behavior analysis via safety engineering, industrial hygiene, industrial engineering, and related programs. We can be cautiously optimistic that behavior analysis will find broad-scale application in occupational health and safety opening an exciting range of opportunities for research and practice.

Notes

1. Personal communication with managers from these service industries.
2. Paid and reserved funds to pay the medical, indemnity, legal, and other expenses of work injuries.
3. Lost time case incidence rates show the number of lost time cases per 100 workers per six months. Lost time case involve the loss of one or more scheduled work days.
4. Loss Ratios are calculated by dividing incurred losses by earned premium x 100.
5. Compensable case incidence rates show the number of cases per 100 workers per six months that involved any incurred expenses.

Reading Objectives

After reading this chapter and selected references, the student will be able to:
1. Outline the key elements of a behavioral safety program.
2. Identify three key outcome measures used to evaluate the effectiveness of safety interventions.
3. Identify key process measures to evaluate the implementation of behavioral safety systems.
4. Articulate how the contingencies of workers' compensation self-insurance systems encourage employers to invest in safety programs.
5. Using an organization with which you are familiar, identify work behaviors at the executive, manager, and employee level that affect safety.
6. Outline a performance feedback system that provides employers, managers, and employees feedback on their safety performances.
7. Outline key elements of a multi-media interactive training program that utilizes behavioral principle to teach managers to practice behavioral safety.
8. Identify circumstances in which punishment would be appropriately used to manage unsafe conduct.
9. Speculate how safety incentives could be effectively arranged to improve and maintain work safety practices.
10. Articulate why COST© should be field-tested with companies in a traditional insurance market.

References

Alavosius, M. P., & Sulzer-Azaroff, B. (1985). An on-the-job method to evaluate patient lifting techniques. *Applied Ergonomics, 16*, 307-311.

Alavosius, M. P., & Sulzer-Azaroff, B. (1986). The effects of performance feedback on the safety of client lifting and transfer. *Journal of Applied Behavior Analysis, 19*, 261-267.

Alavosius, M. P., & Sulzer-Azaroff, B. (1990). Acquisition and maintenance of health-care routines as a function of feedback density. *Journal of Applied Behavior Analysis, 23*, 151-162.

Burton, J., Jr. (Ed.). (1995). *1996 Workers' Compensation Year Book.* LRP Publications.

Chokar, J. S., & Wallin, J. A. (1984). A field study of the effects of feedback frequency on performance. *Journal of Applied Psychology, 69*, 524-530.

Fox, D. K., Hopkins, B. L., & Anger, W. K. (1987). The long-term effects of a token economy on safety performance in open-pit mining. *Journal of Applied Behavior Analysis 22*, 131-141.

Geller, E. S. (1988). *Managing occupational safety.* Blacksburg, VA: Make-A-Difference, Inc.

Harshbarger, D., & Rose T. (1991). New possibilities in safety performance and the control of workers' compensation costs. *Journal of Occupational Rehabilitation, 1*, 133-143.

Hopkins, B. L., Conrad, R. J. & Smith, M. J. (1986). Effective and reliable behavioral control technology. *American Industrial Hygiene Association Journal, 47*, 773-781.

Komaki, J., Barwick K. K., & Scott, L. R. (1978). A behavioral approach to occupational safety: Pinpointing and reinforcing safe performance in a food processing plant. *Journal of Applied Psychology, 63*, 434-445.

Krause, T. R., Hidley, J. H., & Hodson, S. J. (1990). *The behavior-based safety process.* New York: Van Nostrand Reinhold.

Lischeid, W. E., Sulzer-Azaroff, B., & Alavosius, M. P. (1997). Who will train the safety profession? *Professional Safety, 10*, 32-36.

McAfee, R. B., & Winn, A. R. (1978). The use of incentives/feedback to enhance work place safety: A critique of the literature. *Journal of Safety Research, 20*, 7-18.

McSween, T. E. (1995). *The values-based safety process.* New York: Van Norstrand Reinhold.

O'Shea, J., & Madigan, C. (1997). *Dangerous company.* New York: Random House.

Rhoton, W. W. (1980). A procedure to improve compliance with coal mine safety regulations. *Journal of Organizational Behavior Management, 4*, 243-249.

Skinner, B. F. (1953). *Science and Human Behavior.* New York: MacMillan.

Sulzer-Azaroff, B. (1978). Behavioral ecology and accident prevention. *Journal of Organizational Behavior Management, 2*, 11-44.

Sulzer-Azaroff, B., & de Santamaria, C. (1980). Industrial safety hazard reduction through performance feedback. *Journal of Applied Behavior Analysis, 13*, 287-295.

Sulzer-Azaroff B., Harris, T. C., & McCann, K. (1994). Beyond training: Organizational performance management techniques. *Occupational Medicine: State of the Art Reviews, 9*, 321-339.

U. S. Department of Labor, Bureau of Labor Statistics. (1995). *Survey of Occupational Injuries and Illnesses.*

Van den Pol, R., Reid, D., & Fuqua, W. (1983). Peer training of safety-related skills to institutional staff: Benefits for trainers and trainees. *Journal of Applied Behavior Analysis, 16*, 139-156.

Author Notes

Acknowledgments: Significant contributions to the Abacus projects described in this chapter were made by our colleagues including John Rubens, Thomas Sisto, and Kristen Quinn. Portions of the evaluations of the COST© project were supported by grants R43 OH03355 and R44 OH03355 from the National Institute for Occupational Safety and Health of the Centers for Disease Control and Prevention.

Chapter 16

Behavioral Consultation

W. Larry Williams
University of Nevada

Defining Behavioral Consultation

The term behavioral consultation has been used to describe the application of behavioral assessment and change methods in education and other human services settings (Bergan, 1977; Bergan & Kratochwill, 1990; Kratochwill & Bergan 1978, 1990; Martens, 1993). Indeed, in their guide to behavioral consultation in applied settings, Kratochwill and Bergan (1990) describe behavioral consultation as one of the three dominant models including medical/psychological (e.g., Brown, Pryzwansky, & Schulte, 1995) and organizational models (e.g., Benis, 1969; Conyne & O'Neil, 1992) and briefly compare these to seven other established models of consultation originally proposed by West and Idol (1987).

The books by Bergan (1977), Kratochwill & Bergan (1990), and Bergan and Kratochwill (1990) represent the predominant works of the few publications on the specific topic of behavioral consultation and describe many aspects of the process involved in consulting in (primarily educational) human services from a behavioral perspective. A major purpose of this chapter will be to expand the description of behavioral consultation to include several settings and parameters for the appropriate use of behavioral assessment and intervention methods as well as to draw attention to the process (the behaviors of the consultant) of consultation itself as a worthy target for a behavioral analysis.

Consultation

As behavioral consultation involves a consultation process it is best to first address what this means. Consultation is a term that has been used to describe a variety of situations in which individuals voluntarily receive information, advice, assistance or services from a consultant. Presumably the consultant is one with special knowledge, training, or skills that are relevant to the proper identification and solution of a problem with which a consultee is faced. Consultants may be sought out for their known abilities in certain areas, or may promote their employment by others through convincing them that their (the consultant's) services would be beneficial. In either situation, consultation involves a person or organization with a need to respond to a situation and a consultant who is there to assist in getting a response emitted. Consultation therefore occurs across the complete spectrum of human activities. A review of consultation in this broad sense is beyond the scope of this chapter. However some information concerning consultation in human services warrants mentioning.

In terms of consultation in human services, Caplan's (1970) classic mental health consultation model stipulated that consultation involves a voluntary, nonhierarchical relationship between two professionals usually from different occupational groups and is normally initiated by the consultee for the purposes of solving a work-related problem. Since then, various changes and advances in the mental health and human services arenas have initiated the development of several different models for consultation (e.g., Dinkmeyer & Carlson, 1973; Gallessich, 1982; Lippitt & Lippitt, 1986; Brown & Schulte, 1987; Fuqua & Kurpius, 1993). Typical of a current model for human services consultation is that of Brown, Pryzwansky & Schulte (1995). For these authors consultation has the following characteristics: a) It is initiated by either consultee or consultant; b) It is a relationship characterized by authentic communication; c) It involves professionals or non-professionals; d) It provides direct services to consultees, assisting them to develop coping skills that ultimately make them independent of the consultant; e) It is tryadic in that it provides indirect services to third parties; f) It is broadly conceived as work related; g) The consultant's role varies with consultee's needs, h) The consultant may be internal or external, and; i) All communication between consultant and consultee is confidential.

Behavioral Consultation

A behavioral consultation model has been characterized by some (e.g., Kratochwill & Bergan, 1990) as: a) Assuming a behavior analytic approach (e.g., Kazdin, 1989; Martin & Pear, 1996) with its corresponding emphasis on empirical assessment and evaluation of intervention, promotion of adaptive behavior change as integral to the therapeutic process, use of operationalized and therefore replicable treatment methods and, evaluation through multiple response modalities with an emphasis on overt behavior; b) Involving an attempt by a consultant to help a consultee define and intervene to solve a problem, and; c) Typically involving an indirect influence of the consultant on the consultee's client and often direct contact with such clients.

In their description of characteristics that are typically associated with behavioral consultation, Bergan and Kratochwill (1990) included those of problem solving, indirect service to a client, knowledge utilization, and some overlap with counseling. Consulting is very often in mental health and educational settings involving remedial and preventive interventions for children and youth. They also note the difficulties present in defining behavioral consultation. Whereas behavioral consultation shares with other consultation approaches the indirect service to a client via a consultee, so too does a majority of behavioral analysis in applied settings. That is, most applied behavioral interventions involve behavior change in a client group via application of contingencies by others who have been trained or guided by a behavior analyst. Thus the literatures of teacher training, parent training, counselor training, and higher education could all be regarded as part of behavioral consultation. While outcome evaluations of behavioral consultation that would include these larger literatures would be enhanced by their demonstrated results, perhaps a focus on the process of behavioral consultation as suggested by Bergan and Kratochwill (1990) will provide better advancement in all areas of application of behavioral assessment and intervention.

Several behavior analysts have described consultation to organizations using behavioral systems and individual performance levels of analysis (e.g., Austin, this volume; Brethower, 1982; Chase & Smith, 1994; Daniels, 1990; Gilbert, 1978). These examples of consultation also emphasize an initial assessment and definition of problem phase, but typically at an organizational and systems level as they are dealing with the performance of many individuals. This phase is then often followed by specific individual performance management interventions after such performances are pinpointed as crucial to organizational process and outcome needs. Behavioral consultation in organizational settings is often contrasted to traditional consultation in that specific key performances are identified and consultees are helped in actually changing these performances, whereas traditional consultants often only provide diagnostic services and suggest interventions or actions and often do not participate in interventions. It is interesting to observe that this also was a main difference between behavioral psychological services (e.g., Bijou 1970) and traditional psychological services in schools when the former were first introduced. That is, the psychologist would work with the teacher in the classroom, assessing and suggesting methods to correct learning problems or other general behavior problems, as opposed to only testing or counseling students in an office.

As mentioned previously, one could envision many of the activities described in the entire area of applied behavior analysis and their development to date as examples of consultation. That is, most if not all examples to date of applied behavior analysis have involved specialists helping others solve behavioral problems in applied settings. However, whereas the professional literature has documented the effects of a wide variety of behavioral assessment and change methods, less has been described about how the application of such methods by one group to solve the problems of others can be successfully arranged. It would seem that a fundamental aspect of behavioral consultation would be the systematic study of methods that effectively result in consultee's problem solving. This observation leads to the proposition that behavioral consultation would best be defined as that consultation that follows the established dimensions of applied behavior analysis as postulated by Baer, Wolf and Risley (1968, 1987). In this sense, behavioral consultation would be defined as bringing about socially validated solutions to a) others' problems in ways that are b) empirically defined, c) analytical, d) technological, e) conceptually systematic, f) effective, and g) that show generality. Such a definition allows for a clearly behavior analytic approach to the discovery and organization of information relevant to individual and organizational behavior. In addition, it allows for investigation into the behavior of applying the former information to solve others' problems. That is, a crucial feature of the definition lies in "bringing about solutions". Whereas there are numerous examples of applied behavior analytic work in the literature that meet the criteria cited above, few of them would be thought of as examples of behavioral consultation, although many examples of behavior change reported in the literature have included interventions arranged in applied settings through internal or external collaborations that demonstrate important behavior problem solutions. In this sense there may be many demonstrations of procedures and general methods that will be relevant to effective consulting behavior that will not have been labeled as such. It is our purpose here to work toward an elaboration of these.

The Process of Behavioral Consultation

In his book "Flawless Consulting: A guide to getting your expertise used" (Block 1981), Peter Block argues that regardless of the type of consulting one does, one must follow a pre-set order of activities that he describes as phases. Each phase consists of specific activities or tasks that need to be completed before advancing to the next. Reportedly responding from years of experience in corporate consulting in engineering, financial and other technical business areas, Block's formula for flawless consulting is remarkably empirical. His major phases, based on the traditional practice of consultants in the corporate business environment involve: a) defining the problem, b) establishing an information collection method, c) collecting and analyzing information, d) making recommendations for solutions and, e) deciding on actions. His book is a resource for any consultant in that he specifies overall goals and strategies for consulting and emphasizes the "people" problems that are integral to the "technical" problems one is initially called in to consult on, and the many forms of resistance a consultant will face and how to deal with them. More recently (Rosenfield, 1991) has argued that the relationship between consultee and consultant is underestimated in its importance for successful outcomes and is not sufficiently addressed in the formal training of behavioral consultants.

The overriding feature of a behavioral approach has been its adherence to operationally defined phenomena and empirical measures of their existence or variation in occurrence. Thus when it comes to applied problem solving, a mainstay of the behavioral approach has been to define problems and measure behaviors relevant to solutions of those problems. It will be argued later that the teaching of this very practice is possibly the best service a consultant can provide for a consultee. However for the present, I wish to emphasize *that an important feature of behavioral consultation is that it follows a specific course of action*. This course of action is in fact one that applied behavior analysts have used from the beginning: a) define the problem, b) analyze the problem, c) apply an intervention based on the analysis, d) monitor intervention effects and adjust as necessary and, e) arrange for maintenance. A difference or addition to the consultant's course of action is the necessity to assess and train the skills necessary for the consultee to emit the behaviors appropriate to each phase of the consultation. This means skills in defining, assessing, intervening and adjusting an intervention. Of course an integral feature of this approach is the collection of empirical measures of the problem and related variables (usually behavior or behavior products). Indeed, the decision to proceed to the next phase of the process is made from examination of the data that define the relevant issues for the current phase. I like to refer to this as the behavioral clinical decision making model. Its origins in laboratory experimental decision making methods (Sidman, 1960) or the evolved scientist practitioner approach (Hayes, Nelson, & Barlow, 1998) are very clear.

In the major applied fields such as developmental disabilities, the behavioral clinical decision making model has been at the center of virtually all behavioral interventions as is documented in the professional literature (c.f. *Journal of Applied Behavior Analysis, American Journal of Mental Retardation, Research in Developmental Disabilities*). When a behavior analyst consults to individuals or organizations concerning behavioral excesses or deficiencies of consultee's clients, the empirical decision making model is invoked and the above mentioned steps to a solution are followed. Indeed, a recent description of such an endeavor and the problems encountered in maintaining change in consultee's behavior have been described as "ongoing consultation" (Harchik, Sherman, Sheldon, & Strause, 1992).

In a recent presentation at the annual meeting of the Ontario Association for Behavior Analysis (Williams, 1997), I recounted how the behavioral clinical decision making model determined the service delivery parameters of a large metropolitan behavior management service for persons with developmental disability that I directed (Williams, 1995). A large number of consumers (over 500 in a 5 year period) received behavioral consultation services via behavior therapists (Bachelor and Masters degree level individuals) who were supervised by Ph.D. level behavior analysts. All individual therapist interventions followed the steps outlined above for consultation. All cases involved collection of some form of empirical measure. Over the course of several years, we learned that to follow the behavioral consultation process in different settings required different skills. Whereas I will elaborate more on this feature of consultation later, the relevant aspect here is that we eventually used the behavioral clinical decision making approach to teach other agencies to solve their own problems, (Bernicky, Cummings, Drummond, Meagher, & Williams, 1992) and eventually developed a service management and maintenance model for human service settings we called "service review" (Williams, 1995; Williams & Murray, 1993; Williams & Cummings, 1999).

The same process and decision making model can be seen in behavioral approaches to quality assurance and program evaluation (e.g., LaVigna, Willis, Shaull, Abedi, & Sweitzer, 1994). That is, another feature of behavioral consultation is that it involves *the maintenance of empirical measures for relevant features of an operation or process and thus can help individuals to monitor attempts at adjusting performance in desired directions*. It was through this approach that the above-described community behavioral consultation services were able to clinically supervise the case-loads of more than 50 therapists over a five year period, through a procedure described as "binder review" (Williams, Lloyd, Sparks, Crozier, Stanhope, Brown, & Hodges, 1989) in which therapists routinely met with supervisors and presented their cases in terms of the stage of consultation they were at and the intervention change decisions they had made based on client progress, mediator training needs, resistance, and involvement of other professionals, among other things. This resulted in a consistent service delivery capability that over a five year period eliminated the need for any intrusive behavior change methods and successfully treated 571 behaviors of 173 clients for whom long term data were available. "Success" was defined as an 80% change or better from baseline for 83% of all behaviors treated and a 90% reduction for over 73% of all behaviors treated. Maintenance measures of such outcomes averaged 30 weeks and ranged from 1 to more than 200 weeks (Williams, Feldman, Sparks, & Drummond, 1999).

In summary, behavioral consultation involves assistance by an agent with knowledge in the principles and application of behavior analysis who can arrive at effective responses on the part of a consultee in responding to a problem situation. Whereas knowledge and skill in applying behavioral assessment and change methods alone may be sufficient, a consultant will also typically have considerable knowledge of the area of practice of the consultee (e.g., developmental disabilities, elementary school education, manufacturing, personnel, safety, etc.). Behavioral consultation follows a definite course of action or stages derived from the traditional milestones of problem definition and analysis, leading to intervention and its monitoring and culminating in maintaining arrangements for the consultee. The decision to proceed from one phase to another is based on examination of empirical data relevant to the problem being analyzed. The appropriate methods and techniques of behavioral consultation should mirror those that define applied behavior analysis.

The Role of the Behavioral Consultant

The behavior of the behavioral consultant defines such activity and is the main target of our analysis. In attempting to establish parameters for this aspect of behavior analysis I will identify some of the consultant activity most appropriate for specific situations and phases of consulting. While consultant activities have been well described in terms of the tasks and priorities that change as the course of consultation proceeds (Block, 1981; Conyne & O'Neil, 1992; Bergan & Kratochwill, 1990; Kratochwill & Bergan, 1990), there are also features of consultees and their problems that require very different approaches. I will describe how the nature of the consultee's client problem in human services situations, the consultee in any situation, and whether the consultee is operating individually or within an organization are major determinants of appropriate consultant behavior.

Relationship with the Consultee

Block (1981) described three possible roles of a consultant. When in an expert role, the consultant is sought out for his or her technical expertise. When in a pair of hands role, the consultant is hired to perform a specific job or task for management, and when in a collaborative role, the consultant and consultee divide responsibility for defining and addressing a problem. Block asserts that only the latter role is appropriate and one should always resist undertaking the first two. The first instance of expert is rejected as it will typically lead to your expertise being applied without sufficient information or control, or out of context and possibly inappropriately. The second role is rejected as not being consultation by definition, but rather fulfilling a management function (often a highly undesirable one such as firing people).

The collaborative relationship is argued to be the only one that allows the consultant sufficient influence to help bring about change, as well as sufficient responsibility on the part of the consultee for the problem and a commitment to do something about it. The need for a collaborative relationship between consultant and consultee underscores the major tenet of Block's overall position. The position is that although consultees seek out consultants, they often do so as a last resort in getting a solution to a difficult situation that is aversive for them and may additionally expose a weakness or incompetence in how they have managed the problem. This will inevitably lead to the consultee being resistant to giving away control over or exposing information on their operation, their methods, or their performance. This feature of the consultee's problem will also lead to an emphasis in problem identification on the part of the consultee as "technical" as opposed to the often more likely case of the problem being caused or exacerbated by ongoing mismanagement or other inappropriate ways of responding towards the problem.

Related to this general area of the interactions that unfold during the consultation process and the role played by the consultant is the work of Bergan and his colleagues (Bergan 1977; Bergan, Byrnes, & Kratochwill, 1979; Bergan & Tombari, 1975, 1976). Bergan has shown that in leading the consultee through the consulting process the consultant must assert some control via specific forms of verbal interaction. Indeed, by following specific content questioning patterns, the consultant essentially guides the consultee to focus on specific aspects of the relationship of client performance to environmental variables. This guided verbal control over the consultee allows the consultant to proceed with the consultee through the specific stages of the process.

The above work by Bergan and others is relevant to the issue of resistance described by Block (1981). Block maintains that the successful consultant must identify resistance early on, and deal with it head on. In this sense he provides many examples of when and where in the consultation process one can identify resistance (for example in the verbal behavior of consultees during interviews, or meetings to make decisions about the consultation process or direction) and essentially confront the consultee about it through authentic statements that simply identify the situation and provide alternative ways for consultees to behave. Bergan and Kratochwill (1990) provide a sophisticated verbal behavioral analysis of the specific types of statements and questions that a consultant should emit during specific stages of their problem solving behavioral model. The responses are designed to guide the appropriate verbal responses necessary from the consultee in identifying and analyzing the salient behavior-environment relationships involved in their client's problem.

The Nature of the Problem of the Consultee

While Block's suggestions as to the role of the consultant apply to any consulting endeavor, there are specific aspects of a consultee's problem or the nature of the consultee's client's problem that also determine role. Similar to the relatively uncharted area of describing those methods that lead to success in solving highly political problems, human services consultation has its share of unresolved difficult and controversial issues (Riley & Frederiksen, 1983). There is probably no better example of how the nature of the problem changes the role of the consultant than when a consultee's client is engaging in extremely dangerous behavior. Kratochwill and Bergan (1990) differentiated between types of client problems facing a consultant as being developmental- or problem-centered. Whereas developmental problems are long-term and typically involve acquisition of new behavior, problem-centered consultation requires immediate behavior change of typically specific maladaptive or dangerous client behavior.

Williams (1995) described how differences in the referrals from families as opposed to service agencies for community behavioral consultation services required differences in the types of skills that a consultant would require in these situations. Based on over 500 clinical cases, we observed that community-based referrals more often involved older, more aggressive, clients with a history of treatments in residential or day settings that were staffed by relatively transient, younger, less educated and highly opinionated people within often highly political or value biased organizations. Referrals from families on the other hand involved younger clients with a possible compliance, eating or toileting problem but with opportunities for establishing appropriate interactions through training and education through behavioral principles with a few parents or siblings who had strong emotional ties to the client. Whereas the general course of action that the behavioral consultant should follow in assisting consultees to respond effectively to their problem remains the same, it is clear that the nature of the consultee and the client's problem will require different specific skills on the part of the consultant.

Individual versus Organizational Variables

An interesting feature of the various models or approaches to consulting is that regardless of the model, there is an assumed triadic relationship in that consulting is almost always considered as an activity concerning a consultant, a consultee and the consultee's client (Bergan & Kratochwill, 1990). This may be attributable to the origins of the concept of consulting in the practice of medicine and the development of specialists who consulted to or treated other physicians' patients. Consulting by other professionals, especially Psychologists, received impetus with the Community Mental Health Act of 1963 and its call for consultation and educational services to the community. Many of the early examples of consultation (Caplan, 1970; Gallessich, 1982) appear to have been maintained in the mental health and education fields and this perhaps explains their triadic nature and focus on consultee client difficulties.

Although many of our clients' behavioral needs may be challenging, the coordination and motivation of those people (often called mediators) who provide daily living, work, therapeutic or educational environments for them is typically an equal or greater challenge. This aspect of providing community behavioral consultation services is not often practically addressed in training of therapists, or in the literature of clinical behavior service provision. However, utilizing such a "mediator model" approach in behavior therapy has been widely accepted as necessary for any measure of cost effectiveness and/or to promote post intervention generalization and maintenance of behavior change (Baer, Wolf, & Risley, 1968, 1987).

The difficulties involved in mediator training have not been systematically described or studied except in the context of "staff training" or "staff development" (Wu & Williams, 1990). No well documented model is prevalent in the literature from which behavioral practitioners can establish or research different methods of interacting with mediators in order to organize mediator behaviors with respect to referred client programs. How to successfully deal with service mediators is indeed a "grey area" in applied behavior analysis. Our own recent work (Williams & Murray, 1993; Williams 1995; Williams & Cummings, 1999) addresses the issue of the necessity for behavioral consultants to community service organizations to approach the tasks and analyses involved from an organizational approach. Specifically, it is crucial to understand that the "mediator" in an organizational situation involves not just the direct care personnel but their supervisors, the managers of the supervisors, and directors of the managers. Failure to arrange for an appropriate role for all involved in this multi-tiered system can easily lead to frustration on all fronts and consultation failure (including in the solution of the client's problem). Conversely, interventions that are coordinated with an analysis of the organizational levels of a service setting can result in direct client gains via intervention at appropriate management levels (Williams & Lloyd 1992; Methot, Williams, Cummings & Bradshaw, 1996).

In summary, for behavioral consultation in community settings we have seen how client and mediator differences between natural home settings and professional community living settings combine with organizational variables to affect consultant role. At the same time, consultees may be considering behavioral technology to be purely crisis intervention as opposed to ongoing preventive care, and the former situation involves regular staff and supervisory support and development. Given the political and social implications of crises, it follows that a major challenge for behavior analysts as external consultants to such service organizations is to develop ongoing preventive behavioral practices while attending to crises. This in turn, as a result of an analysis of the mediator model in organizational settings, leads to a conclusion that effective, ethical behavioral consultation to community organizational settings must involve organizational level analysis and procedures.

Behavioral Systems Analysis

As the above summary indicates, consulting to organizations is a complex undertaking. To effectively deal with such complexity, behavioral consultants will need to be aware of organizational phenomena that are often described in the area of systems analysis. A good source for behavioral systems analysis, Morasky (1982) defines a behavioral system as "those organizations, programs, groups, and so forth that are dependent upon the behaviors of the people within the system or that have a behavioral component that is critical to system functioning" (p. ix). His book provides clear and practical examples of the basic concepts involved in defining, designing, or analyzing systems at all levels of size and complexity.

The important role of systems analysis is that of context. That is, although the behavior analyst may have knowledge and skills in defining, assessing, and changing individual behavior, such undertakings will always benefit from and often depend on the context in which the individual behaves. Indeed, systems theorists contend that systems behave as an entity in and of themselves. We could understand this from a behavioral perspective if we make use of the concept of metacontingencies (Glenn, 1991; Glenn & Malagodi, 1991). Metacontingencies are literally the contingencies controlling the contingencies in a any situation. For example, a behavioral consultant may be presented with a problem that appears to only involve managing consultee client behavior. The metacontingencies controlling the system, however involve the client and his/her environment and history; the direct caregiver and his/her environment and history with respect to the particular client and the organization; the direct caregiver's supervisor; that person's supervisor, and so on. There are also external influences from the community and funding sources for the organization as a whole that may or may not contribute to the seemingly simple problem of managing consultee client behavior. From this perspective, there is much to be gained by describing events at different organizational levels as they relate to individual performances and products. Much time and energy can be wasted in attempting individual behavior change interventions when the controlling variables of a problem are actually outside of the system or are at a level of the system where the problem is being addressed (Williams & Lloyd, 1992).

Behavioral systems analysis provides a model with which we can make sense of the many levels of contingencies in a situation so that we can then effectively analyze and intervene. Brethower's (1982) Total Performance System (TPS) is perhaps most closely equated with a behavioral systems model, and it has been described elsewhere in detail (Austin, this volume; Brethower, 1982; Redmon 1991). In general, the model depicts a double feedback loop to describe any system. Borrowing from general systems descriptions, the model allows for representation of any processing system (including factors such as input information, process, and output product), an internal quality control or internal process feedback mechanism, as well as a larger market, consumer, or receiving system feedback loop that is external to the process of the organization.

Although the TPS has been typically applied in business situations, we have attempted to utilize it to conceptualize effective provision of clinical behavioral consultation in complex systems as those described above (e.g., for hundreds of consultee clients simultaneously). Indeed the concepts of information and other inputs and outputs from a system, of feedback, and of sub, internal or external systems allow for the pinpointing of specific systems needs at different levels within or between systems that are essential for the pinpointing of the performances of individuals in those systems and their subsequent assessment or change. A version of Brethower's (1982) TPS is seen in Figure 1 as applied to clinical behavioral client service programs (part of the process loop) in an organization.

Examination of Figure 1 reveals four different processing loops, each one consisting of input information (or job/work objectives), some form of job/work activity, and some form of tracking or monitoring how well the job activity is meeting the needs of the job objectives or requests. At the level of services for a given individual client, the "regular service objectives" could represent all or any one of a variety of services that an organization may provide for that client. The "ongoing consumer progress" box represents the results of the service activity that is provided on a regular basis for the client. The "regular program review" represents how the service provider monitors the application of the service for the client to assure that the service is of benefit for the client (as indicated by client progress). These three parts can represent one or all services provided for one client or all clients, depending on the level of analysis one wishes to conduct or review.

A second process loop is seen below the first and it represents specifically a behavioral clinical or training service. As in the previously described loop there are inputs or objectives, activities or services, and a regular monitoring of the effectiveness of those services. (Note that this activity is especially natural and common to any behavioral interventions). A third and more comprehensive loop is represented by the outside lines and their linking of consumer needs to consumer outcomes and the feedback of information on the adequacy of those outcomes to the organization. This feedback loop represents customer satisfaction. Note how the first two loops described are contained within the larger consumer loop. Indeed, they *are the job or activity sector of the larger loop.*

The "service review" line represents a fourth process loop. This loop represents the overall monitoring of all activities related to all client service objectives within the organization. Like the consumer feedback loop, it encompasses all organizational activities and is the overall quality assurance or monitor function of the organization. This feature allows for maintaining or improving lower-level monitoring simply because it represents monitoring of that monitoring (i.e., meta-monitoring) or an organizational metacontingency (Glenn, 1991).

It is important to note that Figure 1 represents a simplified schematic because it summarizes all ongoing regular services for clients in one internal "sub-loop" of the overall organization service (process) loop. If space were not important in this book, we could represent each of the services or programs by their own internal process loop. Figure 1 therefore represents a summary of all service activity for all referral agency clients, and all behavioral programming activities for those clients. This capacity to summarize a great deal of activity (e.g., each of the services or programs are represented by one loop) without losing a great deal of information is still another asset of the TPS.

The application of this model demonstrated its ability to accurately describe the three stages of typical behavioral clinical intervention quality assurance procedures (goals, procedures, and review) in one simple figure. It also allowed for the conceptual description of one intervention with one client, several interventions

TOTAL PERFORMANCE SERVICE REVIEW

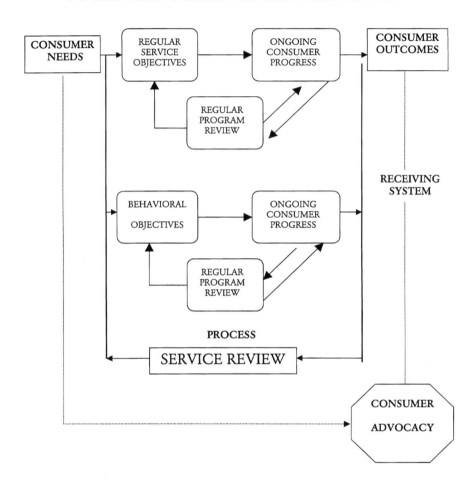

Figure 1. An adaptation of Brethower's (1982) Total Performance System to describe the process and outcome information loops in a human services organization.

with one client, several interventions with several clients, services for several clients at one location, and service across several locations or agencies. The final receiving system includes the clients, consumers, or advocates receiving the service products from the overall organization operation. One observation from such an analysis is that the process loop for any specific category of activity within the organization is part of the process loop for the next level in the organization. In other words, the process loop describing the provision of services to one client receives its input from the outputs of all service process loops for that client. The process loop representing services for a site includes the input from all the services for all clients at the site, and so on. The internal quality review at the organizational level (service review) is therefore an internal receiving system that monitors overall consumer service quality.

By applying the knowledge about levels of the systems within a residential service organization for children with developmental disabilities, (Cummings & Williams, 1995; Williams & Murray, 1993; Williams & Cummings, 1999) we were able to deduce that management decisions about products and their quality and quantity often act as an organizational "conditioned establishing operation" (Michael 1993). This means they have the effect of enhancing the reinforcing effectiveness of products (in this case graphical data summaries of client progress on individual training programs) and strengthening the behaviors that lead to their production. This process that we have termed "Service Review" is essentially a management practice of reviewing a continual baseline of client benefit/outcome data on a regular basis with supervisors of direct service activities. Not only does the maintenance of such a baseline of organizational performance change behavior, it allows for ongoing measurement of the effectiveness of any practice or intervention that is undertaken such as the monitoring of staff skills training or methods of performance maintenance. This model in particular seems to satisfy all of the variety of goals that one could specify for behavioral consultation. It produces client benefits, it changes consultee skills, and it produces enhancement to the overall organization in a self-maintaining fashion.

Research and the Development of Behavioral Consultation

Regardless of the model of consultation that has been practiced, there are few studies of effective practice and very little linking of skills needed for effective practice to the training of consultants (Alpert & Meyers, 1983). Mannino and Shore (1983) reported an analysis of all doctoral dissertations completed from 1968-1978 that mentioned some aspect of consultation in mental health, public organizations or education. They noted that while 209 research articles had been published in the mental health and related literature during that period, 208 dissertations were conducted. The authors suggested that this represented an imbalance and that more research was needed from more senior researchers. It is not clear if this imbalance has persisted as space does not permit such an analysis here.

Research on behavioral consultation has been understandably focused on preparation of consultants (Goodwin, Garvey, & Barclay, 1971; Keeley, Shemberg, & Ferber, 1973), counsellors, (Randolf, 1972; Vernberg & Repucci, 1986), school consultants (Abidin, 1977; Anderson, Kratochwill, & Bergan, 1986; Bergan, 1977; Bergan, Kratochwill & Luiten, 1978; Bergan & Tombari, 1975, 1976), and the activities of behavior analysts operating in the public at large (Fawcett, 1991; Repucci, 1977; Repucci & Saunders, 1974). There is general consensus in the consultation literature that one of the most important aspects of the consultation process is that of problem identification and analysis. In behavioral consultation Bergan and his colleagues have reported on the most developed line of investigations in this area. Bergan and Tombari (1975) demonstrated that the type of verbal behavior emitted by a consultant was directly related to the kinds of information (verbal behavior) emitted by the consultee. They reported on a method to reliably code verbal behavior of consultants and consultees they referred to as the consultation analysis record (CAR). This classification system allows for the coding of verbal behavior into categories of content and process each with several subcategories. The CAR is used together with the consultation analysis checklist (CAC) which is a list of "the types of verbalizations usually required to achieve the purpose of a given interview" (Bergan & Kratochwill, 1990, p. 69). Bergan's research has demonstrated that by practicing the emission and recognition of productive and unproductive verbal statements, consultants can be trained to be more effective at bringing consultees through the steps of behavioral consultation. Bergan and Tombari (1976) trained 11 consultants to work with 806 kindergarten through grade 3 children referred for psychological services by teachers. A multiple regression analysis found that 60% of the variance associated with plan implementation was accounted for by problem identification during that phase of consultation. Not surprisingly, they also found a .977 correlation between problem solution and plan implementation. Thus treatment success is strongly linked to appropriate problem identification which is affected by the consultant's verbal behavior. More recently, research by Witt and Elliot (1983) has further established the significance of appropriately conducted early components of the behavioral consultation model in school consultation. This type of research is an example of the treatment utility or validity studies (Hayes, Nelson, & Jarret, 1986, 1988) and is an area of needed further research in behavioral consultation.

A 1995 special edition in the *Journal of Applied Behavior Analysis* on behavioral consultation represents how the practice of actually intervening, and helping bring about behavior change in real life situations such as suggested by Bijou (1970) has evolved as intricately involved with the area of training and maintaining the performance of others. McGimsey, Greene, and Lutzker (1995) demonstrated that a consultant's proficiency at administering a behavior change procedure (e.g., time out) was not sufficient for that consultant to successfully instruct others in its application. Rather, specific consultant skills such as teaching others in how to apply procedures was necessary for trainees to be effective. Related to these findings, Parsons and Reid (1995) demonstrated that supervisors' teaching of implementation skills were insufficient to have staff, who were receiving on the job feedback, show performance changes. Rather, specific feedback to supervisors on how to provide feedback was required.

Further evidence that the consultation area very often involves and requires knowledge about training was suggested by two additional articles using pyramidal training (Page, Iwata, & Reid, 1982). Shore, et al. (1995) demonstrated that staff's proper implementation of complex behavior reduction programs was achieved only as a result of supervisor training. Similarly, Neef (1995a) demonstrated support for the pyramidal training approach by showing that peer trained parents were as competent as professional trained parents. (Although mediator training is a crucial area for behavioral consultation, space does not permit a review of this literature here. Readers are referred to Reid, Parsons, and Green (1989) for further information on the topic.)

In her introduction to the four articles presented in the special section on behavioral consultation, Neef (1995b) pointed out that "As the scope of investigation expands from treatment recipients to treatment providers, to trainers or supervisors, and to their trainers or supervisors, the complexity of research increases as well" (p. 297). This observation perhaps explains the relatively sparse literature that specifically addresses behavioral consultation. Indeed, as others (Reid, Parsons & Green, 1989; Williams & Lloyd, 1992, Methot et al., 1996) conducting research on staff performance have noted, conducting applied studies such as staff training demonstrations requires cooperation from organizations, is costly and time consuming, and is complex in the controls needed when the dependent variable at one level of analysis functions as the independent variable at another level of analysis. That is, performance of one group of staff or clients is influenced by performance of another group and this is difficult to control and measure. As consulting will typically involve several levels of performance to analyze, we should perhaps not be surprised at the small number of studies that address such issues.

These few demonstrations discussed may only represent a portion of successful behavioral consultation research, for example those with reliable data, that meet publication standards. Unfortunately, a larger number of consultation experiences, including those that are not successful, are not available in the literature. Functionally, we are left without documentation or description of the consultation experience of others which could be used to form a more effective set of procedures and principles important for successful behavioral consultation. This issue is not new, but supports the need for more attempts at dissemination of effective behavior analytic consulting strategies.

Bergan and Kratochwill (1990) called for the standardization of procedures and format in behavioral consultation. They proposed that most behavioral interventions in applied settings suffer from the lack of such standards. If standards of consultation were established this would allow for systematic replication, increased ability to train consultation skills, easier dissemination and use by practitioners in applied settings, and positive effects on legal and ethical issues in applied settings. Descriptive analysis of successful consultation and consultants will be needed to understand consultation. In the work described by Williams (1995) and Williams, Feldman, Sparks, and Drummond (1999) on training and supervision of community behavior consultants to families, agencies schools and hospitals, standardization is a central theme. The performance goals that were sought out and described were based on behavior analytic standards of measurement and procedure. In the consultation model described as "Service Review" (Cummings & Williams, 1995; Williams & Cummings, 1999; Williams & Murray, 1993) the behavioral standards of reliable measurement and graphical representation are the central components to the analysis and decision making procedures that an agency is taught.

Behavioral consultation is still in its infancy although applied behavioral procedures and methods relevant to behavioral consultation have been studied for over forty years. The future of behavioral consultation will undoubtedly be one of productivity and a multitude of methods and refinements of practice. From the above description of its current state, however, three general areas seem reasonable for future research. The first concerns the evaluation of consultation. As previously described, this has involved analysis of outcomes which if related to process will further the description of the relevant features, procedures and methods of behavioral consultation as contrasted to other consultation approaches and other behavioral intervention procedures.

In school consulting the work by Bergan and Kratochwill (1990) appears central as a description of the history and development of behavioral consultation. Although a detailed review of the behavioral consultation model as it has developed in the school systems is not possible here, several citations are here included as representative of some of the work in the area.

Medway (1979) reported that behavioral consultation was the most effective in a review of 29 studies in school consultation. Methodological problems such as failure to control for individual consultant or consultee variables, lack of appropriate experimental control procedures, lack of multiple dependent measures assessing both behavior and attitude change were cited as deficiencies in the generality of these findings. Fuchs, et al. (1992) reviewed the literature on consultation to elementary and secondary schools from 1961-1989. They found that a low number of publications (119) involved evaluating consultation. The literature for the period indicated behavioral consultation to be four times more likely to be studied than other (e.g., mental health) models; group designs were used in two thirds of the studies; and student behavior measures were found in only one quarter of the studies. In research on the evolution of behavioral consultation in schools, Noell and Witt (1996) provide a re-evaluation of five fundamental assumptions underlying behavioral consultation. They argue that the rigidity of the approach may be stifling its growth. Behavioral consultation, they argue, is a model in evolution but is seen as a static approach by less informed consultees and consultants. Lalli, et al. (1993) used a behavioral consultation model to bring about successful interventions by teachers on student problem behaviors. Their intervention focused on the use of descriptive assessments to estimate functions and prescribe interventions.

In addition to the above cited areas, behavioral consulting has been described as an intervention method to day care centers (Twardosz, 1984); extended to language services consultation for speech-language pathologists (Cipani, 1989); and for consulting in nursing homes (MacDonald, 1983). While there has been some development of a consulting method for human service agencies as described above in the service review example (Williams & Cummings, 1999) replication and detailed study of the effective components of the approach are needed.

We are not aware of any systematic descriptions of behavioral consulting procedures or methods in human services or in business settings (although Austin, this volume, describes a methodology to examine performance analysis processes for OBM consultation). As most of the behavioral literature in organizational settings attests, there are many descriptions of individual behavior change procedures, few systems level interventions, and few descriptions of the process used to bring either of the former about. Research is needed on describing the procedures and effectiveness of behavioral consulting.

A second area for research is in the organizational/systems analysis approach to consultation. Few behavior analysts are familiar with systems analysis or behavioral systems analyses. The work developed by Brethower (1982) and applied in our own service review model shows the utility of this approach to consulting. Again, in school consultation Martens and Witt (1988) have proposed systems analysis for interventions in school classroom settings as opposed to just focusing on the individual child and their behavior problems, and Douglas (1982) has similarly called for a systems approach in behavioral school consultation. Not withstanding Brethower's (1982) analysis and the text concerning organizational performance analysis by Chase and Smith (1994) there have been few descriptions of systems analyses interventions. One interesting application would be further examination of the establishing operation role of management review practices at one level within an organization on the relevant performances and products at other levels (presumably subordinate) in the organization. Another example of organizational level analyses would be the development of organizational functional analysis methods as suggested by Austin, Carr, and Agnew (1999) for pinpointing the conditions that result in effective performance by managers, or any specific performance foci in an organization. Such analyses could be developed into methods to diagnose conditions that lead to inappropriate or non functional performance, or in contrast conditions that are associated with appropriate acquisition or stimulus control of desired performances.

A third area of future development is in the continued analysis of teaching behavioral consultation. Although related to the first two areas, there will be specific need for effective and inexpensive training methods. Current research on consultant training indicates that those methods that are criterion-based are easiest to teach to others. These methods are associated with behavioral consultation and have been found to be expensive and require some time commitment. Other methods such as using interactive cases (Austin, 1997), think aloud problem solving (Lindsley, 1996) and using fluency techniques (Johnson & Layng, 1992) need to be better evaluated. If this area of research can be improved, we can produce generations of behavioral consultants who are significantly more effective at making important contributions to our society.

Reading Objectives

After reading this chapter the reader will be able to:
1. Provide a short history of the field of consultation.
2. Provide a definition of behavioral consultation.
3. Provide a general description of the process of behavioral consultation.
4. Describe how the relationship with the consultee will affect the consultant's role.
5. Describe how the nature of the consultee's client problem may affect the role of the consultant.
6. Describe the triadic or mediator model and how it affects consulting to organizations.
7. Describe the general approach to consultation research initiated by Bergan & Kratochwill.
8. Describe the general community agency consultation approach called service review and how it derives from general systems analysis of organizations.
9. Describe several recent studies in training consultants to train others.
10. Describe three areas of research and future development in behavioral consultation.

References

Abidin, R. R. (1977). Operant behavioral consultations as conducted by master's and doctoral level psychologists in Virginia. *Journal of School Psychology, 15,* 225-228.

Alpert, J. L., & Meyers, J. (1983.) *Training in consultation: Perspectives from mental health, behavioral and organizational consultation.* Springfield, IL: Charles C. Thomas.

Anderson, T. K., Kratochwill, T. R., & Bergan, J. R. (1986). Training teachers in behavioral consultation and therapy: An analysis of verbal behaviors. *Journal of School Psychology, 24,* 229-241.

Austin, J. (1997, May). *Using cases to teach OBM.* Paper presented at the 21st Annual conference of the Association for Behavior Analysis, International. Chicago, IL.

Austin, J., Carr, J. E., & Agnew, J. (1999). The need for assessment of maintaining variables in OBM. *Journal of Organizational Behavior Management, 19,* 59-87.

Baer, D. M., Wolf, M. M., & Risley, T. R. (1968). Some current dimensions of applied behavior analysis. *Journal of Applied Behavior Analysis, 1,* 91-97.

Baer, D. M., Wolfe, M. M., & Risley, T. R. (1987). Some still current dimensions of applied behavior analysis. *Journal of Applied Behavior Analysis, 20,* 313 -327.

Benis, W. G. (1969). *Changing organizations.* New York: McGraw-Hill.

Bergan, J. R. (1977). *Behavioral consultation.* Columbus, OH: Charles E. Merrill.

Bergan, J. R., Byrnes, I. M., & Kratochwill, T. R. (1979). Effects of behavioral and medical models of consultation on teacher expectancies and instruction of a hypothetical child. *Journal of School Psychology, 17,* 307-316.

Bergan, J. R., & Kratochwill, T. R. (1990). *Behavioral consultation and therapy.* New York: Plenum Press.

Bergan, J. R., Kratochwill, T. R., & Luiten, J. (1978). Competency based training in behavioral consultation. *Journal of School Psychology, 18*, 91-97.

Bergan, J. R., & Tombari, M. L. (1975). The analysis of verbal interactions occurring during consultation. *Journal of School Psychology, 13*, 209-226.

Bergan, J. R., & Tombari, M. L. (1976). Consultant skill and efficiency and the implementation of outcomes of consultation. *Journal of School Psychology, 14*, 3-14.

Bernicky, G., Cummings, A., Drummond, C., Meagher, S., & Williams, W. L. (1992, March). *The behavioral education and consultation services: Staff, supervisor, and management consultation support for agencies.* Poster presented at the Ontario Association on Developmental Disabilities Conference. Toronto, Ontario.

Bijou, S. W. (1970). What Psychology has to offer education now. *Journal of Applied Behavior Analysis, 3*, 65-72.

Block, P. (1981). *Flawless consulting: A guide to getting your expertise used.* San Diego: University Associates.

Brethower, D. M. (1982). The total performance system. In R. M. O'Brien, A. M. Dickinson, & M. P. Rosow (Eds.), *Industrial Behavior Modification: A management handbook* (pp. 350-369). New York: Pergamon Press.

Brown, D., & Schulte, A. (1987). A social learning model of consultation. *Professional psychology: Research and practice, 18*, 283-287.

Brown, D., Pryzwansky, W. B., & Schulte, A. C. (1995). *Psychological consultation: Introduction to theory and practice.* Boston, MA: Allyn and Bacon

Caplan, G. (1970). *The theory and practice of mental health consultation.* New York: Basic Books.

Chase, P. N., & Smith, J. M. (1994). *Performance analysis: Understanding behavior in organizations.* Morgantown, WV: Envision Development Group, Inc.

Cipani, E. (1989). Providing language consultation in the natural context: A model for delivery of services. *Mental Retardation, 27*, 317-324.

Conoley, J. C. (Ed.). (1981). *Consultation in the schools: Theory, research, procedures.* New York, NY: Academic Press.

Conyne, R. K., & O'Neil, J. M. (1992). *Organizational consultation: A casebook.* London: Sage Publications.

Cummings, A., & Williams, W. L. (1995, May). *Analysis of the contextual effect of a management outcome review process on the programming decision performance of direct care staff in a human services setting.* Paper presented at the 21st annual convention of the Association for Behavior Analysis, Washington, DC.

Curtis, M., & Zins, J. E. (Eds.). (1981). *The theory and practice of school consultation.* Springfield, IL: Charles C. Thomas

Daniels, A. C. (1989). *Performance management: Improving quality productivity through positive reinforcement* (3rd ed.). Tucker, GA: Performance Management Publications.

Dinkmeyer, D., & Carlson, J. (1973). *Consulting: Facilitating human potential and change processes.* Columbus, OH: Charles E. Merrill.

Douglas, J. (1982). A "systems" perspective to behavioral consultation in schools: A personal view. *Bulletin of the British Psychological Society, 35,* 195-197.

Fawcett, S. B. (1991). Some values guiding community research and action. *Journal of Applied Behavior Analysis, 24,* 621-636.

Fuchs, D., Fuchs, L. S., Dulan, J., & Roberts, H. (1992). Where is the research on consultation effectiveness? *Journal of Educational and Psychological Consultation, 3,* 151-174.

Fuqua, D. R., & Kurpius, D. J. (1993). Conceptual models of organizational consultation. *Journal of counseling and development. 71,* 607-618.

Gallessich, J. (1982). *The profession and practice of consultation: A handbook for consultants, trainers of consultants and consumers of consultation services.* San Francisco: Jossey-Bass.

Gilbert, T. F. (1978). *Human competence: Engineering worthy performance.* New York: McGraw-Hill.

Glenn, S. S. (1991) Contingencies and Metacontingencies: Relations among behavioral, cultural, and biological evolution. In P. A. Lamal (Ed.), *Behavioral analysis of societies and cultural practices* (pp. 39-73). Washington, DC: Hemisphere.

Glenn, S. S., & Malagodi, E. F. (1991). Process and content in behavioral and cultural phenomena. *Behavior and Social Issues, 1,* 1-14.

Goodwin, D. L., Garvey, W. P., & Barclay, J. R. (1971). Microconsultation and behavior analysis: A method of training psychologists as behavioral consultants. *Journal of Consulting and Clinical Psychology, 37,* 355-363.

Harchik, A. E., Sherman, J. A., Sheldon, J. B., & Strouse, M. C. (1992). Ongoing consultation as a method of improving performance of staff members in a group home. *Journal of Applied Behavior Analysis, 25,* 599-610.

Hayes, S. C, Nelson, R., & Barlow, M. (1998). *The scientist practitioner: Research and accountability in clinical and educational settings* (5th printing). New York, NY: Pergamon Press.

Hayes, S. C., Nelson, R. O., & Jarrett, R. B. (1986). Evaluating the quality of behavioral assessment. In R. O. Nelson & S. C. Hayes (Eds.), *Conceptual foundations of behavioral assessment* (pp. 463-503). New York: Guilford Press.

Hayes, S. C., Nelson, R. O., & Jarrett, R. B. (1987). The treatment utility of assessment. *American Psychologist, 42,* 963-974.

Johnson, K. R., & Layng, T. V. J. (1992). Breaking the structuralist barrier: Literacy and numeracy with fluency. Special Issue: Reflections on B. F. Skinner and psychology. *American Psychologist, 47,* 1475-1490.

Kazdin, A. E. (1989). *Behavior modification in applied settings* (Rev. ed.). Homewood, IL: Dorsey.

Keeley, S. M., Shemberg, K. M., & Ferber, H. (1973). The training and use of undergraduates as behavior analysts in the consultative process. *Professional Psychology, 4,* 59-63.

Kratochwill, T. R., & Bergan, J. R. (1978). Evaluating programs in applied settings through behavioral consultation. *Journal of School Psychology, 16,* 375-386.

Kratochwill, T. R., & Bergan, J. R. (1990). *Behavioral consultation in applied settings: An individual guide.* New York: Plenum Press.

Kurpius, D. J. (1993). Fundamental issues in defining consultation. *Journal of counseling and Development, 71,* 598-600.

Lalli, J. S., Browder, D. M., Mace, F. C., & Brown, D.K. (1993). Teacher use of descriptive analysis data to implement interventions to decrease student's problem behaviors. *Journal of Applied Behavior Analysis, 26,* 227-238.

LaVigna, G. W., Willis, T. J., Schaull, J. F., Abedi, M., & Sweitzer, M. (1994). *The periodic service review: A total quality assurance system for human services and education.* Baltimore, MD: Paul H. Brookes Publishing Co.

Lindsley, O. R. (1996). Is fluency free-operant response-response chaining? *The Behavior Analyst, 19,* 211-224.

Lippitt, G., & Lippitt, R. (1986). *The consulting process in action* (2nd ed.). San Diego CA: University Associates.

MacDonald, M. L. (1983). Behavioral consultation in geriatric settings. *Behavior Therapist, 6,* 172-174.

Mannino, F. V., & Shore, M. F. (1983). Trainee research in consultation: A study of doctoral dissertations. In J. L. Alpert & J. Meyers (Eds.), *Training in consultation: Perspectives from mental health, behavioral and organizational consultation* (pp. 185-202). Springfield, IL: Charles C. Thomas.

Martens, B. K. (1993). A behavioral approach to consultation. In J. E. Zins, T. R. Kratochwill, & S. E. Elliot (Eds.), *Handbook of consultation services for children.* San Francisco: Jossey-Bass.

Martens, B. K., & Witt, J. C. (1988). Expanding the scope of behavioral consultation: A systems approach to classroom behavior change. *Professional School Psychology, 3,* 271-281.

Martin, G. L., & Pear, J. J. (1996). *Behavior modification: What it is and how to do it* (5th Ed.). Englewood Cliffs, NJ: Prentice-Hall.

McGimsey, J. F., Greene, B. F., & Lutzker, J. L. (1995). Competence in aspects of behavioral treatment and consultation: Implications for service delivery and graduate training. *Journal of Applied Behavior Analysis, 28,* 301-315.

Methot, L., Williams, W. L., Cummings, A. R., & Bradshaw, B. (1996). Measuring the effects of a manager-supervisor training program through generalized performance of managers, supervisors, front-line staff and clients in a human service setting. *Journal of Organizational Behavior Management, 16,* 3-34.

Michael, J. (1993). *Concepts and principles of behavior analysis.* Kalamazoo, MI: Society for the Advancement of Behavior Analysis.

Morasky, R. L. (1982). *Behavioral systems.* New York: Praeger Publishing.

Neef, N. A. (1995a). Pyramidal parent training by peers. *Journal of Applied Behavior Analysis, 28,* 333-337.

Neef, N. A. (1995b). Research on training trainers in program implementation: An introduction and future directions. *Journal of Applied Behavior Analysis, 28,* 297-299.

Noell, G. H., & Witt, J. C. (1996). A critical re-evaluation of five fundamental assumptions underlying behavioral consultation. *School Psychology Quarterly, 11*, 189 -203.

Page, T. J., Iwata, B. A., & Reid, D. H. (1982). Pyramidal training: A large-scale application with institutional staff. *Journal of Applied Behavior Analysis, 15*, 335-351.

Parsons, M. B., & Reid, D. H. (1995). Training residential supervisors to provide feedback for maintaining staff teaching skills with people who have severe disabilities. *Journal of Applied Behavior Analysis, 28*, 317-322.

Randolf, D. L. (1972). Behavioral consultation as a means of improving the quality of a counseling program. *The School Counselor, 20*, 30-35.

Redmon, W. K. (1991). Pinpointing the technological fault in applied behaviour analysis. *Journal of Applied Behavior Analysis, 24*, 441-444.

Reid, D. H., Parsons, M. B., & Green, C. W. (1989). *Staff management in human services: Behavioral research and application.* Springfield, IL: Charles C. Thomas.

Repucci, N. D. (1977). Implementation issues for the behavior modifier as institutional change agent. *Behavior Therapy, 8*, 594-605.

Repucci, N.D., & Saunders, J. T. (1974). Social psychology of behavior modification: Problems of implementation in natural settings. *American Psychologist, 29*, 649-660.

Riley, A. E., & Frederiksen, W. (1983). Organizational behavior management in human service settings: Problems and prospects. *The Journal of Organizational Behavior Management, 5*, 3-18.

Rosenfield, S. (1991). The relationship variable in behavioral consultation. *Journal of Behavioral Education, 1*, 3, 329-335.

Shore, B. A., Iwata, B. A., Vollmer, T. R., Lerman, D. C., & Zarcone, J. R. (1995). Pyramidal staff training in the extension of treatment for severe behavior disorders. *Journal of Applied Behavior Analysis, 28*, 323-332.

Sidman, M. (1960). Tactics of scientific research: Evaluating experimental data in psychology. New York: Basic Books.

Twardosz, S. (1984). Behavioral -organizational consultation to day care centers: The process of implementing change. *The Behavior Therapist, 7*, 193-196.

West, J. F., & Idol, L. (1987). School consultation (Part 1): An interdisciplinary perspective on theory, models and research. *Journal of Learning Disabilities, 7*, 388-408.

Williams, W. L. (1995). Dilemmas in the provision of clinical behavior analysis services in community settings: Individual vs organizational variables. In H. Ayala-Velasquez & J. Urbina Soria (Eds.), *Current fields of application in psychology* (pp. 80-104). Mexico City: National Autonomous University of Mexico.

Williams, W. L. (1997, November). *The way we were.* Paper presented at the annual meeting of the Ontario Association for Behavior Analysis. Toronto, Ontario.

Williams, W. L., & Cummings, A. R. (1999). Service review: Increasing consumer benefits by linking service outcome data to direct-care staff service delivery and decision making. In L. J. Hayes, J. Austin, R. Flemming, & R. Houmanfar (Eds.), *Organizational Change*. Reno, NV: Context Press.

Williams, W. L., Feldman, M., Sparks, B., & Drummond, C. (1999). *Evaluation of a behavioral community clinical outreach service for individuals with developmental disability: Effectiveness, consumer satisfaction and clinical management implications.* Manuscript submitted for publication.

Williams, W. L., Lloyd, M. B., Sparks, B., Crozier, K., Stanhope, J., Brown, D., & Hodges, J. (1989, May). *The effects of self recording and reporting of permanent product service data on the quality and quantity of therapist's consultations to agencies for the developmentally delayed.* Poster presented at the 15th annual meeting of the Association for Behavior Analysis, Milwaukee, Wisconsin.

Williams, W. L., & Lloyd, M. B. (1992). The necessity of managerial arrangements for the regular implementation of behavior analysis skills by supervisors and front line staff. *Developmental Disabilities Bulletin, 20,* 31-62.

Williams, W. L., & Murray, P. (1993, May). *Service review: A management procedure for establishing decision-making under control of service outcome data.* Paper presented at the 19th Annual Association for Behavior Analysis Conference, Chicago, IL.

Witt, J. C., & Elliott, S. N. (1983). Assessment in behavioral consultation: The initial interview. *School Psychology Review, 12,* 1, 42-49.

Wu, B., & Williams, W. L. (1990, May). Trends and a descriptive summary of thirty years of behavioral staff training research. In W. L. Williams (Chair) *Behavioral technology applied to community services for the developmentally delayed.* Symposium conducted at the Annual Meeting of the Association for Behavior Analysis, Nashville, TN.

Vernberg , E. M., & Repucci, N. D. (1986). Behavioral consultation. In F. V. Mannino, E. J. Trickett, M. F. Shore, M. G. Kidder, & G., Levin (Eds.), *Handbook of mental health consultation* (pp. 49-80). Washington, DC: National Institute of Mental Health.

Chapter 17

Behavioral Sport Psychology

Garry L. Martin and Gregg A. Tkachuk
University of Manitoba

Behavioral sport psychology involves the use of behavior analysis principles and techniques to enhance the performance and satisfaction of athletes and others associated with sports. In this chapter, we discuss research and applications in behavioral sport psychology, suggest several ways in which a behavioral approach can enhance more mainstream work in sport psychology, describe some of our own recent involvement in this area, and outline several areas for future study.

Origins and Early Development of Behavioral Sport Psychology

Behavioral sport psychology was launched by Brent Rushall and Daryl Siedentop in 1972 with the publication of their book, *The development and control of behavior in sport and physical education*. Written within an operant framework, their book contains numerous practical strategies for shaping new sport skills, maintaining existing skills at high levels, and generalizing practice skills to competitive settings. The first published research in this area appeared three years earlier when Rushall and Pettinger (1969) described their comparison of several different reinforcement contingencies on the amount of swimming performed by members of an age-group swimming team. Since 1972, Rushall has concentrated mainly on sport (e.g., see Rushall, 1992), first at Dalhousie University and Lakehead University in Canada, and more recently at San Diego State University. Siedentop, on the other hand, while at Ohio State University, pioneered the first behavior analysis research program in physical education (e.g., see Siedentop, 1980). Also, beginning in the 1970s, Ron Smith and Frank Smoll at University of Washington conducted behavioral assessments and interventions in youth sports (for a review, see Smith, Smoll, & Christensen, 1996). Rushall, Siedentop, Smith, and Smoll have provided exemplary leadership for behaviorally-oriented sport psychologists.

During the 1970s and the early '80s, publications in behavioral sport psychology included application guidelines for coaches (e.g., Smoll, Smith, & Curtis, 1978), case histories with before and after data (e.g., Martin, LePage, & Koop, 1983), research using single-subject designs (e.g., McKenzie & Rushall, 1974), and a book that offered an insightful Skinnerian analysis of the contingencies that both promote and deter participation in sports (Dickinson, 1977). Unpublished papers and theses and published reports prior to 1980 were reviewed by Donahue, Gillis, and King (1980), and many of the early studies were contained in a book of readings prepared by Martin and Hrycaiko (1983). A review of applied behavior analysis in sport and physical education during the 1970s and '80s was presented by Martin (1992a). Many of those studies, as well as many of the behavioral studies in sport psychology since that time, are described in the book, *Sport psychology consulting: Practical guidelines from behavior analysis* (Martin, 1997).

Published Research in Behavioral Sport Psychology

Table 1 presents a summary of published research articles in behavioral sport psychology. Articles were included if they conformed to all of the following requirements: (a) use of a single-subject research design; (b) presentation of individual data across observation sessions (vs. just pre-post assessments); (c) reporting of acceptable interobserver reliability data on the dependent measures (or "game statistics" data on objective measures such as free throws made in basketball); and (d) a clear demonstration of a treatment effect.

As can be seen in Table 1, ten studies demonstrated that behavioral interventions applied by coaches and/or researchers were more effective than "standard coaching" for improving a variety of performance measures at practices in a variety of sports. Only one of the studies (Komaki & Barnett, 1977) examined generalization of improved performance from practices to games, and the results were very positive.

Eight studies examined self-management interventions to improve practice performance. These studies fall under three general categories: (a) goal setting, self-monitoring, and feedback to increase the frequency of previously learned skills (Hume, Martin, Gonzalez, Cracklen, & Genthon, 1985; McKenzie & Rushall, 1974; Wanlin, Hrycaiko, Martin, & Mahon, 1997; Wolko, Hrycaiko, & Martin, 1993); (b) stimulus cueing and discrimination training to enhance skill acquisition (Osborne, Rudrud, & Zezoney, 1990; Ziegler, 1987, 1994); and (c) self-talk training to enhance skill acquisition (Ming & Martin, 1996). Only one of the studies (Wanlin et al., 1997) in the self-management category examined generalization of improved practice performance to competitions, and the results were positive for all subjects.

Finally, as indicated in Table 1, two studies (Hamilton & Fremouw, 1985; Kendall, Hrycaiko, Martin, & Kendall, 1990) examined interventions with the primary dependent variable being a measure of competitive performance, and one study (Rushall & Smith, 1979) focused on changing the behavior of a coach.

Collectively, these studies demonstrate the potential of applied behavior analysis for improving a variety of athletic behaviors in a variety of sports and settings. However, several limitations should be noted. First, although the interventions in most cases were described in sufficient detail so that they could be replicated by behaviorally-trained individuals, fewer than half of the studies contained formal procedural reliability assessments of the interventions. Second, very few of the studies have monitored competitive performance as the primary dependent measure. Third, fewer than half of the studies included formal social validity assessments to examine how the athletes felt about the target behaviors, the procedures that were used, and the results that were obtained. Future studies need to rectify these deficits.

In addition to the published research listed in Table 1, there are other studies that, although they did not meet the criteria for inclusion in Table 1, would

Table 1. Summary of Behavioral Sport Psychology Literature.

Study	Participants	Sport-Specific Target Behaviors	Design	Intervention	Percent Change From Baseline[**]
Behavioral Coaching vs. Standard Coaching to Improve Practice Performance					
Komaki & Barnett (1977)	9 male youth football players	3 Offensive plays: Option, Sweep, Counter	Multiple-baseline across plays	Instructions and reinforcement	32%, 51%, 22%
Allison & Ayllon (1980)	5 male youth football players	Offensive blocking	Multiple-baseline across 4 players and ABAB (1 Player)	Instructions, freeze technique, feedback, and modeling	Tenfold; 50%
	6 female youth gymnasts	Backward walkover, front handspring, reverse kip	Multiple-baseline across skills and gymnasts with reversals	Instructions, freeze technique, feedback, and modeling	30-60%
	12 male & female adult novice tennis players	Forehand, backhand, serve	Multiple-baseline across skills and individuals	Instructions, freeze technique, feedback, and modeling	30-50%
Buzas & Ayllon (1981)	3 female youth tennis players	Forehand, backhand, serve	Multiple-baseline across individuals and skills	Differential reinforcement	150-450%
McKenzie & Liskevych (1983)	6 female college volleyball players	Service reception	Multi-element baseline	Monetary reinforcementor private instruction	Private (26%)> Baseline; Money (-75%)< Baseline

Study	Participants	Skills	Design	Intervention	Results
Koop & Martin (1983)	3 female and 2 male youth swimmers	Freestyle stroke, backstroke	Multiple-baseline across swimmers and skills, with follow-up	Instruction, prompting, modeling, reinforcement	50-75% reduction in stroke errors
Fitterling & Ayllon (1983)	4 female youth ballet students battement	Degage, frappe, developpe, grand	Multiple-baseline across skills with reversals	Reinforcement, , instruction, modeling, physical guidance freeze technique	50-80%
Rush & Ayllon (1984)	9 male youth soccer players	Heading, throw-ins, goal kicks	Multiple-baseline across players, reversal, changing criterion	Peer reinforcement, instructions, modeling, freeze technique	50-60%
Shapiro & Shapiro (1985)	1 male and 2 female youth track athletes	Conditioning, form, starts	Multiple-probe across skills	Reinforcement, instructions, modeling, freeze technique	50% 40% 60%
Hazen et al. (1990)	1 male and 6 female youth swimmers	Freestyle flip turn, backstroke spin turn	Multiple-baseline across swimmers	Videotaping feedback package	20-28.6%, 14-300%
	1 male and 5 female youth swimmers	Freestyle swim component	Multiple-baseline across swimmers (AB replication)	Videotaping feedback package	1500%
Hume & Crossman (1992)	6 male and female youth swimmers	Productive behaviors during practice	ABAB reversal	Musical reinforcement	150%

Self-Management Interventions to Improve Practice Performance

Study	Participants	Behavior measured	Design	Intervention	Results
McKenzie & Rushall (1974)	4 male and 4 female youth swimmers	Number of laps completed	ABAB reversal	Instructions and public self-recording	20-34%
Hume et al. (1985)	3 female youth figure skaters	Number of jumps and spins attempted	ABAB reversal	Instructions, public-self-monitoring, and coach feedback	83%
Wolko et al. (1993)	5 female youth gymnasts	Number of balance beam skills attempted and completed	Multi-element alternating treatments	Public vs. private self-recording	Private> Public attempts 22% Completes 15%
Ziegler (1987)	14 female and 10 male college volunteers	Number of successful forehand and backhand returns	Multiple-baseline across groups (individual data presented)	Stimulus cueing strategy	196-220%
Osborne et al. (1990)	5 male college baseball players	Number of "well-hit" curve balls	Alternating treatments	Marked vs. unmarked seams	Marked> Unmarked 5-10%
Ziegler (1994)	4 male college soccer players	4 soccer drills	Multiple-baseline across players	Information, attentional drills	133%
Ming & Martin (1996)	3 female and 1 male youth figure skaters	Correctness of traced figures	Multi-element with multiple-baseline replications	Self-talk package	12-33%

Study	Subjects	Target behavior	Design	Intervention	Results
Wanlin et al. (1997)	4 female youth speed skaters	Number of laps and drills completed; 500m race times	Multiple-baseline across skaters	Goal setting, self-monitoring, self-talk, imagery	Laps 73%, Drills, 15% Races 1.27- 8.08 secs
Interventions to Improve Competitive Performance					
Hamilton & Fremouw (1985)	3 male college basketball players	Free-throw percentage	Multiple-baseline across players	Relaxation, self-talk, mental rehearsal	50-88%
Kendall et al. (1990)	4 female college basketball players	Correct execution of a defensive skill	Multiple-baseline across players	Mental rehearsal, relaxation, self-talk	33%
Changing the Behavior of Coaches					
Rushall & Smith (1979)	1 male age-group swimming coach	Rates of reinforcement, feedback, and reinforcement feedback	Multiple-baseline across behaviors	Self-recording techniques, fading	51-285%

**Note: Unusually large percentage improvements are a result of zero or near-zero rates of baseline target behavior.

nevertheless be of interest to behaviorally-oriented researchers. An important series of studies was conducted by Ron Smith and Frank Smoll and their colleagues at the University of Washington, concerning the assessment and modification of behaviors of Little League baseball coaches. This group has developed a reliable assessment tool called the *Coaching Behavior Assessment System* (CBAS), and have developed a coach effectiveness training program for youth coaches (for a review, see Smith et al., 1996). Other behavioral observation studies have reported that coaches in many sports generally show low rates of positive reinforcement (McKenzie & King, 1982; Rushall, 1977, 1981), and that players of more successful coaches received significantly more of several types of interactions than players of less successful coaches (Claxton, 1988; Marklund & Martinek, 1988). Finally, there are other studies in sport psychology journals (listed later) that are likely to be of interest to behaviorally-oriented researchers, although they did not meet all of the criteria for inclusion in Table 1.

Examples of Mainstream Work in Sport Psychology, and Suggestions for How it might be Enhanced Via a Behavioral Approach

During the past 30 years, mainstream sport psychology has been inching towards professional status. During the 1960s, the International Society of Sport Psychology (1965-), the North American Society for the Psychology of Sport and Physical Activity (1967-), and the Canadian Society for Psychomotor Learning and Sport Psychology (1969-) were established. Since the late 1970s, sport psychology has experienced considerable growth in North America, as evidenced by the development of three journals (*Journal of Sport Psychology*, now called *Journal of Sport and Exercise Psychology*, 1979-; *The Sport Psychologist*, 1986-; and *Journal of Applied Sport Psychology*, 1989-), the appearance of sport psychology articles in other journals (e.g., *Behavior Modification*, *Journal of Applied Behavior Analysis*, *Journal of Sport Behavior*), the publication of numerous books, frequent national and international conferences, the establishment of Sport and Exercise Psychology as Division 47 of the American Psychological Association (APA, 1987-), and the establishment of the Association for the Advancement of Applied Sport Psychology (AAASP, 1986). AAASP is dedicated to the development and professionalization of the field of sport psychology and, in 1997, comprised over 800 professional and student members working in both academic and private settings. Clearly, mainstream sport psychology has come of age. Sport and exercise psychology are frequently combined, as indicated by the title of Division 47 of APA, the title of one of the three sport psychology journals cited above, and the titles of two recent books (Weinberg & Gould, 1995; Van Raalte & Brewer, 1996). Major topic areas include motor learning and skill development, motivation of practice performance and endurance training, leadership and group and team dynamics, mental training for performance enhancement, promoting regular exercise and physical well-being, and psychological issues in specialty areas such as drug abuse, burnout, recovery from injury, aggression, and gender differences in sports. Because of the voluminous literature in these areas, we'll focus just on mental training for performance enhancement. In mainstream sport psychology, mental training (also referred to as psychological skills training) includes (among other things) goal setting, self-talk regulation and imagery rehearsal/visualization. We'll summarize some mainstream research in these areas, and indicate how a behavioral approach might be of value.

Goal-Setting

One of the most well-researched areas in mainstream sport psychology involves goal setting to improve athletic performance (Weinberg, 1994; 1996). In general, a goal describes a level of performance (such as doing 20 push-ups) or an outcome (such as lowering one's time in the 800 meters run by three seconds) toward which an individual should work. A number of between-group studies have indicated that goal setting by athletes is likely to enhance athletic performance. But some results have been equivocal (for reviews, see Burton, 1992; Weinberg, 1994). Weinberg (1994) suggested that some of the inconsistent findings might be attributable to methodological and design considerations such as spontaneous goal setting in control groups to enhance their performance to approximate that of experimental goal setting groups, differences in subject motivation and commitment, and spontaneous competition arising among subjects in the various experiments. While such variables may have affected the outcome of some of the mainstream studies, a behavioral interpretation of goal setting may help to clarify conditions under which goal setting will be effective from those where it is likely to be ineffective.

From a behavioral perspective, goals capitalize on rule-governed control over behavior (Martin, 1997). A rule is a statement that a particular behavior will pay off in a particular situation. A goal typically identifies or implies specific behavior to be performed, the circumstances in which the behavior should occur, and consequences for performing it. For example, if a basketball player says, "I'll practice shooting foul shots until I can make 10 in a row," that player has identified the circumstances (practicing foul shots), the behavior (making 10 in a row), and although the reinforcer is not stated, it is certainly implied (then I'll be a better basketball player and will likely score a higher percentage of foul shots in games). If we conceptualize goals as rules, then an obvious question is: Under what conditions are rules likely to be effective? Rules that describe deadlines for specific behavior that will lead to sizeable and probable outcomes are often effective, even when the outcomes are delayed (Malott, 1989; 1992). On the other hand, rules that describe behavior vaguely, do not identify a deadline for the behavior, and that lead to small or improbable consequences for the behavior are often ineffective. With this analysis in mind, Martin (1997) suggested a summary of guidelines for effective goal setting for influencing athletic behavior (see Table 2). Incorporation of these guidelines in goal setting studies in sports might enhance the efficacy of goal setting interventions.

Self-Talk Regulation

Imagine the thoughts of a young figure skater just before she will step on the ice to skate her program in an important competition. Suppose that the skater thinks, "I hope I don't fall on my double axle. I hope I don't come in last." Are those thoughts likely to elicit some anxiety? And might that anxiety interfere with the skater's performance? Probably yes. On the other hand, suppose that, just before stepping on the ice, the skater repeats to herself, "I've landed all my jumps in practice and I can land them here. I'll focus on the things that I do when I'm skating well, and I'll take it one step at a time." Are these latter thoughts likely to prompt the skater to focus on the sorts of things that she typically focused on when skating well at a practice? And will thoughts of those practice cues enhance transfer of performance from practice to competition? Probably yes.

Much of our thinking is made up of things that we say to ourselves - called self-talk. An important part of mental training in mainstream sport psychology involves teaching athletes to use their self-talk to enhance skill acquisition, change bad habits, improve concentration, enhance self-confidence, and build self-efficacy (Bunker, Williams, & Zinsser, 1993; Williams & Leffingwell, 1996). However, in most cases, supportive research is based on questionnaire studies of athletes (e.g., Orlick & Partington, 1988).

Can a behavioral analysis improve the effectiveness of self-talk interventions? We believe that it can. The first step for improving self-talk interventions would be to carefully analyze the functions that the self-talk is expected to serve. There is evidence, for example, that self-talk can function as a conditioned stimulus (CS) to elicit respondent components of emotions (Staats, 1968; Staats, Staats, & Crawford, 1962). Thus, if a goal is to help a young gymnast feel relaxed just before performing, the psychologist might follow guidelines for respondent conditioning of self-talk as a CS for relaxation (Martin, 1997). We know, for example, that a CS acquires a greater ability to elicit a conditioned response if the CS is always paired with a given unconditioned stimulus (US) than if it is only occasionally paired with the US. Now consider a gymnast who spends two minutes each day practicing a breathing technique that elicits relaxation. Let's suppose that, each time the gymnast exhales while deep center breathing, she repeats the word "e-a-s-y" slowly to herself. After several days, simply reciting the word, "e-a-s-y" will elicit the feelings of relaxation normally elicited by deep center breathing. The gymnast could then recite this word just before performing at a competition to help herself to relax. On the other hand, if, during training, the gymnast had said, "e-a-s-y" on some instances of deep center breathing, but not on others, then saying "e-a-s-y" would be a weaker CS for relaxation.

Another example of how a behavioral analysis might facilitate interventions in this area concerns the problem of transferring learned skills from practices to competitions. Behavioral researchers have identified a number of strategies for programming generalization (Martin & Pear, 1996). One such strategy is programming common stimuli between the training setting and the generalization setting. If athletic performance occurs to a specific stimulus in practice, and if that stimulus can be introduced into a competition, then the likelihood of stimulus generalization to the competitive environment is increased. One way of programming common stimuli would be for an athlete to bring skilled performance under the control of self-talk at practices, and then to rehearse that self-talk just before performing the skill at competitions. Hamilton and Fremouw (1985), for example, described the case of a 20-year-old sophomore college basketball player. In practices, he rarely missed a foul shot. But during games, his foul shooting percentage was less than 40%. Obviously, the problem was not one of skill development, rather it was a problem of transferring a previously learned skill from practices to games. To solve the problem, the player consistently rehearsed specific self-talk and followed a consistent preshot routine just before foul shooting at practices. After using this strategy consistently across several practices, he then used it in games. His foul shooting in games improved to approximately 70%.

In summary, self-talk to control emotions or mood capitalizes on words as CSs to elicit respondent components of emotions. Self-talk to enhance transfer of previously learned skills from practices to competitions can be viewed as programming common stimuli. In a later section, we suggest that self-talk to aid skill development can be analyzed in terms of rule-governed control over behavior. Identifying the intended function of the self-talk, and applying an appropriate behavioral strategy to enhance that function should aid the sport psychologist in improving the effectiveness of his/her advice to athletes.

Imagery Rehearsal/Visualization

Imagery or mental rehearsal refers to the process of imagining and feeling oneself performing an activity. In a survey of 235 Canadian Olympic athletes, 99% claimed to use mental rehearsal to enhance performance (Orlick & Partington, 1988). The majority of mainstream experimental studies on mental imagery and athletic performance can be categorized into three main areas (Gould & Damarjian, 1996; Murphy, 1994): (a) studies of mental practice to improve acquisition of skills at practices; (b) studies of imagery as part of a preperformance routine to improve performance of a previously learned skill; and (c) mediating variables studies. In a comprehensive review of mental practice to improve skills, Weinberg (1981) concluded that mental plus physical practice was better than physical practice alone, which was better than mental practice alone, which was better than no practice. In a review of studies of imagery as part of a preperformance routine just before performing that skill or activity, Tkachuk and Martin (1997) concluded that imagery combined with other preperformance activities improved performance across several analogue and sport tasks, but that imagery alone provided inconsistent or no effects on analogue leg strength tasks, basketball free throw, golf putting, or tennis serving and ground stroke performance. Finally, concerning mediating variables studies, several studies have reported that more successful athletes have higher quality of imagery than less successful athletes, that imagining oneself performing successfully is better than imagining negative results, and that results are equivocal in terms of whether or not it's better to encourage athletes to feel themselves performing or if it's better to encourage athletes to imagine that they are watching themselves performing (Gould & Damarjian, 1996).

How can a behavioral analysis of this area be helpful? First, it may be worthwhile to distinguish between respondent imagery and operant imagery. Consider an example of respondent imagery. If you are told to close your eyes and imagine a clear blue sky, you are probably able to do so. As you grew up, you experienced many trials in which the words "blue sky" were paired with actually looking at and seeing a blue sky. As a result, when you close your eyes and imagine that you are looking at a blue sky, you experience the behavior of "seeing" the actual scene. This has been referred to as "conditioned seeing" (Skinner, 1953). But what about the process of imagining yourself performing some action? That is, rather than "seeing" yourself perform a skill, you might "feel" yourself perform it. Our motor movements involving our skeletal muscles are learned through operant conditioning. One type of internal stimulation generated from movement is referred to as proprioceptive stimuli (also referred to as kinesthetic sensations), which are internal stimuli generated by the position and movement of the body in space, and by the position and movement of parts of the body with respect to other parts. Learning to be responsive to proprioceptive cues is a part of the process of becoming aware of our body positions and movements. For example, if we ask you to close your eyes and raise your left arm to shoulder level, you would be able to do so because you have learned to respond to the proprioceptive cues that are generated when your arm is moved to that position. If we then ask you to close your eyes and to simply imagine raising your left arm to shoulder level, and to try to recapture the feelings as though you were actually performing that act, you would likely be able to do so. Presumably, such covert operant behavior is similar, in terms of its controlling variables, to the behavior of overtly moving your arm to that position (Skinner, 1953).

Now let's reconsider some of the earlier findings concerning imagery rehearsal. Respondent imagery might be useful at practices to simulate the competitive environment. A figure skater practicing in an empty rink, for example, might visualize where the judges will be sitting, where the coach will be standing, and an ice rink full of spectators. Successfully landing certain jumps after visualizing such stimuli might increase the likelihood that the skater will land those jumps in the presence of those actual stimuli at competitions. This is an approximation of the generalization strategy of programming common stimuli. Now consider an instance of mental rehearsal as part of a preperformance routine for a diver just before executing a dive. Her rehearsal is likely to include both respondent and operant imagery. First, she might imagine what she will see as she walks to the end of the diving board (respondent imagery), she might imagine herself experiencing the proprioceptive cues from raising her arms and jumping on the board (operant imagery), she might recall the "feelings" of the proper tuck (operant imagery), and so forth. Analyzing an instance of mental rehearsal in this way should increase the likelihood that all of the senses that are typically used while actually performing the skill will be mentally rehearsed, and should enable researchers to improve the consistency of interventions for examining such activities.

Recent Research Involvement of the Authors in Behavioral Sport Psychology

Planned Self-Talk to Aid Skill Acquisition

Bunker et al. (1993) suggested that, "Simple cues such as 'step, swing' in tennis, 'step, drop, step, kick' for a soccer kick, and 'arms straight, elbows in' for the golf address are designed to foster cognitive associations that will aid the athlete in learning proper physical execution" (p. 227). From a behavioral perspective, such words would function as a partial rule to prompt appropriate body position and movement, and the behavior cued by the partial rule would be rule governed (Martin & Pear, 1996). The full rule might be, "If I tuck my elbows in and swing with a full shoulder turn, then I'm more likely to get a good hit." Some studies that have experimentally assessed the effects of such self-talk on skill acquisition have yielded positive results (Hill & Borden, 1995; Landin & MacDonald, 1990; Ziegler, 1987). Ziegler (1987), for example, demonstrated that attention-focusing self-talk with beginning tennis players enhanced acquisition of forehand and backhand returns of balls shot from a ball projection machine. Two studies (Meyers, Schleser, Cooke, & Cuvillier, 1979; Palmer, 1992) that examined the effects of self-instructions on skill development, however, yielded negative results. However, these latter two studies used pretest-posttest assessments rather than continuous monitoring across sessions, and they did not include procedural reliability assessments of the extent to which the participants actually utilized the self-talk. Also, in the Palmer study, there were no interobserver reliability assessments on the dependent measure.

In one of our studies (Ming & Martin, 1996), Siri Ming examined a self-talk package to improve skill acquisition of compulsory figures by young figure skaters. During a typical figures practice, a skater would attempt to skate a particular figure (such as a figure 8) on the ice with perfectly concentric circles, and would further attempt to trace that figure exactly several times. During a typical practice, subjects practiced each of two figures for approximately 15 minutes each. Objective data collection was made possible by asking a skater to move to a clean patch of ice, and to perform that figure in the presence of observers. When the figure was completed, the observers obtained a score by carefully examining the tracing left on the ice. The final scoring system included 27 different components that assessed aspects of the symmetry of the circles and the quality of turns on the figure that was traced; and that yielded a single score for the entire figure in terms of percent correct.

During an initial baseline phase with each participant, two figures were assessed across several practices. A participant was then trained to utilize a self-talk package for one of the two figures, and was encouraged to practice the other figure as they normally did. One advantage of this type of multi-element design is that, because of the ongoing comparison between the treated and untreated behaviors, it can be used with behaviors that occur at unstable rates (Hrycaiko & Martin, 1996). To learn to use self-talk, a skater:

1. Viewed part 1 of a videotape (Martin, 1989), which portrays national-level figure skaters using key words while performing their figures on the ice, and while walking out their figures off the ice during a simulation.

2. Developed key words for the treated figure as described by Martin (1992b) by:

a) drawing out the targeted figure on a piece of paper;

b) writing in key words at particular points on the drawing to help the skater to skate the figure (for example, a skater might say, "check shoulders" to herself just after a change from a backward to a forward position to remind herself to have her shoulders in the correct position);

c) reviewing and adjusting the key words with the coach;

d) memorizing the key words.

3. Did off-ice walkouts of the figure (as portrayed in Martin, 1989) twice per week in the presence of Siri Ming, in which the skater said the key words out loud while "feeling" the correct movements.

4. Said the key words out loud while practicing the figure on the ice.

5. Said key words out loud while performing the treated figure on the ice during data collection sessions.

For each of the four participants, the self-talk package led to an increase in performance of the treated figure, whereas the untreated figure remained relatively stable across practices. The results for Participants 1 and 2 are presented in Figure 1. Participant 1 improved on the treated figure from a mean of 44% during baseline to a mean of 58% during treatment, for an increase of 14 percentage points and a 32% improvement over baseline. Participant 2 improved on the treated figure from a mean of 58% to a mean of 65%, yielding an increase of 7 percentage points and a 12% improvement over baseline. The results were obtained regardless of whether baseline performance of the treated figure was lower than the control figure (Participant 1) or higher than the control figure (Participant 2). Also, Participants 1 and 2 had the same figures, but they were counterbalanced in terms of the figure that was treated vs. the figure that served as a control. The results were also independent of the length of baseline and treatment phases. Self-report follow-up at one year indicated that the participants continued to use the self-talk during practices, and that they believed that it enhanced their test and/or competitive performance. These results support the view that planned self-talk can aid skill acquisition.

Goal Setting to Improve Practice and Competitive Performance

Studies that have examined goal setting interventions for improving athletic performance have typically involved between-group comparisons of the perfor-mance of subjects who set goals with the performance of various control groups, the results of such studies have been equivocal, and many of the studies suffer from a number of methodological problems (Weinberg, 1994). In order to investigate goal setting for improving individual athletic performance, Connie Wanlin examined

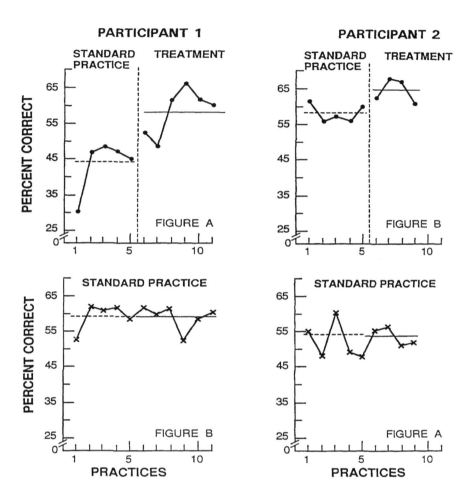

Figure 1. Percent correct performance for figures across practices for Participants 1 and 2. (From "Single-subect evaluation of a self-talk package for improving figure skating performance" by Siri Ming and Garry L. Martin, The Sport Psychologist, 10, 227-238.)

the effectiveness of a goal setting package on objective and subjective measures of speed skating performance in a multiple-baseline design across subjects (Wanlin, et al., 1997).

The participants were four female speed skaters ranging in age from 12 to 17 years who were preparing for the Canada Winter Games. The skaters were selected for study based on the coach's recommendation that they had a high level of off-task behaviors at practices, and were not performing well in races. Dependent variables included the number of laps completed and the frequency of off-task behaviors at practices. The intervention included guidelines for skaters to develop a mission statement, to set long-term goals, to set weekly goals, to use self-talk and visualization to achieve goals, and to record results from daily practices in log books. An additional part of the intervention included individual weekly meetings with Connie in order to check the log books and to prompt the skaters to meet their weekly goals.

The effect of the intervention on laps completed at practices is presented in Figure 2. The goal setting package led to improved performance in all three subjects who experienced it. All three subjects also showed a decrease in off-task behavior, and improved racing times in time trials at practices and during competitions. A social validity assessment provided further support for the effectiveness of the intervention. Also, at the Canada Winter Games, of the skaters who represented Manitoba, the three participants of the study were the most successful.

Sport-Specific Behavioral Checklists

Suppose that you are a behaviorally-oriented sport psychology consultant, and an athlete has asked you for help. One of your first concerns will be to clarify the nature of the problem and identify some target behaviors. If you are a practitioner in private practice, it's unlikely that you and the client will have the time and resources to take extensive baseline observations at several practices and/or competitions. An alternative to direct observation procedures practiced by some behavior therapists has been the use of self-report behavioral checklists (Martin & Pear, 1996). Recently, we developed such behavioral checklists for 21 different sports (Martin, Toogood, & Tkachuk, 1997).

A *sport-specific behavioral checklist* lists, for a particular sport, performance aspects of practices and competitions that an athlete can easily check off or identify in order to provide a quick, convenient, and yet reasonably thorough assessment of those areas in which the athlete would like some help. Such checklists are individualized in the sense that any given checklist would contain items and examples for one specific sport. The jargon in such a checklist reflects the "language" of the sport, and is meant to be user-friendly for athletes (see Figure 3). Consequently, it is often nonbehavioral. Nevertheless, the items in such a checklist can be analyzed behaviorally (Martin, 1997). The goal of such an assessment is to help the athlete select a few areas for which specific target behaviors and goals for improvement can subsequently be identified. In an evaluation of the checklist for swimmers (see Figure 3) with a male and a female university swim team, and a male and a female competitive youth swim team, the checklist was found to have high test-retest reliability, high face validity, and was considered a very useful tool by the coaches and swimmers for identifying areas for improvement (Lines, Tkachuk, & Martin, 1997).

Individualized sport-specific checklists have a number of benefits. Their use of examples for a particular sport gives them face validity with athletes in that sport. They can be completed by the athlete as a homework assignment, saving both time and money. Some athletes who are initially reluctant to discuss their needs may find completion of a sport-specific questionnaire to be somewhat less threatening. Moreover, with the athlete's permission, a questionnaire concerning an athlete's needs could

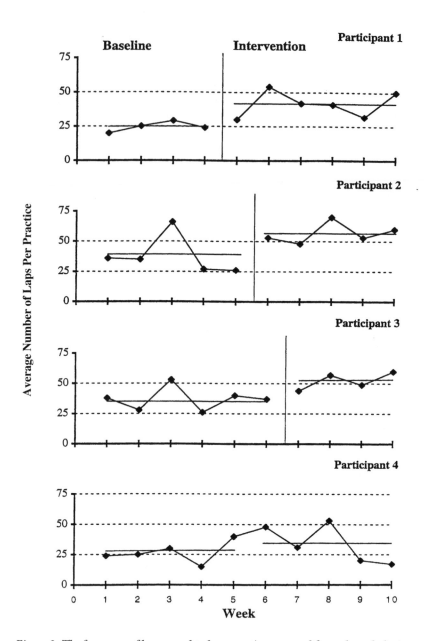

Figure 2. The frequency of laps completed per practice averaged for each week during baseline and intervention phases.
(From "The effects of a goal setting package on the performance of speed skaters" by Connie Wanlin, Dennis Hrycaiko, Garry L. Martin, & Michael Mahon, 1997, Journal of Applied Sport Psychology)

SPORT PSYCHOLOGY QUESTIONNAIRE FOR SWIMMERS

This questionnaire was designed to help you to identify areas in which you would like some help and/or need to improve. All the information will be kept confidential.

Name: _____   Date: _____

COMPETITION Would you say that, just before or during a meet, you need to improve at:	Not Sure	Definitely Don't Need to Improve	Somewhat	Definitely Need to Improve	Check here if you would like help to improve
1. Thinking positive thoughts? *(e.g., "I know I can hit the splits I'm going for", "I'm going for a best time", etc.)*	___	1	2	3	4	5	
2. Tuning out negative thoughts? *(e.g., "I hope I don't come in last", "These swimmers are really fast", etc.)*	___	1	2	3	4	5	
3. Staying loose and not getting too nervous: a) just before a race? b) in pressure situations?	___ ___	1 1	2 2	3 3	4 4	5 5	
4. Maintaining/regaining your confidence in difficult situations? *(e.g., you have a bad start/split, you're behind, you feel really nervous, etc.)*	___	1	2	3	4	5	
5. Maintaining your concentration during a race? *(e.g., focusing on technique, concentrating on turns, etc.)*	___	1	2	3	4	5	
6. Blocking out distractors over which you have no control? *(e.g., the time of day of your race, who you're competing against, etc.)*	___	1	2	3	4	5	
7. Refocusing after you get distracted for any reason? *(e.g., while waiting behind the blocks during the heat before yours, a competitor invades your space, etc.)*	___	1	2	3	4	5	
8. Setting challenging yet attainable goals for each meet?	___	1	2	3	4	5	

Figure 3. A sample of questions from "A Sport Psychology Questionnaire for Swimmers." The complete questionnaire includes 20 items for improving at practices. (From "Behavioral Assessment Forms for Sport Psychology Consulting" by Garry L. Martin, S. Adrienne Toogood, & Gregg A. Tkachuk, 1997, pp. 80-81. Copyright© 1996 by Sport Science Press. Reprinted by permission)

be completed by the athlete, the coach, and perhaps a parent, in order to provide multiple perspectives on potential problems (e.g., see Martin & Toogood, 1997).

Three Areas in which there is Importance and Opportunity for Future Study

Can Self-Talk Improve Generalization from Practices to Competitions?

As indicated by the preceding review of published studies in behavioral sport psychology, a number of studies have demonstrated, using single-subject designs, the effectiveness of various interventions for improving practice performance. However, only two studies (Hamilton & Fremouw, 1985; Kendall et al., 1990) used a measure of competitive performance as the main dependent variable. Both studies included self-talk as part of an intervention package. But neither study clarified the nature of the self-talk that may have contributed to the effectiveness of the intervention. In both studies, the athletes could perform the sport behaviors at a particular level in practices, but did not consistently perform them at that level during competitions. Examples of sport situations where this might occur could involve shooting free throws in basketball, getting first serves in in tennis, keeping a drive on the first fairway in golf, landing certain jumps in a figure skating program or certain moves in a gymnastics routine, hitting the target in archery, pitching in the strike zone in baseball, and performing certain dives in diving. A strategy for helping athletes in such situations might involve programming common stimuli using self-talk. That is, if successful performance can be brought under the control of certain types of self-talk at practice, and if that self-talk is rehearsed in the competitive situation, then the desired athletic performance might more likely generalize from practices to competitions. But what type of self-talk might be most effective: Mood words to elicit respondent components of emotions? Key words or partial rules to prompt particular body positions or attending behavior? Words that increase the likelihood that the skill will occur as a contingency-shaped rather than a rule-governed behavior? Some mixture of these options? Future research might examine these possibilities.

Do Preperformance Routines Enhance Competitive Performance?

A preperformance routine consists of any combination of covert and overt behaviors engaged in immediately prior to the performance of a closed skill or intermittent activity for the purposes of enhancing performance in that skill or activity. Examples of such activities for which preperformance routines are used include serving and receiving in racquet sports and volleyball, basketball free throws, hockey face-offs, penalty shots in a variety of sports, figure skating routines, baton twirling, target shooting, archery, gymnastics routines, diving, and bowling. Components of preperformance routines used by athletes include focusing on specific cues, imagery rehearsal of a skill, use of various types of self-talk, preparatory physiological arousal, and relaxation techniques.

A recent review (Tkachuk & Martin, 1997) indicates that certain preperformance activities are effective in enhancing the performance of analogue tasks, as well as sport tasks in laboratory and practice settings. However, attempts to teach novice and elite competitors to use preperformance routines in competitions have not consistently improved competitive performance of those athletes. Considering the positive effects of preperformance routines on analogue tasks and in practice settings, and considering that olympic-level athletes endorse the value of preperformance routines in questionnaire studies (Orlick & Partington, 1988), future research on preperformance routines during competitions might profitably proceed through several phases. First, the observational methodologies used by Crews and Boutcher (1986), and Southard and Amos (1996), along with video-enhanced recall of elite performers' private behaviors and feelings prior to, and during competitive performances might be used to analyze the preperformance routines of highly successful athletes. Second, such components might then be analyzed behaviorally to identify the operant and respondent behaviors that are involved, and to clarify their probable effects on subsequent athletic performance. Third, intervention studies examining the effects of multiple-component preperformance routines on skilled performance in practice settings could then be conducted. Fourth, if found to be effective in influencing practice performance, then intervention studies of multiple-component preperformance routines could be conducted for improving sport skills in competitive situations. Finally, component analyses designed to reveal the most effective ingredients of the various preperformance routines could be conducted.

Are Seasonal "Mental Training" Programs for Athletes Effective?

Martin and Toogood (1997) described a seasonal psychological skills training program for competitive figure skaters. Strategies included use of self-report behavioral checklists to identify areas in need of improvement at the beginning of the season, a variety of goal setting, self-monitoring and feedback strategies to improve practice performance during the season, and on-site competition strategies to maximize competitive performance. A consumer evaluation of the program by the skaters, their coaches, and their parents was very positive. However, pressure from coaches and parents to make the program available at the start of the season for all skaters precluded the possibility of studying the program in a multiple-baseline design across subjects. Although there have been several published evaluations of other seasonal psychological skills programs, including programs for the U.S. national archery team (Landers, Boutcher, & Wang, 1981), a major college football team (Fenker & Lambiotte, 1987), a university tennis team (Daw & Burton, 1994), the Western Australia cricket team (Gordon, 1990), and a group of competitive skiers in grades 8 to 12 (Hellstedt, 1987), no one has yet examined such a multiple-component treatment program on the behavior of individual athletes in a multiple-baseline design across subjects. Also, the majority of studies have used questionnaire data rather than direct measurement of athletes' performances in competitions during one or more seasons. Considering the increasing popularity of sport psychology consulting with teams as well as individual athletes, research in this area is needed.

Reading Objectives

1. How do goals capitalize on rule-governed control over behavior? Illustrate with an example.
2. Distinguish between effective and ineffective rules. Give examples of each.
3. How might a behavioral analysis of self-talk interventions aid the sport psychologist in improving the effectiveness of his or her advice to athletes?
4. Summarize the findings of mainstream sport psychology concerning mental imagery and athletic performance.
5. Using examples, distinguish between respondent and operant imagery.
6. How might a behavioral analysis of the effects of imagery rehearsal on athletic performance improve research and applications in this area?
7. What are sport-specific behavioral checklists? What are their potential benefits for a sport psychology consultant? What are their potential limitations as a behavioral assessment device?
8. Outline a study to examine whether self-talk might improve generalization of athletic performance from practices to competitions. Justify your choice of the type of self-talk to be examined.
9. What is a preperformance routine? From a behavioral perspective, speculate on reasons why a consistent preperformance routine might enhance competitive performance.
10. What are the likely components of a seasonal psychological skills training program for athletes? Outline how such a program might be researched using a single-subject design.

References

Allison, M. G., & Ayllon, T. (1980). Behavioral coaching in the development of skills in football, gymnastics, and tennis. *Journal of Applied Behavior Analysis, 13*, 297-314.

Bunker, L., Williams, J. M., & Zinsser, N. (1993). Cognitive techniques for improving performance and building confidence. In J. M. Williams (Ed.), *Applied sport psychology: Personal growth to peak performance* (2nd ed.). Mountainview, CA: Mayfield Publishing Co.

Burton, D. (1992). The Jekkyl/Hyde nature of goals: Reconceptualizing goal setting in sport. In T. Horn (Ed.), *Advances in sport psychology* (pp. 267-297). Champaign, IL: Human Kinetics.

Buzas, H. P., & Ayllon, T. (1981). Differential reinforcement in coaching tennis skills. *Behavior Modification, 5*, 372-385.

Claxdon, D. B. (1988). A systematic observation of more and less successful high school tennis coaches. *Journal of Teaching in Physical Education, 7*, 302-310.

Crews, D. J., & Boutcher, S. H. (1986). An exploratory observational behavior analysis of professional golfers during competitions. *Journal of Sport Behavior, 9,* 51-58.

Daw, J., & Burton, D. (1994). Evaluation of a comprehensive psychological skills training program for collegiate tennis players. *The Sport Psychologist, 8,* 37-57.

Dickinson, J. (1977). *A behavior analysis of sport.* Princeton, NJ: Princeton Book Company.

Donahue, J. A., Gillis, J. H., & King, K. (1980). Behavior modification in sport and physical education: A review. *Journal of Sport Psychology, 2,* 311-328.

Fenker, M., & Lambiotte, J. (1987). A sport enhancement program for a college football team: One incredible season. *The Sport Psychologist, 1,* 224-236.

Fitterling, J. M., & Ayllon, T. (1983). Behavioral coaching in classical ballet. *Behavior Modification, 7,* 345-368.

Gordon, S. (1990). A mental skills training program for the Western Australia cricket team. *The Sport Psychologist, 4,* 386-399.

Gould, D., & Damarjian, N. (1996). Imagery training for peak performance. In J. L. Van Raalte & B. W. Brewer (Eds.), *Exploring sport and exercise psychology* (pp. 25-50). Washington, DC: American Psychological Association.

Hamilton, S. A., & Fremouw, W. J. (1985). Cognitive behavioral training for college basketball free-throw performance. *Cognitive Therapy and Research, 9,* 479-483.

Hazen, A., Johnstone, C., Martin, G. L., & Srikameswaran, S. (1990). A videotaping feedback package for improving skills of youth competitive swimmers. *The Sport Psychologist, 4,* 213-227.

Hellstedt, J. (1987). Sport psychology at a ski academy: Teaching mental skills to young athletes. *The Sport Psychologist, 1,* 56-68.

Hill, K. L., & Borden, F. (1995). The effect of attentional cueing scripts on competitive bowling performance. *International Journal of Sport Psychology, 26,* 503-512.

Hrycaiko, D., & Martin, G. L. (1996). Applied research studies with single-subject designs: Why so few? *Journal of Applied Sport Psychology, 8,* 183-199.

Hume, K. M., & Crossman, J. (1992). Musical reinforcement of practice behaviors among competitive swimmers. *Journal of Applied Behavior Analysis, 25,* 665-670.

Hume, K. M., Martin, G. L., Gonzalez, P., Cracklen, C., & Genthon, S. (1985). A self-monitoring feedback package for improving freestyle figure skating practice. *Journal of Sport Psychology, 7,* 333-345.

Kendall, G., Hrycaiko, D., Martin, G. L., & Kendall, T. (1990). The effects of an imagery rehearsal, relaxation, and self-talk package on basketball game performance. *Journal of Sport and Exercise Psychology, 12,* 157-166.

Komaki, J., & Barnett, F. T. (1977). A behavioral approach to coaching football: Improving the play execution of the offensive backfield on a youth football team. *Journal of Applied Behavior Analysis, 7,* 657-664.

Koop, S., & Martin, G. L. (1983). Evaluation of a coaching strategy to reduce swimming stroke errors in beginning age-group swimmers. *Journal of Applied Behavior Analysis, 16,* 447-460.

Landers, D. M., Boutcher, S. H., & Wang, M. Q. (1981). A psychological study of archer performance. *Research Quarterly for Exercise and Sport, 57,* 236-244.

Landin, D. K., & MacDonald, G. (1990). Improving the overheads of collegiate tennis players. *Journal of Applied Research in Coaching and Athletics, 5,* 85-90.

Lines, J., Tkachuk, G., & Martin, G. L. (1997). *A mental skills behavioral checklist for consulting with swimmers.* Paper presented at the Annual Conference of the Association for the Advancement of Applied Sport Psychology, September 24-28.

Malott, R. W. (1989). The achievement of evasive goals: Control by rules describing contingencies that are not direct-acting. In S. C. Hayes (Ed.), *Rule governed behavior: Cognition, contingencies, and instructional control.* New York: Plenum.

Malott, R. W. (1992). A theory of rule-governed behavior and organizational behavior management. *Journal of Organizational Behavior Management, 12,* 45-65.

Markland, R., & Martinek, T. J. (1988). Descriptive analysis of coach augmented feedback given to high school varsity female volleyball players. *Journal of Teaching in Physical Education, 7,* 289-301.

Martin, G. L. (1989). *Sport psyching for figure skaters: A videotape.* Winnipeg, MB, Canada: Communication Systems, University of Manitoba.

Martin, G. L. (1992a). Applied behavior analysis in sport and physical education: Past, present, and future. In R. P. West & L. A. Hamerlynk (Eds.), *Designs for excellence in education: The legacy of B. F. Skinner.* Longmont, CO: Sopris West.

Martin, G. L. (1992b). *Sport psyching for figure skaters.* Winnipeg, MB, Canada: Manitoba Section of the Canadian Figure Skating Association.

Martin, G. L. (1997). *Sport psychology consulting: Practical guidelines from behavior analysis.* Winnipeg, MB, Canada: Sport Science Press.

Martin, G. L., & Hrycaiko, D. (Eds.). (1983). *Behavior modification and coaching: Principles, procedures, and research.* Springfield, IL: Charles C. Thomas.

Martin, G. L., LePage, R., & Koop, S. (1983). Applications of behavior modification for coaching age-group competitive swimmers. In G. L. Martin & D. Hrycaiko (Eds.), *Behavior modification and coaching: Principles, procedures, and research.* Springfield, IL: Charles C. Thomas.

Martin, G. L., & Pear, J. J. (1996). *Behavior modification: What it is and how to do it* (5th ed.). Englewood Cliffs, NJ: Prentice-Hall.

Martin, G. L., & Toogood, A. (1997). Cognitive and behavioral components of a seasonal psychological skills training program for competitive figure skaters. *Cognitive and Behavioral Practice, 4,* 383-404.

Martin, G. L., Toogood, A., & Tkachuk, G. (1997). *Behavioral assessment forms for sport psychology consulting.* Winnipeg, MB, Canada: Sport Science Press.

McKenzie, T. L., & King, H. A. (1982). Analysis of feedback provided by youth baseball coaches. *Education and Treatment of Children, 5,* 179-188.

McKenzie, T. L., & Rushall, B. S. (1974). Effects of self-recording on attendance and performance in a competitive swimming training environment. *Journal of Applied Behavior Analysis, 7,* 199-206.

McKenzie, T. L., & Liskevych, T. N. (1983). Using the multielement baseline design to examine motivation in volleyball training. In G. L. Martin & D. Hrycaiko (Eds.), *Behavior modification and coaching: Principles, procedures, and research* (pp. 203-212). Springfield, IL: Charles C. Thomas.

Meyers, A. W., Schleser, R., Cooke, C. J., & Cuvillier, C. (1979). Cognitive contributions to the development of gymnastics skills. *Cognitive Therapy and Research, 3*, 75-84.

Ming, S., & Martin, G. L. (1996). Single-subject evaluation of a self-talk package for improving figure skating performance. *The Sport Psychologist, 10*, 227-238.

Murphy, S. M. (1994). Imagery interventions in sport. *Medicine and Science in Sports and Exercise, 26*, 486-494.

Orlick, T., & Partington, J. (1988). Mental links to excellence. *The Sport Psychologist, 2*, 105-130.

Osborne, K., Rudrud, E., & Zezoney, F. (1990). Improved curveball hitting through the enhancement of visual cues. *Journal of Applied Behavior Analysis, 23*, 371-377.

Palmer, S. L. (1992). A comparison of mental practice techniques as applied to the developing competitive figure skater. *The Sport Psychologist, 6*, 148-155.

Rush, D. B., & Ayllon, T. (1984). Peer behavioral coaching: Soccer. *Journal of Sport Psychology, 6*, 325-334.

Rushall, B. S. (1977). Two observation schedules for sporting and physical education environments. *Canadian Journal of Applied Sport Sciences, 2*, 15-21.

Rushall, B. S. (1981). Coaching styles: A preliminary investigation. *Behavior Analysis of Motor Activity, 1*, 3-19.

Rushall, B. S. (1992). *Mental skills training for sports: A manual for athletes, coaches, and sport psychologists.* Spring Valley, CA: Sport Science Associates.

Rushall, B. S., & Pettinger, J. (1969). An evaluation of the effects of various reinforcers used as motivators in swimming. *The Research Quarterly, 40*, 540-545.

Rushall, B. S., & Siedentop, D. (1972). *The development and control of behavior in sport and physical education.* Philadelphia: Lea & Febiger.

Rushall, B. S., & Smith, K. C. (1979). The modification of the quality and quantity of behavior categories in a swimming coach. *Journal of Sport Psychology, 1*, 138-150.

Shapiro, E. S., & Shapiro, S. (1985). Behavioral coaching in the development of skills in track. *Behavior Modification, 9*, 211-224.

Siedentop, D. (1980). The Ohio State University behavior analysis research program in physical education and sport, 1973-1978. In P. Klavora & K. Whipper (Eds.), *Psychological and sociological factors in sport* (pp. 188-193). University of Toronto: Publications Division, School of Physical and Health Education.

Skinner, B. F. (1953). *Science and human behavior.* New York: McMillan.

Smith, R. E., Smoll, F. L., & Christensen, D. S. (1996). Behavioral assessment and interventions in youth sports. *Behavior Modification, 20*, 3-44.

Smoll, F. L., Smith, R. E., & Curtis, B. (1978). Behavioral guidelines for youth sport coaches. *Journal of Physical Education and Recreation, 49,* 46-47.

Southard, D., & Amos, B. (1996). Rhythmicity and preperformance ritual: Stabilizing a flexible system. *Research Quarterly for Exercise and Sport, 67,* 288-296.

Staats, A. W. (1968). *Learning, language, and cognition.* New York: Holt, Rinehart, & Winston.

Staats, A. W., Staats, C. K., & Crawford, H. L. (1962). First order conditioning of meaning and the parallel conditioning of a GSR. *Journal of General Psychology, 67,* 159-167.

Tkachuk, G. A., & Martin, G. L. (1997). *Preperformance routines in sport: Current status and future directions.* Paper submitted for publication.

Van Raalte, J. L., & Brewer, B. W. (Eds.). (1996). *Exploring sport and exercise psychology.* Washington, DC: American Psychological Association.

Wanlin, C., Hrycaiko, D., Martin, G. L., & Mahon, M. (1997). The effects of a goal setting package on the performance of young female speed skaters. *Journal of Applied Sport Psychology, 9,* 212-228.

Weinberg, R. S. (1994). Goal setting and performance in sport and exercise settings: A synthesis and critique. *Medicine and Science in Sport and Exercise, 26,* 469-477.

Weinberg, R. S. (1981). The relationship between mental preparation strategies and sport performance: A review and critique. *Quest, 33,* 195-213.

Weinberg, R. S. (1996). Goal setting in sport and exercise: Research to practice. In J. L. Van Raalte & B. W. Brewer (Eds.), *Exploring sport and exercise psychology* (pp. 3-24). Washington, DC: American Psychological Association.

Weinberg, R. S., & Gould, D. (1995). *Foundations of sport and exercise psychology.* Champaign, IL: Human Kinetics.

Williams, J. M., & Leffingwell, T. R. (1996). Cognitive strategies in sport and exercise psychology. In J. L. Van Raalte & B. W. Brewer (Eds.), *Exploring sport and exercise psychology* (pp. 51-73). Washington, DC: American Psychological Association.

Wolko, K. L., Hrycaiko, D. W., & Martin, G. L. (1993). A comparison of two self-management packages to standard coaching for improving practice performance of gymnasts. *Behavior Modification, 17,* 209-223.

Ziegler, S. G. (1987). Effects of stimulus cueing on the acquisition of ground strokes by beginning tennis players. *Journal of Applied Behavior Analysis, 20,* 405-411.

Ziegler, S. G. (1994). The effects of attentional shift training on the execution of soccer skills: A preliminary investigation. *Journal of Applied Behavior Analysis, 27,* 545-552.

Chapter 18

Organizational Behavior Management and Instructional Systems

Dale M. Brethower
Western Michigan University

Overview

Psychologists are in near unanimous agreement about a basic principle of psychology: behavior (what each person does or feels or thinks) is a function of person variables and environment variables. The principle says that a person's behavior, B, in any situation is a function of what the person, P, brings to the situation and what the environment, E, provides at that moment. The basic principle can be stated in symbols, $B = f(P, E)$, and the symbols can be read this way: "Behavior is a function of person variables and environment variables."

The principle provides a focus for the field of psychology. All psychologists study behavior (B). Some psychologists study behavior to identify characteristics of the person, for example, personality variables or intelligence. Other psychologists study behavior to learn about environmental influences, for example, social influences, socio-economic status influences or peer influences. Much of the research in psychology asks broad questions such as "What personality variables are associated with success?" or "What environmental variables are associated with success?" (These questions can also be asked about mental illness or adherence to particular beliefs or other topics of interest.) But whether studying person variables or environmental variables (and arguing endlessly about which set of variables are most important), psychologists agree with the basic principle, $B = f(O, E)$ (where "O"=the organism), and agree that *both* person variables and environmental variables are important in any specific situation.

Behavior analysis is an approach that takes the basic principle very seriously and studies behavior (B) as a function of interactions between person (P) and environment (E) in very specific situations. Behavior analysis is unique in that respect. Behavior analysis is about interactions between a behaving organism and an environment. It is about John Jones and Sally Smith and how each interacts with situations encountered throughout all aspects of life. This chapter focuses on behavior (B) in work and school environments (E). Work and school are two very important aspects of life—by the time John Jones and Sally Smith graduate from college and work for 10 years each one will have logged about 20,000 hours at work and 20,000 hours at school. John and Sally will continue to log thousands of additional hours in the workplace and in workplace classrooms; they will learn completely new sets of tasks many times throughout their adult lives.

What are OBM and Instructional Systems Analysis?

Organizational behavior management (OBM) and instructional systems analysis (ISA) are areas that apply behavior analysis and general systems theory to assure that the interactions between person and environment at work and at school are constructive rather than destructive. Knowledge about constructive and destructive interactions at work and at school is potentially very useful because workplaces and schools are potentially very constructive environments in which people learn and grow and develop. But the interactions can be, and often are, quite destructive.

Workplaces and schools are places of learning. That's always been true of schools and it has become true of necessity in modern workplaces. Along with the modern era knowledge explosion has come a technology explosion, a communications explosion, and, some say, a decline in the quality of education. The demand for a well educated and trained workforce is increasing. Work changes quickly as new products are introduced much more frequently than they were 50 and even 10 years ago. Even the nature of work is changing. At the turn of the last century most people were doing agricultural work. Later, at least in developed countries, there were more jobs in manufacturing than in agriculture; now there are more service jobs than manufacturing jobs.

An even more profound change is occurring than the shift from an agricultural to an industrial economy: People are moving from manual work to knowledge-based work. Much of the labor is done by machines that are operated by workers, using knowledge rather than muscle to do the job. The discrepancy in income between college educated and high school graduates is growing, showing that when we learn more we become more valuable to employers.

How did OBM Originate?

Years ago when I was just beginning to apply behavior analysis in the workplace I thought that working with instructional systems was probably the only kind of work that would be needed. Surely, I thought, executives and managers and supervisors know what performance they want; the only help required from experts in behavior analysis is help in enabling people to learn how to perform well. A brief historical review will disclose just how naïve that thinking was.

OBM grew out of an interest in instructional systems tailored to the workplace. Every workplace requires that people who work there learn to perform in specific ways. People have to learn how to perform, either by picking it up on the job or through planned instructional experiences. While workplace technologies and work practices vary widely, each workplace must have a means for assuring a competent workforce. Thus, being able to operate instructional systems provides the behavior analyst with an entry point into the workplace.

The first work in instructional systems in the workplace grew out of programmed learning, an approach pioneered by a person whose place in the history of psychology is assured, Harvard professor, B. F. Skinner. (The time was 1960;

behavior analysis was called operant conditioning and OBM had yet to be invented.) Research demonstrated, more often than not, that programmed learning outperformed conventional instruction on several measures: total amount learned, percentage of learners reaching mastery, amount of learning time required (programmed learning took less time), and student satisfaction.

These data were important in the workplace and in education but the importance differed in four important ways.

In school, consuming learning time generates revenue; in the workplace it generates cost.

In education, learning more in less time raised the question "What do we do with the children the rest of the time?" As one elementary school teacher told me "You've convinced me that I might be able to teach the curriculum for the entire year by the end of October. But you haven't explained what I'd do with the children for the rest of the year!" (I suggested that the children simply work on the curriculum for the next year but that was not practical because it would require major changes in the way schools are managed.) In both the workplace and school, time is money: Learning more in less time is an economic advantage in the workplace because the employer pays the students for the time they are in the classroom. In school, it's just the opposite: Taxpayers or parents or students pay tuition, essentially paying by the hour. The more hours, the more money the school takes in. In the workplace, the more hours the more money the employer pays out.

In school, failure generates revenue; in the workplace it generates cost.

If students fail in education, they may be retained (generating more dollars) or perhaps be moved into special education classrooms, generating more dollars because states provide more dollars per special education student than per regular education (or gifted) student. If learners fail in workplace courses and have to take a course again, it costs more dollars in wages or salary.

If learners "graduate" and make errors on the job due to poor mastery, those errors cost the company.

If students graduate from public education and make errors on the job because they can't read or do sums, that costs the employer, not the school.

In school, improvements in learner productivity (learning more in less time) threaten teachers' jobs.

That's not a problem for the workplace because there are not hundreds of thousands of people who've earned college degrees in teaching; instead, there are people working full time in training that are also employable in other jobs in the organization. If anything, improvements in learner productivity improve job security for everyone in the company—especially the learners.

The threat to jobs occurs at all levels of education. Within universities, spending time improving instruction is a threat to a professor's job security because it takes time away from research. Universities are a publish or perish environment. Holding the job is contingent on publications because of a quirk in the tenure system; tenure-track professors must be promoted or fired after a very few years. They are promoted if they publish and fired if they do not. Teaching is considered but, unless it is exceptionally and consistently bad, it is not weighted heavily in promotional decisions and pay decisions. (That doesn't mean that a professional should "give in" to such pressures; it just means that the professional should take the dangers into account. See Jennifer Austin's chapter (this volume), for work that has occurred in college teaching in spite of the system. Although this volume doesn't include chapters on behavior analysis in education, that doesn't mean that the work hasn't been done. It can be found in other volumes, for example, Engleman et al., 1988, Gardner et al., 1994).

Economic considerations plus the weight of tradition made schools hostile environments for instructional improvements. It should have been no surprise, then, that programmed learning was well received in the workplace but not in the schoolhouse. (Behavior analysts eventually became more sophisticated about considering systems variables when thinking about improving performance, inventing the area now called behavioral systems analysis, which is also referred to in John Austin, this volume, and Williams, this volume.)

How did OBM and ISA Develop?

Nearly all of the pioneers in programmed learning worked in universities and sought to introduce programmed learning in universities and public schools; however, the workplace was much more receptive to educational innovation. Many of the pioneers in programmed learning were behavior analysts who saw opportunities to apply behavior analysis in the workplace. The Center for Programmed Learning for Business at the University of Michigan began its pioneering and hugely successful programmed learning workshop in 1962, the same year that the National Society for Programmed Instruction (NSPI) was founded. By 1965 the center had enlarged its course offerings to include a workshop on behavior analysis in the workplace and a workshop on a systems approach to improving the performance of individuals and organizations. Many of the pioneers in what we now call OBM (or Human Performance Technology) were involved in the University of Michigan workshops as faculty and as students. (See Dickinson, 1995, for a more complete account).

The NSPI annual conference was the gathering place for pioneers in the field who presented state-of-the-art papers and research papers and talked enthusiastically about the future. (Twenty or so years later, several of the pioneers such as Tom Gilbert, Geary Rummler, and Don Tosti became overnight successes.)

NSPI name changes summarize the development of the field. The change from NSPI, The National Society for Programmed Instruction, to NSPI, The National Society for Performance & Instruction signaled two changes.

1) Putting "performance" in the name signaled the increased attention to workplace performance.

2) The emphasis on instruction had expanded beyond focus on one method of instruction to attention to other instructional methods and, more importantly, to instructional systems.

The change to the current name, ISPI, the International Society for Performance Improvement signaled two additional changes.

1) ISPI and the field had become international in scope.
2) The emphasis had shifted to "performance improvement" so that instructional systems, while still important, focused on improving human performance in systematic and reproducible ways.

The late 60's and early 70's were a time of many publications and an accelerating number of books. The *Journal of the Experimental Analysis of Behavior* was followed by the *Journal of Applied Behavior Analysis* that featured performance applications, including performance of students, teachers, mental health workers and the like, primarily in the public sector.

Another professional association was established, growing naturally out of the Michigan Association for Behavior Analysis to become the International Association for Behavior Analysis (ABA). ABA members are primarily academics, students, and professionals in the public sector and not-for-profit organizations. Many of the academics who had attended NSPI conferences began attending only the ABA conference, in part because of the greater emphasis on research and upon behavior analysis in ABA. As a result, there was a drift in NSPI/ISPI away from its roots in behavior analysis and away from a strong research emphasis. (It is, in 1998, a strategic goal of ISPI to regain the research emphasis.) Beginning in the early 1980's, an increasing number of ABA members who were applying behavior analysis in the for-profit sector formed the OBM Network, imprinting the OBM name on the field. In 1998, both ABA and ISPI have strong emphases in improving workplace performance.

That's a brief look at how the field grew but what about the substance of the field? Where did it come from and how did it develop? There were several pre-cursors to OBM but the major sources have been general systems theory and behavior analysis (cf. Brethower, 1996). Behavior analysts working in the private sector attempted to apply principles of behavior analysis and had to discover general systems theory in order to do so competently. I'll refer to work that explicitly combines behavior analysis and systems analysis as "behavioral systems analysis." Richard Malott (1974) was the among the first to talk about behavioral systems analysis as the area that applies basic principles of behavior and general systems theory to the area now known as OBM and instructional systems design. (OBM is also known as human performance technology or HPT.)

What Does the Research Say?

The research shows that we have had notable successes and are still learning. A clear exposition of the research in OBM can be found in Reid and Parsons, this volume; Poling, Dickinson, Austin, and Normand, this volume; and John Austin, this volume. The research related to the design of instructional systems is quite varied. Some of the best work has been done by people describing themselves as cognitivists, some as behaviorists, and some who have only a nodding acquaintance with theory and refer to themselves as eclectics. I'll mention some of the key findings briefly and then weave more findings into the examples in the section below.

Key findings about concept formation. When learners "acquire" a new concept they acquire 3 skills:

1. The ability to identify differences, that is, to discriminate examples of the concept from something similar that is not an example. For example, in learning the concept of reinforcement students learn to discriminate reinforcement from punishment or extinction or attempts to strengthen behavior by presenting things thought to be rewards that are not rewards or by presenting rewards at the wrong time.
2. The ability to identify similarities, that is, to recognize examples of the concept in spite of seeming differences. For example, students might learn that reinforcement occurs when behavior is strengthened by a stimulus change even though the stimulus change might not seem like a reward.
3. The ability to describe the similarities and differences, perhaps by a rule or definition. For example, students might learn a definition of reinforcement that describes reinforcement as a process in which behavior is strengthened by the consequences of the behavior.

These three properties of conceptual learning (that it requires discrimination of differences, generalization regarding similarities, and the ability to describe or define the concept) are vexing to teachers and students alike. That is because, as research also shows, a substantial array of examples of the concept and an array of items similar to the concept are required for concept formation. If too few examples are given, students will acquire a concept that is too narrow (Tennyson, Woolley, & Merrill, 1972). For example, the concept that rewards are "pleasant" is too narrow. Many things most people would judge "unpleasant" can be rewarding (such as receiving a painful slap on the back in celebration, being yelled at by a parent or boss, experiencing significant pain while exercising, eating a bitter food). Unpleasant events can be used to reward and strengthen behavior under the right conditions.

Researchers have coined the notion of "fuzzy concepts" just because humans are very good at conceptual learning but often learn fuzzy, not well formed, concepts (see McNeil & Freiberger, 1993). Some cultural stereotypes are probably learned this way such as the notions that blondes have more fun, athletes are a bit stupid, and white men cannot jump. We learn by encountering examples of blondes having fun (and brunettes having more fun after dying their hair), of stupid athletes, and non-jumping white men. Our concepts will be fuzzy until we encounter the appropriate counter-examples (researchers call them non-examples). If we observe enough sad blondes and fun-loving brunettes we can learn more accurate concepts. If we encounter examples of brilliant athletes and not very bright engineers or attorneys or high jumping white men or black athletes that cannot jump, our fuzzy concepts can become more accurate.

What we know about the formation of fuzzy and of accurate concepts is quite important. Being able to form fuzzy concepts is a lot better than being unable to learn conceptually. On the other hand, it can give us a false sense of knowing. The "cure" for fuzzy concepts is to experience more and better examples and non-examples but, alas, textbooks have far too few (Markle, 1975). If we imagine that it takes at least three good examples and at least three good non-examples to form a reasonably sharp concept then we can then count the number of new concepts introduced in a text and the number of examples per concept. (Complex concepts require far more examples and non-examples than three; experts have honed their conceptual mastery with hundreds of examples and non-examples.) With the exception of a few texts written by people familiar with the concept formation research, high school and college level texts have far too few examples and non-examples to support accurate conceptual learning. That's one reason some of the best instructors use many examples in class. It's also one reason some of the best students search for additional examples and construct their own "test" examples to get feedback on whether their concepts are accurate (see Heiman & Slomianko, 1992).

Key findings about knowledge of results/intrinsic feedback. The student question "Is this another example of what you are talking about?" is a smart question for two reasons: It focuses on getting more examples to clarify fuzzy concepts and it gets the student more feedback on his or her thinking. The research findings are very clear. Learning is much better with frequent and immediate feedback.

One line of research that supports frequent feedback are studies on the effects of frequent quizzes in instruction. More quizzes tend to translate into more learning (Lloyd & Knutzen, 1969; Keller, 1974). Frequent quizzes support more study time and provide regular feedback on whether or not the study time is paying off in higher test scores. Even so, the feedback from frequent quizzes is infrequent and delayed with respect to learning. It tells the student whether the studying is working but does not provide feedback while studying.

Research has shown that programming the learning process by breaking material down into small chunks, requiring frequent responses from students, and allowing students to find out within a second or so whether their responses are accurate enhances learning. (Many of the best teachers, especially in elementary school and in special education, set up their lesson plans to support learning through active participation and frequent feedback.)

Setting up instruction that is responsive to learners, that is, so that it provides learners with knowledge of the results of their work, corrective feedback, and many good examples, is quite difficult. Fortunately, the technology for doing that has become available during the last few years through computer-based instruction. (Unfortunately, too many of the people cranking out instruction for CBI are quite lacking in knowledge about the learning process and simply put texts or text-like material on the machines or games or gamelike material on the machines.)

We also know that high levels of skill require very precise feedback—it is no accident that the top gymnasts and tennis players have their own coaches, it is no accident that professional football teams have offensive line coaches, defensive line coaches, offensive back coaches, defensive back coaches, quarterback coaches, receiver coaches, and special teams coaches. It is also no accident that researchers learn their craft working in research labs as part of research teams (and thereby get a lot of feedback), that surgeons begin practicing with cadavers and move on to carefully (we hope) coached practice during surgical internships, that pilots receive many hours of coached practice before soloing and many hours of soloing before they carry passengers.

Key findings about transfer of training. "There's no substitute for game experience!" say athletes and coaches and the research says they are right. Transfer of training for surgeons, pilots, researchers, and athletes illustrate what it takes to assure transfer. Realistic practice (starting with cadavers, flight simulators, artificial experiments, and run-throughs without opposition, respectively) is required, supported by guided practice in real operating rooms, airplanes, laboratories, and athletic contests. Just teaching the content is not enough.

The central question in the research on transfer of training is: To what extent does something learned in one setting (e.g., the classroom) transfer to another setting (e.g., the "real world")? All that practice time costs a lot as does the time of the surgeon-coach, the pilot-coach, the researcher-coach, and the other coaching specialists. All those hours practicing cost a lot of student time and energy and someone's money. Is all that money wasted? The professionals don't believe so; they believe that the long hours of practice with feedback and coaching are necessary. The research supports the professionals' views. The shortest summary of the research findings on the question "To what extent does learning transfer?" is "Not a very great extent; very little transfers!" (for further discussion, see Brethower, 1996; Fleming & Sulzer-Azaroff, 1990; Mosel, 1957). Thus all the practice time available, in the real setting or in settings as real as possible, is necessary.

If what we learn in the classroom fails to transfer to life outside the classroom, then we should be concerned about wasted opportunities or wasted resources. Classroom learning can still be valuable to the extent that it prepares us for guided practice in the "real world" but classroom learning doesn't transfer without the "real world" support (Tannenbaum & Yukl, 1992). Some of the reasons for this conclusion are clear on a common sense basis if we just think about it for a bit. Suppose we teach a course on "Investing in the stock market." Most students will not be in a position to do a lot of investing right away and will forget a lot in the meantime. Similarly, a "Family Planning" course will be much more applicable if the people in it are just about to have family planning responsibilities. (On the other hand, if a learner is part of a peer group that's fascinated by what they are learning, animated discussions outside of class support transfer, at least to conversations within the peer group.) One reason material doesn't transfer is that the time gap between learning and application is too large. But how big a gap is too much?

Once something is learned, how long is it remembered? If it is not even remembered, it isn't very likely to transfer. Most people reading this chapter know the answer to this research question from personal experience. Most undergraduates have had the experience of studying for a final exam, earning a high grade on it, and then forgetting most of the material, seemingly within days or even hours. "The more you study, the more you know; the more you know, the more you forget; the more you forget, the less you know—so why study?" is a bit of cogent reasoning that captures the experiences of many undergraduates. McSween (1980) showed that students who earned high scores on quizzes forgot much of the material before the final exam in a psychology course before special review sessions were instituted; similarly, high scores on a final exam were followed by significantly lower scores on a retention test taken early in the next term.

There are a few distinctive experiences that stand out from my undergraduate days (back in the late 1950's). I'll probably remember those experiences forever but I've forgotten even the names of most of the courses I took. (I remember a bit of chemistry and physics and sociology and philosophy and psychology but couldn't pass most of the final exams in most of the courses that I earned A's in.) But are there ways of learning that enhance retention of the material? And enhance transfer of training? There are, but the enhancement is less than educators and students might hope. Guided practice is required during instruction, as are opportunities and support for real world applications (Acosta-Amad & Brethower, 1992).

Key findings about learning-to-learn. In the bad old days, the ability to learn was attributed primarily to genetically endowed aptitude for learning. Those bad old days are still with us to a very large extent as has been thoroughly documented in The Bell Curve (Herrnstein & Murray, 1994). The book has been criticized as "bad scholarship" but not by scholars who have actually read it with reasonable comprehension. The book is good scholarship carrying a message about where we have drifted by not paying attention to what we know about the learning process. As a society we have not done a good job fulfilling our ideals of educating all our citizens: While many people of all skin colors are highly successful in the United States educational system, disproportionate numbers of people with dark skin tones are not. If we don't like the message, we might channel our efforts constructively by showing, for example, that it is possible to learn how to learn effectively enough to meet the challenges of current education, even if measures of "risk" such as academic aptitude predict failure. Behavior analysts such as Heiman (1987), Heiman & Slomianko (1992, 1993) and Johnson and Layng, (1992) have done just that as have a few others who do not take a behavioral systems approach (see Derry & Murphy, 1986; Means et al., 1991).

Why Can Behavioral Approaches Move Us Forward?

Behavioral approaches are especially well suited among the many approaches in psychology for guiding improvement of workplace performance. Oddly enough, most psychologists don't study the individual. That was a shock to me as a student because I had been led to believe that the focus of psychology was the individual. We talk about an individual's intelligence or personality or state of mental health but the research methodology is one in which psychologists don't study individuals. The unit of analysis is the group. Worse still, it's the statistician's group, a sampling of several individuals from a population, not a real group of people who function as a group. That means that the research can tell us only about "tendencies" of people in that population but not about the specific variables that influence the performance of an individual. At the methodological level, the individual is quite literally reduced to a statistic! (A full explanation of the assertions above is both tedious and technical, so I will duck the issues by saying that "a full explanation is beyond the scope of this chapter" and leave the explanation to others, such as Johnston & Pennypacker, 1982.)

One way to explain the power of behavioral approaches is that we study the performance of individuals. We do not study tendencies of populations and then make statistically invalid statements about individuals. There's a second, closely related way to explain the power of behavioral approaches. The explanation goes back to a basic principle of psychology, $B = f(P, E)$. Most approaches to psychology focus on broad characteristics of "P" and "E" that are associated with broad behavior tendencies "B". They don't study the interactions in the more challenging way by studying "this behavior" in "this situation" over long periods of time. In short, what they don't study is precisely what one needs to study to work with individuals to improve performance.

Behaviorists say that, at any moment in time, what the person brings to a specific situation is fixed. Whatever the person's intelligence is, whatever the person's personality is, whatever the person's goals and dreams are, they are what they are. What we can manipulate or change to improve performance is some part of the environment (E). Behavior analysts begin by asking this sort of question: "What aspects of this environment can we change to improve this performance?" We aren't talking about broad brush issues such as changing inner-city neighborhoods, we are talking about specific changes such as altering the frequency of feedback or the rewards or the instructions.

Behaviorists believe, in fact, that if we want to study the person the way to do that is to study the person's behavior in specific situations, looking at the formula this way: $P = f(B, E)$. The person ("who you are") is a result of a long series of interactions between the person's behavior and the environment. Behaviorists know and agree that the characteristics of the person are constrained by the person's genetic inheritance but the characteristics are brought out and supported or suppressed by the environment. Other psychologists agree with that formulation but try very hard to construct specific artificial situations, for example, standardized administration of standardized personality tests or intelligence tests. They are trying to take a snapshot that summarizes the results of all those interactions between person and environment; they hope the snapshot will predict something important about how the person will perform in the future. The logic makes sense but the method is flawed because the only valid predictions that can be made—as pointed out above—are predictions about the population of people with a snapshot like that. The prediction that can be made, for example, on the basis of a college entrance test such as the ACT or SAT is this: "Higher scores are associated positively with success in college. That means that, if we look at all the people that get higher scores than you did and all of those who get lower scores, many of the ones with higher scores will get higher grades than the people with lower scores; some of the people with lower scores will get higher grades than some of the people with higher scores. People with your score sometimes fail and sometimes earn A's. We don't know how you'll do.")

Psychologists who take other approaches are making a contribution but it isn't the sort of contribution behavior analysts seek to make. Behavior analysts would prefer to make statements like this: "If you do X in situation Y, Z will result." "If you do X (identify examples and non-examples of key concepts) in situation Y (your political science class), Z (higher scores on quizzes) will result." "If you do X (provide frequent feedback) in situation Y (a work setting in which there are incentives for good performance), Z (improved work output) will result." But to make statements like those, we must study the behavior of individuals in natural environments. We can't earn the right to make such statements by making tests to predict how workers with such and such a score will perform in a typical workplace; we must study how a specific worker performs in a specific workplace.

How do we do that? To study a specific worker's performance in a specific workplace we look at the performance! We measure the performance, then change a variable, for example, making clearer what good performance is, adding incentives, removing obstacles, providing better tools. If we seek to improve a waiter's performance we might develop a checklist to define good performance. Good performance might involve prompt and accurate service, succinct explanation of specials, average sale per customer, number of customers served per hour, quality ratings made by customers, and such items specified according to the standards at the specific restaurant. We might use the checklist to observe performance to be sure that the items are explicit enough to be meaningful and that customers and restaurant management agree that they add up to "good performance." We would then show the checklist to the waiter—who ordinarily would have helped us make the checklist—as the first intervention: The checklist makes performance standards clearer. We might then remove obstacles to good performance, perhaps by clearing away obstacles in the path from the kitchen to the customer or changing the way orders are relayed to the cook or changing the way tables are arranged. We might provide special recognition such as a small bonus when the waiter improves according to the standards. For examples of the effects of these and other techniques, see Anderson et al., 1982; Bennett, 1988; Fox et al., 1987; Johnson & Masotti, 1990; Rogers et al., 1982; Welsh et al., 1992.

Since we are measuring performance we can readily see which variables influence performance. The logic of the method is quite easy to understand and apply. It can take considerable ingenuity to do it well because there are often many variables that interact with one another but the logic remains simple. For example, if we want to improve the performance of a person who selects the locations for new retail outlets the problem of defining good performance can be quite difficult. There are many variables and it is sometimes several years before anyone knows whether the location selected was a good one. Did the store do well because of a good location or good merchandising? Did the store do poorly because of a bad location or because road construction changed the traffic patterns? Nevertheless, a skillful behavior analyst can help people develop criteria for good performance and then measure performance to determine whether or not it improves. In the case of the location selector, we might agree to a set of criteria based upon the information that is available to the selector at the time of the selection. We'd say that good selection performance is performance that meets the criteria; we'd also validate the criteria, first by applying them to locations already selected so that we know whether they turned out to be successful locations (did the criteria correlate with later success or failure?). Second, we'd continue to validate the criteria by continuing to apply them to store locations this person selects. The details can be complex but the logic of the method is not: Measure, improve variables in the performance environment, and measure improvements if and when they occur.

Behavior analysts take exactly the same approach to performance in school or in a workplace classroom. The way we study learning is to look at the performance of specific learners in specific situations. I'll illustrate how that can be done by describing some of my own work, beginning with my doctoral dissertation, not because my work is the greatest but because it illustrates the power of behavioral systems analysis and shows that the approach, though new by some standards, has been building a track record of success for some time.

Review of Research

My doctoral dissertation was entitled "The Classroom as a Self-Modifying System." The dissertation illustrated each of the three key areas for future study shown below, especially the area of managing individual and organizational performance as a system (Brethower, 1970). I believed then and subsequent experiences and research have supported the belief, that these are key areas for helping individuals and organizations learn and achieve success. The dissertation focused upon instructional systems, taking an approach that is consistent with what was later called OBM.

A main idea in the dissertation was that both learners and teachers function as self-managing systems. Learners and teachers, if they are truly self-managing, will be guided by feedback about their own performance. On the other hand, attempts to provide feedback will be meaningless unless the putative feedback is related to the performance of the individual teacher or student receiving it. Furthermore, the feedback must be relevant to performance decisions that the individual can make.

The major research question in the dissertation was a qualitative question: Can classrooms be described accurately and usefully as self-modifying systems? There were two qualitative sub-questions as well: Can learners be described as self-modifying systems? Can teachers be described as self-modifying systems? In addition, there was a quantitative question: Can learners and teachers improve performance by modifying systemic variables, i.e., can learners and teachers function as self-modifying systems? The question about performance improvement is quantitative because answering it requires quantitative measures of performance improvement. For example, quantitative dependent variables included measures of reading test scores, grades earned, correctly completed homework and in-class assignments, and improved compliance with classroom rules and norms.

The classrooms studied were housed in the Reading Improvement Service at the University of Michigan and in an elementary school in South Lyon, Michigan. Reading Improvement Service students were undergraduates enrolled in non-credit reading classes. Elementary school students were in the 3rd, 4th, or 5th grades. The data support the conclusions that classrooms could be viewed as self-modifying systems. More important, the data showed that when classrooms operated so that teachers, students, or both received performance feedback, classroom performance improved.

The university students were in a reading class that had two aims, first, to improve the reading speed and comprehension of students and, second, to improve their effectiveness in learning academic material. Reading rate and comprehension was measured each time the class met to provide feedback on the effectiveness of reading strategies being taught in the class. Students also learned strategies for mastering course material and practiced the strategies while studying material for their academic classes. Feedback was in the form of coaching from the reading class instructor on attempts to use the strategies and in the form of quiz scores, homework grades, and the like that students received in their academic classes. Reading scores improved significantly, as did student grades.

In another part of the dissertation research, students in 3rd and 4th grade classrooms tracked their own performance relevant to completeness and accuracy of classroom work in several content areas. In all cases, the amount of work completed and the accuracy of the work increased. A 5th grade classroom developed a peer monitoring system to support following classroom rules for good behavior such as getting to work promptly, speaking only when it was appropriate to do so, and the like. Small groups of 5 students took turns monitoring and posting the results of rule following. Rule following increased.

An important feature of the dissertation research was that it was done in real settings and in partnership with the persons responsible for education in those settings. I was both the "executive-in-charge" and the researcher for the research that was done at the Reading Improvement Service. As a matter of policy, benefits to students had to be the primary concern. Similarly, my agreement with the principal in the school in which the other studies were completed was clear: Benefits to the students were the first consideration (as judged by the teacher involved and the principal). Collecting research data was a second priority. (The dissertation reported studies that were completed; it didn't report ideas for studies that the participating teacher or the principal didn't accept because they couldn't see potential benefits to the specific students involved.) A research partnership of this sort is common in the M.A. thesis research and doctoral dissertation research conducted by my students and is something that I believe should be a feature of more research in the future.

The dissertation research has been continued on a variety of fronts. Procedures very similar to those used in the 5th grade classroom have been used repeatedly in the workplace to improve safety related behavior (cf. McSween, 1995). Additional research supports the general notion that adults as well as children tend to respond well to being treated like responsible persons when the goals are clear and self-management is supported with feedback and social reinforcement or other incentives. For example, studies by Smith, et al. (1969) established the effectiveness of providing reinforcement for academic performance of children served at the Reading Improvement Service. Several studies applied similar techniques to improving academic skills of other students (cf. Garcia, Malott, & Brethower, 1988; Abuhmaidan & Brethower, 1990; Daher, Brethower, & Malott, 1991). In addition, research has further clarified, defined, and validated the material taught in the reading classes, making it clear that the approach affects learning, not just reading. The work by Heiman and Slomianko (1992, 1993), discussed above, has built upon the work described in the dissertation to develop a validated system that enables university level students to learn to learn more effectively, improving grades and satisfaction with their work and making it possible for more students to graduate. The Learning-to-Learn® system Heiman and Slomianko developed is currently in use at many universities and remains the only validated system that produces such results. (Study skills classes, taught in most colleges and universities sometimes work, but sometimes they don't and none have been validated to show that the procedures taught are effective and transferable, that is, techniques that can be used in a variety of settings by a variety of people.)

Heiman's work has helped provide a useful answer to the question "How do we learn?" There is a simple answer: We learn by doing what the learning process requires. The simple answer isn't informative but it sets us on the right course to understand the more complex answer. What does the learning process require? A common sense and correct answer is that it requires at least three things: A prepared learner, an opportunity, and action by the learner. Heiman and Slomianko show learners how to prepare, identify opportunities, and take actions that enable them to learn.

Research and validated practice have revealed much that is useful about the actions learners can take to learn effectively. A significant conclusion about which there is no doubt is that learning is an active process. To be sure, learning sometimes "happens," apparently with little effort by the learner. A person might be eavesdropping idly on an idle conversation and hear something that "clicks" and starts the learner on a new line of thinking. Or a person might be sitting idly on the beach when an apparently random thought occurs and starts a new line of thinking. Even learning episodes such as these require a prepared learner, an opportunity, and active thought by the learner.

Learners sometimes try to make learning happen and nothing does, perhaps when studying a textbook. How can learners make learning happen more often, more effectively, and less painfully? How can learners prepare themselves to learn and know what actions to take when learning opportunities occur? There are dozens of "study techniques" that have been suggested over the years, a mixture of extrapolations from research (such as, spaced practice is best—under some conditions; "active" learning is better than "passive" learning) and advice from others who have gone before (such as, get a good night's sleep before major exams, take good notes, go talk to the instructor, form study groups). Study techniques are taught somewhere in most colleges and universities, often in non-credit workshops. The research literature shows that the advice learned in study skills classes sometimes works well enough to enable students to improve their grades slightly, for example, from a 1.9 to a 2.1 on a four point scale (Lipsky & Ender, 1990, Smith & Wood, 1959). Unfortunately, the research literature also shows that, for whatever reason, study skills courses often do not work at all or do not work reliably enough so that the results can be systematically replicated (Chaney & Farris, 1991).

The work by Heiman and Slomianko (1992) is an exception. The approach used by Heiman and Slomianko enables students to acquire very specific learning skills that are learned through carefully guided skill practice. The skills were identified by doing a behavioral analysis of what successful students do to learn. Successful students, of course, are fallible human beings who do some things very well and some things poorly or inconsistently. Consequently, the analysis went beyond identifying successful practices.

As mentioned previously, the research and development effort that yielded the Heiman and Slomianko Learning-to-Learn® system began at the Reading Improvement Service at the University of Michigan. The behavioral analysis of the learning process was done clinically, that is by careful observation of what expert learners do. The validation of the analysis was done, not in the research laboratory, but in the university classroom. The clinical approach was taken, in part, because the research was directed at complex human learning, i.e., the kind that is required for learning the content of university level courses. It would have been very expensive to construct laboratory analogues of such complex learning and it would have been very expensive to hire students to spend hundreds of hours trying to learn the content of the laboratory materials. Furthermore, even after the laboratory studies were done, clinical research would be necessary to assure the real world validity and applicability of the laboratory research.

The clinical research was rigorous. Once a technique for learning was identified as potentially useful it was tested repeatedly. The first test was to assure that the successful practice would really work when used by other students. (That obvious test is rarely used by authors of study skills texts.) The second test was to identify what all the practices that were useful to multiple students had in common. Cognitive psychologists refer to this step as determining the deep structure of the successful practices. The deep structure elements were then taught by modeling the use of the techniques, giving examples and non-examples, and providing guided practice with content assigned in courses the students were taking. This test of the practice continued until it was clear that the technique could be learned and used effectively by a wide array of students, ranging from at-risk students to honors students, from first year undergraduate students to advanced graduate students and faculty members, and ranging from students in the arts programs, in humanities programs, in science programs, and in professional programs.

In addition to the clinical research, much good laboratory research has been conducted during the last twenty years but the laboratory analyses have not yet reached the level of complexity necessary to make their findings directly applicable outside the lab. We have, however, reached the point at which a combination of laboratory research and clinical research would be very beneficial.

The dissertation research showed that instructional systems (using the instructional methods already in use) could be combined with performance management systems to enhance instructional effectiveness. The instructional systems were, thereby, converted from teacher-centered systems in which the teacher attempts to control the learning process into learner-centered systems in which learners set goals and received feedback that enabled them to manage their own learning processes. The learning to learn work went one step further and gave learners effective procedures for learning, thus enabling them to self-manage effective learning strategies and, thereby, improve their own academic performance.

Three Key Areas for Future Study

The Components of Healthy Systems

One very important area for future research is in the identification of components of healthy systems. Applied behavior analysts seek to improve the performance of individuals and of organizations—but the scientific study of behavior has been about how behavior is regulated or acquired, not about what sets of behaviors a person must have to function optimally. Similarly, much of the work in OBM has been about changing performance in organizations. The research has not been about what performance is needed for an organization to function optimally. Consequently, we have many proven techniques for modifying performance but are still struggling with defining what the performances should be. For example, in clinical work we frequently encounter people with behaviors that are, in a sense, dysfunctional. The behaviors serve some functions, for example, acting outrageous gains attention, punching someone out gets them out of the way temporarily. But the same behaviors also create problems, for example, being ostracized by the main streamers, getting punched out or put in jail. Similar examples abound in OBM work. There are dysfunctional performances in organizations such as ignoring data about what works and making decisions politically or rewarding poor performance just as much good performance is rewarded or establishing compensation systems according to what other organizations pay with little regard for how much value the performance adds.

There is great potential value in having knowledge of specific characteristics of healthy performance. If you or I want to help others become psychologically healthy, just what comprises a healthy repertoire? (Clinical psychologists have an elaborate classification system, the DSM-IV, for classifying unhealthy behaviors but have no system for classifying a set of healthy behaviors.) Similarly, the management literature is well supplied with books about what's wrong with organizations but there is little to be found about the characteristics of organizations that work. Two fairly recent best selling books attempt to address characteristics of healthy organizations. Peters and Waterman (1982) wrote *In Search of Excellence* in which they tried to identify a coherent set of characteristics of excellent organizations. The best-selling and influential book, however, lost much of its luster when several of the organizations floundered badly, some into bankruptcy. The Peters and Waterman analysis was brilliant in many ways but simply didn't get to the essential variables. Another best-selling book, *Built to Last*, (Collins & Porras, 1994) attempted to avoid the fate of *In Search of Excellence* by going backwards in time to identify pairs of organizations that had been neck and neck years ago but only one of which had prospered in later years. Armed with these carefully selected examples and non-examples, they attempted to answer the question "What do the successful organizations have in common that's missing from the others?"

"Built to Last" is informative and a good example of this type of research but it does not connect to the general systems literature or the behavior systems analysis literature in an attempt to look at the systemic variables that have been shown by an enormous amount of research to be critical. It was intended to be a good starting point toward identifying the characteristics of healthy organizations, not the final answer.

It is one thing to say that research is needed on characteristics of healthy systems but quite another thing to describe how that research should be conducted. There are several possible approaches to it but my hunch is that healthy systems must be self-managing systems. Thus the research effort that I think would be effective is to do much more work on self-management of individual, group, and organizational performance. As that research is done, the research on characteristics of healthy systems can proceed by meta-analysis of those studies.

Meta-analysis is simply an analysis of research studies to try to identify the variables causing the largest or most reliable effects. Meta-analysis is conceptually very similar to the work done by Peters and Waterman (1982) and by Collins and Porras (1994). The difference is that meta-analysis works on the data collected in well-controlled research studies rather than observations collected as case studies.

In addition to the meta-analytic research, research of the type being done by Kaplan and Norton (1996a, 1996b) is needed. Kaplan and Norton, working with top executives, faced a key problem of measurement. Of the literally hundreds and thousands of measures of organizational performance available to executives, which few are the most important? Executives know that is and important question and each must answer it in practice by focusing on a few measures attached to a few sets of variables. What Kaplan and Norton contributed was a tenacious attempt to find an answer that was broader or more basic than the answer-in-practice given by individual objectives. Had they wanted to know about answers-in-practice they could have surveyed executives to discover which measures many of them say they use. Instead, they worked directly with executives to establish real measures that the executives would use.

Kaplan and Norton answered the question with the concept of a balanced scorecard. The balanced scorecard has financial measures, customer measures, internal business process measures, and learning and growth measures. Rather than overbalancing toward financial measures, the famous "bottom line," or overbalancing toward customer measures (customer is king; market share at any price), or overbalancing toward business process measures (cost cutting, technological excellence), or overbalancing toward learning measures (spending for human resource development, recruiting a highly skilled workforce), the balanced scorecard concept is that all four areas are essential, none can be ignored, and all must be measured and tracked.

The idea is that, if organizations are to be healthy and remain healthy over time, they must manage to a balanced set of measures. The idea is supported by two important general systems theory principles: 1) systems must maintain some set of variables within rather narrow limits if they are to survive, and; 2) systems with better information tend to survive better in a changing environment. The Kaplan and Norton research adds something very important to the systems principles, a practical conceptualization that guides very specific actions. The Kaplan and Norton research, done initially with executives from a few companies, has since been extended, by them, to several other companies (Kaplan and Norton, 1996b). It has also been used and misused by many other companies.

The research by Kaplan and Norton is both very different than and very similar to research commonly reported in the research journals in which applied behavior analysts typically publish such as the *Journal of Applied Behavior Analysis*, the *Journal of Organizational Behavior Management*, the *Performance Improvement Quarterly*, and other journals. The similarity is that the research deals with real cases, the performance of real individuals, work groups, departments, and total organizations. The difference is that behavior analysis articles tend to show changes in specific performances such as decreases in waste, increases in compliance with safety guidelines, or increases in specific behaviors of specific salespersons or specific supervisors. The behavior analyst can look at the performance measures and describe, with reasonable accuracy, the behaviors that produced the measured results. On the other hand, the Kaplan and Norton research deals with much more broadly defined categories of performance, so broadly defined that the behavior analyst would have, at best, a very foggy notion of what behaviors would lead to the business results. To the applied behavior analyst, the Kaplan and Norton research lends little guidance.

Even if a company uses the balanced scorecard and gets performance improvements in all four sets of measures over a two year period, that doesn't give the behavior analyst many clues about how to replicate the results. But it does provide guidance for business people who are experienced in finding ways to achieve clearly defined business goals. And, helping business people attain clearly defined business goals is something that OBM people are getting very good at. Behavior analysts are usually not business people, and business people are usually not behavior analysts. In my view, future research should involve behavior analysts and business people who are working together to, 1) achieve business goals and 2) discover how to achieve the business goals more effectively. While I've never been comfortable helping anyone in single-minded pursuit of the bottom line, I am comfortable with the notion of behavior analysts partnering with business people to achieve a balanced set of goals. Some of the ongoing research described below by my students and colleagues at Western Michigan University does just that.

Managing Individual and Organizational Performance as a System

One thing we know about organizations and about individuals is that they are complex systems. As such, changing one aspect of their performances affects other aspects of their performance. For example, if one person in a family emphasizes her or his own development, for example, by quitting a well-paying job to do something that is more fun, by going to college and drawing money from rather than supplying income to the family, it affects the rest of the family. Similarly, if a very talented person seeks to win a medal at the Olympics, the quest occurs at the cost of many other aspects of the person's life. If an organization seeks to increase sales it affects the resources available to provide service and, if successful, places stress on the parts of the organization that produce the items sold. Thus both individual performance and organizational performance must be viewed and studied as a system.

The chapters in Part One of this book, taken together, describe much of the research needed in assuring that individual performance is healthy. The chapters in Part Two describe much of the research needed to manage workplace performance, both individual and organizational as a system. In addition, more research is needed that is carried out in real organizations while dealing with real organizational problems. For example, Eickhoff (1991) showed that applied behavior analysis and general systems theory could be used in a high technology company to improve performance of individuals, major subsystems, and the company as a whole. Performance measures included measures of accomplishment at the individual level as well as customer satisfaction and overall profitability of the company. The research involved instructional systems and performance management systems within the company. (Eickhoff worked within the company as a manager/researcher and is now the company president.) Another research team at Western Michigan University (LaFleur & Nolan, 1997) is applying behavior systems analysis to a small business owned and operated by one member of the team. The research-in-progress deals with using applied behavior analysis techniques to offer new services to business customers of the company owned by LaFleur. The interventions are designed to improve the health of the businesses, in part so that the customers' businesses will prosper, they will remain customers, and grow, thereby becoming able to purchase more products and services from the researcher's company. The research begins with an organization level assessment to identify specific perfor- mance requirements. LaFleur and Nolan then do a functional assessment to identify variables affecting the targeted performance (similar to the work Austin & LaFleur, 1998 have reported). The interventions are very specific and focused even though the net impact on organizational performance is sometimes quite large.

Research such as that done by Eickhoff and by LaFleur and Nolan is possible because OBM and instructional systems work has progressed to the point where the technology is powerful enough to have a major impact and reliable enough for prudent business people to apply to significant business problems. The approach being taken by the Western Michigan University researchers is similar to that taken by Kaplan and Norton and could easily be combined with balanced scorecard research.

Aligning Individual and Organizational Rewards

One of the many things that the balanced scorecard concept and resulting research can provide is help with an essential problem in organizations: Aligning individual and organizational rewards. The alignment cannot be done properly without knowing what performances will support organizational goals and strategies. People are hired by an organization to serve the organization, to perform some of the work, to add value. At the same time, people's wages, salaries, and benefits are a major cost to the organization. For example, I would like the university to pay me more but that would cost students and taxpayers more money. The university president, the provost, the dean, and the department chair would like me to do more for the university for the dollars I am paid. There is an inherent conflict in that revenue for an employee is a cost to the organization. The cost must be passed on to the customer of for-profit organizations and to the taxpayer or other funding sources in the case of not-for-profit organizations.

A fair day's pay for a fair day's work is an ideal to strive for but what does that mean? The attempt to answer the question has a long history but, from the perspective of behavioral systems analysis, it has rarely been answered well. Several plausible approaches have been taken. To labor and management negotiators it might mean having work standards that can be met by typical union members and wages comparable to what other workers get in comparable organizations. To an individual in a non-union environment it might mean that she can make about as much money in that job as in comparable jobs. To someone doing the hiring it might mean that he can't hire anyone to work for less money. It might mean that most workers perceive the pay as "fair" and not based upon favoritism or unlawful forms of discrimination. It might mean that the people who work hardest and accomplish more don't get upset and leave because non-contributors get equal or greater pay or opportunities for promotion to higher paying work.

But these traditional approaches, please notice, link work very loosely to pay. The approaches seek to define "fair pay" almost independently of "fair work." Part of the reason for not linking the two definitions comes from a fear, well-founded in history, that employers might attempt to get "as much work for as little pay" as possible. Child labor laws grew out of employers offering very small amounts of pay to children. Labor unions grew out of efforts to get a "living wage" from employers who sought to pay as little as possible. Piece-work pay systems were sometimes used in which workers were paid in accordance with the numbers of widgets made; that was "fair" in a sense because there was a clear link between what the employee contributed and what the employee was paid. On the other hand, it's an easy system to exploit by requiring too many widgets and by not having provisions for injured or ill or older workers to continue to earn a living wage. Labor disputes were intense and "negotiated" by violence involving shootings and beatings and loss of property and life on both sides.

These problems came about, partly through misunderstandings, but fundamentally from the inherent conflict stemming from the fact that revenue to the employee is cost to the employer. The enlightened notion that there can be significant and mutual benefits to employee and employer from working together rather than at cross-purposes has been in the background all the time but organizational theory was not worked out well enough to achieve the benefits reliably. Mutual gains bargaining is a concept that now comes up in labor contract bargaining in enlightened organizations but we lack a solid research basis for identifying and working toward mutual gains. Linking pay and performance closely makes sense in both economic and motivational terms. Linking pay to performance can be an effective way to support self-management in the workplace. For example, Lincoln Electric near Cleveland Ohio has done that successfully, yielding an organization that, for many years, has been about three times as productive as other organizations in its industry and yielding pay that is also about three times higher than that received by workers in comparable organizations (Lincoln, 1951). Workers at Lincoln Electric don't require close and costly supervision; the work is supervised and managed and measured but the workers self-manage. People work hard and they work smart.

Aligning individual pay and organizational performance is commonplace at the executive level but, until recently, there has been no practical means of aligning individual pay with organizational performance. But make no mistake—the research question we must answer is not "Is it possible and beneficial to link pay to performance?" We already know that it is, just as we know that it is possible to link pay and performance with disastrous results. For example, linking executive pay to stock prices can overbalance financial considerations and linking individual pay to individual results can encourage costly internal competition. We already know that linking pay to performance well produces good results and doing it badly produces bad results. The research question we should answer is "How can pay be successfully linked to performance?" Key sub-questions for research are: "How can we identify specific performances that improve balanced scorecard results?" and "How can we use pay systems to support workplace learning as well as routine workplace performance?"

The latter question is one that could direct researchers to very significant areas of research. The overwhelming popularity, among human resource development practitioners and managers, of Senge's (1990) book, *The Fifth Discipline: The art and practice of the learning organization,* attests to the timeliness of work on workplace learning. It is important, as we enter the 21st century, to assure that students and workers learn effectively. It was important when my colleagues and I began our research in the 1960s and has become, not only increasingly important but increasingly recognized as important. Thirty years ago it was very important to do research in the nature of the human learning process and in how to enable people to learn more effectively. But the research has born fruit in the form of the findings about concept formation, feedback, transfer of training, and learning-to-learn that are described above.

As we enter the 21st century, the time has come to acknowledge that we know enough about the learning process itself to turn our attention discovering practical ways to support workplace learning. Research on this topic is an important component of research on aligning individual and organizational rewards. In the world of the 21st century organizations that learn how to quickly adapt to a changing economic, social, business, political, and physical environment will be more likely to survive. Learning how to do that is a top priority at the executive level and, many believe, it will require continuous and rapid learning by individuals at all levels of the organization.

Reading Objectives

As you read the chapter, please prepare to answer the following two sets of questions. The first set are factual questions—What does the chapter say about this or that? The second set are essay questions that have strong and weak answers but not right and wrong answers—What conclusions or interpretations can you draw?

Factual Questions

According to the author:
1. Why is the area of organizational behavior management and instructional systems design important?
2. What is organizational behavior management about?
3. How do instructional systems relate to organizational behavior management?
4. What are four differences between learning in the workplace and learning in school?
5. What is one key finding, each, about concept formation, knowledge of results, transfer of training, and learning to learn?
6. What are three key areas for future study?

Interpretation Questions

What do you think about:
1. The major differences between applied behavior analysis and other approaches to psychology?
2. The author's view that future research should, more often, be done in real organizations in which researchers work in partnership with the people in the organization?
3. The potential value of helping people, in school and at work, learn how to learn?
4. The potential for future contributions by applied behavior analysts in education and in the workplace?

References

Abuhmaidan, Y. A., & Brethower, D. M. (1990). Use of study aids to improve comprehension of technical material. *Journal of College and Adult Reading and Learning, 1,* 1-18.

Acosta-Amad, S., & Brethower, D. M. (1992). Training for impact: Improving the quality of staff's performance. *Performance Improvement Quarterly, 5,* 2-11.

Anderson, D. C., Crowell, C., Sucec, J., Gilligan, K. D., & Wikof, M. (1982). Behavior management of client contacts in a real estate brokerage: Getting agents to sell more. *Journal of Organizational Behavior Management, 4,* 67-95.

Austin, J., & LaFleur, D. (1998, May). *Functional assessment in organizations: A case study.* Paper presented at the Association for Behavior Analysis, International, Orlando, FL.

Bennett, R. D. (1988). Improving performance without training: A three step approach. *Performance Improvement Quarterly, 1,* 58-68.

Brethower, D. M. (1970). *The classroom as a self-modifying system.* Unpublished doctoral dissertation, University of Michigan, Ann Arbor, MI.

Brethower, D. M. (1996, February). What do we know about transfer of training? *ISPI News & Notes.* Washington, DC: International Society for Performance Improvement.

Chaney, B., & Farris, E. (1991). Survey on retention at higher education institutions. *Higher Education Surveys Report, Survey #14.*

Collins, J. C., & Porras, J. I. (1994). *Built to last: Successful habits of visionary companies.* NY: Harper Business.

Daher, A., Brethower, D. M., & Malott, R. W. (1991). Techniques for increasing writing and reading proficiency of international students. *Journal of College and Adult Reading and Learning, 2,* 1-11.

Derry, S. J., & Murphy, D. A. (1986). Designing systems that train learning ability: From theory to practice. *Review of Educational Research, 56,* 1-39.

Dickinson, A. M. (1995). *Coming of age in OBM: A celebration of celebrities.* Paper presented at the 19th Association for Behavior Analysis, International, Conference. Washington, DC.

Eickhoff, S. M. (1991). *Organizational development through the implementation of strategic plans.* Unpublished doctoral dissertation, Western Michigan University, Kalamazoo, MI.

Engelmann, S., Becker, W. C., Carnine, D. W., & Gersten, R. (1988). The direct instruction follow through model: Design and outcomes. *Education and Treatment of Children, 11,* 303-317.

Fleming, R. K. & Sulzer-Azaroff, B. (1990, May). *Peer management: Effects of staff teaching performance.* Paper presented at the Association for Behavior Analysis, International Conference, Nashville, TN.

Fox, D. K., Hopkins, B. L., & Anger, W. K. (1987). The long-term effects of a token economy on safety performance in open-pit mining. *Journal of Applied Behavior Analysis, 20,* 215-234.

Garcia, M. E., Malott, R. W., & Brethower, D. (1988). A system of thesis and dissertation supervision: Helping graduate students succeed. *Teaching of Psychology, 15,* 186-191.

Gardner III, R., Sainato, D. M., Cooper, J. O., Heron, T. E., Heward, W. L., Eshleman, J., & Grossi, T. A. (1994). *Behavior analysis in education: Focus on measurably superior instruction.* Pacific Grove, CA: Brooks/Cole Publishing Company.

Heiman, M. (1987). Learning to learn: A behavioral approach to improving thinking. In D. N. Perkins, et al. (Eds.), *Thinking* (pp. 431-452). Hillsdale, NJ: Earlbaun Press.

Heiman, M., & Slomianko, J. (1992). *Success in college and beyond.* Allston, MA: Learning to Learn, Inc.

Heiman, M., & Slomianko, J. (1993). *Learning to learn: Critical thinking skills for the quality workforce.* Allston, MA: Learning to Learn, Inc.

Herrnstein, R. J., & Murray, C. (1994). *The bell curve: Intelligence and class structure in American life.* NY: Free Press.

Johnson, K. R., & Layng, T. V. J. (1992). Breaking the structuralist barrier: Literacy and numeracy with fluency. *American Psychologist, 47,* 1475-1490.

Johnson, C. M., & Masotti, R. M. (1990). Suggestive selling by waitstaff in family-style restaurants: An experiment and multisetting observations. *Journal of Organizational Behavior Management, 11,* 35-54.

Johnston, J. M., & Pennypacker, H. S. (1982). *Strategies and tactics of human behavioral research.* Hillsdale, NY: Lawrence Erlbaum Associates.

Kaplan, R. S., & Norton, D. P. (1996a). Using the balanced scorecard as a strategic management system. *Harvard Business Review, 74,* 75-85.

Kaplan, R. S., & Norton, D. P. (1996b). *The balanced scorecard: Translating strategy into action.* Boston: Harvard Business School Press.

Keller, F. S. (1974). Ten years of personalized instruction. *Teaching of Psychology, 1,* 4-9.

LaFleur, D., & Nolan, T. (1997). *A systems perspective for improving organization-wide performance.* Manuscript in progress. Kalamazoo, MI: Western Michigan University.

Lincoln, J. R. (1951). *Incentive management.* Cleveland: The Lincoln Electric Company.

Lipsky, S. A., & Ender, S. C. (1990). Impact of a study skills course on probationary students' academic performance. *Journal of the Freshman Year Experience, 2,* 7-15.

Lloyd, K., & Knutzen, N. J. (1969). A self-paced programmed undergraduate course in the experimental analysis of behavior. *Journal of Applied Behavior Analysis, 2,* 125-133.

Malott, R. W. (1974). A behavioral systems approach to the design of human services. In D. Harshbarger & R. F. Maley (Eds.), *Behavior analysis and systems analysis: An integrative approach to mental health programs* (pp. 318-343). Kalamazoo, MI: Behaviordelia.

Markle, S. M. (1975). They teach concepts, don't they? *Educational Researcher, 4,* 3-9.

McNeill, D., & Freiberger, P. (1993). *Fuzzy logic: The discovery of a revolutionary computer technology–and how it is changing our world.* NY: Simon and Schuster.

McSween, T. E. (1980). *Programmed review tests in a PSI course.* Unpublished doctoral dissertation, Western Michigan University, Kalamazoo, MI.

McSween, T. E. (1995). *The values-based safety process: Improving your safety culture with a behavioral approach.* New York: Van Nostrand Reinhold.

Means, B., Chelemer, C., & Knapp, M. S. (Eds.). (1991). *Teaching advanced skills to at-risk students.* San Francisco: Jossey-Bass.

Mosel, J. N. (1957). Why training programs fail to carry over. *Personnel, 34,* 56-64.

Peters, T. J., & Waterman, R. H. (1982). *In search of excellence.* NY: Harper and Row.

Rogers, L., Brethower, D. M., Dillon, M. J., Malott, R. W., & Salwey, A. H. (1982). A comparison of behavioral incentive systems in a job search program. *Journal of Organizational Behavior Management, 4,* 5-16.

Senge, P. M. (1990). *The fifth discipline: The art and practice of the learning organization.* NY: Doubleday/Currency.

Smith, D. E. P., Brethower, D. M., & Cabot, R. (1969). Task behavior under various conditions of reinforcement. *Journal of Experimental Child Psychology, 8,* 45-62.

Smith, D. E. P., & Wood, R. L. (1959). Reading improvement and college grades: a follow-up. *Journal of Educational Psychology, 46,* 155-159.

Tennyson, R. D., Woolley, F. R., & Merrill, M. D. (1972). Exemplar and non-exemplar variables which produce correct concept classification behavior and specified classification errors. *Journal of Educational Psychology, 63,* 144-152

Tannenbaum, S. I., & Yukl, G. (1992). Training and development in work organizations. *Annual Review of Psychology, 43,* 399-441.

Welsh, D. H. B., Bernstein, D. J., & Luthans, F. (1992). Application of the premack principle of reinforcement to the quality performance of service employees. *Journal of Organizational Behavior Management, 13,* 9-31.

Chapter 19

Behavioral Approaches to College Teaching

Jennifer L. Austin

Florida State University

Young people are by far the most important natural resource of a nation, and the development of that resource is assigned to education.
B. F. Skinner, 1984, p. 953.

Introduction

Inherent in Skinner's (1984) contention that the development of our greatest natural resource falls in the hands of educators is an obligation to develop that resource to its greatest potential. In order to meet that obligation, educators should use instructional methods which are effective, efficient, and empirically validated. Applied behavior analysis has produced a multitude of strategies which meet these requirements. The actual adoption and use of these strategies, however, has been somewhat limited (Lindsley, 1992). One population that seems to have suffered in particular is college and university students. Although often used as participants in a wide variety of psychological experiments, post-secondary students have been largely neglected in terms of both the application and validation of behavioral education methods. It is difficult to find college classrooms that utilize behavioral methodologies, and with the exception of one specific behavioral education system (i.e., PSI), it is difficult to find empirical support for the use of such methods at the post-secondary level.

This chapter focuses on the application of three behavioral strategies with college and university students. Personalized System of Instruction (PSI), Precision Teaching, and Active Student Responding are discussed in terms of how they may be applied in college classrooms, as well as potential obstacles for their acceptance and use. More importantly, perhaps, the chapter brings to light the relative scarcity of empirical validation for behavioral education methods at the college level and outlines some potential areas for future research.

Personalized System of Instruction

The personalized system of instruction (PSI) method of teaching is perhaps the best known of all the behavioral approaches to college instruction. Often referred to as the "Keller Plan" after its founder and chief proponent, Fred S. Keller, PSI is a teaching method which focuses on establishing contingencies that promote mastery learning. PSI was first formally used as an instructional technique in 1964 in the newly formed Psychology Department at the University of Brasilia, where it attained overwhelming approval from both administrators and students. A year later, Keller and J. G. Sherman began to test the effectiveness of PSI at Arizona State University (Keller, 1968). Since that time, PSI has been one of the most widely researched of all behavioral teaching techniques, sparking both a newsletter (*PSI Newsletter*) and a journal (*Journal of Personalized Instruction*) for reporting research findings[1]. PSI enjoyed its most prominent position as a focus of behavior analytic research in the 1970s (Buskist, Cush, & DeGrandpre, 1991; Lamal, 1984), when it was proven time and again to be superior to traditional methods of instruction on a variety of educational outcome measures (for reviews, see Kulik, Kulik, & Cohen, 1979; Taveggia, 1976). Despite its sound empirical validation as a highly effective educational technique, however, PSI did not gain the wide and encompassing acceptance that Keller had predicted (Keller, 1985; Lloyd & Lloyd, 1986).

This section provides a description of the basic components of PSI, as well as objections to its utility and practicality as a viable method of college instruction. Possible reasons for the overall paucity of full-scale implementation of PSI are also examined.

Basic Components of PSI

PSI is distinguished from traditional pedagogical systems by five key character-istics (Keller, 1968). The first of these characteristics is *self pacing*. Self pacing means that students using PSI may take exams whenever they feel they have sufficient mastery of the material. Testing materials are always available, so that the student decides the schedule on which he or she will take the exams. Usually, the only imposed deadline is that all tests must be completed by the end of the academic term (e.g., semester or quarter). The self pacing component allows students to move through the material at a pace that is comfortable to them. This differs from traditional classes, where one timeline is imposed on all students regardless of individual differences in study habits, understanding of the material, and academic ability.

The second distinguishing characteristic of PSI is a *unit mastery requirement*. Students must demonstrate mastery of a unit of material by achieving a minimum unit test score (usually between 80% and 95%) before being able to attempt a test for a subsequent unit. Students may take tests an unlimited number of times until mastery is attained, and no penalty is imposed for scores lower than the criterion for mastery. The units on which students are tested are typically centered around a few main points, so that the course consists of many units containing limited amounts of information in each. Clearly, the unit mastery requirement differs from tradi-tional educational practices. In typical classrooms, students are allowed only one opportunity per unit to demonstrate how much they have learned, and the class progresses regardless of whether or not individuals in the class have mastered the information. This practice is especially problematic in courses in which understand-ing of new material is contingent upon understanding of previously presented material. In such cases, the student in the traditional classroom who does not achieve mastery of the first unit may struggle to understand all subsequent information that is presented. His or her struggles are exacerbated by the fact that there is a scheduled date for the next test and that new material must be studied within that time frame, thus limiting his or her time to master the information from the previous unit. With PSI, on the other hand, the student may take the time needed to achieve mastery of one unit before moving to the next one, thus ensuring that he or she understands the basic material needed to understand subsequent material in the course.

The third basic component of PSI is the *use of lectures and demonstrations solely for motivational purposes*. In traditional classrooms, lectures are the main vehicle for imparting critical information to students, and instructors want and encourage students to attend lecture sessions. With PSI, attendance to lectures is optional. The lectures, which usually occur only once a week, are typically short (i.e., about 30 minutes) and are used mainly for the purposes of clarifying information that the student has read and motivating further study.

The fourth characteristic which differentiates PSI from traditional instruction is its *focus on written communication*. All critical information required to master individual units is available through readings provided by the instructor, thereby eliminating the need for lectures as modes of information transfer. Typically, detailed study objectives are provided to accompany the text in order to guide the student through the material and assist in identifying the most important points. Requiring students to first obtain information through reading and then to subsequently provide written proof of their mastery of the material (i.e., exams) ensures that students take an active role in acquiring critical information. This differs from traditional classes, where students may fall into the role of passive spectators during lectures, thereby limiting their opportunities to be active participants in the learning process.

The last critical component in PSI is *the use of undergraduate proctors*. Proctors are selected based on several criteria, including superior understanding of the material (demonstrated as students of previous classes), ability to make mature and unbiased judgments about student performance, willingness to help others, and an empathic understanding of being a student in the class. The undergraduates who are selected as proctors play a crucial role in PSI. Without them, repeated testing and scoring would not be possible because such tasks are typically not practical or likely given the constraints on the instructor's time and resources. The proctor assumes primary responsibility for scoring tests, though he or she may defer scoring of particular items to the instructor if he or she can not determine whether or not a student's answer is correct. In addition to supervising and scoring tests, the undergraduate proctors provide a variety of other class-related services to students. These include answering questions and discussing material, usually in terms of what student behaviors may lead to better understanding and more timely mastery of material. Proctors may also meet with individual students to discuss unit tests, at which time a student may challenge the proctor's scoring of particular items. If the student can defend his or her answer to the proctor's satisfaction, the proctor may re-score the item as correct. If the proctor feels unable to make this decision, he or she may defer to the class instructor for final resolution.

In addition to performing various test-related functions, proctors also serve a social function. Because they too are students, they are able to relate to their peers in a way that may be difficult for an instructor. Proctors are naturally more in tune with the issues facing their fellow students, and are in an especially good position to offer assistance and support on class related issues as well as on the general business of being a student. In exchange for their efforts, proctors generally receive academic credit. Additionally, the opportunity to "teach" facilitates greater understanding of the course's material, which will benefit them as they take higher level courses in the same subject area.

Given the multitude of functions performed by PSI proctors, one may wonder why an instructor is even needed. In addition to settling questions regarding test items, the instructor performs several other duties crucial to the success of a PSI-based class. Among these duties are gathering and organizing of appropriate reading materials, designing study objectives and exams, preparing and presenting weekly lectures, and training proctors. In short, the instructor's role is one of an "educational engineer, [and] a contingency manager, with the responsibility of serving the great majority, rather than the small minority, of young men and women who come to him [or her] for schooling in the area of his [or her] competence" (Keller, 1968, p. 88).

Criticisms of the Personalized System of Instruction

Despite the deluge of research supporting PSI's effectiveness as an instructional technique, the system has often come under attack as an inefficient and impractical method of teaching college students. Ironically, one of the first criticisms that has been raised against PSI is based on the educational outcomes it produces. Since students are required to master material and receive no penalties for failed attempts at this effort, the grades of those students who complete all units in the course are at least as high as the mastery criterion. That means that if the criterion for mastery is 85%, then every student who completes every unit in the class will have at least an 85% average. The mastery requirement of PSI, which is so integral to student success, is often its worst enemy in terms of gaining acceptance with faculty and administrators. Any substantial deviation from the normal grade distribution, especially one that is negatively skewed, may be threatening to the instructor or administrator who believes that the hallmark of successful instructor performance is the bell curve. Classes in which the greater majority of students earn A's and B's are often viewed as easy or unchallenging, neither of which an instructor would likely appreciate as a descriptor of his or her class. Since successful teaching (as defined by the organization in which one teaches) is often related to such things as promotion, merit pay, and tenure, instructors in non-behavioral environments may be reluctant to utilize PSI in their classes because of the negative impact it may have on their success in academia (see Brethower, this volume for other restrictive contingencies at the academy). Lloyd and Lloyd (1986) found that many of the instructors who had abandoned PSI did so because of the perceived adverse effects it produced on the instructors' standings in their respective departments. As Lloyd and Lloyd (1986) succinctly stated, when one is deciding whether or not to use PSI "the concern about how well students learn may become secondary" (p. 151).

A second major criticism of PSI is that it promotes rote memorization and surface-level understanding as opposed to higher level processing and critical thinking about the material presented (Hursh, 1976; Meek 1977). Critics argue that PSI is not capable of achieving such outcomes mainly because of its focus on mastery, and that skills like critical thinking, application, and syntheses of ideas can not be evaluated or measured with such a system, if they can be measured at all. Reboy and Semb (1991), however, have argued that this line of reasoning is erroneous in at least three ways. First, the authors explain that PSI is solely a system for delivering instruction; it is not a system for choosing curricula. That is, PSI may dictate **how** material should be presented and **how** students will be evaluated, but it does not dictate **what** should be presented. Course objectives and content are developed at the discretion of the instructor, so that the level of understanding (basic or advanced) that is facilitated in such classes is likewise at the discretion of the instructor. Reboy and Semb (1991) also explain that since mastery-based courses produce higher student achievement, students will have a stronger knowledge base on which to develop skills and more effectively problem solve and apply the information that they have learned. Third, the authors cite evidence that PSI has been used effectively to promote higher order skills such as problem solving and generalization of concepts.

Reboy and Semb's (1991) arguments suggest that while lower level or introductory classes may lend themselves more easily to a PSI structure, they are surely not the only classes which can be taught in such a way. They argue that PSI is an effective delivery system for a wide range of subject areas and can promote a variety of learning outcomes. Unfortunately, there are relatively little data to support their claim. Research aimed at identifying how PSI could significantly influence higher order learning outcomes (e.g., ability to critically analyze and apply information), and specifically, how these outcomes can be effectively measured, are needed in order to remediate PSI's stigma of being a method for teaching students how to memorize and regurgitate basic information.

A variety of other criticisms have been leveled against PSI on various components of the system. One such criticism is that self-pacing results in student procrastination (Born & Moore, 1978), though research has indicated that behavioral contracting (Lamwers & Jazwinski, 1989) or the teaching of time management skills (Glick & Semb, 1978; Keenan, Bono, & Hursh, 1978) can reduce this behavior. Another criticism is that the use of proctors may encourage cheating due to the peer relationship between the grader and the gradee. Caldwell (1985) has suggested that rigorous checks on proctor grading may ameliorate this situation. The use of proctors has also been criticized as a means for building a barrier between the instructor and student (Hobbs, 1987), though no research on this issue has been conducted to date.

A more general criticism, which often leads to failure to adopt PSI systems or to abandon their use (Lloyd & Lloyd, 1986), concerns the amount of time and planning required to effectively run a PSI classroom. In contrast to a traditional lecture class in which the instructor may or may not spend much time preparing for the class, PSI requires a great deal of planning before implementation (e.g., training proctors, collecting readings, developing objectives, etc.), as well as a myriad of management duties once the system is up and running (e.g., supervising proctors, keeping up with scores from multiple tests, etc.). The issue of "teacher as contingency manager" has also fallen under attack from critics who propose that PSI undervalues the role of the instructor in student learning (Martinez & Martinez, 1988).

In addition to the widely published criticisms of various components of PSI, some have suggested that there is a larger, more encompassing reason for the general lack of acceptance and full scale implementation of PSI (e.g., Buskist, Cush, & DeGrandpre, 1991; Sherman, 1992). They suggest that the overall inertia of the educational system is a large factor in the decline of acceptance and use of PSI in colleges and universities. In order for PSI to be effectively implemented, major changes in educational practices must occur. The role of the teacher must be redefined, "normal" grade distributions can no longer be accepted as such, and students must be taught to be responsible for setting their own educational timelines. For faculty and administrators who are entrenched in traditional methods of education, these changes may be too overwhelming, regardless of the supporting data. Perhaps one of the greatest obstacles to wide-range implementation of PSI is that decisions about what is the "best" method of accomplishing educational goals are often made without the support of **any** data. Instead, decisions are made based on tradition or what *should* work. Group lectures with identical timelines for mastery of content for all students have **traditionally** been used in college and university classrooms, and they *should* produce acceptable educational outcomes. The fact of the matter, however, is that often times they do not. As suggested by Buskist et al. (1991), perhaps researchers should begin to focus less on the merits and more on the effective marketing of behavioral education systems like PSI.

Summary of Personalized System of Instruction

The Personalized System of Instruction (PSI) is an instructional delivery system that consists of five basic components which distinguish it from traditional instructional methods: 1) self pacing; 2) unit mastery requirements; 3) use of lectures for clarification and motivation; 4) focus on written communication; and 5) use of undergraduate proctors. Despite the deluge of research supporting its superiority to traditional pedagogical systems, PSI has not attained wide acceptance and has been widely criticized on several fronts. Future research on PSI should focus on increasing the marketability and acceptability of PSI in colleges and universities.

Precision Teaching

Precision teaching is a behavioral education method that helps determine the effectiveness of instructional strategies. Additionally, the use of precision teaching allows students to reach levels of fluent and accurate performance through the use of performance aims, frequent opportunities to respond, and precise performance measurement. Like PSI, precision teaching is mastery-based; unlike PSI, however, it provides detailed strategies for achieving masterful and fluent performance, and is better able to differentiate between mere accuracy and true mastery. The name "precision teaching," however, is somewhat of a misnomer. Precision teaching is not an instructional delivery system as the name might suggest, but rather a method for evaluating the effectiveness of instruction and making instructional decisions based on student competence.

Founded by Ogden R. Lindsley, precision teaching was first implemented in 1965 in a special education classroom at the University of Kansas Medical Center (Lindsley, 1991). Since that time, it has been utilized and researched in a variety of settings with various populations. By far the most common applications of precision teaching have been with developmentally disabled children; however, it has also been used as an effective strategy for building fluent and proficient performance in other populations, including business trainees (Snyder, 1992), pre-college students (Johnson & Layng, 1992), and college students (McDade & Goggans, 1993).

This section describes the basic principles of precision teaching and how these principles can be applied at the college level. Directions for future research are also suggested.

Guiding Principles of Precision Teaching

The development of precision teaching was based on several "policies" Lindsley adopted from his work in free operant conditioning as a student of B. F. Skinner in the 1950s (Lindsley, 1990; White, 1986). Five of these policies became the guiding principles of precision teaching.

The first and most fundamental principle is that *the learner knows best*. This means that the learner knows more about his or her behavior than anyone else does. If one wants to find out the most effective strategies for teaching an individual student, then one must observe that student's behavior and ascertain what contingencies are controlling his or her behavior. If the learner is progressing, then the program of learning is on the right track. If the learner is not progressing, it is the program, not the learner, that is to blame. As stated by White (1986), "only the learner's progress can be fully trusted to guide us in developing and continuously refining appropriate programs" (p. 523).

The second principle of precision teaching is *the use of rate of response* as the standard unit of measurement. This component is quite unlike those found in traditional educational methods, where the majority of focus in placed on the accuracy of responding. The problem with an accuracy-based educational focus is that it makes it impossible to differentiate fluent performance from merely accurate performance. Suppose that two students are given the same test and that both achieve scores of 100% correct. One of these students may have achieved fluent mastery of the material, while the other may have simply achieved completely accurate performance. Based on accuracy scores, however, one could not determine which student was which. Now suppose that both of these students were allowed one minute to complete as many items as they were able. In this situation, which focuses on the **number** of correct responses as opposed to the **percentage** of correct responses, discriminating between the fluent student and the merely accurate student would be much easier. Clearly, the fluent student would have completed a greater number of items because her responding would be much more automatic than the other student, who may have arrived at his accurate answers by such methods as remembering all the parts of a mnemonic, trying to picture the page in his notes that contained the correct answer, or even counting on his fingers. Regardless of his method for arriving at an accurate response, one would hardly characterize his performance as fluent.

It is important to note that fluent performance is characterized by both speed and accuracy of responding. However, in developing fluent performance through precision teaching, the focus is placed predominantly on speed (or rate) of responding. Both accurate and inaccurate responses are considered opportunities to learn, so that emphasis is placed on providing many such opportunities when attempting to build fluent performance. However, as the learner progresses and becomes more fluent in the subject matter, he or she is expected to make fewer and fewer inaccurate responses.

Another guiding principle of precision teaching is *an emphasis on observable behavior* combined with *direct and frequent measurement* of that behavior. An important component of precision teaching is the incorporation of frequent, timed performance trials which provide a representative sample of the learner's behavior. Timed trials are short (e.g., one minute) and require the learner to make as many accurate responses as possible in the allotted time, resulting in a score expressed as responses per minute. Unlike traditional educational settings where performance is assessed every few days, weeks, or months, precision teaching requires that performance be assessed during every class session. One rationale for this practice is that more assessments allow the teacher to better gauge the effectiveness of instruction. Additionally, frequent measurement allows for more accurate and timely detection of improvement across time.

In order to be maximally effective for purposes of feedback and motivation, *data on responding should be graphed*. An important principle of precision teaching is that standard charts be used to display changes in behavior. The conventional graphs typically employed in behavior analysis are adequate for displaying frequency of responding per trial. Precision teaching, however, is also concerned with the celeration of performance; that is, the rate at which performance improves (i.e., acceleration) or decreases (i.e., deceleration). Graphs typically employed in behavior analysis do not provide this information and are therefore insufficient for the needs of precision teaching. Consequently, semi-logarithmic graphs are used. Figure 1 shows an example of a semi-logaritmic graph. Sometimes also referred to as a 6-cycle chart, semi-logarithmic graphs accommodate "a full range of behavior frequencies, from 1 per day to 1000 per minute, on a multiply (or logarithmic) scale up from the left, or short, side of the paper. The long side includes 140 calendar days, or 20 weeks, which is about one school semester" (Lindsley, 1990, p. 11). The example semi-logarithmic graph in Figure 1 contains 50 calender days.

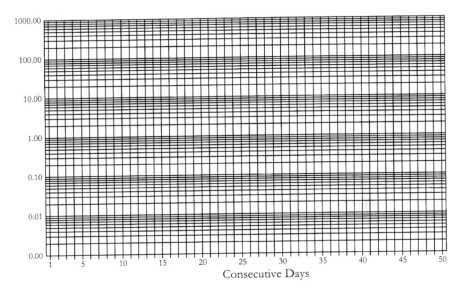

Figure 1. Semilogarithmic chart

There are several advantages of semi-logarithmic graphs over more conventional graphs. Perhaps most important is that semilogarithmic graphs make it possible to see the rate of learning. This is especially important in light of the fact that current rate of learning is predictive of future performance (Lindsley, 1990). Therefore, the rate at which a learner acquires skills becomes an important consideration in evaluating the effectiveness of instruction. If the learning rate is slow, then it may take a great deal of time for a learner to become fluent in a particular skill. In such cases, alternative methods of instruction may need to be considered in order to accelerate learning and produce mastery in a more reasonable time frame. Additional advantages of the semi-logarithmic graphs are that it allows recording of multiple behaviors regardless of disparity between frequencies of those behaviors, and that it permits data from an entire semester to be included in one chart (Lindsley, 1990).

Clearly, precision teaching places a great deal of importance on measuring and charting behavior. Equally important to the success of precision teaching, however, is making instructional decisions based on the data that are collected. As mentioned previously, the learning slope charted on the semi-logarithmic graphs can provide information on the effectiveness of current instruction. During the use of any given instructional strategy, effects on learning become increasingly obvious as the learning slope is charted. If the slope is moving upward at a steeper angle than when other instructional strategies are used, then the current strategy should most likely be maintained. Conversely, if the learning slope under current instructional conditions is less steep or moving in the wrong direction, then the current instructional strategy or the contingencies surrounding that strategy should most likely be changed. Formal guidelines indicating when and how to make these instructional changes have been developed to assist educators in making objective decisions about the efficacy of instructional strategies (e.g., Liberty & Haring, 1990).

The most important consideration in making decisions about changes in the current instructional strategy is whether or not that strategy is effective in helping the student to achieve specified performance aims. Performance aims are "proficiency levels stated in terms of correct and incorrect responding" (Koorland, Keel, & Ueberhorst, 1990, p. 64). The attainment of a particular proficiency level or performance aim is important because it can often provide the foundation for later achievement in a related area. That is, if a student can reach the established performance aim, they are more likely to be proficient in more complex skills which incorporate those behaviors required to attain the performance aim. The reason is that achieving performance aims helps build fluency in the component skills that make up more complex behavior or composite skills (Johnson, 1997). While there is some controversy surrounding the issue of exactly what frequencies represent proficiency in a particular area, some guidelines have nonetheless been developed to assist educators in setting reasonable and effective performance aims for their students (Koorland, Keel, & Ueberhorst, 1990). One of the more simple methods is to use the performance of someone who already demonstrates fluent skills to set the performance standard (Cooper, 1997). For example, one could base the performance aims for students in an Introductory Behavior Analysis class on the performance of the instructor of that class. If the instructor could consistently name 60 behavior analytic terms correctly in one minute, then a frequency of 60 named terms per minute would be an appropriate performance aim for the students.

Implementing Precision Teaching at the College Level

The bulk of research and descriptive articles on precision teaching have focused on its applications in elementary school classrooms with disabled children. Despite the relative paucity of supporting research, precision teaching-based strategies may also be used in college classrooms with normally functioning students to build fluency and mastery of course content (Barbetta & Skaruppa, 1995a). One such strategy is a flashcard system referred to as SAFMEDS or "Say All Fast Minute Every Day Shuffle." Words in the SAFMEDS acronym remind the student how to do the procedure, and also correspond to learning principles derived from a large precision teaching data base (Lindsley, 1993, in Potts et al., 1993). "Say" reminds students to say their answers out loud when they practice, and refers to the fact that actively responding, rather than just thinking about an answer, leads to better learning. "All" reminds students to use all of the cards when they practice, and also refers to the finding that working with all cards at once instead of only learning parts at time increases learning outcomes. "Fast" reminds students to do the exercise as quickly as possible, and corresponds to the fact that steeper celeration slopes are formed when learners start out at a faster pace and use errors as learning opportunities. "Minute" is the amount of time used to do the exercise, and "Every Day" is the frequency with which the learning trials are conducted. Finally, "Shuffle" reminds the students to continually change the order of the cards. This refers to the fact that students learn more when they shuffle the cards prior to the learning trial, because it ensures that students are not just learning the order in which the cards appear.

Students who use SAFMEDS are instructed to practice, do one minute timed trials, and chart their performance on a daily basis until they reach the performance aim. Like other fluency building components of precision teaching, SAFMEDS are intended to help students build mastery of component skills which will make learning more complex skills less difficult in the future. Research has shown that flashcards are effective in teaching a variety of basic skills (Heron, Heward, Cooke, & Hill, 1983; Maheady & Sainato, 1985; Olenik & Pear, 1980; Van Houten & Rolider, 1989; Young, Hecimovic, & Salzburg, 1983). With college students, it may be appropriate to use SAFMEDS to build fluent use of terms presented in the course. Once students are fluent with the use of terms and definitions, applying those terms will be an easier task.

The application of precision teaching techniques at the college level is clearly an area that is in need of further empirical validation. Additionally, research is needed to ascertain what types of modifications would make these techniques more acceptable, practical, and efficacious in the college classroom.

Summary of Precision Teaching

In summary, precision teaching is an instructional assessment strategy guided by four main principles rooted in the experimental analysis of behavior: 1) the learner knows best; 2) rate as the standard measure of responding; 3) emphasis on observable behavior and the frequent measurement of that behavior; and 4) use of a standard chart for displaying data and making instructional decisions. Application of precision teaching techniques have been most commonly implemented with disabled elementary school children, though the procedures are also appropriate and effective with other populations. More research is needed to expand the application of precision teaching to other populations.

Active Student Responding

In his 1916 book *Democracy and Education*, John Dewey provided educators with an interesting insight to instruction: Students learn by doing. Since that time, research has unmistakably proven that Dewey's contention was correct (e.g., Barbetta & Heward, 1993, Barbetta, Heron, & Heward, 1993; Cavanaugh, Heward, & Donelson, 1996; Drevno, Kimball, Possi, Heward, Gardner, & Barbetta, 1994; Gardner, Heward, & Grossi, 1994; Greenwood, Delquadri, & Hall, 1984; Narayan, Heward, Gardner, Courson, & Omness, 1990; Pratton & Hales, 1986; Sterling, Barbetta, Heward, & Heron, 1997). The implication of this and other related research is that instructors who want to maximize the amount of learning that occurs in their classrooms need to establish contingencies that promote the active participation of their students during classroom instruction. When instructors think of increasing active participation, they often think of increasing classroom discussions. Whereas classwide discussions may help students to better understand material, they can be problematic in at least two ways. First, it is unlikely that all students will participate in the discussions. This means that some (usually more confident) students will reap the benefits of active participation while others will not. Second, classwide discussions are often time consuming and may significantly diminish the amount of time that an instructor needs to convey crucial information to his or her students. Given the potential problems with using classroom discussions as the sole method of increasing active participation and the typical constraints on teaching in the typical college lecture class (e.g., large enrollments, diverse learner characteristics, limited time to cover large amounts of material, etc.), instructors may find it difficult to identify methods for increasing student participation which include all students but do not significantly limit the time needed to cover material.

In light of the difficulties associated with increasing active participation in the college classroom, several behavioral methods have been developed which establish effective contingencies to ensure that each student in the class is an active learner. This collection of behavioral methods is often referred to as active student responding (ASR). An active student response is referred to as an observable response to an instructional antecedent (Heward, 1994). Three methods of increasing ASR in college classrooms will be discussed, including guided notes, response cards, and choral responding.

Guided Notes

Most students view notetaking in lecture classes as an essential component to academic success (Palmatier & Bennett, 1974). Students' perceptions of the importance of notetaking with regard to their academic performance explains why the majority of college students engage in notetaking behaviors during their classes. It should be encouraging for students to know that their perceptions of the relationship between notetaking and achievement are not unfounded; research has indicated that students who take notes tend to recall more information than those who do not take notes (Carter & Van Matre, 1975; Fisher & Harris, 1973; Norton, 1981). Additionally, there is evidence to suggest that the quantity and quality of notes are also important factors in predicting academic performance (Baker & Lombardi, 1985; Hartley & Marshall, 1974; Nye, Crooks, Powely, & Tripp, 1984). Research on notetaking in college classes also indicates that taking notes assists students in recalling information by way of two important functions (see Hartley & Davies, 1978 and , 1985 for reviews). First, notetaking serves a "process" function by allowing the student to make active responses in class that are relevant to the material presented. In other words, the very behavior of writing ensures some degree of active participation in class, which aides in later recall of the information presented. Second, notetaking serves a "product" function by providing the student with a permanent record of the topics covered in class so that they may review the information at a later time.

Despite the student-perceived and empirically-proven relationship between notetaking and achievement, the majority of college students are notoriously poor notetakers (Baker & Lombardi, 1985; Hartley & Cameron, 1967; Hartley & Marshall, 1974). It is not uncommon to find that university-level students record largely incomplete and sometimes incorrect representations of material presented in class. Clearly, there are serious implications for these behavioral deficits. Though students who take notes that are deficient in accuracy and content are still making active responses in class (i.e., process function), they may not be making the right responses or maximizing the number of responses that could be made if the proper contingencies were in place. Likewise, incomplete or incorrect notes do not provide a quality permanent record (i.e., product function) from which to recall the content of a particular class.

Why do college students tend to be such poor notetakers? There are at least two plausible explanations. One is that students were probably never trained to take good notes. Palmatier and Bennett (1974) reported that while the majority of students take notes, only a fraction of those students actually received any kind of formal instruction on effective notetaking strategies. Another explanation for deficient notetaking is that the contingencies in the classroom do not support those behaviors which would result in complete and accurate notes. If this is so, then the challenge for instructors is to arrange classroom environments so that effective notetaking behaviors are both prompted and reinforced. Establishing a classroom environment which supports appropriate notetaking behaviors helps students to maximize the benefits of both the process and product of their efforts.

One way to provide students with opportunities to take bet-

Types of Single-Subject Designs	Types of Single-Subject Designs
1. *Reversal (ABAB) Design* Design which shows that when the IV is applied, behavior changes; when the treatment is withdrawn, behavior returns to pre-treatment (baseline) levels. Functional control is demonstrated through replication of effects.	1. *Reversal (ABAB) Design* Design which shows that when the IV is applied, when the treatment is withdrawn, Functional control is demonstrated through replication of effects.
When should reversal designs be used? 1. Behavior is likely to reverse 2. Behavior to be changed is not dangerous to the subject or others	When should reversal designs be used? 1. 2.
Ethical Considerations of ABAB Designs: We have an ethical obligation to return subjects to the best possible condition.	Ethical Considerations of ABAB Designs: We have an ethical obligation to return subjects to the best possible condition.

Figure 2. Samples of overhead transparency (left) and corresponding guided-notes page (right).

ter notes is to present students with clear discriminative stimuli for notetaking behaviors. Using guided notes in the classroom is an effective and practical behavioral teaching technique which provides students with effective antecedents for appropriate notetaking. Guided notes are essentially copies of the instructors notes or overhead transparencies with crucial parts missing. Students are required to complete their notes as the lecture progresses by writing in the missing information. Figure 2 shows an example of a student's guided notes page and the accompanying overhead transparency.

Like any notetaking method, guided notes require students to make active responses (i.e., writing) that are relevant to the material being presented. The benefit of guided notes over traditional methods of notetaking, however, is that they ensure that students are making the **correct** active responses. In a study assessing the effects of various lecture presentation formats on college students' notes, Austin, Carr, Gilbert, and Bailey (1999) found that when students used guided notes they make fewer mistakes in recording lecture information than when they took their own notes. In a related study, Lazarus (1993) found that learning disabled college students who were provided with guided notes achieved higher scores on weekly quizzes in an introductory psychology class than they did when they were not provided guided notes as a supplement to the lecture. These findings suggest that guided notes enhance the benefits of both the process and product of notetaking.

Like many instructional methodologies rooted in behavior analysis, guided notes have not been studied extensively in college classrooms. Their effectiveness has been more solidly validated in other settings and populations, such as secondary schools with learning disabled students (see Heward, 1994 for a review of published and unpublished research). Despite the relative scarcity of published studies on the use of guided notes in college classes, anecdotal evidence attests to their effectiveness and assumptions continue to be made about the appropriateness of their use at the post secondary level. Barbetta and Skaruppa (1995b) suggest that the use of guided notes in college classes not only helps to ensure that students' notes are accurate and organized, but that guided notes may also increase the opportunities that a student has to actively participate in class. The authors contend that students who spend less time writing will presumably have more time to process and think about concepts, resulting in more active responses in class. An additional benefit of guided notes suggested by the authors is a potential increase in the quality of class discussions, due to students' increased confidence in the accuracy of their notes as a basis for asking questions and their increased opportunities to actively process information during the class session.

Empirical support for Barbetta and Scaruppa's (1995b) assumptions is extremely limited, and focuses mainly on the achievement outcomes (i.e., exam scores) associated with the use of guided notes (Hartley, 1976; Klemm, 1976; Lazarus, 1993). Based on the lack of empirical support additional benefits of guided notes, such as enhanced in-class processing of information and increased active participation, Austin, Gilbert, Thiebealt, Carr, and Bailey (in press) conducted a study to ascertain whether students would respond more and demonstrate greater immediate recall when guided notes were used. The number of active responses by students provided an indication of the effects of guided notes on participation, whereas the scores on daily immediate recall quizzes at the end of each lecture were intended to indicate the degree of in-class processing of information. Results indicated that students made more active responses in class (e.g., asking content-relevant questions and comments, answering instructor-posed questions, etc.) when they were given guided notes to supplement the lecture. Results also indicated that mean scores on quizzes given directly after the lecture were higher when guided notes were used. However, the data also suggested that these benefits (i.e., increased responding and active processing) gradually occurred over the course of the semester as opposed to occurring immediately upon receiving and using guided notes. One plausible reason for this pattern was that students were most likely "set" in their notetaking habits, and that the introduction of a new notetaking format may have taken some time for students to learn. The implication is that guided notes should probably be used consistently across the entire course so that students can acclimate to the new note format and obtain maximum benefits from its use.

The use of guided notes at the post-secondary level is an area that is ripe with research opportunities due to the dirge of empirical validation for the benefits of guided notes for college students. Topics to be addressed by future research include ascertaining which types of college students are most likely to benefit from the use of guided notes, what subject areas are best suited for utilizing guided notes, the effect of lecture presentation style on the effectiveness and educational impact of guided notes, which formats of guided notes are most beneficial to students (e.g., Is it better to have to fill in a word here and there or to have to fill in complete sentences?), which types of learning are affected by the use of guided notes (e.g., Can guided notes enhance both recall of factual information and ability to apply concepts?), and the impact of guided notes on teacher behavior.

Response Cards

In 1968, Raymond Wyman introduced the Visual Response System (VRS) for teaching written language to deaf students. The VRS classroom included 8-10 desks arranged in a U-shape around a central overhead projector. On each of the desks, individual built-in projectors allowed each student to individually respond to instructional antecedents. Giving each student the opportunity to respond at once allowed the instructor to check the accuracy of student responses and provide students with immediate feedback. It also allowed students to learn how the system worked by watching their peers, which minimized the amount of instruction that the teacher had to give regarding how and when to respond. The success of the VRS with deaf students prompted its use with a wider range of populations, including juvenile delinquents (Heward, McCormick, & Joynes, 1980; Marshall & Heward, 1979; Test & Heward, 1980), developmentally disabled students (Cooke, Heron, & Heward, 1980), and students with learning disabilities (Test & Heward, 1983). Despite its success in a variety of situations, the equipment and space needed for VRS utilization made it impractical for many schools. In an effort to provide a "lower-tech" alternative to VRS which retained the components that made it so successful as an instructional methodology, Test, Cooke, Heward, and Heron (1983) suggested ways to adapt VRS technology to the typical classroom. Among their suggestions was the utilization of response cards.

Response cards are cards given to students which are used to respond to the instructional antecedents presented in class. Two common types of response cards are color cards and write-on cards. Color cards allow the student to respond in class by holding up the colored card that corresponds to a particular answer. Each student is provided with different colored cards that each correspond to a particular answer. The instructor then presents a question and asks students to hold up the appropriate card. For example, if an instructor provides an example of positive reinforcement, students would hold up the card with the color representing positive reinforcement. The second type of response card is a write-on card (i.e., small dry erase boards). This type of response card requires students to write out their responses and present them to the instructor. In terms of practicality, color cards are easier to use than write-on cards, especially when classes are large and it may be difficult for the instructor to see all the responses on write-on cards and provide appropriate feedback.

Response cards can improve the educational environment in a number of ways. First, they allow all students to respond to every appropriate instructional antecedent with minimal response effort. Traditional classroom settings, where students must raise their hands and wait to be called on, naturally limit the number of students who can actively respond in class. Time constraints make it impossible for teachers to obtain the responses of each student who raises his or her hand, and once the question is answered, obtaining answers from other students is both redundant and a poor use of instructional time. In a similar vein, traditional methods of questioning usually do not result in all students attempting to respond. Instructors often find that the same students typically volunteer to answer questions in class, and that some students never raise their hands. Response cards, however, have been shown not only to increase the number of responses that an individual student makes in class, but also to increase the total number of students who respond to instructional antecedents (Gardner et al., 1994; Narayan et al., 1990). In other words, response cards do not simply increase the response frequency of students who are already likely to participate in class; they also prompt participation from those students who probably would not respond under traditional classroom contingencies.

Consistent with research demonstrating a clear relationship between level of participation and academic success, use of response cards has proven effective in helping students to increase academic achievement on classroom assessment measures. Studies comparing the achievement of students in traditional educational settings with achievement in settings using response cards have consistently found that student performance is better when response cards are used (Cavanaugh et al., 1996; Gardner et al., 1994; Narayan et al., 1990).

A final benefit to utilizing response cards is that they provide an excellent source of feedback to both the students and the instructor. Answering questions which are followed by immediate presentation of a correct answer by the instructor allows students to ascertain how well they comprehend the concepts presented in the lecture. It is not uncommon for students to report that they **think** they understand something until they actually have to answer a question about it on a test. Response cards let students **know** if they understand something before having to use that information to answer test items. Along with providing feedback to students, response cards also provide feedback to instructors on what percentage of the entire class has grasped a particular concept. In traditional situations, instructors merely sample the understanding of the class by calling on one or two students. With response cards, the instructor gains information on the entire class' understanding of the material. This feedback should subsequently affect whether or not a teacher moves on to new material or re-explains a concept until a larger percentage of the class can correctly answer questions about the material.

The published research on response cards has demonstrated their effectiveness as an instructional tool for increasing student performance (Cavanaugh et al., 1996; Gardner et al., 1994; Narayan et al., 1990). However, this support is limited and wrought with various methodological shortcomings that need to be corrected by additional research. First, empirical validation of response cards has been limited to elementary and secondary school settings. While there is anecdotal evidence to support that response cards are effective across all educational levels, no empirical evidence exists to support this contention. Another shortcoming of response card research is that it has focused primarily on assessing the effects of response cards on quiz and test scores. These dependent measures, while common assessment strategies, may or may not represent the actual amount of learning achieved by students. Future research should focus on determining the impact of response cards on other potential measures of learning, including application of information and long term retention of ideas. Lastly, research is needed to determine the effects of response cards on teacher behavior and the extent to which using response cards can help instructors become more effective in presenting material and facilitating learning.

Choral Responding

Choral responding occurs when an entire class simultaneously provides a response to some type of instructional antecedent. There are relatively few studies that have assessed the effects of choral responding on student achievement (some examples include: Kamps, Dugan, Leonard, & Daoust, 1994; McKenzie & Mixon, 1979: Sindelar et al., 1986; Wolery et al., 1992), and most of the published studies have focused on the benefits of choral responding with mildly mentally retarded children. However, despite the limited research, choral responding warrants mention because it is a simple and easy to use method for increasing active student responding in college classrooms. To use choral responding, an instructor need only inform students of the discriminative stimulus for responding and then provide that stimulus. Once the students respond, the instructor then gives feedback on the majority answer.

Like response cards, choral responding can give both students and instructors feedback on the understanding of the information presented. A potential benefit to using choral responding as a method for increasing ASR is that it does not require any outside materials (e.g., cards) in order to use it effectively. However, choral responding does not give as clear an indication of the percentage of students who are answering correctly, nor is it as easy for an instructor to identify students who fail to respond to the antecedent. Clearly, research is needed to ascertain the degree to which choral responding is effective in college classrooms with regard to both student and teacher behavior.

Summary of Active Student Responding

Active Student Responding refers to a variety of behavioral techniques aimed at increasing active learning in the classroom. Three techniques (i.e., guided notes, response cards, and choral responding) have been established as effective methods for increasing student participation in class, however, most studies of these procedures have been conducted in lower-level educational settings. More research is needed to ascertain the benefits of the methodologies at the college level, and to determine modifications which would make these techniques more useful for post-secondary students.

Behavioral Approaches to Teaching: Challenges for the Future

"Education is perhaps the most important branch of scientific technology. It deeply affects the lives of all of us. We can no longer allow the exigencies of a practical situation to suppress the tremendous improvements which are within reach. The practical situation must be changed" (Skinner, 1968, p. 19). This quote from B. F. Skinner's, *The Technology of Teaching* is still probably the most succinct description of the current state of behavioral education. There is no doubt that we have long realized the importance and impact of education. Nonetheless, instructional techniques which are ineffective, inefficient, unvalidated, and non-behavioral continue to be used, despite the fact that applied behavior analysis has provided a multitude of effectual methodologies aimed at improving the quality of instruction and amount of student learning in a variety of educational environments. Clearly, behavioral researchers still have much left to do. One major challenge facing behavioral researchers is to demonstrate the wide range of settings and populations for which these procedures are appropriate and effective. It appears that applications of behavior analysis in education are still focused predominantly in the area where applied behavior analysis got its start: developmental disabilities. A handful of behavioral education researchers have branched out to other populations and settings, and have clearly demonstrated the power of behavior analysis as a foundation for improving education. The acceptance of behaviorally-based methods as valid techniques for mainstream education is dependent upon such researchers and their studies. Continued research on the effectiveness of behavioral approaches to teaching, as well as research on refining these techniques for specific populations, is essential if behavior analysis is to take its place in modern educational systems.

The second major challenge for behavioral educators and researchers is the effective marketing of behavior analysis in educational settings. Binder (1994) has suggested that behavior analysts follow the lead of private sector sales and marketing by engaging in such behaviors as identifying target markets, packaging techniques, and using plain English to promote the use of behavioral teaching methods. While marketing studies may seem unpalatable to some behavioral scientists, research focusing on the effective marketing of behavior analysis could do a great deal to expand the acceptance and use of behavioral teaching methods and behavior analysis in general.

Though this chapter has focused on how behavior analysis may be used at the college level, the aforementioned challenges apply to behavioral educators and researchers at all levels. Any teacher, whether professor, kindergarten instructor, or graduate teaching assistant, has an obligation to his or her students to provide the best possible quality of education. Behavior analysis has provided a strong foundation on which to build and promote educational practices which can help educators effectively meet this obligation, and in the end, produce more educated, satisfied, and successful students.

Reading Objectives

1. Explain the five characteristics of PSI that distinguish it from traditional methods of instruction.
2. What are the major criticisms leveled against the use of PSI?
3. Describe the five policies which guided the development and implementation of precision teaching.
4. Describe the SAFMEDS procedure and the findings on which the development of SAFMEDS was based.
5. Explain the relationship between active responding and learning.
6. What are guided notes, and what are the benefits of their use?
7. What are response cards, and what are the benefits of their use?
8. What is choral responding, and what are the benefits of its use?
9. What research might contribute to establishing behavioral education methods as acceptable and practical for use in college classrooms?
10. Create an outline for what a study might look like in each of the areas for future research.

Notes

1. Both publications were produced by the Center for Personalized Instruction at Georgetown University and published their last issues in 1980.

References

Austin, J. L., Carr, J. P., Gilbert, M., & Bailey, J. S. (1999). Effects of lecture presentation style on the quality of student notes. Manuscript submitted for publication.

Austin, J. L., Gilbert, M., Thiebealt, M., Carr, J. E., & Bailey, J. S. (in press). Effects of guided notes on student responding and recall in a university classroom. *Journal of Behavioral Education.*

Baker, L., & Lombardi, B. R. (1985). Student's lecture notes and their relation to test performance. *Teaching of Psychology, 12,* 28-32.

Barbetta, P. M., & Heward, W. L. (1993). Effects of active student response during error correction on the acquisition and maintenance of geography facts by elementary students with learning disabilities. *Journal of Behavioral Education, 3,* 217-233.

Barbetta, P. M., Heron, T. E., & Heward, W. L. (1993). Effects of active student response during error correction on the acquisition, maintenance, and generalization of sight words by students with developmental handicaps. *Journal of Applied Behavior Analysis, 26,* 111-119.

Barbetta, P. M., & Skaruppa, C. L. (1995a, September). *Practice what you preach: Using behavioral approaches to teach behavior analysis.* Paper presented at the 15th Annual Convention of the Florida Association for Behavior Analysis, Tampa, FL.

Barbetta, P. M., & Skaruppa, C. L. (1995b). Looking for a way to improve your behavior analysis lectures? Try guided notes. *The Behavior Analyst, 18,* 155-160.

Binder, C. (1994). Measurably superior instruction methods: Do we need sales and marketing? In R. Gardner, III, D. M. Sainato, J. O. Cooper, T. E. Heron, W. L. Heward, J. Eshleman, & T. A. Grossi (Eds.), *Behavior analysis in education: Focus on measurably superior instruction* (pp. 21-31). Monterey, CA: Brooks/Cole.

Born, D. G., & Moore, M. C. (1978). Some belated thoughts on pacing. *Journal of Personalized Instruction, 3,* 33-36.

Buskist, W., Cush, D., & DeGrandpre, R. J. (1991). The life and times of PSI. *Journal of Behavioral Education, 1,* 215-234.

Caldwell, E. C. (1985). Dangers of PSI. *Teaching of Psychology, 12,* 9-12.

Carter, J. F., & Van Matre, N. H. (1975). Note taking versus note having. *Journal of Educational Psychology, 67,* 900-904.

Cavanaugh, R. A., Heward, W. L., & Donelson, F. (1996). Effects of response cards during lesson closure on the academic performance of secondary students in an earth science course. *Journal of Applied Behavior Analysis, 29,* 403-406.

Cooke, N. L., Heron, T. E., & Heward, W. L. (1980). Teaching map skills to special education students. *Journal of Geography, 79,* 253-258.

Cooper, J. O. (1997, May). *Precision teaching in the elementary schools.* Paper presented at the 23rd Annual Convention, Association for Behavior Analysis, Chicago, IL.

Dewey, J. (1916). *Democracy and education.* New York, Macmillan.

Drevno, G. E., Kimball, J. W., Possi, M. K., Heward, W. L., Gardner, R., & Barbetta, P. M. (1994). Effects of active student response during error correction on the acquisition, maintenance, and generalization of science vocabulary by elementary students. *Journal of Applied Behavior Analysis, 27,* 179-180.

Fisher, J. L., & Harris, M. B. (1973). Effect of note taking and review on recall. *Journal of Educational Psychology, 65*, 321-325.

Gardner, R., Heward, W. L., & Grossi, T. A. (1994). Effects of response cards on student participation and academic achievement: A systematic replication with inner-city students during whole-class science instruction. *Journal of Applied Behavior Analysis, 27*, 63-71.

Glick, D. M., & Semb, G. (1978). Effects of pacing contingencies in personalized instruction: A review of the evidence. *Journal of Personalized Instruction, 3*, 36-42.

Greenwood, C. R., Delquadri, J., & Hall, R. V. (1984). Opportunity to respond and student academic achievement. In W. L. Heward, T. E., Heron, D. S. Hill, & J. Trap-Porter (Eds.), *Focus on behavior analysis in education* (pp. 58-88). Columbus, OH: Merrill.

Hartley, J. (1976). Lecture-handouts and student notetaking. *Programmed Learning and Educational Technology, 13*, 58-64.

Hartley, J., & Cameron, A. (1967). Some observations on the efficiency of lecturing. *Educational Review, 20*, 30-37.

Hartley, J., & Davies, I. K. (1978). Note-taking: A critical review. *Programmed Learning and Educational Technology, 15*, 207-224.

Hartley, J., & Marshall, S. (1974). On notes and notetaking. *Universities Quarterly, 28*, 225-235.

Heron, T. E., Heward, W. L., Cooke, N. L., & Hill, A. S. (1983). Evaluation of a classwide peer tutoring system: First graders teach each other sight words. *Education and Treatment of Children, 6*, 137-152.

Heward, W. L. (1994). Three "low-tech" strategies for increasing the frequency of active student response during group instruction. In R. Gardner, III, D. M. Sainato, J. O. Cooper, T. E. Heron, W. L. Heward, J. Eshleman, & T. A. Grossi (Eds.), *Behavior analysis in education: Focus on measurably superior instruction* (pp. 283-320). Monterey, CA: Brooks/Cole.

Heward, W. L., McCormick, S., & Joynes, Y. (1980). Completing job applications: Evaluation of an instructional program for mildly retarded juvenile delinquents. *Behavioral Disorders, 5*, 223-234.

Hobbs, S. H. (1987). PSI: Use, misuse, and abuse. *Teaching of Psychology, 14*, 106-107.

Hursh, D. E. (1976). Personalized system of instruction: What do the data indicate? *Journal of Personalized Instruction, 1*, 91-105.

Johnson, K. R. (1997, January). Maximizing fluency at work: Adult literacy and numeracy. Paper presented at the Sixth Florida Association for Behavior Analysis - Organizational Behavior Management Conference, Daytona Beach, FL.

Johnson, K. R., & Layng, T. V. J. (1992). Breaking the structuralist barrier: Literacy and numeracy with fluency. *American Psychologist, 47*, 1475-1490.

Kamps, D. M., Dugan, E. P., Leonard, B. R., & Daoust, P. M. (1994). Enhance small group instruction using choral responding and student interaction for children with autism an developmental disabilities. *American Journal on Mental Retardation, 99*, 60-73.

Keenan, J. B., Bono, S. F., & Hursh, D. E. (1978). Shaping time management skills: Two examples in PSI. *Journal of Personalized Instruction, 3,* 46-49.

Keller, F. S. (1968). Good-bye, teacher. *Journal of Applied Behavior Analysis, 1,* 79-89.

Keller, F. S. (1985). Lightning strikes twice. *Teaching of Psychology, 12,* 4-8.

Kiewra, K. A. (1985). Investigating notetaking and review: A depth of processing alternative. *Educational Psychologist, 20,* 23-32.

Klemm, W. R. (1976). Efficiency of handout "skeleton" notes in student learning. *Improving College and University Teaching, 24,* 10-12.

Koorland, M. A., Keel, M. C., & Ueberhorst, P. (1990). Setting performance aims for precision learning. *Teaching Exceptional Children, 22,* 64-66.

Kulik, J. A., Kulik, C. C., & Cohen, P. A. (1979). A meta-analysis of outcome studies of Keller's personalized system of instruction. *American Psychologist, 34,* 307-318.

Lamal, P. A. (1984). Interest in PSI across sixteen years. *Teaching of Psychology, 11,* 237-238.

Lamwers, L. L., & Jazwinski, C. H. (1989). A comparison of three strategies to reduce student procrastination in PSI. *Teaching of Psychology, 16,* 8-12.

Lazarus, B. D. (1993). Guided notes: Effects with secondary and post-secondary students with mild disabilities. *Education and Treatment of Children, 16,* 272-289.

Liberty, K. A., & Haring, N. G. (1990). Introduction to decision rule systems. *Remedial and Special Education, 11,* 32-41.

Lindsley, O. R. (1990). Precision teaching: By teachers for children. *Teaching Exceptional Children, 22,* 10-15.

Lindsley, O. R. (1991). Precision teaching's unique legacy from B. F. Skinner. *Journal of Behavioral Education, 1,* 253-266.

Lindsley, O. R. (1992). Why aren't effective teaching tools widely adopted? *Journal of Applied Behavior Analysis, 25,* 21-26.

Lindsley, O. R. (1993). Our discoveries over 28 years. *Journal of Precision Teaching, 10,* 11-13.

Lloyd, M. E., & Lloyd, K. E. (1986). Has lightning struck twice? Use of PSI in college classrooms. *Teaching of Psychology, 13,* 149-151.

Maheady, L., & Sainato, D. M. (1985). The effects of peer tutoring upon the social status and social interaction patterns of high and low status elementary school students. *Education and Treatment of Children, 8,* 51-65.

Marshall, A. E., & Heward, W. L. (1979). Teaching self-management to incarcerated youth. *Behavioral Disorders, 4,* 215-226.

Martinez, J. G. R., & Martinez, N. C. (1988). Hello, teacher: An argument for reemphasizing the teacher's role in PSI and mastery learning. *American Journal of Education, 97,* 18-33.

McDade, C. E., & Goggins, L. A. (1993). Computer-based precision learning: Achieving fluency with college students. *Education and Treatment of Children, 16,* 290-305.

McKenzie, G. R., & Mixon, H. (1979). Effects of test-like events on on-task behavior, test anxiety, and achievement in a classroom rule-learning task. *Journal of Educational Psychology, 71*, 370-374.

Meek, R. L. (1977). The traditional in non-traditional learning methods. *Journal of Personalized Instruction, 2*, 114-118.

Narayan, J. S., Heward, W. L., Gardner, R., Courson, F. H., & Omness, C. K. (1990). Using response cards to increase student participation in an elementary classroom. *Journal of Applied Behavior Analysis, 23*, 483-490.

Norton, L. S. (1981). The effects of notetaking and subsequent use on later recall. *Programmed Learning and Educational Technology, 18*, 16-22.

Nye, P. A., Crooks, T. J., Powley, M., & Tripp, G. (1984). Student notetaking related to university performance. *Higher Education, 13*, 85-97.

Olenick, D. L., & Pear, J. J. (1980). Differential reinforcement of correct responses to probes and prompts in picture-naming with retarded children. *Journal of Applied Behavior Analysis, 13*, 77-89.

Palmatier, R. A., & Bennett, J. M. (1974). Notetaking habits of college students. *Journal of Reading, 18*, 215-218.

Potts, L., Eshleman, J. W., & Cooper, J. O. (1993). Ogden R. Lindsley and the historical development of precision teaching. *The Behavior Analyst, 16*, 177-189.

Pratton, J., & Hales, L. W. (1986). The effects of active participation on student learning. *Journal of Educational Research, 79*, 210-215.

Reboy, L. M., & Semb, G. B. (1991). PSI and critical thinking: Compatibility or irreconcilable differences? *Teaching of Psychology, 18*, 212-215.

Sherman, J. G. (1992). Reflections on PSI: Good news and bad. *Journal of Applied Behavior Analysis, 25*, 59-64.

Sindelar, P. T., Bursuck, W. D., & Halle, J. W. (1986). The effects of two variations of teacher questioning on student performance. *Education and Treatment of Children, 9*, 56-66.

Skinner, B. F. (1968). *The technology of teaching*. Englewood Cliffs, NJ: Prentice-Hall.

Skinner, B. F. (1984). The shame of American education. *American Psychologist, 39*, 947-954.

Snyder, G. (1992). Training to fluency: A real return on investment. *Performance Management Magazine, 10*, 16-22.

Sterling, R. M., Barbetta, P. M., Heward, W. L., & Heron, T. E. (1997). A comparison of active student response and on-task instruction on the acquisition and maintenance of health facts by fourth grade special education students. *Journal of Behavioral Education, 7*, 151-165.

Taveggia, T. C. (1976). Personalized instruction: A summary of comparative research, 1967-1974. *American Journal of Physics, 44*, 1028-1033.

Test, D. W., Cooke, N. L., Heward, W. L., & Heron, T. E. (1983). Adapting visual response teaching technology to the conventional classroom. *Journal of Special Education Technology, 6*, 15-26.

Test, D. W., & Heward, W. L. (1980). Photosynthesis: Teaching a complex science concept to juvenile delinquents. *Science Education, 64*, 129-139.

Test, D. W., & Heward, W. L. (1983). Teaching road signs and traffic laws to learning disabled students. *Learning Disability Quarterly, 6*, 80-83.

Van Houten, R., & Rolider, A. (1989). An analysis of several variables influencing the efficacy of flash card instruction. *Journal of Applied Behavior Analysis, 22*, 111-118.

White, O. R. (1986). Precision teaching - precision learning. *Exceptional Children, 52*, 522-534.

Wolery, M., Ault, M. J., Doyle, P. M., & Gast, D. L. (1992). Choral and individual responding during small group instruction: Identification of interactional effects. *Education and Treatment of Children, 15*, 289-309.

Wyman, R. A. (1968). A visual response system for small group instruction. *Audio-Visual Instruction, 13*, 714-717.

Young, C. C., Hecimovic, A., & Salzburg, C. L. (1983). Tutor-tutee behavior of disadvantaged kindergarten children during peer teaching. *Education and Treatment of Children, 6*, 123-135.

Chapter 20

A Futurist Perspective for Applied Behavior Analysis

Jon S. Bailey
Florida State University

In the beginning...

Predicting the future is a perilous activity but may be necessary if, as a field, Applied Behavior Analysis (ABA) is to live up to my expectations. I have had high hopes for this field from the day I was introduced to its predecessor, behavior modification, one warm September day in 1961. Jack Michael was teaching an introductory undergraduate honors course in psychology from (what I only realized later was) a radical perspective. Michael's view was based on Skinner's vision (Skinner, 1948) of a world in which human behavior was understood sufficiently well that routine world conflicts and crises as well as the standard annoying problems of daily living could be eliminated. By applying what we knew about the principles of learning and reinforcement (Skinner, 1953) children would learn rapidly and effortlessly in pleasant, well managed (and certainly safe) classrooms, families would thrive on mutual loving support, businesses would motivate employees to be productive, and communities would manage their human and natural resources so as to promote safe, friendly environments where citizens could enjoy freedom and pursue happiness. It all seemed so reasonable and, as Michael explained so convincingly, the new science of human behavior was off to a great start (Ayllon & Michael, 1959) and the building of a behavioral technology was well underway.

Applied behavior analysis was conceived out of the early dramatic successes of the experimental analysis of behavior (Greenspoon, 1955) and was born in an era of radical social change. Early on when it was referred to as "behavior mod" it somehow caught on and fit with other trappings that were "mod" such as polyester leisure suits, bell bottom trousers, big hair, big government, and acid rock music. No one at the time seemed offended at our terminology of "prediction and control" but soon enough the times changed and we were suddenly psychology's "bad boy" (Hilts, 1974; London, 1969).

"A new breed of post-Skinnerian psychologists (behavior modifiers) assume that man is a soulless machine and seek to control his behavior in schools, prisons, corporations, armies, hospitals, in much the same way they would program a computer. What's more, their techniques are impressively successful. Or are they early warnings of Big Brother and 1984?" Hilts, 1974, jacket cover.

"Computer psychotherapy, radio-activated brain implants, conditioning, hypnotism, psychosurgery, mood-bending drugs: these are the tools of behavior control, the new arsenal of modern psychology, with which some men can make others do their will." London, 1974, jacket cover.

Skinner clearly envisioned a world in which behavior analysis was a very central part of the design of the culture (Skinner, 1948) and one where behavior analysts would play a central role in planning and perhaps implementing social contingencies that would promote the welfare of the culture and it's citizens. But, with this kind of negative publicity from major media outlets, and influential respected scientists, it was clear that we were in for a rough time of it. Later Skinner's *Beyond Freedom and Dignity* (1971) would serve as a lightning rod for criticism of the behavioral perspective.

What Went Wrong?

Now, almost forty years later, I am struck by the appalling lack of understanding of even the most rudimentary principles of learning by experienced teachers, well educated parents, "enlightened" elected leaders, institutions of government, and our otherwise hugely successful multinational business giants. The discrepancy between what could have been (and still could be) and our current state is enough to induce clinical depression in a diehard behavior analyst. What went wrong? How could it happen that an ethical, humane, effective technology based on a sound foundation of science could be so thoroughly ignored and rebuked by so many for so long? I have thought, fretted and worried about this in private and in public for the past few years and have concluded that it is largely our fault (Bailey, 1990, 1991). As a field I believe we have made strategic errors in how we have molded and sculpted our field, in how we present ourselves to the public, and how we view the world. I believe, along with Dick Malott and Aubrey Daniels, that we can save the world but not with the perspective we currently employ. To live up to the potential envisioned in the beginning (Skinner, 1948, 1953; Baer, Wolf & Risley, 1968) we need a new world view; we need to understand paradigm shifts, we need to understand the future.

Understanding Paradigm Shifts

The industrial revolution was a profound paradigm shift (Kuhn, 1970) in the way we viewed human capital and the good life (Toffler & Toffler, 1995). Living in a busy, crowded city, working in a noisy factory dramatically replaced the quiet, stable bucolic (and perhaps romanticized) farm life for millions of Americans. Behaviorism was another significant paradigm shift from the 18th century introspectionism of Wundt and Titchener to a 19th century science of behavior devoid of references to consciousness, mental states, mind, and the like (Baars, 1986; Baum, 1994). Other more recent social/cultural paradigm shifts include civil rights, the women's movement, state-sanctioned terrorism, safe sex, the personal computer, and biotechnology (Barker, 1995). In each case we have an example of revolutionary thinking that replaces old views and raises new concerns. Behaviorists enjoyed a long run, (by some estimates from 1913 to 1960) but many believe that "the cognitive revolution" has now replaced behaviorism with a science intent on exploring underlying factors such as "ideas" and "purposes" explaining behavior (Baars, 1986).

Recent Paradigm Shifts in Service Delivery

Within behavior analysis' short history we have seen other smaller, though no less significant, paradigm shifts. Early "behavior modification" seemed to emphasize the manipulation and control of behavior as though the person was a subject in someone else's experiment (Krasner & Ullmann, 1967; Ullmann & Krasner, 1965; Ulrich, Stachnik & Mabry, 1970). Additionally the use of aversive control procedures was widespread. In the 1970's we saw the emergence of a new value system, a new paradigm, that stressed the value of the person and the need for "less restrictive" modes of treatment. The 1980's brought the "anti-aversives" movement and deinstitutionalization as well. "Behavior mod" was characterized by critics as "inhumane," "manipulative" and "coercive". The new paradigm became "positive behavioral support" which was humane, used strictly positive procedures, and was "citizen" centered. The medical model of the 1950's and 1960's was replaced by the developmental (i.e., training) model of the 1970's and this has been replaced by the "Citizen's Choice" model (shown in Figure 1) of the 1990's (Kimber & Hemingway, 1994). In this model the citizen may choose the setting in which they live and can reject procedures they dislike. Little emphasis is placed on skill acquisition or behavior change. Behavior analysts had little input into this model and the focus on allowing the person to become an active member of the community without acquiring the requisite skills appears in part to be a backlash against the accountability model of the previous 20 years.

This apparent rejection of the behavioral model is due in no small measure to the failure of the behavioral community to be aware of the sea change that was afoot.

Shifting Trends in Supports and Services

Medical Model	Developmental Model	Citizen's Choice
The patient	The client	The citizen
Institutions	Community Placement	Community Member
The Institution	Group Homes	Homes
Low Expectations	Regimented Programs	Supports
Professional Decisions	Habilitation Plans	Individual Support Plan
Out of Community ⟶	Part of Community ⟶	Into Community

Figure 1. Shifting trends in supports and services in developmental disabilities after Kimber & Hemingway, 1994.

Some recipients of behavioral services were apparently unhappy with what they received and in our complacent state we were left out of a series of critical meetings held statewide where these grievances were aired and where the new model evolved. This particular sea change happened over a 12-month period, perhaps a record for societal value drift.

Considering the Social and Cultural Context of Research and Its Adoption

Behavior analysis appears to have had it's heyday (Baars, 1986) and many see it as passe, a technology out of touch and on the wane. And yet, the research base is sound, the fundamentals of science are as strong as ever and the contributions seem even more significant than just a few years ago (Iwata, Bailey, Neef, Wacker, Repp, & Shook, 1997). Stepping back a bit from specific contributions of a particular study and taking in the larger context of cultural change, it is apparent that behavior analysis is not just about certain research findings that can be peer reviewed and published. In the social sciences, of which we are a part, research contributions must increasingly "fit" with societal trends in order to be adopted. In the 1960's, retarded individuals lived in public institutions, received perfunctory custodial care and essentially no training since they were thought to be untrainable. Behavior analysis research was welcomed in this context since the data showed that these individuals could be trained. Hundreds and hundreds of studies were published over the next 20 years establishing an unchallenged claim of the superiority of behaviorally based treatment. Researchers did not have to give a great deal of consideration to the rights of the clients since changing their behavior and improving their performance was paramount. The winds began shifting in the late 1980's however, and advocacy groups began raising a different concern. Behavior change was not the most important gauge of success; the feelings of the person with a "developmental disability" and the concerns of their parents or advocates were now advanced. Aversive procedures in particular might harm or stigmatize a client despite the fact that they "worked".

The research was no less sound but the consumers had changed and they brought a different value system with them. Behavioral research, like any applied endeavor, occurs in a context and the times were changing with a new emphasis on human rights, women's rights, and clients' rights. Had behavior analysts been more aware of this paradigm shift I believe that they would have been able to make adjustments in their research methodology and their communication strategies and as a field, applied behavior analysis would not have become the whipping boy of developmental disabilities.

Creating A Future for Behavior Analysis

It is easy to get caught up in one's work, to be oblivious to trends around us, and it is natural to resist change and deny that cultural context "should" be relevant. However, it is my thesis that for us to survive in the next 20 years, it will be essential that we become acutely aware of cultural trends and super sensitive to sea changes that are taking place all around us. Behavior analysis is the right approach to understanding human behavior but we must adjust our antennae to pick up the signals from a constantly changing society. We need to look around us for shifts in the culture, look for trends, evaluate their likely impact and decide how and where to "position" behavior analysis for optimal effect. To do anything else is folly, since, in this new super-competitive world, there is a good chance that behavior analysis, if it is not properly promoted, will simply disappear from the scene.

What is The Possible Role for Behavior Analysis in Our Society

It seems to me that applied behavior analysis is more relevant than ever before and that it offers our citizens, parents, teachers, and corporate and government leaders advantages that cannot be matched by any other psychological approach. As can be seen in the previous chapters, behavior analysis offers a comprehensive educational and therapeutic technology of treatment. I know of no other approach in psychology that can boast state-of-the-art solutions to the most troubling social ills of the day. We know how to treat brain injury (Jacobs, this volume), emotionally disturbed, neglected and abused adolescents (Friman, this volume) and the mentally ill (Hayes, this volume). We have a thoroughly researched methodology for teaching children in schools (Ehrhardt & Ervin, this volume) and working with them in medical settings (Blum & Friman, this volume). Behavior analysis has made huge contributions in the field of developmental disabilities (Iwata et al., this volume; Ivancic, this volume; Carr et al., this volume) and has been the primary mode of treatment in that field for the past 25 years. We know how to diagnose performance problems in organizational settings (Austin, this volume) and how to improve productivity in virtually any organization (Williams, this volume). Safety (Alavosius, this volume) and instruction (Austin, this volume; Brethower, this volume) are two additional areas where significant gains have been made and generalizable models for improving human productivity have been developed for most any industry or organization. Animal trainers working with the full range of species from dogs to dolphins have adopted the positive reinforcement approach (Pryor, 1985) and there is a steady stream of behaviorally based research in sport psychology (Martin & Tkachuk, this volume).

With all of this potential, why is behavior analysis the best kept secret in all of psychology? The answer is complex and involves choices we have made and strategies we have adopted over the past forty years. It involves unpredictable accidents and unfortunate incidents out of our control, as well as the personal preferences and personality characteristics of early leaders in the field who set the tone for those who would follow. Even to this day there is serious disagreement among the opinion makers in our field as to the proper role of behavior analysis in the culture. We have not clarified our mission nor spoken with one voice. The combined effect of these variables has produced a specialty largely out of touch with larger cultural values and societal trends and almost completely isolated from and ignored by the rest of psychology.

What Do We Have to Offer?

So that the reader will not be unclear on this point, let me state categorically that I believe that behavior analysis can and should be the primary orientation of parents who wish to raise happy, intelligent, curious, responsible, children; the coda for teachers who wish to motivate their students to be active learners who cooperate with and support their peers; the bible for corporate executives who wish to encourage their employees to work productively, show initiative, and seek new ways to grow the business; and the textbook for therapists who desire to help their clients overcome almost any crippling disorder from anxiety to Tourette Syndrome.

Behavior analysis offers solutions for everyday, contemporary problems that plague us; solutions that are humane, effective and, if given the chance, chosen by consumers. Behavior analysis solutions match the values of the culture, it is democratic, it supports moral behavior. We know, based on research findings, that if you want a behavior to occur more often it is necessary to reinforce it. The culture supports the use of rewards for creativity, hard work, and initiative. Behavior analysts believe in making data-based decisions; government in particular and society in general are increasingly supporting accountability; the business community is daily becoming comfortable with statistical process measures. Note that I am not suggesting we try to sell the "no free will" philosophy of behaviorism. I believe this is futile and self-defeating. Rather than push determinism, we need to promote a new philosophy of understanding human behavior in practical terms; a philosophy that encourages everyone to look closely at determining variables for behavior and seeks to make changes that will encourage the use of proven procedures to enhance the welfare of our citizens. Our emphasis should be on the use of positive, humane, data-based, effective procedures which benefit the individuals involved as well as society. We need to encourage consumers to be skeptical of approaches that sound too good to be true (Sagan, 1996) whether in business (Micklethwait & Wooldridge, 1996), education (Lehmann, 1997) or therapy (Singer & Lalich, 1996). Our philosophy which we need to actively promote should embrace the notion that "a behavioral approach to social problems can enhance democracy and promote moral behavior." (Baum, 1994, p. 15).

Who Should Our Consumers Be?

Up to this point, I contend, we have had a very restricted audience for this burgeoning behavioral technology. We speak almost entirely to ourselves, using our own special brand of technical jargon, through our own journals and to each other at our own conferences. This not effective public relations and is self-defeating if we are to have a broad cultural impact. We will need to rethink our audience, perhaps rework our product, and certainly develop a systematic strategy for bringing our solutions to public awareness. Currently, our audience is behavior analysts but in the future we will need to target the general public, decision-makers at the local, state and national level and the media. All of the work in classroom management and teaching technology has been largely ignored, I believe, because we have not packaged this information for presentation to school superintendents, members of local school boards and concerned parents. We now know how to solve, I would argue, the number one education problem in this country—discipline. We have known how to deal effectively with this issue since the late 1970's. And yet, for lack of an effective method of communicating these findings to those with authority who can make a difference, we have allowed our schools to disintegrate and our classrooms to become battlegrounds between students and teachers. We need to systematically rework all our findings and make sure that our message is tailored to key decision-makers at the state and local level as well as those in the federal government. Other consumers who need to know about effective methods of behavior change include decision makers in insurance companies, managed care institutions, and major business and consulting firms. Reaching a popular audience with our message as Aubrey Daniels (Daniels, 1994) has recently done and as Karen Pryor has for years is clearly an essential part of any strategy of public awareness and acceptance (Pryor, 1985). Most recently, Catherine Maurice has probably done more to boost the image of behavior analysts than all of us have collectively over a 25 year period (Maurice, 1993).

Current Trends to Watch

Watching trends and predicting cultural changes has become increasingly important in recent years for governments as they attempt to anticipate critically needed services and businesses as they try to stay one step ahead of the competition. Professional trendwatchers (Davis, 1996; Popcorn & Marigold, 1996; Morrison & Schmid, 1994; the World Futurist Society, 1997) are developing a science of the prediction business and sell their services through direct consultation (with company names like BrainReserve and Institute for the Future) and via highly priced newsletters (e.g., the BrainReserve newsletter CLICKTIME is $199 per year). Using information gleaned from the Census Bureau and the Bureau of Labor Statistics as well as "softer" sources such as annual Gallup polls and household surveys and articles in the popular media, trendwatchers make observations about current tendencies and short- and long-term predictions regarding their implications.

Here are just a few trends that have implications for future human behavior in a variety of ways:

• the aging of our US population

• the increasing number of working mothers

• the proliferation of managed care

• the growing service economy

• the US as leader in the knowledge creation and dissemination business

• increasing global competition

• the disparity of wealth in the culture

•easy access to information via desktop computers
•virtual reality simulations

•virtual relationships via cyberspace
•distance learning
•less government, more privatization
•less federal government influence, more decisions at state and local government level
•the decline in civic America– "bowling alone"
•working at home
•mass customization
•the technology revolution–personal digital assistants for all
•"cocooning"–the tendency to stay home for entertainment, shop via catalog and the home shopping network, provide home security systems, etc.
•the shift from "mass marketing" to "micro marketing"
•"clanning"–the tendency to seek out others with similar interests
•working in groups
•access to any person, any time, anywhere via cell phones
•the proliferation of satellite and cable TV offerings
•fewer people watching the major TV networks

The list goes on and on. It is not certain, of course, whether all these trends will continue or how long they will last. It is clear to me that the environment that spawned behavior analysis in the early and mid 1960's does not exist today.

Positioning Behavior Analysis in the Near-Future Culture

How do we "package" behavior analysis findings for maximum impact? My suggestion is that we employ business professionals who make this their specialty. Marketing and advertising companies exist solely to represent products and services in a very competitive world. They can determine how best to present concepts and ideas (e.g. recycling as an aspect of environmentalism) as well as new products (e.g. digital cameras) to consumers. They understand which media and advertising combinations work best for maximum exposure and optimal impact. These companies will no doubt extensively employ focus groups to determine what potential consumers currently think of our field and then devise a variety of marketing strategies to correct mis-impressions and present our case effectively. Our part will be to work with current trends and make sure that our field has been optimally formulated to address them as well as to plan future research that will be timely and relevant. Here are just a few examples:

Dealing with Our Aging population

While we are currently devoting a huge percentage of our resources and a significant proportion of our researchers to dealing with issues of developmental disabilities, the major social problem of the future is how to deal with our aging and middle aging citizens. We will see an increase of 50 percent in those between the ages of 45 and 55 in the period from 1990 to 2000 (Morrison & Schmid, 1994).

While we have some limited amount of research going on with older citizens, it is clear that behavior analysis could make major contributions to the placement, training and support of this older group of workers (i.e., work environments and workplace contingencies will probably have to be totally redesigned). Behavior analysts know how to measure performance to a very fine degree and with great precision; we know how to design reinforcement systems to promote high motivation and optimal performance (Abernathy, 1996; Daniels, 1994; Rummler & Brache, 1995). Now the challenge is to adapt these settings to people who are 45 (and well educated–25% will have college education) instead of 18.

Another easy to predict situation is that this aging population will need nursing care at some point. A brain trust of creative behavior analysts could meet to analyze the current state of our understanding of residential treatment based on our experience in developmental disabilities and make suggestions for those in the private sector to will be developing these environments. I believe we have the beginning knowledge of how to make such settings interesting and challenging so as to maintain the health and vitality of senior citizens but unless we take the initiative our findings will again be unappreciated or ignored. Just as the school system is increasingly beginning to appreciate the value of behavior analysts in the schools (Reiss, M. R., personal communication, August 5, 1997) residences and nursing homes may also find it valuable to employ behavior analysts to help develop effective training and motivational systems to keep elders active, alert and responsive to their environment.

Competing in Managed-Care

We are in the middle of a revolution in how we receive medical services. Only ten years ago most Americans had a family doctor whose services were paid on a fee for service basis through private insurance. It is now far more common that they belong to a for-profit HMO and have their healthcare brokered by accountants who determine which services they will receive and how much money will be allotted for each instance. Under traditional health insurance plans it was not unusual for coverage to include 20 days of mental health services. Now most managed-care plans will require psychologists and psychiatrists to justify any treatment more than 6-8 days in length (Greene, 1997). Managed-care embraces focused, goal-oriented therapy, which is cost-effective. Long drawn out traditional psychotherapy is being replaced with short-term therapy which focuses on specific problems of patients rather than "rummaging through their pasts to link the problems to earlier events in their lives" (Greene, 1997). This trend could be a tremendous boon to behavior analysts and behavior therapists who have argued for years for just such accountability in therapy. Without analyzing the unique advantages of our behavioral approach and packaging the elements in a way that it will be understood by HMO managers we will likely be overlooked as a treatment option. Again, it would be useful to employ professionals to help us determine how this information should be prepared and presented. Information alone may not be sufficient. Lobbyists (like those who work for the Florida Association for Behavior Analysis to protect the Certified

Behavior Analyst program) may have to be hired to advocate for our inclusion in services covered by HMOs.

The recent explosion in demand for behavior analysts to treat autistic children has raised another related treatment issue. How do we respond if we are recognized as having the only available expertise? Currently the need for trained therapists in autism far outstrips the supply of qualified individuals, and further, parents are unaware of the requirements they should look for in a therapist. Had we been on top of the trend we would have quickly put together guides for parents and made this information readily available via all media sources. Unfortunately, having been unaware, we are caught in a situation where many totally unqualified individuals are claiming expertise and demanding top dollar for their services (Green, G., personal communication, Oct. 18, 1997). In addition, we are in a rather desperate situation with regard to providing trained therapists. We have too few behavior analysis graduate programs in this country to ever meet the need that is apparent from the current demand.

New Models of Child Care

With the increase in working mothers (from 38% to 57% over the past 30 years) and the two-income family (Morrison & Schmid, 1994) the dependence on care delivered by others becomes increasingly important. Behavior analysts at the University of Kansas have studied this critical delivery system for over twenty-five years (Baer & Wolf, 1970; Risley & Hart, 1968) and very concrete recommendations can be made about all aspects of early childhood care and education. Such findings are available to those who read the *Journal of Applied Behavior Analysis* but parents or preschool directors would be hard pressed to find a way to get access to this treasure trove of important information. If they were to stumble across this journal few would be able to understand it given the proliferation of technical jargon and the emphasis on behavioral methodology. The development of books, brochures and video tapes on behaviorally designed day care and preschool environments will be essential to reach the key markets.

In addition, future research might focus on effective ways of training preschool staff, "au pair" and "nannies" to decrease the likelihood that child abuse will occur when parents are at work. In keeping with other current educational and electronic communication trends, such training might focus on the Internet and distance learning strategies. A "Nanny Channel" might be developed that would run tips for day care personnel covering child development, the design of activities and games for children of early ages, advice from experts, comments from parents and so on.

Hi-Tech Education

With the advent of small, portable, relatively inexpensive and readily available personal computers and personal "assistants", education and training can take on a completely different character. Teachers, long seen as the source of information become "managers" of information instead. Behavior analysts need to become actively involved in research in this new arena. With our knowledge of the new technology of fluency (Binder, 1996) and contingencies of reinforcement it should be possible to design effective virtual educational settings where students learn information gathering and research skills and bring those skills together in new forward-looking, problem-solving repertoires.

Behavior analysts may need to team up with instructional designers and computer engineers to produce new applied research to meet this need. Instructional designers typically are expert in the design of effective strategies and the development of state-of-the-art media but lack a background in contingencies of reinforcement that can motivate students to peak performance. Computer engineers who can develop realistic virtual simulations of most any setting or environment from a classroom to an aircraft carrier give us the possibility of virtual shaping of behavior. Therapists might work with "virtual patients" in virtual clinical settings where they can try out their clinical skills at no risk. The Army and Air Force have used this technology for years training soldiers to drive tanks and pilots to fly and land jet aircraft at no risk to life or limb or big budget hardware. Combining our knowledge of behavior with their resources should result in an educational technology that matches the computer technology revolution that we have experienced in the past ten years (Moore, Murdock, Harrington, & Bostow, 1997).

As alluded to earlier our previous research on effective educational contingencies also needs to repackaged for educators, administrators and parents. Very few of these individuals have any knowledge of the early work in classroom management or realize the immense size of the body of work that has accumulated (Sulzer-Azaroff, Drabman, Greer, Hall, Iwata & O'Leary, 1988). A recent encounter with a staff director for the president of the Florida House of Representatives in which this book of readings was presented resulted in astonishment. Though he had been "researching" this topic for months he was totally unaware of the work that had been done in behavior analysis and yet was advising key legislators on a new bill that was to redirect some education funding for the purpose of "motivating students". I realized at the time that a companion volume that translated this voluminous and impressive work for the lay person was badly needed. Catherine Maurice (Maurice, 1997) has complained publicly about the same problem in getting information for parents of autistic children who are seeking therapy.

A New Research Strategy for Applied Behavior Analysis

In order for applied behavior analysis to continue making substantial contributions to the culture it will be necessary to adopt a new research strategy. Rather than basing new research ideas on previous published studies or on applied needs that present themselves, we need to look at the driving forces in contemporary society and attempt to predict needed behavioral technology at least five years out. Then we need to pursue creative lines of applied research that, when combined with an effective dissemination strategy, will clearly have an impact. As shown in Figure 2 some variables that we might consider include: advances in computer/information technology, shifting demographics of our aging society, environmental changes,

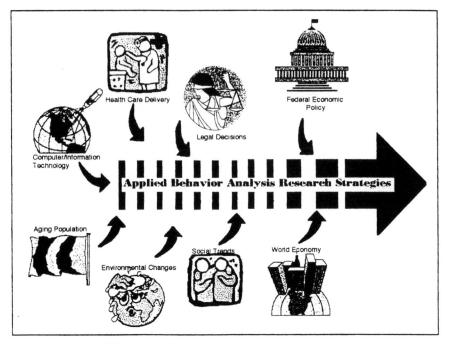

Figure 2. A new behavior analysis research strategy which takes into account current variables such as advances in computer/ information technology, shifting demographics of our aging society, environmental changes, social trends, the world economy, changing federal economic policies, the effect of legal decisions, and modifications in health care delivery systems.

social trends, the world economy, changing federal economic policies, the effect of legal decisions, and modifications in health care delivery systems.

Next Steps

There is much work to be done and very little time. Collectively we need to urge our professional associations to take immediate steps to address some pressing issues. Time at national meetings could be used to confer on the vision of our field's future. Where would we like it to be in 20 years? What resources can we bring to bear? What strategies must we employ? These and many other questions will require us to look around us and then look ahead. Bringing in professional trendwatchers to work with us and help us understand what to look for and how to interpret it might be a way to jump start the process.

Research teams might begin to employ consumers in a much more active way on the front end of projects that are in the planning stages. By expanding our notion of social validity we might discover that we are simply asking questions they have little interest in. Probing consumers to determine what value they put on certain behaviors and to what extent they would be willing to pay for services to remediate them could be a valuable exercise in strategic planning and resource management. Similar exercises with consumers might be carried out with the findings of existing research that has never been put to use. Behavior analysts might add professional writers, who know how to reach the public, to their research and dissemination teams.

Liaisons with other organizations such as insurance companies or health maintenance organizations is another step to consider. I feel certain that these organizations are totally unaware that we have research showing how to change human behavior in a positive direction with positive means. Punitive contingencies now used to cajole and threaten might be replaced with far more effective incentive systems that energize and motivate individuals to adopt healthy lifestyles.

We need to make far better use of the electronic media to get our message out. By developing web pages devoted to all aspects of behavior analysis we can reach a world-wide audience. Animated, full color sites with functional links to research studies as well as professionals who can provide behavioral services is probably the fastest way we can communicate the many advantages of behavior analysis.

Finally, we need to devote extra time to promote the next generation of behavior analysts who will inherit this field. My own personal assessment is that we are not training anywhere near enough students to take up the behavioral challenges of the next millennium. New graduate programs, especially at the master's level, need to be created and current programs expanded. If our most recent experience with the needs of parents of autistic children for trainers is any indication, we may fade as a field simply because we could not meet the demand. A similar phenomenon is currently occurring in business where the need is for computer literate employees by the thousands. The need to develop fast-track training methods to meet a need in our culture for literally thousands of behaviorally trained specialists could be the highest priority of all.

The Decade of Behavior: 2000-2010

It appears that we may have one of the most unique and opportune windows of opportunity to come our way in 50 years. The incoming Executive Director of APA's Science Directorate has just announced that upon taking his position in January 1998 the Science Directorate " ... will work cooperatively with academic departments, scientific societies, government agencies and private foundations to launch the DECADE OF BEHAVIOR for the period 2000-2010." (McCarty, 1997).

"The programs and activities associated with the DECADE OF BEHAVIOR will focus attention on the many contributions of the behavioral and social sciences to address in part the problems facing our society... For too long, behavioral scientists have been on the outside looking in when it comes to federal funding for basic and applied research. In addition, we are still not viewed as serious scientists by many segments of our society. The DECADE OF BEHAVIOR has the potential to address many of these problems facing scientific psychology and in the process it will bring our knowledge and skills to the forefront in addressing many of our society's most daunting problems." (McCarty, 1997).

Reading Objectives

1. What was Skinner's vision of a culture based on behavior analysis? What fears were raised by Hilts and London?
2. How was the shift from introspectionism to behaviorism an example of "paradigm shift"?
3. Describe a recent paradigm shift in the human services.
4. What possible role does Bailey see for behavior analysis in our society?
5. Why does the author recommend we push "understanding human behavior" as opposed to the philosophy of behaviorism?
6. What are five important trends to watch that have implications for behavior analysis?
7. How might marketing and advertising professionals assist behavior analysis in promoting our "product"?
8. How does the shift in funding in health care possibly give behavioral approaches an edge?
9. How might the cutting edge technology of virtual reality be used in training behavior analysts?
10. How is the research strategy suggested by the author different from our current strategies? What influences does he say we should take into account?

References

Abernathy, W. B. (1996). *The sin of wages*. Memphis: PerfSys Press.

Ayllon, T., & Michael, J. (1959). The psychiatric nurse as behavioral engineer. *Journal of the Experimental Analysis of Behavior, 2*, 323-334.

Baars, B. J. (1986). *The cognitive revolution in psychology*. New York: The Guilford Press.

Baer, D. M., & Wolf, M. M. (1970). The entry into natural communities of reinforcement. In R. Ulrich, T. Stachnik, & J. Mabry (Eds.), *Control of human behavior: Volume II* (319-324). Glenview, IL: Scott, Foresman.

Baer, D. M., Wolf, M. M., & Risley, T. R. (1968). Some current dimensions of applied behavior analysis. *Journal of Applied Behavior Analysis, 1*, 91-97.

Bailey, J. S. (1990, April). *Please don't do behavior modification on me: Toward behavioral ethics*. Paper presented at the University of Georgia University Affiliated Program on Developmental Disabilities, Athens, GA.

Bailey, J. S. (1991). Marketing behavior analysis requires different talk. *Journal of Applied Behavior Analysis, 24,* 445-448.

Barker, J. A. (1992). *Paradigms: The business of discovering the future.* New York: HarperCollins.

Baum, W. M. (1994). *Understanding behaviorism.* New York: HarperCollins.

Binder, C. (1996). Behavioral fluency: evolution of a new paradigm. *The Behavior Analyst, 19,* 163-197.

Daniels, A. (1994). *Bringing out the best in people.* New York: McGraw-Hill.

Davis, S. (1996). *Future perfect.* Reading, MA: Addison-Wesley.

Greene, J. (1997, July 27). To some, HMO policies on mental illness make little sense. *The Orange County Register,* p. A01.

Greenspoon, J. (1955). The reinforcing effect of two spoken sounds on the frequency of two responses. *American Journal of Psychology, 68,* 409-416.

Hilts, P. J. (1974). *Behavior mod.* New York: Harper & Row.

Institute for the Future. (1997). Web page: www.iftf.org.

Iwata, B. A., Bailey, J. S., Neef, N. A., Wacker, D. P., Repp, A. C., & Shook, G. L. (Eds.). (1997). *Behavior Analysis in Developmental Disabilities, 3rd ed., 1968-1995.* Lawrence, Kansas: The Society for the Experimental Analysis of Behavior.

Kimber, C., & Hemingway, M. (1994). New directions for developmental services. *Florida Association for Behavior Analysis Newsletter, 14*(3), 3-5.

Krasner, L., & Ullmann, L. P. (1967). *Research in behavior modification.* New York: Holt, Rinehart and Winston.

Kuhn, T. (1970). *The structure of scientific revolutions* (2nd ed.). Chicago: University of Chicago Press.

Lehmann, N. (1997). The reading wars. *The Atlantic Monthly, Nov.,* 128-134.

London, P. (1969). *Behavior control.* New York: Harper & Row.

Maurice, C. (1993). *Let me hear your voice.* New York: Fawcett Columbine.

Maurice, C. (1997, September). *ABA and us: One parent's reflections on persuasion and perceptions.* Paper presented at the 17th annual meeting of the Florida Association for Behavior Analysis, Sarasota, FL.

McCarty, R. C (1997). *The Decade of Behavior 2000-2010.* Available by e-mail: rcm@virginia.edu.

Mickelthwait, J., & Wooldridge, A. (1996). *The witch hunters.* New York: Random House Books.

Moore, B., Murdock, K., Harrington, S., & Bostow, D. (1997, September). *Technologies for teaching with computers: Authoring tools, distance learning issues and experimental results.* Paper presented at the 17th annual meeting of the Florida Association for Behavior Analysis, Sarasota, FL.

Morrison, I., & Schmid, G. (1994). *Future tense: The business realities of the next ten years.* New York: William Morrow and Company.

Popcorn, F., & Marigold, L. (1996). *Clicking: 16 trends to future fit your life, your work, and your business.* New York: HarperCollins.

Pryor, K. (1985). *Don't shoot the dog.* New York: Bantam Books.

Risley, T. R., & Hart, B. M. (1968). Developing correspondence between the nonverbal and verbal behavior of preschool children. *Journal of Applied Behavior Analysis, 1*, 267-281.

Rummler, G., & Brache, J. (1995). *Improving performance: How to manage the white space on the organizational chart.* San Francisco: Jossey-Bass.

Sagan, C. (1996). *The demon-haunted world.* New York: Ballentine Books.

Singer, M. T., & Lalich, J. (1996). *Crazy therapies.* San Francisco: Jossey-Bass.

Skinner, B. F. (1948). *Walden two.* New York: The Macmillan Company.

Skinner, B. F. (1953). *Science and human behavior.* New York: The Macmillan Company.

Skinner, B. F. (1971). *Beyond freedom and dignity.* New York: Knopf.

Sulzer-Azaroff, B., Drabman, R.M., Greer, R. D., Hall, R.V., Iwata, B.A., & O'Leary, S.G. (Eds.). (1988). *Behavior Analysis in Education 1968-1987.* Lawrence, Kansas: The Society for the Experimental Analysis of Behavior.

Toffler, A., & Toffler, H. (1995). *Creating a new civilization.* Atlanta: Turner Publishing.

Ullmann, L. P., & Krasner, L. (1965). *Case studies in behavior modification.* New York: Holt, Rinehart and Winston, Inc.

Ulrich, R., Stachnik, T., & Mabry, J. (1970). *Control of human behavior: Volume two.* Glenview, IL: Scott, Foresman and Co.

World Futurist Society. (1997). Web page: www.wfs.org/wfs